THE LIVING WORD™

LEADING RCIA DISMISSALS

YEAR B

LEISA ANSLINGER

MARY A. EHLE

BIAGIO MAZZA

VICTORIA M. TUFANO

LTP

LITURGY
TRAINING
PUBLICATIONS

Nihil Obstat
Very Reverend Daniel A. Smilanic, JCD
Vicar for Canonical Services
Archdiocese of Chicago
May 8, 2017

Imprimatur
Very Reverend Ronald A. Hicks
Vicar General
Archdiocese of Chicago
May 8, 2017

The *Nihil Obstat* and *Imprimatur* are declarations that the material is free from doctrinal or moral error, and thus is granted permission to publish in accordance with c. 827. No legal responsibility is assumed by the grant of this permission. No implication is contained herein that those who have granted the *Nihil Obstat* and *Imprimatur* agree with the content, opinions, or statements expressed.

The overview of the Gospel according to Mark was originally written by Charles A. Bobertz and published in *Sourcebook for Sundays, Seasons, and Weekdays* © Archdiocese of Chicago, Liturgy Training Publications, 3949 South Racine Avenue, Chicago, IL 60609. It was adapted for *The Living Word: Leading RCIA Dismissals, Year B* by Mary A. Ehle © Archdiocese of Chicago, Liturgy Training Publications. All rights reserved. Dismissal texts were compiled and adapted from material written by: Ward Johnson, Corinna Laughlin, Maria Laughlin, Graziano Marcheschi, Paul Turner, Jill Maria Murdy, Stephen S. Wilbricht, CSC, and D. Todd Williamson © Archdiocese of Chicago, Liturgy Training Publications. All rights reserved. Explanations of the rites included in the "Overview of the Appendix" were written by Victoria M. Tufano and D. Todd Williamson © Archdiocese of Chicago, Liturgy Training Publications. All rights reserved.

Scripture backgrounds in this book were previously published in *Celebrating the Lectionary*® 1997, 2000, 2003, 2004, 2005, 2006, 2009, and 2010 and *Foundations for Preaching and Teaching*® 2011, 2012, 2014, 2015, and 2016 © Archdiocese of Chicago, Liturgy Training Publications, 3949 South Racine Avenue, Chicago, IL 60609. All rights reserved. Authors include Mary A. Ehle, Peg Ekerdt, Jean Marie Hiesberger, Biagio Mazza, Mary M. McGlone, CSJ, Abbot Gregory J. Polan, OSB, Denise Simeone, George Smiga, and Paul Turner. Advent seasonal environment suggestions were originally published in *The Living Word 2015–2016* © 2016 Archdiocese of Chicago, Liturgy Training Publications, 3949 South Racine Avenue, Chicago, IL 60609. All rights reserved.

Special thanks to Leisa Anslinger, Mary A. Ehle, Michael Ruzicki, and Victoria M. Tufano for their generous and pastoral guidance in the development of this resource.

THE LIVING WORD™: LEADING RCIA DISMISSALS, YEAR B © 2017 Archdiocese of Chicago: Liturgy Training Publications, 3949 South Racine Avenue, Chicago, IL 60609, 800-933-1800; fax 800-933-7094; e-mail orders@ltp.org. Website: www.LTP.org. All rights reserved.

This book was edited by Danielle A. Noe, MDIV. Michael A. Dodd was the production editor, Anna Manhart was the designer, and Juan Alberto Castillo was the production artist. The Scripture Backgrounds were edited by Victoria M. Tufano and copyedited by Víctor R. Pérez.

Cover art by James B. Janknegt; back cover and interior icons by Steve Musgrave.

21 20 19 18 17   1 2 3 4 5

Printed in the United States of America.

Library of Congress Control Number: 2017948560

ISBN 978-1-61671-366-9

LWLDB

CONTENTS

INTRODUCTION

"By his words our Lord won over the hearts of the people; they came to hear him from all parts (see Mark 1:45); they were amazed at his teachings (see Mark 6:2), and they sensed that he spoke to them as one with authority (see Mark 1:27)."

—Pope Francis, *Evangelii gaudium*, 136

Welcome

Jesus loved stories—stories that revealed a way of life. He taught in synagogues. On the mountain, he instructed his disciples about the essence of holiness in the Beatitudes. On the road to Jerusalem, his healing encounters with the sick and the possessed gave the Gospel writers the basis for the healing narratives on which we now reflect. Jesus, the Messiah, the Risen One, opened the Word and broke bread with his disciples as they came to Emmaus. Perhaps we could, in a way, consider him the first dismissal catechist. Following Jesus' example, then, we invite you to embark on the journey of faith with the catechumens you guide to discover the Living Word and how it forms their relationship with Jesus and continually draws them to a life of discipleship.

Whether you are a pastor, pastoral associate, catechumenate director, catechist, or another initiation minister involved with the Rite of Christian Initiation of Adults (RCIA), especially the dismissal on Sundays and other holy days, *The Living Word™: Leading RCIA Dismissals, Year B* will support and direct you as you explore the Lectionary readings with catechumens throughout the liturgical year. This resource serves to draw dismissal catechists and their catechumens into the Living Word. Use it to reflect on the many wonders of the Word of God as it applies to their deepening lives of faith in the Church and the world. May the Spirit of the Living God—the Spirit of the Living Word—breathe in you, in all those who lead catechumens into the Word, and in the catechumens and elect.

About this Resource

The Living Word™: Leading RCIA Dismissals, Year B provides initiation ministers with an understanding of the purpose of the dismissal, how it takes place, and what dismissal catechists should be concerned with when leading meaningful discussions about the Word of God throughout the liturgical year. Following the organization of the Sunday *Lectionary for Mass*, this resource provides both preparatory material for the cate-chists and step-by-step guides for the same catechists to facilitate discussion on the day's Scripture readings. The "Catechist's Preparation" consists of:

- **Seasonal Overviews:** Each seasonal chapter is preceded by an overview which explains the theological meaning of the season, gives suggestions for preparing a seasonal environment in the space where the dismissal session will take place, and provides brief summaries of the readings for that season.

- **Dated Entries with Focus Statements:** A dismissal session guide is provided for each Sunday, Holyday of Obligation, and each solemnity and feast of the Lord and solemnity of the saints that could take the place of Sunday. To make it easy for the dismissal catechist, the name of each day (for example, First Sunday of Advent) appears at the beginning of each session followed by a concise focus statement providing direction for the catechist.

- **Overview of the Day:** This short overview provides the dismissal catechist with a general, pastoral overview of the day's readings. On days that are special solemnities or feasts, the backgrounds include a biography of the saint or more information about the day itself (for example, the Most Holy Trinity).

- **Scripture Backgrounds:** The Scripture backgrounds offer an overarching commentary on how the Lectionary knits the Scriptures readings together over the course of a liturgical year. Written in a pastoral tone, the backgrounds offer a historical-critical overview of the readings and underscore their relevance to life today. The overviews give particular attention to the major evangelist or Gospel writer for the liturgical year and the theological and spiritual emphases of the writer.

- **Reflection Questions for the Catechist:** A set of reflection questions concludes the preparatory material. The questions are intended to assist the catechist in centering himself or herself on the Word before leading the dismissal.

The "Catechist's Guide" is used by catechists to effectively lead the dismissal session conversation. The guides are meant to be the catechist's script; however, they can be adapted to the particular needs of the catechumens. Each guide includes the following elements:

- **Dismissal and Procession:** Instructions are given for the dismissal rite and the procession to the place where the dismissal session will occur. Sample dismissal texts are provided for priest celebrants.

- **Centering:** Suggestions are provided transitioning from the body of the church to the sacred space where the catechumens and catechists will gather.

- **Reflection and Discussion:** The reflection and discussion section provides the dismissal catechist with a general framework for leading the conversation around the day's Scripture readings. The reflection and discussion section connects directly with the Scripture backgrounds, the focus statement, and the themes that arise in the texts for the day.

- **Wrapping It Up:** The bullet points are intended to help the catechist recap the discussion and move it forward by making the connection between liturgy and life.

- **Closing Prayer:** A prayer is provided to conclude each dismissal session guide. Pray the prayer given, or adapt it to the thoughts and comments that arose in the day's conversation.

- **Readings for the Next Dismissal:** This section directs the catechist to the readings for the next Mass in which the dismissal will take place. It will be helpful to give the citations of the readings to the catechumens so that they can prepare during the week to hear the Word at Mass and reflect on the Word as a group. Questions are also provided to help catechumens prepare for the next dismissal session by providing a thought process to connect the readings from one Sunday to the next or from one dismissal session to the next at the end of this section.

Because this resource can be used every time Year B occurs, and the liturgical year is fluid (that is, the First Sunday of Advent does not take place on the same calendar date each year), a chart is provided on page xvi noting the name of the Sunday or special feast day, and the date on which it occurs from 2018 through 2028. Reference this chart so that you know what dismissal guide to use for a particular Sunday or feast day (note that only those feast days that could fall on a Sunday are included in this resource).

- **Extended Catechesis:** The final section of the dismissal guide lists relevant topics on which you might base the extended catechesis session. These are doctrinal topics that relate to the Lectionary readings and the time in the liturgical year. The list provided is not intended to be exhaustive, but is rather a starting point.

- **Appendix:** In addition to the session guides for each Sunday and special feast day, this resource provides an appendix with dismissal session guides for particular rites that occur during the initiation process.

UNDERSTANDING THE DISMISSAL OF CATECHUMENS

Why Are Catechumens Dismissed?

Ordinarily, however, when [catechumens] are present in the assembly of the faithful they should be kindly dismissed before the liturgy of the eucharist begins (unless their dismissal would present practical or pastoral problems). For they must await their baptism, which will join them to God's priestly people and empower them to participate in Christ's new worship (RCIA, 75.3).

Catechumens are formally and "kindly dismissed" from the liturgical assembly for a specific purpose—to go forth "with the help of some of the faithful" to share their "joy and spiritual experience" and reflect more deeply upon the Word of God they heard proclaimed at Mass (RCIA, 67). The Church dismisses catechumens not because they are unwelcome in the assembly, but because they are preparing for Baptism. The catechumens are dismissed after the homily and before the Profession of Faith because that prayer and the prayers and rites that follow (the Universal Prayer, Eucharistic Prayer, reception of Holy Communion, and so on) are specific to those who are baptized.

At Baptism, God embraces us as part of his priestly people and empowers us to participate in Christ's new worship and feast at the table of the Eucharist. The faithful can learn about the meaning of their Baptism and their call to live as disciples from the words of dismissal. In the Universal Prayer, they undertake Christ's priestly role and approach God with the needs of the world and the Christian community. In the Eucharistic Prayer, the faithful participate in the Church's great prayer of thanksgiving to the Father through Christ. By receiving the Body and Blood of Christ, they embrace their profound relationship of communion with him through this sacrament of the Church. When they are dismissed, they are sent out to live as disciples in the Word and to carry on Jesus' own mission of preaching the Kingdom of God in words and actions of love. Not yet joined to the Christian community through Baptism and participation in the Eucharist, the catechumens are formed through the Word in the requirements of discipleship.

The Church begins to dismiss those seeking Baptism after these inquirers have been accepted into the Order of Catechumens. This formal ritual is the Rite of Acceptance into the Order of Catechumens. This rite may take place at any time during the year (see RCIA, 41–74). (A dismissal session guide to reflect upon this rite is found on page 313 in the appendix.) Catechumens continue to be dismissed from the liturgical assembly to reflect on the Word until they are fully initiated at the Easter Vigil (see RCIA, 83.2). Those who are baptized are not dismissed from the liturgical assembly. Candidates for reception into the full communion of the Roman Catholic Church and uncatechized Catholics seeking Confirmation and/or Eucharist should not take part in rites and formation that resemble the catechumenate since the candidates have already been baptized (see the *National Statutes for the Catechumenate*, 30–31). Although they will not receive the Eucharist, candidates should remain in the assembly and participate in the liturgical life of the parish.

How Does the Dismissal Rite Take Place?

The phrase "dismissal rite" refers to the ritual words and actions that comprise the sending forth of the catechumens from the assembly of the faithful. The RCIA provides some guidance for how the dismissal rite and the reflection on the Word that follows (hereafter, called the dismissal session) is to occur; that is, when it takes place, who is involved, and what the priest celebrant is to say when the catechumens are formally dismissed (see RCIA, 67 and 83.2).

When it is time to dismiss the catechumens from the liturgical assembly, the priest celebrant calls them forward with their catechists. Before Mass, catechists should tell those participating in the dismissal that they should bring their coats, purses, and other belongings with them. Sponsors usually remain at Mass. The priest celebrant is responsible for speaking the words of dis-

missal, while the community in its entirety will send the catechumens forth (see RCIA, 67). The RCIA provides two formulary options for the celebrant to speak when dismissing the catechumens. The rubric for option A instructs the celebrant to urge the catechumens to "live according to the word of God they have just heard," while the text of option B notes that the community sends the catechumens forth "to reflect more deeply upon the word of God which you have shared with us today" (RCIA, 67). The peace, support, and prayers of the community go with the catechumens as they leave the liturgical assembly to reflect more deeply on the Word of God. The texts provided in the RCIA may be used as is, or similar words may be said. Each dismissal guide in this resource provides seasonal texts that the priest celebrant may use.

Although this is not noted in the RCIA, the priest celebrant might hand the Lectionary to the dismissal catechist to carry when leading the catechumens to the place where they will discuss the Word. Your parish liturgical staff might encourage the dismissal catechist to hold the Lectionary in a reverent manner with both hands, if they are able, and at about mid-torso height as he or she leads the catechumens in procession out of the main liturgical assembly. (As per the *General Instruction of the Roman Missal*, the *Book of the Gospels* is elevated, not the Lectionary [see GIRM, 120, D].)

The RCIA provides the option for the assembly to sing a song after the priest celebrant formally dismisses the catechumens (see RCIA, 67). It has become a custom in many parishes to sing a short acclamation or refrain until the procession with the catechumens exits the church. Parishes might select a different antiphon or refrain for each liturgical season or keep it consistent throughout the liturgical year. The chosen piece should keep the assembly focused on the ritual of dismissal and the fact that the catechumens are leaving to reflect more deeply on the Word of God they have just shared with the faithful. Your parish music director might consider using "Listen to God's Word" by David Haas (GIA Publications), "Go in Peace" by Kevin Keil (Oregon Catholic Press), or *Chosen by Christ/Elegidos en Cristo,* a bilingual collection by Jerry Galipeau (World Library Publications).

What Happens after Catechumens Are Dismissed?

In this resource, the terms "dismissal session" and "dismissal catechesis" refer to the time of reflection and surfacing of insights about the Lectionary readings, the Christian life, and our relationship with God in Jesus Christ which takes place after the catechumens are dismissed from the parish's liturgical worship. "Extended catechesis" refers to catechetical sessions that delves more deeply and specifically into the catechumens' questions around Catholic dogmas, doctrines, and teachings.

After the catechumens are dismissed, they gather in another location to "reflect more deeply upon the word of God" (RCIA, 67, B). The RCIA states, "after the dismissal formulary" (that is, the text the priest celebrant uses to dismiss the catechumens), "the group of catechumens goes out but does not disperse" (67, A). The RCIA presumes they are dismissed together and remain together with the assistance of some of the faithful "to share their joy and spiritual experiences" (RCIA, 67, A). This is the time for "dismissal catechesis."

The RCIA does not specify how the dismissal session is to take place. However, guidance can be taken from the RCIA's emphasis on the celebrations of the Word that occur during the Period of the Catechumenate. The RCIA emphasizes that celebrations of the Word of God are essential for the catechumens' preparation for Baptism. "During the period of the catechumenate there should be celebrations of the word of God that accord with the liturgical season and contribute to the instruction of the catechumens and the needs of the community" (RCIA, 81). The spiritual reflection and catechesis that takes place in the dismissal session extends the catechumens' participation in the Liturgy of the Word. When catechumens participate in celebrations of the Word and reflect upon this experience they are able to:

1. implant in their hearts the teachings they are receiving;

2. receive instruction and experience in the different aspects and ways of prayer;

3. obtain a beginning level of experience and skill in listening to, reading, and reflecting on the readings at Mass and Scripture in general;

4. begin to understand the signs, celebrations, and seasons;

5. prepare to gradually enter the worship assembly of the entire community (see RCIA, 82).

This time of unlocking the mysteries of the Lectionary readings in light of personal and communal experiences of faith provides the catechumens with opportunities to develop their relationship with Christ by internalizing the Word, concentrating their prayer around the Scriptures and the liturgical year, and becoming familiar with the teachings of the Church. This "suitable pastoral formation and guidance" (RCIA, 75) is given to the catechumens in four ways:

1. catechesis that is "planned to be gradual and complete in its coverage, accommodated to the liturgical year, and solidly supported by celebrations of the word. This catechesis leads the catechumens not only to an appropriate acquaintance with dogmas and precepts but also to a profound sense of the mystery of salvation in which they will participate" (RCIA, 75.1);

2. familiarity with the Christian way of life, "helped by the example and support of sponsors, godparents, and the entire Christian community," to turn to God in prayer and witness to the faith, to hope in Christ, follow divine guidance in their actions, and to love their neighbor (RCIA, 75.2);

3. participation in suitable liturgical rites, including celebrations of the Word of God and the Liturgy of the Word at Mass, which purify and strengthen the catechumens with God's blessing (RCIA, 75.3);

4. actively working to spread the Gospel and build up the Church by the witness of their lives and profession of their faith (RCIA, 75.4).

How Long Does the Dismissal Session Last?

The formation that takes place during the dismissal session will vary from parish to parish. Some parishes combine extended catechesis with dismissal catechesis (see above). They choose to have the dismissal session with the catechumens until Mass ends, take a break (and perhaps join the parish community for coffee and donuts), and then regather for a time of extended catechesis that focuses more on Church teachings that arise from the Sunday's readings. Other parishes choose to have a separate time for extended catechesis on a different day of the week. The makeup of the group of catechumens and their availability should determine which model your parish chooses. Never simply impose a model that solely meets the needs of the parish staff and not of the catechumens. Larger parishes with many catechumens might need to offer multiple options, including celebrating the dismissal at more than one liturgy and ensuring that the dismissal catechists are available for the various sessions. If the dismissal catechesis lasts until the conclusion of Mass, carefully consider the amount of time you have for the session, and perhaps even have someone take responsibility for being aware of the progress of the Mass, alerting the primary dismissal catechist five to ten minutes before Mass will end so he or she can begin to draw the session to a close (see below under "involving assistants").

THE ROLE OF THE DISMISSAL CATECHIST

Who Leads the Dismissal Session?

The RCIA gives no other identifying information about the catechist who leads the dismissal sessions other than "some of the faithful" (RCIA, 67). Yet what it does say presumes that those present are comfortable with facilitating conversations around spiritual experiences arising from the Liturgy of the Word as celebrated within the faith community.

One or two catechists will be needed to facilitate the dismissal session. The dismissal session catechists need to be good listeners and strong spiritual guides. As spiritual guides, they too open themselves up to continually grow in faith. A dismissal session catechist accompanies the catechumens on their journey to the heart of the Word—walking with them as they journey to Jerusalem this time, this year—and reminding them that this journey into the Word continues to take place each year, even after they are members of the baptized community of the faithful. As followers of Jesus, we continually grow in our relationship with him and our knowledge of what it means to live as his disciples.

Leading the dismissal session with catechumens is more spiritual facilitation than academic exercise—it is not the time for a lecture or longer presentation. Catechists need to be comfortable moving conversations forward and helping participants draw connections to the liturgical season and the Scripture readings. You want people of the Word—people who themselves strive to live their lives in accord with the message of Scripture.

Involving Assistants

The number of catechumens attending a particular dismissal session will greatly determine how a session will be facilitated. For example, realistic decisions will need to be made about how many assistants will be necessary. Remember that when the RCIA describes the dismissal, it mentions that "some of the faithful" (RCIA, 67) participate in the reflection on the Word with the catechumens. Aside from the dismissal catechesis leader, one assistant is always helpful and practical. There really shouldn't be more members of the faithful than there are catechumens (unless there are only a few). It is a fine balance between not overwhelming the catechumens, so they feel comfortable contributing the discussion, and having enough community members present to assure a good flow to the conversation and to the session as a whole.

Along with participating in the discussion, an assistant can also help keep track of the progression of the Mass or simply the time frame you have for the session. This will help the dismissal catechist transition through different parts of the session and not have to rush to draw it to a conclusion. If your dismissal session concludes at the same time as Mass, an assistant could give a heads up when there is approximately five minutes or so left in the Mass—or when the Communion Rite has concluded.

Assistants could also help with setting up the prayer space, making sure Bibles are available, helping catechumens locate the readings if a Bible is used, leading the music, or making sure audio is set up if you need to play a recorded piece. Assistants can also offer hospitality and a warm send-off when the session concludes, reminding catechumens of the time to meet back for extended catechesis or of the day and time during the coming week when it will take place. Music ministers might also be available to help lead sung refrains if music will be included in the dismissal session.

Preparing to Lead the Dismissal Session

As with any Bible study, catechetical session, or faith formation session, you will want to prepare ahead of time in order to facilitate the conversation. Ideally, gather together with any assistants you will have and with the catechist(s) who will be leading the time of extended catechesis so as to assure continuity. Spend some time together, or by yourself if you are unable to meet, reading and praying with the Scriptures for the Sunday, solemnity, feast, or Holyday of Obligation. Go over the Sunday backgrounds, the Sunday and seasonal overviews, and reflection questions. Always bring yourself back to the Scripture text, as you will do with the catechumens. As you prepare, perhaps write down the approximate time you want to spend on each part of the dismissal session. Allow room for surprises and for unexpected comments by catechumens! The Holy Spirit will move them in ways we will not or cannot anticipate! Flexibility is key in spiritual conversations around the Word of God.

Consult with the parish music director or other musicians who may be assisting you with music that you will sing or play during the session. Choosing short refrains that the catechumens will sing during the liturgy and the liturgical seasons will help them make connections between the liturgy and their journey of faith during the week.

A small, minor detail is to make sure the room you will use for the dismissal session is available. Depending on your parish, this means reserving the time and space well ahead of time—perhaps even months ahead when the parish's annual calendar takes shape. Lest a minor detail become a major issue, plan ahead! Room conflicts can be challenging to resolve on the spot.

You might want to jot down a few notes during the homily so you can integrate comments and questions that stem from it. If you can speak to the homilist during the week, you could ask about key points that he will bring up, or perhaps if he could give you a one or two sentence synopsis of the homily so you could integrate some thoughts ahead of your dismissal session. Another way to integrate the homily into the dismissal session is to pose a question to the catechumens about it in relation to the readings and allow them to make connections. Whenever posing questions, do so in an open-ended format that invites discussion. Question that lead to yes or no answers tend to stifle discussion rather than open dialogue.

Preparing a Prayerful Space

Dismissal sessions may take place in a variety of locations depending on what the parish has available. The location could be a small chapel, a meeting room, or a classroom. Whatever the location, you will want to create a prayerful environment. Some spaces are intentionally more functional than prayerful to begin with, and they will pose some creative challenges in setting up a prayerful environment.

Creating an environment of prayer—a prayer space —sets the tone for the dismissal session. It says to us that something other than a business meeting is going to take place. It reminds us that what we will experience in here connects with the prayer of the liturgical assembly from which we came.

If you are able to set up the room in a circle of chairs without tables for the number of participants you will have (leader, assistants, and catechumens), this will create a sense of community and help open people to conversation and sharing more than sitting around tables or in desks would. If the Lectionary was not carried out of the worship space, place it or a Bible on a stand on a small table in the center of the circle. Drape the table with fabrics that reflect the color of the liturgical season. Choose to mirror the liturgical environment in the main assembly to the extent possible, although on a much smaller scale. Place a candle on the table to draw attention to the Word, or near the table if the candle is on a floor stand. The assistant can be responsible for lighting and extinguishing the candle. When you proclaim a reading, do so from the Lectionary or Bible. Refer to the seasonal overviews in this resource for other environment suggestions.

Interacting with Catechumens

Discussion of faith or faith-sharing is new to many people. It might even be new to you as a dismissal catechist. For catechumens and the elect, their faith journey toward initiation is both a personal and communal experience. Each catechumen comes with unique life experiences that he or she attempts to integrate with his or her faith during the time of the catechumenate. We never want to force anyone to publicly discuss the intersection of his or her faith and life. We do, however, want them to feel the love and support of the Christian community as they journey in faith and live the Word. The dismissal sessions can and should empower us all to become more comfortable discussing Scripture and its application to our life of faith in the Church.

Set a positive and encouraging tone as you open the dismissal sessions. Let everyone know that all contributions are equally valued. You never know how the Spirit will move within the community gathered to reflect and open eyes, hearts, and minds to the Living Word. An effective dismissal session will have led catechumens more deeply into the Word. The Lectionary texts should be the focus so that the catechumens will walk away with the tools needed to apply the texts to their daily life in the coming week. In the end, your group might generate more questions than answers about the readings and how they apply to their lives. That is good. It means the Spirit has given more food for thought. Our faith journey never ends—and neither does our journey into the Word. If you have led the catechumens to dig deeper and deeper into the Word and to begin to unwrap the many layers of meaning of the Word, you can say your session achieved its goal.

But you will encounter challenges in breaking open the Word. What if no one talks? It is okay if it takes a while for people to respond. As a facilitator of conversation, your task is to lead the catechumens deeper into the Word. To do this, consistently remind yourself that the Spirit works in the silence as well as through words. Become comfortable with silence. You might have a group of catechumens who are mostly introverts. Introverts need time to process and think. Know your time frame and where you are at in the session. You will need to judge how much silence is too much in your group. You might rephrase a question that seems not to have stimulated any comment or discussion. You might have to inject a small thought of your own to get the discussion going. But try not to dominate the discussion. You will be able to tell if you are talking too much!

On the flip side, be mindful of a catechumen who might tend to be the first to respond to a question or continuously want to share his or her extensive thoughts or personal experiences. Gently remind him or her, though not in front of the entire group, that others need to have some process time before they speak and that we want to provide everyone an opportunity to contribute. Some in your group may be reticent to speak if there is a single person who tends to always talk. Remember the uncomfortable experience of being in a classroom and having the teacher call on a student whose body language clearly showed that he or she did not want to speak. As a dismissal catechist, be careful not to single people out who are not talking or sharing. Introverts especially, but even some extraverts, do not like to be called upon. Calling on someone to speak when they might not have anything to say, or are still processing, can be embarrassing and might deter them from speaking in the future. It is okay if there are times when a catechumen is quiet and reserved. Such can be the nature of a person and the nature of reflective listening.

If you have a large group of catechumens, you might consider breaking them into a few small groups for parts of the conversation. While a dismissal session might only be twenty-five to forty minutes in length, this is still enough time to pose a few questions to small groups and then gather back together as a large group. Your assistant can help watch the time if you choose to do this. You will also want to consider time as you prepare the session.

What if someone poses a challenging question? If the question is on topic and you are comfortable, you could choose to allow the conversation to flow. If the question is about Church teaching, you have the option to say that this is a question more appropriate for the time of extended and in-depth catechesis. If it is a question requiring a direct answer about Church teaching, and you are not sure how to present a response, it is also fair for you to say you will look into the question and get input from the pastor or the RCIA coordinator. You could also look at the *Catechism of the Catholic Church* and other Church documents. Similarly, if it is a question of textual interpretation and translation, it is also fair to say you will consult biblical commentaries and dictionaries or speak with pastoral leaders educated in the field.

You do not need to be an expert, but you always need to let people know you will get information, not necessarily "answers," to their questions so that you together can grow in your understanding of the faith, and your relationship with God can deepen.

Keeping conversations on track when you are with a group of catechumens can often challenge one's facilitation skills—especially when reflecting on the Lectionary readings and connecting life experiences to the readings or the telling of life stories, which can become lengthy. At certain points, you will have to redirect the conversation, draw it to a close, and move on to the next part of the dismissal session. Do this directly, but gently, with grace. Let the person speaking, and the group, know you are not simply cutting them off, but that the group needs to proceed. Offer them the opportunity to continue the conversation and story telling informally over coffee and donuts, should your group break for a parish hospitality time, or revisit the conversation before the time of extended catechesis.

Always move to the next section of the conversation gently and with grace. If the conversation gets way off track, draw the group back to the Scripture reading that has become your focus. Summarize the reflections so far or restate the main theme from the Scripture backgrounds. Most adults will realize when the conversation has gone far afield, so you are not telling them anything they are not already aware of!

Scripts to help facilitate this discussion have been included in this resource under "Reflection and Discussion" in each dismissal guide. You should feel free to adapt the discussion based on the group of catechumens you lead. Be cognizant of how the size of the group affects the amount of time necessary for an adequate discussion. If your group wants to spend more time on a specific question, choose to do so. A dismissal session is not so much about the amount of content covered, but rather more about facilitating a process of reflection and discussion on the readings that will lead catechumens to grow in their faith and deepen their identity as followers of Christ. It is about guiding them to know Jesus and to develop a profound relationship with him as the source of their life and faith, as the One who saves through the grace of his life, Death, and Resurrection.

If you have both elect and catechumens who participate in the dismissal rite, ideally they should meet separately for dismissal catechesis, especially when the elect have celebrated a rite particular to their journey, such as a Scrutiny. The elect will benefit from an opportunity to reflect in a more focused way on their ritual experience of the Scrutiny as it pertains to their coming celebration of the sacraments of initiation. Separate dismissal guides that reflect upon the elects' experience of particular rituals are provided in the appendix to this resource.

Depending on your people resources, however, there might be times when you find yourself leading dismissal sessions with both catechumens and the elect. This will most likely happen if a few catechumens are not ready to celebrate the sacraments of initiation, or your parish has a year-round Period of the Catechumenate. You will want to be mindful of the mixed group especially on the Third, Fourth, and Fifth Sundays of Lent, when the Church celebrates the Scrutinies with the elect. Allow some time for reflecting on the experience of the Scrutinies from both the vantage point of the catechumens and the elect.

You might consider encouraging the catechumens to keep a faith journal in which they jot down significant words or phrases from the readings, thoughts that come to mind in relation to the readings, and any questions about the readings, the liturgy or liturgical season, or Church teaching that arise during the week.

Here is one final note about facilitating the dismissal session. In order to facilitate the dismissal session well, you need neither be a Scripture scholar nor a doctrinal expert. You do, however, need to be a person of the Word, a person of faith who year after year journeys through the Lectionary readings with an open heart and mind, seeking ever new and deeper ways to connect the Word with your life of faith as a Catholic and life in the communion of faith, the Church, and the world. You yourself must hunger to learn more about the Word, to understand it more deeply. Your hunger for the Word is an example to the catechumens.

FAMILIARITY WITH THE SCRIPTURES

What Is the *Lectionary for Mass?*

Catechists who lead the dismissal session will need to have familiarity with the *Lectionary for Mass* and the Bible. The readings that we hear whenever we gather for Mass are found in and proclaimed from a ritual book called the *Lectionary for Mass*. The Lectionary is an ordered selection of readings, chosen from both testaments of the Bible, for proclamation in the assembly gathered for worship. Lectionaries have been used for Christian worship since the fourth century. The *Lectionary for Mass* includes the readings for every day of the liturgical year: weekdays (a two-year cycle) and Sundays (a three-year cycle), saints' days, Ritual Masses, Votive Masses, Masses for Various Needs and Occasions, and Masses for the Dead. No wonder Lectionaries are divided into several volumes!

Dismissal catechists will use the Lectionary for Sundays for Years A, B, and C. These volumes include the readings for Advent, Christmas Time, Lent, Sacred Paschal Triduum, Easter Time, Ordinary Time, as well as solemnities and feasts of the Lord and the saints. The three-year cycle of readings allows a fuller selection of readings from the Bible. During Year A, the Gospel readings for Ordinary Time are taken from Matthew, for Year B from Mark, and for Year C from Luke.

If the catechumens themselves do not raise the question, occasionally remind them that the Lectionary readings come from the Bible. Often people think that the readings proclaimed at Mass do not come from the Bible. But indeed they do! The biblical texts that are included in the Lectionary used in dioceses of the United States of America are based on the *New American Bible* (NAB) translation of Scripture. The Lectionary texts have been adapted so that the selections read at Mass are easier to proclaim and to understand.

How to Use the Sunday Lectionary

To find the readings for a Sunday Mass, you need to know whether you are in Year A, Year B, or Year C. Here is a quick guide to the Lectionary for the next few years. Notice that the Lectionary year begins with the First Sunday of Advent, which usually falls in late November or very early December, and ends with the Solemnity of Our Lord Jesus Christ, King of the Universe in late November of the following year. A list of the Sundays and special solemnities and feasts with calendar dates are noted on the chart on page xvi.

Advent 2018 – Christ the King 2019	Year C
Advent 2019 – Christ the King 2020	Year A
Advent 2020 – Christ the King 2021	Year B
Advent 2021 – Christ the King 2022	Year C

Once you know which year of the Lectionary you are in, it is easy to mark the Sunday Lectionary. You'll notice that every Sunday and special feast day is assigned a distinctive number. The dismissal guides in this resource provide the Lectionary numbers. For example, if you turn to page 3, the First Sunday of Advent, you will see Lectionary #2B in the heading. You will find the readings for this Sunday at #2B in the Lectionary.

It will be helpful for catechists to have access to the Lectionary so that they can prepare to facilitate discussion at the dismissal session. Parishes might have extra copies on hand or even purchase study editions for catechists to use. As a tool for your preparation, you might choose to use LTP's study edition of the *Lectionary for Mass*. You also might choose to have Bibles available for the catechumens for the dismissal session. Or, if they were presented a Bible during the Rite of Acceptance, encourage them to bring their Bible to both the dismissal session and the extended catechesis session. Through the use of the Bible, they will familiarize themselves more and more with the ordering of the books.

How Do Catholics Interpret Scripture?

Catholics view Scripture as God's Living Word pre sent among us. Literary genres such as biography or history help us to understand the Bible, but they do not define the genres of literature present in the Bible. The Scriptures—Old and New Testaments together—recount God's covenantal relationship with his people from creation forward through the New Covenant Jesus made with us, which carries forward today and will exist in years to come.

Catholics look to the historical context of the work and seek to understand the original language in which the authors wrote the texts. We ask questions about the philosophical and scientific background of the texts at the time the authors penned them. We note differences in translations. Yet—and most importantly—we read Scripture as God's story of love and care for his people—for us. We interpret Scripture neither literally nor as a science or history textbook. Think about the story of creation in Genesis. We first notice there are two vastly different creation accounts that we cannot reconcile scientifically or historically. Creation did not necessarily happen exactly as the passages state. Yet both accounts together teach us the *truth* about what God reveals to us about salvation. God created the world and all that is in it *good*. God created us in the divine image and likeness. We are God's good people. This means the creation narratives are not fictional stories, but true faith accounts about what God has done for his people.

Though we can and do read the Bible privately, by ourselves, as Catholics we believe we always read and pray the Scripture united with the Church, with the entire communion of the faithful. Together, in communion with the Church, we discern the meaning of Scripture for our lives and the life of the Church. We read not fundamentalistically, but with a fundamental concern for how the allegories, metaphors, stories, miracles, parables, struggles, and adventures of God, Jesus, the Israelites, and the disciples become ours. How will we live as Jesus' disciples here and now? How will we grow our relationship with God in Jesus Christ through the Holy Spirit in union with the Church? How will the Scriptures help the catechumens in their journey and guide us as we accompany each other in the journey of faith?

Catholics believe and interpret Scripture as God's divinely inspired Word. God, as he has always done, worked through the authors of the biblical texts to convey the truth about his ongoing relationship with men, women, and children of all time. Dictation was not God's method. But faith was and is. How we will participate in God's ongoing story of love and care is a question we as Catholics bring to our reading of Scripture. Each time we read and pray with Scripture, we see God's amazing care for his people—God's grace made available to us.

We might have questions about what is scientifically and historically true and fact in Scripture. We might recognize inconsistencies in the texts. These are important questions for Catholics, but we always return to the truth about life reigning over death, and how the early Christian communities proclaimed the message of the Gospel (kerygma) to the ends of the known earth to contextualize our response. When we accept our responsibility to respond to questions in this manner, we form catechumens in God's Living Word and the Catholic interpretation of it.

THE EVANGELISTS FOR YEAR B

The Gospel according to Mark

Mark is the primary evangelist for Year B of the three-year Lectionary cycle. His account is the earliest of the four canonical Gospel accounts, although it is second to Matthew in its placement in the New Testament. The evangelist wrote for an audience composed primarily of non-Jewish people living outside of the Holy Land. We can date the Gospel according to Mark somewhere between AD 60 and 70, most likely around the time of Peter's death in Rome under the Emperor Nero in AD 64. Mark's work is the primary source for Matthew and Luke, the other two synoptic Gospel accounts, composed approximately two decades after Mark.

"A creative and fascinating theologian" would be an apt description of this Gospel writer. His account of the Good News begins with the baptism of Jesus. Mark immediately connects the story of Jesus' baptism to the story of the Cross at the end of the Gospel. From beginning to end, the evangelist communicates to us Jesus' identity as the Son of God (see Mark 1:1, 15:39). Peter's confession midway through the narrative reveals Jesus' identity as the Messiah (see Mark 8:29). This turning point leads his disciples and us to the Cross.

From the opening of the Gospel, Mark invites us—catechumens and initiation ministers alike—to consider what it means to be baptized into the Death of Jesus. We must not take Baptism lightly, but must recognize the depths of its demands. These demands are nothing less than following Jesus to the Cross. In Baptism, we become disciples of the Cross, disciples of the Death and Resurrection of Jesus, the Son of God, the Messiah who gave his life as a "ransom for the many" (Mark 10:45).

Our suffering and participating in Jesus' Death leads to our glorification, just as the Messiah's suffering and Death led to his (see Mark 8:35; 10:38–39). In Mark, we also learn that ours is a share in the mission of the disciples. Just as Jesus sent his disciples forth for the Gentile mission, so too he sends us who follow him out to become "fishes of men" (1:17). Like Jesus and his dis-

ciples who fed others with five loaves and two fish (6:38) and had twelve baskets of leftovers, the Son of God calls us to feed the hungry—Jewish people and Gentiles alike—all who hunger to participate in Jesus' family as doers of the will of God (see Mark 3:31).

The second feeding narrative in Mark helps to emphasize the centrality of the Lord's Supper, what we know as the Eucharist, for the evangelist's narrative (see Mark 8:1–11). Jesus' mission of feeding and nourishing extends to all—Gentiles, men, women, and children. It is a mission of including everyone in the message of new life in the family of God through Jesus. In this household we eat and are satisfied (see Mark 6:42) and we invite others to do the same.

The two feeding narratives in Mark are overtures to the Last Supper that occurs immediately prior to the Passion and Death of Jesus (see Mark 14:22–26). During the Last Supper, Jesus takes up the one loaf—which we now know includes Jewish people, Gentiles, men, women, and children—and declares it to be his Body. This is the Body that will suffer and die, and which God will restore in the new creation in the Resurrection of his Son, the Messiah. Mark's story of the Good News instructs us that this restoration also avails itself to us through our Baptism and participation in the Eucharist. Jesus joins us to himself as disciples in the new creation of the Resurrection celebrated in the meal of the Eucharist.

Ours is the lifelong journey of discipleship. Each Year B we immerse ourselves in Mark's always relevant and brilliant theological narrative. Baptism unites us to Christ. We celebrate together at the Eucharistic table. We experience new life in Christ and live as part of a new creation united forever with God. Would that our confession year after year mirror Peter's! Would that we accept the commission of the Risen Christ found in the longer ending of Mark, probably penned by someone other than the evangelist, to "Go into the whole world and proclaim the gospel to every creature" (Mark 16:15). For "Whoever believes and is baptized will be saved; whoever does not believe will be condemned" (Mark 16:16). We go forth and preach, trusting the Risen Lord works with us (see Mark 16:21).

The Gospel according to John

"And the Word became flesh and made his dwelling among us" (John 1:14). The Word's glory we beheld. People witnessed to the glory then, as now, for it was the glory of the only Son of the Father. The Gospel according to John comes alive for us as we hear it proclaimed almost fifty times over the course of the three-year Lectionary cycle of readings. During Year B of the Lectionary cycle, we hear a semicontinuous selection of John's Bread of Life Discourse from the Seventeenth through the Twenty-First Sundays in Ordinary Time. The Gospel according to John is also important during the Period of Purification and Enlightenment, as we will hear the Year A Gospel accounts from John on the Third, Fourth, and Fifth Sundays of Lent in connection with the three Scrutinies.

Written between AD 80 and 110 in Ephesus, the Gospel according to John stands as a testimony to the developing Christian community's understanding and lived experience of faith. We know that at the time John's Gospel account was written the community of believers faced internal challenges from other Christians who denied the fullness of Jesus' divinity and external challenges from the Jewish leadership who were expelling from the synagogues those who believed in Jesus. People in the late first century simply wanted to bring the story of Jesus to bear on the life of their community and the world. We have the same desire today—the same mission.

Like the other Gospel accounts, the same person who provides the Gospel's main ideas may, in fact, not be responsible for writing the ideas. The "disciple whom Jesus loved" (John 20:2), the Beloved Disciple, is perhaps the source of the Gospel's ideas and unity. His followers probably composed and edited the written Gospel. The author of John knew the synoptic Gospel accounts. Sayings in John parallel sayings in Mark. Yet even though John had knowledge of the synoptic accounts, the differences between his account and the other three show that John developed independently.

In John, Jesus speaks in lengthy discourses, engages in extensive conversations, and uses symbolic language. Seven signs or miracle stories form the heart of John: (1) the changing of water into wine at Cana, (2) the cure of the royal official's son, (3) the cure of the paralytic at the pool, (4) the multiplication of loaves, (5) walking on water, (6) the healing of the man born blind, and (7) the raising of Lazarus. John derived these miraculous signs from a "Sign Source."

Jesus' lengthy discourses come from a different source, perhaps an earlier account of the Passion coupled together with other traditions about Jesus' post-Resurrection appearances. The well-known Prologue comes from an early hymn into which an editor inserted comments on John the Baptist.

John does not include a narrative of the institution of the Eucharist in his Last Supper account. Rather, as we know from the liturgy on Holy Thursday, John's account of this meal focuses on Jesus' example of service and humility. The evangelist narrates Jesus' actions of washing his disciples' feet and his instructions to the disciples to do the same. Jesus' moving, lengthy discourses find him conversing with his disciples about grief and loss, his departure and return, and the coming of the Advocate (the Spirit). Through his words, Jesus prepares them for how to live and love as his disciples before he comes again in glory.

You will hear people refer to John's account of the Gospel as the *Hellenistic* (Greek) Gospel because of Greek philosophical influences from Platonism, Stoicism, and Gnosticism, especially the contrasts between above/below, spirit/flesh, natural world/eternal world, light/dark, truth/falsehood, and the use of *logos* (word). The Gospel writer used these philosophies to serve his purpose of proclaiming the truth of Jesus, the Son of God who descended from heaven to earth and ascended back from earth to heaven.

The Gospel writer wants to lead people to faith in Jesus (see John 20:30–31). He knows his primarily Christian audience is familiar with prophetic sayings and major themes of the Old Testament. Christians versed in Judaism would hearken back to the divine Word in Genesis when he speaks of the Word becoming flesh. They would know Jewish feasts such as Passover and have familiarity with leadership institutions of Judaism. Yet others do not yet believe in the Son of God, and the Gospel's author deeply desires their conversion to Jesus, who uniquely reveals the Father in his triumph on the Cross to those who believe.

Perhaps in the Gospel writer's call to conversion to those who do not yet believe, you can find similarities with your own faith journey or the journeys of the catechumens with whom you minister. Belief in Jesus brings life and salvation. Belief means acceptance of Jesus. Belief is a gift the Father gives. Belief leads to eternal life.

Those who believe serve together as Jesus' disciples, taking as their model Jesus' own humility and service. Their mission in the world will not be without struggle, even persecution. This is why they must intentionally choose to stay together as a community of believers—the Church. The waters of Baptism, for John, are waters of eternal life born of Jesus' own Death and Resurrection. The Eucharist is the Bread of Life. Jesus feeds us now and eternally. The Sacraments of Baptism and Eucharist form the heart of the Christian community for John.

John used the phrase "the Jews" as a functional device to develop his theme of belief and unbelief. "The Jews" were antagonizing characters to Jesus and set in opposition to those who believed in him. Most often, the term related to Jewish leadership, not the entire Jewish people as a particular ethnic or religious people. In either case, it is necessary to remember the historical context of John's time, when Christians faced expulsion from synagogues, and not in any way to extend this situation to our present context to justify anti-Semitism.

The early Church Father St. Clement of Alexandria called John the "spiritual Gospel." We must, however, not think of John as "spiritual" in the sense of being unconcerned with the world. John's is a Gospel account entirely grounded in the reality of the Incarnation. John's account of the Good News affords us the opportunity to reflect on the questions "Who is Jesus for us?" and "Who are we as his disciples?" in light of our world today—a world longing for the life and food only Jesus can give.

— Mary A. Ehle
With additional contributions by
Charles A. Bobertz, Martin Connell,
and Corinna Laughlin

About the Authors

Leisa Anslinger brings extensive experience in parishes and schools to her ministry as an author, speaker, and consultant. She is the director of Catholic Life and Faith, a center for leadership development to help pastoral leaders engage their people in living faith. She is the author of books, articles, and numerous e-resources for evangelization, catechesis, and stewardship, and is a regular contributor to the International Catholic Stewardship Council's e-newsletter and *Catechetical Leader*, the journal of the National Conference for Catechetical Leadership. Leisa is a frequent presenter at national and diocesan gatherings as well as parish leadership days and parish missions. She holds a bachelor of arts in music education from St. Mary-of-the-Woods College, a master of arts in secondary school counseling

from Purdue University, and a master of arts in religion from Athenaeum of Ohio.

Mary A. Ehle holds a doctorate in religious studies from Marquette University in Milwaukee, Wisconsin, as well as degrees from St. John's University in Collegeville, Minnesota, and St. Norbert College in De Pere, Wisconsin. She is an experienced liturgist, pastoral associate, and director of faith formation. Mary is a contributing author to many LTP resources. She resides in Albuquerque, New Mexico, where she is a member of St. John XXIII Catholic Community.

Biagio Mazza is pastoral associate at St. Sabina's Parish in Belton, Missouri, coordinating and facilitating adult faith formation, including RCIA. For more than seventeen years, Biagio was a staff member of the Center for Pastoral Life and Ministry in the Diocese of Kansas City–St. Joseph, where he facilitated ministry formation for the diocese. A contributor to *The Catholic Bible, Personal Study Edition* published by Oxford University Press, Biagio is also a contributor to *Foundations for Preaching and Teaching and Scripture Backgrounds for the Sunday Lectionary* published by LTP. Biagio has authored a book in the Paulist Press Catechist Guide Series called *A Catechist Guide: How to Teach Scripture*. Biagio Mazza has a master's degree in theology from Fordham University, Bronx, New York, with post graduate work at Maryknoll School of Theology, Maryknoll, New York.

Victoria M. Tufano is senior editor and liturgical consultant at LTP. She served as pastoral associate and director of liturgy at Ascension Catholic Church in Oak Park, Illinois, and as director of liturgy for the Diocese of Des Moines, Iowa. She was a team member of the North American Forum on the Catechumenate and served as a member and chair of the board of directors for that organization. Vicky holds a master of arts degree in liturgical studies and a master of divinity, both from the University of Notre Dame.

Liturgical Calendar

Advent	2018 – Year B	2019 – Year C	2020 – Year A	2021 – Year B	2022 – Year C
First Sunday of Advent	December 3, 2017	December 2, 2018	December 1, 2019	November 29, 2020	November 28, 2021
Solemnity of the Immaculate Conception of the Blessed Virgin Mary	December 8, 2017 (Friday)	December 8, 2018 (Saturday)	December 9, 2019 (transferred to Monday)	December 8, 2020 (Tuesday)	December 8, 2021 (Wednesday)
Second Sunday of Advent	December 10, 2017	December 9, 2018	December 8, 2019	December 6, 2020	December 5, 2021
Third Sunday of Advent	December 17, 2017	December 16, 2018	Decmeber 15, 2019	December 13, 2020	December 12, 2021
Fourth Sunday of Advent	December 24, 2017	December 23, 2018	December 22, 2019	December 20, 2020	December 19, 2021

Christmas Time	2018 – Year B	2019 – Year C	2020 – Year A	2021 – Year B	2022 – Year C
Solemnity of the Nativity of the Lord	December 24/25, 2017 (Sunday/Monday)	December 24/25, 2018 (Monday/Tuesday)	December 24/25, 2019 (Tuesday/Wednesday)	December 24/25, 2020 (Thursday/Friday)	December 24/25, 2021 (Friday/Saturday)
Feast of the Holy Family of Jesus, Mary, and Joseph	December 31, 2017	December 30, 2018	December 29, 2019	December 27, 2020	December 26, 2021
Solemnity of Mary, the Holy Mother of God	January 1, 2018 (Monday)	January 1, 2019 (Tuesday)	January 1, 2020 (Wednesday)	January 1, 2021 (Friday)	1/1/2022 (Saturday)
Solemnity of the Epiphany of the Lord	January 7, 2018	January 6, 2019	January 5, 2020	January 3, 2021	January 2, 2022
Feast of the Baptism of the Lord	January 8, 2018 (Monday)	January 13, 2019	January 12, 2020	January 10, 2021	January 9, 2022

Lent	2018 – Year B	2019 – Year C	2020 – Year A	2021 – Year B	2022 – Year C
First Sunday of Lent	February 18, 2018	March 10, 2019	March 1, 2020	February 21, 2021	March 6, 2022
Second Sunday of Lent	February 25, 2018	March 17, 2019	March 8, 2020	February 28, 2021	March 13, 2022
Third Sunday of Lent	March 4, 2018	March 24, 2019	March 15, 2020	March 7, 2021	March 20, 2022
Fourth Sunday of Lent	March 11, 2018	March 31, 2019	March 22, 2020	March 14, 2021	March 27, 2022
Fifth Sunday of Lent	March 18, 2018	April 7, 2019	March 29, 2020	March 21, 2021	April 3, 2022
Palm Sunday of the Passion of the Lord	March 25, 2018	April 14, 2019	April 5, 2020	March 28, 2021	April 10, 2022

Sacred Paschal Triduum	2018 – Year B	2019 – Year C	2020 – Year A	2021 – Year B	2022 – Year C
Evening Mass of Lord's Supper (Holy Thursday)	March 29, 2018	April 18, 2019	April 9, 2020	April 1, 2021	April 4, 2022
Good Friday of the Passion of the Lord (Good Friday)	March 30, 2018	April 19, 2019	April 10, 2020	April 2, 2021	April 15, 2022
Easter Sunday of the Resurrection of the Lord	April 1, 2018	April 21, 2019	April 12, 2020	April 4, 2021	April 17, 2022

Easter Time	2018 – Year B	2019 – Year C	2020 – Year A	2021 – Year B	2022 – Year C
Second Sunday of Easter / Sunday of Divine Mercy	April 8, 2018	April 28, 2019	April 19, 2020	April 11, 2021	April 24, 2022
Third Sunday of Easter	April 15, 2018	May 5, 2019	April 26, 2020	April 18, 2021	May 1, 2022
Fourth Sunday of Easter	April 22, 2018	May 12, 2019	May 3, 2020	April 25, 2021	May 8, 2022
Fifth Sunday of Easter	April 29, 2018	May 19, 2019	May 10, 2020	May 2, 2021	May 15, 2022
Sixth Sunday of Easter	May 6, 2018	May 26, 2019	May 17, 2020	May 9, 2021	May 22, 2022

2023 – Year A	2024 – Year B	2025 – Year C	2026 – Year A	2027 – Year B	2028 – Year C
November 27 2022	December 3 2023	December 1 2024	November 30 2025	November 29 2026	November 28 2027
December 8, 2022 (Thursday)	December 8, 2023 (Friday)	December 9, 2024 (transferred to Monday)	December 8, 2025 (Monday)	December 8, 2026 (Tuesday)	Decmeber 8, 2027 (Wednesday)
December 4 2022	December 10 2023	December 8 2024	December 7 2025	December 6 2026	December 5 2027
December 11 2022	December 17 2023	December 15 2024	December 14 2025	December 13 2026	December 12 2027
December 18 2022	December 24 2023	December 22 2024	December 21 2025	December 20 2026	December 19 2027

2023 – Year A	2024 – Year B	2025 – Year C	2026 – Year A	2027 – Year B	2028 – Year C
December 24/25, 2022 (Saturday/Sunday)	December 24/25, 2023 (Sunday/Monday)	December 24/25, 2024 (Tuesday/Wednesday)	December 24/25, 2025 (Wednesday/Thursday)	December 24/25, 2026 (Thursday/Friday)	December 24/25, 2027 (Friday/Saturday)
December 30, 2022 (Friday)	December 31, 2023	December 29, 2024	December 28, 2025	December 27, 2026	December 26, 2027
January 1, 2023 (Sunday)	January 1, 2024 (Monday)	January 1, 2025 (Wednesday)	January 1, 2026 (Thursday)	January 1, 2027 (Friday)	January 1, 2028 (Saturday)
January 8, 2023	January 7, 2024	January 5, 2025	January 4, 2026	January 3, 2027	January 2, 2028
January 9, 2023 (Monday)	January 8, 2024 (Monday)	January 12, 2025	January 11, 2026	January 10, 2027	January 9, 2028

2023 – Year A	2024 – Year B	2025 – Year C	2026 – Year A	2027 – Year B	2028 – Year C
February 26, 2023	February 18, 2024	March 9, 2025	February 22, 2026	February 14, 2027	March 5, 2028
March 5, 2023	February 25, 2024	March 16, 2025	March 1, 2026	February 21, 2027	March 12, 2028
March 12, 2023	March 3, 2024	March 23, 2025	March 8, 2026	February 28, 2027	March 19, 2028
March 19, 2023	March 10, 2024	March 30, 2025	March 15, 2026	March 7, 2027	March 26, 2028
March 26, 2023	March 17, 2024	April 6, 2025	March 22, 2026	March 14, 2027	April 2, 2028
April 2, 2023	March 24, 2024	April 13, 2025	March 29, 2026	March 21, 2027	April 9, 2028

2023 – Year A	2024 – Year B	2025 – Year C	2026 – Year A	2027 – Year B	2028 – Year C
April 6, 2023	March 28, 2024	April 15, 2025	April 2, 2026	March 25, 2027	April 13, 2028
April 7, 2023	March 29, 2024	April 18, 2025	April 3 2026	March 26, 2027	April 14, 2028
April 9, 2023	March 31, 2024	April 20, 2025	April 5, 2026	March 28, 2027	April 16, 2028

2023 – Year A	2024 – Year B	2025 – Year C	2026 – Year A	2027 – Year B	2028 – Year C
April 16, 2023	April 7, 2024	April 27, 2025	April 12, 2026	April 4, 2027	April 23, 2028
April 23, 2023	April 14, 2024	May 4, 2025	April 19, 2026	April 11, 2027	April 30, 2028
April 30, 2023	April 21, 2024	May 11, 2025	April 26 2026	April 18, 2027	May 7, 2028
May 7, 2023	April 28, 2024	May 18, 2025	May 3, 2026	April 25, 2027	May 14, 2028
May 14,, 2023	May 5, 2024	May 25, 2025	May 10, 2026	May 2, 2027	May 2,1 2028

Solemnity of the Ascension of the Lord	May 10/13, 2018	May 30 or June 2, 2019	May 21 or 24, 2020	May 13 or 16, 2021	May 26 or 29, 2022
Seventh Sunday of Easter	May 13, 2018	June 2, 2019	May 24, 2020	May 16, 2021	May 29, 2022
Solemnity of Pentecost	May 20, 2018	June 9, 2019	May 31, 2020	May 23, 2021	June 5, 2022

Ordinary Time	2018 – Year B	2019 – Year C	2020 – Year A	2021 – Year B	2022 – Year C
Second Sunday in Ordinary Time	January 14, 2018	January 20, 2019	January 19, 2020	January 17, 2021	January 16, 2022
Third Sunday in Ordinary Time	January 21, 2018	January 27, 2019	January 26, 2020	January 24, 2021	January 23, 2022
Fourth Sunday in Ordinary Time	January 28, 2018	February 3, 2019	OMITTED in 2020 (see Presentation)	January 31, 2021	January 30, 2022
Fifth Sunday in Ordinary Time	February 4, 2018	February 10, 2019	February 9, 2020	February 7, 2021	February 6, 2022
Sixth Sunday in Ordinary Time	February 11, 2018	February 17, 2019	February 16, 2020	February 14, 2021	February 13, 2022
Seventh Sunday in Ordinary Time	OMITTED	February 24, 2019	February 23, 2020	OMITTED	February 20, 2022
Eighth Sunday in Ordinary Time	OMITTED (see Trinity)	March 3 2019	OMITTED	OMITTED	February 27 2022
Ninth Sunday in Ordinary Time	OMITTED (See Most Holy Body and Blood)	OMITTED	OMITTED	OMITTED (see Most Holy Trinity)	OMITTED
Tenth Sunday in Ordinary Time	June 10, 2018	OMITTED	OMITTED (see Most Holy Trinity)	OMITTED (see Most Holy Body and Blood)	OMITTED
Eleventh Sunday in Ordinary Time	June 17, 2018	OMITTED (see Most Holy Trinity)	OMITTED (see Most Holy Body and Blood)	June 13 2021	OMITTED (see Most Holy Trinity)
Twelfth Sunday in Ordinary Time	OMITTED (see Nativity of St. John the Baptist)	OMITTED (see Most Holy Body and Blood)	June 21, 2020	June 20, 2021	OMITTED (see Most Holy Body and Blood)
Thirteenth Sunday in Ordinary Time	July 1, 2018	June 30, 2019	June 28, 2020	June 27, 2021	July 26, 2022
Fourteenth Sunday in Ordinary Time	July 8, 2018	July 7, 2019	July 5, 2020	July 4, 2021	July 3, 2022
Fifteenth Sunday in Ordinary Time	July 15, 2018	July 14, 2019	July 12, 2020	July 11, 2021	July 10, 2022
Sixteenth Sunday in Ordinary Time	July 22, 2018	July 21, 2019	July 19, 2020	July 18, 2021	July 17, 2022
Seventeenth Sunday in Ordinary Time	July 29, 2018	July 28, 2019	July 26, 2020	July 25, 2021	July 24, 2022
Eighteenth Sunday in Ordinary Time	August 5, 2018	August 4, 2016	August 2, 2020	August 1, 2021	July 31, 2022
Nineteenth Sunday in Ordinary Time	August 12, 2018	August 11, 2019	August 9, 2020	August 8, 2021	August 7, 2022
Twentieth Sunday in Ordinary Time	August 19, 2018	August 18, 2019	August 16, 2020	OMITTED (see Assumption)	August 14, 2022
Twenty-First Sunday in Ordinary Time	August 26 ,2018	August 25, 2019	August 23, 2020	August 22, 2021	August 21, 2022
Twenty-Second Sunday in Ordinary Time	September 2, 2018	September 1, 2019	August 30, 2020	August 29, 2021	August 28, 2022
Twenty-Third Sunday in Ordinary Time	September 9, 2018	September 8, 2019	September 6, 2020	September 5, 2021	September 4, 2022

May 18 or 21, 2023	May 9 or 12, 2024	May 29 or June 1, 2025	May 14 or 17, 2026	May 6 or 9, 2027	May 25 or 28, 2028
May 21, 2023	May 12, 2024	June 1, 2025	May 17, 2026	May 9, 2027	May 28, 2028
May 28, 2023	May 19, 2024	June 8, 2025	May 24, 2026	May 16, 2027	June 4, 2028

2023 – Year A	2024 – Year B	2025 – Year C	2026 – Year A	2027 – Year B	2028 – Year C
January 15, 2023	January 14, 2024	January 19, 2025	January 18, 2026	January 17, 2027	January 16, 2028
January 22, 2023	January 21, 2024	January 26, 2025	January 25, 2026	January 24, 2027	January 23, 2028
January 29, 2023	January 28, 2024	OMITTED (see Presentation)	February 1, 2026	January 31, 2027	January 30, 2028
February 5, 2023	February 4, 2024	February 9, 2025	February 8, 2026	February 7, 2027	February 6, 2028
February 12, 2023	February 11, 2024	February 16, 2025	February 15, 2026	OMITTED	February 13, 2028
February 19, 2023	OMITTED	February 23, 2025	OMITTED	OMITTED	February 20, 2028
OMITTED	OMITTED (see Most Holy Trinity)	March 2, 2025	OMITTED	OMITTED (see Most Holy Trinity)	February 27 2028
OMITTED (see Most Holy Trinity)	OMITTED (see Most Holy Body and Blood)	OMITTED	OMITTED (see Most Holy Trinity)	OMITTED (see Most Holy Body and Blood)	OMITTED
OMITTED (see Most Holy Body and Blood)	June 9, 2024	OMITTED	OMITTED (see Most Holy Body and Blood)	June 6, 2027	OMITTED (see Most Holy Trinity)
June 18, 2023	June 16, 2024	OMITTED (see Most Holy Trinity)	June 14, 2026	June 13, 2027	OMITTED (see Most Holy Body and Blood)
June 25, 2023	June 23, 2024	OMITTED (see Most Holy Body and Blood)	June 21, 2026	June 20, 2027	June 25, 2028
July 2 ,2023	June 30, 2024	OMITTED (see Sts. Peter and Paul)	June 28, 2026	June 27, 2027	July 2, 2028
July 9, 2023	July 7, 2024	July 6, 2025	July 5, 2026	July 4, 2027	July 9, 2028
July 16, 2023	July 14, 2024	July 13, 2025	July 12, 2026	July 11, 2027	July 16, 2028
July 23, 2023	July 21, 2024	July 20, 2025	July 19, 2026	July 18, 2027	July 23, 2028
July 30, 2023	July 28, 2024	July 27, 2025	July 26, 2026	July 25, 2027	July 30, 2028
OMITTED (see Transfiguration)	August 4, 2024	August 3, 2025	August 2, 2026	August 1, 2027	OMITTED (see Transfiguration)
August 13, 2023	August 11, 2024	August 10, 2025	August 9, 2026	August 8, 2027	August 13, 2028
August 20, 2023	August 18, 2024	August 17, 2025	August 16, 2026	OMITTED (see Assumption)	August 20, 2028
August 27, 2023	August 25, 2024	August 24, 2025	August 23, 2026	August 22, 2027	August 27, 2028
September 3, 2023	September 1, 2024	August 31, 2025	August 30, 2026	August 29, 2027	September 3, 2028
September 10, 2023	September 8, 2024	September 17, 2025	September 6, 2026	September 5, 2027	September 10, 2028

Ordinary Time *cont.*	2018 – Year B	2019 – Year C	2020 – Year A	2021 – Year B	2022 – Year C
Twenty-Fourth Sunday in Ordinary Time	September 16, 2018	September 15, 2019	September 13, 2020	September 12, 2021	September 11, 2022
Twenty-Fifth Sunday in Ordinary Time	September 23, 2018	September 22, 2019	September 20, 2020	September 19, 2021	September 18, 2022
Twenty-Sixth Sunday in Ordinary Time	September 30, 2018	September 29, 2019	September 27, 2020	September 26, 2021	September 25, 2022
Twenty-Seventh Sunday in Ordinary Time	October 7, 2018	October 6, 2019	October 4, 2020	October 3, 2021	October 2, 2022
Twenty-Eighth Sunday in Ordinary Time	October 14, 2018	October 13, 2019	October 11, 2020	October 10, 2021	October 9, 2022
Twenty-Ninth Sunday in Ordinary Time	October 21, 2018	October 20, 2019	October 18, 2020	October 17, 2021	October 16, 2022
Thirtieth Sunday in Ordinary Time	October 28, 2018	October 27, 2019	October 25, 2020	October 24, 2021	October 23, 2022
Thirty-First Sunday in Ordinary Time	November 4, 2018	November 3, 2019	OMITTED (see All Saints)	October 31, 2021	October 30, 2022
Thirty-Second Sunday in Ordinary Time	November 11, 2018	November 10, 2019	November 8, 2020	November 7, 2021	November 6, 2022
Thirty-Third Sunday in Ordinary Time	November 18, 2018	November 17, 2019	November 15, 2020	November 14, 2021	November 13, 2022
Solemnity of Our Lord Jesus Christ, King of the Universe/ Thirty-Fourth or Last Sunday in Ordinary Time	November 25, 2018	November 24, 2019	November 22, 2020	November 21, 2021	November 20, 2022

Solemnities/Feasts of the Lord/Saints	2018 – Year B	2019 – Year C	2020 – Year A	2021 – Year B	2022 – Year C
Solemnity of the Most Holy Trinity	May 27, 2018	June 16, 2019	June 7, 2020	May 30, 2021	June 12, 2022
Solemnity of the Most Holy Body and Blood of Christ (Corpus Christi)	June 3, 2018	June 23, 2019	June 14, 2020	June 6, 2021	June 19, 2022
Feast of the Presentation of the Lord	February 2, 2018 (Friday)	February 2, 2019 (Saturday)	February 2, 2020 (Sunday)	February 2, 2021 (Tuesday)	February 2, 2022 (Wednesday)
Solemnity of the Nativity of St. John the Baptist	June 24, 2018 (Sunday)	June 24, 2019 (Monday)	June 24, 2020 (Wednesday)	June 24, 2021 (Thursday)	June 24, 2022 (Friday)
Solemnity of Sts. Peter and Paul, Apostles	June 29, 2018 (Friday)	June 29, 2019 (Saturday)	June 29, 2020 (Monday)	June 29, 2021 (Tuesday)	June 29, 2022 (Wednesday)
Solemnity of the Assumption of the Blessed Virgin Mary	August 15, 2018 (Wednesday)	August 15, 2019 (Thursday)	August 15, 2020 (Saturday)	August 15, 2021 (Sunday)	August 15, 2022 (Monday)
Feast of the Exaltation of the Holy Cross	September 14, 2018 (Friday)	September 14, 2019 (Saturday)	September 14, 2020 (Monday)	September 14, 2021 (Tuesday)	September 14, 2022 (Wednesday)
Solemnity of All Saints	November 1, 2018 (Thursday)	November 1, 2019 (Friday)	November 1, 2020 (Sunday)	November 1, 2021 (Monday)	November 1, 2022 (Tuesday)
Commemoration of All the Faithful Departed (All Souls' Day)	November 2, 2018 (Friday)	November 2, 2019 (Saturday)	November 2, 2020 (Monday)	November 2, 2021 (Tuesday)	November 2, 2022 (Wednesday)
Feast of the Dedication of the Lateran Basilica	November 9, 2018 (Friday)	November 9, 2019 (Saturday)	November 9, 2020 (Monday)	November 9, 2021 (Tuesday)	November 9, 2022 (Wednesday)

2023 – Year A	2024 – Year B	2025 – Year C	2026 – Year A	2027 – Year B	2028 – Year C
September 17, 2023	September 15, 2024	OMITTED (see Exaltation of the Holy Cross)	September 13, 2026	September 12, 2027	September 17, 2028
September 24, 2023	September 22, 2024	September 21, 2025	September 20, 2026	September 19, 2027	September 24, 2028
October 1, 2023	September 29, 2024	September 28, 2025	September 27, 2026	September 26, 2027	October 1, 2028
October 8, 2023	October 6, 2024	October 5, 2025	October 4, 2026	October 3, 2027	October 8, 2028
October 15, 2023	October 13, 2024	October 12, 2025	October 11, 2026	October 10, 2027	October 15, 2028
October 22, 2023	October 20, 2024	October 19, 2025	October 18, 2026	October 17, 2027	October 22, 2028
October 29, 2023	October 27, 2024	October 26, 2025	October 25, 2026	October 24, 2027	October 29, 2028
November 5, 2023	November 3, 2024	OMITTED (see All Souls' Day)	OMITTED (see All Saints)	October 31, 2027	November 5, 2028
November 12, 2023	November 10, 2024	OMITTED (see Lateran Basilica)	November 8, 2026	November 7, 2027	November 12, 2028
November 19, 2023	November 17, 2024	November 16 2025	November 15, 2026	November 14, 2027	November 19, 2028
November 26, 2023	November 24, 2024	November 23, 2025	November 22, 2026	November 21, 2027	November 26, 2028

2023 – Year A	2024 – Year B	2025 – Year C	2026 – Year A	2027 – Year B	2028 – Year C
June 4, 2023	May 26, 2024	June 15, 2025	May 31, 2026	May 23, 2027	June 11, 2028
June 11, 2023	June 2, 2024	June 22, 2025	June 7, 2026	May 30, 2027	June 18, 2028
February 2, 2023 (Thursday)	February 2, 2024 (Friday)	February 2, 2025 (Sunday)	February 2, 2026 (Monday)	February 2, 2027 (Tuesday)	February 2, 2028 (Wednesday)
June 24, 2023 (Saturday)	June 24, 2024 (Monday)	June 24, 2025 (Tuesday)	June 24, 2026 (Wednesday)	June 24, 2027 (Thursday)	June 24, 2028 (Saturday)
June 29, 2023 (Thursday)	June 29, 2024 (Saturday)	June 29, 2025 (Sunday)	June 29, 2026 (Monday)	June 29, 2027 (Tuesday)	June 29, 2028 (Thursday)
August 15, 2023 (Tuesday)	August 15, 2024 (Thursday)	August 15, 2025 (Fridsay)	August 15, 2026 (Saturday)	August 15, 2027 (Sunday)	August 15, 2028 (Tuesday)
September 14, 2023 (Thursday)	September 14, 2024 (Saturday)	September 14, 2025 (Sunday)	September 14, 2026 (Monday)	September 14, 2027 (Tuesday)	September 14, 2028 (Thursday)
November 1, 2023 (Wednesday)	November 1, 2024 (Friday)	November 1, 2025 (Saturday)	November 1, 2026 (Sunday)	November 1, 2027 (Monday)	November 1, 2028 (Wednesday)
November 2, 2023 (Thursday)	November 2, 2024 (Saturday)	November 2, 2025 (Sunday)	November 2, 2026 (Monday)	November 2, 2027 (Tuesday)	November 2, 2028 (Thursday)
November 9, 2023 (Thursday)	November 9, 2024 (Saturday)	November 9, 2025 (Sunday)	November 9, 2026 (Monday)	November 9, 2027 (Tuesday)	November 9, 2028 (Thursday)

INTRODUCTION TO ADVENT

Overview of Advent

Prepare. Wait. Watch. While brief in duration, Advent is a season that is rich in potential for spiritual attentiveness and growth. The two-fold emphasis of preparing for the coming of Christ at the end of time and his birth at Christmas provides much upon which to reflect. Throughout Advent, we are struck with the recognition that Christ has come, is with us now, and will come again. For many, thinking about what happens at the end of our lives or at the end of time prompts discomfort, perhaps even anxiousness. This is understandable, and is precisely why the beginning of Advent is so important—an annual spiritual checkup, through which we become more attentive to God's presence with us now as we anticipate the fullness of life with God for eternity. This reflection on our readiness for the end of time leads to the later focus of preparation for Christmas, through which we take to heart the depths of God's love for us in Jesus Christ.

Keeping Advent is often a challenge, knowing that the surrounding culture bombards us with the sights, sounds, and activities of what many experience as the "Christmas season." The rhythm of the liturgical seasons may be unfamiliar to some of the catechumens. They and all who journey with them will benefit from intentional immersion in the prayerful preparation of Advent. The Sunday liturgy, time during dismissal and catechetical sessions, and daily prayer at home focus our minds and hearts on the things that last, the great gift of faith, and the hope that is found in Jesus Christ.

Preparing a Seasonal Environment

Consider making your Advent environment simple, in keeping with the simple nature of the season. Incorporate the seasonal violet (and rose) through the use of fabric. Include an Advent wreath and make lighting the candles of the wreath part of your session, or have a single candle with a few sprigs of evergreen in your space. Set an Advent mood by dimming the lighting so that the focus is on the Advent wreath. Keep a space available for the Lectionary (or a Bible) such as a lectern or table. Keep a candle near the Lectionary (or Bible) and light this candle before the session begins.

Be sure to hold off putting any Christmas decorations in your space until the late afternoon or early evening of December 24. The space where you gather may be the only opportunity catechumens have to get away from the commercial merrymaking in order to enter into the spirit of Advent. Make every effort to make this a prayerful, quiet, and expectant place. Slow down the pace of your gathering in order to give catechumens time to reflect. If catechumens question the contrast between the Advent environment and the commercial Christmas encountered each day, ask: What value does Advent hold in your life?

In everything you do to create the environment for Advent in the dismissal space, take your lead from the environment in the sanctuary of the main assembly. Consistency between what the catechumens see in the environment in that space and in the environment in the dismissal space is important. You do not want to create divergent messages about the day and season and thus generate unnecessary questions or confusion within the group. Keep the environment simple but not simplistic, understated but not minimized. Colors, light, images, and other added elements should all assist the catechumens in their reflection on the significance of the day and the Word of God.

Overview of the Readings

The readings during Advent set before us the call to watch, wait, and be prepared for the advent of the Lord at Christ's Second Coming and for the celebration of the birth of Christ Jesus at Christmas. The readings reflect this two-fold focus of the season, with the early weeks much more somber in tone, turning to joyful anticipation in Gaudete Sunday and the Fourth Sunday of Advent.

First Readings   During the first three weeks of Advent, the First Reading in Year B is from the book of the prophet Isaiah. These passages take place from the time of exile and of the people's return. They invite us to place our hope and trust in God. Isaiah reminds the people that God has been with them in the difficulties of the past and will be with them in the unknown future. God is always ready to renew the covenant, and is always faithful, bringing light in darkness, comfort to those who are burdened, and healing, liberty, and vindication. These readings from Isaiah are particularly appropriate during Advent, as we wait in hope for the Second Coming of Christ and anticipate the celebration of the birth of Jesus at Christmas. Christians see the depictions of God's love, mercy, forgiveness, and consolation come to life in Jesus.

On the Fourth Sunday of Advent, we hear from the second book of Samuel. King David wants to build a house for God. Through the prophet Nathan, David is told that God will set the time for the establishment of the Kingdom of God. This reading prepares us for the Nativity narratives in which we are reminded that Jesus is born into the house of David, the ultimate and perfect fulfillment of God's promise.

Responsorial Psalms   While the Responsorial Psalm always flows from the First Reading and toward the Gospel, the psalms selected for the Sundays of Advent also echo the primary themes of the season: salvation, justice, mercy, covenant, God's goodness. It is important to note that in the third Sunday in Year B, Mary's song of praise, the Magnificat, from the Gospel according Luke, is proclaimed in lieu of a psalm. We rejoice at the greatness of the Lord with Mary, whose fiat models the faithful living to which we are called.

Second Readings   Unlike the Second Readings during Ordinary Time, which often offer a continuous reading from one book or letter over a period of time, the passages during Advent have been selected in relationship to the First Reading and Gospel for the day. In Year B, the readings are taken from 1 Corinthians, 2 Peter, 1 Thessalonians, and Romans. Each instructs us to hold fast to faith in God who is always faithful, to live according to that faith, and to rejoice in the great gift of salvation, which is offered to us through Jesus Christ.

Gospel Readings   We begin Advent with the beginning of the Gospel according to Mark, in which Jesus tells us to be watchful and alert. We do not know when the Lord will return. In weeks two and three of the season, we meet John the Baptist, who calls us to prepare our hearts for the coming of Christ through humble repentance. On the second Sunday of the season, we read from the Gospel according to Mark, and on the third Sunday, from the beginning of the Gospel according John. The progression of these Gospel readings seemingly reverses our understanding of chronological order. We begin with a focus on Christ's coming at the end of time. After that, we have two presentations of John the Baptist's witness to Jesus, the one who will come after him. Finally, we hear the narrative of the Annunciation in which Mary speaks the words that summarize her life: "May it be done to me according to your word" (Luke 1:38). Mary's encounter with the angel Gabriel readies us for the celebration of the Nativity. From beginning to end, the message is clear: the Christ who came will return, and his Kingdom will have no end.

First Sunday of Advent

Focus: Be alert! The Messiah is coming.

Lectionary #2B

Catechist's Preparation

Overview of the Sunday

During the season of Advent, we wait for the "advent," or "coming," of the Lord. In the early days of the season, our focus is on the coming of Christ at the end of time. Today's readings invite us to be alert to God's saving presence in our midst now and to the ways in which we are called to live as God's people. In your preparation for this dismissal session, think about the catechumens you lead. How are they already showing signs of putting their lives in God's hands, growing in faith, and trusting in the Lord? Keep these things in mind as you lead the catechumens to reflect on the ways their growing faith is directing the way they live.

Scripture Background

Isaiah 63:16b–17, 19b; 64:2–7 The prophet Isaiah was writing to the Israelites at a time of national disaster, as they returned to rebuild their community after long years of exile in Babylon. Isaiah admonished them to remember that God had saved them in the past and would do so again. In return, they must be faithful, crying out to God to lead them to salvation. By confessing their guilt and putting themselves into God's hands, they will know God's presence among them again. As God's people, they must lead lives that are faithful and holy as they fulfill their part of the covenant with God.

The concluding verses are a well-known image: "we are the clay and you our potter: / we are all the work of your hand" (64:7). By remembering the covenant and entrusting their lives to God's hands, the people of Israel would know the joy of redemption. This Advent, we, too, can place our lives in God's hands and invite him to shape us into faithful followers.

Psalm 80:2–3, 15–16, 18–19 (4) The refrain of this Sunday's psalm, "Lord, make us turn to you; let us see your face and we shall be saved" (80:4) calls upon God to make us do two things: return to him and be faithful, and turn our lives around in order to improve our situation. We hear in the psalm how this will happen. We ask God to show compassion to us, be kind to us, protect us, and save us.

Psalm 80 is a prayer of a nation that has been beset by calamity and disaster. Yet, the image in the first stanza of God as the guiding shepherd reminds us that we are not abandoned, but saved. God has saved his people in the past and he will do so again. It remains for us to offer our faithful response by turning toward the God who saves us.

1 Corinthians 1:3–9 Paul assures us of God's faithful initiative and action. Paul's words, written around 54 AD from Ephesus to the community of believers at Corinth, are assuring to us, too, as we await God's revelation in our lives this Advent. Paul's letters to the Corinthians are characterized by their explanations of how the members of a community of brothers and sisters are to treat one another. A community that acts with love for others is a reflection and a sign to the world of God's love. Such a community is a true witness to Jesus Christ, who gave his very life for all and who showed us the kind of love we are to offer one another through his suffering, Death, and Resurrection. As communities, we are called to remind ourselves at Advent to pay attention to how we act in the world; in essence, to be alert every moment for God's reign of peace and justice in order to fulfill Paul's prodding to love. When we do this, we are signs of God's love to the world.

Mark 13:33–37 This passage sounds like the last judgment and end of the world, and indeed it is sometimes referred to as "the little apocalypse." No one knows when the Messiah will come; therefore, Jesus is clear in his warnings to disciples to watch, stay awake, and be alert. These are Jesus' last words to his disciples before the beginning of his Passion.

There are many times in our lives when we are alert and watchful, such as when we are cooking something that can burn easily, patrolling on guard duty, hovering over a sick child, or trying to drive and follow directions. We know what it feels like to stay alert because if we don't, we may miss a crucial moment. Jesus does not want disciples to miss the opportunity; he does not want distractions to get in the way of our seeing the presence of God in our midst. Seeing God and knowing that he is present despite perils or hardships gives us hope that God's saving power can be found clearly among his people. We read this passage with anticipation, reminding ourselves that once again we remember that the Messiah comes to save. As we proclaim in the refrain of today's psalm, our response is to turn our face to God and be saved.

Reflection Questions for the Catechist

⑨ How have you placed yourself as clay in the hands of the potter (God)?

⑨ In what ways do you perceive the grace of God, alive and active, in your life?

⑨ What difference does watchful waiting make in your daily actions and interactions with others?

Catechist's Guide

Objectives

▷ To take to heart God's steadfast love for humanity.

▷ Recognizing that we are created to freely accept or reject God's love, participants will reflect on what it means to be faithful to God, through all circumstances.

▷ To grasp the meaning of Jesus' call to be watchful and alert.

Dismissal and Procession

Following the homily, the priest celebrant picks up the Lectionary and invites the catechumens to come forward with the catechist(s) who will lead today's dismissal session. Holding the Lectionary so that all can see, the priest celebrant sends the catechumens and catechist(s) forward using RCIA, 67, his own words, or the following:

PRIEST: **My dear friends, this community now sends you forth that you may continue to reflect on the Living Word of God, which has been proclaimed in our midst. With you, we watch and wait for the coming of the Lord. May he come quickly and not delay! Go now in the peace of Christ!**

All process to where the dismissal session will take place. The catechist holds the Lectionary in a reverent manner. The assembly may sing an acclamation to accompany the procession.

Centering

Upon reaching the place where the dismissal occurs, place the Lectionary on the ambo, lectern, or other dignified place (or hold the book reverently). Light the candle that is in the place of gathering and reread Isaiah 63:16b–17, 19b; 64: 2–7 in order to refocus the group's attention. Consider singing the Responsorial Psalm or have a recording of it available to use as part of the centering, either before or after the reading.

Reflection and Discussion

The following "script" may be used or adapted to help facilitate discussion on today's readings. Begin the discussion by asking the catechumens if any words or phrases from today's readings spoke to them.

God always loves us. In God's wisdom, we are created with the freedom to respond to God's love or to walk away from it. This freedom is a sign of God's love, which does not coerce or demand, but rather invites the response of open minds and hearts, through which faith grows and is lived. In the passage from Isaiah, which we heard today, the writer offers an extended prayer to God, in which his steadfast love is acknowledged.

⑨ What difference does it make in your life to know that God always loves you? What experience comes to mind in which you were made aware of God's constant love for you?

⑨ Is there a moment that stands out, in which you were filled with awe at the wonder of God's faithfulness?

We do not always respond to God's love, however. Sometimes, we overtly fail to live as we should, or we become complacent in our commitment to live and grow in faith. Yet no matter how often we fail, God remains with us, ready for our return.

🌀 What is the greatest temptation you face at this time?

🌀 Who supports you when you need encouragement to live in faith?

In moments of temptation, we must increase our commitment to place ourselves in God's hands. The writer of Isaiah gives us a powerful image of this: we are like clay in the hands of the potter. As the potter works with clay, it becomes malleable, allowing the potter to work with it, to shape it over time, into the form that the potter desires. The clay does not offer resistance, and, once formed, is known as the work of the potter.

🌀 How are you growing in trust of God?

🌀 What daily or weekly actions help you to put your life and self in God's hands?

Jesus tells us we must be watchful and alert. Most of us have moments in which we go about our daily lives blind to the many signs of God's loving presence with and for us. We lose concentration. We may fall back on earlier patterns of living that are not directed by our faith. Perhaps a situation occurs and we make a decision in haste or fail to recognize an opportunity to respond as a Christian. The psalm for today echoes the reading from Isaiah and points toward this Gospel passage. In the psalm, we sing together, "Lord, make us turn to you; let us see your face and we shall be saved."

🌀 What recent experience comes to mind, in which you reacted in a manner that was not in keeping with your faith in Jesus Christ?

🌀 What recent experience comes to mind in which you turned toward God and responded in a manner that reflected God's love?

We do not know when our final hour of life will be. We do not know when Christ will return at the end of time. Living with such awareness is not intended to frighten us, but rather to focus our attention, to wake us up. We know that salvation is ours in Christ Jesus. The salvation offered to us in Christ is a great gift. Our response to this gift is to grow in holiness, as God's good and faithful people. Advent is a time of waiting watchfulness.

🌀 How will you be watchful and alert to God's love and Christ's call to discipleship during this season?

Wrapping It Up

Consider these points to conclude the dismissal. Integrate the thoughts and ideas that surfaced during the discussion.

- God is always with us, offering salvation and the grace to respond to God's love. We may freely choose to do so, or to turn away from God.

- When we place our lives in God's hands, as the clay in the hands of the potter, we allow God to direct our daily decisions, growing and living as faithful people.

- Advent is a time of waiting and watchfulness. In this season, we wait for Christ's return in glory and for the celebration of the Incarnation at Christmas.

Closing Prayer

Conclude with prayer. If time permits, sing the psalm refrain a few times before or after the following prayer.

> O Lord, you are our Father,
> we are the clay and you the potter.
> We are all the work of your hands.
> Turn our face to you in this season of watchfulness.
> Direct our lives so that we will be ready,
> as servants who remain awake,
> watching for their Master's return.
> May we be awake to your presence within and among us.
> Make us attentive to the opportunities we have to live as your people,
> acting with love as people who have been shaped by your great love.
> Through Christ our Lord.
> Amen.

Closing Prayer

Provide catechumens with a list of the readings for the next dismissal session. Consult the liturgical calendar on page xvi to find out what day will be observed next week. Give catechumens the questions below to guide their reflection through the week.

⑥ What connections are you seeing in the readings of this liturgical season? As you pray with the readings, around what themes do your thoughts seem to be coming together?

⑥ Where do the readings intersect with your journey of faith? What questions do they raise for you?

Extended Catechesis

Based on today's readings and liturgical observance, the following topics may be covered for extended catechesis:

❋ God's covenant love

❋ Free will

❋ Christ's return in glory

❋ Advent as a season that immerses us in the here-and-not-yet of the reign of God

Second Sunday of Advent

Focus: To humble ourselves before the truth.

Lectionary #5B

Catechist's Preparation

Overview of the Sunday

We do not celebrate Advent as though we do not know the Good News of the Gospel. One of the richest dynamics of our liturgical prayer and the liturgical year is that every celebration acknowledges the Paschal Mystery of Christ's birth, ministry, Passion, Death, and Resurrection. So while we anticipate the Second Coming of Christ in glory and the celebration of his birth in Bethlehem, we also prepare our hearts for a deeper relationship with Christ in our lives in this time, in this place. With John the Baptist, we come to the Lord in humility, ready to encounter the truth of God's love for us in Jesus Christ.

Scripture Background

Isaiah 40:1–5, 9–11 God brings comfort to those who have toiled in work and felt burdened by sin. Nothing will stop the advent of this mighty God. No rugged pathway, no plunging valley, no insurmountable height will keep God from coming to a beloved people who prepare the earth—and themselves—to meet him. The same passage portrays God as a loving shepherd who feeds the hungry flock and scoops into his arms those who crave a gentle sign of his love.

The tenderness and unmitigated joy of this prophecy shows why Advent is beloved by many Christians. As the calendar year draws to its close and the pressures of the holidays are heaped upon the usual burdens and demands of life, the faithful hear prodigious words of consolation. God knows of their struggles and rushes to lift their burdens.

Psalm 85:9–10, 11–12, 13–14 (8) God comes into the world with a message of justice and peace. The particular verses of Psalm 85 chosen for today provoke the same emotional release offered in the First Reading. Kindness, truth, justice, and peace are all meeting as the Lord who created the world renews the many benefits he provides it.

The refrain this week uses the word *salvation*— another key word for Advent. Because the name Jesus means "Savior," when the refrain has the community sing, "grant us your salvation," it is praying for the coming of Christ.

The meeting of heaven and earth in verse 12—"Truth shall spring out of the earth, / and justice shall look down from heaven"—serves as a prophecy for the Incarnation of Jesus Christ, the Word of God, who will take flesh to advance the salvation of the faithful.

2 Peter 3:8–14 In contrast to the messages of comfort emanating from the First Reading and the psalm, the Second Letter of Peter carries a more disturbing message: the day of the Lord is coming like a thief. The heavens will pass away with a mighty roar and elements will be dissolved in fire. To drive home this harrowing message, the writer asks, "What sort of persons ought you to be?" (2 Peter 3:11).

This passage explores the moral implications of the anticipated return of Christ. Echoing Jesus' own admonition in last Sunday's Gospel, this reading aims to put the reader on notice. Advent serves as a kind of alarm clock for the faithful. It disturbs the restful sleep of a complacent people.

Mark 1:1–8 John the Baptist makes his Advent entrance in the proclamation of today's Gospel. St. Mark quotes the prophecy of Isaiah that served as today's First Reading. It was not just any voice encouraging people to prepare the way for the Lord. That voice was fulfilled on the lips of John.

John proclaims "a baptism of repentance for the forgiveness of sins" (1:4). He is asking people to make themselves ready for the appearance of Jesus. If they wish to hear his message and follow after him, it will take some preparation on their part.

John's clothing and diet also place him in the ambit of prophets. He bridges the Old and New Testaments—the last of the great prophets, appearing a step ahead of the sacred feet of Jesus.

As the First Sunday of Advent prepares the faithful for the Second Coming of the glorified Christ, the Second Sunday recalls how John prepared people for the first coming of the adult Christ. This basic theme will recur next week. The Gospel for the Fourth Sunday of Advent tells of the events leading up to the birth of the infant Christ. The message this week helps us see how people in Jesus' own day prepared for his coming. The readings encourage us to reform our lives while maintaining the joyful expectation that Christ will bring the salvation for which we long. Whatever our struggles, his coming brings peace.

Reflection Questions for the Catechist	🌀 In what ways do you need the comfort and tender care of God in your life at this time?
	🌀 What personal valley, mountain, or rugged country needs to be touched by the truth of God's love?
	🌀 How are you preparing your heart and life for a deep encounter with Christ?

Catechist's Guide

Objectives

▷ To reflect on humility as a necessary virtue in the spiritual life.

▷ With a humble heart and willing spirit, participants will examine the obstacles (self-created or through life circumstance) to growing acceptance of the truth of the Gospel.

▷ Catechumens will acknowledge the areas of their lives in which God's tender love and comfort are needed.

Dismissal and Procession

Following the homily, the priest celebrant picks up the Lectionary and invites the catechumens to come forward with the catechist(s) who will lead today's dismissal session. Holding the Lectionary so that all can see, the priest celebrant sends the catechumens and catechist(s) forward using RCIA, 67, his own words, or the following:

PRIEST: John the Baptist yearned for the coming of God's Kingdom and made himself ready for it by repentance. During this time of Advent waiting, you are called to journey with the Lord and to give him room to fill your heart with joy. Listen to God's Word this day in confidence and hope; make straight the path for the Lord's coming, and know that this faith community accompanies you in joy. Go in peace.

All process to where the dismissal session will take place. The catechist holds the Lectionary in a reverent manner. The assembly may sing an acclamation to accompany the procession.

Centering

Upon reaching the place where the dismissal occurs, place the Lectionary on the ambo, lectern, or other dignified place (or hold the book reverently). Light the candle that is in the place of gathering and reread Mark 1:1–8 in order to refocus the group's attention. Consider singing the Responsorial Psalm or have a recording of it available to use as part of the centering, either before or after the reading.

Reflection and Discussion

The following "script" may be used or adapted to help facilitate discussion on today's readings. Begin the discussion by asking the catechumens if any words or phrases from today's readings spoke to them.

Today is the Second Sunday of Advent. We continue our watchful waiting in anticipation of Christ's return in glory and the celebration of Christmas.

🌀 In what ways are you celebrating Advent each day?

🌀 Do you have an Advent wreath or calendar at home?

🌀 Are you using a devotional book, the daily readings, or an Advent reflection to guide your prayer?

🌀 How might you describe your experience of Advent thus far?

🌀 Is your spiritual preparation in sync with the practical preparation for Christmas (gift-giving, social gatherings, and so on), or do these sometimes seem at odds?

🌀 If your spiritual preparation seems to be getting lost in the practical preparations for Christmas, what helps you to get back on track?

During Advent, we hear from the prophet Isaiah. Isaiah spoke to the generations of people who longed for the coming of the Messiah. His message speaks to us, too, as we prepare our hearts for a deeper encounter with the Lord. Today's First Reading speaks of finding comfort and tender care in the arms of God. Accepting such comfort calls us to humbly acknowledge that we are in need of God's tenderness, which surpasses our understanding.

- How do you experience God's tenderness and comfort?
- In what ways does this comfort in God's love shape your faith?
- How does such consolation shape the way in which you interact with others?

God loves us in every circumstance, including the times in which we face obstacles in our spiritual lives. In Isaiah we hear: "A voice cries out: / In the desert prepare the way of the LORD! / Make straight in the wasteland a highway for our God! / Every valley shall be filled in, / every mountain and hill shall be made low; / the rugged land shall be made a plain, / the rough country, a broad valley. / Then the glory of the LORD shall be revealed, / and all people shall see it together; / for the mouth of the LORD has spoken" (Isaiah 40:3–5).

- What in your life feels like a desert, a wasteland, a valley, mountain, or rugged land at this time?
- How does the consoling comfort of God's presence bring hope to these situations?
- Is the obstacle of your own making, or is it the result of circumstances that are beyond your control?
- Knowing that God is with you, do you feel called to a particular action or change in the midst of these obstacles?

In today's Second Reading, St. Peter invites us to take the long view in our spiritual lives: "with the Lord one day is like a thousand years and a thousand years like one day" (2 Peter 3:8). We are reminded again to be watchful, to remember that we do not know when the Lord will return in glory. St. Peter's question is appropriate for us, as it was for those to whom he wrote in the first century: "What sort of persons ought you to be, conducting yourselves in holiness and devotion, waiting for and hastening the coming of the day of God?" (2 Peter 3:11).

- In what ways is this perspective reassuring?
- What is the challenge of waiting in trust, knowing that God's time is not our time?

In today's Gospel, John the Baptist calls people to prepare their hearts and lives for the arrival of the Messiah through repentance. He clearly understands that his ministry is to point people to Christ. He does not confuse himself as the messenger with the one whom he prepares people to encounter. His message is one of humility in the face of the truth, which he knows Christ is and will bring to the world.

- In what aspect of your life do you need to exercise greater humility?
- How are you growing in humble faith, acknowledging your need for salvation?

Wrapping It Up

Consider these points to conclude the dismissal. Integrate the thoughts and ideas that surfaced during the discussion.

- Preparing the way of the Lord requires us to open our hearts in humble faith.
- Isaiah and John witness to the truth of God's love and offer of salvation; our acceptance of this truth requires an open, humble heart and spirit.
- Humility in prayer is a requisite for healthy spiritual growth.

Closing Prayer

Conclude with prayer. If time permits, sing the psalm refrain a few times before or after the following prayer.

> Merciful God,
> you offer tender comfort in our time of need,
> strength as we face obstacles and challenges in our lives and faith,
> and the assurance of your love.
> Open our hearts in true humility,
> so that we will recognize our need for your salvation.
> Prepare our minds, hearts, and lives
> for the truth of your way of love, justice, and peace
> in this Advent time and throughout our lives.
> Through Christ our Lord.
> Amen.

Readings for the Next Dismissal

Provide catechumens with a list of the readings for the next dismissal session. Consult the liturgical calendar on page xvi to find out what day will be observed next week. Give catechumens the questions below to guide their reflection through the week.

- What connections are you seeing in the readings of this liturgical season? As you pray with the readings, around what themes do your thoughts seem to be coming together?
- Where do the readings intersect with your journey of faith? What questions do they raise for you?

Extended Catechesis

Based on today's readings and liturgical observance, the following topics may be covered for extended catechesis:

- The call to holiness
- Repentance offered in Baptism
- Ongoing conversion in and conformity to Christ
- Acceptance of the deposit of faith and formation of conscience in moral decision making

THIRD SUNDAY OF ADVENT

Focus: To rejoice at the presence of the Spirit of the Lord.

Lectionary #8B

Catechist's Preparation

Overview of the Sunday

Rejoice! The Third Sunday of Advent is traditionally known as *Gaudete*, or "Rejoice," Sunday. *Gaudete* is the first word of the Mass if said in Latin (Entrance Antiphon/Introit), which is how today received its name. We rejoice in knowing that Christ has come and will return; we rejoice in knowing Christ's offer of salvation for all; we rejoice in the presence of the Spirit of the Lord who calls us to share the Good News through our actions. We hear familiar and powerful passages of Sacred Scripture today. Each raises our hearts in praise, rejoicing in the saving action of God who heals, brings liberty and justice, and calls us to live in holiness. As you lead the catechumens today, invite them to be attentive to their reasons for rejoicing as we await the coming of the Lord.

Scripture Background

Isaiah 61:1-2a, 10-11 As ancient Israel saw the end of its exile, a glorious future opened before the Chosen People. Those who refused to lose hope saw their dreams fulfilled. The spirit of the Lord fell upon the prophet who faithfully announced the good tidings of healing, liberty, and vindication.

God makes justice and praise spring up. Justice signifies the restoration of a community in its social dignity, and also in its spiritual union. Praise results from these actions. It is the only fitting response of a people redeemed.

Many Christians recognize this passage as the one that Jesus read in the synagogue at the beginning of his ministry in Luke's account of the Gospel. Today it stands on its own to further the character of Advent.

Luke 1:46-48, 49-50, 53-54 (Isaiah 61:10 b) Mary's canticle, the Magnificat, proclaims the greatness of a God who has upended the injustices of the world. The hungry are filled; the rich are empty. God has returned to lift Israel from slavery to mercy.

Normally the response that follows the First Reading is drawn from the Book of Psalms, but there are occasions when a canticle from another book fills in. Today's passage might seem more fitting as a Gospel for the Fourth Sunday of Advent, which recounts the events immediately preceding the birth of Christ. In fact, it is the Gospel whenever December 22 falls on a weekday. Today, however, it joins with the First Reading to serve as a prophecy for the significance of the coming of Jesus Christ. He will bring justice to a world in need.

1 Thessalonians 5:16-24 St. Paul encourages the Thessalonians to rejoice always and constantly give thanks. By retaining what is good and refraining from evil, the Thessalonians may be preserved "blameless for the coming of our Lord Jesus Christ" (5:23). That phrase explains why this passage has been chosen for our meditation this weekend. The people were awaiting the coming of the Lord, just as Christians today do. As Paul encouraged his readers to be blameless, so we receive the same advice.

This letter is possibly the very first piece of literature composed for the New Testament—the oldest of Paul's epistles, older than each of the four Gospel accounts. In it can be seen the early anticipation of the imminence of Christ's return.

John 1:6-8, 19-28 Today's passage from John parallels the account heard last week from Mark. It is in two parts—the body following a brief introduction. The introduction is taken from the prologue of the Gospel according to John, a poetic proclamation of the mystery of the divine Word. Embedded into the prologue is a narrative about John, distinguishing him from Christ. Those few verses are proclaimed today ahead of the actual appearance of John in the unfolding account of Jesus' ministry. John the evangelist provides information about the conversation between John the Baptist and the priests and Levites from Jerusalem. They probe to find out just who he is. John cannot answer that without proclaiming who Jesus is.

The Third Sunday of Advent sounds two concurrent themes. One of them is *Gaudete* (rejoice), as seen in the other elements of today's Liturgy of the Word. The other is the message of John (the Fourth Gospel account never calls him "John the Baptist"). So central is John's preaching to Advent that the Gospel readings for both the Second and Third Sundays always tell of him. Historically, he was preparing his contemporaries for the arrival of Jesus. Biblically, he prepares us to meet Christ at the end of time.

Reflection Questions for the Catechist

- How do you perceive the presence of the Spirit in your life?
- What does the Spirit of God call you to be and to do?
- In what ways do you make straight the way of the Lord for those you lead?

Catechist's Guide

Objectives

- ▷ To gain an appreciation for the joy of salvation in Christ Jesus.
- ▷ To reflect upon the presence of the Spirit, who calls us to witness to God's love through our attitudes, words, and actions.
- ▷ To consider the difference that faith makes in daily living.

Dismissal and Procession

Following the homily, the priest celebrant picks up the Lectionary and invites the catechumens to come forward with the catechist(s) who will lead today's dismissal session. Holding the Lectionary so that all can see, the priest celebrant sends the catechumens and catechist(s) forward using RCIA, 67, his own words, or the following:

PRIEST: **John the Baptist yearned for the coming of God's Kingdom and made himself ready for it by repentance. During this time of Advent waiting, you are called to journey with the Lord and to give him room to fill your heart with joy. Listen to God's Word this day in confidence and hope. Make straight the path for the Lord's coming, and know that this faith community accompanies you in joy. Go in peace.**

All process to where the dismissal session will take place. The catechist holds the Lectionary in a reverent manner. The assembly may sing an acclamation to accompany the procession.

Centering

Upon reaching the place where the dismissal occurs, place the Lectionary on the ambo, lectern, or other dignified place (or hold the book reverently). Light the candle that is in the place of gathering and reread Isaiah 61:1–2a, 10–11 in order to refocus the group's attention. Consider singing the Responsorial Psalm or have a recording of it available to use as part of the centering, either before or after the reading.

Reflection and Discussion

The following "script" may be used or adapted to help facilitate discussion on today's readings. Begin the discussion by asking the catechumens if any words or phrases from today's readings spoke to them.

Today is the Third Sunday of Advent, which we call *Gaudete*, or "Rejoice," Sunday. Our readings are filled with the call to rejoice in the knowledge of God's saving action in the world. As we continue to celebrate this season of Advent, we allow our hearts to dwell on the gift of God's love and mercy. In these later days of Advent, we more deeply anticipate Christmas, in which we celebrate the birth of Jesus in Bethlehem.

- How does the continuing celebration of Advent lead you to a greater sense of wonder and awe in the love of God for you?
- For what do you have reason to rejoice?

In today's First Reading, from Isaiah, we hear of the anointing of the Spirit of the Lord.The Spirit instills in us the living presence of God, inspiring us to live as God's people in the world.

- In what ways do you perceive the presence of the Spirit of the Lord?
- How does this awareness of the Spirit enhance your anticipation of the deepening of the gifts of the Holy Spirit in the Sacraments of Baptism and Confirmation?

The prophecy of Isaiah proclaims glad tidings of healing, liberty, and vindication for God's people. This section of Isaiah was written as the people of Israel were returning from captivity in Babylon. They saw God's action in the freedom of returning to their homeland. As Christians, we read Isaiah's proclamation (see 61:1) in the context of Jesus' ministry to "bring glad tidings to the poor, / to heal the broken hearted," and so on. In fact, we know this passage as one that Jesus read in the synagogue, after which he announced "today, this scripture is fulfilled in your hearing" (Luke 4:21).

- In what ways does the Holy Spirit urge you to reach out to others with healing, presence, and care?

- How does your assurance of the presence of God make you more willing to reach out to others in service or to advocate for justice?

- What example comes to mind of an experience attending to or serving others through which you shared God's love or mercy with another?

Mary's song of praise, which we heard at Mass today, continues this announcement: God's mercy is for every generation; the hungry are filled and our spirits rejoice. We will hear in next week's Gospel how, when the angel Gabriel announces the news to Mary that she is to be the Mother of God, she is also told that her cousin Elizabeth, who is advanced in age, is expecting a child. Later in the Gospel according to Luke, we learn that Mary goes "in haste" to visit Elizabeth (see Luke 1:39). Upon arriving, she proclaims God's greatness. We know this proclamation of praise as the Magnificat. Filled with the Holy Spirit, Mary sings of God's goodness.

- What "great things" has the Lord done for you (Luke 1:49)?

- Mary proclaims that God has filled the hungry with good things and has sent the rich away empty. Is there an aspect of your life in which your richness causes separation from God or his ways?

- How does this cause you to "quench the Spirit" (1 Thessalonians 5:19)?

- In what ways might you empty yourself of this, in order to be filled with the goodness of God?

In St. Paul's letter to the Thessalonians, likely the earliest Christian writing, he prays that the people will be made perfectly holy in spirit, soul, and body.

- How does your faith affect your daily living—spiritually and practically?

We hear again today of John the Baptist, who is questioned by religious leaders about his identity. Who is he who is baptizing people and calling them to repentance? Is he a prophet like those who have come before him? Is he the long-awaited Messiah?

John makes it clear he is not the Messiah, and he humbly acknowledges his role in preparing the way for the Christ. He is not the light, but testifies to the light; he calls us to make straight the way of the Lord.

- What in your life needs straightening?

- How is faith accomplishing this?

- In what ways does the Spirit inspire or guide you to live for Christ and others?

Wrapping It Up

Consider these points to conclude the dismissal. Integrate the thoughts and ideas that surfaced during the discussion.

- The Spirit of the Lord is present within us.

- The Spirit urges us to live as people for others.

- The Spirit strengthens us to live as people of faith spiritually and practically.

Closing Prayer

Conclude with prayer. If time permits, sing the psalm refrain a few times before or after the following prayer.

God our Savior,
in you we have cause for great rejoicing!
Fill us with your Holy Spirit.
Instill in us a true desire to bring glad tidings to the poor,
to heal the brokenhearted, and proclaim your liberty to all.
Banish all that separates us from you.
Make us perfectly holy, so that we may reflect your love,
making straight your way in our lives
and in the lives of all we touch with your love.
Through Christ our Lord.
Amen.

Readings for the Next Dismissal

Provide catechumens with a list of the readings for the next dismissal session. Consult the liturgical calendar on page xvi to find out what day will be observed next week. Give catechumens the questions below to guide their reflection through the week.

- What connections are you seeing in the readings of this liturgical season? As you pray with the readings, around what themes do your thoughts seem to be coming together?

- Where do the readings intersect with your journey of faith? What questions do they raise for you?

Extended Catechesis

Based on today's readings and liturgical observance, the following topics may be covered for extended catechesis:

- The Holy Spirit, third Person of the Trinity

- The prophets as bearers of God's message

- Right relationship with God

Fourth Sunday of Advent

Focus: God's Kingdom endures forever.

Lectionary #11B

Catechist's Preparation

Overview of the Sunday

The Fourth Sunday of Advent reminds us that the celebration of the Incarnation is almost upon us, and that the in-breaking of God's love in Christ has eternal implications. In Christ, the Kingdom of God is made visible and through Christ, we are drawn to live in the knowledge that this Kingdom endures forever. It is good for us to keep this greater vision in our minds and hearts as we prepare for Christmas. As you lead your catechumens to reflect on the Kingdom of God today, consider what it means to have a king who enters the world as a child in a manger, as one who came to be among us in humility and compassion, and who draws us to live this way of love in our lives.

Scripture Background

2 Samuel 7:1–5, 8b–12, 14a, 16 The words in Samuel are like an epic sketch of the history of God's promise. David wants to build a house for God, but instead God responds that he will build the house: "I will fix a place for my people Israel; I will plant them so that they may dwell in their place" (2 Samuel 7:10). God promises David that this house and kingdom will be firm forever. We hear the fulfillment of that promise in the Gospel story of Mary's obedience.

The house of David also means the household, family, or relations of David. David's salvation does not come to him as an individual or even as a king. Rather, it comes in community, among people who are in relationship with one another. In God's decision to tell David that it is he who will build the house, God expanded the relationships within the house. In our relationship to God as daughters and sons, we find that we are locked in an embrace with all God's sons and daughters, making us all sisters and brothers. This family relationship will be all the more emphasized by Jesus' image of how we treat our brothers and sisters.

Psalm 89:2–3, 4–5, 27, 29 (2a) Psalm 89, a royal psalm, includes prayers for the king because it is through him that the people of God are blessed. Therefore, how the king behaved as a servant of the Lord was significant. Prophets often approached the king, calling upon him to change his behavior to be more faithful to his royal heritage. The full text of Psalm 89 laments over the suffering of the king, possibly because of his defeat and disgrace in battle. Yet in the verses we hear on this Advent Sunday, we hear no laments but only praise for the God of the covenant.

The opening line announces the theme of God's faithfulness over all time. Terms like forever and all generations convey the lasting depth of the covenant and reflect God's continual promise to David's house. Seen in light of a possible military loss, it is certain that despite defeat, God's love for David does not change. This Sunday, we sing praise and proclaim the faithfulness of God for the entire world to know.

Romans 16:25–27 Found at the end of Paul's epistle, these verses are a doxology or a benediction, a hymn of praise and glory to God. This reading echoes connections to the other readings in images of the endless mystery of God to be proclaimed to all nations. Paul emphasizes that all Jews and Gentiles now share in the promise of salvation fulfilled in Jesus Christ. In proclaiming this gracious and generous message of covenantal relationship and compassion to all, it will become known to the world that God is indeed faithful. While this message may seem impossible to some, to others this Good News of Jesus Christ will be seen as the fulfillment of the enormous capacity and power of the Lord.

Luke 1:26–38 The revelation in this Sunday's Gospel must have seemed unimaginable to Mary. It was impossible for her to conceive a child and impossible for her barren cousin, Elizabeth, to bear a child. Yet, she believed: "Nothing will be impossible for God" (1:37). God has promised salvation to his people, and it has begun with these two women with their willingness to accept impossibly good news.

In telling Mary's story, the Church highlights her response to the overwhelming power of God's Spirit. In her acceptance and trust of God's promise, Mary responded as a faithful servant of the line of David. There had been no kings in the Davidic line for over five centuries, since before the Babylonian exile, yet God is faithful and has found a way to allow the Son of the Most High to inherit David's throne.

Mary's simple statement of obedience did not come without fear or anxiety or challenge, yet it came (see 1:38). Mary has responded as a faithful disciple and, because of her willingness to allow God to enter into her very self, salvation will be seen upon the earth.

Reflection Questions for the Catechist

🌀 How does Jesus show you the essence of the Kingdom of God?

🌀 In what ways is Advent a time to prepare to announce God's reign through your actions?

🌀 What impossible thing in your life needs the presence of God at this time?

Catechist's Guide

Objectives

▷ To develop a greater grasp of the concept of the Kingdom of God.

▷ To better understand the promise of God's covenant love as expressed in the coming of the Messiah.

▷ To reflect on Mary's fiat (her yes) and the catechumen's call to say yes to God.

Dismissal and Procession

Following the homily, the priest celebrant picks up the Lectionary and invites the catechumens to come forward with the catechist(s) who will lead today's dismissal session. Holding the Lectionary so that all can see, the priest celebrant sends the catechumens and catechist(s) forward using RCIA, 67, his own words, or the following:

> PRIEST: **My dear friends, Advent is a time of darkness and waiting, but also a season of great hope. As you continue your reflection on the Word of God and your journey toward initiation, may your body, mind, and soul be filled with hope, as you prepare for Christ Jesus to be born a new within you. Go forth in peace.**

All process to where the dismissal session will take place. The catechist holds the Lectionary in a reverent manner. The assembly may sing an acclamation to accompany the procession.

Centering

Upon reaching the place where the dismissal occurs, place the Lectionary on the ambo, lectern, or other dignified place (or hold the book reverently). Light the candle that is in the place of gathering and reread Luke 1:26–38 in order to refocus the group's attention. Consider singing the Responsorial Psalm or have a recording of it available to use as part of the centering, either before or after the reading.

Reflection and Discussion

The following "script" may be used or adapted to help facilitate discussion on today's readings. You might choose to begin your discussion with the catechumens by asking if any words or phrases from today's readings spoke to them.

The celebration of Christmas is almost upon us. It may seem odd to focus our attention today on the Kingdom of God. Shouldn't we be thinking about the meaning of the birth of Jesus? Our readings today do lead us to prepare more deeply for the celebration of the Incarnation. Through the Incarnation, we grasp more fully what God's Kingdom is all about. Yet most of us have difficulty thinking about a kingdom of any sort. We do not have many monarchies in our world today, and of the ones that exist, most are not absolute, in the manner of ancient kingdoms.

🌀 How has the season of Advent helped you to prepare your heart for a more profound celebration of Christmas?

🌀 Has your daily prayer included a seasonal reflection?

🌀 Have you adopted particular Advent practices that have shaped your spiritual life this season?

🌀 What first comes to mind when you hear the word *kingdom*?

In the First Reading, from the second book of Samuel, King David wants to build a house for God. Through Nathan the prophet, the Lord reminds David that God has acted in making David king and in the protection of the people. God has acted in the past, and will continue to act; it is up to God to set the time for the establishment of the kingdom. David's kingdom is a temporal kingdom; God's Kingdom is eternal.

David initially thought he would give glory to God by building a house for the Ark of the Covenant. Nathan helps David to hear the voice of the Lord, however, and understand this was not what he was called to do.

🌀 How do you perceive God's voice?

🌀 Who helps you to discern the will of God?

The Responsorial Psalm today highlights God's faithfulness, even when we are experiencing difficulty. The covenant between God and humanity insures that God will always be with us. We sometimes walk away; our faith may waver. God's love does not waver. God's care and mercy are constant in the face of an always-changing world.

🌀 How do you experience this constancy of God's love?

🌀 In what ways does God's eternal faithfulness call you to be faithful?

In today's Gospel, we hear of Mary's encounter with the angel Gabriel. Gabriel's announcement must have been perplexing to Mary. She was "greatly troubled at what was said and pondered what sort of greeting this might be" (Luke 1:29). Gabriel reassures her, telling her to not be afraid. We hear this often in Sacred Scripture. God knows, we may be struck with fear as we put our faith into action! Yet God's Kingdom is not about fear.

🌀 Think about an experience in which you were afraid to act on your faith. What happened? How did you overcome the fear? What sort of growth resulted from this experience?

We hear Mary's astonishment at the angel's message in her reply, "How can this be, since I have no relations with a man" (Luke 1:34)? Yet Mary finds the grace to say yes to God's plan. She trusts that "nothing will be impossible for God" (Luke 1:37).

🌀 What seemingly impossible thing do you need God to act upon at this time?

🌀 Is there something to which you feel called that seems impossible?

🌀 How will you find the strength to say yes to this call?

In today's Gospel we are led to a growing understanding that God's eternal Kingdom is not temporal. Nor is the Kingdom about power, earthly authority, or might. God's reign is shown to us in the birth of the Son of God in the manger in Bethlehem. In this way, today's readings are the perfect reflection for us as we prepare to celebrate Christmas.

Wrapping It Up

Consider these points to conclude the dismissal. Integrate the thoughts and ideas that surfaced during the discussion.

- God's Kingdom is eternal and is shown to us in the coming of the Christ child.
- The covenant which God has established assures us that he will always be faithful. We are called to respond in faithfulness to God.
- We are called to discern God's will for us. We do this with the help of the community of faith.

Closing Prayer

Conclude with prayer. If time permits, sing the psalm refrain a few times before or after the following prayer.

God our King,
you have established with us a covenant,
through which we are assured of your faithfulness.
Let us be your people,
willingly responding to your love by saying yes to your plan for our lives
and for the world.
Let us not be filled with fear, but with awe in your presence,
trusting that with you, all things are possible.
May we, like Mary, be your servants,
giving you glory through the obedience of faith,
as we await your advent among us.
Through Christ our Lord.
Amen.

Readings for the Next Dismissal

Provide catechumens with a list of the readings for the next dismissal session. Consult the liturgical calendar on page xvi to find out what day will be observed next week. Give catechumens the questions below to guide their reflection through the week.

- What connections are you seeing in the readings of this liturgical season? As you pray with the readings, around what themes do your thoughts seem to be coming together?
- Where do the readings intersect with your journey of faith? What questions do they raise for you?

Extended Catechesis

Based on today's readings and liturgical observance, the following topics may be covered for extended catechesis:

- Covenant
- Mary
- Kingdom of God
- Jesus, Son of God, Son of Mary

INTRODUCTION TO CHRISTMAS TIME

Overview of Christmas Time

"Joy to the world! The Lord is come." The celebration of Christmas Time is a season filled with wonder and awe at the incredible love of God for humanity. The mystery and miracle of the Incarnation is so great that it requires a season in which to reflect and take to heart the Good News that God has come to be one with us. Throughout the season, the story of the Nativity and infancy of Jesus unfolds. Christ's light shines, dispelling every darkness. With angels, shepherds, and Magi, we praise and glorify God. We are inspired by the witness of holy men and women like Abraham and Sarah, Simeon and Anna, and of course, Mary and Joseph. Their response to God's love is a model for each of us—to embrace the gift of God's love, to be transformed by it, and to share the light of Christ with the world.

For catechumens, the Christmas season is a time in which to become immersed in the assurance that God is with us in the daily moments of our lives. Those catechumens who are new to the rhythm of the liturgical seasons may find the extended season of Christmas refreshing. After the many practical as well as spiritual preparations during Advent, they will welcome the opportunity to linger in the season as they grow in understanding of the true meaning of Christmas.

Preparing a Seasonal Environment

The liturgical color for Christmas Time is white, although gold and silver may also be used. Pine boughs and candles are often used to accent the environment. The evergreens remind us of the hope we have in the birth of Jesus; the candles call to mind the light of Christ, which shines in our hearts. Incorporate a crèche as a prominent feature of the environment for the season.

Keep a space available to place the Lectionary (or Bible) such as a lectern or table. Keep a candle near the Lectionary (or the Bible) and light this candle before the session begins. In everything you do to create the environment for Christmas Time in the dismissal space, take your lead from the environment in the sanctuary of the main assembly. Consistency between what the catechumens see in the environment in that space and in the environment in the dismissal space is important. You do not want to create divergent messages about the day and season and thus generate unnecessary questions or confusion within the group. Keep the environment simple but not simplistic, understated but not minimized. Colors, light, images, and other added elements should all assist the catechumens in their reflection on the significance of the day and the Word of God.

Overview of the Readings

On each Sunday and special day that occurs during Christmas Time, we are invited to reflect upon a particular aspect of the Good News of the Incarnation. The readings lead us to encounter Christ through multiple manifestations: the Nativity, Epiphany, and the Baptism of the Lord. We are invited to look to

Mary and Joseph as models of faithful living, and as we strive to grow in holiness, we consider how we may share the light of Christ with others. The Gospel accounts tell the story of the birth and infancy of Jesus, with the season concluding with Jesus' baptism in the Jordan. The other readings are fitting accompaniments to the story of the Incarnation, providing context, insight and wisdom to our reflections throughout the season.

First Readings   "The people who walked in darkness / have seen a great light; / upon those who dwelt in the land of gloom / a light has shown / . . . For a child is born to us, a son is given us; / upon his shoulder dominion rests" (Isaiah 9:1, 5). This passage from the book of the prophet Isaiah, which we hear at the Mass during the Night in our celebration of the Nativity of the Lord, is a fitting beginning to the entirety of Christmas Time. Throughout the season, we will be drawn to the light and allow it to illumine our hearts and minds. We pick up this theme again in the celebration of the Epiphany, hearing again from Isaiah, "Rise up in splendor, Jerusalem! Your light has come" (Isaiah 60:1). The First Readings for the celebration of the Holy Family of Jesus, Mary, and Joseph, and that of the Blessed Virgin Mary, the Holy Mother of God, lead us to reflect on the example of holy people who are our ancestors in the faith: Abraham and Sarah, Moses and Aaron. We hear again from Isaiah as we conclude the season, in which we are told that the Lord spreads before us a banquet, a rich feast for all who come to God.

Responsorial Psalms   Throughout Christmas Time, the Responsorial Psalms are filled with proclamations of praise and thanksgiving for God's great goodness, mercy, and faithfulness. The psalms during this season focus our attention on the primary themes for the day: During Mass during the Night at Christmas, we sing to the Lord a new song and tell the nations of God's wondrous deeds. In Psalm 105, as we celebrate the Holy Family, we remember God's covenant love. We recall God's mercy in Psalm 67, which we sing as we reflect on the Blessed Virgin Mary, the Holy Mother of God, who herself sang of God's mercy when visiting her kinswoman Elizabeth. Psalm 72, which we sing at the Epiphany, tells us that every nation on earth will adore the Lord. And as we celebrate the Baptism of the Lord, we sing a canticle from Isaiah, drawing water at the fountain of salvation.

Second Readings   The Second Readings throughout the season, from Titus, Hebrews, Galatians, Ephesians, and 1 John, lead us to reflect upon ourselves as heirs of God's eternal Kingdom, sons and daughters of God. As children of God, we are called to respond in faith, as people who live in right relationship with God and others.

Gospel Readings   It is in the Gospel each Sunday of Christmas Time that we hear and reflect upon the story of the Incarnation. At Christmas (Mass during the Night), Holy Family, and the Blessed Virgin Mary, the Holy Mother of God, the Gospel accounts are from Luke. We hear the story of Jesus' birth, his presentation at the Temple, and the shepherds who come to see the Christ child in the manger. On Epiphany, we hear the story of the Magi from the Gospel according to Matthew, and we return to the Gospel according to Mark, from which we read throughout Year B, to hear of Jesus' baptism in the Jordan River. The Gospel at Christmas Time provides the narrative through which we encounter Emmanuel, God-with-us.

SOLEMNITY OF THE NATIVITY OF THE LORD (CHRISTMAS)

Focus: There is nothing to fear, for God is with us.

Lectionary #14ABC (Mass during the Night)

🌿 Separate readings are provided in the Lectionary for the Vigil Mass (Lectionary #13ABC), the Mass at Dawn (Lectionary #15ABC), and the Mass during the Day (Lectionary #16ABC). Because the readings from the Mass during the Night are the most familiar, and these readings are most often proclaimed at the other Masses, they have been included in this resource.

Catechist's Preparation

Overview of the Solemnity

Merry Christmas! The Lord is come! As you prepare to celebrate Christmas with your catechumens, take a few moments to reflect on the miracle of the Incarnation, the astounding news that God is with us. Throughout Christmas Time, we allow this mystery to sink in and to have a place deep in our hearts. Christ's light shines through all darkness, illuminating God's great love for humanity. With the shepherds and angels, we praise God, finding hope in the child who is born to us, the son who is given us. Fear is cast aside, as we sing, "Glory to God in the highest / and on earth peace to those on whom his favor rests" (Luke 2:14).

Scripture Background

Isaiah 9:1–6 When hearing this reading, some will undoubtedly recall the words sung in George Frederic Handel's *Messiah*, a tribute to the evangelizing power of music. The words are Isaiah's, somewhat influenced by other cultures' descriptions of an ideal ruler. The historical circumstances surrounding this composition, however, were far from ideal: the people were undergoing deportation and enslavement. The only way for them to describe themselves was as living in a land of gloom. The horror of their abject darkness included their captors' brutality, which involved putting out the eyes of some of them, both as a warning and as a way to debilitate and humiliate would-be leaders.

When Isaiah speaks of light, he is not talking about the decorations that offset the dark of winter in December in the northern hemisphere. For Isaiah, light is a symbol of desperately needed salvation and liberation. The light is coming from God in person and in a person, a child to be born who would deliver the people. In Isaiah's day, that presaged a king. But no king lived up to the promise. Rather than abandon hope, the people came to understand the prophecy as referring to a Messiah to come. For the early Church, the prophecy fit the person of Jesus perfectly, who came offering light and liberation.

Psalm 96:1–2, 2–3, 11–12, 13 (Luke 2:11) This psalm, so appropriate for Christmas, sings out a core message of the Psalter: Rejoice, for God reigns! The song celebrates and recalls Israel's many experiences of rescue. For us it sings the joy of the Nativity and invites us to ask how the Good News of Christ's birth sheds new light on our lives today. When we strive to let our daily lives be permeated with Christ's presence, we will know how to "announce his salvation, day after day" (96:2).

Titus 2:11–14 This short reading reminds us that the coming of Christ at Christmas was only the beginning. The Epiphany has happened; God has appeared definitively in our history. As a result, Christ's presence enables us to live a new way. Even more, we look toward that future when Isaiah's prophecy of peace will come true; not only will there be peace, but every person will know the love of God that Christians have found in Christ. We proclaim that belief with the Lord's Prayer in every liturgy, as we remember the "blessed hope" (2:13) we share as we await the coming of our Savior, our Lord Jesus Christ. This perspective on Christ's presence invites us to let that hope be the guiding beacon of our entire life.

Luke 2:1–14 This selection from Luke's account of the Gospel portrays three distinct scenes. In the first we hear of Mary and Joseph, who undertook a journey of approximately ninety miles in the last days of Mary's pregnancy. That journey was necessary because the people of occupied Israel had to register for the purpose of taxation. The opening scene depicts a time of oppression for God's people.

In the second scene, Luke uses very few words to announce the birth of the Messiah. He simply tells us that Mary's time was completed and she gave birth to her son. There is no great drama, no miracles, just a simple birth. To emphasize the ordinariness of it all, Luke mentions that the baby was wrapped in swaddling clothes—a sign as spectacular as someone today saying that the baby was diapered. Finally, as if the birth were not unostentatious enough, Luke adds a crucial detail and the rationale for it. The child was laid in a manger because there was no room for him among his own people. In those few lines, Luke orients us to the entire Gospel he is about to recount. God's son comes among us unobtrusively, in adverse conditions, and not even the members of God's own people make room for him.

The third scene underlines the simplicity of God's involvement in human history. The first to hear of the birth of the child are poor shepherds—either hired hands or those who had not the means to hire others to work the night shift for them. They were often stigmatized as dishonest and for being unable to fulfill the strict requirements of the law. It was to them that the announcement came, with the assurance that they had nothing to fear from this great event that God was working among them.

Reflection Questions for the Catechist

- What is most striking to you about the Incarnation?
- What darkness or fear is on your mind or in your heart at this time? How does the assurance that God is with us give you hope in the midst of this darkness?
- What Christmas tradition in your family speaks most powerfully to the message of God's love for us in Christ?

Catechist's Guide

Objectives

- ▷ To grasp more fully the mystery of the Incarnation.
- ▷ To gain appreciation for the longing for the Messiah for God's people, and for the hope we have in Christ, who meets the longing of our hearts.
- ▷ To reflect upon the simplicity and wonder of the birth of Jesus.

Dismissal and Procession

Following the homily, the priest celebrant picks up the Lectionary and invites the catechumens to come forward with the catechist(s) who will lead today's dismissal session. Holding the Lectionary so that all can see, the priest celebrant sends the catechumens and catechist(s) forward using RCIA, 67, his own words, or the following:

PRIEST: **The birth of the Lord is announced to shepherds, those whose job it is to keep watch over their flocks. God's message of peace falls upon the hearts of the humble and seeks to topple the mighty from their thrones. As you go forth to explore God's Word more deeply, consider what needs to be purified in your hearts so that you might more easily behold the Lord's manifestation. Open God's Word with tremendous joy this day. Go in peace.**

All process to where the dismissal session will take place. The catechist holds the Lectionary in a reverent manner. The assembly may sing an acclamation to accompany the procession.

Centering

Upon reaching the place where the dismissal occurs, place the Lectionary on the ambo, lectern, or other dignified place (or hold the book reverently). Light the candle that is in the place of gathering and reread Luke 2:1–14 in order to refocus the group's attention. Consider singing the Responsorial Psalm or have a recording of it available to use as part of the centering, either before or after the reading.

Reflection and Discussion

The following "script" may be used or adapted to help facilitate discussion on today's readings. Begin the discussion by asking the catechumens if any words or phrases from today's readings spoke to them.

It is Christmas! Our Advent watchful waiting has ended. Today we begin the season of Christmas, a time in which to dwell on the miracle and mystery of the Incarnation, the incredible news that God has come to be with us, as one with us.

Before we reflect on Christmas, take a moment to consider the Advent season we have just completed.

- What image, thought, or insight do you take with you as the fruit of this Advent season?
- How did your Advent prayer and practice prepare you for Christmas?

We hear again from the prophet Isaiah in the First Reading. Isaiah speaks of hope to people who were living in very difficult times. God's people longed for the Messiah, for one who would bring peace and freedom, who would take their burdens and would rule with justice. Christians read Isaiah and hear expressed what they have found in the Lord: light in darkness, joy, and peace. The psalm response gives voice to this Good News: "Today is born our Savior, Christ the Lord."

- What darkness in your life or in the world needs the great light of God's love?
- What signs of this light glimmer, even in the midst of the darkness?

The passage we heard from the Gospel according to Luke is familiar to many. We hear the story of Jesus' birth in Bethlehem and in our mind's eye we envision a Nativity display, television show, or children's play. Yet there is so much more than these expressions to consider! The great mystery of Christmas is that God loves us so deeply that he came to humanity as a child, Emmanuel, God-with-us. This incredible story is the story of our salvation. God has removed all barriers between humanity and God. In Jesus, God entered into the humble, fragile circumstances of human life and transforms them into something sacred.

- What image or tradition captures Christmas for you? How does this speak to the meaning of Christmas?

The Gospel according to Luke tells the story of Jesus' birth very simply: Mary and Joseph journeyed to Bethlehem; while there, the baby was born; he was swaddled and laid in a manger. Yet each of these details points to a larger story: Mary and Joseph had to undertake a difficult journey at a tenuous time, as people who were under Roman rule; they were unable to find lodging—even though Mary was obviously very pregnant, no one would take them in; the baby was born in a place where animals were kept and was laid in the trough from which animals were fed. From the very beginning of the story, we see that this is not the story of a God who is distant from humanity. This is the story of God who desires to meet us in the most humble and vulnerable of human circumstances.

- What does it mean to you that Jesus was born at a time of oppression for God's people?
- What do the circumstances of Jesus' birth in Bethlehem say to you about God's relationship with humanity? About the sanctity of creation?
- How do Mary and Joseph's roles in the birth of the baby Jesus provide insight into who we are called to be as Christian people?
- Are there situations in today's world that are similar to the plight of Mary and Joseph? What is the Christian response?

The Gospel continues with the angel's announcement of the birth of Jesus to shepherds in the fields. Imagine their reaction! We are told they were struck with great fear. This sounds reasonable to us. These simple, poor, working people did not expect to experience God's presence firsthand! Like Mary at the Annunciation, the shepherds are told to not be afraid. They are invited to put aside their fear in order to encounter Jesus.

- What fear must you cast aside in order to encounter Jesus?

Wrapping It Up

Consider these points to conclude the dismissal. Integrate the thoughts and ideas that surfaced during the discussion.

- God is not distant from us, but is with us in every moment and circumstance.
- Jesus' birth is the turning point in salvation history.
- Through the Incarnation, God shows his great love for and desire to be with humanity.

Closing Prayer

Conclude the dismissal session with prayer. If time permits, you might choose to sing the psalm refrain a few times before or after the closing prayer.

Glory to God in the highest
and on earth peace to those on whom his favor rests!
Gracious God, through the birth of Jesus, your Son,
you bring light to every darkness, and cast out all fear.
Like the shepherds who were drawn to the manger,
we are struck with awe and wonder at Jesus' birth.
May this Christmas Time lead us to be joyful people
whose lives reflect your great love for all.
Through Christ our Lord.
Amen.

Readings for the Next Dismissal

Provide catechumens with a list of the readings for the next dismissal session. Consult the liturgical calendar on page xvi to find out what day will be observed next week. Give catechumens the questions below to guide their reflection through the week.

- What connections are you seeing in the readings of this liturgical season? As you pray with the readings, around what themes do your thoughts seem to be coming together?
- Where do the readings intersect with your journey of faith? What questions do they raise for you?

Extended Catechesis

Based on today's readings and liturgical observance, the following topics may be covered for extended catechesis:

- Incarnation
- Messiah
- Salvation history

FEAST OF THE HOLY FAMILY OF JESUS, MARY, AND JOSEPH

Focus: To be a light for the family of all nations.

Lectionary #17B

🌿 The First Reading, Responsorial Psalm, and Second Reading from Year A may also be used.

Catechist's Preparation

Overview of the Feast

While much of the world celebrates Christmas as a single day, the Church lingers to reflect upon the Incarnation through a season of celebrations. Today we pause to reflect upon the Holy Family of Jesus, Mary, and Joseph. For some of your catechumens, it may be easy to think of their family growing in holiness. For others, "family" may be a painful experience of death, grief, separation, or conflict. Yet, we know that God acts in and can transform us in the midst of such pain. Through the stories of Abraham and Sarah, Jesus, Mary, and Joseph, and Simeon and Anna, we reflect on the ways in which faith may transform the uncertainties of family life, leading us to live and grow in holiness.

Scripture Background

Genesis 15:1–6; 21:1–3 Today's feast extends to every Christian family a model: the Holy Family of Jesus, Mary, and Joseph. Children are a blessing to a married couple, as can be seen in the fulfillment of the promise God made to Abram. Abram, a childless old man, pleaded with God for an heir, and God promised him more descendants than he could count—more than the stars of the sky.

In the Lectionary, this reading leaps from chapter 15 to chapter 21 of Genesis, in order to condense the promise and its fulfillment. To this elderly couple is given a great gift of God's compassion, a son, an only son, Isaac, whom they loved. Not every couple is blessed with a child, and not every child receives the care of father and mother. But, in the ideal, the arrival of a child turns a couple into a family. It is happiness indeed.

Psalm 105:1–2, 3–4, 5–6, 8–9 (7a, 8a) Psalm 105 celebrates the history of Israel as a variation on the theme of God's covenant. The Lectionary offers the opening verses of this somewhat lengthy psalm. This excerpt summons the descendants of Abraham to glory in God's holy name.

Hebrews 11:8, 11–12, 17–19. The full drama of Abraham's life with Isaac is recalled in the Letter to the Hebrews. This section of the letter holds up examples of faith, among which Abraham shines bright. He trusted that God would provide a son, though he himself was old and Sarah was sterile. But even more, Abraham trusted that God could raise Isaac from the dead, since God had commanded Abraham to slay his son.

Family life is an unpredictable mix of love and death, trust and faith, hopes and fears. It is holy ground. This passage continues the Lectionary's reflection on Abraham's family in the light of the Holy Family. Abraham's son was a miracle baby, and, before growing up, Isaac came close to death. Mary and Joseph's son was another miracle baby, and Mary watched him die.

Luke 2:22–40 or 2:22, 39–40 Mary and Joseph present Jesus to the Lord in the Temple on the fortieth day of his life, in accordance with Jewish tradition of the time. Two prophets, Simeon and Anna, behold Jesus as he enters the Temple. They both realize who he is, and Simeon sings blissfully of the event. The message of his song is something like, "Now I've seen everything. I can die happy." But, it also proclaims one of the biggest messages of the Christmas season: Christ is the light of the nations.

A shorter form of this Gospel may be proclaimed, but it removes both Simeon and Anna from the narrative. Without their prophetic presence, the reading dwindles to a report of the parents taking the child to Jerusalem in fulfillment of the Law of Moses. It proclaims a simpler, yet important message: parents hand down values to their children. Children will discern the rules that matter to parents, and they will begin to form their lives according to these values. In Jesus' case, he developed a great love for Jerusalem and its Temple, and both became key symbols in his life. St. Luke, more than the other evangelists, links the themes of Jesus and Jerusalem in anticipation of his Death. Even in the sequence of the temptation in the desert, the Devil takes Jesus to Jerusalem for the final temptation. Matthew places that temptation second, but Luke sees it as a climax. Just as Jesus' infancy reaches its climax on the fortieth day in Jerusalem, so will the final days of his entire earthly life.

Reflection Questions for the Catechist	⑨ What is your experience of family? In what ways is your experience of family that of striving for holiness?
	⑨ How have you experienced the fulfillment of a promise of God?
	⑨ In what ways do you live in faith, even when there seems no hope of resolution to a situation?

Dismissal Session Guide

Objectives	▷ To reflect upon Abram as an example of faith.
	▷ Through reflection on the readings, catechumens will better understand that God desires that every person live in loving relationship with others.
	▷ To reflect upon the stories of Abram and Sarah, Mary and Joseph in thinking about their own experience of family.

Dismissal and Procession

Following the homily, the priest celebrant picks up the Lectionary and invites the catechumens to come forward with the catechist(s) who will lead today's dismissal session. Holding the Lectionary so that all can see, the priest celebrant sends the catechumens and catechist(s) forward using RCIA, 67, his own words, or the following:

> PRIEST: My dear friends, you have feasted with us at the table of God's word. May the Lord Jesus, who is the Word made flesh, be with you as you continue your journey toward Baptism. Go now in the peace of Christ.

All process to where the dismissal session will take place. The catechist holds the Lectionary in a reverent manner. The assembly may sing an acclamation to accompany the procession.

Centering

Upon reaching the place where the dismissal occurs, place the Lectionary on the ambo, lectern, or other dignified place (or hold the book reverently). Light the candle that is in the place of gathering and reread Luke 2:22–40 in order to refocus the group's attention. Consider singing the Responsorial Psalm or have a recording of it available to use as part of the centering, either before or after the reading.

Reflection and Discussion

The following "script" may be used or adapted to help facilitate discussion on today's readings. Begin the discussion by asking the catechumens if any words or phrases from today's readings spoke to them.

While much of the world celebrates Christmas as a single day, the Church lingers to reflect upon the Incarnation through a season of celebrations. Each Sunday and holy day in this season focuses on a particular aspect of the story of Jesus' birth and the early moments of his life. Our focus today is on the life of the family in relationship to God. For many, Christmas is a time for families to be together, share a meal, gifts, and one another's presence. Not all families can be together physically, however, and for some families, the season is one that highlights conflict or painful separation among family members. Today's readings help us to know that God is present in the midst of every family circumstance.

⑨ What part of your family's Christmas celebration most reflects the joy and love of the Incarnation?

⑨ Is there an aspect of your family circumstances or tradition that is painful, awkward, or frustrating?

In the First Reading, from the Book of Genesis, we hear the story of Abram and Sarah. Both are advanced in age, and Sarah is unable to conceive. Abram is honest with God:

What good are the gifts of God without a child who will be Abram's heir? Many who wish to conceive understand Abram's cry to God. Their longing for a child is given voice through Abram's plea. Abram shows us that honesty with God is necessary for growth in faith.

God assures Abram that he will have a child. Not only this, but his descendants will be as numerous as the stars in the sky! Abram puts his faith in God, in spite of the improbability of a child at his age. Sarah and Abram put God at the center of their lives. Sarah conceives and bears a son, whom they name Isaac. All this is done in God's time.

- How does Abram's faith inspire you?
- What improbable thing do you bring to God in faith?

The Second Reading, from the letter to the Hebrews, highlights Abraham's faith and continues the story with the account of Abraham's willingness to offer up Isaac as a sacrifice. Our lives in family are at times filled with trial. We experience death, illness, separation, unemployment, disappointment, disillusionment. The witness of Abraham and Sarah is that in faith, we know that God is with us through it all.

- What circumstance or experience have you endured through faith?

In today's Gospel, we hear how Mary and Joseph present the child Jesus at the Temple in Jerusalem, in fulfillment of the Jewish custom. Throughout the Gospel, Mary and Joseph stand as models of holiness for us. They place their trust in God, and their faith guides their response to God's grace, even in (especially in) the uncertain moments of their lives as family. The Holy Family of Jesus, Mary, and Joseph encourages us to make our lives in family holy, centered on God and God's ways.

- How is (or is) God the center of life for your family?
- What example comes to mind of making a faith-directed decision or choosing an action for your family?

In the Gospel reading, Simeon and Anna are people of strong faith who have awaited the coming of the Messiah. Simeon's insight that Jesus is a light for all surely rang in the ears of Mary and Joseph as their family lived and grew in holiness throughout Jesus' early life with them.

- In what ways does your faith in Jesus bring light to your life?
- What family stands as a witness to Christ's light for you?
- How is your family a witness to the light of Christ for those with whom you interact or serve?

Wrapping It Up

Consider these points to conclude the dismissal. Integrate the thoughts and ideas that surfaced during the discussion.

- Abram and Sarah's faith in the midst of uncertainty inspires us to put faith at the center of our lives.
- Mary, Joseph, and Jesus are models of holiness for us and for all families.
- Jesus grew and was filled with wisdom during his life with Mary and Joseph. Faith is passed through family, from one generation to the next.

Closing Prayer

Conclude with prayer. If time permits, sing the psalm refrain a few times before or after the following prayer.

> Loving God,
> you give us to one another to share your great love in our family and in our community.
> We have many examples of living faith to guide us:
> Mary and Joseph, Abraham and Sarah, Simeon and Anna,
> people in our own families and in our faith community.
> Lead us to put you at the center of our life
> so that our family may be rooted in faith and love.
> Guide us, as we strive to grow in holiness throughout our lives,
> so that Christ's light may shine among and through us.
> Who lives and reigns for ever and ever.
> Amen.

Readings for the Next Dismissal

Provide catechumens with a list of the readings for the next dismissal session. Consult the liturgical calendar on page xvi to find out what day will be observed next week. Give catechumens the questions below to guide their reflection through the week.

⑨ What connections are you seeing in the readings of this liturgical season? As you pray with the readings, around what themes do your thoughts seem to be coming together?

⑨ Where do the readings intersect with your journey of faith? What questions do they raise for you?

Extended Catechesis

Based on today's readings and liturgical observance, the following topics may be covered for extended catechesis:

❋ Incarnation (continued)   ❋ Faith

❋ The early life of Jesus

SOLEMNITY OF MARY, THE HOLY MOTHER OF GOD

OCTAVE DAY OF THE NATIVITY OF THE LORD (CHRISTMAS)

January 1

Focus: To profess Mary as the Mother of God.

Lectionary #18ABC

Catechist's Preparation

Overview of the Solemnity

As we continue to celebrate Christmas Time, we reflect on Mary, who is the Mother of God. It is New Year's Day, and our reflection on Mary as the holy Mother of God—a model of holiness and Christian life—is particularly appropriate for us as we begin a new year. As you prepare to lead your catechumens today, take a few moments to reflect on your time with them thus far. How are they responding to the many blessings of their lives? How is their growing faith a sign for you of God's mercy and love? In what ways may this new year be a time of grace for you? Like Mary, ponder these things in your heart today and throughout the coming year.

Scripture Background

Numbers 6:22–27 God teaches Moses how to bless Aaron and his progeny. The prayer is for protection, happiness, and peace. In three parts, it became a model for the solemn blessing that may precede the dismissal at Mass.

In the present liturgical calendar, the Church reflects today on the motherhood of Mary. We also observe a world day of prayer for peace. Some people come to Mass with a more secular instinct: Prayer is a great way to start the new year. This passage from the Book of Numbers supports that motive. As we flip over the calendar and embrace a new beginning, we hear the blessing that God taught Moses. It has little to do with the motherhood of Mary, but it starts the year on the right foot, reminding us that all time and every season of our lives belong to God.

Psalm 67:2–3, 5, 6, 8 (2a) Another prayer of blessing serves as the Responsorial Psalm. Psalm 67 asks for God's mercy. To motivate God's favorable response, it suggests that all the nations will rejoice when they see what God has done. Blessing the people with peace will bring God the benefit of more praise. The psalm recognizes that God rules the nations, and does so in equity. The justice that God can bring will return praise from the earth.

Crossing the threshold of a new year, praying for the peace and justice of the world, today's psalm makes a fitting start to the Scripture readings that open a new year.

Galatians 4:4–7 The coming of Jesus as the only begotten Son of God has made it possible for us to become God's children by adoption, with the right to call God "Father" (see 4:6). This reading appears in the Lectionary today because it says that Jesus was "born of a woman" (4:4). In all the letters of St. Paul, he never mentions the name of Jesus' mother. (St. John doesn't, either.) Without the synoptic Gospel accounts, we would never know that her name is Mary. In fact, this is the only reference to Jesus' mother in the entire Pauline corpus. So, this passage from Galatians is used as the Second Reading many times throughout the year on Marian liturgical observances, since there are not many other choices.

The thrust of the argument in Paul's letter is that we have become adopted into God's family because Jesus entered the world as the Son of God. The words "God sent his Son" (4:4) and the repeated word born makes this reading especially appropriate for Christmas Time.

Some may feel that this translation is gender-exclusive when it repeats the word "sons" to comment on God's adoption of believers. There is another argument to be made, though. In Paul's day, sons received the inheritance of families. Daughters did not. To be adopted as a son was to be eligible for full inheritance. Paul's message reassured all of the Galatians that they would receive the full adoption that only sons could claim in his day. After all, this is the epistle where Paul says that there is neither male nor female in Christ (see 3:28).

Luke 2:16–21 Today is the Octave of Christmas. On the Octave of Easter, the Lectionary offers the account of Jesus appearing to the incredulous Thomas on the eighth day of the Resurrection, and this passage fits the Christmas Octave.

Happily, this passage also includes a depiction of Mary reflecting on the events in her heart. For this reason, the liturgical title of this day refers to her motherhood. This makes it a good day for the entire Church to reflect on the mystery of the Incarnation and its implications. For ordinary Christians, who have just completed Christmas responsibilities, closed one year, and are greeting a new one, this becomes a beautiful day to do what Mary did: reflect.

Mary's title as Mother of God caused quite a stir in the past. Many people rightly wondered, "How can God have a Mother?" The title says as much about Jesus as it does about Mary. It proclaims that Jesus is indivisibly God and human, and that Mary is his Mother. It makes no attempt to claim the divinity of Mary. She is human, one of us, but given a unique role in the history of salvation. The first Eucharistic Prayer refers to Mary as the "Mother of our God and Lord, Jesus Christ."

Reflection Questions for the Catechist

⑨ What great blessing have you experienced recently? What has been your response to this blessing?

⑨ In what ways is Mary a model of holiness and Christian discipleship for you?

⑨ What does it mean to you to be an adopted son or daughter of God?

Catechist's Guide

Objectives

▷ Recognizing Mary as singularly blessed by God, catechumens will reflect upon the blessings of their lives.

▷ To come to a deeper appreciation of Jesus, Son of God and Son of Mary.

▷ To reflect upon the meaning of being adopted sons and daughters of God.

Dismissal and Procession

Following the homily, the priest celebrant picks up the Lectionary and invites the catechumens to come forward with the catechist(s) who will lead today's dismissal session. Holding the Lectionary so that all can see, the priest celebrant sends the catechumens and catechist(s) forward using RCIA, 67, his own words, or the following:

PRIEST: **My dear friends, those who seek full membership in the Church of Christ have experienced the joy of proclaiming Emmanuel, "God-with-us!" Go forth to ponder this great mystery, supported by our sincere prayer that the one who was born in a stable will lead you to eternal glory in his heavenly kingdom. Go in peace.**

All process to where the dismissal session will take place. The catechist holds the Lectionary in a reverent manner. The assembly may sing an acclamation to accompany the procession.

Centering

Upon reaching the place where the dismissal occurs, place the Lectionary on the ambo, lectern, or other dignified place (or hold the book reverently). Light the candle that is in the place of gathering and reread Luke 2:16–21 in order to refocus the group's attention. Consider singing the Responsorial Psalm or have a recording of it available to use as part of the centering, either before or after the reading.

Reflection and Discussion

The following "script" may be used or adapted to help facilitate discussion on today's readings. Begin the discussion by asking the catechumens if any words or phrases from today's readings spoke to them.

As we continue to celebrate the Christmas season, we take time today to reflect on Mary, who is the Mother of God. It is New Year's Day, and our reflection on Mary as a model of holiness and Christian life is particularly appropriate for us as we begin a new year. Each of the readings today helps us to focus on the blessing of a deep relationship with God. Mary points the way to a life that is open to God's grace and mercy. Take a moment to look back at the year that has just passed.

⑨ What experiences of God's grace and blessing stand out for you?

In today's First Reading, God teaches Moses how to bless Aaron and the people of God. The blessing is threefold, asking for protection, a close, intimate relationship with God, and peace. Pause for a moment and think about these things. These are the desires, the blessings hoped for, among people who have God at their center. We might say that when these three things are given us, all is right with the world! The blessings in this prayer are not for material things, or comfortable living, or even for an easy life. The blessing comprises what it means to live in right relationship with God and others. Today's psalm is a similar prayer of blessing. When we experience God's mercy, we are compelled to share it, raising all of creation in a song of praise.

- In what ways do you know the blessing of protection by God? For example, protection in moments of fear, worry, or anxiety.

- How do you experience the blessing of an intimate relationship with God?

- In what ways does God's love and mercy give you peace?

- How does Mary show you the life of one who is in such an intimate, blessed relationship with God?

In the Second Reading from St. Paul's letter to the Galatians, we are invited to reflect on the dramatic nature of being drawn deeply to Christ in the waters of Baptism. As people who are united to Christ, we become adopted sons and daughters of God, who will inherit eternal life with God in heaven. Through the Holy Spirit, we call God "Abba, Father!" (Galatians 4:6). Through her participation in the mystery of the Incarnation, Mary shows us what it is to live as a child of God—her total openness and acceptance of God's will is instrumental in God becoming one of us in the "fullness of time" (Galatians 4:4).

- What does it mean to you to be an adopted son or daughter of God? In what ways does this inform your anticipation of the grace of Baptism?

- How does knowing Mary as the Mother of God help you to grasp who Christ is and what belonging to Christ means for us?

Today's Gospel reading picks up where we left off on Christmas, with the shepherds going in haste to Bethlehem. Do you remember when Mary "went in haste" to visit her cousin Elizabeth (see Luke 1:39)? Mary visited Elizabeth after she was visited by the angel Gabriel. The shepherds' anxiousness in visiting Mary, Joseph, and Jesus also happens after an announcement of an angel. They put aside their fear and responded to the message of Jesus' birth by going to him. Shepherds were among the poor and outcast of society. Yet they are among the first to witness the miracle of the baby in the manger, a lowly place for the Son of Mary who is the Son of God! The shepherds could not help but share what they experienced with others. Through their evangelizing, others were drawn to Jesus.

- What significance do you see in the message of the Christ child being told to the shepherds?

- What does their response teach you about what we are called to do as people who have been drawn to Christ? To whom are you called to share the impact of your faith?

Mary ponders all of these things in her heart.

- What in your relationship with Christ do you hold closely in your heart, taking time to reflect and allow your experience to deepen and grow?

Wrapping It Up

Consider these points to conclude the dismissal. Integrate the thoughts and ideas that surfaced during the discussion.

- Jesus is the Son of God and Son of Mary—fully divine and fully human.

- Mary is a model for us of openness to and acceptance of God's will.

- Growing in an intimate relationship with God is a blessing.

Closing Prayer

Conclude with prayer. If time permits, sing the psalm refrain a few times before or after the following prayer.

Gracious and ever-merciful God,
bless us and keep us in your protective arms.
Let your face shine upon us in closeness and love.
Look upon us kindly and teach us your will for our lives
and give us peace in our interactions with others, and peace in our world.
With Mary as our intercessor, mother, and guide,
give us the strength and wisdom to live in response to your great blessings
by showing and sharing your great love with others.
Through Christ our Lord.
Amen.

Readings for the Next Dismissal

Provide catechumens with a list of the readings for the next dismissal session. Consult the liturgical calendar on page xvi to find out what day will be observed next week. Give catechumens the questions below to guide their reflection through the week.

- What connections are you seeing in the readings of this liturgical season? As you pray with the readings, around what themes do your thoughts seem to be coming together?

- Where do the readings intersect with your journey of faith? What questions do they raise for you?

Extended Catechesis

Based on today's readings and liturgical observance, the following topics may be covered for extended catechesis:

❋ Incarnation

❋ Jesus, fully human and fully divine

❋ Mary, Mother of God and Mother of the Church

SOLEMNITY OF THE EPIPHANY OF THE LORD

Focus: A light shines in the darkness for the upright and the strong.

Lectionary #20ABC

Catechist's Preparation

Overview of the Solemnity

We are still immersed in Christmas Time, and again we hear about the manger and reflect on the implications of Jesus' birth in Bethlehem. On this Solemnity of the Epiphany of the Lord, we ponder the truth that the story of God's love and desire to be with all of humanity cannot—should not—be contained by select group of people. Jesus did not come for a few, but for all. So while we have thought about the Incarnation—about who Jesus is (Son of God and Son of Mary) and who we are as adopted sons and daughters of God, now we take time to recognize that this Good News is for everyone. We are called to share this light with all whom we meet.

Scripture Background

Isaiah 60:1–6 Isaiah 60 has long been associated with the Solemnity of the Epiphany, and with good reason. It not only includes traditional Epiphany imagery, it also describes Isaiah's vision of an actual epiphany of God.

The first thing Isaiah saw was the appearance of God's light rising to shine on the fallen people of Israel. Even though darkness might cover the rest of the earth, the glory of God was beginning to dawn in Zion. Then Isaiah saw a great throng of pilgrims approaching Jerusalem. Leading the procession were all the exiled children of Israel. Following them were representatives from all the nations of the world bearing gifts for Israel and Israel's God. Attracted by God's light, they, too, had come to worship.

The most significant feature of this epiphany is its breadth. Given that Isaiah was writing at a time when Israel was obsessed with the pains of reconstructing its national life following the exile, Isaiah could have focused primarily on his own people. But he didn't. In Isaiah's vision, God's light shone not only on Israel but on all the nations of the world. This epiphany, Isaiah says, is for everyone. It is a feast of reconciliation, bringing together all the cultures and races of the world.

Psalm 72:1–2, 7–8, 10–11, 12–13 (see 11) This psalm epitomizes the royal theology that was popular in ancient Israel. The psalm itself may have been written for a coronation of one of Israel's kings or for one of the regular festivals celebrating the king's coronation. Today we might call Psalm 72 a prayer of invocation. Like many invocations written for official occasions, it sought God's blessings for both the king and the nation he led. The psalmist prayed that the king would rule justly, that he would see to the needs of the most vulnerable, that he would bring prosperity to the nation, and that his rule would increase even to the ends of the earth.

Although it may not seem like it at first, this psalm also describes an epiphany of God. At least that is how the ancient Israelites might have seen it, for in the eyes of the royal theology the king was a very real manifestation of God. The king was God's anointed. He was God's adopted son. He was the bridge that connected the people to God. Christian theology, too, has seen this psalm as an epiphany of God's rule on earth, not in the person of the king but in the person of Jesus.

Ephesians 3:2–3a, 5–6 What Isaiah had only dreamed of, the author of Ephesians now proclaims has already happened. Gentiles are coming to God. In fact, by the time Ephesians was written, most everyone knew that Paul's mission to welcome Gentiles into the church had been successful. That was no mystery. What everyone didn't know, however, was that God had intended the inclusion of Gentiles from the very beginning. What is more, God also intended that Gentiles would be included as full coheirs, not just as guests in the household of God.

Since most of us in the Church today are Gentiles, this revelation does not seem to be much of an epiphany for us. But in Paul's day, God's secret plan for the Gentiles would have been shocking. If we are willing to apply it to our own day, the universality of God's plan can still shock us. It challenges our human tendency to put up barriers against those we perceive as different. It particularly challenges our long-standing practice of drawing theological lines between those who are acceptable and those who are not.

Matthew 2:1–12 Of all the Gospel writers, Matthew is the most meticulous about tying Old Testament stories and prophecies to the life of Jesus. For Matthew, the visit from the Magi fulfills a number of prophecies. He quotes two of them, but the prophecy he has most in mind is the one we saw from Isaiah 60.

As if on cue, the Gentile Magi arrive in Bethlehem, bearing gifts and talking about the light of a great star. But after that, the plot thickens. Not everyone welcomes this new epiphany of God. Herod fears that a rival has come to claim his ill-gotten throne. The people of Jerusalem are "troubled" (2:3). Even the Magi themselves end up sneaking away, having been warned in a dream not to return to Herod.

This is surely not what Isaiah had in mind, but Matthew is determined to speak the truth. Epiphanies of God are not all sweetness and light. They also announce a new order and, as such, they threaten people like Herod, people who have a stake in maintaining the status quo. Jesus threatened the power structure from the very beginning. But to those who seek him, like those star-gazing Magi, he is the very light of God.

Reflection Questions for the Catechist

⑨ How has salvation been made manifest for you?

⑨ To whom are you called to share the light of Christ?

⑨ What experience comes to mind in which you were challenged to expand your view beyond the status quo?

Catechist's Guide

Objectives

▷ To grasp how startling and challenging it was for the early Christians to take to heart that the message of the Gospel is for all.

▷ To grow in self-understanding as people who are called to evangelize.

▷ Catechumens will be able to integrate the Christmas story into a cohesive narrative that expresses God's love for humanity.

Dismissal and Procession

Following the homily, the priest celebrant picks up the Lectionary and invites the catechumens to come forward with the catechist(s) who will lead today's dismissal session. Holding the Lectionary so that all can see, the priest celebrant sends the catechumens and catechist(s) forward using RCIA, 67, his own words, or the following:

PRIEST: My dear friends, like the Magi, you have seen the star of Bethlehem, for you have begun to walk in the light of Christ. We send you forth so that you may reflect more deeply on the Word of God you have shared with us today. We look forward to the day when you will remain here with us at the Lord's table. Go in peace.

All process to where the dismissal session will take place. The catechist holds the Lectionary in a reverent manner. The assembly may sing an acclamation to accompany the procession.

Centering

Upon reaching the place where the dismissal occurs, place the Lectionary on the ambo, lectern, or other dignified place (or hold the book reverently). Light the candle that is in the place of gathering and reread Matthew 2:1–12 in order to refocus the group's attention. Consider singing the Responsorial Psalm or have a recording of it available to use as part of the centering, either before or after the reading.

Reflection and Discussion

The following "script" may be used or adapted to help facilitate discussion on today's readings. Begin the discussion by asking the catechumens if any words or phrases from today's readings spoke to them.

The magnitude of Christmas is so great that it takes a season to adequately express and reflect upon the message. Today we celebrate the Epiphany. *Epiphany* means "manifestation." Through today's celebration, we recognize that salvation is offered to all through Jesus Christ. The gift of God's love is for everyone.

⑨ How are you continuing to celebrate Christmas Time?

⑨ In what ways does the extended season invite you to more fully understand the meaning of Christmas Time?

“Rise up in splendor, Jerusalem, your light has come, / the glory of the LORD shines upon you!” (Isaiah 60:1). The people of Israel were living in exile. It seemed that all around them was darkness and despair. Isaiah gives the Israelites a message of hope. God is with them, no matter how desperate their situation may be. God’s light will shine! The Israelites scattered and taken away from their home will be united in God’s presence. In time, people of all nations will come to them, proclaiming the praises of the One God who is their Lord.

- Have you or someone close to you experienced a moment of desperation or despair?
- Have you ever been separated from your loved ones due to physical necessity such as a job or school, or as a result of conflict or disagreement?
- In what ways did the assurance of God’s love get you through this time?
- In what ways does Isaiah’s message of hope speak to your experience?

In today’s reading from Isaiah and the psalm, we are provided images of rulers of nations in caravans of camels carrying gifts to present to the Lord. For the people of Israel, these images powerfully told of a future in which all peoples would declare their belief in the One God. Not only was this a theological hope, but there were also temporal implications to this great dream. The Israelites would live in a time of justice; the poor and lowly would receive care; God’s ways would be the way of life for the world.

- Are there times in which it seems Christianity is in exile in our surrounding culture?
- Is it difficult for you to express your faith and its impact among family or friends?

In the letter to the Ephesians, we hear that the promise of salvation is for Gentiles as well as for the people of Israel. Keep in mind that before Jesus, the Jewish people knew themselves to be the *only* chosen people. Yet, as the early Christians reflected on Jesus’ interactions with Gentiles and on the revelation to Peter and Paul, they began to recognize that the Gentiles are “coheirs, members of the same body, and copartners in the promise in Christ Jesus through the gospel” (Ephesians 3:6). This expanded understanding of the universality of the Gospel message is for us as well. Not only are we challenged to share the Good News of God’s love with those who have not yet experienced it, we are also charged with inviting one another into a deeper encounter with Christ, through which the lives of all are to be transformed. Christ’s light is for everyone!

- Who in your life needs to know God’s love in a special way at this time?
- How might you bring the Good News to this person?

The story of the Magi who bring their gifts to pay homage to the baby Jesus powerfully illustrates how the child in the manger challenged the existing expectations for the Messiah. The child, born in poverty and simplicity, as well as the arrival of the Gentile Magi to pay him homage, would certainly challenge all that the people expected of the anointed one of God and would overturn existing structures of power.

- What gifts do you bring to share Christ’s light through your actions and interactions with others?

Wrapping It Up

Consider these points to conclude the dismissal. Integrate the thoughts and ideas that surfaced during the discussion.

- Salvation in Christ is offered to all people.
- We are called to share Christ's light through our actions and interactions with others.
- Each of us has gifts through which we may share the light of Christ in the world.

Closing Prayer

Conclude with prayer. If time permits, sing the psalm refrain a few times before or after the following prayer.

God of splendor and light,
your glory shines through every darkness,
bringing hope to all who are in despair.
Your love is made manifest through the child Jesus in the manger,
whose birth announced your love for all.
May we, like the Magi, bring our gifts to share Christ's light with the world
so that all may come to know your love, justice, mercy, and peace.
Through Christ our Lord.
Amen.

Readings for the Next Dismissal

Provide catechumens with a list of the readings for the next dismissal session. Consult the liturgical calendar on page xvi to find out what day will be observed next week. Give catechumens the questions below to guide their reflection through the week.

- What connections are you seeing in the readings of this liturgical season? As you pray with the readings, around what themes do your thoughts seem to be coming together?
- Where do the readings intersect with your journey of faith? What questions do they raise for you?

Extended Catechesis

Based on today's readings and liturgical observance, the following topics may be covered for extended catechesis:

- Call to evangelize
- Universal offer of salvation
- Christ's light shown through acts of faith, hope, and love

FEAST OF THE BAPTISM OF THE LORD

Focus: Come to the Lord through the springs of salvation.

Lectionary #21B

❧ The First Reading, Responsorial Psalm, and Second Reading from Year A may also be used.

Catechist's Preparation

Overview of the Feast

With today's celebration of the Feast of the Baptism of the Lord, we conclude Christmas Time. Jesus' baptism shows us that, while sinless, he identifies with humanity, opening for us the springs of salvation. Jesus' baptism is also an occasion for a manifestation of the Triune God: as Jesus comes up from the water, the Holy Spirit descends upon him and a voice comes from the heavens declaring, "You are my beloved Son; with you I am well pleased" (Mark 1:11). As you lead your catechumens today, consider what it means to them to prepare for Baptism, through which they will know themselves as the beloved sons and daughters of God.

Scripture Background

Isaiah 55:1–11 The First Reading begins with the image of a banquet to describe the richness of God's blessings. In this section of Isaiah, the long exile is ending; the people are returning to their homeland and to the free practice of worship and living of the covenant between God and the people. Abundant riches await all who come to the Lord. God, the Holy One, always awaits all who come, regardless of wealth or status, with the offer of mercy and forgiveness. God is ready to renew the covenant with the chosen people. The faithfulness of God is beyond our comprehension, for God's ways are above our ways, God's thoughts above our thoughts. This reading seems especially appropriate when paired with the narrative of Jesus' baptism, and is also among the readings for the Easter Vigil, providing a fitting reflection for those who will enter the waters of Baptism that night.

Isaiah 12:2–3, 4bcd, 5–6 (3) This song of thanksgiving uses images and phrases similar to the psalms. With knowledge of the saving God, the people find confidence and courage. Those who are thankful to the Lord for salvation fittingly give praise, making God's great deeds known to all. The response which we sing, taken from this section of Isaiah ties the First Reading with the Gospel, the "springs of salvation" offered in Baptism (refrain).

1 John 5:1–9 The first letter of John is a theological reflection on the divine and human nature of Jesus. All who believe that Jesus is the Son of God are themselves loved by the Father. This relationship calls the believer into right relationship with God. Belief is carried out in action as a faith response to the love one has for God.

It is not necessary to rely solely on the testimony of humans in recognizing Jesus' divine and human nature. The Spirit, as well as the water of Baptism and the blood of the Eucharist, are testimony to the truth of Christ's identity. Spirit, water, and blood are God's testimony. To put faith in Christ is to accept the testimony of God that Jesus is the Son of God.

Mark 1:7–11 From its first verse, the Gospel according to Mark gets right to the point about who Jesus is and what it means to follow him. In today's reading from this Gospel, beginning with verse 7 of the first chapter, we meet John the Baptist who baptizes people in the Jordan. John clearly understands his role in preparing people for the Christ. We hear today that Jesus came from Nazareth and was baptized by John. While John is the vessel for Jesus' baptism, it is God who blesses and affirms Jesus. As in all of the gospel narratives of Jesus' baptism, as Jesus comes out of the water, the Holy Spirit descends upon him, and a voice from heaven speaks, "You are my beloved Son; with you I am well pleased" (Mark 1:11). Thus, God blesses and affirms Jesus and his ministry as the Christ, the anointed one of God.

The Baptism of the Lord is known as the third manifestation narrative, following the accounts of the Nativity and the Epiphany. Through these narratives, we come to see who Jesus is, the Divine Son of God, Son of Mary, who has come to be one with humanity, Emmanuel.

Reflection Questions for the Catechist

- What does it mean to you to be the beloved of God?
- What consolation do you find in knowing that God's thoughts and ways are beyond your own?
- What is in your heart at this time about the grace of Baptism?

Catechist's Guide

Objectives

- ▷ To reflect on the abundant life of the children of God.
- ▷ To deepen the catechumen's understanding of Jesus, who enters fully into our human state and draws us toward life with God.
- ▷ To reflect on the grace of Baptism.

Dismissal and Procession

Following the homily, the priest celebrant picks up the Lectionary and invites the catechumens to come forward with the catechist(s) who will lead today's dismissal session. Holding the Lectionary so that all can see, the priest celebrant sends the catechumens and catechist(s) forward using RCIA, 67, his own words, or the following:

PRIEST: **My dear friends, as we send forth the catechumens, let us continue to pray for them as they seek a fuller relationship with Jesus and with Holy Mother Church. May the harsh reality of cradle and Cross only deepen their awareness of God, and his overwhelming love, in sending us Jesus, his beloved Son. Go now in peace.**

All process to where the dismissal session will take place. The catechist holds the Lectionary in a reverent manner. The assembly may sing an acclamation to accompany the procession.

Centering

Upon reaching the place where the dismissal occurs, place the Lectionary on the ambo, lectern, or other dignified place (or hold the book reverently). Light the candle that is in the place of gathering and reread Isaiah 55:1–11 in order to refocus the group's attention. Consider singing the Responsorial Psalm or have a recording of it available to use as part of the centering, either before or after the reading.

Reflection and Discussion

The following "script" may be used or adapted to help facilitate discussion on today's readings. Begin the discussion by asking the catechumens if any words or phrases from today's readings spoke to them.

Today we celebrate the final Sunday of Christmas Time, the Feast of the Baptism of the Lord. Throughout the weeks of the season, we have reflected upon the mystery of the Incarnation. We have gained understanding about God's great love for humanity, about the meaning of Jesus' birth, and the ways in which we are called to witness to and share Christ's love through the manner in which we live our lives.

- What stands out for you about Christmas Time?
- How has the celebration of Christmas Time in worship, in our time together, and at home led you to ponder the love of God more deeply?

We hear again from the prophet Isaiah in today's First Reading. This passage paints vivid images of life with God as a banquet. The thirsty are invited to come to the water; those who are hungry receive food; all will delight in rich food, regardless of wealth or status (or lack thereof). God is ready to renew the covenant, through which God's people are assured of God's faithfulness and mercy.

⑤ For what do you thirst?

⑤ For what are you hungry?

⑤ In what ways does Christ meet you in your need?

Isaiah invites us to seek the Lord, to turn to God with repentant hearts. It is sometimes difficult for us to comprehend God's great mercy and forgiveness. We may hesitate to acknowledge our failings to God, yet we must remember that, for God, "as high as the heavens are above the earth / so high are my ways above your ways / and my thoughts above your thoughts" (Isaiah 55:9). With this assurance, we can sing, "God indeed is my savior; / I am confident and unafraid" (Isaiah 12:2).

⑤ In what ways are you growing in confident faith?

⑤ How is your life changing through finding strength and courage in the Lord?

In the Second Reading, from the first letter of John, we deepen the recognition of security in God's love. We are promised that those who love God keep his commandments and that these commandments are not burdensome. Those who have faith and act on it do so in response to God's great love, not from a sense of duty, but out of a desire to live in right relationship with God and with others.

⑤ Is this a shift in thinking for you?

⑤ How does your faith lead you to respond by striving to keep God's commandments, to live in right relationship with God?

We see this great love of God come to life in the Gospel story of Jesus' baptism in the Jordan. Jesus is sinless and therefore does not "need" a baptism of repentance. Yet Jesus comes to John for baptism. Jesus fully identifies with humanity, and through his entry into the waters of baptism, he opens to us the fullness of life with him. Through Christ, the wellsprings of salvation are prepared for us.

⑤ As you continue to prepare for Baptism, what does it mean to you that Jesus so identifies with us that he himself was baptized?

As Jesus comes up out of the water, the Holy Spirit descends upon him and a voice comes from the heavens, saying, "You are my beloved Son; with you I am well pleased" (Matthew 1:11). This manifestation of the Triune God gives us increased insight. At this moment, we are shown that Jesus is the anointed One of God, the Messiah. Through Baptism, we are drawn deeply to Christ, united to God as beloved sons and daughters.

⑤ What in your life must change if you are to embrace life as a baptized member of Christ's body?

⑤ What does it mean to you to be known as the beloved of God?

Wrapping It Up

Consider these points to conclude the dismissal. Integrate the thoughts and ideas that surfaced during the discussion.

- Jesus' baptism opens for us the fullness of life with God in Christ.
- Living in deep relationship with God leads to accepting and keeping God's commandments.
- We can be assured of God's constant offer of mercy and forgiveness.

Closing Prayer

Conclude with prayer. If time permits, sing the psalm refrain a few times before or after the following prayer.

God our Father,
you are always ready to offer mercy and forgiveness.
Help us to trust in your goodness and to come to you, confident of your love.
Our of your great love,
you sent your Son to enter into human weakness
to raise us toward the fullness of life with you.
Show us the way to live as your disciples in the days and years of our lives.
In the presence of your Holy Spirit, we find courage and strength.
Fill our hearts with insight and wisdom
that we may accept and live as your beloved sons and daughters.
Through Christ our Lord.
Amen.

Readings for the Next Dismissal

Provide catechumens with a list of the readings for the next dismissal session. Consult the liturgical calendar on page xvi to find out what day will be observed next week. Give catechumens the questions below to guide their reflection through the week.

- What connections are you seeing in the readings of this liturgical season? As you pray with the readings, around what themes do your thoughts seem to be coming together?

- Where do the readings intersect with your journey of faith? What questions do they raise for you?

Extended Catechesis

Based on today's readings and liturgical observance, the following topics may be covered for extended catechesis:

✳ Baptism

✳ Trinity

✳ Commandments

INTRODUCTION TO LENT

Overview of Lent

From the experience of early Christian communities to the present time, the weeks leading to the celebration of the Triduum have been set aside for intense reflection on the meaning of the Paschal Mystery of Jesus Christ, in whose life, Passion, Death, and Resurrection we are joined in Baptism, Confirmation, and Eucharist. While this is true for all disciples, it is particularly rich with meaning and the potential for spiritual growth for catechumens who continue their journey and the elect who will be initiated at the Easter Vigil. The roots of the season as preparation for initiation and the participation of the elect as they journey toward the Easter Vigil help to bring the season to life—as they prepare for initiation (or completion of initiation), we grasp more fully the blessing and challenge of our own Baptism and commit ourselves to Christ to a greater degree with our lives.

For those catechumens who will not be initiated this year, the discipline of the Lenten practices of prayer, fasting, and almsgiving/works of charity, while continuing to be dismissed from the Sunday liturgy and taking part in catechetical sessions, provides enriched spiritual nourishment and encourages their growth in faith. With the whole Christian community, they consider Jesus' identity as the Messiah and learn what it means to be a disciple. Taking to heart the seasonal call to turn away from sin, and turn toward God, the catechumens journey with the community, discovering and taking to heart Christ's mission of love. Those who journey with the catechumens may continue to use this resource throughout the season, leading them to reflect deeply upon Christ's Paschal Mystery and the hope of the Resurrection.

The elect embrace the season as a time of purification and enlightenment, a final, intense period of preparation for initiation and the commencement of a lifetime of membership in Christ's Body. The dismissals for the elect are ideally separate from those of the catechumens. Those who walk with the elect may still use this resource to guide their dismissal from the Sunday liturgy, while also leading the elect to prepare for, break open, and reflect upon the various rites (dismissal guides for these rites have been prepared for you and are found in the appendix, beginning on page 311). All who walk with them as sponsors and leaders recommit themselves to living as disciples who embrace the Cross and look forward to the joy of the Resurrection at Easter.

Preparing a Seasonal Environment

Lent is typically austere in environmental design. Use violet cloths and perhaps one single candle, reminding all that nothing extinguishes the light of Christ. Some parishes use a few sparse palm branches or thorns in the environment, as a reminder of the celebration on Palm Sunday of the Lord's Passion. A large crucifix adds a simple but dramatic element to your gathering space during Lent. The crucifix reminds catechumens of Jesus' journey and our invitation to walk with him. It calls to mind the suffering of those today who carry their own difficult crosses. A table could hold a bowl of unblessed ashes or sand, reminiscent of the desert. Either of these basic materials helps focus the mind during prayer, imparts an atmosphere of simplicity, and invites us to strip away pretenses.

Keep a space available for the Lectionary (or Bible) such as a lectern or table. Keep a candle near the Lectionary (or Bible) and light this candle before the session begins. In everything you do to create the environment for Lent in the dismissal space, take your lead from the environment in the sanctuary of the main assembly. Consistency between what the catechumens see in the environment in that space and in the environment in the dismissal space is important. You do not want to create divergent messages about the day and season and thus generate unnecessary questions or confusion within the group. Keep the environment simple but not simplistic, understated but not minimized. Colors, light, images, and other added elements should all assist the catechumens in their reflection on the significance of the day and the Word of God.

Overview of the Readings: Year B

First Readings   We begin the season with narratives from Genesis, in which we hear the stories of the covenant with Noah and the promise of God to Abraham following Abraham's willingness to sacrifice his son, Isaac. On the Third Sunday of Lent, we read from the book of Exodus, in which the people of God are given the Ten Commandments. (Note the readings for Masses in which the Scrutinies are celebrated are taken from Year A in weeks 3, 4, and 5, and are summarized below). On the Fourth Sunday, we hear the story of the exile of the Israelites from 2 Chronicles, and on the Fifth Sunday, the people are promised that God will renew the covenant, placing the law within us, writing it on our hearts. The First Reading on Palm Sunday of the Lord's Passion is one of the suffering servant songs of Isaiah, in which the prophet declares love for God even in the face of adversity.

Responsorial Psalms   Throughout the season, we sing Psalms 25, 116, 19, 137, 51, and 22. Each invites us to open our hearts to God and his ways, assured that he is with us through every trial, steadfast in love, mercy, and forgiveness.

Second Readings   During Year B, we hear from 1 Peter that through water, we are drawn to life in Christ; from Romans, if God is for us, no one can triumph against us; from 1 Corinthians, that God's wisdom defies human reason; from Ephesians, that God is rich in mercy, by grace we are saved; from Hebrews, that Jesus was made perfect through obedience to the will of the Father. These readings culminate in the great proclamation on Palm Sunday of the Lord's Passion, from Philippians, that Jesus Christ is Lord, to the glory of God the Father.

Gospel Readings   During Year B on the first two Sunday, we hear from Mark's account of Jesus' temptation in the desert and his Transfiguration on the mountain. We also hear familiar passages from the Gospel according to John on the Third, Fourth, and Fifth Sundays of the season: On the Third Sunday, Jesus cleanses the Temple; on the Fourth, we hear that "God so loved the world that he gave his only Son" (John 3:16); and on the Fifth, "whoever hates his life in this world will preserve it for eternal life" (John 12:25). And, of course, we conclude the season in hearing the tremendous narrative of Jesus' institution of the Eucharist, his Passion, Death, and burial.

Please refer to pages 55, 63, and 71 for commentary on the Year A Scrutiny readings for the Third, Fourth, and Fifth Sundays of Lent.

First Sunday of Lent

Focus: To remember and keep God's covenant.

Lectionary #23B

❧ Today is the usual date for the Rite of Election. If you wish to discuss this ritual during the dismissal session, a dismissal guide is provided in the appendix on page 319. If your parish celebrated the optional Rite of Sending of the Catechumens for Election, and you wish to discuss this ritual, a dismissal guide is found in the appendix on page 316. A separate dismissal session should take place with the elect.

Catechist's Preparation

Overview of the Sunday

"Repent, and believe in the gospel" (imposition of Ashes; *The Roman Missal*). On Ash Wednesday, we began the season of Lent, through which we turn away from all that keeps us from God and turn toward Christ's way of love. We begin the season by recalling the covenant between God and Noah, a rebirth of relationship between humanity and God. As you prepare to lead your catechumens through the Period of Purification and Enlightenment, consider what it means to live in covenant with God. How will you lead them to more fully believe in the Gospel? How will you embrace Gospel living yourself? In what ways will your time together lead each of you to renounce sin and embrace new life in Christ, in preparation for or renewal of the waters of Baptism?

Scripture Background

Genesis 9:8–15 God's statement to Noah and his family in this reading is profound: "I will establish my covenant with you, that never again shall all bodily creatures be destroyed by the waters of a flood" (9:11). Never again will God destroy humanity. It is a wonderful promise on God's part because, while Noah and his family may deserve to be rewarded for their faithfulness, human beings will certainly continue to sin. Yet, in spite of the infidelity of subsequent generations of humans, God has promised never to send destruction again. This is God's covenant: to remain in a loving, compassionate, and merciful relationship with all human beings, no matter what.

After the flood, God once again invited human beings to recognize the beauty of creation. The flood waters released humanity from sin and revealed the possibility of a new Eden, a new garden of life. This new earth, birthed from the flood waters, is where humans could be faithful partners in their loving relationship with God. God's creatures are welcomed, once again, to enter the waters of rebirth. In those waters, they can remember their part in keeping the covenant and relearn the ways of God. During Lent, we join with those who move toward the waters of Baptism at the Easter Vigil.

With them, we are invited to seek a rebirth from sin and recognize our possibility of new life.

The bow suspended in the sky in Genesis is a sign of peace and God's faithfulness. It is a new dawn for humans who are, once again, invited to learn and live by God's ways. Like Noah, we see the sign of a new dawn as we begin this Lenten season.

Psalm 25:4–5, 6–7, 8–9 (see 10) We pray this same psalm and verses on the Third Sunday in Ordinary Time, but with a different refrain. In today's refrain, we pray for the courage and trust to learn the ways of the Lord: "Your ways, O Lord, are love and truth to those who keep your covenant" (25:10). Learning the ways of God means being willing to be attentive to what God offers to teach us. In the psalm, we plead for God to make known, teach, guide, and remember. We ask God to be active in our lives. Despite our sinfulness, which we acknowledge as Lent begins, God does remember. God does make it known. God does teach and guide. The way to the Lord is set before us.

1 Peter 3:18–22 The passage from Peter's epistle sounds like a creedal statement: Christ suffered, died, and rose, brought to life in the Spirit. His imagery reminded listeners of God's patience while Noah obeyed in building the ark. Peter linked the flood to the saving water of Baptism. His message is clear: Christ suffered that he might lead us to God.

Some Scripture commentators suggest that because this early community was living the true ways of the Gospel message, they were being derided and maligned. Peter encourages them to continue to live in ways that are faithful to Christ, no matter the cost. The author points to Jesus, who also suffered at the hands of those who abused him for his witness and message of God's reign. Yet, death was not the end. Jesus' Resurrection and new life in the spirit enabled his message and ministry to continue. All other powers are subject to the Risen Lord.

Mark 1:12–15 Mark gives the briefest account of Jesus' temptation in the desert of the three synoptic Gospel accounts. Its brevity drives home the most important points. The Spirit drives Jesus into the desert. There he encounters Satan, wild beasts, and angels. It is an otherworldly experience, but he is not alone. The Spirit is with him. When he emerges after forty days, the message he proclaims is clear: God's reign is at hand. Repent and believe the Gospel. Jesus was willing to submit to learning the ways of God in the desert for forty days, and came out preaching the Good News of God's covenant love.

As we begin our Lenten journey, we are invited to spend these forty days learning the ways of God. We are not alone. The Spirit is with us. During this time, we will need to confront the sinfulness, emptiness, and infidelity of our own lives in response to Jesus' exhortation to repent and believe in the Gospel. In our encounter with the Lord and with the Gospel message, we can learn the saving ways of God and remember our promise to keep God's covenant.

Reflection Questions for the Catechist

⑨ From what must you turn away during this Lenten season?

⑨ How will you more faithfully turn toward Christ?

⑨ What practice or promise will make this Lent a fruitful season for you?

Catechist's Guide

Objectives

▷ To develop an appreciation for Lent as a season of spiritual renewal.

▷ To reflect on the covenant love of God for humanity.

▷ To recognize the Lenten call to repentance as a way to grow in Christian living of covenant love.

Dismissal and Procession

Following the homily, the priest celebrant picks up the Lectionary and invites the catechumens to come forward with the catechist(s) who will lead today's dismissal session. Holding the Lectionary so that all can see, the priest celebrant sends the catechumens and catechist(s) forward using RCIA, 67, his own words, or the following:

PRIEST: **During Lent, we enter the desert with the Lord Jesus to fast, to pray, and to engage in works of mercy. This is our sacred pilgrimage, when the Church journeys together, striving to become more like her Master. We give thanks that you, our sisters and brothers, remind us of the Lord's daily call to conversion. May your ears be open to God's Word this day, and may your hearts be eager to share his love with others. Soon we shall all be one around the table of the Lord. Go in peace.**

All process to where the dismissal session will take place. The catechist holds the Lectionary in a reverent manner. The assembly may sing an acclamation to accompany the procession.

Centering

Upon reaching the place where the dismissal occurs, place the Lectionary on the ambo, lectern, or other dignified place (or hold the book reverently). Light the candle that is in the place of gathering and reread Genesis 9:8–5 in order to refocus the group's attention. Consider singing the Responsorial Psalm or have a recording of it available to use as part of the centering, either before or after the reading.

Reflection and Discussion

The following "script" may be used or adapted to help facilitate discussion on today's readings. Begin the discussion by asking the catechumens if any words or phrases from today's readings spoke to them.

Today is the First Sunday of Lent. Lent is a season of renewal through repentance, reflection, and spiritual practices. Lent is also a time of immediate preparation for those/you who will be initiated at the Easter Vigil, a time in which they/you anticipate the waters of Baptism. The baptized prepare to renew their baptismal commitment to Christ. During Lent, we turn away from all that is counter to our relationship with God and commitment to Christ, and turn toward that to which Christ calls us. The traditional practices of prayer, fasting, and almsgiving or works of charity are concrete ways in which to put our Lenten resolve into action.

- What is on your mind or in your heart as you begin Lent this year?
- In what ways do you look forward to a season in which to turn more intentionally away from sin and toward Jesus?

In the First Reading, from the Book of Genesis, we hear of the establishment of a covenant between God and Noah and all who follow after the time of the flood. God promises to never bring destruction upon the whole earth again. This is striking because God does not presume we will never sin. Rather, knowing that we will surely sin, God establishes a covenant with humanity. God's covenant is to remain in a merciful and loving relationship for all ages to come.

- In your own words, what does it mean to live in covenant relationship with God?

In today's Responsorial Psalm, we ask God to teach us how to live in the Lord's ways. The Lord shows sinners the way and guides the humble to justice. In a particular way during Lent, we acknowledge our sinfulness. Rather than hiding our failings from God and from ourselves, we reflect on the ways in which we fail to live as God's children and as followers of Jesus, and we resolve to do better in the future.

- What is the relationship between humility and the repentance to which Lent calls us?
- Are there aspects of Catholic teaching or Christian living that you find especially challenging?

The Second Reading, from the first letter of Peter, presents a summary of Christian faith: Jesus suffered and was put to death, he rose, and is now at the right hand of God in heaven. Those who are baptized have been drawn into Christ's Death and Resurrection. The author sees the flood of Noah as a prefigurement of Baptism—in the waters of the flood, Noah and those who were with him were offered new life. Through the waters of Baptism, we are given new life in Christ.

- What is different in your daily living that results from your commitment to follow Christ?
- What change(s) do you need to make in order to more fully embrace new life in Christ?

The passage we heard today from the Gospel according to Mark immediately follows Jesus' baptism in the Jordan. The Spirit drove Jesus out into the desert, where he stayed for forty days. The forty day time in the desert is reminiscent of the forty years in the desert of Moses and the Israelites, and it is from this forty day period that we embrace the forty days of Lent. Going out to the desert, Jesus would have been alone and would have faced physical as well as spiritual discomfort. Jesus was tempted by Satan. Remember that Jesus is fully human as well as fully divine. It is very reasonable to understand that he faced temptation as he prepared to begin his earthly ministry. Following his desert time, Jesus is ready to proclaim the Good News (Gospel) of God's covenant love and mercy. He calls us to repentance, through which we will be prepared to live as Christ's people in the reign of God.

- What tempts you to turn away from Jesus and your commitment to Christ?

Wrapping It Up

Consider these points to conclude the dismissal. Integrate the thoughts and ideas that surfaced during the discussion.

- God's covenant relationship is an invitation to respond to God's constant love, mercy, and forgiveness.
- Lent is a season for spiritual renewal through repentance and spiritual practice.
- Jesus is the covenant love of God in human form; following Jesus is a living of covenant in daily life.

Closing Prayer

Conclude with prayer. If time permits, sing the psalm refrain a few times before or after the following prayer.

Gracious and merciful God,
you created a covenant between yourself, Noah, and people for ages to come.
Noah and those with him on the ark,
were offered new life beyond the waters of the flood.
In the waters of Baptism, you call us to new life in Christ.
Be with us as we enter into the forty days of Lent.
Teach us your ways, guide us to your truth,
show us your way of justice and mercy.
May we see this time as a gift,
through which we will turn away from all that is not of you
and toward fruitful faithfulness to Christ and his way of love.
Who lives and reigns for ever and ever.
Amen.

Readings for the Next Dismissal

Provide catechumens with a list of the readings for the next dismissal session. Consult the liturgical calendar on page xvi to find out what day will be observed next week. Give catechumens the questions below to guide their reflection through the week.

- What connections are you seeing in the readings of this liturgical season? As you pray with the readings, around what themes do your thoughts seem to be coming together?
- Where do the readings intersect with your journey of faith? What questions do they raise for you?

Extended Catechesis

Based on today's readings and liturgical observance, the following topics may be covered for extended catechesis with catechumens who will not be initiated this coming Easter:

- Covenant
- Lent
- Repentance
- Forgiveness
- Mercy
- Reconciliation

SECOND SUNDAY OF LENT

Focus: To discern God's desire for his beloved.

Lectionary #26B

Catechist's Preparation

Overview of the Sunday

Sacrifice. Transfiguration. Discerning. Doing God's will. On this Second Sunday of Lent, we hear the dramatic story of Abraham, who was willing to sacrifice his only son, Isaac. We hear this great story alongside the account of Jesus' Transfiguration on the mountain, in which the disciples hear God say, "This is my beloved Son. Listen to him" (Mark 9:7). Abraham's willingness to answer God's call, paired with our reflection the sacrifice of Jesus, God's beloved Son, leads us to grapple with our own readiness to hear and answer the call of the Lord. As you lead your catechumens in reflection on this Second Sunday of Lent, help them discern God's desire for them—to be beloved in God's sight.

Scripture Background

Genesis 22:1–2, 9a, 10–13, 15–18 The sacrifice of Isaac focuses more on Abraham's obedience to God's desire than it does on the sacrifice itself. God had promised Abraham that he would be the father of many nations. All hope of the promise's fulfillment rested on Isaac, who embodied all that Abraham loved and all that would ensure his posterity. Isaac was not just any son. He was Abraham's only son, the one "whom you love" (22:2). Without Isaac, Abraham's own meaning and identity would cease. This makes God's demand a true test of faith.

Abraham immediately demonstrates his readiness by responding, "Here I am!" (22:7). As Abraham is about to sacrifice his only son, the Lord's messenger intervenes. Abraham is praised for being willing to sacrifice "[his] own beloved son" (22:12) simply because the Lord so desired. Because of his willingness and obedience to God's word, Abraham is blessed abundantly with many descendants, and becomes the means by which "all the nations of the earth shall find blessing" (22:18).

Psalm 116:10, 15, 16–17, 18–19 (116:9) Trust in the face of great suffering and pain is the central message of this psalm. The refrain portrays God as a God of the living. Trust in God, no matter how difficult and challenging, always has life-giving consequences. Walking before the Lord brings assurance that we will always walk "in the land of the living" (116:9). The psalm verses emphasize how "Precious in the eyes of the Lord / is the death

of his faithful ones" (116:15). God works at loosening the bonds of death from "your servant, the son of your handmaid" (116:16). This bountiful love moves the psalmist to praise the Lord, to offer sacrifices, and to "pay" his vows in the sight of all. With Abraham, Isaac, and Jesus, our desire should always be to trust the Lord no matter how difficult, knowing this to be the path that leads to life.

Romans 8:31b–34 Paul's argument and rhetorical questions stress God's bountiful love for humanity. Rhetorically, Paul states that if "God is for us" (8:31), there is nothing we need fear. Whatever God does is ultimately for our benefit. The ultimate proof of God's love is Jesus, the offering of the "beloved Son" (Mark 9:7) "for us all" (Romans 8:32). If God was willing to gift us with the beloved, is there nothing that God would not give us? In arguments typical of his day, Paul highlights God's bountiful love for all. God acquits us through Jesus who died, was raised, and sits at the right hand of God interceding on our behalf.

Mark 9:2–10 Mark presents a select group of disciples witnessing the transfigured Jesus conversing with two towering Old Testament figures, Moses and Elijah. The symbolic elements that the evangelist Mark incorporates into the narrative convey truths about Jesus' identity and mission. In Jewish tradition, a person's transformation was connected with messianic end times. Moses and Elijah are Jewish precursors to messianic times. Having these two converse with Jesus is Mark's way of saying that both Moses and Elijah acknowledge Jesus as Messiah. The voice from the cloud, symbolic of God, proclaims Jesus as "my beloved Son," thus linking Jesus with Isaac in the First Reading. God directs all of us to "listen to him" (9:7).

The disciples are fearful and confused about Jesus' identity and mission. Mark's Transfiguration account clearly identifies Jesus as God's beloved, the Messiah, who would die but would be raised up. Mark uses the Transfiguration as God's way of offering hope to Jesus' followers as they experienced opposition and Jesus' eventual Death. They still needed to learn how to discern God's direction and purpose in their lives, even in the face of death. They had to learn that life, and not death, is God's desire for all his beloved sons and daughters.

<table>
<tr>
<td>

**Reflection
Questions for
the Catechist**

</td>
<td>

⑤ When you think about your catechumens, how do you see each of them discerning God's call?

⑤ What recent experience comes to mind in which you felt compelled to sacrifice something? How did you discern God's will in this experience? What happened as a result?

⑤ Who helps you to discern God's call?

</td>
</tr>
</table>

Catechist's Guide

Objectives

▷ To reflect on the story of Abraham in light of the sacrifice of Jesus, God's beloved Son.

▷ To deepen the catechumens' appreciation of themselves as the beloved of God.

▷ To reflect on the continuing call to discern and do God's will.

**Dismissal and
Procession**

Following the homily, the priest celebrant picks up the Lectionary and invites the catechumens to come forward with the catechist(s) who will lead today's dismissal session. Holding the Lectionary so that all can see, the priest celebrant sends the catechumens and catechist(s) forward using RCIA, 67, his own words, or the following:

PRIEST: For those of you participating in the rites of Christian Initiation, you have already experienced a long journey this year. You have nearly reached the fullness of your journey toward full communion in the Catholic, Christian tradition. Do not weary now or let the devil tempt you. Continue on your way. May you always find blessings now and in every day as you continue to turn toward God in your life. Trust in Jesus and the Cross to lead you home safely. Go in peace.

All process to where the dismissal session will take place. The catechist holds the Lectionary in a reverent manner. The assembly may sing an acclamation to accompany the procession.

Centering

Upon reaching the place where the dismissal occurs, place the Lectionary on the ambo, lectern, or other dignified place (or hold the book reverently). Light the candle that is in the place of gathering and reread Genesis 22:1–2, 9a, 10–13, 15–18 in order to refocus the group's attention. Consider singing the Responsorial Psalm or have a recording of it available to use as part of the centering, either before or after the reading.

**Reflection and
Discussion**

The following "script" may be used or adapted to help facilitate discussion on today's readings. Begin the discussion by asking the catechumens if any words or phrases from today's readings spoke to them.

It is the Second Sunday of Lent. Today we hear powerful stories of sacrifice, transfiguration, and God's desire that we live in newness of life. It is still early in the season of Lent, and yet our readings already reflect upon God's sacrifice of his beloved Son, and of our call to discern ourselves as the beloved of God.

⑤ In what ways is this Lenten season a time for you to listen more intently to the Lord?

⑤ What Lenten practice is the most difficult for you at this time?

⑤ What practice is bearing fruit in your life?

In the First Reading, from the Book of Genesis, we hear the dramatic story of Abraham. We recall that God had promised Abraham that his descendants would be more numerous than the stars in the sky. The birth of Isaac in Abraham and Sarah's old age was the fulfillment of that promise, the proof that they had found favor in the eyes of God. Today we hear that God put Abraham to the test, telling him to sacrifice Isaac. We cannot imagine the pain of this request by God. Yet Abraham acts in faith, responding "Here I am!" (Genesis 22:1) and taking Isaac to slaughter him on an altar which he made.

- In what ways do you sacrifice for the sake of another?

- How is this sacrifice a reflection of, or enriched by, your faith?

- In what ways do you respond to God by saying, "Here I am!" (Genesis 22:1)?

The Lord's messenger intervenes and tells Abraham not to kill Isaac. God saw Abraham's devotion through his willingness to sacrifice Isaac, and God repeats the promise that Abraham's descendants will be as countless as the stars in the sky and the sands of the seashore. "In your descendants all the nations of the earth shall find blessing—all this because you obeyed my command" (Genesis 22:18). We hear this story of Abraham in light of our knowledge of Christ's Passion and Death on the Cross. As we hear in the Second Reading, from the letter to the Romans, God "did not spare his own Son but handed him over for us all" (Romans 8:32). Abraham's willingness to offer Isaac was a reflection of his love of God. God's love for humanity is what leads to the acceptance of the suffering and Death of Jesus on the Cross. We will return to our reflection of Jesus' Passion and Death throughout Lent. For now, it is good for us to reflect on God's acceptance of Abraham's faith and to know that we, too, are called to discern, accept, and carry out God's will.

- Who or what helps you to place your faith and trust in God?

- In what ways are you consoled by the story of Abraham and Isaac?

- How does the story challenge you?

On the Second Sunday of Lent, the Gospel reading is always an account of Jesus' Transfiguration. Jesus took Peter, James, and John to the mountain and was transfigured before them. Elijah and Moses appeared to them, and they speak to Jesus. The disciples are understandably awestruck. Then they hear a voice from a cloud, "This is my beloved Son. Listen to him" (Mark 9:7). We remember the voice from the heavens that spoke at Jesus' baptism. We are mindful that through Christ we are adopted sons and daughters, the beloved of God. Like the disciples on the mountain, we also learn to listen to the Lord.

- How do you listen to the Lord?

- Who helps you in this discernment and in the carrying out of the things to which you are called?

Wrapping It Up

Consider these points to conclude the dismissal. Integrate the thoughts and ideas that surfaced during the discussion.

- Abraham teaches us to put our faith and trust in God, even when doing so is difficult.

- Christ's sacrifice shows us the depths of God's love for humanity.

- The disciples grew in their understanding of Jesus and what it meant to follow him, and so must we.

Closing Prayer

Conclude with prayer. If time permits, sing the psalm refrain a few times before or after the following prayer.

> God of power and might,
> you put Abraham to the test, and you delighted in his faithful, trusting response.
> Guide us to always listen to your Son, Jesus,
> and give us wisdom as we discern the ways
> in which you call us as your beloved sons and daughters.
> Strengthen us as we strive to place our trust in you;
> give us courage to be bold in answering your call,
> even when you ask us to sacrifice for the sake of another.
> In all things, may we give you glory, finding joy in saying, "Here I am!"
> Through Christ our Lord.
> Amen.

Readings for the Next Dismissal

Provide catechumens with a list of the readings for the next dismissal session. Consult the liturgical calendar on page xvi to find out what day will be observed next week. Give catechumens the questions below to guide their reflection through the week.

🌀 What connections are you seeing in the readings of this liturgical season? As you pray with the readings, around what themes do your thoughts seem to be coming together?

🌀 Where do the readings intersect with your journey of faith? What questions do they raise for you?

Extended Catechesis

Based on today's readings and liturgical observance, the following topics may be covered for extended catechesis with catechumens who will not be initiated this coming Easter:

❄ Discipleship

❄ Sacrifice

❄ Discernment of God's will

❄ Jesus' sacrifice and acceptance of Passion and Death out of love for humanity

If there are elect in your parish, today should be spent preparing them for the First Scrutiny and for reflecting upon the nature of sin rather than egaging in extended catechesis.

THIRD SUNDAY OF LENT, YEAR B

Focus: To find joy in the Gospel.

Lectionary #29B

❦ When the First Scrutiny is celebrated with the elect, the Year A readings are proclaimed instead of those for Year B. See page 55 for the Year A dismissal guide. A separate dismissal session should take place with the elect.

Catechist's Preparation

Overview of the Sunday

On this Third Sunday of Lent, we contemplate the perfect law of God's truth. We reflect upon our response to the passionate love of God for us which is most fully expressed in the Paschal Mystery of Jesus Christ. As you prepare for this dismissal session, reflect on your own appreciation of the power and wisdom of God, which is expressed in self-giving and sacrificial love. Think about your catechumens: In what way is their emerging faith expressed through giving of self for others? How is their conversion to Christ leading them toward joyful acceptance of the truth of the Gospel?

Scripture Background

Exodus 20:1–17 or 20:1–3, 7–8, 12–17 God convenes the Hebrew people and gives them a set of rules, and in doing so, he draws them more deeply into relationship with himself. He addresses them with the familiar second person pronoun ("I am . . . your God . . . " [20:2]), establishing an intimacy that did not exist before. He reminds them that he brought them safely out of Egypt and that he is passionate (jealous) in his commitment to them. In return he asks that they be his and his alone. This first commandment and the next two are new to the people. The remaining seven have been part of the communal wisdom that protects the common good. This time it is God, however, and not a tribal elder, who proclaims them, giving them a new authority. Though some might see the law as restrictive, God's commandments tell the people who they are—a people set aside and chosen. They provide the security of an eternal promise of faithfulness that frees them to embrace the law as a means of knowing more deeply the God who loves them with a jealous passion.

Psalm 19:8, 9, 10, 11 (John 6:68c) The Exodus reading illustrates the power of the law to transform and define a relationship between God and his people. That said, Psalm 19 as we sing it today provides its own glorious affirmation of the gift of the law of the Lord. This psalm is a poem of praise, divided into three stanzas. The first stanza, which we do not hear today, proclaims the silent majesty of God's creation. The third stanza requests freedom from sin and merciful cleansing from unknown faults. But it is the second stanza, which we sing at today's liturgy, that magnifies this hymn of praise. With its first words, "The law of the LORD is perfect, / refreshing the soul," the psalmist begins a love song that cherishes the law of the Lord (19:8). "The law of the LORD is perfect," "trustworthy," "right," "clear," "pure," and "true" (19:8, 9, 10). It enlightens the people and is the source of wisdom. It is more precious than gold. It is the law that forms God's people and draws them near. It is the law that defines this newly established covenant. In short, it is the law that gives life to the people.

1 Corinthians 1:22–25 Paul makes it clear that those Jews and Greeks saw beyond the limits of human imagination and recognized that Jesus Christ is the power and wisdom of God. They didn't necessarily understand it, but they accepted that God's wisdom defied human reason. What seemed like weakness was really strength; what seemed like abject loss was the story of victory. In the view of the faithful, Christ crucified was and is not the figure of shame, but the source of new life.

John 2:13–25 John's is the only account of the Gospel that places the cleansing of the temple at the beginning rather than at the end of the narrative. Each of the evangelists has a theological point to make and orders events accordingly. Thus, we presume that John wanted to depict the raising of Lazarus as the event that propelled Jesus from his public life toward his own suffering and death. Early on, John deems it important to describe the temple incident through a post-Resurrection lens (see 2:22). Not only does he make it clear that the temple is not a marketplace, but in addition, because the temple has been destroyed by the time John writes, he wants his readers to know that Jesus is the new temple, the place where humans meet the presence of God. Mindful of the invitation of Lent to grow more deeply in faith, we pray with Jesus, who leads us to the presence of God and the gift of new life.

Reflection Questions for the Catechist

⑨ In what ways does your love of God direct your life?

⑨ How does your commitment to Christ call you to be a person for others?

⑨ What meaning do you find in the paradox that the foolishness of God is wiser than human wisdom, and the weakness of God is stronger that human strength?

Catechist's Guide

Objectives

▷ Through reflection on the readings, catechumens will deepen their desire to live as God commands.

▷ To ponder the deep satisfaction and joy of living as a disciple.

▷ Catechumens will grow in their understanding of the Gospel call of self-giving love.

Dismissal and Procession

Following the homily, the priest celebrant picks up the Lectionary and invites the catechumens to come forward with the catechist(s) who will lead today's dismissal session. Holding the Lectionary so that all can see, the priest celebrant sends the catechumens and catechist(s) forward using RCIA, 67, his own words, or the following:

PRIEST: As you ponder the Scriptures more deeply, we pray that you will be strengthened on your journey to conversion. We ask you to keep us in prayer as well. Remember that we look forward to the day when you will remain here to share in the Eucharist. Go in peace.

All process to where the dismissal session will take place. The catechist holds the Lectionary in a reverent manner. The assembly may sing an acclamation to accompany the procession.

Centering

Upon reaching the place where the dismissal occurs, place the Lectionary on the ambo, lectern, or other dignified place (or hold the book reverently). Light the candle that is in the place of gathering and reread 1 Corinthians 1:22–25 in order to refocus the group's attention. Consider singing the Responsorial Psalm or have a recording of it available to use as part of the centering, either before or after the reading.

Readings for the Next Dismissal

The following "script" may be used or adapted to help facilitate discussion on today's readings. Begin the discussion by asking the catechumens if any words or phrases from today's readings spoke to them.

On this Third Sunday of Lent, we will reflect upon the ways in which God's love directs our lives. As we begin, let us take a few moments to pause and take stock of the progress of our Lenten journey.

⑨ How has this Lent been a time of growth in faith for you thus far?

⑨ Have you promised to carry out some action that has been particularly beneficial to someone else or to your own spiritual growth?

⑨ Is there a resolution you have not kept? How might you return to that promise with renewed commitment?

Today's First Reading is from the book of Exodus. As we hear God give the commandments to the people of Israel, we also hear God instructing us. Notice that God wants to be the center of our lives, and he promises mercy to those who love him and keep his commandments. Think about this: Living as God desires is a response to his love for us. The commandments are not meant to be burdensome, but they rather reflect the life of one who has experienced the great love of God—when we know God's love in our lives, we will respect and reverence others. Right relationship with God leads to right relationship with others. Today's Responsorial Psalm captures this well: our hearts rejoice when we live in the perfect law of the Lord.

🌀 What moments in your daily life reflect your commitment to put God first?

🌀 In what ways does your love of God direct your interactions with others?

The Second Reading, from 1 Corinthians, expresses the paradox of the Paschal Mystery. The "foolishness of God is wiser than human wisdom, and the weakness of God is stronger than human strength" (1 Corinthians 1:25). Throughout his life, ministry, Passion, Death, and Resurrection Jesus confounded the people he encountered. He showed us that when our lives are rooted in the love of God, love will direct our relationships and actions with and for others. Jesus' way of sacrificial, self-giving love is confounding and leads to life filled with meaning.

🌀 How have you found wisdom in God's way of self-giving love?

🌀 How is Jesus' love for humanity a deepening of what is reflected in the Ten Commandments?

In today's passage from the Gospel according to John, we are given a vivid depiction of Jesus as he reacted to the presence of vendors and money changers in the Temple area. Some commentators note that the portion of the Temple in which we find Jesus was known as the Court of the Gentiles. This Court was outside the sanctuary of the Temple and was set aside for Gentiles to worship. It represented the openness of God to all peoples. Jesus is dismayed because this place was to represent God's desire to reach all of humanity. Instead it was being used as a marketplace. Jesus drove those selling animals and changing money out with a whip made of cords, spilling the coins of the moneychangers and overturning tables. We might say he is overturning expectations again—the Jewish authorities demand an explanation for his actions. His response to them was as perplexing as his actions: "Destroy this temple and in three days I will raise it up" (John 2:19). The Gospel author explains that the disciples came to understand that Jesus meant the Temple of his body, and was foretelling the Resurrection.

Today's Gospel invites us to consider the perspective and direction that comes from life rooted in the Gospel. Jesus shows us what life that is centered on God is to be. So often we see in the Gospel that Jesus was filled with compassion and mercy. He was also strong in the face of injustice, exclusion, and hypocrisy.

🌀 Upon what do you want to further reflect following today's session?

Wrapping It Up   *Consider these points to conclude the dismissal. Integrate the thoughts and ideas that surfaced during the discussion.*

- The Paschal Mystery of Jesus' life, ministry, Passion, Death, and Resurrection shows us what it means to live in right relationship with God and others.

- Our response to God's love is to live as he desires.

- The power and wisdom of Christ is found in sacrificial, self-giving love.

Closing Prayer

Conclude with prayer. If time permits, sing the psalm refrain a few times before or after the following prayer.

> Merciful God,
> your foolishness is wiser than human wisdom,
> your weakness is stronger than human strength.
> At times, we find your immense love confounding, beyond our understanding.
> We know that the commands you give us flow from your love for humanity,
> and we see in Jesus the fulfillment and ultimate expression of your law of love.
> Guide us through our Lenten journey as we grow in willingness to follow Jesus,
> who through his life, Death, and Resurrection shows us your wisdom and power.
> Who lives and reigns for ever and ever.
> Amen.

Readings for the Next Dismissal

Provide catechumens with a list of the readings for the next dismissal session. Consult the liturgical calendar on page xvi to find out what day will be observed next week. Give catechumens the questions below to guide their reflection through the week.

⑥ What connections are you seeing in the readings of this liturgical season? As you pray with the readings, around what themes do your thoughts seem to be coming together?

⑥ Where do the readings intersect with your journey of faith? What questions do they raise for you?

Extended Catechesis

Based on today's readings and liturgical observance, the following topics may be covered:

❋ Paschal Mystery

❋ Commandments

❋ Kenosis (self-emptying)

THIRD SUNDAY OF LENT, YEAR A

Focus: Christ is the Living Water.

Lectionary #28A

❧ When the First Scrutiny is celebrated with the elect, the Year A readings are proclaimed instead of those for Year B. If you wish to incorporate a discussion on the Scrutiny in your dismissal session, a dismissal guide is provided in the appendix on page 322. A separate dismissal session should take place with the elect.

Catechist's Preparation

Overview of the Sunday

On this Third Sunday of Lent, we are drawn to the living water of Christ. With the Israelites and the Samaritan woman at the well, we recognize our thirst of our hearts, which only God can quench. For the elect who are preparing for initiation at the Easter Vigil, this Sunday of Lent is a time of scrutiny, and a further step toward the waters of Baptism. For catechumens who are early in their journey toward initiation (those who will not be baptized this year), it is a moment in which to be more deeply joined to Christ, who is the living water. For the sponsors and leaders, this is a day in which to more fully appreciate the grace and power of Baptism, in which we will be renewed at Easter.

Scripture Background

Exodus 17:3–7 As a squeaky wheel gets its grease, so a cranky people get their water. Moses and God react differently to the thirsty people strewing complaints across the desert. Moses is exasperated, but God comes up with a practical solution. This passage tells the classic story of Moses striking a rock with his staff, and God opening the rock with a burst of water. The elders of Israel witnessed the event, lending credibility to an otherwise implausible story. God invited the people into this journey, wanted them to complete it, and offered them every aid. This episode serves as a prelude to the Gospel of the day, which in turn foreshadows the mystery of Baptism.

Psalm 95:1–2, 6–7, 8–9 (8) This psalm recalls the same event told in the First Reading. Here, though, God's response is not as bemused as it seems to be in Exodus. Instead of casually cooperating with the people's request, God issues a different command to a later generation: "'Harden not your hearts . . . / as in the day of Massah in the desert, / Where your fathers . . . / tested me though they had seen my works'" (95:8, 9). Basically, the psalm is asking a later generation of beleaguered people to have a better attitude than their forebears had.

Romans 5:1–2, 5–8 Just as God poured forth water for the people in the desert, so God pours love into the hearts of Christians through the gift of the Holy Spirit.

St. Paul's challenging letter to the Romans has some of its meatiest material in chapter 5. He explores what came to be known as the theological virtues: Christians are justified by faith, which gives them hope, because they have received the love of God. By comparing this gift of the Spirit to something "poured out" (5:5), Paul uses a metaphor that the Lectionary puts to eloquent purpose. It links this passage with the love of God in the First Reading and the Gospel's promise of the Spirit.

John 4:5–42 OR 4:5–15, 19B–26, 39A, 40–42 A woman who comes to perform an ordinary task finds herself in an extraordinary conversation. The story is one of the most vivid in the Gospel according to John. In the time of Christ, Jews and Samaritans did not get along, partly because many generations earlier, upon their release from the Babylonian captivity, the Jews rebuilt the Temple without inviting the Samaritans to help. So, when Jesus, a Jew, asks a woman, a Samaritan, for a drink, he was already testing boundaries. That their conversation climaxed in a discussion on places of true worship showed their willingness to step right into the heart of a centuries old conflict, played out in the ordinary lives of two people needing water on a hot, sunny day. Jesus wants something more than water. He wants the woman's faith. He probes and parries, demonstrating his prophetic knowledge of her life and his willingness to satisfy the deepest thirst in her heart. He offers her living water. He is that water, the one who can so slake those who receive him that they will never be thirsty, lifeless, and aimless again. He wants her to drink him in.

The woman herself shifts the discussion to faith, as she identifies the unrewarded thirst of the ancients: the coming of the Messiah, the one called Christ. Already she is wondering, could this be the one? At a well of water, echoing words Moses heard at a bush of fire, Jesus says to her, "I am he" (John 4:26). Now, the woman acts like an apostle. She invites others to believe in Jesus, and they do, not just because of her testimony, but because they come to know Christ.

This entire story has long been associated with the Third Sunday of Lent. There is strong circumstantial evidence that it was proclaimed with the scrutiny rites in the early Church, in order to prepare catechumens for Baptism. This story, then, provides a paradigm in which those seeking the waters of Baptism today can find hope in the woman's story. Lent is observed not just by catechumens but also by the faithful. Those who mark the disciplines of Lent in order to renew their commitment to Christ will come to the end of their spiritual journey when they renew their baptismal promises at the Easter Vigil. Then they will be sprinkled with the blessed water of Baptism, living water that enables them to tell the world that Jesus is the Christ.

Reflection Questions for the Catechist

⑨ For what do you thirst?

⑨ How does Christ quench the thirsts of your heart?

⑨ In what ways does the grace of Baptism draw you to live as a disciple of the living water?

Catechist's Guide

Objectives

▷ Catechumens will reflect upon the thirsts of their hearts.

▷ To connect the story of Moses with the people in the desert and the Samaritan woman who recognized her thirst in her encounter with Jesus.

▷ To recognize in the woman's story the catechumens' own journey toward Christ and to lead others to Christ.

Dismissal and Procession

Following the homily, the priest celebrant picks up the Lectionary and invites the catechumens to come forward with the catechist(s) who will lead today's dismissal session. Holding the Lectionary so that all can see, the priest celebrant sends the catechumens and catechist(s) forward using RCIA, 67, his own words, or the following:

PRIEST: **Each day of Lent brings you closer to the waters of Baptism that will claim you for Christ and incorporate you into his holy body, the Church. God's Word becomes richer fare during these days of penitence challenging us to consider our choices and renew our commitments. May your reflection on God's holy Word deepen your conviction to surrender your whole life to him and strengthen you for the mission of discipleship you will undertake at the great Vigil when we celebrate Christ's victory and God's incomprehensible love. Go in peace.**

All process to where the dismissal session will take place. The catechist holds the Lectionary in a reverent manner. The assembly may sing an acclamation to accompany the procession.

Centering

Upon reaching the place where the dismissal occurs, place the Lectionary on the ambo, lectern, or other dignified place (or hold the book reverently). Light the candle that is in the place of gathering and reread John 4:5–42 in order to refocus the group's attention. Consider singing the Responsorial Psalm or have a recording of it available to use as part of the centering, either before or after the reading.

Reflection and Discussion

The following "script" may be used or adapted to help facilitate discussion on today's readings. Begin the discussion by asking the catechumens if any words or phrases from today's readings spoke to them.

On this Third Sunday of Lent, we are drawn to the living water of Christ. We hear stories of the Israelites in the desert and the Samaritan woman at the well. We recognize the thirst of our hearts, which only God can quench.

⑨ What strikes you in what you heard in the readings and homily today? (If leading this dismissal with the elect, and the First Scrutiny was celebrated, take time to break open the prayers and experience of the rite [see page 322].)

In the First Reading, the Israelites, who had been led out of captivity in Egypt and are now journeying through the desert, grumble because they are thirsty. Their physical thirst is only part of the story, as it leads them to question Moses, and ultimately is a sign of their doubt of God. In spite of their deliverance from slavery, they still question God's attentiveness to them. As we hear in today's Responsorial Psalm, they had hardened their hearts, grumbling, asking why if God had truly delivered them out of slavery in Egypt they would be allowed to die of thirst in the desert. God hears the cries of the people through Moses and provides water from a rock.

⑨ Are there times when you grumble to God through impatience or hardness of heart?

⑨ How do you turn yourself around and remember God's faithfulness and love?

⑨ What experience comes to mind in which God provided something that you needed, perhaps in an unexpected or unusual way, like water from a rock?

Faith. Hope. Love. In the Second Reading, St. Paul helps the Romans to grow in an appreciation of these key virtues. Faith is a gift, and it is a response to the gift of grace with which God blesses us. We know this grace, this saving love, most especially in and through Jesus Christ. Christ's Death on the Cross was not due to worthiness on our part, but is proof of God's great love for humanity, even in our sinfulness. Through faith, we have hope; and "hope does not disappoint, because the love of God has been poured out into our hearts through the Holy Spirit" (Romans 5:5).

⑨ In what ways does God's love which is shown through Christ's sacrifice on the Cross lead you to desire Baptism?

All of this leads us to the story of the Samaritan woman at the well. Jews and Samaritans held each other in great disdain. So much so that Jews would often take a longer journey in order to avoid going through Samaria. Men would typically not talk to women who were not family members. Yet Jesus speaks to the Samaritan woman. He seeks her out. He offers her the living water of himself, and in doing so she recognizes a thirst she may not have been aware of, a thirst within her heart for the living water of God.

⑨ What spiritual thirst is within you?

⑨ How does your growing faith in Christ quench the thirsts of your heart?

⑨ How does the woman's response to her encounter with Jesus inspire you to respond to the living water who is Jesus?

The encounter between the woman and Jesus leads her to recognize the longing of her heart for the Messiah. She wonders if Jesus might be the Christ, and in her wonder he acknowledges his identity. Through their dialogue, the woman comes to believe in Jesus. She goes back into the town and tells others about him. Through her testimony and their experience of Jesus, many others come to believe in him as well.

⑨ In what ways are you drawn to fullness of life in Christ in the waters of Baptism?

⑨ How does your belief in Christ lead you to share your belief, and the impact of belief, with others?

Wrapping It Up

Consider these points to conclude the dismissal. Integrate the thoughts and ideas that surfaced during the discussion.

- God listens to the longing of our hearts.

- Jesus seeks us out in order to draw us to the living water of Baptism.

- Belief in Christ leads us to evangelize, to share the Good News with others.

Closing Prayer

Conclude with prayer. If time permits, sing the psalm refrain a few times before or after the following prayer.

Lord Jesus Christ,
you are the living water, the source of our spiritual refreshment.
In you, every thirst is quenched, every hunger is filled.
Through your Holy Spirit, pour out your love on us today.
Show us the way to you, in the assurance that you desire that we come to you
with every need, every longing of our hearts.
Guide us to more deeply encounter your love and to lead others to you.
Who live and reign for ever and ever.
Amen.

Readings for the Next Dismissal

Provide catechumens with a list of the readings for the next dismissal session. Consult the liturgical calendar on page xvi to find out what day will be observed next week. Give catechumens the questions below to guide their reflection through the week.

🌀 What connections are you seeing in the readings of this liturgical season? As you pray with the readings, around what themes do your thoughts seem to be coming together?

🌀 Where do the readings intersect with your journey of faith? What questions do they raise for you?

Extended Catechesis

Based on today's readings and liturgical observance, the following topics may be covered for extended catechesis with catechumens who will not be initiated this coming Easter:

❊ Baptism

❊ Sins forgiven in Baptism

❊ Union with Christ in Baptism

❊ The Holy Spirit given in Baptism

❊ Faith, a gift from God

❊ The theological virtues of faith, hope, love

If there are elect in your parish, today should be spent preparing them for the Second Scrutiny and for reflecting upon the nature of sin rather than engaging in extended catechesis.

FOURTH SUNDAY OF LENT, YEAR B

Focus: To respond to God's expansive love.

Lectionary #32B

❧ When the Second Scrutiny is celebrated with the elect, the Year A readings are proclaimed instead of those for Year B. See page 63 for the Year A dismissal guide. A separate dismissal session should take place with the elect.

Catechist's Preparation

Overview of the Sunday

We call this Sunday, *Laetare* Sunday. *Laetare* is Latin for "rejoice," and is taken from the first word of the Mass if prayed in Latin. *Laetare* Sunday in Lent is similar to *Gaudete* Sunday in Advent, a mid-season moment in which to be reminded that we have much for which to rejoice, even as we prepare to celebrate Christ's Passion and Death on the Cross during Holy Week. On this Fourth Sunday of Lent, we face our sinfulness and rejoice again in God's expansive love. There is no doubt that we sin. We fail to live as God's good and holy people. Throughout the history of humankind, we have turned away from God and hurt each other.

Scripture Background

2 Chronicles 36:14–16, 19–23 Second Chronicles, the last book in Jewish Scripture, concludes with these thoughts. God's Chosen People, along with their leaders and priests, are found guilty of infidelity to covenant promises, practicing abominations, and polluting the Jerusalem Temple. God continually had compassion on them and sent messengers to turn their hearts back to God. But the people refused to listen and change their hearts. God's anger flared, bringing destruction and ruin upon the land, the Temple, and the people, exiling the survivors to slavery in Babylon. Sabbath infidelity resulted in seventy years of punishment until all lost Sabbaths were retrieved.

Darkness covered the land and the people, yet the Lord did not forget the covenant promises. God's compassion empowers a foreign king, Cyrus the Persian, to defeat the Babylonians and to restore the people to their land. Seeing himself as God's instrument, Cyrus exhorts God's people to return home and build a house for the Lord in Jerusalem. In the midst of darkness, God's compassion shines bright. God's expansive love overcomes the rejection and the darkness, offering another opportunity for the people to turn back and renew fidelity to covenant promises. We are invited once more to respond to God's expansive love.

Psalm 137:1–2, 3, 4–5, 6 (6ab) The psalm reveals the anguish and pain of an exiled people separated from all that gave meaning and purpose to life. Their captors even tormented them by forcing them to sing joyously about the land and Temple that had been polluted and destroyed. In the midst of such anguish and sorrow, how does one maintain identity and balance? The psalmist's response challenges all to remember who they are and to whom they belong. Jerusalem, the Temple and the land, must never be forgotten. That active recollection keeps hope alive, and enables the people to endure much. God must never be forgotten or ignored, because covenant love endures forever, no matter how difficult and challenging life becomes. In the midst of darkness, God never forgets us and we must never forget God. This is the eternal bond that covenant love creates and sustains.

Ephesians 2:4–10 The depth and richness of God's mercy in Christ suffuses these verses from Ephesians. The perennial biblical theme of God's love and mercy, manifested most clearly in the darkness of sin and death, shines brightly here, offering all life-giving hope and joy. We are saved not by any merit of our own, but as a totally free and gracious gift from God. In Christ, not only did God save us from sin and death, but he raised us up, and even seats us at the honored place with Christ.

Ephesians emphasizes that we are God's handiwork, created anew in Christ Jesus for the "good works that God has prepared in advance" (2:10). God calls us out of our sinful darkness and saves and creates us anew in Christ, the model of good works that God desires of all believers. We do good works not to gain salvation, but in faithful response to the marvelous saving deeds God has accomplished for us in Christ Jesus. In acknowledging God's expansive love, we commit ourselves to taking on the mind and heart of Jesus, living as God desires.

John 3:14–21 John's account of the Gospel consistently plays with the images of light and darkness as a means of getting at the core of what God is about in the person of Jesus. Darkness is associated with sinfulness and evil, while light is associated with the person of Jesus and with what God is doing in the world. Jesus is God's light come into a sinful, evil world, to manifest God's love, care, and concern for all. All that God desires is that we believe in Jesus, and love one another in the same expansive manner that God has loved us.

John 3:16, which we commonly see on signs at sporting events and on bumper stickers, is the core of John's message and portrait of Jesus. "For God so loved the world that he gave his only Son, so that everyone who believes in him might not perish but might have eternal life." In Jesus, God has called us out of darkness. God asks that we respond to that expansive love by believing in Jesus. For John, believing is not only a head, lip, and heart event, it is also an action event, leading us to live and act like Jesus. This way of acting will demand much of Jesus and of us. Our coming into the light demands that we take up that challenge, knowing that God will always be with us, and like Jesus, we will be lifted up into God's expansive love.

Reflection Questions for the Catechist

⑨ What sign has recently reminded you of God's expansive love?

⑨ In what ways does the Sacrament of Penance communicate God's mercy and love to you?

⑨ How do you offer mercy and forgiveness to others?

Catechist's Guide

Objectives

▷ Catechumens will recognize themselves as loved sinners.

▷ To see in the story of the exile the story of all people, who are offered love and salvation in Jesus Christ.

▷ Catechumens will more deeply appreciate God's expansive love, which we do not earn, but which is a gift of God.

Dismissal and Procession

Following the homily, the priest celebrant picks up the Lectionary and invites the catechumens to come forward with the catechist(s) who will lead today's dismissal session. Holding the Lectionary so that all can see, the priest celebrant sends the catechumens and catechist(s) forward using RCIA, 67, his own words, or the following:

PRIEST: **Sisters and brothers, your faith journey reminds us all that conversion is to be our Christian way of life. Listen intently to God's Word, and ponder it carefully in your hearts. Persevere in the disciplines of fasting, praying, and almsgiving. The day draws near when you will be one with us around the table of the Lord. Go now in peace.**

All process to where the dismissal session will take place. The catechist holds the Lectionary in a reverent manner. The assembly may sing an acclamation to accompany the procession.

Centering

Upon reaching the place where the dismissal occurs, place the Lectionary on the ambo, lectern, or other dignified place (or hold the book reverently). Light the candle that is in the place of gathering and reread John 3:14–21 in order to refocus the group's attention. Consider singing the Responsorial Psalm or have a recording of it available to use as part of the centering, either before or after the reading.

Reflection and Discussion

The following "script" may be used or adapted to help facilitate discussion on today's readings. Begin the discussion by asking the catechumens if any words or phrases from today's readings spoke to them.

Today is referred to as *Laetare* Sunday. *Laetare* is Latin for "rejoice," and is taken from the first word of the Mass if prayed in Latin. *Laetare* Sunday in Lent is similar to *Gaudete* Sunday in Advent (the Third Sunday of Advent), a mid-season moment in which we are reminded we have much for which to rejoice—even as we prepare to celebrate Christ's Passion and Death on the Cross during Holy Week. On this Fourth Sunday of Lent, we face our sinfulness and rejoice again in God's expansive love. There is no doubt that we sin. We fail to live as God's good and holy people. Throughout the history of humankind, we have turned away from God and hurt each other. Pause to consider your Lenten journey for a moment.

⑨ In what ways is Lent leading you to turn away from sin and toward God's expansive love?

⑨ How are Lenten practices of prayer, fasting, and almsgiving or works of charity helping you to grow in your relationship with God and your love of others?

Today's First Reading from the second book of Chronicles tells the dramatic story of the Israelites' exile to Babylon, which is attributed to their lack of fidelity to God. God had compassion on them and sent prophets to lead them back to him. But, the Israelites mocked the prophets and failed to listen to what they had to say. The Responsorial Psalm captures their grief as they endured exile. They have failed God and are living in captivity. Still, God is with them. "By the streams of Babylon / we sat and wept / when we remembered Zion" (Psalm 137:1).

⑨ In what ways do you fail to live and grow in holiness? (*Share only as you are comfortable.*)

⑨ In what ways are you consoled by God's expansive love, which offers mercy in the face of our sin?

We do not earn God's forgiveness. God *is* love. God *is* mercy. It is "by grace you have been saved through faith, and this is not from you; it is the gift of God; it is not from works, so no one may boast" (Ephesians 2:8–9). In the Second Reading, from the letter to the Ephesians, we are struck with the reality that "even when we were dead in our transgressions" (Ephesians 2:5), we were brought to life through Christ's Resurrection.

⑨ What does it mean to you to be a loved sinner?

God's mercy awaits us every step of the way. We are created as God's handiwork. Each of us has been "created in Christ Jesus for the good works that God has prepared in advance, that we should live in them" (Ephesians 2:10). God calls us to turn aside sinfulness, to live in the light of Christ, and to bring this light to the world through our actions and interactions.

⑨ To what "good work" are you called at this time?

⑨ How do your daily actions and interactions share with others the expansive love of God?

Many of us recognize John 3:16 from signs at sporting events and billboards: "For God so loved the world that he gave his only Son, so that everyone who believes in him might not perish but might have eternal life." In many ways, this powerful statement sums up the essence of the Paschal Mystery. As wondrous as this love of Christ is, it also constitutes a call: "But whoever lives the truth comes to the light, so that his works may be clearly seen as done in God" (John 3:21). God offers expansive love—always and everywhere. Our response is to live as loving people so that God's glory and salvation may be known.

⑨ In what ways do you see Lent as a time in which to deepen your commitment to come to Christ's light?

⑨ What one thing do you need to do in order to more fully live Christ's call at this time?

Wrapping It Up

Consider these points to conclude the dismissal. Integrate the thoughts and ideas that surfaced during the discussion.

- We do not earn God's love. Salvation, forgiveness, and mercy are gifts.

- Each of us is created in God's image and is called to contribute our gifts in response to his expansive love.

- It is important to acknowledge our sinfulness and to rely on the strength of the Holy Spirit in seeking forgiveness.

Closing Prayer

Conclude with prayer. If time permits, sing the psalm refrain a few times before or after the following prayer.

Loving and merciful God,
we know that we sometimes fail to live as we ought.
We lose sight of you and forget your constant love.
Yet you are faithful to us.
You are not willing for us to remain separate from you.
In Christ, you have stretched your arms out to us,
reaching for us in your expansive love.
Guide us this day to live as your handwork,
as your holy people, redeemed in Christ Jesus, our Lord and Savior.
Who lives and reigns for ever and ever.
Amen.

Readings for the Next Dismissal

Provide catechumens with a list of the readings for the next dismissal session. Consult the liturgical calendar on page xvi to find out what day will be observed next week. Give catechumens the questions below to guide their reflection through the week.

- What connections are you seeing in the readings of this liturgical season? As you pray with the readings, around what themes do your thoughts seem to be coming together?

- Where do the readings intersect with your journey of faith? What questions do they raise for you?

Extended Catechesis

Based on today's readings and liturgical observance, the following topics may be covered:

❄ The Sacrament of Penance and Reconciliation

❄ Mercy

❄ Sin

❄ Salvation

FOURTH SUNDAY OF LENT, YEAR A

Focus: Christ is the true light.

Lectionary #31A

❧ When the Second Scrutiny is celebrated with the elect, the Year A readings are proclaimed instead of those for Year B. If you wish to incorporate a discussion on the Scrutiny in your dismissal session, a dismissal guide is provided in the appendix on page 325. A separate dismissal session should take place with the elect.

Catechist's Preparation

Overview of the Sunday

Today's readings present memorable stories of people who were chosen by God: David, the young shepherd boy, son of Jesse, and the man who was born blind, whom Jesus healed without his asking. We, too, are chosen by God, called to turn away from all that blinds us and to turn toward the light of Christ which banishes darkness and illumines the path toward eternal life. The elect who are in the final weeks of preparation before initiation at the Easter Vigil celebrate the Second Scrutiny today. All of us join with them in examining our lives, to see with new eyes, claim Christ as our light, and share the light with others.

We call this *Laetare* Sunday. *Laetare* is Latin for "rejoice," and is taken from the first word of the Mass if prayed in Latin. *Laetare* Sunday in Lent is similar to *Gaudete* Sunday in Advent, a mid-season moment when we are reminded that we have much for which to rejoice, even as we prepare to celebrate Christ's Passion and Death on the Cross during Holy Week.

Scripture Background

1 Samuel 16:1B, 6–7, 10–13A God chooses David as the king of Israel, and Samuel anoints him. This reading serves two purposes in today's liturgy. When lifted out of its context here, it can be placed in sequence with the other First Readings of the season; it then becomes one in a series of markers in the history of Israel. One workable method of preaching and catechizing during Lent focuses just on the First Readings of the six weeks, which together show how God was preparing for the salvation of the human race step by step throughout the generations of Israel. One of those milestones is the anointing of David.

The other reason this reading fits today's liturgy is its relationship to the Gospel account of the man born blind. Basically a story of how people who have physical sight may lack spiritual sight, this First Reading carries a similar message. Those who were looking for a likely candidate to be king overlooked the best of them all. Note how dramatically the writer of 1 Samuel keeps the reader in suspense. The name of the future king is not revealed until the very last lines. A skilled reader of this passage will pause before announcing the name, as if to say, "And the winner is [*pause for excruciating suspense*] . . . David!"

Psalm 23:1–3A, 3B–4, 5, 6 (1) Unquestionably the most popular psalm in the Bible, Psalm 23 appears today because of its idyllic picture of the shepherd with his peaceful sheep. It looks back to the First Reading with reassuring confidence that David will shepherd God's people as no one has before. The psalmist at Mass can imagine David singing these words—he who is the shepherd acknowledging that the Lord is his shepherd. Then will come alive this phrase: "You anoint my head with oil" (23:5). This psalm has little to do with the theme of the Gospel, but matches up nicely with the story about the anointing of Israel's first king.

Ephesians 5:8–14 Addressing a Gentile community in words not complimentary about its past, Paul says, "You were once darkness, but now you are light in the Lord" (5:8). Paul affirms the beautiful brightness that shines from the hearts of these believers and encourages them to shine their light upon others. The closing verses probably come from an early Christian hymn, summoning those who sleep—and those who have died—to greet Christ who gives them light.

Obviously, this passage is chosen for today's liturgy because of its strong link to the theme of the Gospel. Whereas the Gospel will tell of a man born blind, Paul refers to a people born blind, but who now see with the eyes of faith.

John 9:1–41 OR 9:1, 6–9, 13–17, 34–38 Jesus gives sight to a man born blind. But that is not even half the story. The miracle is dispatched rather quickly in the early verses of this chapter, and the rest of today's proclamation explores the effect this miracle has on the family, acquaintances, and the very person of the man born blind. John does not conceal his main point. He contrasts physical blindness with spiritual blindness. This miracle story lies behind the opening verse of the popular hymn "Amazing Grace": "I once was lost, but now am found, / was blind, but now I see."

Like last week's Gospel, this one has a long history associated with the catechumenate. As catechumens elected for the Easter sacraments make their final preparations for Baptism, they experience scrutiny rites intended to drive out whatever keeps them from Christ and to strengthen their resolve to follow him. As did the woman at the well, so does the man born blind. Surprisingly, the man never asked Jesus for this miracle. His gift of faith came after, not before, his healing. Yet, it comes in a powerful statement: "I do believe, Lord," he says.

This story still strengthens those preparing for Baptism, even as it reminds those already baptized that following Christ means removing blindness. At this stage of Lent, the faithful should be more aware of their weaknesses, their dependencies, their addictions, and their sin. They may not have asked for the healing that Lent offers, but here it is, ready to open their eyes, that they might believe.

Reflection Questions for the Catechist

- What darkness threatens to overcome you?
- In what ways does your faith in Christ bring light to those dark places?
- What must you do in order to live in the light of Christ?

Catechist's Guide

Objectives

- ▷ Catechumens will examine their lives and acknowledge the areas of sin, doubt, or trial which need the light of Christ.
- ▷ In reflecting on the readings, catechumens will know themselves as chosen by God and drawn to Christ's light.
- ▷ To see anew with eyes of faith and recognize how faith brings light to life situations.

Dismissal and Procession

Following the homily, the priest celebrant picks up the Lectionary and invites the catechumens to come forward with the catechist(s) who will lead today's dismissal session. Holding the Lectionary so that all can see, the priest celebrant sends the catechumens and catechist(s) forward using RCIA, 67, his own words, or the following:

PRIEST: **In today's Gospel you heard how the Lord Jesus Christ gave sight to the blind man who in turn became a fearless follower of the Lord. As you go forth today to reflect more deeply on the Word, may you become aware of your own blindness and afflictions so that you may rejoice with us one day at the table of the Lord. Go in peace.**

All process to where the dismissal session will take place. The catechist holds the Lectionary in a reverent manner. The assembly may sing an acclamation to accompany the procession.

Centering

Upon reaching the place where the dismissal occurs, place the Lectionary on the ambo, lectern, or other dignified place (or hold the book reverently). Light the candle that is in the place of gathering and reread John 9:1–41 in order to refocus the group's attention. Consider singing the Responsorial Psalm or have a recording of it available to use as part of the centering, either before or after the reading.

Reflection and Discussion

The following "script" may be used or adapted to help facilitate discussion on today's readings. Begin the discussion by asking the catechumens if any words or phrases from today's readings spoke to them.

We call this *Laetare* Sunday. *Laetare* is Latin for "rejoice," and is taken from the the first word of Mass if prayed in Latin. Today is a mid-season moment in which to be reminded that we have much for which to rejoice. The elect, who are preparing for initiation at the Easter Vigil, participated in the Second Scrutiny today and, with them, each of us examines our lives, asking Christ to bring to light any darkness of sin, doubt, and trial; that we may see with the eyes of faith and be transformed by the light of Christ.

⑨ What strikes you in what you heard in the readings and homily today? (If the Second Scrutiny was celebrated, take time to break open the prayers and experience of the rite; see page 325.)

In the First Reading, from the first book of the prophet Samuel, we hear the story of the anointing of David. It is only when David comes out of the fields that Samuel sees the one God has chosen. "Not as man sees does God see" (1 Samuel 16:7), we hear. God sees through the depths of our hearts and leads us to see ourselves as the chosen of God, called to be anointed and to live in God's love.

⑨ How do you know yourself to be chosen by God?

⑨ What does God see in the depths of your heart?

Psalm 23 is one of the most beloved of all psalms. We sing, "The LORD is my shepherd, I shall not want" (23:1), and we recognize our longing to trust God with our lives as the sheep do the shepherd. Even when we walk in the dark valleys of life, we have nothing to fear because we know God is with us.

⑨ How have you known God's presence and care in times of darkness?

In the Second Reading, from the letter to the Ephesians, we are told to "Live as children of light, for light produces every kind of goodness and righteousness and truth" (Ephesians 5:9). Taking to heart Christ's way of love and sacrifice, we touch the people around us with goodness. When others do "what is pleasing to the Lord" (Ephesians 5:10), they touch us with the light of Christ.

⑨ How have you been touched by the light of another?

⑨ In what ways do you recognize Christ's light in the community of faith, in family members, friends, and in the world?

In today's Gospel reading, we hear the story of a man who was born blind. It is important to understand that in Jesus' time, people who were disabled were shunned by society as sinners. It was thought that those who were born with disabilities bore the sin of a parent. Jesus reaches out to the man without his asking. His actions bring light to a place of darkness. In opening the eyes of the blind man, he brings the light of God's love to the man and all who will see it as a result. Consider life at this time:

⑨ What darkness lingers within you or your life circumstances?

⑨ What continues to plague you (*possible answers: death of a loved one, sin, addiction, doubt, conflict with family or friends, negative habits or thoughts*)?

⑨ In what ways does faith bring light to these places of darkness? How may you allow Christ's light to dispel the darkness?

The Pharisees in the story refuse to see the light. They cannot or will not see beyond the fact that Jesus healed the man on the Sabbath. The Pharisees judge the blind man and Jesus to be sinners. Their determination to remain blind to this action of God in their midst is striking. People are divided; even the man's parents are afraid to acknowledge the truth of their son's healing. Only the man who was blind sees the truth in front of them all and, through the eyes of faith, comes to believe in Jesus.

⑨ Is there an aspect of your life in which you have been blind to the action of God?

⑨ How might you open your eyes more fully to God's presence and love?

Wrapping It Up

Consider these points to conclude the dismissal. Integrate the thoughts and ideas that surfaced during the discussion.

- God chooses each of us.
- Through the eyes of faith, we see our life situations more clearly and find strength to face any darkness that remains.
- We bear responsibility to share Christ's light with others.

Closing Prayer

Conclude with prayer. If time permits, sing the psalm refrain a few times before or after the following prayer.

Christ, who is our light and life,
you cast away the darkness of death, sin, and doubt.
Call us into your light this day.
Bring hope to despair, healing to illness, and strength to weakness.
Remove the blindness of stubbornness, judgment, and worry,
so that we may see clearly with the eyes of faith.
Transform our hearts, so that we may bear your light,
transforming the lives of the people we touch.
Who live and reign for ever and ever.
Amen.

Readings for the Next Dismissal

Provide catechumens with a list of the readings for the next dismissal session. Consult the liturgical calendar on page xvi to find out what day will be observed next week. Give catechumens the questions below to guide their reflection through the week.

- What connections are you seeing in the readings of this liturgical season? As you pray with the readings, around what themes do your thoughts seem to be coming together?

- Where do the readings intersect with your journey of faith? What questions do they raise for you?

Extended Catechesis

Based on today's readings and liturgical observance, the following topics may be covered for extended catechesis with catechumens who will not be initiated this coming Easter:

- ❊ Faith
- ❊ Belief
- ❊ Anointing in Baptism

If there are elect in your parish, today should be spent preparing them for the Third Scrutiny and for reflecting upon the nature of sin, rather than engaging in extended catechesis.

Fifth Sunday of Lent, Year B

Focus: To share God's glory through Jesus.

Lectionary #35B

✤ When the Third Scrutiny is celebrated with the elect, the Year A readings are proclaimed instead of those for Year B. See page 71 for the Year A dismissal guide. A separate dismissal session should take place with the elect.

Catechist's Preparation

Overview of the Sunday

On this Fifth Sunday of Lent, we, with Jesus, journey toward Christ's Passion, Death, and Resurrection. In today's Gospel, Jesus uses the image of a grain of wheat, which falls to the ground and dies, and in doing so, produces much fruit. There are many ways in which we die—we die to self, to the ideals of a perfect body, to the things of this world. We hear Jesus say today, "Whoever loves his life loses it, and whoever hates his life in this world will preserve it for eternal life" (John 12:25). Be mindful that, in laying down our lives as Christ's servants, we will be lifted up with him. We will share God's glory with Jesus.

Scripture Background

Jeremiah 31:3-34 Jeremiah's career as a prophet began in Judah about 627 BC and ended about 580 BC. His life spanned the tragic last days of Judah, the final defeat by the Babylonians, the destruction of the Temple and the exile. In most of his preaching, Jeremiah was an uncompromising prophet of judgment. He called his people to repentance. They would not listen. The message people needed to hear after defeat by the Babylonians was different. Jeremiah began to preach wonderful words of hope.

The opening phrase "the days are coming" (31:27, 31) looks forward to a new time. This phrase, used throughout the Book of Jeremiah, sometimes refers to the period after the exile and other times projects into the future messianic period. At this future time, which is near at hand, there will be a new covenant with the house of Judah and Israel (see 31:31).

The first covenant, made with Moses and the people in the desert, had obviously been broken. Jeremiah says that God will offer a new beginning and a new covenant. Unlike the first, etched in stone and external, this new bond between God and Israel will be written on the heart of every Israelite. It will be an interior covenant accessible to each person without intermediaries.

The result of the covenant written on the heart is knowledge of God (see 31:34). The Hebrew word for "knowing" is the same one used to describe the intimate relationship between a man and a woman. Knowing God is not intellectual knowledge but a close, unique bond. Finally, the new covenant will not be based upon judgment but upon God's love and forgiveness (see 31:34). The hope kindled by this prophecy must have been a source of great comfort to a nation facing exile in a foreign land.

Psalm 51:3-4, 12-13, 14-15 (12a) Psalm 51 is one of the penitential psalms. This psalm focuses on the heart, the same place Jeremiah focused. Conversion begins in the inner part of a person and is possible only with the help of God. The psalmist readily acknowledges sin and prays that God will restore all the things damaged by sin. In return, the psalmist promises to help others with the conversion process by offering instruction in God's ways.

Hebrews 5:7-9 Hebrews is a complex book. It was probably a sermon that circulated among the Church communities directed to Christians of Jewish origin who were weak in faith. The main argument centers on a comparison between the temporary and therefore imperfect priesthood of the people of Israel and the permanent and perfect priesthood of Christ.

In this pericope, the author wants to assure the hearers that Christ was truly human. The reference to prayers made with a loud voice and with tears may refer to the agony in the garden. This suffering is meant to console the hearers, who are undergoing their own persecution. Suffering is not foreign to Christ and therefore will not be foreign to his followers. Likewise, as Christ was resurrected (saved from death; see 5:5), so too will be those who remain faithful to God.

Being Son of God in no way saved Jesus from the realities of human life. What was unique about his life is that he remained completely and perfectly obedient to God in the midst of his trials. Because he remained faithful, all have access to the salvation his faithfulness accomplished: eternal life. He is the model of the new covenant.

John 12:20-33 This Gospel passage comes just after Jesus' entry into Jerusalem when he was welcomed as a Messiah into the city. This discourse stands in contrast to that joyous welcome (see 12:12–13). Jesus is the Messiah who suffers, who dies and who surrenders his life.

The arrival of some Greek inquirers becomes an occasion for Jesus to announce that his hour has come (see 12:23). These are the Gentiles who are attracted to the faith of Israel. In the Gospel according to John, seeing is a metaphor for faith; their desire "to see Jesus" (12:21) is an expression of their faith in Jesus. In response to their request, Jesus teaches the meaning of his messiahship. (John's account of the Gospel uses Jesus' speeches to explain the significance of his life, Death, and Resurrection.) It is clear that Jesus' "hour" refers to his Passion. His glorification will take place through the cross. John then interrupts the glorification theme with a parable about wheat (see 12:24). Death is necessary for new life. The rich harvest of a single death may refer to the fruit of Jesus' Death: the faith of the Gentiles. Then Jesus applies the parable to his followers. They must be willing to imitate his suffering and Death if they are to bear fruit; they must be willing to carry a cross.

In verse 27, Jesus resumes the discussion of his own Death. While Jesus is troubled, he accepts his sacrificial Death as the purpose for his coming into the world. According to John, Jesus was not the unwilling victim of human plots against him nor was he coerced by divine power. He was not even a victim of Satan's power. The Passion was a deliberate but difficult choice made by Jesus for the glory of the Father (see 12:28). Jesus expresses grief and anguish when making this choice; he is truly human.

In the other Gospel accounts, a voice from heaven speaks at Jesus' baptism and Transfiguration. Here, the voice from heaven confirms Jesus' choice to accept the hour of his passion. It is a foreshadowing of the future: Jesus will one day be glorified by God because of his willingness to suffer and die. Some will understand this sign, and others will misunderstand God's voice and misinterpret it.

The final verses express the meaning of Jesus' Death and Resurrection in cosmic terms. Jesus tells the people that through his Death, the ruler of this world (Satan) will be driven out (see 12:31). This does not mean there will be no more evil but that the decisive victory will be won on the Cross; death is defeated for those who believe. There is still time to examine our lives and reflect on the heart of the matter—eternal life with Jesus.

Reflection Questions for the Catechist

- To what must you die?
- In what ways is your life shaped by the call to serve and follow Jesus?
- Pause and allow God's love to sink into your heart. In what ways does this awareness of God's love guide your life?

Catechist's Guide

Objectives

- ▷ To reflect upon the intimate relationship which God desires with us.
- ▷ Catechumens will more deeply appreciate Jesus' call to serve and follow him.
- ▷ To take to heart that being united to Christ makes us sharers in God's glory.

Dismissal and Procession

Following the homily, the priest celebrant picks up the Lectionary and invites the catechumens to come forward with the catechist(s) who will lead today's dismissal session. Holding the Lectionary so that all can see, the priest celebrant sends the catechumens and catechist(s) forward using RCIA, 67, his own words, or the following:

PRIEST: **My dear friends, we send you now to another place where you may gather and reflect on the words from Scripture you have heard today. We pray that your reflections on the Word will carry you ever deeper into the mysteries of our faith, preparing you to celebrate the great Easter sacraments with us. Go in peace.**

All process to where the dismissal session will take place. The catechist holds the Lectionary in a reverent manner. The assembly may sing an acclamation to accompany the procession.

Centering

Upon reaching the place where the dismissal occurs, place the Lectionary on the ambo, lectern, or other dignified place (or hold the book reverently). Light the candle that is in the place of gathering and reread John 12:20–33 in order to refocus the group's attention. Consider singing the Responsorial Psalm or have a recording of it available to use as part of the centering, either before or after the reading.

Reflection and Discussion

The following "script" may be used or adapted to help facilitate discussion on today's readings. Begin the discussion by asking the catechumens if any words or phrases from today's readings spoke to them.

On this Fifth Sunday of Lent, we journey toward Christ's Passion, Death, and Resurrection. We are mindful that Lent is a time in which to focus more intently on our journey of ongoing conversion to Christ. Throughout this season, we have spent additional time in prayer, fasting, and offering service to others (almsgiving). Not only do these practices focus our time and attention, they lead us to deeper spirituality as well. Today's readings invite us to take to heart the full scope of this life with God.

🌀 In what ways has this Lent helped you to grow in your relationship with God?

🌀 What stands out as an example of a Lenten practice bearing fruit in your life?

🌀 What are you learning from this Lenten time?

In today's First Reading, from the book of the prophet Jeremiah, we hear of God's deep desire to live in an intimate relationship with us. When Jeremiah spoke these words to the people of Israel, he did so in order to give them hope in a time of uncertainty. God promises a new covenant, not written in stone which the people violated, but written in their hearts. God acknowledges the sinfulness of the people, but does not let this come between humanity and God.

🌀 How do you know yourself to be in intimate relationship with God?

🌀 In what ways are you growing as a person in whose heart God's law of love is written?

In today's Responsorial Psalm, we sing, "Create a clean heart in me, O God" (Psalm 51:10; refrain). In order for God to write the law of love in our hearts, our hearts must be made clean and whole. Only God can accomplish this in us. We cooperate with the Holy Spirit in order to be renewed, willingly turning away from sin, returning to God and his ways.

🌀 How has this Lent been a time of turning away from sin for you?

🌀 What experience comes to mind which is an example of your changing heart and life?

In order to fully grasp the message in the Second Reading from the letter to the Hebrews, we must remember that Jesus was fully human as well as fully divine. We may otherwise struggle to understand that Jesus "learned obedience" (Hebrews 5:8). Jesus "offered prayers and supplications with loud cries and tears" (Hebrews 5:7), we read today. In the Gospel, we hear that Jesus was "troubled" (John 12:27) in his acceptance of the suffering that was to come. Yet he became obedient. The word obedient comes from root words which mean to listen deeply. Jesus listened deeply to God and his desire to live intimately with us. He accepted the suffering that was to come, in order to become "the source of eternal salvation for all who obey him" (Hebrews 5:9). Notice that Jesus' obedience leads to our obedience. When we obey—to listen deeply to Christ—we grow in deep relationship with God who loves us.

🌀 In what ways are you learning to listen to God?

🌀 How does Jesus' obedience to his ultimate mission call you to be obedient to God?

In today's Gospel, Jesus uses the image of a grain of wheat which falls to the ground and dies. In doing so, it produces much fruit. There are many ways in which we die—we die to self, to the ideals of a perfect body, to the things of this world. We hear Jesus say today, "Whoever loves his life loses it, and whoever hates his life in this world will preserve it for eternal life" (John 12:25). In laying down our lives as Christ's servants, we will be lifted up with him. We will share God's glory with Jesus.

🌀 To what do you need to die?

🌀 What do you need to let go of in order to more fully live as Christ's servant and follower?

Wrapping It Up

Consider these points to conclude the dismissal. Integrate the thoughts and ideas that surfaced during the discussion.

- We are drawn deeply to Christ through whom we are drawn toward God's glory.

- When we cooperate with the Holy Spirit God will renew our hearts.

- In accepting his hour, Jesus became the source of eternal salvation.

Closing Prayer

Conclude with prayer. If time permits, sing the psalm refrain a few times before or after the following prayer.

Good and gracious God,
you place your law of love in our hearts
and draw us to a deep relationship with you.
Create in us clean hearts.
Through your Holy Spirit, renew us,
so that we may be willing to die to all that separates us from you.
Teach us to listen deeply to you, so that, like Jesus,
we may be ready to fulfill your mission of love in the world.
Through Christ our Lord.
Amen.

Readings for the Next Dismissal

Provide catechumens with a list of the readings for the next dismissal session. Consult the liturgical calendar on page xvi to find out what day will be observed next week. Give catechumens the questions below to guide their reflection through the week.

🌀 What connections are you seeing in the readings of this liturgical season? As you pray with the readings, around what themes do your thoughts seem to be coming together?

🌀 Where do the readings intersect with your journey of faith? What questions do they raise for you?

Extended Catechesis

Based on today's readings and liturgical observance, the following topics may be covered for extended catechesis with catechumens who will not be initiated this coming Easter:

❄ Suffering   ❄ Glory of God, glorify God

❄ Obedience to God's will

FIFTH SUNDAY OF LENT, YEAR A

Focus: Christ is the Resurrection and the Life.

Lectionary #34A

❦ When the Third Scrutiny is celebrated with the elect, the Year A readings are proclaimed instead of those for Year B. If you wish to incorporate a discussion on the Scrutiny in your dismissal session, a dismissal guide is provided in the appendix on page 328. A separate dismissal session should take place with the elect.

Catechist's Preparation

Overview of the Sunday

On this Fifth Sunday of Lent, Jesus' announcement, "I am the resurrection and the life" (John 11:25) rings in our ears. We near the end of our Lenten journey with the recognition that death will not be victorious over Christ, and that, joined with Christ in Baptism, we are drawn to life beyond the bounds of death in all its forms. The elect celebrate the Third Scrutiny today. With them, we peer deeply into our lives and acknowledge the dead places that are in need of Christ, who is the Resurrection and the Life. Through the power of the Holy Spirit, we too proclaim, "I have come to believe that you are the Christ, the Son of God, the one who is coming into the world" (John 11:27).

Scripture Background

Ezekiel 37:12-14 Through the prophet Ezekiel, God announces to captive Israel that freedom will come, as surely and miraculously as the dead shall rise from their graves. This short passage concludes a famous prophecy in which Ezekiel sees dry bones in a field coming to life as a mighty army, stirred by spirit—and not just any spirit—by God's Spirit. This powerful conclusion places a mighty prophecy before a dispirited people. God's comparison would have stunned even the prophet: captive Israel's future resembles the liberty of the dead from their graves.

On this particular Sunday, this passage lifts a veil from the miracle that caps Jesus' career in John's account of the Gospel: the raising of Lazarus from the dead.

Psalm 130:1–2, 3–4, 5–6, 7–8 (7) The psalm today carries a refrain about God's mercy that prophetically pairs it with the "fullness of redemption" (130:7). God's mercy is not just a compassionate feeling of pain, but one that intervenes to offer complete salvation. The faint drumbeat of the coming Easter victory can already be heard. More importantly, this psalm opens with the famous line, "Out of the depths I cry to you, O Lord" (130:1).

Well known by its Latin title, *De profundis,* this prayer for mercy stresses the depths from which the psalmist cries out. In the light of the other readings today, Psalm 130 brings to the ears of the faithful the chilling voice of the dead, calling out from the depths of the grave for forgiveness, confident that God will redeem. This psalm has a classic position in the Catholic funeral rites for the same reason. Although the original psalmist was alive but feeling lonely, the psalm can be heard as the voice of the souls of the faithful departed, expressing their confident plea for forgiveness and life.

Romans 8:8-11 The Spirit of Christ gives life to those who are dead. Paul applies this statement in two ways, both to the living and to the dead. Those who are "in the flesh" live in sin, but those in whom the Spirit of God dwells are "in the spirit" (8:9). So throughout a Christian's days, the Spirit bestows righteousness. It does not end with death. Through the Spirit, God, who raised Jesus from the dead, gives life to bodies claimed by death.

Throughout this central passage of the letter to the Romans, Paul is building his case about the triumph of spirit over flesh, life over sin and death. Because of the thematic content of the other readings today, this passage helps the Christian understand how the powers of Christ over death apply very personally to the lives of believers.

John 11:1-45 OR 11:3-7, 17, 20-27, 33b-45 Jesus raises his friend Lazarus from the dead. John's dramatic account of this episode has Jesus appear indifferent to the sickness, but he is more interested in life than death, in preaching than in illness. When he tells the disciples that Lazarus has died, he adds, "I am glad for you that I was not there" (11:15). Illness and death are merely the substance upon which Jesus builds the greatest prophetic stance of his career. This is the last of the great signs Jesus works in John's account of the Gospel.

After showing his power over death here in chapter 11, the story of his Passion gets underway in chapter 12. The conversation with Martha carries the most important teaching. Jesus tells her, "I am the resurrection and the life." The Resurrection is not just something that happened to him; he is the Resurrection, the one in whom all souls find hope.

This Gospel is the climax of three Johannine passages that build through the latter part of Lent. They were probably first associated with scrutinies in the early Church. The post–Vatican II lectionary recovered them, to be used even in Years B and C whenever there are elect present with whom to celebrate scrutinies. The images increase in drama: first water, the source of life; then light, the sign of faith; and now life, the fulfillment of the promise of birth. The elect can be brought to a deeper appreciation of the sacraments to which they are called, even as they leave behind whatever keeps them from Christ.

These readings also draw the faithful more deeply into the expectations of the Christian life. More aware of their sin, they seek God's forgiveness. Many will celebrate the Sacrament of Reconciliation before Easter. With today's reading they encounter the ultimate mysteries of life. God who summoned them through their birth now shows power over death. Those who repent die to their past, that they may rise as new people on Easter Day.

Reflection Questions for the Catechist

- What within you is dead? Are you bound by old habits or destructive patterns?
- In what ways does the assurance of life in Christ give you strength?
- How will you give witness to the power of the Resurrection to your elect, catechumens, and candidates, and to all who journey with them?

Catechist's Guide

Objectives

- ▷ Catechumens will reflect upon the places in their lives that feel dead and will claim the Resurrection of Christ over these points of pain.
- ▷ To grasp more fully the transformative power of faith in Jesus Christ in the catechumens' lives.
- ▷ Catechumens will consider the implications of Baptism, through which they will be immersed in Christ's life and become members of Christ's Body.

Dismissal and Procession

Following the homily, the priest celebrant picks up the Lectionary and invites the catechumens to come forward with the catechist(s) who will lead today's dismissal session. Holding the Lectionary so that all can see, the priest celebrant sends the catechumens and catechist(s) forward using RCIA, 67, his own words, or the following:

PRIEST: **As Lent draws to a close, the Church gives us the Gospel of the raising of Lazarus. At Christ's word, the dead man comes forth, bound in burial cloths, a reminder that it is never too late to seek new life that comes from Christ. My dear [catechumens/elect], this is the new life that you seek! May your reflection on God's holy Word deepen your conviction to surrender your whole life to him and strengthen you for the mission of discipleship you will undertake at the great Vigil when we celebrate Christ's victory and God's incomprehensible love. Go in peace.**

All process to where the dismissal session will take place. The catechist holds the Lectionary in a reverent manner. The assembly may sing an acclamation to accompany the procession.

Centering

Upon reaching the place where the dismissal occurs, place the Lectionary on the ambo, lectern, or other dignified place (or hold the book reverently). Light the candle that is in the place of gathering and reread John 11:1–45 in order to refocus the group's attention. Consider singing the Responsorial Psalm or have a recording of it available to use as part of the centering, either before or after the reading.

Reflection and Discussion

The following "script" may be used or adapted to help facilitate discussion on today's readings. Begin the discussion by asking the catechumens if any words or phrases from today's readings spoke to them.

On this Fifth Sunday of Lent, we reflect upon the stunning understanding at the heart of our faith in Jesus Christ: in him, even death does not have the last word. In Christ, all that is dead is brought to life. We who put our faith in Christ experience life when all seems lost; when there appears no outcome other than to give up hope. The elect celebrated the Third Scrutiny today, and with them we reflect deeply upon the points of death in our lives, knowing through faith that Christ is the Resurrection and offers life in the shadow of death.

🌀 What strikes you in what you heard in the readings and homily today? (If the Third Scrutiny was celebrated, take time to break open the prayers and experience of the rite; see page 328.)

Our reflection today begins with wisdom from the prophet Ezekiel. Ezekiel speaks to the Israelites during exile, at a time in which they have lost all hope for the future. Their exile was the result of their sinfulness. Their sin caused their separation from God, the Temple, and the Promised Land. Through Ezekiel, God offers a powerful image: their graves will be opened and they will rise. They will be given God's spirit so that they may have life in its fullness. Their sin will no longer separate them from the life of God and his ways. In today's Responsorial Psalm, we cry out to God from the depths of our hearts. We place our hope and trust in the mercy of God, through whom we have redemption.

🌀 What feels dead within you?

🌀 What binds you to old habits or destructive patterns?

🌀 What seems beyond the power of Christ to overcome?

🌀 What would it mean to have this grave opened, to find life there instead?

The passage we hear today from the Gospel according to John is a powerful story of death and life, of faith, and of the truth of Jesus' identity as the Christ. Martha, Mary, and Lazarus are good friends of Jesus. We know from the beginning of this story that Lazarus is ill. The disciples are confused that, while knowing that Lazarus is sick, Jesus remains where he was for two days. Jesus clearly has a larger purpose in mind. He is focused on life in the face of death, and he knows that God will be glorified through what will take place. This is the last of Jesus' signs in John's account of the Gospel, and it leads to his Passion and Death. Put yourself in the place of the disciples for a moment:

🌀 What would you think or feel as you struggle to understand Jesus' decision to stay put rather than to hurry to Lazarus and his sisters?

🌀 Do you ever feel that God is not acting quickly enough for you?

🌀 What experience comes to mind in which you have struggled to have faith that God is with you in the midst of difficulty?

In the encounter between Martha and Jesus, Jesus declares himself to be the Resurrection and the Life. Martha declares her faith in Jesus as the Christ, the anointed one of God. Mary and Martha both proclaim their faith, "Lord, if you had been here, my brother would not have died" (John 11:21). Jesus is touched by the grief of the sisters, and in his own grief, he wept. Again, he assures Martha that she will see the glory of God, as he tells them to take away the stone from the tomb. Lazarus is raised. Many who had come to Mary and Martha in their grief come to believe in Jesus.

⑨ In what ways are you consoled that Jesus wept with Mary and Martha and is with you in the turmoil of your life?

Jesus said to Mary and Martha: "Untie him and let him go" (John 11:44).

⑨ What do you need Jesus to untie?

⑨ What do you need to let go of in order to live fully in the Spirit of Christ?

Wrapping It Up

Consider these points to conclude the dismissal. Integrate the thoughts and ideas that surfaced during the discussion.

- Jesus has power over death in all its forms.
- Jesus Christ is the Resurrection and the Life. In Christ, we have the hope of everlasting life.
- In the waters of Baptism, we are immersed in Christ's life as members of Christ's body.

Closing Prayer

Conclude with prayer. If time permits, sing the psalm refrain a few times before or after the following prayer.

Christ, the Resurrection and the Life,
in you, we know that nothing, not even death, is beyond your power.
We cry out to you today and place our trust in your goodness.
Give us the abundance of your life,
and free us from the bonds of all that is counter to your life and love.
Guide us as we continue our Lenten journey with you
toward your Passion, Death, and Resurrection.
Who live and reign for ever and ever.
Amen.

Readings for the Next Dismissal

Provide catechumens with a list of the readings for the next dismissal session. Consult the liturgical calendar on page xvi to find out what day will be observed next week. Give catechumens the questions below to guide their reflection through the week.

⑨ What connections are you seeing in the readings of this liturgical season? As you pray with the readings, around what themes do your thoughts seem to be coming together?

⑨ Where do the readings intersect with your journey of faith? What questions do they raise for you?

Extended Catechesis

Based on today's readings and liturgical observance, the following topics may be covered:

☀ Redemption   ☀ The indwelling of the Holy Spirit

☀ Resurrection

PALM SUNDAY OF THE PASSION OF THE LORD

Focus: Christ is obedient to the point of death.

Lectionary #37B (Blessing of the Palms); #38ABC (Readings at Mass)

Catechist's Preparation

Overview of the Sunday

How do we begin to take it all in? On this Palm Sunday of the Passion of the Lord, we begin Holy Week. We are with Jesus as he is mocked, scourged, and crucified. We hear the centurion who declares, "Truly, this man was the Son of God" (Mark 15:39), and we are with Mary Magdalene and Mary the mother of Joses who watched where the crucified body of our Lord was laid. On this day, we confess that Jesus Christ is Lord, to the glory of God the Father.

Scripture Background

Mark 11:1–10 In Mark, the story begins in an exchange between Jesus and two of his disciples. He sends them into Jerusalem to find a colt in a particular place and bring it back to him. It is unclear if these instructions reflect Jesus' supernatural power or if they reflect arrangements he had made in advance, but the disciples do as they are told and find the colt in exactly the way Jesus predicted. They bring it to him and spread their cloaks, and Jesus sits atop the colt. The procession begins as people put branches from the fields along the road and Jesus rides among them, their thunderous greeting resounding.

OR

John 12:12–16 Unlike the other three accounts of the Gospel, there is no set of instructions to disciples sent in pursuit of a colt. Rather, the scene begins with a statement that a crowd has gathered because they heard Jesus was coming to town. For John, it is the Lazarus miracle that sealed Jesus' fate among the chief priests. As a result of it, they wanted both Jesus and Lazarus dead. So the very adulation of the crowds on that first Palm Sunday (only John's account identifies the branches as palms) had the opposite effect on the authorities, who feared his power and the loss of their own. Certainly not oblivious, but obedient to his mission, Jesus secures his own colt and enters the city.

Isaiah 50:4–7 This third servant song of Isaiah exhibits a kind of resignation and acceptance of his fate that will be echoed in today's Passion proclamation. Whether the prophet is describing his own lot in life or, as some scholars suggest, that of the community of Israel, the message is clear: adversity and difficulty do not deter a true disciple.

Psalm 22:8–9, 17–18, 19–20, 23–24 (2a) The psalmist's cry of lament is filled with complaint and self-pity. He is mocked, scoffed at, and insulted by those around him, Fearful, angry, and in great need, the psalmist turns to the Lord, whose name he will ever praise and proclaim. It is thus that the relationship between human and divine grows richer and deeper so that we can pray with the psalmist, "hasten to aid me" (22:20).

Philippians 2:6–11 Paul writes of Christ, who "though he was in the form of God," (2:6) emptied himself and freely took on the form of a powerless slave. He who was immortal paradoxically took on human form, facing inevitable death. He was obedient to the point of death. One can get lost in the poetry of the reading, but savoring each line makes it clear that the powerlessness and death of Christ reversed all human expectations. God, who named Jesus Christ as Lord, exalted the crucified Christ.

Mark 14:1—15:47 or 15:1–39 It is an account of the preparations for Jesus' Death, his instructions to friends at a final meal, a betrayal in Gethsemane, a trial that cannot find cause to condemn him, and finally, a crucifixion that ultimately leads to life. One could focus on those who betrayed Jesus: Peter, Judas, James, and John, those passing by, the bystanders at the Cross, and the revolutionaries crucified with him. Or one could reflect on those who stood with him: Simon the leper, the woman who anointed him with costly oil, Simon of Cyrene, Mary of Magdala, Salome, Mary the mother of the younger James and Joses, and the women who watched from a distance. Finally, one could preach an entire homily on the two who seem to have had a conversion of heart: the centurion who announced at Jesus' Death, "Truly this man was the Son of God" (15:39), and Joseph of Arimathea, a "distinguished member of the council" (15:43) that had just condemned Jesus, who came forward to claim his broken body for burial. We wonder if we would have stood among the faithful women, spoken out bravely like the centurion, or condemned him out of fear like the bystanders. As this Holy Week begins, gratitude runs deep for those who remind us that hearts can be changed and action can be taken to make amends.

Reflection Questions for the Catechist

- What is in your heart today?
- What most strikes you as you reflect upon Jesus' Passion and Death?
- What images, experiences, and hopes for your elect do you carry with you as you enter into Holy Week?

Catechist's Guide

Objectives

▷ To more deeply grasp the meaning of Jesus' Passion and Death on the Cross.

▷ Catechumens will reflect on Jesus' union with them as they face the crosses in their lives.

▷ To reflect upon Jesus' obedience to the point of Death on the Cross.

Dismissal and Procession

Following the homily, the priest celebrant picks up the Lectionary and invites the catechumens to come forward with the catechist(s) who will lead today's dismissal session. Holding the Lectionary so that all can see, the priest celebrant sends the catechumens and catechist(s) forward using RCIA, 67, his own words, or the following:

PRIEST: **The Lord Jesus willingly embraced human likeness and was obedient to God, even unto a shameful Death. "Because of this" he was exalted by God. As you continue to follow Jesus on the journey that will lead you to the heart of the saving mysteries of his Passion, Death, and Resurrection, may you come him better than ever before and to embrace him as your brother and friend, teacher and master, and Lord and Savior. Go in peace.**

All process to where the dismissal session will take place. The catechist holds the Lectionary in a reverent manner. The assembly may sing an acclamation to accompany the procession.

Centering

Upon reaching the place where the dismissal occurs, place the Lectionary on the ambo, lectern, or other dignified place (or hold the book reverently). Light the candle that is in the place of gathering and reread Philippians 2:6–11 in order to refocus the group's attention. Consider singing the Responsorial Psalm or have a recording of it available to use as part of the centering, either before or after the reading.

Reflection and Discussion

The following "script" may be used or adapted to help facilitate discussion on today's readings. Begin the discussion by asking the catechumens if any words or phrases from today's readings spoke to them. In order to facilitate the reflection on the Passion narrative, it may be helpful for participants to have their Bibles open to Mark 14:1—15:47.

- How do we begin to take in all that we have just heard?

Today is Palm Sunday of the Passion of the Lord and the beginning of Holy Week. Throughout this week we will immerse ourselves in the mystery of God's great love for humanity, to the point of accepting Death on a Cross. We cannot fully comprehend all that we celebrate this week!

We begin our reflection with the proclamation of the Gospel and procession of palms. Jesus entered Jerusalem with people shouting "Hosanna in the highest!" (Mark 11:9). If we did not know what was to come, we might be filled with anticipation of God's glory with a victorious Christ reigning over the world with justice and love. We now know that this is what is to come, but in a very different way than what the people who shouted Hosanna were thinking in that moment.

- What is the difference between what the people expected as Jesus entered into Jerusalem and the Kingdom of God as we understand it?

🌀 What meaning does this have for you in your life?

The First and Second Readings and the Responsorial Psalm all help us to prepare our minds and hearts to hear the proclamation of Christ's Passion. Each invites us to trust in God through every trial, as did Jesus during his Passion and Death on the Cross.

🌀 As you participated in the Liturgy of the Word today, what personal experiences came to mind?

🌀 What trials have you faced, what crosses do you bear, trusting that God is with you and will strengthen you to endure?

There is so much to consider as we reflect on the Passion narrative, which we heard proclaimed in today's Gospel. We will focus our attention here on four moments in the story of Jesus' Passion and Crucifixion: the Last Supper, Garden of Gethsemane, Jesus' arrest and Crucifixion, and Jesus' burial in the tomb. There is much more upon which to reflect, of course, and it is hoped that you will read and pray with the Gospel often during this Holy Week.

Read Mark 14:1–25. Highlight key points: The woman in Bethany who anoints Jesus with expensive oil; Judas' agreement to betray Jesus; the Passover meal.

🌀 How is your anticipation of receiving Holy Communion deepened in hearing the narrative of the Last Supper?

Read Mark 14:26–72. Highlight key points: Jesus is troubled while praying in the garden of Gethsemane yet remains steadfast in fulfilling his mission; the disciples cannot stay awake during Jesus' time of prayer; they flee when he is arrested; Peter denies Jesus, just as Jesus foretold he would.

Jesus willingly gives himself over to certain suffering and death, even when those closest to him cannot stay awake to pray with him in the garden.

🌀 What does this teach you about the extent of God's love for humanity? In what ways do you deny Christ?

Read Mark 15:1–47. Highlight key points: Jesus suffers with humility; he is mocked, scourged, and crucified; Mary Magdalene and Mary, the mother of James, Joses and Solome, along with other women, remain with Jesus during the crucifixion; Joseph of Arimathea asks for the body of Jesus and lays him in the tomb, which the women see.

🌀 What most strikes you in reflecting on the Passion, Crucifixion, and burial of Jesus?

Wrapping It Up   *Consider these points to conclude the dismissal. Integrate the thoughts and ideas that surfaced during the discussion.*

- Our participation in the Eucharist is a participation in the Paschal Mystery of Christ.

- Christ's acceptance of his Passion and Crucifixion is a witness to the extent of God's love for humanity.

- Christ suffers with us as one who has known the extreme suffering of betrayal, Passion, and Crucifixion.

Closing Prayer

Conclude with prayer. If time permits, sing the psalm refrain a few times before or after the following prayer.

Lord Jesus Christ,
you entered willingly into your Passion and Crucifixion,
and in doing so, you show us the depths of God's love for humanity.
We cannot comprehend this love, and yet we rely upon it
in all of our moments of trial, suffering, and grief.
As we enter into this Holy Week, lead us to accept and embrace your love
with humble and contrite hearts as people who walk your way of the Cross.
Who live and reign for ever and ever.
Amen.

Readings for the Next Dismissal

Provide catechumens with a list of the readings for the next dismissal session. Consult the liturgical calendar on page xvi to find out what day will be observed next week. Give catechumens the questions below to guide their reflection through the week.

⑥ What connections are you seeing in the readings of this liturgical season? As you pray with the readings, around what themes do your thoughts seem to be coming together?

⑥ Where do the readings intersect with your journey of faith? What questions do they raise for you?

Extended Catechesis

Based on today's readings and liturgical observance, the following topics may be covered for extended catechesis with catechumens who will not be initiated this coming Easter:

※ Eucharist

※ Crucifixion

※ Passion

※ Discipleship

※ Suffering

INTRODUCTION TO THE SACRED PASCHAL TRIDUUM

Overview of the Sacred Paschal Triduum

Our Lenten observance is complete. We now prepare to enter into the three most sacred days of the liturgical year, the Sacred Paschal Triduum. The Triduum is one continuous liturgy which spans three days, beginning with the evening Mass on Holy Thursday and concludes after Evening Prayer on Easter Sunday. We begin the Holy Thursday liturgy with the Sign of the Cross and do not sign ourselves again until the beginning of the Easter Vigil liturgy. Each of the three days draws us into some particular aspect of the Paschal Mystery. Holy Thursday: the institution of the Eucharist and washing of feet; Good Friday: the Passion of Jesus Christ, including the Adoration of the Cross; the great Easter Vigil and Easter Sunday: the celebration of Christ's Resurrection and beginning of Easter Time.

While the Triduum is to be time set apart for all of us, it is even more so for the elect, who will be initiated at the Easter Vigil. For the catechumens, this may be their first real immersion into the Paschal Mystery of Christ. The Triduum invites all of us to participate in the sacred mysteries of Christ's life, Passion, Death, and Resurrection, through the liturgy as well as extended prayer, fasting, and reflection.

It is beneficial to continue the pattern of dismissals for the elect and the catechumens throughout the Triduum. These are the most important days of our liturgical year, and while it will require some additional preparation for the catechist, these dismissal sessions offer too much depth and spiritual nourishment to be curtailed. If only one liturgy is celebrated on Holy Thursday or Good Friday, a member of the elect may be invited to lead the discussion and sharing, using this resource to provide the framework for the session, so that the regular catechist may attend the full Triduum liturgy. The catechist may prepare these people (one for each dismissal, and separate sessions for the elect and the catechumens) and use time after Easter to continue to allow the grace and insights from the Triduum to unfold. It seems most appropriate for catechumens who are not among the elect to participate in Easter Sunday Mass rather than the Easter Vigil. In this way, they may enter into and reflect upon the Good News of the Resurrection while their participation in the great Vigil will wait for their eventual initiation. It is helpful to remember that the dismissal sessions with the elect and catechumens are not the final word. The elect will have time for mystagogical reflection during Easter Time and throughout the rest of their lives. The catechumens will continue to learn and grow in faith as the seasons unfold. For leaders and for all the faithful, Triduum invites us to linger with the knowledge of God's love, which is shown to us and shared through Jesus Christ.

Preparing a Seasonal Environment

The liturgical color for Holy Thursday is white. Consider having bread and wine within the environment, as well as a Bible opened to the Last Supper narrative. Keep the environment simple, free from unnecessary elements. The liturgical color for Good Friday is red. Perhaps include palms, a crucifix, and a thorny branch in the environment, as well as a Bible opened to the passion narrative from the Gospel according to John. The liturgical color of Easter is white and sometimes includes silver or gold embellishments. In the environment for the season, give prominent place to a candle, whose light shines throughout the season. Keep a space available for the Lectionary (or Bible) such as a lectern or table. Keep a candle near the Lectionary (or Bible) and light this candle before the session begins. Consider also a vessel for water, Easter flowers, green plants, and a Bible.

Overview of the Readings

First Readings On Holy Thursday, the First Reading from Exodus is the remembrance of the Passover meal preceding the Exodus, and on Good Friday, the First Reading is from another of the Servant Songs in Isaiah. At the Easter Vigil, there are seven Old Testament readings. Their proclamation makes the saving works of God throughout history present and real to us. On Easter Sunday, Peter summarizes the mission, Death, and Resurrection of Jesus.

Responsorial Psalms The psalms of Triduum are suitable to each of the three days. On Holy Thursday, the antiphon used with Psalm 110 comes from the New Testament's first letter of Paul to the Corinthians; it speaks of the blessing cup as participation in the Blood of Christ. Good Friday's Responsorial Psalm is Psalm 22; its antiphon contains the words spoken by Jesus as he hangs on the Cross: "Father, into your hands I commend my spirit," according to Luke 23:46. The seven Responsorial Psalms of the Easter Vigil, which correspond with the seven Old Testament readings, abound with themes of the glorious nature of the earth and the Lord himself, the Lord's faithfulness to his people, the salvation the Lord offers, and the joyful nourishment that comes from following the Lord and his word. Easter Sunday we pray from Psalm 118 for the first of three times (also on the Second Sunday of Easter, Fourth Sunday of Easter), repeating its Paschal acclamation: "The stone which the builders rejected / has become the cornerstone" (118:22).

Second Readings On Holy Thursday, the Second Reading from Paul's First Letter to the Corinthians gives the oldest written account of the Eucharist; it reminds us of what we celebrate each time we gather to pray the Eucharistic liturgy. On Good Friday, the Second Reading is from the Letter to the Hebrews. The letter speaks of the high priesthood of Jesus Christ. In particular, Good Friday's passage emphasizes the sacrifice of the High Priest's own life as an offering for sin. At the Easter Vigil, the letter to the Romans points to the relationship of Christ's Death and Resurrection to our own, through Baptism. On Easter Sunday morning, the letter to the Colossians directs us to keep our minds on where Christ has gone and where we shall be; the first letter to the Corinthian's hearkens back to the Passover roots of our Easter celebration.

Gospel Readings The Gospel readings present Jesus' example in his washing the feet of his disciples on Holy Thursday; John's account of the Passion, emphasizing Jesus as Isaiah's servant of the Lord who is the One High Priest, on Good Friday; and Mark's account of the women at the empty tomb and their encounter with the angel, on the Easter Vigil. On Easter Sunday morning, we journey once again with Mary and then Peter and the disciple to the inexplicably empty tomb, reminding us that even for those of us who know how the events progressed, Easter calls us to contemplate mystery.

Evening Mass of the Lord's Supper (Holy Thursday)

Focus: To wash one another's feet.

Lectionary #39ABC

🌿 Please note that another catechumen may volunteer to lead this session so that the catechist(s) who normally lead the dismissal may participate in the entire Mass of the Lord's Supper.

Catechist's Preparation

Overview of Holy Thursday

Our Lenten observance is complete. We now prepare to enter into the three most sacred days of the liturgical year, the Sacred Paschal Triduum. The celebration of the evening Mass of the Lord's Supper commences the Triduum liturgy, through which we enter deeply into the heart of all we believe about Jesus Christ and to reflect upon who we are called to be as disciples of the Lord Jesus. The three celebrations of Holy Thursday, Good Friday, and the Easter Vigil is one liturgy, which draws us into the Paschal Mystery of Jesus' life, Passion, Death, and Resurrection. As you prepare to reflect with your catechumens, be mindful that through the Triduum they will be presented with the essential mysteries of our faith. Consider their current understanding and grasp of the Paschal Mystery and the call to discipleship as you prepare to lead them in reflection tonight.

Scripture Background

Exodus 12:1–8, 11–14 While the community of Israel suffered bondage in Egypt, God sends the ten plagues through which the Pharaoh became convinced to free the people of Israel from their captivity. In the midst of these plagues God commands Moses and Aaron to prepare for the night of their freedom, and institutes the feast that would be known as Passover.

Passover came to mean the meal and the date fixed on the Jewish calendar. For the first observance, a family slaughtered a lamb or a goat, eating the meat but sprinkling the blood on the two door posts of each home. The blood became a sign for the angel responsible for the tenth plague to "pass over" (12:13) the homes and spare the life of the firstborn.

Psalm 116:12–13, 15–16bc, 17–18 (see 1 Corinthians 10:16) Several verses from a psalm of thanksgiving supply the Responsorial Psalm. The overall purpose of this psalm is to give thanks to God, but the Lectionary designates these verses because they especially fit the themes of Holy Thursday. The psalmist gives thanks by taking up "the cup of salvation" (116:13). The psalm pro-

claims, "Precious in the eyes of the Lord / is the death of his faithful ones" (116:15). These verses foreshadow the Eucharistic cup that Jesus shared at the Last Supper, as well as his own death looming on Good Friday.

The refrain is taken from the same epistle that gives us the Second Reading. As Christians experiencing anew the last days of Jesus, and familiar with the meal traditions of our ancestors in faith, we sing, "Our blessing-cup is a communion with the Blood of Christ" (refrain). Normally, the Responsorial Psalm echoes a theme from the First Reading or the Gospel. This is a rare instance when it pertains to the Second Reading, which has not yet been proclaimed.

1 Corinthians 11:23–26 St. Paul tells how Jesus instituted the Eucharist. With minor variations, this account also appears in Gospel accounts of Matthew, Mark, and Luke, but Paul wrote his epistles before the evangelists wrote their Gospel narratives. Therefore, this is the oldest account of what happened at the Last Supper, the version that lies closest to the years of Jesus' life.

At this point in his letter, Paul is probably responding to some specific questions from the Corinthians. Apparently, they had asked about the proper way to celebrate the Eucharist. Paul hands on to them what others had told him. Paul says that the supper took place on the night before Jesus was betrayed, that Jesus took bread, gave thanks, and said, "This is my body that is for you"; then he commanded his followers to "do this in remembrance of me" (11:24). Jesus repeated this command upon taking up the cup, which he called "the new covenant in my blood" (11:25). Paul says we proclaim the Death of the Lord until he comes whenever we "eat this bread and drink the cup" (11:26).

These words address the heart of Catholic faith. We believe that the Eucharist is the Body and Blood of Christ, that Jesus told us this, and that he commanded us to eat and drink in remembrance of him. This passage is the key that unlocks the meaning of Holy Thursday.

John 13:1–15 Jesus gives his followers a model of discipleship when he washes their feet. In John's account of the Last Supper, the institution of the Eucharist as it appears in the synoptic Gospel accounts, and even in Paul's First Letter to the Corinthians, is not there. Instead, John gives a mystical interpretation of the Eucharist in the washing of the feet. Just as Paul's letter unlocks the meaning of Holy Thursday, John's narrative of the Gospel unlocks its implications. As Jesus stoops to wash his feet, Simon Peter resists until Jesus warns him, "Unless I wash you, you will have no inheritance with me" (13:8). His statement probably alludes to Baptism. Importantly, Jesus advises the disciples, "If I, therefore, the master and teacher, have washed your feet, you ought to wash one another's feet" (13:14). Whenever we engage in selfless, humble service of our neighbor, we follow the model that Jesus gave.

Reflection Questions for the Catechist

- What is in your heart and mind as you prepare to enter into the Triduum?
- In what ways does the yearly immersion into the Paschal Mystery through the Triduum shape your faith and life?
- What do you most hope to share with your catechumens in these holy days of the Triduum?

Catechist's Guide

Objectives

- ▷ To grasp more deeply the mystery of the Eucharist.
- ▷ To reflect upon the significance of Jesus' washing the feet of the disciples and the ritual with which we participate.
- ▷ To experience the Triduum as an immersion into the Paschal Mystery of Christ and the call to discipleship.

Dismissal and Procession

Following the homily, the priest celebrant picks up the Lectionary and invites the catechumens to come forward with the catechist(s) who will lead today's dismissal session. Holding the Lectionary so that all can see, the priest celebrant sends the catechumens and catechist(s) forward using RCIA, 67, his own words, or the following:

PRIEST: **My dear friends, you have feasted together with us at the table of God's Word. We now send you forth that you may reflect on the Gospel of the one who gave himself for you and for all. We look forward to the day, so near at hand, when you will share fully with us at the table of the Lord's Body and Blood. Go in the peace of Christ.**

All process to where the dismissal session will take place. The catechist holds the Lectionary in a reverent manner. The assembly may sing an acclamation to accompany the procession.

Centering

Upon reaching the place where the dismissal occurs, place the Lectionary on the ambo, lectern, or other dignified place (or hold the book reverently). Light the candle that is in the place of gathering and reread John 13:1–15 in order to refocus the group's attention. Consider singing the Responsorial Psalm or have a recording of it available to use as part of the centering, either before or after the reading.

Reflection and Discussion

The following "script" may be used or adapted to help facilitate discussion on today's readings. Begin the discussion by asking the catechumens if any words or phrases from today's readings spoke to them.

Tonight we conclude our Lenten observance and begin the three most sacred days of the liturgical year, the Sacred Paschal Triduum. As we do so, let us first reflect on your experience of Lent.

🌀 In what ways did Lent bring you closer to Christ and to more fully understand yourself as a follower of Jesus?

🌀 In what ways will your Lenten practices, especially those of prayer, fasting, and almsgiving, lead you to live faith more fully in the future?

The Triduum begins with the celebration of the Evening Mass of the Lord's Supper, which we commonly call Holy Thursday. During the Holy Thursday liturgy, we hear three key stories of our faith. In the First Reading, we hear God give Moses and Aaron instructions for the Passover meal. While the Israelites are in exile in Egypt, Pharaoh is convinced to free the Israelites from their captivity through a series of plagues. The Passover takes place before the final plague, in which the firstborn children of the Egyptians will be killed. The angel of the Lord will pass over the children of the Israelites who have placed the blood of the lamb on their doorposts.

🌀 What is the meaning for you in hearing the story of the Passover on this particular night?

🌀 What comes to mind when you hear of the Passover lamb, whose flesh is food and whose blood is poured out in protection of the Israelites?

While the Responsorial Psalm usually connects the First Reading with the Gospel, tonight's Responsorial Psalm and the text used for the response lead in a special way to the proclamation of the Second Reading, from St. Paul's first letter to the Corinthians. The response text is taken from 1 Corinthians 10:16 and is a direct connection to the Second Reading and the institution of the Eucharist, which we celebrate tonight. The brief, yet powerful passage from 1 Corinthians expresses what we know and believe about the Eucharist St. Paul shared what he was told, that on the night before he died, Jesus took bread, blessed and broke it, and said, "This is my body that is for you. Do this in remembrance of me" (1 Corinthians 11:24). After supper, Jesus took the cup, saying, "This cup is the new covenant in my blood. Do this, as often as you drink it, in remembrance of me" (1 Corinthians 11:25). In the Eucharist, the bread and wine are transformed into Christ's Body and Blood. We share in Christ's Passion, Death, and Resurrection; we take into our bodies the Body and Blood of the Lord; nourished by this sacrificial meal, we are sent out as members of Christ's Body into the world.

🌀 What does the Eucharist mean to you? Why are you excited to receive?

🌀 What do you anticipate in receiving Holy Communion?

🌀 How is the new covenant in Jesus' blood a fulfillment and deepening of the covenant between God and the people through Abraham, Noah, and Moses?

In tonight's Gospel from John's account, we hear of Jesus' Last Supper with his disciples before his Passion and Crucifixion. Jesus knew that his hour had come, and he loved his own until the very end. During supper, Jesus rose from the table and began to wash his disciples' feet. Washing another's feet was considered a very dirty, humbling task, usually left to the lowest of the servants. Peter's response helps us understand how stunned the disciples would have been at having their feet washed by Jesus.

🌀 How is Jesus' washing the feet of the disciples an expression of all that Jesus has shown them in his life and will show them in his acceptance of his Passion and Crucifixion?

"If I, therefore, the master and teacher, have washed your feet, you ought to wash one another's feet. I have given you a model to follow, so that as I have done for you, you should also do" (John 13:14–15). The Holy Thursday liturgy includes a foot washing ritual, which follows the proclamation of the Gospel and the homily.

⑨ Think about what you experienced this evening. How does the ritual draw us into Christ's action and command to wash one another's feet?

⑨ What does it mean to wash another's feet?

⑨ How is foot washing part of what it means to be a disciple?

Wrapping It Up

Consider these points to conclude the dismissal. Integrate the thoughts and ideas that surfaced during the discussion.

- The Triduum is the most sacred liturgy of the year.

- In the Evening Mass of the Lord's Supper, we celebrate the institution of the Eucharist.

- As disciples, we are called to wash the feet of others, to love them as Jesus loves.

Closing Prayer

Conclude the dismissal session with prayer. Consider using Psalm 116 (see Lectionary, 39ABC) or the prayer below. If time permits, you might choose to sing the psalm refrain a few times before or after the closing prayer.

> Lord Jesus Christ, on the night before you died,
> you washed the feet of your disciples
> and command us to take up your ministry of washing the feet of others.
> Teach us to look upon our brothers and sisters with your tender, merciful care.
> Strengthen us to follow your example of self-giving love
> so that you may be known and shared throughout the world.
> Who live and reign for ever and ever.
> Amen.

Readings for the Next Dismissal

Provide catechumens with a list of the readings for the next dismissal session. Consult the liturgical calendar on page xvi to find out what day will be observed next week. Give catechumens the questions below to guide their reflection through the week.

⑨ What connections are you seeing in the readings of this liturgical season? As you pray with the readings, around what themes do your thoughts seem to be coming together?

⑨ Where do the readings intersect with your journey of faith? What questions do they raise for you?

Extended Catechesis

Based on today's readings and liturgical observance, the following topics may be covered for extended catechesis:

❄ Passover

❄ Eucharist

❄ Discipleship

❄ Paschal Mystery

❄ Sacred Paschal Triduum

FRIDAY OF THE PASSION OF THE LORD (GOOD FRIDAY)

Focus: For our sake, Jesus became obedient to Death on the Cross.

Lectionary #40ABC

Catechist's Preparation

Overview of Good Friday

Today we celebrate Good Friday of the Passion of the Lord. We call this Friday "good" in that, while we enter into Christ's Passion and Death, we know that through this ultimate act of sacrifice, humanity is offered salvation and eternal life. For this one day of the year, we thoroughly immerse ourselves in the reality of Jesus' Passion and Death. Yet throughout the liturgy of this day, we know that death does not have the final word.

Scripture Background

Isaiah 52:13–53:12 The Lectionary subtitles this passage the "Fourth oracle of the Servant of the Lord," but it is often called the fourth song of the Suffering Servant. Near the end of the book of the prophet Isaiah, we meet a figure called God's servant, who represents God but suffers greatly for the sins of others. The figure may have been a historical person at the time of Isaiah or a representation of the people of Israel. Christians read these four passages with a very specific insight: they prophesy Jesus, the servant of the Father, who suffered for our salvation.

The passage presents a startling description of this servant. He was "spurned and avoided by people, / a man of suffering, accustomed to infirmity" (53:3). In the most moving verses, we realize that the servant's suffering should have been ours: "Yet it was our infirmities that he bore, / our sufferings that he endured . . . / We had all gone astray like sheep . . . / but the Lord laid upon him / the guilt of us all" (53:4, 6). On Good Friday, these verses come to fulfillment in the crucified Jesus.

Psalm 31: 2, 6, 12–13, 15–16, 17, 25 (Luke 23:46) Psalm 31 appeals to God for rescue. The psalmist is desperate, "an object of reproach, / a laughingstock to my neighbors, and a dread to my friends" (31:6). But the psalm does not dwell in despair. It trusts that God will redeem the one in distress. This singer is so convinced of salvation that the psalm concludes with an exhortation to the hearer: "Take courage and be stouthearted, / all you who hope in the Lord" (31:25). The refrain "Father, into your hands I commend my spirit" (31:6) was spoken by Jesus on the Cross as he breathes his last (see Luke 23:46).

Hebrews 4:14–16; 5:7–9 The sufferings of Jesus enabled him to sympathize with our weakness, making him a powerful mediator of mercy and grace. The Letter to the Hebrews explains the role of Jesus as the greatest of all high priests. This passage describes the events of Jesus' Passion: "In the days when Christ was in the flesh, he offered prayers and supplications with loud cries and tears to the one who was able to save him from death" (5:7). These words resemble the Gospel accounts of Jesus suffering his agony in the garden of Gethsemane. But the passage does not linger on Jesus' suffering. "[H]e was heard" (5:7). The Father, who could save Jesus from death, did, by raising him from the dead.

John 18:1–19:42 This passage in the Gospel according to John is one of the most sublime testimonies to the glory of God. The narrative moves through several scenes, but it constantly teaches the meaning of Jesus' life, Death, and Resurrection. Early on, John presents "Jesus, knowing everything that was going to happen to him" (18:4). Jesus is no innocent bystander. He is the omniscient God in control of the events that follow. Three times in the opening confrontation he says, "I AM," boldly claiming the name that God revealed to Moses in the burning bush. His enemies end up proclaiming the truth about Jesus in spite of themselves. Caiaphas had told the Jews that, "it was better that one man should die rather than the people" (18:14), fulfilling Isaiah's fourth oracle. Pilate, unable to get a straight answer from Jesus about his identity, asks, "What is truth?" (18:38). But it is Pilate who has an inscription made for the Cross that calls Jesus, in three languages, the King of the Jews. The soldiers plait a crown from thorns and wrap Jesus' aching body in purple cloth, intending to mock, but handing over the signs of his kingship.

While the enemies of Jesus unintentionally speak the truth, his friend Peter intentionally denies Jesus three times. From the Cross, Jesus takes matters into his own hands, entrusting his mother and the disciple whom he loved to each other. From these faithful disciples the Church will be born. Before he dies, Jesus says, "It is finished" (19:30). That doesn't mean "It's over." It means "It is accomplished" or "It is perfected." He has completed the task he was given. He hands himself over to God. John has Jesus dying on the Cross on preparation day, the day before Passover, so that we will see in the slaughtering of the Passover lambs a contemporary symbol of the One who gave his life that others might live.

85

Reflection Questions for the Catechist

- What does it mean for you that Jesus accepted Passion and Death for the sake of humanity?
- What does it mean that Jesus did this for all of creation?
- In what ways are Christ's Passion and Death a sign and instrument of God's love?

Catechist's Guide

Objectives

▷ Participants will experience the Triduum as an immersion into the Paschal Mystery of Christ and the call to discipleship.

▷ Participants will more fully grasp the sacrifice of Jesus on the Cross.

▷ Participants will more deeply take to heart the love of God, which is shown and shared through Christ's Passion.

Dismissal and Procession

Following the homily and before the Solemn Intercessions, the priest celebrant picks up the Lectionary and invites the catechumens to come forward with the catechist(s) who will lead today's dismissal session. Holding the Lectionary so that all can see, the priest celebrant sends the catechumens and catechist(s) forward using RCIA, 67, his own words, or the following:

PRIEST: **My dear friends, soon you will join us at our feast of thanks and praise, where the table is laid with the Bread of Life, and the cup is filled with the Precious Blood of our Lord. But at this time we send you forth to another place once again to ponder and discuss our Lord's Passion which you have heard in our midst. Go in the peace of Christ.**

All process to where the dismissal session will take place. The catechist holds the Lectionary in a reverent manner. The assembly may sing an acclamation to accompany the procession.

Centering

Upon reaching the place where the dismissal occurs, place the Lectionary on the ambo, lectern, or other dignified place (or hold the book reverently). Light the candle that is in the place of gathering and reread Isaiah 52:13—53:12 in order to refocus the group's attention. Consider singing the Responsorial Psalm or have a recording of it available to use as part of the centering, either before or after the reading.

Reflection and Discussion

The following "script" may be used or adapted to help facilitate discussion on today's readings. Begin the discussion by asking the catechumens if any words or phrases from today's readings spoke to them. Today's reflection includes a guided meditation on the Passion reading. Be sure to prepare your reflection in advance, using the following to guide you. Use the Lectionary to incorporate Scripture passages during the reflection.

We continue the Triduum liturgy with the celebration of Good Friday of the Lord's Passion. Notice that the three days of the Triduum are one liturgy, through which we are immersed in Christ's Paschal Mystery. Today, we take to heart the reality of Christ's Passion and Death on the Cross. In today's First Reading, we hear a passage from Isaiah which is known as the Fourth Song of the Suffering Servant. When it was written, at the time nearing the end of Israel's Babylonian exile, the song may have referred to a particular person or the people of Israel. We hear the verses and see in them a profound prophecy of the Passion of Jesus Christ.

- What is in your heart as you hear, "We had all gone astray like sheep, / each following his own way; / but the LORD laid upon him / the guilt of us all" (Isaiah 53:6). In what ways do you see the Passion of Christ in this passage?

Through today's Responsorial Psalm, we sing the psalm that Jesus had on his lips and in his heart during his Crucifixion. We sing his final words on the Cross as the psalm refrain, "Father, into your hands I commend my spirit." With Jesus' words in our hearts and minds, we hear the Second Reading, from the letter to the Hebrews, which helps us reflect on Christ as the great high priest, who willingly accepted his suffering and sacrifice, and became the source of eternal salvation.

⑨ In what ways do you place your trust in God?

We now turn our minds and hearts to the story of Jesus' Passion and Death on the Cross. Pause for a moment to recall all that you heard.

[**From the beginning of the Gospel to Peter's third denial:**] Jesus knew everything that was going to happen to him, and yet he did not run from the ordeal that was to come. He knew his betrayer. He faced those sent to arrest him, declaring his identity as "I AM." Recall that, when Moses asked for God's name at the burning bush, God declared, "I AM." Remember that, at the Last Supper, Jesus foretold Peter's denial, and recall Peter's firm commitment to remain faithful to the Lord. Yet, as Jesus faces his accusers, Peter denies Jesus three times. Jesus is and shows God's love.

⑨ What does it mean to you that he was betrayed by one of his own followers and denied by another?

⑨ Do you ever deny Christ through your words or actions?

⑨ How does Jesus' love for humanity stand in stark contrast to the betrayal and denial of Judas and Peter?

[**From Jesus' interrogation by Pilate to his handing Jesus over to be crucified:**] The Jewish leaders take Jesus to Pontius Pilate, who questions Jesus. While Pilate believes himself to be in control, Jesus makes it clear that true authority comes from God. Pilate tries to release Jesus, but Pilate succumbs to pressure to convict him and hands him over to be crucified.

⑨ How do Jesus' responses to Pilate give witness to the depths of God's love? What does it mean to you that Jesus willingly accepted suffering, scourge, and the horror of crucifixion?

[**To the end of the passage:**] Jesus is crucified. The witnesses of his crucifixion include his mother and his mother's sister, Mary the wife of Clopas, Mary of Magdala, and the beloved disciple. Other followers take his body to a nearby tomb in keeping with Jewish Passover and burial customs.

The Good Friday liturgy includes the ritual Adoration of the Cross. In kissing or caressing the Cross, we place ourselves alongside those who witnessed his Crucifixion. We pray silently, acknowledging Christ's sacrifice for us and for all of humanity.

⑨ What is most prominently in your heart at this time?

Wrapping It Up

Consider these points to conclude the dismissal. Integrate the thoughts and ideas that surfaced during the discussion.

- Jesus obediently accepted suffering and Death, and in doing so he broke the bonds of sin and death.
- God has power and authority over all that is not loving, merciful, and forgiving in our lives and in the world.
- Christians throughout the world hold the Passion and Death of Christ in their hearts, taking to heart God's love for humanity.

Closing Prayer

Conclude the dismissal session with prayer. Consider using Psalm 131 (see Lectionary, 40ABC) or the prayer below. If time permits, you might choose to sing the psalm refrain a few times before or after the closing prayer.

Lord Jesus Christ,
you willingly entered into your Passion and Death,
accepting suffering for the sake of humanity.
We often fail to live as people who know you.
We sometimes betray you, at times deny you,
falling short of your call to bear your love in our broken world.
Guide us so that we may bear witness to your Passion
through our daily thoughts, words, and deeds.
Who live and reign for ever and ever.
Amen.

Readings for the Next Dismissal

Provide catechumens with a list of the readings for the next dismissal session. Consult the liturgical calendar on page xvi to find out what day will be observed next week. Give catechumens the questions below to guide their reflection through the week.

- What connections are you seeing in the readings of this liturgical season? As you pray with the readings, around what themes do your thoughts seem to be coming together?
- Where do the readings intersect with your journey of faith? What questions do they raise for you?

Extended Catechesis

Based on today's readings and liturgical observance, the following topics may be covered for extended catechesis:

- Christ's Passion and Death
- Salvation
- Paschal Mystery

EASTER SUNDAY OF THE RESURRECTION OF THE LORD

Focus: To intensify our witness as resurrection people.

Lectionary #42ABC (Mass during the Day)

❧ If your parish has year-round catechumenate, and catechumens are present for the Easter Masses,
it is better for them to attend the Easter Sunday liturgy and be dismissed rather than the Easter Vigil. In this way,
they will be able to experience for the first time the rituals of the Vigil while they are initiated and can
mystagocically reflect on their experience.

Catechist's Preparation

Overview of the Sunday

He is risen! "This is the day the Lord has made!" (today's psalm refrain). Our Lenten journey has led us to the joy of Easter, a season in which to ponder the meaning of the Resurrection, of Christ's victory over sin and death. As you prepare to lead your catechumens to reflect on this Easter Sunday, pause to allow the mystery of the Resurrection to come to life in your mind and heart, so that you may give witness to the Risen Christ for those who are learning to follow him, as disciples who themselves will witness to the power of the Resurrection. Since "the duration of the catechumenate will depend on the grace of God and on various circumstances," and knowing that "the time spent in the catechumenate should be long enough . . . for the conversion in faith of the catechumens to become strong," (RCIA, 76) it is very possible that there will be catechumens who were not initiated at the Easter Vigil, and who will continue their formation throughout the coming year; therefore, those catechumens who were not initiated at last night's Vigil should continue to be dismissed today.

Scripture Background

Acts of the Apostles 10:34a, 37–43 Peter's preaching coincides with the baptism of Cornelius, a Gentile who desires to follow Jesus. The speech to this Gentile audience is a testimony to the life and ministry of Jesus, who was crucified and died, but whom God raised up. Peter and the others are living witnesses to the marvelous things that God accomplished through Jesus during his lifetime, from his baptism to his risen presence. As witnesses to and believers in the Risen Lord, they were "commissioned" by Christ to "preach . . . and testify" that "everyone who believes in him will receive forgiveness" (10:42–43).

Peter emphasizes the inclusive nature of Jesus' ministry: "Everyone who believes . . . will receive forgiveness," (10:43) Jew and Gentile alike. As believers in the Risen Lord, we are all called to witness to what the Lord has done for us in raising us up from death in sin to new life in Christ. In the Risen Christ, we live as Resurrection people, always ready to witness to the marvelous deeds the Lord has done on our behalf.

Psalm 118:1–2, 16–17, 22–23 (24) This thanksgiving psalm, the common psalm of Easter Time, praises God for having rescued the psalmist from death. The psalm throws an interpretive lens on God's rescue of Jesus from death. Calling upon all people to praise the Lord, the psalm reminds us that, like Jesus, we have been rescued by God's mercy and power exercised on our behalf. Our responsibility is to let all know "the works of the Lord" (118:17). The rejected stone becoming the cornerstone resonates with Peter's inclusive understanding of Jesus' mission. Jesus was rejected for his inclusive embrace of Gentiles, outcasts, and sinners, and was ultimately put to death. God raised Jesus from the dead and made him the cornerstone of inclusivity, marked by forgiveness and reconciliation toward all who believe in the Risen Lord. Today, our gladness and joy is unbounded because the Lord continues to carry out that ministry through us.

Colossians 3:1–4 or 1 Corinthians 5:6b–8 Both readings reflect on the new awareness that is required if we are truly Resurrection believers. Colossians calls believers to "seek what is above, where Christ is," and not to focus on "what is on earth" (3:1–2). As believers, we approach life on earth from the perspective of the Risen Christ, namely, as witnesses to the new life of inclusive forgiveness and reconciliation toward all. Jesus' ministry is now ours, and we are called to look at life through that lens. In so doing, we too will one day "appear with him in glory" (3:4).

First Corinthians challenges believers to "clear out the old yeast, so that you may become a fresh batch of dough" (5:7). In the sacrificed and Risen Christ, we have been made "unleavened," (5:7) clean and undefiled once more. In Christ, we have been forgiven and reconciled to God. Therefore, we are no longer to live in "malice and wickedness" but in "sincerity and truth" (5:8) our witness, and continue the ministry of the Risen Lord.

Sequence This Sunday, the Church sings a sequence—an ancient, poetic song that precedes the singing of the Gospel Acclamation. The Easter sequence, Victimae paschali laudes, is a song of praise to the Paschal victim that also reflects the Gospel account of Mary's encounter with the Risen Lord.

John 20:1–9 On Easter, we proclaim not the presence of the Risen Christ, but the empty tomb. Mary of Magdala, Peter, and the "other disciple whom Jesus loved" (20:2) are the key characters, as is the empty tomb. Mary can only surmise that the body has been stolen as she rushes to Peter. Peter and the beloved disciple run to the tomb. The beloved disciple gets there first, but waits for Peter to arrive before entering. Both Mary and the beloved dis-ciple seem to acknowledge Peter's priority status among the disciples. Peter arrives and enters the tomb followed by the beloved disciple. Both see the burial cloths but no body. The beloved disciple sees and believes. Peter does not yet appear to believe for "they did not yet understand the Scripture that he had to rise from the dead" (20:9). Like the disciples, we acknowledge that belief in the Resurrection is a mystery. Scripture continues to sustain us in that belief. And the living witness of those whose faith is concretized in lives of care, concern, and reconciliation, is the clearest proof that the Lord is risen and active among us. Let us always continue to intensify our witness to the Resurrection by continuing the Risen Lord's ministry.

Reflection Questions for the Catechist

⑨ What difference does it make in your life that Christ rose from the dead?

⑨ In what ways do you witness to the power of the Resurrection?

⑨ How is your life shaped in the knowledge that "your life is hidden with Christ in God" (Colossians 3:3)?

Catechist's Guide

Objectives

▷ To develop a greater understanding of the Paschal Mystery.

▷ To more fully grasp the meaning of Christ's Resurrection.

▷ To reflect upon the call to witness to Christ through word and deed.

Dismissal and Procession

Following the homily, the priest celebrant picks up the Lectionary and invites the catechumens to come forward with the catechist(s) who will lead today's dismissal session. Holding the Lectionary so that all can see, the priest celebrant sends the catechumens and catechist(s) forward using RCIA, 67, his own words, or the following:

> PRIEST: My dear friends, we in the assembly now send you forth to another place, where you may gather to consider and discuss the scriptures you have heard proclaimed. We pray that the words you have heard will inspire you, drawing you closer to the light of the Risen Lord. Go now in his name, our Lord Jesus Christ. Alleluia.

All process to where the dismissal session will take place. The catechist holds the Lectionary in a reverent manner. The assembly may sing an acclamation to accompany the procession.

Centering

Upon reaching the place where the dismissal occurs, place the Lectionary on the ambo, lectern, or other dignified place (or hold the book reverently). Light the candle that is in the place of gathering and reread John 20:1–9 in order to refocus the group's attention. Consider singing the Responsorial Psalm or have a recording of it available to use as part of the centering, either before or after the reading.

Reflection and Discussion

The following "script" may be used or adapted to help facilitate discussion on today's readings. Begin the discussion by asking the catechumens if any words or phrases from today's readings spoke to them.

He is risen! Today we celebrate Easter and begin a season in which we reflect upon the meaning of the Resurrection. We will hear the story of the early community of believers in the Acts of the Apostles, and we will think about who we are called to be as disciples of the Risen Christ. As we begin our reflection today, take a few moments to look back on the Lenten season that has just concluded, and on your experience of Triduum (the evening of Holy Thursday through this evening):

⟳ What stands out for you spiritually and practically as you look back on Lent? What most powerfully captures your experience of Lent?

⟳ What is in your heart as you reflect upon the Triduum?

⟳ Upon what will you continue to reflect during Easter Time?

Throughout Easter Time, the First Reading comes from the Acts of the Apostles. We will hear how the Church grew from the initial gathering of Apostles and those who had followed Jesus, and how the Good News of Jesus Christ was proclaimed to people throughout the world. In today's First Reading, Peter speaks to the household of a Gentile man, Cornelius, who has come to believe in Jesus. Peter summarizes the essence of the Paschal Mystery: Jesus' life and ministry, his Passion and Death, his Resurrection and post-Resurrection time with those witnesses who were chosen by God. Those witnesses now preach and share the Good News of Christ with others.

⟳ What of the Paschal Mystery would you share with others? What meaning does this have for you in your life?

In today's Responsorial Psalm, we sing that "the stone which the builders rejected / has become the cornerstone" (118:22). During Jesus' life and ministry, he was often rejected by the Jewish leaders and yet was sought out by and reached out to outcasts, sinners, and Gentiles. The early communities of Christians followed Jesus' example of inclusion of others, sharing the Good News with all who would hear it.

⟳ In what ways do you see the Church extending the ministry and care of Christ to all?

⟳ How does this mission of sharing the life of Christ with others compel you to live?

Today's Second Reading is taken either from the letter to the Colossians or from the first letter to the Corinthians. Both speak of the new life in Christ of the baptized. In the waters of Baptism, we die with Christ and anticipate eternal life with God in glory. Those who are Baptized are unleavened bread, made clean and living in sincerity and truth.

⟳ As you continue on your journey of faith, what grace do you anticipate through initiation?

Today we heard an ancient text sung just before the Gospel. Known as a Sequence, the particular text we hear today proclaims the Good News of the Resurrection. It helps us to prepare to hear the Gospel with an appreciation for the mystery we will hear proclaimed. Each of the Gospel accounts of the Resurrection differs somewhat in detail, yet all tell of the amazing news that Christ is Risen. The narrative we hear today is from the Gospel according to John. In it, Mary Magdalene discovers the empty tomb and runs to tell Simon Peter and the other disciple. They in turn run to the tomb, find it empty as Mary had said, and see the burial cloths cast aside, with the cloth that had covered Jesus' head rolled up in a separate place. The other disciple saw the empty tomb and believed; they did not yet understand the Scripture that Jesus had to rise from the dead. Put yourself in Mary Magdalene's place.

🌀 What might you think and feel in discovering the empty tomb?

🌀 Upon what might you reflect as you ran to tell Peter and the other disciple the news?

🌀 What is the meaning of the Resurrection for you?

🌀 How are you called to be a witness to the Resurrection?

Wrapping It Up

Consider these points to conclude the dismissal. Integrate the thoughts and ideas that surfaced during the discussion.

- The early Church reflected upon their experience of Jesus in order to fully grasp the Paschal Mystery.

- In Baptism, we are drawn into Christ's Death and Resurrection.

- We are called to witness to the fullness of life in Christ through our words and deeds.

Closing Prayer

Conclude with prayer. If time permits, sing the psalm refrain a few times before or after the following prayer.

> Risen Lord Jesus Christ,
> through your Passion and Death,
> you sacrificed yourself
> so that all might be drawn to life with God in glory.
> Through your Resurrection, you conquered death, destroying its power over us.
> In Easter Time, help us to more fully grasp the fullness of life with you,
> for you live and reign with the Father in the unity of the Holy Spirit,
> one God, for ever and ever.
> Amen. Alleluia!

Readings for the Next Dismissal

Provide catechumens with a list of the readings for the next dismissal session. Consult the liturgical calendar on page xvi to find out what day will be observed next week. Give catechumens the questions below to guide their reflection through the week.

🌀 What connections are you seeing in the readings of this liturgical season? As you pray with the readings, around what themes do your thoughts seem to be coming together?

🌀 Where do the readings intersect with your journey of faith? What questions do they raise for you?

Extended Catechesis

Based on today's readings and liturgical observance, the following topics may be covered for extended catechesis:

❉ Paschal Mystery   ❉ Discipleship

❉ Resurrection   ❉ Witness

❉ Belief

INTRODUCTION TO EASTER TIME

Overview of Easter Time

Alleluia! Christ is Risen! Easter Time leads us to delve into the meaning of the Resurrection, hear the story of the early community of believers, and consider the call to continue Christ's ministry of love. Beginning with the great Easter Vigil, the fifty-day Easter season begins with the Resurrection of the Lord, includes post-Resurrection narratives, explores the love and unity with God which is given through Christ, and culminates with Christ's Ascension and the advent of the Holy Spirit on Pentecost Sunday. The season is one of great joy, in which the elect reflect deeply on their initiation into the fullness of the Christian life and on Christ's Paschal Mystery. Those who have already been baptized renew their Baptism throughout the season and consider their call to share in Christ's mission of love.

Since "the duration of the catechumenate depends on the grace of God and on various circumstances," and knowing that "the time spent in the catechumenate should be long enough . . . for the conversion and faith of the catechumens to become strong" (RCIA, 76), it is very possible that there will be catechumens who were not initiated at the Easter Vigil and who will continue their formation throughout the coming year. These catechumens may initially be unfamiliar with Easter as a season, especially since the experience of the surrounding culture is of Easter as a single day. Keeping Easter as a season in which to reflect upon the Good News of Christ's Resurrection has the potential to make a lasting impact in the ways in which the catechumens grasp the fullness of life in Christ now and for eternity. Following the austerity of the season of Lent, Easter is a time to celebrate the abundance of grace, peace, and life to which we are drawn in Christ. This is a season in which the catechumens come to a greater appreciation of and longing for the waters of Baptism, the gifts of the Holy Spirit, and inclusion in the Eucharistic table. This anticipation of initiation in the future is mediated by the reflection on the call of disciples to share in Christ's way of self-giving love.

Preparing a Seasonal Environment

After the dark violet color of Lent, we transition to the liturgical colors of white and gold. Think of the stark difference in the church environment during Lent and Easter. What brings Easter joy and new life to the eye in your gathering space? The liturgical color of Easter Time is white and sometimes includes silver or gold embellishments. In the environment for the season, give prominent place to a candle, whose light shines throughout the season. Consider also adding a vessel with water that was blessed at the great Easter Vigil as well as green plants or other colorful flowers. Keep a space available for the Lectionary (or Bible) such as a lectern or table. Keep a candle near the Lectionary (or Bible) and light this candle before the session begins.

In everything you do to create the environment for Easter Time in the dismissal space, take your lead from the environment in the sanctuary of the main assembly. Consistency between what the catechumens see in the environment in that space and in the environment in the dismissal space is important. You do not want to create divergent messages about the day and season and thus generate unnecessary questions or confusion within the group. Keep the environment simple but not simplistic, understated but not minimized. Colors, light, images, and other added elements should all assist the catechumens in their reflection on the significance of the day and the Word of God.

Overview of the Readings

First Readings The First Readings throughout the season are from the Acts of the Apostles. The passage on the Second Sunday focuses on the Christian community, which was of one heart and mind. On the Third Sunday, Peter calls those who were present during Jesus' Passion to repent and be converted, declaring that he knows that they acted out of ignorance. On the Fourth Sunday, Peter, filled with the Holy Spirit, addresses the Jewish leaders and elders who have arrested Peter and John, following the healing of a man who was crippled from birth. On the Fifth Sunday, we learn of the arrival of Saul to Jerusalem, and of Barnabas witnessing to the Jerusalem community of Saul's conversion. On the Sixth Sunday, we hear of the conversion, outpouring of the Holy Spirit, and subsequent Baptism of Cornelius and his household. As we celebrate the Ascension of the Lord, the First Reading includes Jesus' promise of the Holy Spirit and his Ascension. On the Seventh Sunday, the Apostles and other disciples gather in prayer and discern Matthias as the twelfth Apostle, replacing Judas, Jesus' betrayer. On the Solemnity of Pentecost, we hear how the Spirit was received by those who were gathered, who immediately proclaim the Good News of Christ.

Responsorial Psalms An optional communal response to every psalm of this season is "Alleluia," which could also summarize the message and mood of these psalms. Three times, we pray from Psalm 118, repeating its Paschal acclamation: "The stone which the builders rejected / has become the cornerstone" (118:22). Three additional themes dominate the Easter psalms: the plea for God's light and spirit, the proclamation that God's power has been shown to the nations, and joy in Christ's Ascension to the heavenly throne. They all offer variations on the theme expressed in the response to the Easter psalm: "Give thanks to the Lord, for he is good, / for his mercy endures forever" (118:1).

Second Readings Throughout Easter Time, we hear from the first letter of John as the Second Reading. Through this letter, we reflect on God as love and our call to love one another as united in Christ through the power of the Holy Spirit. The Second Readings also include passages from the letters to the Colossians, Ephesians, and Galatians, through which we are called to seek what is above, to carry out Christ's mission through the gifts given by the Holy Spirit, and to live as people of love in community.

Gospel Readings Throughout Easter Time, we hear primarily from the Gospel according to John. We hear the narrative of the Risen Lord offering peace and declaring "Blessed are those who have not seen and have believed" (John 20:29) on the Second Sunday. We hear again from the Gospel according to John during the Fourth (Good Shepherd), Fifth (vine and branches), Sixth ("remain in my love"; "love one another as I have loved you" [15:9, 10, 12]), and Seventh Sundays (Jesus' prayer during the Last Supper). On the Third Sunday, we read from the Gospel according to Luke, in which the Risen Christ offered peace, ate with the disciples, and opened their minds to understand what was written in the Scriptures. On the Ascension, Christ tells the disciples to go out to all the world and proclaim the Gospel just before he ascended into heaven. On Pentecost, Jesus tells the disciples that "the Spirit of truth . . . will guide you to all truth" (John 16:13).

SECOND SUNDAY OF EASTER / SUNDAY OF DIVINE MERCY

Focus: To believe without seeing.

Lectionary #44B

🌿 Please note that the dismissal guide for Easter Sunday is found in the Triduum section, p. 89.

Catechist's Preparation

Overview of the Sunday

It is the Second Sunday of Easter, and as we will throughout the season, we reflect on the encounters of the Apostles with the Risen Christ, the spread of the Gospel to all nations, and the meaning of all of this for us in our time and place. Today is also the Sunday of Divine Mercy, in which we highlight in a particular way the great mercy of God shown to us especially in the Paschal Mystery of our Lord. The readings today are always taken from those prescribed for the Second Sunday of Easter. Today, we are challenged to believe without seeing, and we will think about how we make Christ seen and known through our belief. Think about and pray for your catechumens today. How are they coming to belief in Jesus Christ? What challenges them as they continue to journey toward belief? In what ways will you bear God's enduring love today so that the catechumens you lead may believe?

Scripture Background

Acts of the Apostles 4:32–35 Luke presents various idealized descriptions of the early communities established by Christ's followers, all centered on the Apostles' role as witnesses to the resurrected Jesus. The Risen Christ, present through his Spirit, empowers believers to live out Jesus' mission and ministry. Witness to the Risen Christ is manifested in the communal lifestyle evidenced in his followers. They are of "one heart and mind" (4:32), sharing their possessions with others in need, as the Apostles administer their distribution.

Whether these communities were real or idealized by Luke, one thing is certain. Belief in the Risen Christ motivates his followers to manifest the same sacrificial love for others that Christ modeled for them. Empowered by the Spirit of the Christ, they carry on that lifestyle for all to see and experience. Others who have not seen or known Christ can now experience him in his followers. In their self-giving, they are living manifestations of the Risen Lord.

Psalm 118:2–4, 13–15, 22–24 (1) The psalm invites all to thank God, who is good and whose love is forever faithful and enduring. All are called to acclaim God's *hesed*, translated as "mercy," but literally meaning deep, faithful, enduring covenant love. God is attuned to the cry of the beloved with whom he has made this covenant, reaching out to save them and restore their courage and strength. Suffering and pain lead to experiences of loneliness, rejection, or abandonment by others. Such feelings of abandonment increase their suffering. God's covenant love restores and gives new life to the rejected ones, bringing back their sense of dignity and self-worth. This is the essence of covenant love. Such love "is wonderful in our eyes" (118:23), as we joyfully acknowledge that "This is the day the Lord has made; / let us be glad and rejoice in it" (118:24). Faithful love does ultimately conquer all.

1 John 5:1–6 John makes the bold statement that all who believe Jesus to be the Christ, God's anointed, are begotten by God. This includes us, who believe without having seen. Believing in and loving Christ also means loving God. Love of God is clearly manifested in loving God's children and obeying the Commandments. God's Commandments are not burdensome. John's letter asserts that love of God manifests itself in love of others, while love of others clearly manifests love of God. No matter where one starts, the other necessarily follows.

Such love ultimately conquers the world, understood as the place where love of God and others is severely lacking. Faith in Jesus as God's Son empowers us, through God's Spirit, to overcome the world by loving God and neighbor. Jesus came to model total, self-giving love through water and blood, his total self-sacrifice. Belief in Jesus empowers us, through the testimony of his Spirit, to live in self-giving love toward God and others.

John 20:19–31 Two Johannine Resurrection appearances are proclaimed every Second Sunday of Easter. The first one takes place on Easter Sunday evening, as the Risen Christ appears through locked doors and imparts peace to his fearful followers. Having been shown his hands and feet, they rejoice in seeing that it really is the Lord, as he breathes on them and gifts them with his Spirit. He commissions them to practice forgiveness and reconciliation with all. Being Spirit-filled demands that disciples take up Jesus' mission of reconciling the world to God and one another.

Thomas, who was not present for this first appearance, refuses to believe what he has been told unless he sees and touches Jesus for himself. A week later, Jesus appears, imparts peace once again, and invites Thomas to see and touch. We do not know whether Thomas follows through or not. What he does do is make the boldest affirmation of belief in the Risen Christ, "My Lord and my God!" (20:28). Jesus responds by saying "Have you come to believe because you have seen me? Blessed are those who have not seen and have believed" (20:29).

John's community, some three generations removed from the Risen Christ, are like us. We all seek to know where and how to experience the Risen Christ. The Gospel ending asserts that the Scriptures are written that "you may come to believe that Jesus is the Christ" and so believing, "you may have life in his name" (20:31). Faith in Jesus empowers us to live as disciples who have come to know and experience the Risen Christ through Scripture and through lives of self-giving, reconciling love.

Reflection Questions for the Catechist

⑨ When have you experienced doubt?

⑨ What helped you to believe in the face of doubt?

⑨ What is the role of the community in helping you to live in faith?

Catechist's Guide

Objectives

▷ To reflect upon the role of the community in drawing one another to live as disciples.

▷ To reflect upon the gift of faith.

▷ To grasp more fully the impact of faith in daily life.

Dismissal and Procession

Following the homily, the priest celebrant picks up the Lectionary and invites the catechumens to come forward with the catechist(s) who will lead today's dismissal session. Holding the Lectionary so that all can see, the priest celebrant sends the catechumens and catechist(s) forward using RCIA, 67, his own words, or the following:

PRIEST: **My dear friends, the Church is renewed in the living waters of Baptism, as Easter joy resounds in our hearts and upon our lips. As you grow to know Christ more and more each day and follow in his footsteps, you will long for these waters and the newness of life they contain. We, your brothers and sisters, join with you in prayer, as you share with each other the Word of God. We patiently wait for the day when you too will share fully in the Paschal feast of the Lord. Go in peace. Alleluia!**

All process to where the dismissal session will take place. The catechist holds the Lectionary in a reverent manner. The assembly may sing an acclamation to accompany the procession.

Centering

Upon reaching the place where the dismissal occurs, place the Lectionary on the ambo, lectern, or other dignified place (or hold the book reverently). Light the candle that is in the place of gathering and reread John 20:19–31 in order to refocus the group's attention. Consider singing the Responsorial Psalm or have a recording of it available to use as part of the centering, either before or after the reading.

Reflection and Discussion

The following "script" may be used or adapted to help facilitate discussion on today's readings. Begin the discussion by asking the catechumens if any words or phrases from today's readings spoke to them.

It is the Second Sunday of Easter, and as we will throughout the season, we reflect on the encounters of the Apostles with the Risen Christ, the spread of the Gospel to all nations, and the meaning of all of this for us in our time and place. Today is also designated as the Sunday of Divine Mercy, a day in which we reflect in a particular way on the enduring love of God for humanity, which we know through Jesus Christ.

🌀 What most powerfully strikes you as you continue to reflect upon the Resurrection?

🌀 How is Jesus' life, Death, and Resurrection a sign and instrument of God's mercy?

In today's First Reading from the Acts of the Apostles, we hear about the community of believers. Scripture scholars do not know if the descriptions of the community are idealized—the vision for what the Christian community can be—or if they are actually descriptive of life in the early Church. Either way, what a beautiful witness to Christ's love we see in this passage! We know that the early communities of faith did witness to Christ's love powerfully, and through them others came to believe. Their being in community with one another helped others to see Christ, whose life they bore through their life together.

🌀 How does the community of faith help you to grow as a believer?

🌀 In what ways do you see the community witnessing to Christ's love through its ministries, outreach, care for others, and attention to those who need to know God's love?

Again today, the Responsorial Psalm is Psalm 118. Today we sing, "Give thanks to the Lord, for he is good, his love is everlasting" (refrain). God has established a covenant with us, through which we are assured that God's love never fails. We know this love most perfectly in Jesus Christ, whose sacrifice shows us how we are to live as Christian people. The early community in the Acts of the Apostles gave of themselves for others in response to what they knew and experienced in Jesus' life and ministry, his Passion and Death. It can be difficult for us to embrace such self-giving love, which is counter to the individualism and materialism that is championed in the world. Yet as followers of Jesus we are called to embrace self-giving love together with others in community. As we grow in belief and acceptance of Christ's way of self-giving love, we grow in our desire to keep God's commandments as an expression of our faith.

🌀 In what ways are you growing as a person who gives of self for others?

🌀 How are you becoming a fuller member of the community of believers?

🌀 In what ways does your faith direct the ways in which you live in relationship with God and others?

In today's Gospel, we hear two stories of encounters with the Risen Lord. In the first story, Jesus stands in the midst of the disciples, who were locked away out of fear. He offers his peace and shows them his hands and side. The disciples were filled with joy as they recognized him. He breathes on them, giving them the Holy Spirit and telling them to share his reconciliation and forgiveness with others.

🌀 Of what are you afraid?

🌀 How does Jesus tear down the walls that you place around yourself, inviting you to put aside your fear and put your faith in him?

We also hear of Thomas, who cannot believe without seeing and touching Christ, and we are told, "Blessed are those who have not seen and have believed" (John 20:29). None of us have physically seen the Lord. Yet, we are drawn to belief through the testimony of Sacred Scripture and the witness of believers today and throughout the centuries.

§ Faith is a gift from God. Who helps you to accept this gift and to grow in belief of Christ?

Wrapping It Up

Consider these points to conclude the dismissal. Integrate the thoughts and ideas that surfaced during the discussion.

- Christ calls us to be with and for others.

- Faith is a gift from God.

- We grow in faith through the testimony of Sacred Scripture and the witness of believers.

Closing Prayer

Conclude with prayer. If time permits, sing the psalm refrain a few times before or after the following prayer.

> Loving God,
> we come to know and to believe in your enduring mercy
> through your only begotten Son, Jesus, who offers us peace
> and draws us into his mission of self-giving love.
> Be with us as we accept your gift of faith and grow in belief.
> For while we have not seen, we do believe;
> and in our belief, we become more committed each day
> to living your commandments as your people in the world.
> Through Christ our Lord.
> Amen.

Readings for the Next Dismissal

Provide catechumens with a list of the readings for the next dismissal session. Consult the liturgical calendar on page xvi to find out what day will be observed next week. Give catechumens the questions below to guide their reflection through the week.

§ What connections are you seeing in the readings of this liturgical season? As you pray with the readings, around what themes do your thoughts seem to be coming together?

§ Where do the readings intersect with your journey of faith? What questions do they raise for you?

Extended Catechesis

Based on today's readings and liturgical observance, the following topics may be covered for extended catechesis:

❇ Faith, doubt, and belief   ❇ Union with Christ in Baptism

❇ Christian community   ❇ Christian life in response to God's love

THIRD SUNDAY OF EASTER

Focus: To know Christ's peace through the forgiveness of sin.

Lectionary #47B

Catechist's Preparation

Overview of the Sunday

Can we imagine the world as God intends and desires it to be? Is it possible for us to grasp the extent of God's love for humanity and for all of creation? Throughout the centuries, humanity has often fallen short of the love and purpose for which we are made. Yet God never walks away from us. God remains faithful to the covenant; God's law of love endures. Through Jesus' perseverance in his mission, to the point of Death on the Cross, we are offered the way back to the fullness of life with God. Christ is victorious over sin and death. In Jesus, we are offered the path of repentance and forgiveness of sin. In this forgiveness, we find Christ's peace.

Scripture Background

Acts of the Apostles 3:13–15, 17–19 It is fitting that we hear this sermon just after we have celebrated Christ's Resurrection. Peter reviews with his listeners how the people freed Barabbas, a murderer, and had Jesus put to death. This injustice was done even though the God of Abraham, Isaac, and Jacob had glorified Jesus. The audience to whom he is preaching includes some people who participated in these events and some from the general population. Peter declares that the people "denied the Holy and Righteous One" (3:14) but God raised him from the dead. Peter's accusations in this sermon are strong but true. Jesus suffered because of ungodly elements such as human ignorance, ruthlessness, selfishness, and sinfulness. Peter recognizes that they did this terrible deed out of ignorance, but his goal is to call everyone to repentance and conversion. Nothing is too great to be forgiven. God will forgive, he proclaims, if you reform your lives and turn to God.

Psalm 4:2, 4, 7–8, 9 (7a) Psalm 4 is linked closely to Psalm 3, as an individual lament with the theme of trust in the Lord. This psalm paints a picture of a wonderful God, one who listens to us, hears our cries, and relieves our distress. Ours is a God who smiles with love on us even though we continue to need to be called to repentance. How fitting and comforting it is to be reminded of this gracious and protecting God just after the strong accusations we just heard from Peter. We can rejoice knowing that this is still how God relates to us today. The Lord will heal us and will answer us when we call.

1 John 2:1–5a The same message found in today's psalm continues in this passage from 1 John. The original context of these particular verses seems to have been initiation into the Christian community. During the initiation rites, each person was to make a public confession of his or her sinfulness. Following that, they were reminded that Christ, whose Death and Resurrection were expiation for all sins, is our advocate. In this context, as elsewhere, the community is reminded that "to know [God] is to keep his commandments" (2:3). It is a timeless message, true for us today as it was for the early Christians: one's behavior must reflect his or her knowledge of God. To know Christ is to be obedient to his commands. Knowledge of God cannot be separated from ethical conduct. This is the price of the privilege of being called a follower of Christ.

Luke 24:35–48 The first words out of Jesus' mouth when he appears to the disciples are "Peace be with you" (24:36). This is the greeting, *shalom*, Jesus had taught the disciples to say whenever they entered a house. These are words that he had spoken over and over during his public life. Peace is at the heart of his message, the epitomes of how the followers of Christ are to live. Gathered as they were, listening to the report of the disciples on the way to Emmaus, the disciples were startled and, indeed, terrified when Jesus suddenly appeared in their midst. Once he showed them proof that it was he, the disciples' terror turned to incredulous joy.

In this appearance, Jesus does three things that are integral to his life: he greets them with peace, he shares a meal, and he teaches them. He asked for food and ate it in front of them, we are told. Eating together was significant throughout Jesus' life on earth, and he shared meals many times, including at the Last Supper. Here, again, he is showing us the importance of shared meals. Then he begins to teach. He uses the Law of Moses to emphasize that he is the Messiah. He points out specifically how what the prophets and psalms taught had now been fulfilled in him. The Apostles were able to understand because they opened their hearts and minds to his message. Everything about this Gospel makes his message so clear. Christ came to fulfill the law, and now that he has risen, those who follow him are to continue preaching his message, especially his message of peace.

Reflection Questions for the Catechist

🌀 What sinful tendency did you recognize during Lent? How will you fight this temptation in the future?

🌀 How do you experience the peace of Christ?

🌀 How do you offer Christ's peace to others?

Catechist's Guide

Objectives

▷ To acknowledge our weakness and temptation to sin.

▷ To grasp more fully the gift of God's grace.

▷ To develop a greater appreciation for the peace that comes from offering and receiving forgiveness.

Dismissal and Procession

Following the homily, the priest celebrant picks up the Lectionary and invites the catechumens to come forward with the catechist(s) who will lead today's dismissal session. Holding the Lectionary so that all can see, the priest celebrant sends the catechumens and catechist(s) forward using RCIA, 67, his own words, or the following:

> PRIEST: **The Easter mysteries reminded us of who we want to be: faithful disciples washed in the Blood of the Lamb fully incorporated into his Body the Church. As you continue your journey of preparation, we rejoice in your commitment and long for the time when you will share with us in the supper of the Lamb. Go in peace. Alleluia!**

All process to where the dismissal session will take place. The catechist holds the Lectionary in a reverent manner. The assembly may sing an acclamation to accompany the procession.

Centering

Upon reaching the place where the dismissal occurs, place the Lectionary on the ambo, lectern, or other dignified place (or hold the book reverently). Light the candle that is in the place of gathering and reread Luke 24:35–48 in order to refocus the group's attention. Consider singing the Responsorial Psalm or have a recording of it available to use as part of the centering, either before or after the reading.

Reflection and Discussion

The following "script" may be used or adapted to help facilitate discussion on today's readings. Begin the discussion by asking the catechumens if any words or phrases from today's readings spoke to them.

Can you imagine the world as God intends and desires it to be? Is it possible for us to grasp the extent of God's love for humanity and for all of creation? Throughout the centuries, humanity has often fallen short of the love and purpose for which we are made. Yet, God never walks away from us. God remains faithful to the covenant; God's law of love endures. Through Jesus' endurance to his mission, to the point of Death on the Cross, we are offered the way back to the fullness of life with God.

🌀 What do you think of when you hear the word *sin*?

🌀 When have you offered forgiveness to another person? When have you been offered forgiveness? What happened, and what was the impact?

In today's First Reading, from the Acts of the Apostles, Peter speaks to a group of Jewish people. Some of them would have been in the crowds that shouted for the release of Barabbas and for Jesus to be crucified. Peter witnesses to Jesus' true identity as the Son of God, driving home the point that it was the author of life who was put to Death on the Cross.

Peter goes on to say that he knows that the people who participated in Jesus' Crucifixion acted out of ignorance, and he urges them to repent of this grievous sin.

⑨ What does Peter's testimony say to you about Christ? What does Peter's call for repentance and assurance of forgiveness teach you?

In today's Responsorial Psalm, we sing a heartfelt prayer to God, "When I call, answer me, O my just God, / you who relieve me when I am in distress" (4:2). As the prayer continues, we sing of the wonders God does and of the peaceful sleep of one who rests in the love of God.

⑨ Think of a time in which you were troubled by a conflict with a family member or friend. How does such an experience affect other aspects of life?

⑨ How would you describe the peace that comes when a difficult situation or interpersonal conflict is resolved?

In the first letter of John, from which we hear in today's Second Reading, we are told that Christ is "expiation for our sins, and not for our sins only but for those of the whole world" (2:2).

⑨ What does it mean to you that in bringing God's great love to the world, Jesus was put to death?

⑨ How is his sacrifice "expiation" for our sins (1 John 2:2)?

⑨ How is keeping God's commandments a response to the grace and love of Christ?

We hear another post-Resurrection account today, from the Gospel according to Luke. The beginning of the passage refers to the encounter of two disciples with the Risen Lord on the road to Emmaus. In this encounter, the disciples recognized Christ in the breaking of bread, and they ran back to Jerusalem to share their experience with the eleven Apostles and those who were with them. Christ is suddenly in their midst, offering his peace to them. He shows them his hands and feet so that they will know it is him, and with this physical proof, their fear turns to joy. He eats with them, sharing a meal as he so often had before the Crucifixion, and offering more physical proof that it is him. Christ understands that the disciples are frightened and confused. Some of them had run away during his arrest and Passion. The disciples are afraid that they will be arrested because they are Christ's followers. He greets them with peace, the greeting he had taught them to use when they entered a house. And he eats with them. Then, he teaches them. He shows them how he fulfilled all that had been written in the Scriptures. Disciples, then and now, are witnesses to this Good News of Christ's offer of forgiveness and peace.

⑨ In what ways is following Christ a bit frightening or uncertain for you?

⑨ What reassurance do you find in hearing Christ's greeting, "Peace be with you" (Luke 24:36). How is Christ's offer of forgiveness also an offer of peace?

Wrapping It Up   *Consider these points to conclude the dismissal. Integrate the thoughts and ideas that surfaced during the discussion.*

- Christ repairs the divide between God and humanity.

- In Jesus' Death and Resurrection, we recognize him as the Christ, the Messiah.

- In Christ, forgiveness and peace are indelibly intertwined.

Closing Prayer

Conclude with prayer. If time permits, sing the psalm refrain a few times before or after the following prayer.

Risen Lord,
through your Death and Resurrection,
you claim victory over sin and death,
offering peace in the face of fear and confusion, forgiveness for repentant hearts.
Guide us to acknowledge the times in which we fail to be God's loving people,
to seek your forgiveness, and to be assured of your love and peace,
which we celebrate in this Easter time.
Who live and reign for ever and ever.
Amen.

Readings for the Next Dismissal

Provide catechumens with a list of the readings for the next dismissal session. Consult the liturgical calendar on page xvi to find out what day will be observed next week. Give catechumens the questions below to guide their reflection through the week.

- What connections are you seeing in the readings of this liturgical season? As you pray with the readings, around what themes do your thoughts seem to be coming together?
- Where do the readings intersect with your journey of faith? What questions do they raise for you?

Extended Catechesis

Based on today's readings and liturgical observance, the following topics may be covered for extended catechesis:

- Original Sin
- The Resurrection is a victory over sin and death
- Christ's presence in the Sacrament of Penance and Reconciliation
- Risen Christ
- Christ is the fulfillment of the law and prophets

FOURTH SUNDAY OF EASTER

Focus: To find God in the rejected.

Lectionary #50B

Catechist's Preparation

Overview of the Sunday

Those of us who do not live on or near a farm may have a limited understanding of sheep and shepherds. On the Fourth Sunday of Easter, the Gospel always includes a passage in which Jesus describes himself as the Good Shepherd. Therefore, this Sunday is often known as Good Shepherd Sunday. Not only does he care for his own, he seeks out, welcomes, and cares for those who are lost. The shepherd is not only called to make sure that the sheep are fed and have water, they also must protect the sheep. Sheep that have a good shepherd follow the shepherd's call, sure that where the shepherd goes, all will be well. On this Good Shepherd Sunday, reflect with your catechumens on what it means to be sheep who have the best shepherd of all, Jesus Christ, who lays down his life for the sheep.

Scripture Background

Acts of the Apostles 4:8–12 All the readings reflect this aspect of Jesus' identity. In Acts of the Apostles, Peter explains to the Jewish leaders that the crippled person he cured was healed in Jesus' name. They had rejected and crucified Jesus, he reminds them, but God raised him up. As a result, the Risen Christ is now the means of healing and salvation for all who believe. Peter connects Jesus with the stone rejected by the builders in Psalm 118. The Jewish leaders—the builders—rejected Jesus, but God raised him up, making him the cornerstone of the building.

The Risen Christ, the Good Shepherd, is now the ultimate and exclusive source of healing and salvation for all. God's love for humanity, incarnate in Jesus, is extended to all. God's concern for the rejected stone is the essence of that love, which Jesus clearly manifested in his ministry. His disciples follow through on their master's call to bring healing and salvation to all, especially the weak, the rejected, and the needy.

Psalm 118:1, 8–9, 21–23, 26, 28, 29 (22) The refrain from Psalm 118 echoes the theme of the stone rejected by the builders. The readings connect Jesus with the rejected stone, whom God raised up and made the cornerstone. As disciples of Jesus, we also are caught up into God's covenant love and saving actions. The psalm invites all to give thanks to God whose covenant love (mercy, kindness) endures forever. God alone can be trusted, and we

are to take refuge in him. When we are in trouble or feel lonely and rejected, God is there to save and restore us. The Lord accomplishes such wonders before our eyes. The psalm blesses all who come in the name of the Lord, asking all to give thanks to God for being our Savior and restoring us. In the context of Good Shepherd Sunday, the psalm looks to the Risen Lord, raised from death by God, as the living presence of God who cares for all, especially the lost, the rejected, and the oppressed.

1 John 3:1–2 God's love in Christ has recreated us and made us children of God once more. As a new creation in the Risen Christ, we are called to know and live like him, to take on his values, his mind and heart, and make them our own. The world, understood as the place where God is not known or acknowledged, "does not know us" (1 John 3:1) because it does not know Christ. The manner of Christian living is often in opposition to the manner of the world. As a result, those who live in Christ will be misunderstood, opposed, and rejected. No matter the world's reaction, we are challenged to remember that we are God's children now.

John 10:11–18 Biblically, shepherds were the leaders, the kings, priests, and prophets who were supposed to facilitate justice and right relationship with God and others. Many were bad shepherds, more concerned with themselves than with God or others. Jesus asserts that he is the Good Shepherd, and that he knows his sheep and they know him.

The biblical meaning of the word *know* is related to the intimacy of the marriage covenant, in which one knows the other so intimately that one is willing to give all for the other, even one's life. Jesus' love is inclusive of all. There are other sheep that do not yet belong to his circle of love. His mission is to search them out and manifest his care and concern for them also, so that all may be one in him. Jesus' deep love is manifested in his desire to give his life for all. Such love does not end in death, but is raised up by God so that all people can experience the reconciling power and intimacy of love. We are called to be good shepherds modeled on Jesus, so that all can experience God's love, ultimately leading to total union with our Good Shepherd forever.

Reflection Questions for the Catechist

- In what ways do you rely on the care and protection of Jesus, the Good Shepherd?
- How do you, like a shepherd, lead your catechumens to the water of Baptism and the food of the Eucharist?
- In what ways do you seek out, welcome, and care for the outcast, lonely, and marginalized?

Catechist's Guide

Objectives

- ▷ To more fully appreciate the image of the Good Shepherd.
- ▷ To better understand that Jesus came for the sake of all, especially those who are outcast, rejected, and marginalized.
- ▷ To more deeply reflect on the call to see God's face in the faces of the rejected.

Dismissal and Procession

Following the homily, the priest celebrant picks up the Lectionary and invites the catechumens to come forward with the catechist(s) who will lead today's dismissal session. Holding the Lectionary so that all can see, the priest celebrant sends the catechumens and catechist(s) forward using RCIA, 67, his own words, or the following:

PRIEST: **My dear friends, in this time of Easter joy, the Church renews her faith in the waters of Baptism and seals our resolve to give our lives in service as the Lord gave his life up for us. As you continue to progress on your journey of coming to know the Lord, may you reveal to us all God transforming power. Open your eyes to the wonders of God's Kingdom and free your ears to discern his will. Go in peace to share God's Word. Alleluia!**

All process to where the dismissal session will take place. The catechist holds the Lectionary in a reverent manner. The assembly may sing an acclamation to accompany the procession.

Centering

Upon reaching the place where the dismissal occurs, place the Lectionary on the ambo, lectern, or other dignified place (or hold the book reverently). Light the candle that is in the place of gathering and reread John 10:11–18 in order to refocus the group's attention. Consider singing the Responsorial Psalm or have a recording of it available to use as part of the centering, either before or after the reading.

Reflection and Discussion

The following "script" may be used or adapted to help facilitate discussion on today's readings. Begin the discussion by asking the catechumens if any words or phrases from today's readings spoke to them.

We continue to celebrate Easter by reflecting on who Jesus is and who he calls us to be as his followers. Those of us who do not live on or near a farm may have limited understanding of sheep and shepherds. In today's Gospel, Jesus describes himself as the Good Shepherd. Not only does he care for his own, he seeks out, welcomes, and cares for those who are lost. Shepherds are not only called to make sure that the sheep are fed and have water, they also must protect the sheep. Sheep that have a good shepherd follow the shepherd's call, sure that where the shepherd goes, all will be well.

- In what ways do you need the nourishment and care of Jesus, the Good Shepherd? How do you rely on Christ for protection, help, and guidance?
- In what ways are you growing in willingness to follow Christ?

In today's First Reading, Peter and John have been arrested and have been brought before the Jewish leaders for questioning. At issue is the healing of a man who was lame from birth (and therefore an outcast) and Peter's proclamation of the Risen Christ following the man's healing. Now, Peter addresses the leaders and elders: It was in Christ's name that the man was healed. Throughout his life and ministry, Jesus had reached out to and identified with those who were rejected and marginalized, and he was himself rejected. Peter uses the image found in Psalm 118, which we sing today, of the stone (Jesus) which the builders (the Jewish leaders) rejected, which has become the cornerstone. Name the people (individuals or groups of people) who are the rejected of today.

- How do you recognize them as God's beloved, through whom we see God's face?
- What does this recognition call you to do?
- Have you experienced rejection?
- How does Jesus' commitment to and identification with the rejected bring hope in times when you or a loved one are rejected?

Through Christ, we are drawn into a deep and lasting relationship with God as his children. As we grow in faith, we become more like Christ and may find ourselves at odds with the elements of the surrounding culture, "the world" (1 John 3:1), which values things that are counter to God's ways. Jesus reached out to the outcast and to sinners, and so must we; Jesus identified himself with the rejected and the lonely, and so must we; Jesus sacrificed himself in order to bear God's love in the world, and so must we.

- What would need to change in order for you to more closely resemble Christ and to live as a child of God in your daily life?

This leads us to today's Gospel and Jesus' description of himself as the Good Shepherd. Jesus points out that a hired man, whose sheep are not his own, will abandon the sheep at the first sign of trouble. The Good Shepherd, on the other hand, lays down his life for his sheep. Sheep learn to distinguish the voice of their shepherd in the midst of many voices calling out to them. "I am the good shepherd, and I know mine and mine know me" (John 10:14). Christ wants an intimate relationship with us, in which we know one another in a sacrificial, self-giving way, in which we favor this way over all other ways of life.

- In what ways are you learning to listen to and follow the voice of the Good Shepherd?
- How are you coming to know Christ intimately?

Jesus describes himself as having other sheep who must be brought into the fold—one flock, one shepherd. The Gospel writer reminds us of Jesus' inclusion of Gentiles as he carried out his mission. We read this and think of the people whom Jesus longs to draw in now, through us. In Christ, we, too, are to be good shepherds, who extend God's forgiveness, mercy, and love to all.

- To whom will you reach out with the love of Christ?

Wrapping It Up *Consider these points to conclude the dismissal. Integrate the thoughts and ideas that surfaced during the discussion.*

- Jesus came to draw all people to God's love.
- In his rejection, which led to the Crucifixion, Jesus identifies with the rejected of the world, whom we are called to recognize as the beloved of God.
- Christ is the cornerstone of our faith.

Closing Prayer *Conclude with prayer. If time permits, sing the psalm refrain a few times before or after the following prayer.*

> Jesus, Good Shepherd,
> you lay down your life willingly for all.
> Teach us to hear your voice, to trust in your loving care,
> to find refreshment in the waters of Baptism,
> and nourishment in the saving Body and Blood of the Eucharist.
> Draw us to yourself.
> Teach us to hear your voice and to follow you,
> knowing that in you, all will be well.
> Who live and reign for ever and ever.
> Amen.

Readings for the Next Dismissal *Provide catechumens with a list of the readings for the next dismissal session. Consult the liturgical calendar on page xvi to find out what day will be observed next week. Give catechumens the questions below to guide their reflection through the week.*

⑥ What connections are you seeing in the readings of this liturgical season? As you pray with the readings, around what themes do your thoughts seem to be coming together?

⑥ Where do the readings intersect with your journey of faith? What questions do they raise for you?

Extended Catechesis *Based on today's readings and liturgical observance, the following topics may be covered for extended catechesis:*

❋ Salvation

❋ Mercy

❋ Solidarity with the poor, rejected, and marginalized

❋ Sacrificial love

FIFTH SUNDAY OF EASTER

Focus: We are connected as parts of the vine.

Lectionary #53B

Catechist's Preparation

Overview of the Sunday

As members of Christ's Body, the Church, we are called to be in communion with Christ and one another. Being in community is not always easy, especially in a time such as ours, in which individualism is prized by so many. Members of the "me" generations are not always comfortable with the give and take of being members of a community. On this Fifth Sunday of Easter, we reflect upon what it means to be branches on the vine that is Jesus Christ. As you prepare to reflect with your catechumens, think about how they are growing in unity with one another and the community of faith, and consider how this unity is a sign of their growing union with Christ.

Scripture Background

Acts of the Apostles 9:26–31 Paul, formerly a persecutor and rabid member of the Pharisee sect, has undergone a remarkable change in his conversion to Christianity. The members of the mother Church in Jerusalem did not trust his conversion and were afraid of Paul when he returned to Jerusalem. It had been a few years since Paul had become a follower of Christ and, although he changed in his belief, his theological style was still forceful and argumentative. Barnabas intervened and brought about change in the community so that they came to accept Paul. Barnabas was trusted. He was kind and forgiving, and explained that Paul had undergone a dramatic conversion and was now preaching the Good News. In fact, Barnabas became something of a mentor to Paul and helped launch him on his extraordinary ministry (see Acts of the Apostles 15:36–39). Unity was not easy for the early Church, which was often faced with controversy. Yet, it remained one body and, as the reading tells us, grew in numbers. Paul returned to Jerusalem six times and became equal to the other Apostles.

Psalm 22:26–27, 28, 30, 31–32 (26a) We are reminded that, on an individual level, we are expected to praise the Lord through our words and habitual actions. We are also to remain part of the assembly of God's people, praising and living the Gospel precepts as a community.

1 John 3:18–24 The opening sentence of this reading summarizes so well what is expected of each follower of Christ. We are not just to give lip service to what we believe, we are to live it out in deed. It is not enough to say that we love one another. We must take it to the next level, so to speak, and show it in our actions. God knows what is in our hearts. God's commandment is that we believe in his Son, Jesus Christ, and love one another. Not one without the other. It is in living out the love we profess that we stay connected to Christ. We know this through the Holy Spirit.

John 15:1–8 This Gospel about the vine and branches is rich with meaning and levels of analogy. At the heart of it, John shows the cost of Church unity and the intimacy and interconnectedness of her members. Jesus is the vine—that is, the main stem, also called the vine-stock—that provides life and sustenance to the whole plant. Apart from the vine we can do nothing. If we stay connected, however, we will produce abundant fruit. We will be part of the source of life because we share the same lifeblood that flows through the interconnected veins and arteries. Jesus is the heart and gives us life and strength. We are warned, however, that those who become separated will wither and die. Like rejected branches, they are thrown into the fire.

Just as vines need to be pruned in order to remain as fruitful as possible, so does the Church. For example, practices or organizations that do not serve the life of the whole Church may to be ended or redirected. Pruning is important for the health of the vine, but it is not enough. A vine must be nurtured, fed, and watered. Jesus teaches that it is his word that nourishes all those connected to the vine. At the beginning of the reading he reassures the disciples that they are not in danger of pruning because they are already pruned due to hearing the word.

At the end of the reading Jesus makes the connection between following his teachings and glorifying the Father. If you do what he teaches, you can ask in confidence for what you need. If you follow him, you will bear much fruit. As members of the vine, we are called to put aside our own wants and look to the needs of the larger community.

Reflection Questions for the Catechist

⑨ How does being an active member of your faith community help you to grow faith?

⑨ What is the most demanding thing in being a member of the Body of Christ?

⑨ In what ways do you encourage your catechumens to grow in unity with one another and the faith community as they are growing in faith?

Catechist's Guide

Objectives

▷ To develop a deeper understanding of what it means to be a member of the Body of Christ.

▷ To reflect upon the example of St. Paul, who stayed closely tied to the Church, even in times of disagreement.

▷ In reflecting on the readings, catechumens will consider the ways they are being pruned as they continue to grow in faith.

Dismissal and Procession

Following the homily, the priest celebrant picks up the Lectionary and invites the catechumens to come forward with the catechist(s) who will lead today's dismissal session. Holding the Lectionary so that all can see, the priest celebrant sends the catechumens and catechist(s) forward using RCIA, 67, his own words, or the following:

PRIEST: **My dear friends, as we move through Easter Time, you will indeed encounter the Risen Christ in the Scriptures and in those around you. Marvel at this mystery, and find your hope within it as you go forth with an "Alleluia" on your tongue and in your heart. Go in peace. Alleluia!**

All process to where the dismissal session will take place. The catechist holds the Lectionary in a reverent manner. The assembly may sing an acclamation to accompany the procession.

Centering

Upon reaching the place where the dismissal occurs, place the Lectionary on the ambo, lectern, or other dignified place (or hold the book reverently). Light the candle that is in the place of gathering and reread John 15:1–8 in order to refocus the group's attention. Consider singing the Responsorial Psalm or have a recording of it available to use as part of the centering, either before or after the reading.

Reflection and Discussion

The following "script" may be used or adapted to help facilitate discussion on today's readings. Begin the discussion by asking the catechumens if any words or phrases from today's readings spoke to them.

It is the Fifth Sunday of Easter. Just as we take forty days of Lent to immerse ourselves in Jesus' life and ministry, and to prepare our minds and hearts for the celebration of the Triduum and the fullness of the Paschal Mystery, we now take fifty days to reflect upon and take to heart all that the Resurrection means for us as believers in Jesus Christ. Today, we will reflect particulary on the ways being united to Christ in faith draws us to unity with other believers.

⑨ How are you growing in unity with others in the faith community?

⑨ In what ways is the community a sign of Christ's life, love, and mercy?

⑨ How is being called to unity with others challenging?

Today's First Reading, from the Acts of the Apostles, tells of Saul, whose dramatic conversion to Christ was initially doubted by the Apostles and Christians in Jerusalem. It is important to understand that Saul, who came to be known as Paul, had been a Pharisee who had persecuted Christians. So it is understandable that the community in Jerusalem would be hesitant to trust that he had changed. Barnabas was a respected member of the community, and it is his testimony that convinces the Apostles to accept Paul. We hear in this story how the early Church strove for unity, even when it was not easily accomplished.

- ⑨ Have you been or are you now a part of a strong community? (*Perhaps your family is very close, or you have a tight-knit group of friends. Maybe you are closely connected to your neighbors or coworkers, or you have grown in relationship with others in the faith community.*)

- ⑨ How has your belonging to this community influenced your life?

- ⑨ Have you been warmly welcomed by the faith community?

- ⑨ Are there ways in which you feel as though you are on the outside, or in which you desire deeper connections with people in the parish?

Those who believe in Christ grow in the ways they take on the values, teaching, and character of the Lord. The Second Reading, from the first letter of St. John, tells us that we know that Christ remains with us as we grow in faith and live as people of faith in the world. The Holy Spirit assures us of this. With one another, we sing in Responsorial Psalm 22, "I will praise you, Lord, in the assembly of your people" (refrain).

- ⑨ What is the impact of faith in your daily life?

- ⑨ In what ways do you perceive that God is with you as you strive to direct your daily actions and decisions through your faith in Jesus Christ?

Anyone who has ever grown a plant can appreciate Jesus' analogy of the vine and branches, which we hear in today's Gospel. Jesus is the vine; God the Father is the vine grower; we are the branches on the vine. Without the vine, we will wither and die. We need to be nourished by the vine in order to grow and bear fruit. Branches that do not bear fruit will be pruned. We have already been pruned because we have heard the Word of God. If we remain in Christ and in his Word, we may come to God in prayer, asking for what we need.

- ⑨ What does it mean to you to be growing on the vine that is Christ Jesus?

- ⑨ How is your faith nourished through your union with other members of the vine?

- ⑨ In what ways are you living in fruitful faith?

Living as disciples of Christ who bear good fruit gives glory to God the Father, just as Jesus, in his union with the Father throughout his life, ministry, Passion, Death, and Resurrection glorified the Father.

- ⑨ What fruit do you bear that gives glory to God?

Wrapping It Up   *Consider these points to conclude the dismissal. Integrate the thoughts and ideas that surfaced during the discussion.*

- As members of Christ's Body, we are drawn into communion with Christ and one another.

- The Church strives for unity with all Christians; the Church also longs to bring the message of God's love in Christ to all.

- Being part of the community of believers leads us to grow in faith and the way we live as disciples.

Closing Prayer

Conclude with prayer. If time permits, sing the psalm refrain a few times before or after the following prayer.

> Lord Jesus Christ,
> you are the true vine, we are the branches.
> You nourish us through your Word,
> leading us to grow as your good and holy people.
> By holding fast to the vine, which you are,
> we are given all that we need to bear good fruit.
> Remain with us today, so that our lives and actions
> will be fruitful expressions of discipleship,
> giving glory to God the Father, who is one with you and the Holy Spirit,
> for ever and ever.
> Amen.

Readings for the Next Dismissal

Provide catechumens with a list of the readings for the next dismissal session. Consult the liturgical calendar on page xvi to find out what day will be observed next week. Give catechumens the questions below to guide their reflection through the week.

⑥ What connections are you seeing in the readings of this liturgical season? As you pray with the readings, around what themes do your thoughts seem to be coming together?

⑥ Where do the readings intersect with your journey of faith? What questions do they raise for you?

Extended Catechesis

Based on today's readings and liturgical observance, the following topics may be covered for extended catechesis:

❋ Christian unity ❋ Body of Christ

❋ Ecumenism ❋ Communion

❋ Christian community

SIXTH SUNDAY OF EASTER

Focus: Christians are called to love one another.

Lectionary #56B

Catechist's Preparation

Overview of the Sunday

As we continue to journey through Easter Time, we take to heart the true nature of discipleship. In his life and ministry, Jesus reached out to the poor, sick, marginalized, and sinners with healing, mercy, and forgiveness. He gave his life so that we might have eternal life. In brief, Jesus loved. Jesus *is* love. In today's Gospel, Jesus says to his disciples, "This is my commandment: love one another as I love you" (John 15:12). As you prepare to reflect with your catechumens on this Sixth Sunday of Easter, think about Jesus' command to love one another. How are they already showing signs of such love? In what ways may they be called to grow as Christians who love one another?

Scripture Background

Acts of the Apostles 10:25–26, 34–35, 44–48 In an amazing sequence of events, the doors of the Chosen People are opened to Gentiles as well as to Jews. Two messengers came to Peter as he was preaching and invited him to go with them to the house of Cornelius. This was very significant, since Cornelius was a Roman soldier, not a Jew. Cornelius was a good man, however, and his whole house hold was God-fearing. When Peter entered the house, Cornelius knelt before him in reverence. Peter, however, insisted that Cornelius stand, saying that he himself was also human, not a god.

In what transpired, Peter saw that God accepts not only Jews but all nations who act uprightly or lead God-fearing lives. Not only did Peter sense this but the Holy Spirit made it perfectly clear. While Peter was preaching, the Holy Spirit came upon everyone there, uncircumcised Gentiles included. It must have been quite a joyous sight as the whole household praised God and spoke in tongues. Peter immediately ordered that these Gentiles could be baptized, since God clearly showed that all were welcome in the name of Jesus Christ.

Psalm 98:1, 2–3, 3–4 (see 2b) This psalm continues the theme of God's love for all peoples. God's saving power is revealed to all nations. A new song can be sung, for the Lord has revealed his salvation. He has come to the house of Israel; however, "all the ends of the earth have seen / the salvation by our God" (98:3). Surely, this universal gift is worthy of the song of praise we offer. Surely this is a wonderful thing for us to sing about.

1 John 4:7-10 The message from John in this brief pericope couldn't be clearer or more direct. God is love. Everything flows from him. The focus is on the second part of the double commandment. We are to love God and we are to love our neighbor. We are to love one another because of God's love. If we do not love one another, John tells us, we do not know God. In fact, love is what distinguishes those who know God from those who don't. We are reminded of just how great God's love for us is, as he sent his only Son. Love is clearly God's initiative, and while God's love is revealed to Christians in Jesus, the Christian community, which now has life through that love, also reveals God's love (see John 5:26; 6:57).

John 15:9-17 Having just taught his disciples that they are connected to him and to each other as branches on the vine, Jesus now deepens the relationship. He preaches the importance of love, the centrality of love, and the interconnectedness that comes about as a result of love. He has proved his love by his death, and his love provides not just the example but also the very foundation for love among his followers. We remain in his love by keeping his commandments, just as Jesus keeps his Father's commands.

Christian love is traced to the Father as its source. It is expressed in the redemption of Jesus and then in the mission of all his followers who are to love one another as God loves us. This passage also points to the upward direction of obedience. Jesus' response to the love of the Father is lived out in his obedience to the Father's commands. Likewise, Jesus' followers are to respond to his love through obedience to his commands. Love is more than a feeling. Love is action. Jesus' standard of perfection makes that perfectly clear.

In John 8:31–33, Jesus has taught the disciples about the transition from being a slave to being free. Slaves do not belong to the family permanently; they will be set free by the truth that he brings. Thus, he will no longer call his disciples slaves. He has taught them what the father taught him. Unlike slaves, they know what the master is doing. They are now friends, rather than slaves. This reading ends with the same straightforward imperative that the previous reading begins, "Love one another" (15:17).

Reflection Questions for the Catechist

- How do you know the love of Christ?
- What recent experience comes to mind in which someone extended themselves to show you Christ's love?
- How are you called to love others with Christ's love?

Catechist's Guide

Objectives

- ▷ To appreciate what it means to be a friend of Jesus.
- ▷ To grow in understanding of the call to self-giving love.
- ▷ To reflect upon the ways in which they are called to love others.

Dismissal and Procession

Following the homily, the priest celebrant picks up the Lectionary and invites the catechumens to come forward with the catechist(s) who will lead today's dismissal session. Holding the Lectionary so that all can see, the priest celebrant sends the catechumens and catechist(s) forward using RCIA, 67, his own words, or the following:

PRIEST: **My dear friends, the Church is renewed in the living waters of Baptism, as Easter joy resounds in our hearts and upon our lips. As you grow to know Christ more and more each day and follow in his footsteps, you will long for these waters and the newness of life they contain. We, your brothers and sisters, join with you in prayer as you share with each other the Word of God. We patiently wait for the day when you too will share fully in the Paschal feast of the Lord. Go in peace. Alleluia!**

All process to where the dismissal session will take place. The catechist holds the Lectionary in a reverent manner. The assembly may sing an acclamation to accompany the procession.

Centering

Upon reaching the place where the dismissal occurs, place the Lectionary on the ambo, lectern, or other dignified place (or hold the book reverently). Light the candle that is in the place of gathering and reread John 15:9–17 in order to refocus the group's attention. Consider singing the Responsorial Psalm or have a recording of it available to use as part of the centering, either before or after the reading.

Reflection and Discussion

The following "script" may be used or adapted to help facilitate discussion on today's readings. Begin the discussion by asking the catechumens if any words or phrases from today's readings spoke to them.

What is true love all about? We use the word "love" in many ways. At times, when we speak of love we refer to the intimate love of spouses for each other; we love family; we love friends. Sometimes we "love" the idea of a vacation, or an object, a movie, or television show. With all of these various meanings of the word "love" in mind, let us reflect upon the tremendous love of Jesus Christ and the love to which Christ calls us.

- How do you describe the love of God? In what ways is God's love different from the love of humans?

In today's First Reading, from the Acts of the Apostles, Peter is driven by the love of Christ to respond to Cornelius in his search for God. Cornelius is not a Jew. In fact, he is a Roman soldier, but he is an upright man who seeks to follow God's ways. As Peter responds to Cornelius, the Holy Spirit fell upon those who were gathered, Jews and Gentiles alike. This would have been an occasion for great joy for all who were there. "The circumcised believers who had accompanied Peter were astounded that the gift of the Holy Spirit should have been poured out on the Gentiles also" (Acts 10:45). As Peter declares, "I see that God shows no partiality" (Acts 10:34). God's love is for everyone. With the recognition that the Holy Spirit has been given to the Gentiles who were there, Peter orders them baptized in the name of Jesus Christ. The Responsorial Psalm seems a particularly fitting song following this story of Christ's love being manifested in Cornelius and his household: "The Lord has revealed to the nations his saving power" (refrain).

- What does Peter's response teach you about Christ's love?

- How might you seek to listen to and understand others as a result of hearing this account?

Today's Second Reading, from the first letter of John, and the Gospel passage, from John's account, guide us to reflect upon the love that God is and offers and our call to respond to this love by loving one another. The Gospel today immediately follows the passage we heard last week, in which Jesus describes himself as the vine and we as the branches. Now we are invited to think about this more deeply. God is love. Jesus' way of being in the world is to love. As branches on the vine that is love, we are nourished to love, and the fruit we are called to bear is love. Jesus said, "Remain in my love. If you keep my commandments, you will remain in my love, just as I have kept my Father's commandments and remain in his love" (John 15:9b–10). Think for a moment about the vine and branch analogy.

- What does it mean to "remain" in Christ's love?

- What happens to branches that are separated from the vine?

- What would separate the branch (you) from the vine (Christ)?

Jesus says, "This is my commandment: love one another as I love you. No one has greater love than this, to lay down one's life for one's friends" (John 15:12–13). In accepting Death on the Cross, Jesus gave love totally and perfectly. Jesus chose us and appointed us to go and bear fruit. We do so by loving one another with the same love with which Jesus loves us.

- To what sort of love do you know yourself to be called as a result of reflecting on Jesus' gift of self on the cross?

- What is the challenge of loving others with the love of Christ?

- In what ways does Christ's assurance of God's presence strengthen you to offer such love?

Wrapping It Up   *Consider these points to conclude the dismissal. Integrate the thoughts and ideas that surfaced during the discussion.*

- God is love.

- God's love is revealed through Christ.

- We have been chosen to bear Christ's love.

Closing Prayer

Conclude with prayer. If time permits, sing the psalm refrain a few times before or after the following prayer.

> God of love,
> you sent your Son into the world
> that we might have life through him.
> He laid down his life for us,
> calling us friends and showing us your great love.
> As we remain in Christ's love, we are drawn more deeply to you.
> Show us the way to keep your commandments,
> so that we may give you glory by loving one another as a sign of our love for you.
> Through Christ our Lord.
> Amen.

Readings for the Next Dismissal

Provide catechumens with a list of the readings for the next dismissal session. Consult the liturgical calendar on page xvi to find out what day will be observed next week. Give catechumens the questions below to guide their reflection through the week.

🌀 What connections are you seeing in the readings of this liturgical season? As you pray with the readings, around what themes do your thoughts seem to be coming together?

🌀 Where do the readings intersect with your journey of faith? What questions do they raise for you?

Extended Catechesis

Based on today's readings and liturgical observance, the following topics may be covered for extended catechesis:

❋ Trinity

❋ Call to holiness

❋ Christ's sacrifice

SOLEMNITY OF THE ASCENSION OF THE LORD

Focus: To continue Jesus' ministry.

Lectionary #58B

❦ Depending on your diocese, today's solemnity may take place on the Thursday following the Sixth Sunday of Easter or in place of the Seventh Sunday of Easter. The Second Reading from Year A may also be used.

Catechist's Preparation

Overview of the Solemnity

Jesus Christ is Lord of heaven and earth. While no longer physically here on earth, Christ is with us through the power and presence of the Holy Spirit. The Risen Christ taught the disciples how his life, Death, and Resurrection fulfilled what had been written in Scripture. As he prepared to ascend, he instructed them to wait together for the descent of the Holy Spirit upon them. Through the Spirit's presence, they will understand what they must do and will be given the power to share the Good News through word and deed. On this Solemnity of the Ascension of the Lord, we will consider the call of every Christian to continue Jesus' ministry of love.

Scripture Background

Acts of the Apostles 1:1–11 Jesus' Ascension frames Luke's two-volume work. Luke ends his Gospel account and begins Acts of the Apostles with the Ascension narrative. The Ascension functions differently in each work. In the Gospel, it gives closure to Jesus' ministry. In Acts, it signals the beginning of the disciples' ministry. The passage begins with the prologue to Theophilus, giving the Ascension a forty-day time frame; in the Gospel it takes place late on Easter Sunday. Luke uses the biblical time frame of forty days to indicate a period of transition as the disciples are prepared to receive the Spirit, and begin their ministry.

The disciples' focus on restoring "the kingdom to Israel" (1:6) is readily dismissed by Jesus as he instructs them to await the Spirit's power. This will signal the beginning of their ministry as witnesses to the Risen Lord in Jerusalem and, from there, to the entire world. As Jesus is lifted up from them, they fix their gaze to the heavens, longing for Jesus. Reprimanded for gazing at the heavens, they are assured that he will return just as he left. Their focus should now be on preparing to welcome the Spirit and begin their ministry. From now on, the Spirit will guide and support them in their ministry as they go about loving others the way Jesus loved them.

Psalm 47:2–3, 6–7, 8–9 (6) The psalm highlights God's enthronement as king over all the nations, a most fitting psalm to celebrate Jesus' Ascension as he is lifted up and made king over all creation. Shouts of joy and blasts of the trumpet rise from the people as they acknowledge and celebrate God, "the great king over all the earth" (47:3). The psalm's setting envisions the ark, symbol of God's presence, being processed into the Temple and taking its place in the Temple throne room. The Ascension celebrates the lifting up of the Risen Christ to the heavenly throne as king of all creation. For the psalmist, the only fitting response to such a glorious event is to "sing praise . . . sing hymns of praise" (47:7–8).

Ephesians 4:1–13 or 4:1–7, 11–13 Ephesians speaks of God lifting up Jesus, both from death and in the Ascension, where the Risen Christ is now seated at the right hand of God. Being so exalted, God "put all things beneath his feet and gave him as head over all things" (1:22). Both readings affirm that Jesus, now exalted, "fills all things" (1:23; 4:10).

As disciples, we have been filled with Christ's Spirit, who has showered upon all a diversity of gifts that we may more effectively witness to Jesus, and carry on the ministry that he initiated. The Spirit empowers us to live according to Jesus' standards. Both readings offer guidance on how we are to act and live. We witness to the Risen Lord both in our actions and with our words, continuing Jesus' ministry of loving others as he loved us. As we work to build up the Body of Christ, we strive for unity among all, waiting in hope for the day when we will be fully united with Christ.

Mark 16:15–20 This longer ending added to the Gospel according to Mark references similar events from accounts of the Gospel, or even earlier traditions. The Ascension links to the Gospel according to Luke, while Jesus' great commission to his disciples references the ending of the Gospel according to Matthew. The Gospel according to Mark surfaces in the assertion that "Whoever believes and is baptized will be saved; whoever does not believe will be condemned" (16:16). This longer ending was probably added after Mark's original text was completed. Even though Mark's original text ended with chapter 16:8, this later addition is still considered to be the inspired Word of God.

While the Ascension is the key focus of the First Reading from Acts, Mark's account of the Gospel clearly mentions Jesus taking "his seat at the right hand of God" (16:19). Jesus is honored by God and given authority over all things. Mark speaks of the many signs that accompany the disciples, seeing them as a confirmation of the word they are proclaiming. They are to "go into the whole world and . . . to every creature" (16:15) proclaiming the Good News. Clear signs will witness to the validity of their testimony. These signs highlight the Spirit's power to unite, heal, and establish harmony. Having received from the Spirit the ability to confront all sorts of dangers, the disciples are assured that they are not alone, that the "Lord worked with them" (16:20).

Reflection Questions for the Catechist

- In what ways do you recognize Christ's presence with you?
- How do you continue Jesus' ministry through your words and deeds?
- In what ways are your catechumens embracing Jesus' teaching and life?

Catechist's Guide

Objectives

- ▷ To reflect upon Jesus' words to the Apostles at the time of his Ascension.
- ▷ To grasp the call to continue Jesus' ministry.
- ▷ To come to a greater understanding of the Church as continuing the ministry of Christ.

Dismissal and Procession

Following the homily, the priest celebrant picks up the Lectionary and invites the catechumens to come forward with the catechist(s) who will lead today's dismissal session. Holding the Lectionary so that all can see, the priest celebrant sends the catechumens and catechist(s) forward using RCIA, 67, his own words, or the following:

PRIEST: **My dear friends, this community now sends you forth, that you may continue to reflect on the Word of God that we have shared with you today. May the Holy Spirit grant insight and understanding as you learn to walk in the way of the Gospel. Go in the peace of Christ. Alleluia!**

All process to where the dismissal session will take place. The catechist holds the Lectionary in a reverent manner. The assembly may sing an acclamation to accompany the procession.

Centering

Upon reaching the place where the dismissal occurs, place the Lectionary on the ambo, lectern, or other dignified place (or hold the book reverently). Light the candle that is in the place of gathering and reread Mark 16:15–20 in order to refocus the group's attention. Consider singing the Responsorial Psalm or have a recording of it available to use as part of the centering, either before or after the reading.

Reflection and Discussion

The following "script" may be used or adapted to help facilitate discussion on today's readings. Begin the discussion by asking the catechumens if any words or phrases from today's readings spoke to them.

We continue to celebrate Easter Time, and today we will reflect on Christ's Ascension into heaven.

- In what ways does celebrating Easter Time lead you to a deeper reflection upon the Resurrection of Jesus Christ?
- How does this reflection guide you to grow in faith and to live as a disciple?

We hear in today's First Reading, from the Acts of the Apostles, how, through the Holy Spirit, Jesus gave the Apostles instructions, appearing to them and speaking to them about the Kingdom of God. While meeting with them, he told them not to leave Jerusalem, but to remain there and wait to be "baptized with the Holy Spirit" (Acts 1:5). It is good for us to remember that, even with Christ's Resurrection, the Apostles were still unsure of their safety in Jerusalem, where Jesus had been crucified. They were uncertain, afraid, and still trying to understand all that had taken place in Jesus' arrest, Passion, Death, and Resurrection. Jesus' promise of the Holy Spirit surely consoled the Apostles in their uncertainty.

- In what ways do you anticipate the outpouring of the Holy Spirit in Baptism?

The Apostles still wondered if Jesus's Kingdom was about temporal, political rule. "Lord, are you at this time going to restore the kingdom to Israel" (Acts 1:6)? Jesus' response may have disappointed those who were still hoping for the return of self-rule over Israel. "It is not for you to know the times or seasons that the Father has established" (Acts 1:7).

- What is the difference between the kingdom that the Apostles asked about and the Kingdom of God?
- How does Christ reign in your heart, mind, and life?

While the Apostles were looking on, Jesus was taken up from them. They look "intently at the sky as he was going" (Acts 1:10), and suddenly, two men dressed in white garments stood beside them. "They said, 'Men of Galilee, why are you standing there looking at the sky? This Jesus who has been taken up from you into heaven will return in the same way as you have seen him going into heaven'" (Acts 1:11). The Apostles are not to linger, longing for the Lord, but rather are now to wait to welcome the Holy Spirit and prepare to witness to Christ's life and love.

- What does it mean to you that Christ will return?
- In what ways does our response to Christ's call to live as a witness to God's love prepare us for Christ's return in glory?

In the Second Reading, from the letter to the Ephesians, we hear that through the Holy Spirit we are drawn together as members of Christ's Body. We are given gifts, with which we carry out the call of Christ in which we find lasting hope.

- What gifts have you been given that you may use in service, sharing of faith, and growing as a disciple?

In today's Gospel, we hear the account of Jesus' Ascension from the Gospel according to Mark. Jesus instructs the Apostles to "Go into the whole world and proclaim the gospel to every creature" (Mark 16:15). While in their presence, he was taken up away from them. While we never fully understand God's ways, in our personal lives and in the whole of salvation history, the deposit of faith is clear: in Christ's Ascension, his disciples, including we who are here, are called to continue his ministry of love in the world.

- In what ways are you called to continue Christ's ministry? How does this call affect your daily decisions and actions?
- How do you proclaim the Good News of Jesus Christ? In what ways are you called to more fully live and grow as a disciple?

Wrapping It Up

Consider these points to conclude the dismissal. Integrate the thoughts and ideas that surfaced during the discussion.

- Disciples are called to share in Christ's mission.
- The more deeply we grow in faith, the more fully we are to live as people of faith in the world.
- Following the Ascension, the disciples waited for the Holy Spirit.

Closing Prayer

Conclude with prayer. If time permits, sing the psalm refrain a few times before or after the following prayer.

Risen Lord Jesus,
you were raised up in the Resurrection and in your Ascension into heaven,
promising the Holy Spirit to your disciples
as you called them to continue your ministry of love.
Be with us and strengthen us as we grow in commitment to you
and to your mission of forgiveness, peace, service, justice, mercy, and love.
Guide us as we discern the ways in which you call us to live as your disciples.
Who live and reign for ever and ever.
Amen.

Readings for the Next Dismissal

Provide catechumens with a list of the readings for the next dismissal session. Consult the liturgical calendar on page xvi to find out what day will be observed next week. Give catechumens the questions below to guide their reflection through the week.

- What connections are you seeing in the readings of this liturgical season? As you pray with the readings, around what themes do your thoughts seem to be coming together?

- Where do the readings intersect with your journey of faith? What questions do they raise for you?

Extended Catechesis

Based on today's readings and liturgical observance, the following topics may be covered for extended catechesis:

☀ Ascension   ☀ Christian unity

☀ Discipleship

SEVENTH SUNDAY OF EASTER

Focus: To love as God loves.

Lectionary #60B

Catechist's Preparation

Overview of the Sunday

In this final week of Easter Time, we allow the life and message of God's love for us in Christ to sink into our minds and hearts. Today we are presented with a model for Christian discernment and decision-making, we bless and thank God for his everlasting kindness, and we reflect on the gift of union with God in Christ through the Holy Spirit. As we anticipate the celebration of Pentecost next Sunday, it will be good to draw your catechumens to reflect on the mystery of God's abiding love, knowing more deeply that "if we love one another, God remains in us and his love is brought to perfection in us" (1 John 4:12).

Scripture Background

Acts of the Apostles 1:15–17, 20a, 20c–26 God's overwhelming love for all manifests itself in today's readings. On Pentecost, we celebrate God's active presence with us always in the gift of the Spirit. As the "brothers," 120 of them, wait for the gift of the Spirit, they focus on finding a replacement for Judas, so that the Twelve who knew and walked with Jesus would be complete. Jesus had more than twelve men following him, as the presence of 120 gathered testifies. But Luke's desire to show continuity with Israel has him focus on the Twelve as the link between the earthly life of Jesus and the community that now gathers in his name.

The selection process used presents a model of effective Christian decision making. The Apostles focus on two people who walked and witnessed with them from Jesus' baptism to his Resurrection. Either would have been suitable. But, acknowledging God's presence with them, they pray for guidance. Ultimately, using the very human process of casting lots, the lot falls to Matthias, who "was counted with the eleven" (1:26). All Christian decision making should be based on the acknowledgement of God's presence and guidance with us as we go about our human deliberations. God works through all our humanness, ensuring that all things do good work for the Lord.

Psalm 103:1–2, 11–12, 19–20 (19a) God's *hesed*, or faithful covenant love, suffuses this psalm. The refrain proclaims that God's throne is set in heaven, asserting that God's Kingdom of love is what governs the universe. As is typical in Jewish prayer, the psalm calls us to bless the Lord with all our being, remembering all that God has done. Those benefits are specified in terms of kindness, or covenant love, and forgiveness of transgressions. Those who fear the Lord, those who revere, trust, and hope in the Lord, experience the vastness of God's love and mercy, a vastness as wide as the universe.

God's love and mercy are the inherent qualities of the Kingdom established in heaven that rules over all. All who fear the Lord are called to live in God's Kingdom and to love and forgive as we have been loved and forgiven. The psalm concludes by calling upon all those who do the Lord's bidding, whose might and strength comes from living according to kingdom love and mercy, to bless the Lord at all times.

1 John 4:11–16 John's consistent theme through his letters is the realization that God has "so loved us," (1 John 4:11) clearly manifested in Jesus' total self-giving love. If God has so loved us, then we "must love one another" (4:11). In this manner, God remains in us and love is perfected in us. The assurance of God with us and the bond of that love and presence is the gift of the Spirit. In Jesus' self-giving love and saving actions on our behalf, we have come to know and believe in God's love. In affirming Jesus as Son of God, John assures us that God remains in us in mutual indwelling. God is love. All who remain, act, and live in love, modeled for us by Jesus, remain in God and God in them. Psalm 103 asserts this to be the essence of God's Kingdom. We are to live and act in the world as citizens of God's Kingdom, manifesting to all that vast love and mercy that God has shown us.

John 17:11b–19 John's account of the Last Supper has Jesus deliver a farewell address to his disciples. In this passage, part of Jesus' priestly prayer, Jesus prays that God keep his disciples together "so that they may be one just as we are one" (17:11). As Jesus' disciples, we are made as intimate with God as Jesus is with his Father. Because we believe that Jesus is God, we are made one with God in Jesus. We are consecrated in God's truth through Jesus because we have chosen to believe the truth about God that Jesus delivered both in his life and message.

Jesus is aware that "the world," (17:11) those not open to hearing or believing the truth, has rejected him, and he knows that his followers will also be rejected. He prays not that they be taken from the world, the world that God loves and sent Jesus to redeem, but that his disciples be protected from the evils of the world. In such a manner, they will be able to carry on his mission and ministry once he is no longer with them. Jesus' intimacy with the Father is extended to all who love Jesus and continue the work he began by loving others the way he loved us. Jesus prays that God will be with and protect his disciples. God's gift of the Spirit ensures that intimacy and presence to be ours always.

Reflection Questions for the Catechist

- How do you prayerfully discern decisions?
- In what ways do you rely on the Holy Spirit and the community of faith in your discernment?
- How does the assurance of God's in-dwelling presence strengthen you as you reach out in love to others?

Catechist's Guide

Objectives

- ▷ To more fully understand prayerful discernment in making decisions.
- ▷ To recognize love as the guiding force in all Christian action.
- ▷ To more fully understand that, in Christ, we remain in God and God remains in us.

Dismissal and Procession

Following the homily, the priest celebrant picks up the Lectionary and invites the catechumens to come forward with the catechist(s) who will lead today's dismissal session. Holding the Lectionary so that all can see, the priest celebrant sends the catechumens and catechist(s) forward using RCIA, 67, his own words, or the following:

PRIEST: **My dear friends, this community now sends you forth, that you may continue to reflect on the Word of God that we have shared with you today. May the Holy Spirit grant insight and understanding as you learn to walk in the way of the Gospel. Go in the peace of Christ. Alleluia!**

All process to where the dismissal session will take place. The catechist holds the Lectionary in a reverent manner. The assembly may sing an acclamation to accompany the procession.

Centering

Upon reaching the place where the dismissal occurs, place the Lectionary on the ambo, lectern, or other dignified place (or hold the book reverently). Light the candle that is in the place of gathering and reread John 17:11b–19 in order to refocus the group's attention. Consider singing the Responsorial Psalm or have a recording of it available to use as part of the centering, either before or after the reading.

Reflection and Discussion

The following "script" may be used or adapted to help facilitate discussion on today's readings. Begin the discussion by asking the catechumens if any words or phrases from today's readings spoke to them.

In this final week of the Easter Time, we allow the life and message of God's love for us, which is expressed and modeled most fully in Jesus Christ, to sink into our minds and hearts. As we begin our reflection, think about your experience of love, especially the love of God.

- How do you know that God loves you?
- Who helps you to perceive God's love?
- How does this love shape you?

In today's First Reading, from the Acts of the Apostles, Peter calls those present to discern who will be counted among the Twelve Apostles, replacing Judas who betrayed Jesus. The community proposes two men and they pray, putting the decision in the hands of God. Following their time of prayer, they cast lots, and the lot falls upon Matthias. We have much to learn in reflecting upon this process of prayerful discernment. When making decisions, it is important to pray, asking God to illumine our hearts and minds. We also consult members of the community who have wisdom or insight about the situation, and we take into account those who will be affected by the decision. In other words, discerning action through our faith is not just a "me and Jesus" thing. Christian discernment involves prayer and other Christians who help us to see the way of love in whatever situation we find ourselves. Today's Responsorial Psalm seems especially fitting as an expression of such a prayerful, trusting relationship with God: "Bless the LORD, O my soul; / and all my being, bless his holy name" (103:1).

- How have you experienced prayerful discernment?
- Who helps you to discern God's call?
- In what ways does prayer guide your day-to-day life?

With this understanding of prayerful discernment of Christian life and action in our hearts, we hear again of the call to love one another in today's Second Reading, from the first letter of John. If we love one another with the love of God, which Christ most fully shows and shares with us, God will remain with us, and his love is brought to perfection in us. We can do this through the indwelling presence of the Holy Spirit.

- What experience comes to mind in which you heard the call to live in love, even if challenging? What did you do? What happened as a result? In what ways did this experience lead you to recognize and express God's love in a particular way?

In the Gospel according to John, from which we hear today, Jesus prays for his disciples just before his Passion. He prays that they and the disciples who will follow (including us) will be united with God, just as Jesus and the Father are one. Jesus protected the disciples, and as he prepares to return to the Father, he prays that his disciples may share in the joy of Christ's love and mission.

- What does it mean to you to be united with God as intimately as Jesus and the Father are united?
- In what ways do you anticipate being immersed in Christ's Death and Resurrection in Baptism as a means for greater union with the Father and the Son?

In his life on earth Jesus was rejected, and he knew that his disciples would also be rejected. "The world" (John 17:11) of which he speaks are those who refuse to accept the love of God which Jesus offers. As disciples, we do not belong to the world, but rather are sent into the world in order to share Christ's love through the ways in which we live our lives. Jesus prays that we will be consecrated in the truth of God's word. To consecrate is to be made holy. We are consecrated in the truth of Christ's eternal love.

- How does growing in understanding of the truth of the Gospel draw you towards holiness?

Wrapping It Up

Consider these points to conclude the dismissal. Integrate the thoughts and ideas that surfaced during the discussion.

- Jesus and his Father are one.

- We who are united with Christ through Baptism are united with God the Father and the Holy Spirit.

- Living in love is a lifetime expression of the truth of Christ through which we are consecrated.

Closing Prayer

Conclude with prayer. If time permits, sing the psalm refrain a few times before or after the following prayer.

Heavenly Father,
you are one with your Son, Jesus Christ,
whom you sent as Savior of the world.
Draw us close to you in love.
Protect us as we witness to the mission of Christ.
Consecrate us in the truth of your word
so that, growing in holiness, your love may be made perfect.
Through Christ our Lord.
Amen.

Readings for the Next Dismissal

Provide catechumens with a list of the readings for the next dismissal session. Consult the liturgical calendar on page xvi to find out what day will be observed next week. Give catechumens the questions below to guide their reflection through the week.

- What connections are you seeing in the readings of this liturgical season? As you pray with the readings, around what themes do your thoughts seem to be coming together?

- Where do the readings intersect with your journey of faith? What questions do they raise for you?

Extended Catechesis

Based on today's readings and liturgical observance, the following topics may be covered for extended catechesis:

- ☀ Sacrificial love
- ☀ Holiness
- ☀ Love in action

- ☀ Discernment
- ☀ Christian community
- ☀ Apostolic succession

Solemnity of Pentecost

Focus: The Holy Spirit will guide you.

Lectionary #63B (Mass during the Day)

❦ The Second Reading and the Gospel from Year A may also be used.

Catechist's Preparation

Overview of the Sunday

Blessings on this Solemnity of Pentecost! Today we celebrate the gift of the Holy Spirit and the ways in which the Spirit inspires, guides, and strengthens us to live as Christian disciples. Especially in the later weeks of Easter Time, we have anticipated the advent of the Holy Spirit in the lives of the disciples and in the Church. Now we hear the account of the first Pentecost, when, through the presence and power of the Holy Spirit, the Good News of Christ was shared with people from throughout the world. Those who heard the disciples speaking were amazed and astonished at the power of God. Invite the Holy Spirit to inspire you as you prepare to reflect with your catechumens today.

Scripture Background

Acts of the Apostles 2:1–11 In Luke's account of the event of Pentecost, the only account we have in our Scriptures, we hear more about the response of the people who witnessed the event than about the event itself. Earlier, the disciples had chosen Matthias to fill out the symbolic number of twelve patriarchs who represented people of Israel. On the day of Pentecost, we hear that there were Jews from "every nation under heaven," (2:5) in other words, people representing the ends of the earth.

Although the account of the coming of the Spirit is spare, it is laden with symbolism. Luke indicates that the 120 people mentioned earlier (see 1:15) were gathered as a community. The imagery of the wind and the fire remind us of Exodus 19:18, when God came in fire; Ezekiel 37:9, where the spirit came from the four winds; and 2 Samuel 22:8–16, when God appears with all the forces of nature. In recording the detail that "tongues as of fire" (2:3) rested on the gathered disciples, Luke is emphasizing the fact that the Spirit came to each individual in the community.

In the Old Testament, being filled with the Spirit of God indicated that an individual was called to prophecy. In this experience it was an entire community who received the Spirit and began to speak the prophetic word so that all could understand it.

Psalm 104:1, 24, 29–30, 31, 34 (see 30) Today we sing part of the same psalm that we prayed in yesterday's vigil Mass. Again, we praise God for the diversity of creation and recognize the dependence of every creature on God. On this day of Pentecost, we conclude the singing of the psalm with the stanza that praises God's glory and asks that the Lord be glad with all of creation, especially with our song of praise. Most of all, we repeatedly cry out, "Lord, send out your Spirit!" (refrain).

Galatians 5:16–25 We need to take care not to allow a dualistic mindset fashion our interpretation of Paul's message to the Galatians. In Paul's day, there were two particular words that could refer to the physical dimension of people and animals. One of them, here translated as "flesh," (5:16) could emphasize human frailty and ego-driven desire. The other, usually translated as "body," had a range of meanings, but the word was consistently used for the flesh that is redeemed and will undergo resurrection. Paul is not opposing body and spirit, but warning of the dangers of a lifestyle of self-indulgence.

When we read the list of fruits of the Spirit, we note that, with the possible exception of self-control, all of them are social virtues; they are practiced only in relationship to others. Paul is not speaking primarily to individuals. Rather, he is instructing the community about how to be a community living under the influence of the Spirit.

Sequence This Sunday, the Church sings one of four sequences—ancient, poetic songs that precede the singing of the Gospel acclamation. In the Pentecost Sequence, Veni, Sancte Spiritus, the Church prays for the Holy Spirit to come. Using beautifully poetic titles, the sequence calls on the Father of the Poor, the Comforter, Divine Light, Sweet Rest, and Healer, emphasizing that if the Holy Spirit is absent, we have nothing. When the Holy Spirit is present, we have the salvation of the Lord.

John 15:26–27; 16:12–15 There are two key ideas in this selection from Jesus' farewell discourse. The first is that Jesus will send the Advocate, the Spirit of truth, to testify through the disciples. Earlier in the discourse, John indicated that the role of the Advocate would be to judge the world (see 16:8), to help the disciples remember all that Jesus taught (see 14:26), and to dwell in the disciples (see 14:17).

The second key teaching of this reading is that the Spirit of truth will continue to impart the revelation Jesus has given. The truth that the Spirit teaches is more than intellectual; it also implies the grace needed to put Jesus' teaching into daily communal practice. All of this points to the idea that as time moves on, the Spirit will continue to guide the Christian community into knowing how to live the truth that Jesus revealed: how to live as disciples, and how to give witness to his message in each era.

Reflection Questions for the Catechist

- In what ways does the Holy Spirit inspire and guide you?
- How do you bear the fruit of the Spirit?
- In what ways do you bring to mind and heart the presence of the Holy Spirit within and for you?

Catechist's Guide

Objectives

- ▷ To reflect upon the change in the disciples with the advent of the Holy Spirit at Pentecost.
- ▷ To take to heart the call to rely on the Holy Spirit in the midst of daily life.
- ▷ To understand more fully the presence of the Spirit in the ongoing proclamation of the Gospel.

Dismissal and Procession

Following the homily, the priest celebrant picks up the Lectionary and invites the catechumens to come forward with the catechist(s) who will lead today's dismissal session. Holding the Lectionary so that all can see, the priest celebrant sends the catechumens and catechist(s) forward using RCIA, 67, his own words, or the following:

PRIEST: **My dear friends, this community now sends you forth, that you may continue to reflect on the Word of God that we have shared with you today. May the Holy Spirit grant insight and understanding as you learn to walk in the way of the Gospel. Go in the peace of Christ. Alleluia!**

All process to where the dismissal session will take place. The catechist holds the Lectionary in a reverent manner. The assembly may sing an acclamation to accompany the procession.

Centering

Upon reaching the place where the dismissal occurs, place the Lectionary on the ambo, lectern, or other dignified place (or hold the book reverently). Light the candle that is in the place of gathering and reread Act 2:1–11 in order to refocus the group's attention. Consider singing the Responsorial Psalm or have a recording of it available to use as part of the centering, either before or after the reading.

Reflection and Discussion

The following "script" may be used or adapted to help facilitate discussion on today's readings. Begin the discussion by asking the catechumens if any words or phrases from today's readings spoke to them.

Blessings on this Solemnity of Pentecost! Today we celebrate the presence of the Holy Spirit with us and with the Church. We acknowledge our need to rely on the Spirit to guide and strengthen our resolve to live as disciples, and we recognize the fruit of living and following the Spirit.

- When you think of the Holy Spirit, what comes to mind?
- How do you picture or understand the Spirit?

In the First Reading, from the Acts of the Apostles, we hear of the first Pentecost. A number of Jesus' followers were together, and suddenly they were all filled with the Holy Spirit. The Jewish feast of Pentecost was a commemoration of God's giving of the Ten Commandments to Moses on the fiftieth day following the exodus from Egypt. The word *Pentecost* is derived from the word which means "fiftieth." Because of the feast, Jews from throughout the world would have been in Jerusalem. The naming of the regions from which the people who heard the Good News came signifies that the Gospel was proclaimed to all nations. The disciples, who had stayed together following Jesus' ascension, were suddenly able to proclaim the Good News of Jesus Christ through the power of the Holy Spirit.

- What strikes you in this account of the first Pentecost?
- In what ways does the Church continue to proclaim the Good News through the power of the Holy Spirit?

In today's Responsorial Psalm, we sing, "Lord, send out your Spirit, and renew the face of the earth" (refrain). Today, we praise God that it is through the breath of God, the Spirit, that all creation is brought into being, and through which creation is sustained. As Christians, we are to rely on this powerful presence of the Spirit in our daily living. In the Second Reading, from St. Paul's letter to the Galatians, we are shown what living in the Spirit of God is to be about. St. Paul cautions us to not fall into a lifestyle of self-indulgence, but rather urges us to live in and follow the Holy Spirit. We can see the differences in the lists of the "works of the flesh" and the "fruit of the Spirit." The fruit of the Spirit is holiness. In our commitment to Christ, we are to crucify our desire for inappropriate self-indulgent behavior. In living in the Spirit, we follow the Spirit's guidance and inspiration in order to bear the fruit of God's love in the world.

- In what ways do you rely on the Spirit to guide and strengthen you to live as you know God desires?
- What strikes you in St. Paul's list of the works of the flesh?
- In what ways are such self-indulgent behaviors also self- and other-destructive?
- In what ways does life in the Spirit build up people and relationships, bearing God's love in the world?

Before the proclamation of the Gospel today, we sing an ancient Sequence, "Come, Holy Spirit." In this prayer, we hear that without the Spirit, we have nothing. We invite the Spirit to heal our wounds, renew our strength, bend our heart and will toward God, guide our steps, and give salvation. Through the Holy Spirit, life is filled with joy that never ends.

In today's Gospel, we hear Jesus' promise of the Holy Spirit, the Advocate, who testifies to the truth of Christ. Jesus understands that his disciples cannot comprehend all that has taken place in his Paschal Mystery—they need time in order to understand their experience. The Spirit will guide disciples to all truth, revealing the ways in which we are to live as disciples and to proclaim the Good News in every time and place.

- How does the Holy Spirit guide individual Christians and the Church to proclaim the Good News in every time and place? The way you answer Christ's call?

Wrapping It Up

Consider these points to conclude the dismissal. Integrate the thoughts and ideas that surfaced during the discussion.

- The Holy Spirit proceeds from the Father and the Son.
- The Holy Spirit is one with the Father and the Son.
- In Pentecost, we recognize the birth of the Church.

Closing Prayer

Conclude with prayer. If time permits, sing the psalm refrain a few times before or after the following prayer.

> Come, Holy Spirit, fill the hearts of your faithful,
> and kindle in them the fire of your love.
> Through your indwelling presence, guide our thoughts and actions,
> so that we may bear your fruit in the world.
> May we live as people of love, joy, peace, patience, kindness, generosity,
>   faithfulness, gentleness, and self-control,
> so that your life and love will be known by all.
> You are one with the Father and the Son, now and forever.
> Amen.

Readings for the Next Dismissal

Provide catechumens with a list of the readings for the next dismissal session. Consult the liturgical calendar on page xvi to find out what day will be observed next week. Give catechumens the questions below to guide their reflection through the week.

Ⓢ What connections are you seeing in the readings of this liturgical season? As you pray with the readings, around what themes do your thoughts seem to be coming together?

Ⓢ Where do the readings intersect with your journey of faith? What questions do they raise for you?

Extended Catechesis

Based on today's readings and liturgical observance, the following topics may be covered for extended catechesis:

❋ Holy Spirit　　　　　　　　❋ Fruit of the Holy Spirit

❋ Gifts of the Holy Spirit　　　❋ Church

INTRODUCTION TO ORDINARY TIME

Overview of Ordinary Time

Ordinary Time is the lengthy time of counted time in the liturgical year. A shorter segment falls between Christmas Time and Lent and a lengthier segment falls after Pentecost and Advent of the next liturgical year. You could think of these segments as Ordinary Time during Winter and Ordinary Time during Summer and Fall, although this is not an official distinction.

Nestled between the major seasons of the liturgical year, Ordinary Time affords us the opportunity to embrace the journey of discipleship from start to finish each year. Catechumens might participate in part or all of Ordinary Time, or even in multiple years of Ordinary Time depending on their progress in the catechumenate and their discernment for readiness to celebrate the sacraments of initiation.

The lengthy season of Ordinary Time gifts us with a simple, yet profound time of well-needed respite from the intensity of Advent and Christmas Time and Lent, Triduum, and Easter Time. This is true for catechumens as well as pastors, initiation ministers, liturgists, and music ministers. Take your time exploring the Word of God in this season and allow it to enter deeply into your heart and the hearts of the catechumens. In our humanity as God's children, we need this time to grow in the length and breadth and depth of our relationship with God in Jesus Christ through the Spirit.

Preparing a Seasonal Environment

The liturgical color for Ordinary Time is green. Green symbolizes life. Green reveals to us the abundance of God's life surrounding us in nature. In the depths of winter in the northern hemisphere the color green gives us hope in this holy time that spring and summer will come. In fall, green leads us to know the changing times of the season will not be the end of the story. Life will come again.

Mirror the Ordinary Time environment of the worship space in the space where catechumens gather for dismissal catechesis. Carry forward into your space the simplicity of the varying textures and shades of green fabric in the sanctuary. You might choose to coordinate with your parish's environment team to see if they could help design additional pieces for the dismissal space that are similar to those in the main body of the Church.

Do not overdo the dismissal space environment. Less is more. To distinguish the segments of Ordinary Time, you could incorporate a green plant or two, or fall leaves, or other harvest symbols. Keep a space available for the Lectionary (or a Bible), such as a lectern or table. Keep a candle near the Lectionary (or Bible), and light this candle before the session begins. Keep the Lectionary open to the passage you will read during the dismissal session. When solemnities or feasts of the saints or a particular aspect of Jesus' life occur on Sunday, you might choose to augment the environment with an image or icon reflective of the day. Again, let your direction come from the environment in the main liturgical assembly.

Overview of the Readings

First Readings The First Readings in Ordinary Time complement the Gospel readings and familiarize us with Old Testament history and theology. These readings may be linked thematically, they may provide context, or they may introduce us to characters and stories whose importance echo throughout salvation history and into our own time. A number of these readings focus on the covenant; others, on God's providence. All of them remind us of our shared roots with the Jewish people.

Responsorial Psalms The Responsorial Psalms help us to respond to the Living Word proclaimed in the First Readings. The psalms of Ordinary Time lead us to praise God for his ongoing and everlasting care for his people throughout all time. The psalms we sing and pray in Ordinary Time complement the Sunday theme and still convey a message of their own. If we meditate on them as a group, their overwhelming message is God's compassionate care for us. Some of the psalms, such as Psalm 95, invite us not to harden our hearts, as the Israelites did, when we hear God's voice. The well-known and beloved Psalm 23 is our response to the First Reading on the Sixteenth Sunday in Ordinary Time, in which the prophet Jeremiah chastises the shepherds who mislead their flocks and proclaims to us how the Lord will raise up the true shepherd as the king who will govern with wisdom and justice.

Second Readings In Year B, the Second Readings are a semicontinuous reading from 1 Corinthians, 2 Corinthians, Ephesians, James, and Hebrews. *Semicontinuous* means that the passages we read as the Second Reading follow the general order of the chapters and verses in these books, but that occasionally some verses or even a chapter or two might not be read. The Second Readings help us to see the struggles and efforts the early Christian community had to endure in order to solidify itself and grow together as a people of faith. The Corinthians faced deep division in their community around bringing together Jewish and Gentile believers. Paul addresses these by speaking to them about how they are one body in Christ. Each member of the body contributes significantly to the body of Christ.

In Ephesians, James, and Hebrews, letters that were written late in the first century and even perhaps early into the second century, we hear of the development of the early Christian community as it came to understand its beliefs and how they contrasted with those who wanted to deny the fullness of Jesus' humanity and divinity. Passages from Ephesians encourage us to love each other as Christ loves the Church. Passages from James call us to explore how we are to be doers of the Word. And, on the Sundays during the final months of Ordinary Time, the letter to the Hebrews gives us ample opportunity to reflect on Jesus' high priesthood and how there has been and never will be another high priest like him.

Gospel Readings Mark is the primary evangelist for Year B. The work of this Gospel writer is short and to the point. Mark never provides us a lot of detail; rather, he is straightforward about the centrality of a disciple's task. As disciples, our call and the call that you form catechumens in, is the call to take up the Cross and follow Jesus. We are to preach repentance, proclaim the nearness of the Kingdom of God—already present in Jesus, yet still to come at the end of time when Christ comes again. We are to heal, do away with demons, and in general, love as Jesus loved. In Mark's concept of discipleship, there is no room for the hypocrisy Jesus saw in the scribes and Pharisees. Jesus calls his disciples to live the two commandments: to love God with your whole heart, mind, and soul and to love your neighbor as yourself. A disciple does not choose one commandment over the other. Disciples live both commandments.

On occasion in Year B, we hear and reflect on passages from John's account of the Gospel. This occurs on the Second Sunday in Ordinary Time, when John the Baptist acclaims Jesus as the Lamb of God, and two of his disciples immediately follow the Lord. Then, from the Seventeenth Sunday in Ordinary Time through the Twenty-First Sunday in Ordinary Time, the Gospel readings come from John 6, the chapter known as the Bread of Life discourse. The Gospel readings these Sundays invite us to explore with catechumens the connection between the Jesus as the Bread of Life and the Eucharist. The liturgical year also ends with a Gospel reading from John. In this passage, Pilate interrogates Jesus about his kingship. Jesus tells Pilate that his kingdom surely is not of this world. If we belong to Jesus, we belong to the truth. We listen to Jesus' voice. We work as disciples to transform this world into the Kingdom of God.

SECOND SUNDAY IN ORDINARY TIME

Focus: To belong to God through Jesus, the Lamb of God.

Lectionary #65B

Catechist's Preparation

Overview of the Sunday

As we begin the season of Ordinary Time, the readings invite us to reflect on God's call. We encounter God's personal invitation to us—to respond in faith to him. In the First Reading, God so unexpectedly calls Samuel that the young man does not recognize God's voice until the third time God calls him. In the Gospel reading, John the Baptist's acclamation of Jesus as the Lamb of God compels Andrew and Simon Peter to follow the Messiah. Paul's words in the Second Reading instruct us how closely we belong to Christ—through Baptism, we live as members of Christ. What will be our response to God's call at this point in our faith journey? Will we continue to follow the Lord?

Scripture Background

1 Samuel 3:3–10, 19 Before kings ruled the tribes of Israel, judges governed the people who "did what was right in their own eyes" (Judges 21:25). Samuel, who serves as priest and prophet, is a bridge between the two ages. Samuel's birth was an answer to the prayers of his mother, who was barren, like many other women in Scriptures. In gratitude, Samuel was dedicated to God and taken to be of service to Eli, an elderly priest in the Temple at Shiloh (1 Samuel 2:11). Like Jesus, "Samuel continued to grow both in stature and in favor with the Lord and with the people" (1 Samuel: 26). Unlike Eli's sons, who disobeyed the voice of their father and the commands of the Lord, Samuel is found worthy to receive God's revelation. At night while Eli sleeps, Samuel is awake and listening. Three times he hears God's voice, and each time he goes to Eli, saying, "Here I am, for you called me" (1 Samuel: 5, 6, 8), thinking it was Eli's voice he heard. The third time, Eli tells the boy to answer, "Speak, Lord, for your servant is listening" (1 Samuel 3:9–10) Samuel's submission to God's Word prepares him for the role he would later play in Israel's history.

Psalm 40:2, 4, 7–8, 8–9, 10 (8a and 9a) This psalm is a prayer of trust; it may have been two separate psalms and later combined into one. The psalmist's life was in danger, perhaps from an enemy or sickness. He found himself in a "desolate pit," a "miry bog" (40:2). But God heard his cry and drew him out, setting his feet on solid rock. A new song of praise is given to him, and he publicly declares his confidence in God. Israel's worship depended on the many sacrifices offered by the people. The psalmist's sacrifice is not one of burnt offerings, but one of a listening heart and contrite spirit obedient to do God's will.

1 Corinthians 6:13c–15a, 17–20 Rivalries developed in the Christian community at Corinth. Each faction claimed to belong to an important figure: Paul, Apollos, or Cephas (Peter's Aramaic name). Paul reminds them that they should not boast about any human leader, because in Baptism, they all "belong to Christ" (1 Corinthians 3:23). Paul then takes up the matters of sexual immorality (see 1 Corinthians 5) and lawsuits among Christians (see 1 Corinthians 6:1–11), which bring shame to the community. Some believed that the Law of Moses no longer bound them, and misquoted Paul to back their claim: "All things are lawful for me" (1 Corinthians 6:12). Paul strongly disagreed: While all things might be lawful, not everything is beneficial. Because the body belongs to the Lord, it must be treated as the sacred "temple of the Holy Spirit" (1 Corinthians 6:19). The word Paul uses is *naos* the innermost sanctuary of the Temple.

John 1:35–42 The day after Jesus' baptism, John the Baptist is no longer the focus of attention. John points to Jesus as the "Lamb of God" (John 1:36). Just as the blood of the Passover lamb saved the Israelites from death (see Exodus 12), Jesus, the new paschal lamb, sheds his blood for the sins of the world. Two of the Baptist's disciples follow Jesus out of curiosity. On seeing them, Jesus asks what they are looking for, and they ask him, "Where are you staying?" (John 1:38). The Greek word also means "abiding," which is not a geographical place but a state of being in relationship with someone. Jesus invites them to "come and see" (John 1:39). The two came, saw, and stayed with Jesus from that day. The new disciples address Jesus as their "rabbi" (teacher), but they soon discover that Jesus is the "Messiah" which is translated "Anointed" (v. 41; *Christos* in Greek). Andrew, the brother of Simon Peter, is one of these new disciples. Andrew brings his brother to Jesus, who changes Simon's name to Peter, meaning "rock" (*Petros* in Greek). Changing a person's name signifies a new relationship and function. Peter will be the foundation on which Jesus will build his Church.

Reflection Questions for the Catechist

- ֍ At what times in your life has God called you? What were the circumstances surrounding God's call?
- ֍ How does God work through you, like he worked through John the Baptist, to call others to follow Jesus?
- ֍ How do you respond to God's call by glorifying the Lord in your body?

Catechist's Guide

Objectives

- ▷ To appreciate that God calls us at various times in our lives, even when we might not expect God to call.
- ▷ As we begin Ordinary Time, to reflectively consider what our initial response to God's call is and how we will follow the Lord at this point in our faith journey.
- ▷ To prayerfully contemplate how we embody the truth that we are Temples of the Holy Spirit, who lives within us and unites us to Christ.

Dismissal and Procession

Following the homily, the priest celebrant picks up the Lectionary and invites the catechumens to come forward with the catechist(s) who will lead today's dismissal session. Holding the Lectionary so that all can see, the priest celebrant sends the catechumens and catechist(s) forward using RCIA, 67, his own words, or the following:

PRIEST: **My dear friends, you have heard the Word of God proclaimed; we now send you forth to another place where you may reflect on these Scriptures. We pray that you will come to know the abundance of God's grace in our world, and that you will come to yearn for the blessings that await you around the Lord's table. Go now in the peace of Christ.**

All process to where the dismissal session will take place. The catechist holds the Lectionary in a reverent manner. The assembly may sing an acclamation to accompany the procession.

Centering

Upon reaching the place where the dismissal occurs, place the Lectionary on the ambo, lectern, or other dignified place (or hold the book reverently). Light the candle that is in the place of gathering and reread John 1:35–42 in order to refocus the group's attention. Consider singing the Responsorial Psalm or have a recording of it available to use as part of the centering, either before or after the reading.

Reflection and Discussion

The following "script" may be used or adapted to help facilitate discussion on today's readings. Begin the discussion by asking the catechumens if any words or phrases from today's readings spoke to them.

Samuel was sleeping when the Lord called. Not once, but three times, did the Lord call. Each time Samuel responded, "Here I am." But it was not until the third and final time after Eli's instruction that Samuel recognized it was the Lord who was calling him and that the Lord's call was the call to servanthood.

- ֍ When have you encountered the Lord's call in your life?
- ֍ How many times did the Lord call you before you recognized it was actually the Lord calling you?
- ֍ Did others help you to see it was the Lord who was calling, like Eli helped Samuel?

Samuel's response the last time the Lord called teaches us that we are the Lord's servants. Ours is a call to first listen to the Lord and to hear the Lord's voice. Then, we live. We grow in our faith, trusting and knowing that the Lord is with us. The Lord calls us, like Samuel, to make his Word effective.

🌀 Mindful that often the Lord calls in unexpected ways, how have you already accepted the Lord's call to make the Word effective—alive and present in the world?

In the Gospel reading, John the Baptist immediately recognizes Jesus and acclaims him as the Lamb of God. John's testimony led two of his own disciples to follow Jesus. The immediacy of their decision to follow Jesus stands out to us. Jesus notices, too, that they follow, and he poses to them the question, "What are you looking for?" (John 1:38). The disciples respond to his question with one of their own: "Where are you staying?" (John 1:38). Jesus' invitation to "Come, and you will see" (John 1:39) follows.

🌀 Whose testimony about Jesus has led you to see the Lamb of God?

🌀 How has your decision to "Come and see" deepened your relationship with Jesus?

🌀 Who are the others who have followed the Lamb of God because of your decision to follow?

When Andrew finds his brother, Simon Peter, the message he conveys is straight to the point. He has found the Messiah, the Christ. Simon does not go on his own to Jesus; rather, Andrew brings him. That Jesus declares Simon will now be called Cephas—or Peter, signifies how radically Jesus transforms Simon's life, even though he first follows because his brother brought him to Jesus.

🌀 When did you recognize Jesus as the Messiah?

🌀 How has Jesus transformed your life because of your decision to follow him?

When we choose to follow Jesus, we accept the responsibility to live our faith with our whole being—body, mind, and soul. Paul teaches the Corinthians, who struggled mightily with glorifying God in their bodies, to do just that. Our whole bodies belong to Christ. Everything we do, the choices we make, the way we interact with others, reflects our commitment to follow the Messiah. Our body is a Temple of the Holy Spirit because the Holy Spirit lives within us, in every cell of our being. The Holy Spirit lives within us and within each and every person God creates. No one is perfect, but God calls each of us to glorify him in our body.

🌀 How do you glorify God in your body?

🌀 How do you avoid immorality?

🌀 What role does the faith community play in helping you to uphold your body as a Temple of the Holy Spirit?

Wrapping It Up

Consider these points to conclude the dismissal. Integrate the thoughts and ideas that surfaced during the discussion.

- God calls us continually through Jesus, the Messiah—the Christ—God's only Son. As you go about your week, open yourself to the people and situations in which God might be calling you to draw closer to him.

- God frequently acts through other people to bring us closer to him. Notice the opportunities God offers you to lead others to faith. Be patient, as the Lord was with Samuel, if others do not respond on the first occasion that God works through you. Listening to God's Word is challenging work.

- Perhaps the most difficult challenge from today's readings comes from how you will make the Lord's Word effective. In silent prayer, consider how you will live out the reality that your body is a Temple of the Holy Spirit and that the body of every single person on earth is the same. Consider one action you will take this week to signify you belong to Christ.

Closing Prayer

Conclude with prayer. If time permits, sing the psalm refrain a few times before or after the following prayer.

O patient and loving God,
our gratitude abounds for your continuous invitation
to come and see the mysteries of faith.
For eras and centuries you have revealed yourself to your people.
Gift us now with the richness of grace to glorify you in our bodies,
to live as the Temples of the Holy Spirit you created us to be,
to companion others on their journey to you,
and to make your Word active in all of creation.
Through Christ the Lord—the Messiah—who is the Lamb of God.
Amen.

Readings for the Next Dismissal

Provide catechumens with a list of the readings for the next dismissal session. Consult the liturgical calendar on page xvi to find out what day will be observed next week. Give catechumens the questions below to guide their reflection through the week.

- What connections are you seeing in the readings of this liturgical season? As you pray with the readings, around what themes do your thoughts seem to be coming together?

- Where do the readings intersect with your journey of faith? What questions do they raise for you?

Extended Catechesis

Based on today's readings and liturgical observance, the following topics may be covered for extended catechesis:

- Discerning God's call
- Responding to God's call
- Jesus as the Lamb of God
- Church as a community of disciples

- Peter's place and role in the Roman Catholic Church
- Morality and immorality in the body
- Temple of the Holy Spirit
- Theology of the body

Third Sunday in Ordinary Time

Focus: God's Kingdom is fulfilled in Jesus.

Lectionary #68B

Catechist's Preparation

Overview of the Sunday

We hear Jesus' call of Andrew and Simon from the Gospel according to Mark. Mark introduces his call story with Jesus' proclamation of the nearness of the Kingdom of God and his command to repent and believe in the Gospel. In the First Reading, the Word of the Lord instructs the prophet Jonah to go to the large city of Nineveh where he must try to turn its people from their evil ways lest God destroy their city. The prophet succeeds. We hear how God, too, repents. Surely, we are God's Kingdom people when we mirror our repentance on God's very own. Our fidelity to God in the face of his coming again is Paul's reminder to us in the Second Reading.

Scripture Background

Jonah 3:1–5, 10 The Book of Jonah was written in the postexilic period and later placed among the prophets in the Bible. Actually, it is a lengthy parable on the history of prophets told with wisdom and humor. Like Moses, Isaiah, and Jeremiah, Jonah expresses misgivings when God calls him to be a prophet. When God commands him to go preach against Israel's ancient adversary, the Assyrians of Nineveh, Jonah sets sail to Tarshish in the far west of the Mediterranean Sea. But this reluctant prophet will not thwart God. When a violent storm threatens to break up the ship, the crew discovers that Jonah is fleeing from God. They blame Jonah for their plight and throw him overboard. A giant fish swallows him, and after three days and three nights ("the sign of the prophet Jonah," used by Jesus concerning his Death and Resurrection, Matthew 12:39), God commands the fish to spew Jonah up on the very shore he attempted to avoid. When Jonah announces God's plan to destroy Nineveh in forty days, much to the prophet's dismay, the people turn away from their sins in repentance. The story ends with Jonah sulking under a bush because God had mercy on a people who "did not know their right hand from their left" (Jonah 4:11).

The Book of Jonah is an indictment against Israel's narrow-minded attitude and their unwillingness to share God's message with other nations. Unlike Jonah and Israel, God has compassion toward people they regard as their enemies.

Psalm 25:4–5, 6–7, 8–9 (4a) This psalm is arranged alphabetically, allowing for easy memorization. Each verse begins with a successive letter of the Hebrew alphabet. It is also a Wisdom psalm, a meditation on the way (*hallakah* in Hebrew) to God. The psalmist realizes his own sinfulness and knows he cannot find the path to God on his own. He invokes God seven times (a number that stands for completeness), asking God to reveal the correct path that leads to God's compassion and goodness.

1 Corinthians 7:29–31 Paul continues to answer questions people ask as they try to follow God's call. One question regards the choice between the married or celibate state of life. If the world they know is passing away, does marriage serve any purpose? Paul, like many in his day, believes the return of Christ is imminent. Some in the community devalued marriage, believing it only concerned the flesh and had no place in the coming Kingdom. While Paul clearly favors the celibate state because it left him free to minister, he insists this is a personal choice and not a command of the Lord. Whether married or unmarried, each person should continue to live a life of fidelity until the coming of the Lord.

Mark 1:14–20 After the arrest of John the Baptist, Jesus leaves the Judean countryside where John baptized him in the Jordan River. He travels north to a small fishing village along the Sea of Galilee. This area is the center of his ministry for the first half of Mark's account of the Gospel. Jesus begins preaching with a continuation of John's call to repent and believe in the Good News. While John merely announced the Kingdom, Jesus declares that the time of fulfillment for God's reign is at hand. Jesus calls his first disciples, two pairs of brothers who are fishermen. With the invitation, "Follow me" (1:17), Jesus makes a radical demand of his disciples to turn away from their former way of life and turn toward the Kingdom of God. Simon Peter and his brother Andrew immediately forsake their boats and nets to become fishers of souls. James and his brother John also leave their family and fishing business to follow Jesus. Jesus promises the new disciples they will be instruments to spread the Gospel throughout the world. During their journey together, they will discover that there are no half measures to serving the Lord. Jesus' disciples must leave everything behind and accompany him on the road to his Death and Rising.

Reflection Questions for the Catechist

🌀 When has God called you, like Jonah, to carry out a difficult mission?

🌀 In what areas of your life is God encouraging you to repent and believe to show the Kingdom is at hand?

🌀 What have you had to leave behind to follow Jesus?

🌀 What are the challenges you face in living faithfully until Jesus comes again?

Catechist's Guide

Objectives

▷ To acknowledge how the Kingdom of God is at hand and how today is the time of fulfillment.

▷ To contemplate the way in which Jesus invites us to follow him and fish for people.

▷ To grasp the reality that the mission of faithfulness before Jesus comes again is, at times, a demanding mission we might hesitate to accept.

Dismissal and Procession

Following the homily, the priest celebrant picks up the Lectionary and invites the catechumens to come forward with the catechist(s) who will lead today's dismissal session. Holding the Lectionary so that all can see, the priest celebrant sends the catechumens and catechist(s) forward using RCIA, 67, his own words, or the following:

> **PRIEST:** My dear friends, you have heard the Word of God proclaimed; we now send you forth to another place where you may reflect on these Scriptures. We pray that you will come to know the abundance of God's grace in our world, and that you will come to yearn for the blessings that await you around the Lord's table. Go now in the peace of Christ.

All process to where the dismissal session will take place. The catechist holds the Lectionary in a reverent manner. The assembly may sing an acclamation to accompany the procession.

Centering

Upon reaching the place where the dismissal occurs, place the Lectionary on the ambo, lectern, or other dignified place (or hold the book reverently). Light the candle that is in the place of gathering and reread Mark 1:14–20 in order to refocus the group's attention. Consider singing the Responsorial Psalm or have a recording of it available to use as part of the centering, either before or after the reading.

Reflection and Discussion

The following "script" may be used or adapted to help facilitate discussion on today's readings. Begin the discussion by asking the catechumens if any words or phrases from today's readings spoke to them.

In the First Reading, from Jonah, the Lord instructs Jonah to go to Nineveh, a large city filled with people desperately needing to repent of their evil ways. Should the people decide not to turn back to God in forty days despite the prophet's words of warning, God would destroy Nineveh.

🌀 When has someone communicated to you the Lord's Word to repent and turn back to the Lord?

God saw how the people of Nineveh changed. Their new way of living—their actions—provided evidence of their conversion. God returned repentance in kind to the people. No longer would God destroy their city.

🌀 After you repented, how did your actions change?

⑨ How did you sense God acknowledged your repentance and deepened God's love for you?

God daily calls us to change. Jesus began his mission in Galilee proclaiming repentance and belief in the Gospel. In him, the Kingdom of God arrived. The response of those Jesus invites to follow him is nothing less than the changing of their very lives. The Greek word for "change" or "conversion" is *metanoia*. Metanoia is a deep profound change. It gets at the heart of who we are as people of God, of who God wants us to be, and of how God desires us to live.

⑨ Where in your life have you heard Jesus announce the nearness of the Kingdom of God?

⑨ What have you learned about needing to repent and believe in the Gospel in order to show others the presence of God's Kingdom?

The disciples respond with utter abandonment to Jesus' invitation to come after him. What was attractive to the disciples about Jesus' promise to make them fishers of people, we will never know for sure. Since we know the promise of the Resurrection and the hope of God's Kingdom, we have an idea of how compelling Jesus' invitation was to them.

⑨ What have you abandoned in order to accept Jesus' invitation to follow him?

⑨ What is compelling to you about following him and becoming a fisher of people?

Jesus invites not only Simon and his brother Andrew to follow him, but also James and John, sons of Zebedee. So drawn are the brothers to Jesus, they leave their father and his coworkers behind in the boat.

⑨ Who or what have you had to leave behind in order to come after Jesus?

⑨ How difficult was it for you to make the decision to follow the One in whom the Kingdom is fulfilled?

⑨ What is Jesus calling you to leave behind at this time in your faith journey to draw closer to him in love?

Faithfulness to Jesus' invitation to come after him requires a daily, even hourly, or minute-by-minute commitment. We speak of living a life of fidelity to the Lord. We live this life in a community of faithful disciples who trust the Lord is always with us. We believe Jesus will come again, although we do not know when he will return. St. Paul teaches the Corinthians to remain faithful to their way of life in this world as they await what they believe will be the imminent Second Coming of the Lord. Remaining faithful is not always easy. The world presents many challenges to us. Yet God is always faithful.

⑨ What challenges does the world present to you as you seek to live a life of faithfulness?

⑨ What helps you to remain faithful?

⑨ How does the community of believers in the Church sustain you on your faith journey?

⑨ How do you as a catechumen companion others in faith?

Wrapping It Up

Consider these points to conclude the dismissal. Integrate the thoughts and ideas that surfaced during the discussion.

- God is loving and forgiving. As you live this week, model your actions on God's own example of repentance in the First Reading, from Jonah. Embrace change in one area of your life that will lead you to live in loving relationship with God and others as God lives with you.

- Accept Jesus' invitation to follow him and become fishers of people, which includes the mission of proclaiming the Kingdom of God. Reflect this week on your responsibility to proclaim the Kingdom and announce the need for others to repent and believe in the Gospel. Consider ways in which your actions proclaim the Kingdom.

- Take some time each day to ponder today's readings so they remain with you throughout the week. Notice the other chatter and clutter in your life that you need to abandon in order to focus on responding to Jesus' invitation to come after him this week.

Closing Prayer

Conclude with prayer. If time permits, sing the psalm refrain a few times before or after the following prayer.

Loving and forgiving God,
your mercy and kindness prevailed as the people of Nineveh came back to you.
We seek to repent and believe in the Gospel.
Grace us with the courage to live as repentant and believing disciples.
We desire to remain faithful to your Word, and invite others to live as disciples.
Grace us with steadfastness to persist in our mission.
Constantly and gently guide us as we follow the One in whom the Kingdom is at hand—
our Lord who lives and reigns forever and ever.
Amen.

Readings for the Next Dismissal

Provide catechumens with a list of the readings for the next dismissal session. Consult the liturgical calendar on page xvi to find out what day will be observed next week. Give catechumens the questions below to guide their reflection through the week.

- What connections are you seeing in the readings of this liturgical season? As you pray with the readings, around what themes do your thoughts seem to be coming together?

- Where do the readings intersect with your journey of faith? What questions do they raise for you?

Extended Catechesis

Based on today's readings and liturgical observance, the following topics may be covered for extended catechesis:

- ☀ Conversion, repentance
- ☀ Faithfulness/fidelity
- ☀ Kingdom of God, here and now, already and not yet

- ☀ Belief in the Gospel
- ☀ Initial call discipleship and the mission to call others
- ☀ Second Coming of Jesus

FOURTH SUNDAY IN ORDINARY TIME

Focus: To speak God's prophetic Word.

Lectionary #71B

Catechist's Preparation

Overview of the Sunday

Moses' prophetic words inform us that God will raise up a prophet from among their kin. This reveals to us that the prophet is Jesus, the Holy One of God, who teaches and exorcises with divine authority. He is the One to whom God desires us to wholly devote ourselves to, as St. Paul instructs the Corinthians and us in the Second Reading.

Scripture Background

Deuteronomy 18:15–20 We do not know much about the author of Deuteronomy except that he lived in about the seventh century BC and was very concerned about the negative influence of the monarchy on Israel's faith. This concern led him to reinterpret some of Israel's earlier traditions in order to make them more relevant for his own time. In the First Reading, the author incorporates two specific strands of Israel's past. The most obvious is the Exodus-Moses tradition. Indeed, most of Deuteronomy, including this passage, was written as if it were a farewell speech by Moses. The second strand of tradition, that of Elijah, is less obvious. The phrase "I will raise up for them a prophet like you" (18:18) is a reference to the prophet Elijah's resemblance to Moses.

The literary context for these words is a warning against using divination or other means of fortune telling to predict and control the future. For the author of Deuteronomy, such things were wrong on two counts. First, they were pagan practices borrowed from Israel's neighbors; second, they were veiled attempts to manipulate the power of the one true God. Although divination is not as enticing today as it might have been in the days of Deuteronomy, most of us are still not entirely free from the desire to play God on occasion. However, the author of Deuteronomy shows us that the Lord our God already knows our need to communicate with the divine. Indeed, that is why he often spoke through prophets like Moses and Elijah to communicate his word, drawing his people close to him. Christians believe that God sent his only Son, Jesus, a great prophet, but also true God and true man, to draw us into communion with him.

Psalm 95:1–2, 6–7, 7–9 (8) The words of this psalm might have originally been a processional song sung to remind the people of whom they were coming to worship as they made their way to the Temple. The psalmist says that the Lord is a "great God," a "great King above all gods" (95:3). All of creation belongs to him, and he has the authority and power to do whatever he wants. He is the "rock of our salvation" and because of this his people can make a "joyful noise" (95:1). As the exuberant procession approaches the Temple, another voice is heard, perhaps that of a priest. It is not enough to acknowledge God with our words, he warns; we must also acknowledge his authority and power by the way we live. Thus, the psalmist exhorts the people to hear the Lord's voice and not harden their hearts as the Israelites had at Meribah and Massah in the desert.

1 Corinthians 7:32–35 This Sunday, Paul continues his reflection on the question of marriage and in the process reveals a decided preference for the single life. It is not that marriage is wrong, he says, it is that singleness promotes more focused attention to the work of God. Married persons, he argues, have to concern themselves with the needs of their spouse and family. Single people are free to devote themselves to God. For Paul, singleness is a charism, a gift that enables a person to be more fully available to God and to other people. Ultimately, though, whether single or married, Paul's desire is that a Christian be as totally devoted to God as Jesus was.

Mark 1:21–28 According to Mark, the appearance of Jesus on earth set off a spiritual battle between the powers of good and the powers of evil. Today's Gospel records the first of four specific conflicts. Jesus enters the synagogue and is immediately challenged by the man with an unclean spirit. The unclean spirit even knows Jesus' name, which in that day was a sign that this unclean spirit had power over Jesus. But Jesus is in control. He rebukes the unclean spirit, and the man it has tormented is healed. Astonished, the people in the synagogue marvel, "What is this? A new teaching—with authority! He commands even the unclean spirits, and they obey him" (1:27). Although Mark often depicts Jesus as a teacher, he records very little of what Jesus actually said. Instead, Mark prefers to concentrate on the authority of Jesus as evidenced in his works, such as the healing in today's Gospel. For Mark, however, both Jesus' teaching and his power to heal confirm that he is indeed the Son of God. Even in the unexpected words of the unclean spirit, "I know who you are, the Holy One of God," is a confession of Jesus' true identity (see 1:24).

Reflection Questions for the Catechist

- How is Jesus' authority evident in your life?
- What practices do you adopt that help you remain devoted to the Lord in the face of distractions?
- How does your life proclaim the Lord's prophetic words of life and healing to others?

Catechist's Guide

Objectives

▷ To grasp Jesus' relation to the prophets who came before him in the divine words he proclaims.

▷ To welcome Jesus' words and actions that bring life to us and to the world and destroy evil.

▷ To reflect on our responsibility to devote ourselves to the Lord and how our devotion leads us to proclaim life to the world through Jesus' teachings.

Dismissal and Procession

Following the homily, the priest celebrant picks up the Lectionary and invites the catechumens to come forward with the catechist(s) who will lead today's dismissal session. Holding the Lectionary so that all can see, the priest celebrant sends the catechumens and catechist(s) forward using RCIA, 67, his own words, or the following:

PRIEST: **My dear friends, you have heard the Word of God proclaimed; we now send you forth to another place where you may reflect on these Scriptures. We pray that you will come to know the abundance of God's grace in our world, and that you will come to yearn for the blessings that await you around the Lord's table. Go now in the peace of Christ.**

All process to where the dismissal session will take place. The catechist holds the Lectionary in a reverent manner. The assembly may sing an acclamation to accompany the procession.

Centering

Upon reaching the place where the dismissal occurs, place the Lectionary on the ambo, lectern, or other dignified place (or hold the book reverently). Light the candle that is in the place of gathering and reread Deuteronomy 18:15–20 in order to refocus the group's attention. Consider singing the Responsorial Psalm or have a recording of it available to use as part of the centering, either before or after the reading.

Reflection and Discussion

The following "script" may be used or adapted to help facilitate discussion on today's readings. Begin the discussion by asking the catechumens if any words or phrases from today's readings spoke to them.

We hear so many words each day. We speak our share of words. We read enormous amounts of electronic words online, in texts, in emails, and on web pages, each day. We believe the Bible, from where the Lectionary readings come, is the Word of God, living and active. Our First Reading begins with Moses communicating the divine Word to God's people, as prophets do. Not once, but twice, we hear Moses say that the Lord will raise up a prophet like him from among the people. The people are to listen to this prophet for the prophet will speak in God's name.

- When have you experienced God speaking through someone in your life?
- How did you know and discern God spoke through this person?

Ours is the choice to hear and listen to God speaking in our lives, or to ignore his voice and harden our hearts as the Responsorial Psalm reminds us.

- What causes you to harden your heart in response to God's voice?

֍ What helps you to open your heart and receive God's Word?

We believe Jesus is God's Word incarnate. He is the Word made flesh. He is the fulfillment of all the prophets. In today's Gospel reading we see Jesus teaching on the Sabbath in the synagogue. Astonished. Amazed. Bewildered. These all could be apt descriptions of the people's response to Jesus' words. The people in the synagogue do not respond with their own words; rather, the evangelist Mark only has the man with an unclean spirit speak. The man asks whether Jesus' purpose is destruction. The same man identifies Jesus as the "Holy One of God" (Mark 1:24). The juxtaposition of the question about destruction and the man's revelation of Jesus' identity could not be more ironic as Jesus' exorcism of the man's unclean spirit shows.

֍ When have Jesus' words brought life to you?

֍ How have you come to know Jesus' identity as the "Holy One of God" who speaks and acts with divine authority?

֍ What has Jesus done in your own life to reveal he offers—indeed he is—God's life-giving Word?

֍ What helps you to understand the new teaching with authority that Jesus brings?

֍ How do you express your own amazement at Jesus' Word? How do you in turn proclaim his Word to others?

Jesus' "fame" grew throughout the whole region of Galilee. Many craved to see him, to take in his Word. They yearned for the life he was bringing.

֍ Where do you desire Jesus' word in your life?

֍ Where do you see others longing for him?

֍ In what areas does the world stand in need of the life his teaching brings?

As disciples, we devote ourselves to the Lord and his life-giving Word. Some days this devotion comes easily. At other times, devotion can seem quite challenging, perhaps even impossible to us. In the Second Reading, St. Paul refocuses the Corinthians on their need to steadfastly devote themselves to the Lord. Soon the Lord will come again. Adhere to the Lord without distraction. Be free of the anxieties this world produces. This is St. Paul's teaching in light of the Corinthians' belief in the immanence of Jesus' Second Coming.

֍ How does your own faith help you handle life's anxieties?

֍ How do we as a community of disciples support one another in our devotion to the Lord?

Discerning who speaks in the Lord's name can be a daunting task today as it was in Moses' and Jesus' time.

֍ How do we know we are hearing God's voice?

This is the question Moses refers to at the conclusion of the First Reading. Together with the guidance of the Church and the Church's teaching authority, we assist each other in recognizing when a prophet only presumes to speak in the Lord's name and to ascertain when someone speaks in the name of other gods. In doing so, we live as a communion of believers who proclaim the Word of truth and life and whose actions show forth this Word.

- When have you been uncertain about God's voice in your life?
- What helped you clarify that it was or was not God speaking?

Wrapping It Up

Consider these points to conclude the dismissal. Integrate the thoughts and ideas that surfaced during the discussion.

- Jesus fulfills the words of the prophets who came before him. His Word is always the Word of life which destroys evils. Reflect on the importantance of your own words. Before you speak, consider how your words will bring life and not death.
- Jesus' words and actions destroyed evil. They revealed God's tremendous love for the world and its people—for us—for you. Be open to the ways Jesus seeks to destroy evil in your own life and reveal his love for you. Take some time to ponder how you harden your own heart to God's Word.
- The Lord utterly devotes himself to us in Jesus, his Son. Devotion to the Lord deepens our relationship with God. Focus on one or two actions you can take this week that will intensify your devotion to the Lord.

Closing Prayer

Conclude with prayer. If time permits, sing the psalm refrain a few times before or after the following prayer.

God of life,
you spoke your divine Word through the prophets
who dared us not to harden our hearts, but to hear your voice.
You speak your Word in a myriad of ways and through many and diverse peoples.
May your Son lead us to discern your true voice in our world today.
May we support each other as a community of disciples in the Church
as we strive to devote ourselves wholeheartedly to you.
Through Christ our Lord.
Amen.

Readings for the Next Dismissal

Provide catechumens with a list of the readings for the next dismissal session. Consult the liturgical calendar on page xvi to find out what day will be observed next week. Give catechumens the questions below to guide their reflection through the week.

- What connections are you seeing in the readings of this liturgical season? As you pray with the readings, around what themes do your thoughts seem to be coming together?
- Where do the readings intersect with your journey of faith? What questions do they raise for you?

Extended Catechesis

Based on today's readings and liturgical observance, the following topics may be covered for extended catechesis:

- Prophets and prophecy
- Discerning, hearing, and listening to God's voice
- The Word of God, the Word of Life
- Divine authority
- Exorcism
- Vocation

Fifth Sunday in Ordinary Time

Focus: To act for the sake of the Gospel.

Lectionary #74B

Catechist's Preparation

Overview of the Sunday

As we continue our journey through Ordinary Time, and on the verge of completing a month of the counted Sundays in the liturgical year, our readings reveal to us that discipleship is not in name only. We must act for the sake of the Gospel. The First Reading, from Job, reminds us of the truth we already know: life on earth is not always easy. We will have days where we feel life's drudgery. Yet our hope is in the Lord. The Gospel reading narrates the beauty of God's healing power present in Jesus who cured many who were sick and exorcised demons from many others. The Word he preached is a word of healing and hope. When we act for the sake of the Gospel, we choose to offer healing and hope to the world. St. Paul tells the Corinthians in the Second Reading that the Gospel he preaches is this Gospel of Jesus Christ.

Scripture Background

Job 7:1–4, 6–7 Many people find it easy to think of all the blessings God offers until they go through a difficult time. When troubling times hit, people's faith can waver. We realize that good things don't just happen to good people, and that bad things don't just happen to bad people. Life is much more mysterious and complicated than that. In Job's time, people took a more simplistic view of things. If you were being punished, it must be as a result of sin.

Job's suffering is mysterious. What does God want him to learn? How is this supposed to help him to grow? In spite of his troubles, Job's faith is constant. Job complains to God about his treatment, he never curses God, even though his friends advise him to do so. Job's friends insist that he must have sinned, but Job remains adamant that he has not. He stays resilient and reliant upon God.

Psalm 147:1–2, 3–4, 5–6 (see 3a) The first stanza of Psalm 147 speaks of a God who understands life at the level of loss and pain. God gathers, rebuilds, heals, binds up wounds, and gives sustenance. God is present to the brokenhearted, lost, wounded, and lowly. God has a personal relationship with human beings, yet he also numbers each star and knows them by name. This God, with his immense power and tender love, is unlike all of the other gods that the Israelites and their pagan neighbors had ever worshipped. Those who are lost and scattered are gathered together, and that which has been torn down is rebuilt—such is the attentiveness of this God.

1 Corinthians 9:16–19, 22–23 Paul faced criticism from others, who said that he had no right to preach the Gospel and act as an Apostle because he was not a true follower. But, Paul knew the call to act for the sake of the Gospel. He had experienced the call in the person of Jesus Christ. Nothing could dissuade him from that mission. Paul's sense of his own vocation speaks to us of ours. Our Baptism initiates us into the community of Christian believers. We are to respond individually to our vocational call to follow Jesus Christ. This means finding ways to live out our baptismal promise by proclaiming the Good News, not just in our words but also in our actions.

Like Job and Paul, we are invited to a faithful response in the circumstances of our lives. We, too, seek to find the brokenhearted, lost, wounded, and lowly. We help people by gathering them, rebuilding them, healing them, binding up their wounds, giving them sustenance, and teaching them. We may not always have Job's patience or the psalmist's eloquence of poetic prayer. We may not always have Paul's zeal or Jesus' strength. But, we always have God's steadfast love and grace, and that is enough.

Mark 1:29–39 Jesus clearly states his mission in the Gospel according to Mark. He comes to bring a message about God's reign and invites a decision from followers to change their lives and believe the Good News. In today's passage, he reiterates his mission: "Let us go on to the nearby villages that I may preach there also. For this purpose have I come" (1:38). Even after his preaching in the synagogue, he did not choose to rest at Simon's house, but healed Simon's mother-in-law instead. After days of curing the sick and driving out demons, he continued traveling throughout Galilee, helping people. Jesus knows the need is great and his message and ministry is urgent, and he calls his followers to act with the same passion for the sake of the Gospel.

Reflection Questions for the Catechist

- When have you sensed life's drudgery like Job?
- What effect did your hopelessness and restlessness have on your faith?
- What does it mean to you to do everything for the sake of the Gospel?
- How do you offer God's healing, life, and love to the catechumens on their faith journey?

Catechist's Guide

Objectives

- ▷ To trust in the hope faith brings even in the face of life's difficulties.
- ▷ To affirm that as people of faith, we find our hope in God who offers healing and life in the face of suffering.
- ▷ To recognize that God calls us to live out the Gospel of Jesus Christ in our daily lives, proclaiming and offering healing, life, and hope as he did.

Dismissal and Procession

Following the homily, the priest celebrant picks up the Lectionary and invites the catechumens to come forward with the catechist(s) who will lead today's dismissal session. Holding the Lectionary so that all can see, the priest celebrant sends the catechumens and catechist(s) forward using RCIA, 67, his own words, or the following:

PRIEST: **My dear friends, you have heard the Word of God proclaimed; we now send you forth to another place where you may reflect on these Scriptures. We pray that you will come to know the abundance of God's grace in our world, and that you will come to yearn for the blessings that await you around the Lord's table. Go now in the peace of Christ.**

All process to where the dismissal session will take place. The catechist holds the Lectionary in a reverent manner. The assembly may sing an acclamation to accompany the procession.

Centering

Upon reaching the place where the dismissal occurs, place the Lectionary on the ambo, lectern, or other dignified place (or hold the book reverently). Light the candle that is in the place of gathering and reread 1 Corinthians 9:16–19 in order to refocus the group's attention. Consider singing the Responsorial Psalm or have a recording of it available to use as part of the centering, either before or after the reading.

Reflection and Discussion

The following "script" may be used or adapted to help facilitate discussion on today's readings. Begin the discussion by asking the catechumens if any words or phrases from today's readings spoke to them.

The Gospel is the heart of the matter. Paul preaches the Gospel and recognizes that even the Gospel does not give him a reason to boast. Neither arrogance nor bragging has any place in a disciple's heart. All we do is "for the sake of the gospel" (1 Corinthians 9:23). In this we find our satisfaction, our hope, our life, our happiness. Paul feels compelled to preach the Gospel.

- How does God compel you to do the same?
- What satisfaction do you receive when you do everything for the sake of the Gospel?

Living life according to the Gospel is not always easy. Trials and suffering—hardships and crises—these come with human life. No one—not even God—promises us that our life will be free from difficulties and that everything will be smooth sailing. The prophet Job stands as an example for many because of how he acknowledges the pain and misery of his suffering. In today's First Reading, we are at a point in Job's story where he does not know when the dawn will come and when he will rise above his suffering. He is hopeless. Reflect on an experience in your own life or the life of someone close to you, when hopelessness in the face of suffering was the reality.

- How did the suffering affect your faith or his/her faith?

- What role did God and other people of faith have in helping you to see the dawn?

Even in our pain and suffering, even in the midst of sickness and disease, even amid the evil and demons that find (or attempt to find) their place within us and in the world, God holds out the healing love and life brought to us in Jesus, his Son. Jesus offers hope and healing to us individually—personally and to the whole world. The Gospel reading begins with Jesus entering not just any building, but a *home*, the home of four of his disciples who have already chosen to follow him. It was the home where Simon's mother-in-law lay sick with a fever.

- When has Jesus personally come to you and entered into your home to offer healing?

Jesus healed Simon's mother-in-law with a healing touch. She did not have to get up by herself. Jesus helped her to rise. Her response was service.

- How does Jesus accompany you week in and week out in your day-to-day living and extend his personal healing touch, helping you to rise above life's struggles and illnesses?

- What is your response to Jesus' healing touch?

Recall from last Sunday's readings how amazement filled the people in the synagogue when they heard Jesus teach. Perhaps Simon, Andrew, James, and John experienced a similar amazement upon Jesus' healing of Simon's mother-in-law. They went into action going out of the house and gathering up those who were ill or possessed by demons. Even though it was after sunset, they brought the people in need of healing back to Jesus. They acted for the sake of the Gospel—and not just a few people, but the *whole* town gathered at the doorstep to the home where Jesus was.

- When has your experience of healing compelled you to bring others to experience Jesus' healing?

The Gospel knows no geographical bounds. It is available to all. This is why Jesus needs to move on from the comfort of the home where he was. Others needed to hear the Good News and experience new life in him.

- Where is Jesus calling you to go to preach the Good News and to offer healing and new life in his name?

Wrapping It Up

Consider these points to conclude the dismissal. Integrate the thoughts and ideas that surfaced during the discussion.

- Prayer plays an important role in helping us to trust in the midst of life's difficulties. Consider the kinds of prayer that are most helpful to you when you experience suffering or hopelessness in a particular situation. Know that when you pray, whether in the privacy of your own heart and home, or within the liturgy of the Church, you pray in communion with the Church.
- When you experience a challenging situation or interaction with coworkers or family members this week, take a moment to recognize your hope is in God.

- God calls all of us who follow Jesus to bring others to him so they might experience the healing and life he offers. This is our responsibility as disciples. It is how we evangelize and act so that the Gospel might be known to all peoples. Consider one way, large or small, you will act for the sake of the Gospel this week. Write it down in your journal and commit to it.

Closing Prayer

Conclude with prayer. If time permits, sing the psalm refrain a few times before or after the following prayer.

> God of life and love,
> you were with Job in his suffering and when he cried out in hopelessness.
> You invite us to hold steadfastly to hope in you in our sufferings
> and what can seem the drudgery of daily life.
> Grant us grace and courage to continue on the journey of faith.
> Make us willing to act for the Gospel, taking the Apostle Paul as our example,
> as we proclaim in word and deed your salvation.
> Through Christ our Lord.
> Amen.

Readings for the Next Dismissal

Provide catechumens with a list of the readings for the next dismissal session. Consult the liturgical calendar on page xvi to find out what day will be observed next week. Give catechumens the questions below to guide their reflection through the week.

⑨ What connections are you seeing in the readings of this liturgical season? As you pray with the readings, around what themes do your thoughts seem to be coming together?

⑨ Where do the readings intersect with your journey of faith? What questions do they raise for you?

Extended Catechesis

Based on today's readings and liturgical observance, the following topics may be covered for extended catechesis:

❋ Suffering and faith

❋ Trust in God's abiding presence

❋ Happiness in the life of faith

❋ Preaching and spreading the Gospel

❋ Extending healing and hope to others

❋ Evangelization

❋ Healing and exorcism

❋ Anointing of the Sick

SIXTH SUNDAY IN ORDINARY TIME

Focus: Do everything for the glory of God.

Lectionary #77B

Catechist's Preparation

Overview of the Sunday

We dedicate our whole lives, everything we do—all our words and all our actions—to God's glory. Each day, we strive to imitate Christ. Paul did this. As followers of Christ, we are to do the same. In the Gospel reading, a leper comes to Jesus begging Jesus to make him clean. Jesus heals him but inexplicably warns him to not say a word to anyone about his glorious healing. The man publicizes everything and shows us the impossibility of remaining silent in the face of God's glory. God calls us to lead others to Jesus so that they, too, might experience divine glory and wholeness. Jesus changes lives forever so that one is no longer unclean but holy and whole in the Lord.

Scripture Background

Leviticus 13:1–2, 44–46 As the Israelites began to understand their role as the people of God, they worked to understand what it meant to be holy, faithful, and free of sin in the eyes of the Lord. They created rituals to cleanse themselves and to show signs of repentance. They established laws and practices to keep themselves holy and pure. They saw these practices as ways to uphold their part of the covenant to be faithful to the Lord. One such prescription in Leviticus allowed that a priest, such as Aaron, could declare a person clean from sin and so able to return to the community. But, in their legislation, they began to practice extremes and see external diseases such as leprosy, or physical irregularities such as blindness or deafness, as a sign that a person was unclean. They thought that the outward appearance must mirror the internal, so they interpreted illness and deformity as signs of sin. People avoided the sick and handicapped, and relegated them to staying outside the community that was so important to the Israelites. In the First Reading, we hear of the leper: "He shall dwell apart, making his abode outside the camp" (13:46). It was a terrible fate for people to be cast out from the community. This story sets the scene for us to hear of Jesus' cure of the leper in the Gospel.

Psalm 32:1–2, 5, 11 (7) Psalm 32 is a hymn for those who know they have sinned and are overjoyed by God's forgiveness. The final verse of the selection of today's psalm calls upon others to join in the praise. The just and upright of heart are invited by the psalmist to exult in the song. It is significant to call upon the community to sing praise together in light of the stories we hear today of lepers separated from their community because they were considered unclean. One can imagine the joy of a leper, or a sinner, who is restored to the bonds of community and those whom they love. Such is the joy of salvation!

1 Corinthians 10:31—11:1 In chapter 10 of Paul's letter to the Corinthians, he recounts the story of the Israelites and their Exodus in the desert. He reminds them that the Israelites were tempted and they failed. They worshipped other idols, blamed God for their troubles, and complained about their situation. Paul reminds Corinth about the potential for this to happen there, too.

In today's reading, Paul tells the Corinthians what kind of example they should be: they should do everything for the glory of God, and avoid things that would cause offense. Another translation of this reading says that they should avoid doing anything that would cause another to stumble. Paul says that they should avoid causing Jews, Greeks, or members of the Church of God—basically, everyone—to stumble. Clearly, Paul expects that Christians are to be examples to the world.

Mark 1:40–45 Today's medical science has classified leprosy as a single skin condition, also known as Hansen's disease. In Jesus' time, though, leprosy was a term that referred to multiple skin disorders. As we hear in today's First Reading, leprosy made a person unclean and unfit for life within the community. We read in Leviticus that lepers wore torn clothes, and had to announce themselves with cries of "Unclean!" Lepers were not allowed to participate in public worship and were banished from the community. This practice continued even into the Middle Ages, when lepers were forbidden to attend any religious service, and had to watch through holes in cathedral walls. It was a terrible fate.

The leper in today's Gospel should not have been anywhere near Jesus nor close enough to speak with him. He broke the law. Yet Jesus did not shun the man. Instead, he listened when the man approached him. Then, Jesus broke the law by touching him. By breaking that law, Jesus showed his disciples and followers that God does not shun. We are not to shut anyone out from the community of the People of God, no matter what. This is the Good News of salvation that Jesus preached.

Reflection Questions for the Catechist

- When have you approached the Lord seeking healing and wholeness?
- How do you respond to God's healing in Jesus when you experience it?
- Where do you see and sense God's glory present in your life? In others? In the world around you?

Catechist's Guide

Objectives

- ▷ To witness God's glory present in life.
- ▷ To recognize ways others have led us to see God's glory and how we have done the same for them.
- ▷ To contemplate what it means to imitate Christ and reflect God's glory in our own lives.

Dismissal and Procession

Following the homily, the priest celebrant picks up the Lectionary and invites the catechumens to come forward with the catechist(s) who will lead today's dismissal session. Holding the Lectionary so that all can see, the priest celebrant sends the catechumens and catechist(s) forward using RCIA, 67, his own words, or the following:

PRIEST: **My dear friends, you have heard the Word of God proclaimed; we now send you forth to another place where you may reflect on these Scriptures. We pray that you will come to know the abundance of God's grace in our world, and that you will come to yearn for the blessings that await you around the Lord's table. Go now in the peace of Christ.**

All process to where the dismissal session will take place. The catechist holds the Lectionary in a reverent manner. The assembly may sing an acclamation to accompany the procession.

Centering

Upon reaching the place where the dismissal occurs, place the Lectionary on the ambo, lectern, or other dignified place (or hold the book reverently). Light the candle that is in the place of gathering and reread 1 Corinthians 10:31—11:1 in order to refocus the group's attention. Consider singing the Responsorial Psalm or have a recording of it available to use as part of the centering, either before or after the reading.

Reflection and Discussion

The following "script" may be used or adapted to help facilitate discussion on today's readings. Begin the discussion by asking the catechumens if any words or phrases from today's readings spoke to them.

To do everything for the glory of God. That is no small task St. Paul instructs the Corinthians to undertake. As follows of Christ, it is our task as well. We are to be mindful of the weak—those who are on the outskirts of society as well as the community of faith—in everything we do. St. Paul himself tried to please everyone in that regard, not to reap any benefits himself, but to bring others to the gift of salvation in Christ. We know it is humanly impossible to please everyone, but ours is the responsibility to care for all to the best of our ability.

- What does it mean to do everything for God's glory? What motivates you to serve others unselfishly as Paul did?

Live as an imitator the Apostle Paul, who after his conversion lived his life in imitation of Christ. Surely we will fall short of perfect imitation of Christ. We sin. God forgives. God's call to follow his Son always remains.

- What helps you to live in imitation of Christ? To continue to do so even after you sin?

Part of living in imitation of Christ includes welcoming those whom society shuns. Think about those whom others consider as unclean in today's world. Perhaps you even think less of a coworker or family member for one reason or another.

Name some people considered unclean by human standards in the world today. After naming them, sit for a moment in silence to consider how Jesus would welcome them.

The leper in the Gospel had the courage to come to Jesus on his own and kneel before him begging Jesus to make him clean. Jesus responds to his wish in a personal manner. Jesus stretches out his hand and touches him. Jesus' words are direct and to the point. He accepts the responsibility to make the leper clean and simply commands the man to be made clean. The miracle of healing occurs. Outside of being a medical doctor, many of us will not have the responsibility or ability to physically heal someone. Our call might not be to heal a person physically but simply to offer an invitation to seek the healing of body, mind, and soul in Jesus—to seek wholeness and salvation in him.

⑨ When have you approached Jesus begging for healing? What was your experience like?

⑨ How do you invite others to come to Jesus to experience healing?

The man with leprosy whom Jesus healed failed to heed Jesus' warning not to tell anyone. He publicized everything that happened. Surely the report he gave about his healing included many details! He probably was so amazed, so excited, so happy with the gift he received, he just had to tell others. He evangelized! He proclaimed Jesus the healer, although the evangelist Mark does not have the man testify that Jesus is the Messiah, the Son of God.

⑨ What is usually your response after you experience Jesus' healing, love, and compassion?

⑨ How does your response attest to the glory of God you have experienced?

The Church's liturgy each Sunday provides us an opportunity to praise God in songs, hymns, and prayers that express our gratitude for all that God does in Jesus. Our participation in liturgy is one way we proclaim our joy for all the Lord gives us. When we are sent forth from liturgy, we take God's Word of salvation with us as we go. We publicize the Gospel of salvation in Jesus Christ so that others keep coming to him.

⑨ What does it mean to publicize your experience of Jesus in this day and age?

⑨ Where will you publicize God's healing glory and the joy of salvation?

Wrapping It Up

Consider these points to conclude the dismissal. Integrate the thoughts and ideas that surfaced during the discussion.

- The wonder of God's glory is immense, beyond human comprehension. Yet we see signs, small and large, day in and day out, which reflect divine glory.

- Jesus often welcomes and acts compassionately to those the world puts asunder. Who will you reach out to that the world berates and pushes aside? Pray to let your human interactions this week reflect God's glory.

- Imitating Christ as Paul did is hard work. It is holy work. It involves living a life of faith and holiness not just when we come to Church and reflect on the Word but throughout our day-to-day journey of faith. Remember that we always have the example of people of faith throughout the centuries to buoy us on our journey. Find ways to support one another this week as you strive to be imitators of Christ and reflect God's glory. Pray with and for each other in words, in song, and in silence.

Closing Prayer

Conclude with prayer. If time permits, sing the psalm refrain a few times before or after the following prayer.

Holy God,
throughout all time you heal those who suffer from illness
and offer compassion to those the world's people deem unworthy.
You sent prophets and Apostles, teachers and disciples,
to show us how to live as imitators of Christ.
We pray today for their example to guide us
as we choose to reach out to those society shuns
and to act for your glory.
May our words and actions compel others
to live in imitation of your Son, Jesus Christ our Lord.
Who lives and reigns for ever and ever.
Amen.

Readings for the Next Dismissal

Provide catechumens with a list of the readings for the next dismissal session. Consult the liturgical calendar on page xvi to find out what day will be observed next week. Give catechumens the questions below to guide their reflection through the week.

- What connections are you seeing in the readings of this liturgical season? As you pray with the readings, around what themes do your thoughts seem to be coming together?
- Where do the readings intersect with your journey of faith? What questions do they raise for you?

Extended Catechesis

Based on today's readings and liturgical observance, the following topics may be covered for extended catechesis:

- Divine glory
- Jesus' healing and compassion
- Outreach to the marginalized
- Corporal and Spiritual Works of Mercy
- Imitation of Christ
- New life and salvation in Christ
- Proclamation of the Gospel and evangelization

SEVENTH SUNDAY IN ORDINARY TIME

Focus: God makes everything new.

Lectionary #80B

Catechist's Preparation

Overview of the Sunday

The prophet Isaiah's message is poignant: the Lord is doing something new here and now. We have only to notice the newness the Lord brings forth through the forgiveness of sin. In the Gospel reading, Jesus makes real this newness as he heals a paralytic whose friends so desperately wanted to bring him Jesus that they lowered him through a roof. Jesus forgave the sins of this child of God and he walked home. Jesus indeed is God's Yes incarnate, as St. Paul writes in the Second Reading.

Scripture Background

Isaiah 43:18–19, 21–22, 24b–25 In this passage, Isaiah writes to comfort his people in exile. He declares that God is changing history: "Remember not the events of the past" (43:18). Even while the passage clearly recalls the past, it proclaims that what is to come will be like a new Exodus: "In the desert I make a way" (43:19). But this new way will be even more marvelous. In Exodus 15:23–27, God taught Moses how to sweeten brackish water and led the people to springs. Now, God will give them nothing less than rivers in the wasteland.

And, lest they forget their unworthiness of all of this, Isaiah makes it absolutely clear that it is all God's free action. This people who wearies God is forgiven, not because of their merit but, as God says, "for my own sake" (43:25). The new thing, the free and forgiven status of the forsaken people, is a revelation of God's goodness.

Psalm 41:2–3, 4–5, 13–14 (5b) In Psalm 141 the blessed is the one who has regard for the lowly and poor. Although this psalm begins with a beatitude, it is actually a prayer for help, which the psalmist admits is not fully deserved. In the psalmist's worldview, sin and illness are intimately connected; lack of moral integrity results in lack of physical integrity. By the time we reach the last verses, the penitent psalmist makes a proclamation of faith: Those who place all their trust in God will be healed and will bless God for all eternity.

2 Corinthians 1:18–22 In this first selection from 2 Corinthians, from which the Second Readings are taken from the Seventh to the Fourteenth Sundays in Ordinary Time, Paul refutes a charge that he has been capricious about visiting Corinth. Later, he will say that

he did not go there to cause grief. But before he explains his travel plans, he moves from self-defense into a theological proclamation. Paul insists that he is as reliable as the word he preached to them, and that Word was Jesus Christ, in whom all of God's promises have been fulfilled. Beyond affirming the absolute yes of God's Word and his own steadfastness, the closing verses of the reading reveal Paul's Trinitarian theology and the anthropology that flows from it. He reminds his readers that it is God who has brought them together in Christ, and it is God who has given them the first installment of the Spirit in their hearts. This would quite likely remind them of the theme of unity and love he expounded in 1 Corinthians 12—13. Thus, as Paul begins what many see as his most personal letter, he calls the community to express the forbearance and self-awareness that should spring from their unity with and in Christ.

Mark 2:1–12 The crowds originally responded to Jesus' words and deeds with amazement and astonishment. Now, for the first time, people come to Jesus with faith. Judging by all they did, the friends who brought the paralytic to Jesus believed that he could and would heal. Jesus' immediate response to that faith was to forgive the man's sins.

Those were audacious words; everyone knew that only God can forgive sin. The scribes correctly understood that Jesus was assuming a divine right. It should come as no surprise that Jesus would perceive their thoughts and respond with a question that would trap them. Because both healing and forgiving were considered divine prerogatives, Jesus' healing activity was a sign that he was acting with God's power (see Isaiah 35:6, Micah 3:6).

While the scribes sulked, the crowds glorified the God who makes all things new. Some were beginning to recognize Jesus as one who made God's healing love and forgiveness present among them. Finally, it should be noted that while Jesus both forgave and healed, he did not link illness and guilt. In fact, when he broached the topic, he contradicted the accepted wisdom about it, denying that victims of calamity or illness were more sinful than others (see John 9:2–3, Luke 13:2).

Reflection Questions for the Catechist

⑨ When have you come to Jesus in faith asking for healing and forgiveness?

⑨ What is God making new in your life and in the world around you?

⑨ How do you see God's newness evident in the lives of the catechumens and the initiation team members? How does God make new your parish community through the witness of the catechumens?

Catechist's Guide

Objectives

▷ To acknowledge that God does not hold onto the sins of our past but continuously makes all things new.

▷ To examine the areas in our lives where God calls us to make our word consistently yes to a life of faith.

▷ To contemplate how our response to God's forgiveness in Jesus will lead others to glorify the new things God is doing.

Dismissal and Procession

Following the homily, the priest celebrant picks up the Lectionary and invites the catechumens to come forward with the catechist(s) who will lead today's dismissal session. Holding the Lectionary so that all can see, the priest celebrant sends the catechumens and catechist(s) forward using RCIA, 67, his own words, or the following:

PRIEST: **My dear friends, you have heard the Word of God proclaimed; we now send you forth to another place where you may reflect on these Scriptures. We pray that you will come to know the abundance of God's grace in our world, and that you will come to yearn for the blessings that await you around the Lord's table. Go now in the peace of Christ.**

All process to where the dismissal session will take place. The catechist holds the Lectionary in a reverent manner. The assembly may sing an acclamation to accompany the procession.

Centering

Upon reaching the place where the dismissal occurs, place the Lectionary on the ambo, lectern, or other dignified place (or hold the book reverently). Light the candle that is in the place of gathering and reread Isaiah 43:18–19, 21–22, 24b–25 in order to refocus the group's attention. Consider singing the Responsorial Psalm or have a recording of it available to use as part of the centering, either before or after the reading.

Reflection and Discussion

The following "script" may be used or adapted to help facilitate discussion on today's readings. Begin the discussion by asking the catechumens if any words or phrases from today's readings spoke to them.

The people of Israel were in exile, and they heard the promise that God was doing something new. Life in exile was tremendously difficult. Many of us will not experience geographical exile, but at some point in life we might experience exile from a job, our family, our friends, or even our faith and our relationship with God. We might feel lost, and in need of hearing God's promise that he is doing something new.

⑨ When have you been in exile—in need of God's assistance in changing your life situation and creating new possibilities?

⑨ What was it like to place your trust in God's promise of newness?

Newness became incarnate, became flesh like never before in the person of Jesus, God's Son. God certainly did something new! Freedom from sin is ours in Jesus. Healing and wholeness is God's gift to us. Our faith brings us to Jesus. And often it is the faith of others who care so deeply for us that accompanies us along the path to Jesus just as the friends lowered their paralyzed companion through the roof.

⑨ When has someone accompanied you and gone to great lengths for you to experience forgiveness and be made whole? How did their faith influence you?

The scribes in the Gospel reading questioned Jesus' authority. They could not grasp why he told the paralyzed child his sins were forgiven. Only God could do that. Jesus knew what was in their hearts and responded accordingly, healing the paralytic so that he could walk. His authority was clear. Presumably even the scribes were among those who were astounded! Maybe even some glorified God in recognition of the marvelous new thing God has done in Jesus! Sometimes we question, too. Your faith has led you to Jesus, to the Cross, to discipleship, to this point in your faith journey as a catechumen.

⑨ What is a "scribe moment" you have had along the way in your faith journey?

⑨ How did God in Jesus respond to that moment?

⑨ Where did the experience lead you in your faith?

When we are in touch with our need for forgiveness, we come face-to-face with our humanity. We recognize that we are not God *and* that we desperately need God. And, we find that God is there for us. God always has been present with us. Each day we reaffirm this and voice a resolute yes to God's amazing, ever-new love in our lives. We accept our call to discipleship and to follow Jesus. We commit to making known the forgiveness and healing he offers, just as the paralytic publicized the Good News of his healing.

Describe a time when you came face-to-face with your humanity, your need for forgiveness, and your need for God.

⑨ How have you already made known the newness of God's love in Jesus to someone?

Often we experience God's love for us in Jesus in community, gathered together with other people of faith. In the call stories of the first disciples on the early Sundays of Ordinary Time, we heard how Jesus invited individuals to follow him. The call was personal. But the call was also a call to discipleship with others who accepted the same call. The community of disciples—what we know as the communion of the Church—is also God's gift to us. Together, we walk the road of discipleship, supporting one another in our yes to God's Word, Jesus Christ.

⑨ In what ways do you experience the support of the Christian community as you deepen your commitment, your yes to God's Word?

⑨ In what ways do you need more support and love from the Christian community?

⑨ How can you return this support in kind and accompany others in the community?

Wrapping It Up

Consider these points to conclude the dismissal. Integrate the thoughts and ideas that surfaced during the discussion.

- Seeing how God makes all things new day in and day out requires mindfulness. It takes being willing to shed the past and have faith that God truly is at work in our lives and in the world.

- God's forgiveness and healing love and compassion is always available to us in Jesus. Allow your faith to lead you toward experiences of newness in Christ. You will probably end up saying you have never seen anything like this just as those who witnessed the healing of the paralytic in the Gospel reading said.

- Our life of discipleship requires a faith response that includes both our words and actions. Our yes to God must mean yes, not yes and no, and our actions must carry others to the source of new life.

Closing Prayer

Conclude with prayer. If time permits, sing the psalm refrain a few times before or after the following prayer.

> God of all things new,
> you did something astoundingly new in Jesus.
> Give us the humility to know the sins for which we need forgiveness.
> Open our hearts to our need for healing.
> With faith, lead us to your Son to be made whole,
> and then enliven us with the Spirit in our hearts to go out to others,
> glorifying you for the blessing of our new home in your Son, our Lord.
> Who lives and reigns for ever and ever.
> Amen.

Readings for the Next Dismissal

Provide catechumens with a list of the readings for the next dismissal session. Consult the liturgical calendar on page xvi to find out what day will be observed next week. Give catechumens the questions below to guide their reflection through the week.

⑨ What connections are you seeing in the readings of this liturgical season? As you pray with the readings, around what themes do your thoughts seem to be coming together?

⑨ Where do the readings intersect with your journey of faith? What questions do they raise for you?

Extended Catechesis

Based on today's readings and liturgical observance, the following topics may be covered for extended catechesis:

❋ Forgiveness of sins/healing from our sins/sin

❋ Sacrament of Reconciliation

❋ The relationship between Eucharist and forgiveness

❋ Faith and healing

❋ Leading others to healing in Jesus

❋ Our response to receiving God's forgiveness

❋ God's definitive yes to us in the Incarnation of Jesus, his Son

❋ New life in Christ

EIGHTH SUNDAY IN ORDINARY TIME

Focus: God's new love for us in Jesus is written on our hearts.

Lectionary #83B

Catechist's Preparation

Overview of the Sunday

The message of love and mercy is clear in today's readings. In the First Reading, the Lord leads us on a journey in the desert where he speaks intimately to us in our hearts. We see justice and right, love, and mercy as the basis of the Lord's relationship with us. The Lord will remain faithful, will we? Even the psalm focuses us on the Lord's kindness and mercy. Paul's words move us to recognize how God's intimate love for us compels us to heed the Spirit of life at work in us to live as a letter of Christ to others. We learn from the Gospel reading that in Jesus exists a radically new way of life that is ours to accept or not. New wine in new wineskins describes the wonder of life in Christ available to all who choose to follow him to the Cross.

Scripture Background

Hosea 2:16b; 17b, 21–22 Hosea prophesied in the last years of the Northern Kingdom (Israel). Like most of Israel's prophets, he anguished over his people's failure to keep the Sinai Covenant. His approach, however, was unique. Instead of scrupulously avoiding the sexual imagery characteristic of Canaanite religion, Hosea borrowed that imagery and applied it to Israel's relationship to God. Hosea pictured the Exodus as Israel's marriage to God and their sojourn in the wilderness as their honeymoon. Unfortunately, Israel did not stay faithful. They committed adultery with other gods, most notably the gods of Canaan.

In Sunday's reading, God tries to win Israel back with long walks together in the desert where they first met, with thoughtful gifts and tender words of affection. God even engages in a bit of wordplay in hopes of wooing the errant Israel. (The Hebrew word for "husband" is also the word for Canaan's chief deity, Ba'al.)

Tradition has often described God's invitation as if it were an "offer we can't refuse." Hosea, however, prefers to think of God's invitation more in terms of a valentine. For Hosea, God is a long-lost lover seeking to win back our hearts. There is no coercion here, only tenderness and love.

Psalm 103:1–2, 3–4, 8, 10, 12–13 (8a) By genre, Psalm 103 is an individual hymn of praise. Interestingly, however, the psalmist does not sing it to God nor does he sing it for the worshiping congregation. Instead, he sings it to himself, lest he forget God's benefits. These benefits are many: forgiveness, healing, redemption, steadfast love, mercy, goodness, vindication, compassion, and righteousness. Only in the last strophe does the psalmist then think to turn to others, inviting them, too, to praise the God who has been so gracious to the psalmist.

Like Hosea, the psalmist describes God's invitation to us in terms of tenderness and love. Perhaps because he has experienced it firsthand, the psalmist is particularly mindful of God's enduring mercy. It doesn't matter that we are rather frail creatures. It doesn't matter that we often feel woebegone. It doesn't even matter that we are not perfect and often make mistakes. God still sets a table before us, overflowing with an abundance of good things.

2 Corinthians 3:1b–6 Once again Paul is defending his version of the Gospel and his style of ministry to the Corinthians. This time he addresses the charge that he had come to Corinth without any recommendation from other believers. Such recommendations were common Greek business practice and had become commonplace among traveling preachers in the early Church, too. Because Paul's opponents in Corinth had no doubt come highly recommended, Paul was under strong pressure to explain himself. He doesn't need written letters of recommendation, he says. Why? Because the Corinthians themselves are his letters of recommendation. Their faith is living proof that his Gospel is true and his ministry genuine. It is also proof that God, not Paul, is at work in Corinth. No paper letters of recommendation can compare with that any more than the tablets of the law could compare to the life of the Spirit.

According to Paul, our invitation to God's new life is not written on some piece of paper, however fancy. It isn't even carved in stone. Instead, Paul says, God's invitation is a living one that the Spirit has inscribed on our hearts by faith.

Mark 2:18–22 When this reading opens, Jesus has just called the tax collector, Levi. The religious leaders immediately grumbled, "Why does he eat with tax collectors and sinners?" (see 2:18). Now they grumble because he doesn't encourage his disciples to fast. In fine rabbinic fashion, Jesus responds to their grumbling with a question of his own, "Can the wedding guests fast while the bridegroom is with them?" (2:19).

Originally, the story probably ended there. Mark, however, has a few more points he wants to make, so he adds several other stories of Jesus that he is familiar with. To make sure that no one forgets the Cross, Mark adds a prediction of Jesus' death (see 2:20). (That prediction also served to explain why Mark's Church had now begun to fast again.) Then, to make sure his readers would understand how radically different the way of Jesus was to the ways of their religious leaders, he adds two parables. Both maintain that the new order inaugurated by Jesus was not just a patched-up or remodeled version of the old. It was indeed a "new teaching." When Jesus invites Levi to follow him that day, Mark says, he is calling him to an entirely new way of life. The same is true when Jesus invites us to follow him today. Now that the bridegroom has come, everything is new—so new that it often breaks the boundaries and limits of our old way of life.

Reflection Questions for the Catechist

⑨ What was a desert journey the Lord has led you on? What did the Lord speak to your heart on the journey?

⑨ What is a challenge you find in following the Spirit of life, rather than only the letter of the law?

⑨ What is an area of your life in which you desire to experience the new wine in new wineskins Jesus offers?

Catechist's Guide

Objectives

▷ To absorb the depths of the Lord's love, mercy, and faithfulness. (If before Lent, link this concept to the season.)

▷ To cherish how Christ writes his letter on each of our hearts, for us and others, so we might know the Spirit of life.

▷ To explore the radical wonders of newness available to us and the world in Jesus.

Dismissal and Procession

Following the homily, the priest celebrant picks up the Lectionary and invites the catechumens to come forward with the catechist(s) who will lead today's dismissal session. Holding the Lectionary so that all can see, the priest celebrant sends the catechumens and catechist(s) forward using RCIA, 67, his own words, or the following:

PRIEST: **My dear friends, you have heard the Word of God proclaimed; we now send you forth to another place where you may reflect on these Scriptures. We pray that you will come to know the abundance of God's grace in our world, and that you will come to yearn for the blessings that await you around the Lord's table. Go now in the peace of Christ.**

All process to where the dismissal session will take place. The catechist holds the Lectionary in a reverent manner. The assembly may sing an acclamation to accompany the procession.

Centering

Upon reaching the place where the dismissal occurs, place the Lectionary on the ambo, lectern, or other dignified place (or hold the book reverently). Light the candle that is in the place of gathering and reread 2 Corinthians 3:1b–6 in order to refocus the group's attention. Consider singing the Responsorial Psalm or have a recording of it available to use as part of the centering, either before or after the reading.

Reflection and Discussion

The following "script" may be used or adapted to help facilitate discussion on today's readings. Begin the discussion by asking the catechumens if any words or phrases from today's readings spoke to them.

The new covenant Paul speaks of is a covenant of spirit not of letter. It is a covenant of the heart. It is a relationship between the heart of God and our heart. God draws us into his heart through his Son, Jesus Christ. Heart speaks to heart. The covenant is no longer on stone tablets, but on hearts.

🌀 What is the covenant God writes on your heart in Jesus Christ?

Nothing qualifies us for this covenant. God in Christ freely enters into relationship with us. There is nothing we need to do to make us worthy to be in relationship with God. We are God's creation. Our inherent goodness comes from God, who created us in his image and likeness. We are to be the letter of his Son, Jesus Christ, to the world holding the Spirit's life out to all people.

🌀 How can you bring life, not death, to the world by serving as a minister of the new covenant?

Remaining faithful to the covenant—to our relationship with God—is a journey, a process. Yes, it requires an initial commitment. But that commitment is not the end of the story. The journey of discipleship is a life-long journey in which God in Jesus Christ continuously makes us new, forgives us our sins, extends divine mercy to us, and invites us into mission for the sake of the world. Sometimes the journey is a desert journey where we need to dig deep in our souls to name those places in our hearts still in need of conversion.

🌀 Is the Lord currently inviting you to embark on a desert journey of the heart?

🌀 What are the areas of your heart in need of conversion, of turning back to the Lord?

Often our desert journeys involve discerning where we have held too tightly to the letter of the law that brings death and failed to open ourselves to the Spirit who gives life. The old wineskins of the letter of the law will burst if we refuse to open ourselves to change, to newness, to divine life.

🌀 When have you tried to mix the new with the old and found the two did not work well together?

🌀 What completely new wineskins must you have to welcome the Spirit of life into your heart?

When we live in relationship with God in Christian community, every now and then our relationship can become strained because of the human interactions and relationships. Sometimes our Christian community, its committees, and its groups need new life. It is just like relationships in families. They need work. Relationships do not just happen. Faithfulness is important, as is loving kindness and mercy, as is desiring new life, not death, for others and for the communities to which we belong.

🌀 In what ways do you, or can you, live out God's covenant with you in your family? In the Christian community?

🌀 What are challenges that you face to living God's covenant?

🌀 In what ways does the radical newness brought in Jesus needs to take root?

🌀 What might your role be in bringing this newness and life?

The work of faithfulness to the covenant is work that we do not do alone. God remains always with us, ever-faithful to the covenant. God holds out righteousness and justice, love and mercy to us. God's sincere desire is for us to know him.

🌀 How will you draw closer to the heart of God this week?

🌀 What helps you when you are unable to sense God's love and mercy so you might find your way back to God and experience newness in his Son?

Wrapping It Up

Consider these points to conclude the dismissal. Integrate the thoughts and ideas that surfaced during the discussion.

- God's love for us is right, just, merciful, faithful, and deeply personal; it endures forever, despite the times when we move away from him and harm the intimate relationship he has with us.

- It is our responsibility to hold God's love out to others. The letter of Christ on our hearts is not a letter of law, but of love and life. The Spirit gives life. This is the message we communicate with others.

- Jesus bears ultimate newness for us and for the world in his very person and mission. Opting for the newness Jesus offers—the newness we know as the Cross—means fundamental and deep-seated change. We name this change *conversion*. (*If before Lent: The forty days of Lent present disciples the time to engage in this work of the heart.*)

Closing Prayer

Conclude with prayer. If time permits, sing the psalm refrain a few times before or after the following prayer.

God of love,
you led your people in the desert to speak to their hearts.
You invite us to a journey in the desert with you.
Empower us to live as the love letter of your Son, Jesus Christ, in the world,
making your love available to people near and far.
Through Christ our Lord.
Amen.

Readings for the Next Dismissal

Provide catechumens with a list of the readings for the next dismissal session. Consult the liturgical calendar on page xvi to find out what day will be observed next week. Give catechumens the questions below to guide their reflection through the week.

- What connections are you seeing in the readings of this liturgical season? As you pray with the readings, around what themes do your thoughts seem to be coming together?

- Where do the readings intersect with your journey of faith? What questions do they raise for you?

Extended Catechesis

Based on today's readings and liturgical observance, the following topics may be covered for extended catechesis:

- God's love for us
- Covenant faithfulness
- God's loving kindness and mercy
- The relationship between the Spirit of life and letter of the law

- The relationship between the old covenant and the new covenant in Jesus
- Lent (*if before the season*)

NINTH SUNDAY IN ORDINARY TIME

Focus: God frees us in Jesus Christ to keep holy the Sabbath in new ways.

Lectionary #86B

Catechist's Preparation

Overview of the Sunday

The Pharisees truly did not understand Jesus' mission. With Jesus, we are no longer to merely observe the Sabbath legally and ritualistically. We are to live the Sabbath as Jesus did. As Lord of the Sabbath, Jesus shows us how we are to work to feed others. We are to offer healing to those in need. We are to live for others and, in doing so, we live for God to whom everything and everyone belongs. In God, true freedom from restrictive laws exists. God's amazing power manifest in Jesus reveals to us the hope of the Resurrection just as Lent dawns and we journey to Jerusalem, trusting in the promise of the Resurrection. Holy is the Sabbath day. Holy are all days lived in confidence that the Lord is God.

Scripture Background

Deuteronomy 5:12–15 To prepare us for the Sabbath controversy found in Sunday's Gospel, the Lectionary has chosen the original Sabbath law itself for our First Reading. Two versions of this law are in the Pentateuch, one in Exodus and this one, in Deuteronomy. Though the intent of the law is the same, the emphasis in each is slightly different. In Exodus, the Sabbath was instituted as a memorial of the creation and as a foretaste of the world to come. Deuteronomy grounds the Sabbath in the Exodus from Egypt.

As such it is primarily a sign of God's grace and a reminder of our dependence on God. By including slaves, visitors, even farm animals in its provision, the Sabbath law was also seen by Deuteronomy as a sign of God's justice. Time is valuable and how we spend it reveals our values.

Psalm 81:3–4, 5–6, 6–8, 10–11 (2a) Psalm 81 was written as a festival song, most likely for the Feast of Tabernacles. It begins with a stirring call to worship complete with musical accompaniment. Then a voice speaks, probably the voice of a priest speaking for God. Apparently it is a voice Israel has not listened to for a while. As the song continues, God reminds the people that they were saved out of the hands of the Pharaoh in Egypt. God urges them to listen and to obey the words they were given at Sinai.

If they do, God promises to take care of them and guide them, but if they choose to go another way, they are unfortunately on their own. Again we find the commandments of God inviting us to a Sabbath style of living. The psalmist is very specific about what this means. It means a close relationship with God and a willingness to walk in God's ways.

2 Corinthians 4:6–11 In this reading, Paul replies to another charge leveled at him by opponents in Corinth: that he is not very impressive in person. Not only that, he always seems to be in trouble—hardly the marks of a true apostle.

Paul admits that he and his coworkers are not impressive. But, he says, this is exactly what God intended. If Paul had been impressive and if things always went well for him, it would be easy for people to think he had done it all himself. But because he is in fact weak and unimpressive, there can be no doubt that whatever he achieves is achieved through the power of God. Indeed, the less impressive Paul is, the clearer it is that God is working through him.

Mark 2:23–3:6 or 2:23–2 With this reading, we come to the final two controversies in this section of Mark's account of the Gospel. Both are controversies over the Sabbath law and both assert the power and authority of Jesus. In the first, Jesus and his disciples are traveling on the Sabbath and stop in a grain field to glean some food. Immediately the religious leaders accuse them of breaking the Sabbath. Jesus counters with a story about King David. The story offers a perfect precedent, for just like Jesus, David was rightfully king at the time but he was not recognized as such. In the second story, Jesus is the one who issues the challenge: "Is it lawful on the Sabbath to do good?" To illustrate his point, he immediately turns to a man with a withered hand and heals him. The religious leaders are appalled. Of course it is lawful to do good on the Sabbath, but this was no emergency. It was, however, the proverbial last straw that seals Jesus' fate.

Like many of us, the religious leaders thought of the Sabbath in terms of what one was not supposed to do. Jesus, however, thought of the Sabbath in terms of relationship. For him, that was the whole point of the Sabbath. It was meant to nurture our relationship with God and with those around us, particularly those in need.

🌀 What does it mean to you to keep holy the Sabbath?

🌀 What is the song of joy you to offer to God for his help in your life? Specifically in leading the dismissal sessions?

🌀 What will you do to prepare yourself to enter the season of Lent ?

Catechist's Guide

Objectives

▷ To contemplate the ways God invites us to keep holy the Sabbath.

▷ To come to know the freedom Jesus extends to us to hold out his Word of life to others.

▷ To cherish Jesus as the Lord of all in whom neither death nor the law have power over.

Dismissal and Procession

Following the homily, the priest celebrant picks up the Lectionary and invites the catechumens to come forward with the catechist(s) who will lead today's dismissal session. Holding the Lectionary so that all can see, the priest celebrant sends the catechumens and catechist(s) forward using RCIA, 67, his own words, or the following:

> **Priest:** Dear friends, you have heard the Word of God proclaimed; we now send you forth to another place where you may reflect on these Scriptures. We pray that you will come to know the abundance of God's grace in our world and that you will come to yearn for the blessings that await you around the Lord's table. Go now in the peace of Christ.

All process to where the dismissal session will take place. The catechist holds the Lectionary in a reverent manner. The assembly may sing an acclamation to accompany the procession.

Centering

Upon reaching the place where the dismissal occurs, place the Lectionary on the ambo, lectern, or other dignified place (or hold the book reverently). Light the candle that is in the place of gathering and reread Mark 2:23–28 or Mark 2:23—3:6 in order to refocus the group's attention. Consider singing the Responsorial Psalm or have a recording of it available to use as part of the centering, either before or after the reading.

Reflection and Discussion

The following "script" may be used or adapted to help facilitate discussion on today's readings. Begin the discussion by asking the catechumens if any words or phrases from today's readings spoke to them.

We work. We play. We deal with our finances. We raise children. We care for sick relatives. We go to school. We participate in Church activities. We resolve family arguments and disagreements among friends. We worship. We pray. We set aside time on Saturday or Sunday to celebrate the Liturgy of the Word with the community of friends who gathers together as Church in this particular place. We seek to grow in our relationship with God. We are holy, as is everything God has created. Today's readings invite us to honor this holiness.

🌀 How do you keep holy the Sabbath?

🌀 How do you observe the holiness of each day?

Sometimes our legalistic interpretation of the law, even religious laws, get in the way of our recognition of the holiness of the day of worship, the Sabbath, or the Sunday on which we gather to do God's work in the liturgy. Jesus, the Son of Man, shows us in the Gospel reading how he is indeed Lord over all, even over the Sabbath, even over the day we set aside for worship. He is the Lord of life. He never ceases to bring life to others, even on a day of rest, despite the Pharisees who wanted to hold the law against him.

- What can you do to bring life to others on the day you worship with the Christian community?

- When do you have a tendency to interpret rules or principles too strictly rather than extend life to others?

- When have you experienced others' overly literal interpretation of the rules to be death dealing rather than life giving to you?

In the Second Reading, from 2 Corinthians, St. Paul focuses us on the amazing treasure we have in God's power. We might be afflicted or confused. We might suffer, and others might persecute us for our faith. But God never abandons us. In Jesus, who himself experienced suffering and death in the fullness of his humanity, we have a Savior who extends life to us. He frees us. His life lives in us.

- How would you describe this amazing treasure of life we have in God's power in Jesus Christ?

- In your journey as a catechumen so far, how have you grown in your experience of the freedom and life of Jesus?

Jesus acted out of love in healing the man with a withered hand. His disciples who picked heads of grain in order to feed others acted too despite the fact that work was not permitted on the Sabbath. Through their actions they intended to bring life to others. The Pharisees, so mortified by what they said and did, chose to garner support from the Herodians to plot again Jesus. Most of us will not need to face death or extreme persecution for our faith, but we will experience challenges because of what we believe.

- What types of challenges or struggles have already occurred for you on your faith journey?

- How have they affected your relationship with God in Jesus Christ? What questions have they raised for you?

As people of faith, ours is a song of joy to God, who helps us and who accompanies us on each holy day. The psalm speaks of finding a melody that is ours to sing and of playing instruments that reflect joy for all that God has done for us. God led the people of Israel forth from bondage in Egypt, and God continues to free us today.

- What would be some of the text in your song of joy to the Lord?

- What instruments would accompany your song?

- How does the music in the liturgy help you to grow closer to the Lord? To know God's power to overcome death and bring life?

Wrapping It Up   *Consider these points to conclude the dismissal. Integrate the thoughts and ideas that surfaced during the discussion.*

- Jesus' mission is to show us how to do good rather than evil, and to save life rather than destroy it. As his disciples, it is the mission to which he also calls us.

- There are times when we will not carry out the mission to which God calls us. We will sin. We will act in ways that hurt our relationships with others and with God. Yet as the psalm reminds us, we can still sing with joy to God because God is our help.

- As part of our spiritual practice, it is important that we reflect on how we do, in fact, keep holy the Sabbath. How we honor the Lord's Day on Sundays and throughout the week, for every day is holy in God's eyes. Every day is ours to be a Sabbath disciple.

Closing Prayer

Conclude with prayer. If time permits, sing the psalm refrain a few times before or after the following prayer.

Lord of all,
you command us to keep holy the Sabbath day.
Through Jesus you freed us to go beyond the laws of this holy day
to embrace the mission of your Son
and to bring life and nourishment and healing to your people.
Place your song of joy on our lips as we draw closer to our initiation,
for we live in confidence that Resurrection life is ours.
Through Christ our Lord.
Amen.

Readings for the Next Dismissal

Provide catechumens with a list of the readings for the next dismissal session. Consult the liturgical calendar on page xvi to find out what day will be observed next week. Give catechumens the questions below to guide their reflection through the week.

⑥ What connections are you seeing in the readings of this liturgical season? As you pray with the readings, around what themes do your thoughts seem to be coming together?

⑥ Where do the readings intersect with your journey of faith? What questions do they raise for you?

Extended Catechesis

Based on today's readings and liturgical observance, the following topics may be covered for extended catechesis:

※ Keeping holy the Sabbath

※ Commandments

※ Freedom in the Law through Jesus

※ Sunday Mass

※ Jesus conquers death and brings life

※ Holy work

※ The Lord is Lord of all creation

※ Mass and mission

TENTH SUNDAY IN ORDINARY TIME

Focus: To have hope in the midst of chaos.

Lectionary #89B

Catechist's Preparation

Overview of the Sunday

Faith in the Risen Lord sustained Paul. It compelled him to speak of hope and grace. It encouraged him in the midst of his transitory, earthly life. We, too, believe our eternal and lasting home is in God. This is the Easter promise to which we look forward in the coming days. Confusion about Jesus' identity might fill the world's people as it did the scribes who think Beelzebul possesses Jesus in the Gospel reading. Confusion might fill us as it did the man and woman as they passed responsibility for evil off to the serpent in the First Reading, from Genesis. Despite the chaos that inevitably enters our human lives, our hope lies in belonging to Jesus by doing God's will.

Scripture Background

Genesis 3:9–15 The first eleven chapters of Genesis contain two creation stories. Ancient peoples often dealt with abstract concepts through story. Who are we and where did we come from? Who is God? Why are there problems in the world? These are some of the questions answered in the two creation stories, stories that were handed down from one generation to another through a strong oral tradition. The events and people are symbolic of the broad questions of humanity.

In addition, these first chapters of Genesis are similar to a number of ancient stories from other cultures, stories that also attempt to answer the questions of where and how we began, such as the Babylonian stories of Enuma Elish and Gilgamesh, the stories of Etana and Adapa, the myth of Baal. In contrast to these stories, however, Genesis introduces one God, a creator and sustainer, with whom it is possible to have an intimate relationship.

The reading for this Sunday is part of the second creation story. At the heart of this section are the questions: Why is there evil in the world? How did it get here? It is clear that Adam and Eve had a choice; they were not manipulated by the serpent. Their immediate response to God's query was to blame each other. Adam and Eve misused God's gift and are guilty and ashamed. Verse 15 verifies the consequences of the first parents' choice of personal desire over God's will: disharmony and conflict. The punishment of the serpent (not necessarily the devil) has been interpreted by Christians to mean the triumph of good over evil in the person of Jesus. But it can

be translated literally as the disdain of all her offspring for snakes.

Psalm 130:1-2, 3-4, 5-6, 7-8 (7bc) Psalm 130 is a lament. Laments are different from psalms of petition because they often cry out to God in frustration and desperation. These complaining psalms reveal intimacy with God as a very human response to suffering or adversity. The psalmist acknowledges personal sin and yet is confident that God who has taken care of things in the past will do so again. Imagine the first parents pleading this psalm. Psalm 130 is a personal rather than a community psalm. Yet the community enters in because the psalmist witnesses to the community that God will indeed "hear my voice!" (130:1b) The psalmist trusts that there is nothing God will not forgive (see 130:4), and with God there is "plenteous redemption" (130:7). The psalm reflects the cry of humanity after the devastation of sin and evil.

2 Corinthians 4:13—5:1 In this passage from Paul's letter, it is again clear what sustained Paul. He had a faith that carried him through every difficulty and, in fact, impelled him into dangerous situations by his need to proclaim his faith in Jesus Christ. To explain himself, he quoted from Psalm 116:10, "I believed, and so I spoke."

Contrary to the beliefs of his Greek contemporaries, Paul did not believe in the duality of human nature. He did not believe that the body was the evil jailer of the soul. Rather, Paul called for an appreciation of the body as created and blessed by God, and as raised from the dead in Jesus Christ. Paul believed that with body and soul he would one day experience and enjoy an eternal resurrection with his Savior. And it is that vision that sustains him in all things.

Mark 3:20-35 The reading from Mark could reflect a personal low point in Jesus' ministry. Instead Jesus uses it as a starting point for a message on relationships.

Mark uses a parallel structure to draw together and relate two or more topics. Beginning (see 3:20–21) and ending (see 3:3–35) with reflections on family and familial ties, Mark explores the question of Jesus' authority in the middle verses.

In verse 21 *hoi par' autou*, literally, "those around him," can mean "family" or "neighbors" or even "friends." These people come to take Jesus away. They think he is out of his mind. They cannot understand or accept him any more than his enemies. Maybe he is even possessed. Why else would he abandon the security of a good trade in their village to go about preaching a message that only brings abuse and ridicule?

In contrast, the scribes took the message of Jesus to heart and conscience. To deflect the truth of his words, they accuse him of being possessed by Beelzebub and of acting by the power of evil. Jesus refutes their accusations with supreme logic: If Jesus' power was from Satan, why would he undermine Satan's power by driving out demons?

Jesus concludes his lesson to the scribes with a teaching about the one unforgivable sin, the sin against the Holy Spirit. How does Mark interpret that sin? He returns to the context of the scribes' accusation. By accusing Jesus of demonic possession, they deny the presence of the Holy Spirit and the reign of God in Jesus. Mark sees this sin as perpetuating a habitual refusal to accept Jesus, a refusal that ultimately perverts the mind and heart until they cannot recognize Jesus and the reign of God. And so there is no wish for forgiveness.

Returning to the earlier familial references, Mark concludes this chapter with a final word about the acceptance of Jesus. Acceptance of Jesus and all that this entails, entitles one to a relationship that takes precedence over relationship by blood. That is a promise of hope in the midst of chaos.

Reflection Questions for the Catechist

- When have you chosen evil instead of good and had difficulty taking responsibility for your actions?
- How does the spirit of faith compel you to speak hope in the midst of chaos?
- How will you as a dismissal catechist assist the catechumens in the coming weeks of Ordinary Time to accept their identity as "relatives" of Jesus (Mark 3:21)?

Catechist's Guide

Objectives

- ▷ To accept that belonging to God's family involves doing God's will and following the example Jesus set for his disciples.
- ▷ To grasp the meaning of Christian hope in the midst of chaos.
- ▷ To examine how the spirit of hope makes God's mercy transparent in the face of evil and sin.

Dismissal and Procession

Following the homily, the priest celebrant picks up the Lectionary and invites the catechumens to come forward with the catechist(s) who will lead today's dismissal session. Holding the Lectionary so that all can see, the priest celebrant sends the catechumens and catechist(s) forward using RCIA, 67, his own words, or the following:

PRIEST: **My dear friends, you have heard the Word of God proclaimed; we now send you forth to another place where you may reflect on these Scriptures. We pray that you will come to know the abundance of God's grace in our world, and that you will come to yearn for the blessings that await you around the Lord's table. Go now in the peace of Christ.**

All process to where the dismissal session will take place. The catechist holds the Lectionary in a reverent manner. The assembly may sing an acclamation to accompany the procession.

Centering

Upon reaching the place where the dismissal occurs, place the Lectionary on the ambo, lectern, or other dignified place (or hold the book reverently). Light the candle that is in the place of gathering and reread Mark 3:20–35 in order to refocus the group's attention. Consider singing the Responsorial Psalm or have a recording of it available to use as part of the centering, either before or after the reading.

Reflection and Discussion

The following "script" may be used or adapted to help facilitate discussion on today's readings. Begin the discussion by asking the catechumens if any words or phrases from today's readings spoke to them.

Adam blames the woman. The woman blames the serpent. No one wants to take responsibility for the sin committed. This is human nature, is it not? It is humbling when we have to admit our wrongdoing. It is humbling to face the consequences of unhealthy choices we make. These choices can throw our lives and the lives of those around us into chaos. The serpent certainly experienced chaos as part of God's punishment as the serpent now must slither along, belly to the ground, cut off from humanity.

 ⑥ What is an occasion when you did not want to take responsibility for your sinful choice?

 ⑥ What were you afraid might happen if you were to take responsibility?

 ⑥ Where was God in your experience?

We believe that in his Death and Resurrection Jesus brings the end to evil. We know this is the truth of faith evidenced in the Gospel. Today's Gospel reading begins with the utter chaos of crowds making it impossible for Jesus and his disciples to eat. There was so much going on around them. They had done so much good. They had preached a life-giving word. They had healed people. They had left people astonished and amazed. Yet the chaos led his relatives to think he was "out of his mind" (Mark 3:21) and scribes to think he was possessed by the prince of demons. Jesus' relatives and the scribes appeared afraid of him and wanted to control him, to put him down.

 ⑥ When have you been afraid of the power of Jesus to bring life and healing to you in those areas of your life that needed to be healed?

Change is never easy. Our human nature would rather control things and keep things the same, to endure the status quo rather than risk newness. Perhaps it was newness that the relatives and scribes feared. Jesus was doing something new. He was bringing hope into the midst of a chaotic world.

 ⑥ How do you respond to change?

 ⑥ How have you changed throughout your faith journey in the initiation process so far?

 ⑥ What have been sources of hope for you in the midst of the faith changes you have experienced?

By the end of the Gospel reading, Jesus has taught us that his relatives are those who do the will of God. His relatives stand as a house united in God with a clean spirit. They do not blaspheme against the Holy Spirit. They stand for life in the face of authorities who stand for sin and death.

 ⑥ What does it mean to do the will of God?

 ⑥ What are some ways you can discern or perceive God's will for you?

 ⑥ How does participating in the Sunday liturgy and in the community of faith help you to know God's desire for your life?

Once Paul experienced his conversion to Jesus Christ, he remained steadfast in his faith. He struggled and he faced persecution. Yet he never wavered in his proclamation of the Gospel. The spirit of faith he possessed empowered him to speak the truth that we who believe will be raised with Jesus and live in God's presence forever. Hope in the midst of the chaos of suffering remained with Paul. He knew there was something beyond this transitory earthly life.

⑨ What is it like to have the spirit of faith inside of you?

⑨ How does the spirit of faith empower you to hold onto hope in the face of suffering and not to despair?

⑨ Who has spoken hope in Jesus Christ to you on your faith journey?

⑨ How is God calling you to speak hope to others?

Wrapping It Up

Consider these points to conclude the dismissal. Integrate the thoughts and ideas that surfaced during the discussion.

- God's mercy prevails in the face of sin. From this our hope arises. Our belief in the Resurrection of Jesus is also a belief that one day God will raise us up with Jesus. Sin will no longer hold sway over us. Ours, too, is the victory of Resurrection. Each time we experience God's mercy, our hope in the Resurrection is reaffirmed.

- Belonging to God's family entails doing God's will. When we live as Jesus' disciples, we acknowledge the choices we make to follow him. To us belongs the challenge to be consciously aware of how God calls us to act in each and every situation we face. This is the demanding work of discernment.

Closing Prayer

Conclude with prayer. If time permits, sing the psalm refrain a few times before or after the following prayer.

> God of mercy and hope,
> you punished the serpent for its evil choice,
> yet still brought hope in the midst of chaos through your mercy and salvation.
> Give us the spirit of faith that leads us to hope in your forgiveness.
> Encourage us to do your will,
> for you intensely desire us to belong to your family.
> Through Christ our Lord.
> Amen.

Readings for the Next Dismissal

Provide catechumens with a list of the readings for the next dismissal session. Consult the liturgical calendar on page xvi to find out what day will be observed next week. Give catechumens the questions below to guide their reflection through the week.

⑨ What connections are you seeing in the readings of this liturgical season? As you pray with the readings, around what themes do your thoughts seem to be coming together?

⑨ Where do the readings intersect with your journey of faith? What questions do they raise for you?

Extended Catechesis

Based on today's readings and liturgical observance, the following topics may be covered for extended catechesis:

❋ God's mercy

❋ Christian hope

❋ Sin and evil

❋ Blasphemy

❋ God's will

❋ Discernment

❋ Participation in Christ's Resurrection

ELEVENTH SUNDAY IN ORDINARY TIME

Focus: To understand God's life-giving care.

Lectionary #92B

Catechist's Preparation

Overview of the Sunday

God's care for us brings life. Even when we experience our darkest days, as did the Israelites in exile, God remains with us. God's promise forever remains to make withered trees bloom. At times, this promise surpasses our limited human ability to comprehend it, especially when deep and profound suffering impacts us. In the Gospel reading, Jesus speaks in a parable to teach his disciples and us that God cares so immensely for the smallest of seeds—the mustard seed—that the life God gives it causes the seed to burst forth and become the largest of plants. Such is God's tremendous care for us that helps us to blossom forth with a new life that shows forth the Kingdom to others.

Scripture Background

Ezekiel 17:22–24 Believers often tell the story of faith in hindsight. In painful times it may be difficult to see the hand of God. This is true in the story from Ezekiel the prophet. When the Israelites experienced many of their people being taken off into exile by the Babylonians, they were desolate and turned to Egypt rather than to God to be saved. They experienced another destruction of their land and people by Babylon and finally began to realize that it was their unfaithfulness that caused their suffering and loss. The prophet reminded them that God promised never to abandon them. Using the image of a cedar tree, he told them God would save a remnant of the exiles, placing a tender shoot high on the mountain to dwell in majesty. Their God is so powerful that even a withered, lowly, almost dead branch will prosper and bloom.

Psalm 92:2–3, 13–14, 15–16 (see 2a) Birthday greetings often wish people many more years of life. The Responsorial Psalm conveys that image of anticipating the promise of long life like palms and cedars. The symbolic connection of these trees to royalty is found in Ezekiel, 1 Kings, and Isaiah. They convey longevity, loyalty, and strength. The psalm says those who practice justice will bear fruit like these trees, even in old age.

Echoing the tree metaphor of the First Reading, the psalm invites us to join our voices in thanksgiving to God for all he has done. The righteous and just are like trees planted in royal courts, giving witness to the king's splendor. Yet the king is called to serve God's people with the righteousness and justice that the Lord bestows. The steadfast compassion that God so freely gives must be rooted in the king's actions. We, too, are called to bear these same fruits as witness to the justice and peace of God's kingdom on earth in how we act toward the children of God, our brothers and sisters.

2 Corinthians 5:6–10 St. Paul's image of being at home in the body and away from the Lord conveys his acknowledgment that we are not completely united to Christ at the moment; we are separated. Only death will bring us to the fullness of that union and ability to be at home with the Lord. In their earthly time, believers are to walk in faith. Paul uses that often-quoted phrase "we walk by faith, not by sight" (2 Corinthians 5:7). Faith acknowledges our belief here and now even though we do not see. Faith allows us, like the Israelites, to stay rooted in our belief in God and in the covenant as fulfilled in his Son, Jesus Christ. Paul says all will be judged according to the good or evil they have done. Followers of Christ are urged to live their lives well, with courage and confidence, so they will live with Christ for eternity.

Mark 4:26–34 Jesus often used common experiences to help people understand his teachings, and he used images for God and his Kingdom. In the first parable we do not understand how a seed grows and produces, but that is how the reign of God manifests itself. In the second, the Kingdom of God is like the smallest of seeds but becomes so large that birds build nests in the shades of its branches.

Jesus speaks about the Kingdom of God as a way of being or following God's way: if we believe and practice a way of life, then God's reign would look like this. The image helps us understand our role in this. Our work is to proclaim this Kingdom of God by demonstrating through our actions toward God and one another that we are true followers. Like the palm and cedar trees, like the mustard seed and the seed upon the ground, we show the fruits of our belief here on earth in our treatment of one another, in the way we practice justice and peace, and in the way we right our relationships with our sisters and brothers.

Reflection Questions for the Catechist

- Where is God's life-giving care evident in your life?
- How have you seen God's life-giving care present in the lives of the catechumens whose growth in faith you facilitate during the dismissal sessions?
- When in your faith journey have you realized you were walking by faith and not by sight?

Catechist's Guide

Objectives

- ▷ To acknowledge where God's life-giving care is and has been active in our lives.
- ▷ To describe what it is like to let our faith, rather than sight, guide our life journey.
- ▷ To reflect on the many ways we can reveal God's Kingdom to others.

Dismissal and Procession

Following the homily, the priest celebrant picks up the Lectionary and invites the catechumens to come forward with the catechist(s) who will lead today's dismissal session. Holding the Lectionary so that all can see, the priest celebrant sends the catechumens and catechist(s) forward using RCIA, 67, his own words, or the following:

PRIEST: **My dear friends, you have shared with us at the table of God's Word. Now, you go forth to explore the beauty of God's Word that you might be freed to become the beautiful creation God calls you to be. Supported by our prayer and encouraged by our fellowship, go seek together the meaning of God's saving Word. May it sustain you until the day when you can feast with us at the table of his Body and his Blood. Go in peace.**

All process to where the dismissal session will take place. The catechist holds the Lectionary in a reverent manner. The assembly may sing an acclamation to accompany the procession.

Centering

Upon reaching the place where the dismissal occurs, place the Lectionary on the ambo, lectern, or other dignified place (or hold the book reverently). Light the candle that is in the place of gathering and reread Mark 4:26–34 in order to refocus the group's attention. Consider singing the Responsorial Psalm or have a recording of it available to use as part of the centering, either before or after the reading.

Reflection and Discussion

The following "script" may be used or adapted to help facilitate discussion on today's readings. Begin the discussion by asking the catechumens if any words or phrases from today's readings spoke to them.

God lifts up the lowly. God lifts us up when we are in need of God's life-giving care. We all experience times in our lives when we feel like the withered tree. Perhaps we wonder when or if we will bloom again. During these times we might even ask, where is God?

- When has God made you bloom again in life?
- How were you able to remain hopeful that God would indeed act to bring you new life?

In the First Reading, from Ezekiel, we hear God also promise that the high trees will be brought low and the lowly trees will be lifted high. God lives and speaks in and through his people to proclaim a message of new life and hope and goodness.

- What are the "trees" in society that need to be brought low? That need to be lifted high?
- How is God inviting you to help bring forth new life in the world?

Often we do not know the way to bring God's grace and life to the world. We do not know what path lies ahead. St. Paul's words to the Corinthians remind us that we take one step at a time by faith, not by sight. We walk with the courage of faith. We want to serve God and to please him.

🕉 What does it mean to let faith, rather than sight, guide your steps?

🕉 How would you describe the courage of faith that it takes to bring God's life to bear on the world?

We all want to draw closer to the Lord. This is at the heart of the catechumenate journey. This is the lifelong journey of a person of faith. Our life of faith is about deepening our relationship with the Lord and then living out that relationship in the world among friends, family, and strangers. It is about growing the Kingdom of God from its beginning as the smallest of seeds—a mustard seed—into the largest of plants. It is about creating a home for God's people everywhere and tending to his creation.

🕉 How do you work together with God to sow his Kingdom here on earth?

🕉 What actions do you take to enable the seed to grow into a large plant?

🕉 How would you characterize your interaction with God in your endeavor to bring forth the Kingdom?

Christ is the sower of the seed who helps us to realize the Kingdom here and now. His life of teaching and healing revealed God's Word to those who were willing to hear and to act on the Word. His Death and Resurrection made God's Kingdom a reality. We live in the hope that one day we will go home to the Lord, to the Kingdom, to live forever.

While we reside here on earth, ours is the responsibility to hold the hope of the Kingdom out to *all* people, to extend God's life-giving care to them. As God has loved us, so must we love others. Doing so is the work of discipleship, the work of sowing the seeds of the Kingdom. We cannot get around it. This is the hard work and mission of choosing to be a disciple, a follower of Jesus. It is the lesson that the end of today's Gospel reading tells us Jesus would explain to his disciples in private.

🕉 In what areas of your life are you ready to accept the responsibility to build up the Kingdom of God from the smallest of seeds to the largest of plants?

🕉 What spiritual work do you need to do in your own life to understand better God's life-giving care for you?

We speak of making our home in the Lord. We speak of eternally residing in God's Kingdom. We know it is a journey we are on. Yet we speak of the Kingdom of God that is already, and yet to come. We believe the Kingdom of God was present in Jesus. When he returns, the Kingdom's gift of love will be known in all its glory. We will be at home. This home is available to us now. Each day we walk by faith, as St. Paul noted in the Second Reading, we make our home in the Lord. The Lord guides us and cares for us as we take steps into places we have not seen before.

🕉 How has walking by faith helped you to know you are already making your home in the Lord and that the Lord makes a home in you?

Wrapping It Up   *Consider these points to conclude the dismissal. Integrate the thoughts and ideas that surfaced during the discussion.*

- Even when we fail to notice it, God's life abides in us. God never abandons us, even though we might feel like he does, especially in times of intense need, suffering, and loneliness. Yet God is always present, helping us to bloom once again.

- We take the steps of our life's journey in faith. Every step you take in the catechumenate is a step of faith, not sight. How good is God that he strengthens us with the courage of faith to press onward in joy toward him, making our home in him.

- What way will you reveal God's Kingdom to others this week? As disciples, our very lives, the way we live out our faith commitment, makes the Kingdom visible to others. In the sixteenth century, St. Teresa of Avila reminded us that Christ has no other hands and feet now but ours. We lead others to their home in God as they do for us.

Closing Prayer   *Conclude with prayer. If time permits, sing the psalm refrain a few times before or after the following prayer.*

> Compassionate God,
> from the beginning of time you have extended
> your life-giving care to your people.
> Through exile and boundless suffering,
> you showed them how you would never abandon them.
> You sent your Son, Jesus,
> so that we might know your offer of life is available to everyone who walks by faith.
> Accompany us now as we embrace our mission
> to grow your Kingdom into a welcoming home where all can find refuge.
> Through Christ our Lord.
> Amen.

Readings for the Next Dismissal   *Provide catechumens with a list of the readings for the next dismissal session. Consult the liturgical calendar on page xvi to find out what day will be observed next week. Give catechumens the questions below to guide their reflection through the week.*

- What connections are you seeing in the readings of this liturgical season? As you pray with the readings, around what themes do your thoughts seem to be coming together?

- Where do the readings intersect with your journey of faith? What questions do they raise for you?

Extended Catechesis   *Based on today's readings and liturgical observance, the following topics may be covered for extended catechesis:*

- ❋ Parable
- ❋ Faith
- ❋ Kingdom of God—already present, but also yet to come
- ❋ The disciple's role in proclaiming and living the Kingdom of God
- ❋ Making our home in the Lord
- ❋ Relationship between the Kingdom of God and the tree of the Cross
- ❋ Judgment seat of Christ
- ❋ Care for creation
- ❋ To be Christ-like in the world

TWELFTH SUNDAY IN ORDINARY TIME

Focus: To perceive everything in the light of Jesus.

Lectionary #95B

Catechist's Preparation

Overview of the Sunday

The darkness of life's storms can often overwhelm us. Job experienced this in his sea travels. Terror gripped the disciples crossing the Sea of Galilee during the storm. The Lord's words to Job, and Jesus' message to the disciples, point to the power of God in their midst. God in Jesus Christ calms the wind and stills the stormy seas of life. On this Twelfth Sunday of Ordinary Time, the readings lead us to reflect on how faith leads us to perceive the light of Christ in the midst of stormy darkness. The Apostle Paul's words to the Corinthians proclaim to us how Christ's love urges us forward, for Christ makes the old things of sin and death new in his light.

Scripture Background

Job 38:1, 8–11 The Book of Job deals with the mystery of human suffering. Job was a righteous man afflicted with numerous difficulties. His friends told him he suffered because he sinned. These friends represent a traditional, religious point of view: obedience to God brings blessing; disobedience brings suffering. Job vehemently disagreed because he knew he was a good man. He couldn't believe his sin caused him to suffer.

Job turned to God and repeatedly asked why he was afflicted. God does not answer his questions or tell Job that his sins caused his misfortune. Instead, God portrays the great mystery and marvels of the universe. In verses 8–11, the creation of the sea is described as if it were the birth of a baby. The waters that burst forth are controlled by God's activity and word. Like a tender parent, God clothes the sea with clouds and darkness. The tone of God's response to Job is "Can you match divine activity? Can you even understand it? I, God, control the force you fear most, the sea. What do you know about the order of the universe?" The truth is that God's order is more mysterious than Job will ever understand. What Job can understand is that God, not he, is in charge.

Psalm 107:23–24, 25–26, 28–29, 30–31 (1b) The Israelites considered the desert and the sea to be the two most dangerous and mysterious places on earth. They experienced the vastness, power, and overwhelming intensity of the desert and sea and knew that only God could control them.

The psalm response focuses on the experience of sailors who ventured forth from safe shores and encountered a storm. The sailors recognize God's authority when they call out, and God responds by bringing them to a safe harbor. The psalmist invites everyone to praise this loving God, the one who rescues those near drowning.

2 Corinthians 5:14–17 Paul wants the Corinthians to understand what a true Apostle is, because his authority is questioned by some in Corinth. He defines a true Apostle as one who has been transformed by faith in Christ. A true Apostle is someone who lives not for himself, but for Christ. Paul explains, using a creed-like statement, that because "one died for all; therefore, all have died" (2 Corinthians 5:14). Christ's Death enables true Apostles to die to themselves and to live in a completely new way for Christ. Unlike some, who judge with ordinary human understanding, true Apostles have a Christ-like perspective. Believers are not simply improved, they are totally changed. Paul urges the Corinthians to convert and be reborn.

Mark 4:35–41 In the first century, the Sea of Galilee was a boundary between the Jews and the Gentiles. Jesus challenged his followers to cross the sea and enter the unknown territory of the Gentiles. The sea symbolized the fear and doubts the disciples and the early Church must have felt when faced with outreach to the Gentiles. Although Jesus was with them, they felt as if they faced the journey alone. It might have seemed that Jesus was asleep.

In their fear, the disciples cry out and awaken Jesus. They believe Jesus will let them drown. Jesus' words are enough to calm the waters. Like the God of Israel, Jesus has authority over the sea, over chaos, and over the entire world.

Jesus questions the disciples: "Why are you terrified? Do you not yet have faith?" (4:40). The little band in the boat does not understand. They only respond with awe that their teacher has power over the water. For those with faith, this miracle is a clear sign that Jesus is the one from God.

The early Church, like the boat—battered and blown about—will not sink. Jesus will not let any of his followers sink into chaos. With Jesus, we can survive any storm.

Reflection Questions for the Catechist

- When was a stormy time in your life? How was God present in the storm?
- What old things have passed away and become new in your life through Christ?
- How do you see the catechumens growing in their faith in Jesus Christ and coming to know him as the one whom the wind and sea obey?

Catechist's Guide

Objectives

- ▷ To consider how our faith guides us forward in life's stormy times to perceive the light of Christ.
- ▷ To ponder how our relationship with Jesus, like that of the disciples in the Gospel reading, is moving from responding in awe to expressing curiosity about Jesus' authority to recognizing God's power at work in Jesus.
- ▷ To express gratitude to God for his everlasting love in Christ at work in our lives and in the lives of those around us.

Dismissal and Procession

Following the homily, the priest celebrant picks up the Lectionary and invites the catechumens to come forward with the catechist(s) who will lead today's dismissal session. Holding the Lectionary so that all can see, the priest celebrant sends the catechumens and catechist(s) forward using RCIA, 67, his own words, or the following:

PRIEST: **My dear friends, you have shared with us at the table of God's Word. Now, you go forth to explore the beauty of God's Word that you might be freed to become the beautiful creation God calls you to be. Supported by our prayer and encouraged by our fellowship, go seek together the meaning of God's saving Word. May it sustain you until the day when you can feast with us at the table of his Body and his Blood. Go in peace.**

All process to where the dismissal session will take place. The catechist holds the Lectionary in a reverent manner. The assembly may sing an acclamation to accompany the procession.

Centering

Upon reaching the place where the dismissal occurs, place the Lectionary on the ambo, lectern, or other dignified place (or hold the book reverently). Light the candle that is in the place of gathering and reread Job 38:1, 8–11 in order to refocus the group's attention. Consider singing the Responsorial Psalm or have a recording of it available to use as part of the centering, either before or after the reading.

Reflection and Discussion

The following "script" may be used or adapted to help facilitate discussion on today's readings. Begin the discussion by asking the catechumens if any words or phrases from today's readings spoke to them.

No doubt we all can relate to Job and his travels on the stormy seas of life.

- When have you felt overcome by the darkness of a storm in life?

The Lord's words to Job communicate God's power over the darkness. The darkness will never have the final say. The pride of the waves will never win out over God. God stills the waves brought on by life's storms. This might not happen at the time we want nor in the manner we desire, but it will happen. Darkness only covers so much ground in our life and in the world.

- What words has the Lord spoken to you during difficult times in your life?
- How were you able to see that the darkness could only advance so far before the Lord helped you to see light?

In the Gospel reading, Jesus and his disciples encounter stormy seas. The disciples wake Jesus up to express what comes across as their lack of faith, even doubt. Their question expresses their fear that Jesus does not care that they all might die. In the stormy seas of our lives, sometimes we might need to bring that question to Jesus, too.

🌀 What questions have you asked Jesus during difficult times in your life?

🌀 Have there been times when you have felt and thought that he was not with you, when your faith needed to be buoyed up?

The disciples' question to Jesus helps us to see that we need only approach Jesus, to come to him, to draw closer to him. Jesus' immediate response to the disciples' question shows us how real and effective his power is over the storms of life, over our fears, and over what poses danger to us. The power of the Word living and active in Jesus is the power present in our lives.

🌀 How has Jesus calmed a storm in your life?

🌀 What did Jesus' words and actions to calm that storm reveal to you about who he is?

🌀 How did it deepen your faith? Your understanding of who he is?

God in Jesus Christ is Lord of all creation. Like the disciples, we might respond in awe to Jesus. We might be curious about his identity, his presence in our lives. This is what our faith journey is about. Faith is not something tangible we receive only once. Rather, we grow in faith through our experiences in life. Jesus accompanies us in this journey. What might seem as a rebuke of the disciples for not yet having faith is really a question about coming to know who Jesus is. Jesus wants to know why they are terrified. He desires that they come to know his power and authority. He wants his disciples to perceive the light of the newness and life in him.

🌀 When do you find yourself wanting to know more about who Jesus is? What questions to do have about him?

In the Second Reading, St. Paul teaches the Corinthians that the love of Christ is what pushes us forward. We believe that Christ died for all. When we believe this, we truly live not for ourselves but for others so that they, too, might know the light of Christ triumphs over darkness. When we believe that Christ died for all, we are a new creation. What is new wins victory over old. Joy replaces sadness. Hope reigns. Love always defeats hate.

🌀 What new things have come in your life because of Christ's love and triumph over death?

🌀 How do you live for others so that they might know love?

Wrapping It Up

Consider these points to conclude the dismissal. Integrate the thoughts and ideas that surfaced during the discussion.

- Wherever your faith is when a challenging time arises in your life, if you need to express frustration as Job did or fear as the disciples did, God still remains with you leading you to overcome darkness through the light of Christ.

- Our understanding of Jesus Christ never solidifies itself once and for all. We are always growing in our relationship with him. Our awe in his love persists, yet our discipleship requires that we also develop a deep understanding of him as the Son of God.

- We go forth this week, as we always do, wrapped in the love of God in Jesus Christ. Consider various ways during the week you might express your praise and gratitude for this love and share Christ's love with others.

Closing Prayer

Conclude with prayer. If time permits, sing the psalm refrain a few times before or after the following prayer.

Loving God,
you companion us on the stormy seas of life as you did Job and the disciples.
Accompany us as we seek to find our peace in you in the midst of struggle.
Changed by the power of Jesus and arriving on solid ground at the shore,
strengthen us to companion others
with the love of your Son, Jesus Christ our Lord.
Who lives and reigns for ever and ever.
Amen.

Readings for the Next Dismissal

Provide catechumens with a list of the readings for the next dismissal session. Consult the liturgical calendar on page xvi to find out what day will be observed next week. Give catechumens the questions below to guide their reflection through the week.

- What connections are you seeing in the readings of this liturgical season? As you pray with the readings, around what themes do your thoughts seem to be coming together?

- Where do the readings intersect with your journey of faith? What questions do they raise for you?

Extended Catechesis

Based on today's readings and liturgical observance, the following topics may be covered for extended catechesis:

- ☀ Power of God in Jesus overcomes darkness

- ☀ Seeing, acknowledging, and responding the authority of Jesus

- ☀ Love of Christ

- ☀ Gratitude for God's love

- ☀ Becoming a new creation in Christ

- ☀ Faith in times of struggle

- ☀ Becoming a new creation in Baptism

THIRTEENTH SUNDAY IN ORDINARY TIME

Focus: To have faith in God's care.

Lectionary #98B

Catechist's Preparation

Overview of the Sunday

The readings during this part of Ordinary Time proclaim to us in so many ways God's care and love for us. The First Reading, from Wisdom, communicates that God is the author of justice and life, not evil and death. God gives us the possibility of living eternally. Jesus' two healings in the Gospel provide a strong affirmation of God's desire that we share in divine life. We are only to believe to have faith, in the God of Jesus Christ, and to be able to reach out to him in trust as the woman with a hemorrhage does. Paul's words in the Second Reading show us that faith involves knowledge of Jesus Christ but also the embodiment of his gracious act of love to others so others might share in the abundance we have.

Scripture Background

Wisdom 1:13–15; 2:23–24 The Book of Wisdom, written approximately one hundred years before the birth of Jesus, may well have been the last Old Testament book written. This passage combines insights from both Jewish and Greek thought, affirming that all humans are created for immortality because we are all created in the image and likeness of God. By reinterpreting Genesis 3, the author asserts that God created us for eternal life. Death entered the world through the serpent, who is equated with Satan. Those who cooperate and live the way God created us will never die, despite the ravages of physical death. Those who do not live in this manner will not experience eternal life. The author, in the tradition of Wisdom literature, is presenting us with a choice: eternal life or everlasting death. We trust in God and pray that God helps us to choose rightly.

Psalm 30:2, 4, 5–6, 11, 12, 13 (2a) Psalm 30 is a song of praise and thanksgiving to God, who has rescued the psalmist from some horrendous fate, comparable to going down to the netherworld or the pit of death. God is a God of life who desires not death but life. Calling upon and trusting in the Lord results in reliable deliverance by God. Having experienced God's deliverance, the psalmist invites the whole community to praise and thank, whose good will lasts a lifetime. God acts on our behalf to change our weeping into rejoicing and our mourning into dancing. God is ever gracious and reliable, ready to answer whenever we call. Praise and thanksgiving to God are always appropriate and fitting.

2 Corinthians 8:7, 9, 13–15 Paul encourages the Christian community in Corinth to share with others their material abundance. He praises them for excelling in following Christ, and for the many gifts they have received through the Spirit. Other communities are in need, and Paul asks the Corinthians to share so that all may have life's necessities. Paul exhorts the Corinthians to imitate Jesus, who, as God, was rich beyond all measure yet chose to become poor, to become human, for their sake. So, too, they are to share their riches with others in need, thus being true imitators of Jesus. Those helped would, in return, be motivated to share whatever riches they possess. In this fashion all would experience the graciousness of God, richly expressed in Christ Jesus.

Mark 5:21–43 or 5:21–24, 35b–43 This passage speaks of faith in God, which enables us to cross boundaries and reach out to one another. In doing this, we become living witnesses to God's compassion and healing touch. Mark's Jesus confronts the powers of evil, sickness, and death, while affirming life. In sandwiching one healing event within another, Jesus highlights the essence of discipleship. The request by Jairus, a synagogue official, that Jesus come to heal his daughter surrounds the healing of the hemorrhaging woman. The woman, long afflicted with hemorrhages, dares to reach out and touch Jesus in public, without his knowledge or consent. In so doing, she violates both social custom and religious purity laws. Yet, her trust in God and in Jesus' healing powers emboldens her to act. Jesus, deeply touched by her faith, restores her to community life by calling her "daughter" (5:23) and sends her on her way both healed and at peace.

As Jesus continues on to Jairus' home, news of the daughter's death reaches them. Jesus counsels Jairus not to fear but to have faith. In the midst of the crowd's ridicule and doubt, Jesus approaches the dead girl and touches her, calling her to rise. Jesus breaks both social custom and ritual purity laws by touching the dead body of a woman he does not know. This daughter of God is brought to life by Jesus, and he encourages her parents to give her something to eat. Jairus and the hemorrhaging woman call us to have faith in God's life-giving touch. Like Jesus, disciples are called to cross boundaries so that God's healing touch assickness, and the powers of evil, to God and the life-giving support of family and community.

173

Reflection Questions for the Catechist

- When was a time you had to consciously remind yourself that God has nothing to do with sin and death, but God made you to experience life?
- How does Jesus' gracious act of becoming poor through Death on the Cross lead you to reach out to others with gracious acts of your own?
- Where have you experienced the healing touch of Jesus in your life?
- Where have you witnessed Jesus healing the catechumens with whom you reflect on the Scriptures?

Catechist's Guide

Objectives

- ▷ To deepen our faith in God's loving care of us as the author of life, not death.
- ▷ To contemplate those times when we have approached Jesus in faith for healing.
- ▷ To consider the relationship between Jesus' gracious act of suffering and death that led to new life and how our faith compels us to give out of abundance to meet others' needs.

Dismissal and Procession

Following the homily, the priest celebrant picks up the Lectionary and invites the catechumens to come forward with the catechist(s) who will lead today's dismissal session. Holding the Lectionary so that all can see, the priest celebrant sends the catechumens and catechist(s) forward using RCIA, 67, his own words, or the following:

PRIEST: **My dear friends, you have shared with us at the table of God's Word. Now, you go forth to explore the beauty of God's Word that you might be freed to become the beautiful creation God calls you to be. Supported by our prayer and encouraged by our fellowship, go seek together the meaning of God's saving Word. May it sustain you until the day when you can feast with us at the table of his Body and his Blood. Go in peace.**

All process to where the dismissal session will take place. The catechist holds the Lectionary in a reverent manner. The assembly may sing an acclamation to accompany the procession.

Centering

Upon reaching the place where the dismissal occurs, place the Lectionary on the ambo, lectern, or other dignified place (or hold the book reverently). Light the candle that is in the place of gathering and reread Mark 5:21–24, 35b–43 in order to refocus the group's attention. Consider singing the Responsorial Psalm or have a recording of it available to use as part of the centering, either before or after the reading.

Reflection and Discussion

The following "script" may be used or adapted to help facilitate discussion on today's readings. Begin the discussion by asking the catechumens if any words or phrases from today's readings spoke to them.

Jairus had faith in the healing and life-giving power of Jesus. The woman who suffered for twelve years from hemorrhages had faith that if she would touch Jesus' clothes, his healing power would cure her. They came to Jesus. They trusted in him and in God's power active in him.

- When have you approached Jesus in faith, trusting in his life-giving power?
- How did Jesus respond?

Jesus addresses the woman with the personal, relational, and familial term "daughter" (Mark 5:23) and tells her that her faith has saved her. He encourages Jairus, the synagogue official, to not be afraid, but to have faith.

⑨ What does it mean to you to have faith?

Both of Jesus' healings were personal. In the case of Jairus' daughter, no one accompanied Jesus into Jairus' home except a few disciples. People inside the house mocked Jesus when he told them Jairus' daughter was only asleep, not dead. Jesus sent those who ridiculed him out of the house but went to heal the child accompanied by her parents and the few disciples. He grasped the child's hand and commanded her to arise.

⑨ How have you come to experience Jesus' healing in a personal way?

⑨ Have others ridiculed you for your faith in his healing power?

God's life-giving power exists in all its fullness in Jesus Christ. The First Reading from Wisdom, communicates how God created us to be imperishable. We are made in the image of God's own nature. Life is ours. God created us to share in divine life. Yet evil and death are part of our world. They do not come from God. Jesus Christ has overcome them in his own Death and Resurrection.

⑨ How do you see yourself and others as created in the image of God?

⑨ How do you share in God's life?

St. Paul speaks about the "gracious act" (2 Corinthians 8:6) of Jesus Christ in the Second Reading. This "gracious act" is Christ humbling himself to accept Death on a Cross and, through the power of God, overcoming death in the Resurrection. What love Christ has for us! What grace he freely offers to us! What abundance is ours when we see what God has done for us in Jesus Christ.

⑨ What is it like for you to share in God's abundant life-giving care in Jesus Christ?

⑨ Where do you experience the abundance of grace most?

Often we are astonished by the way God acts in Jesus Christ in our lives. In the Gospel, Jesus instructs the woman he healed from hemorrhages to go forth in peace. He strictly orders those who witness the healing of Jairus' daughter not to let anyone else know what had happened, but to feed the girl.

⑨ How does Jesus' healing grace bring your peace?

⑨ What is your response to the abundance of life you receive from him?

⑨ How do you nourish others as a response to Jesus' loving care for you?

The abundance we have is ours to share. Paul tells us it is a "matter of equality" (2 Corinthians 8:13). Out of what we have, we should take care of others' needs and their abundance should help meet our needs.

⑨ How have you seen the mutual sharing of our abundance at work in the faith community? In the world?

⑨ What challenges does the mutual sharing pose for you? How does it stretch you to broaden and deepen your relationship with Jesus Christ?

Wrapping It Up

Consider these points to conclude the dismissal. Integrate the thoughts and ideas that surfaced during the discussion.

- Be patient with yourself as your deepen your faith in God's loving care for you. Sometimes our life experiences can lead us to mistrust others, even God. God, however, always invites us to experience his life-giving care. Our faith journeys ebb and flow throughout life. Our faith matures.

- Embrace the times when you have approached Jesus for healing or seen others do so. Take time in prayer to ponder the heartfelt nature of your experiences and those of others you know. Jesus' offer of life and care is constant. His loving touch is always available to us.

- God's love in Jesus Christ extends to all people. We have the responsibility to extend a share in our abundance to those who suffer from material lack. In doing so, we make the gracious act of Jesus Christ available to them here and now.

Closing Prayer

Conclude with prayer. If time permits, sing the psalm refrain a few times before or after the following prayer.

Life-giving God,
your care for us is compassionate and personal.
Inspire us to approach your Son in faith as did the woman fraught with hemorrhages.
May our faith lead us to rise anew in Jesus with Jairus' daughter.
May we walk boldly once again in our renewed faith.
Compel us to share with others our material abundance
and the richness of the gracious act of Christ our Lord,
always trusting in our participation in eternal life.
Through Christ our Lord.
Amen.

Readings for the Next Dismissal

Provide catechumens with a list of the readings for the next dismissal session. Consult the liturgical calendar on page xvi to find out what day will be observed next week. Give catechumens the questions below to guide their reflection through the week.

- What connections are you seeing in the readings of this liturgical season? As you pray with the readings, around what themes do your thoughts seem to be coming together?

- Where do the readings intersect with your journey of faith? What questions do they raise for you?

Extended Catechesis

Based on today's readings and liturgical observance, the following topics may be covered for extended catechesis:

- ☀ Eternal life

- ☀ Jesus' gracious act of his life, suffering, Death, and Resurrection

- ☀ Our share in Jesus' Death and Resurrection

- ☀ Sharing our abundance

- ☀ The relationship between faith and salvation

- ☀ Jesus' healing miracles

FOURTEENTH SUNDAY IN ORDINARY TIME

Focus: Who is amazed?

Lectionary #101B

Catechist's Preparation

Overview of the Sunday

The Fourteenth Sunday in Ordinary Time comes near the beginning of summer when amazement at summer's beauty surrounds us. On this Sunday, we hear God call the prophet Ezekiel to proclaim the divine Word to a recalcitrant people. We, like the Israelites, sometimes close our hearts off to God. But one day amazement will fill our hardened hearts because we will know of God's abiding presence. Or, will amazement fill Jesus at the lack of faith he finds in us? Paul knows how sufficient the Lord's grace is for him. May amazement fill us on this Sunday as it did Paul—for God's sufficient grace is truly amazing grace! It is more than enough for us.

Scripture Background

Ezekiel 2:2–5 Nebuchadnezzar, the notorious Babylonian king, sacked Jerusalem in 598 and took the king of Judah, Jehoiachin, captive along with members of the royal family and other important Judeans. The new king of Judah, Zedekiah, whom Nebuchadnezzar had placed on the throne, and the remaining residents of Judah later rebelled against Babylon, but Judah and Jerusalem were ultimately destroyed. During this turbulent period, Ezekiel received his prophetic call.

The Lord spoke to Ezekiel and the spirit entered him, giving him the strength and power to respond to his call. Ezekiel accepts the responsibility of preaching the Word of God to the Israelites at a time when few are interested in listening. The people turned rebellious, and they hardened themselves against God.

God reassures Ezekiel that whether the people listen to him and repent, or reject his message, they will know that God was among them (see 2:5). The rejection of the message does not mean that the message is false. Ezekiel is assured that he is truly God's messenger.

Psalm 123:1–2, 2, 3–4 (2cd) The psalm response stands in contrast to the First Reading. Here the faithful seek God, watching for any gesture that God might make toward them. The tragic events of Israel's past subjected them to human scorn but increased their trust and dependence on God (see 123:3–4).

2 Corinthians 12:7–10 In this section of Paul's letter, he wants to convince the Corinthians that he is the true apostle, in contrast to some "false apostles, deceitful workers" (2 Corinthians 11:13) who have been promoting themselves in the community. To this end, Paul described his trials and tribulations for the sake of the Gospel (see 2 Corinthians 11:23–30) and shared the story of his conversion (see 2 Corinthians 12:1–6).

Paul sees his malady, the mysterious "thorn . . . in the flesh" (12:7), as something that enables him to keep a proper perspective. No one knows what this thorn is. Some scholars speculate that it is a physical disability; others claim it is the persecution he endured as an apostle. Whatever it is, Paul understands it to be a reminder that the good he accomplishes is not due to his efforts but to God. His disability is a window into the power of God, for the weaker Paul is, the more receptive he is to God's strength.

Mark 6:1–6 John the Baptist, the last of the Old Testament prophets, is persecuted for proclaiming an unpopular message. Although Jesus will share the same fate, Jesus is the best example of God's power made perfect in weakness. Jesus' birth, his friendship with outcasts, and his crucifixion were not typical signs of glory. He was not a powerful person in the world's view, yet the power and glory of God were manifested in him.

The reading is a rehearsal of the Passion story. The hometown folks are amazed at Jesus' teaching. The next step would be for them to affirm or deny their faith in him. Are their hearts softened enough by his teaching to accept him? No. They could not grasp the fact that the Messiah seems to be an ordinary person, a carpenter in their neighborhood. Further, they know his relatives well and, presumably, these people were not remarkable in their eyes. Ironically, the people who think they know him fail to recognize him. Like the prophets of old, Jesus, too, will go without acknowledgment of his role in God's plan. At Nazareth the stark reaction of Jesus' neighbors foreshadows his rejection and Death on the Cross.

Reflection Questions for the Catechist

◈ When has God called you to serve as a prophet to someone who was rebellious?

◈ Do you think Jesus has ever been amazed at your lack of faith? Why or why not?

◈ When have you been amazed at Jesus' wisdom and grace?

Catechist's Guide

Objectives

▷ To experience wonder and amazement at how God is at work in our lives.

▷ To respond when God calls us to serve as a prophet.

▷ To know that God's grace is sufficient for us, even when we are weak.

Dismissal and Procession

Following the homily, the priest celebrant picks up the Lectionary and invites the catechumens to come forward with the catechist(s) who will lead today's dismissal session. Holding the Lectionary so that all can see, the priest celebrant sends the catechumens and catechist(s) forward using RCIA, 67, his own words, or the following:

PRIEST: **My dear friends, you have shared with us at the table of God's Word. Now, you go forth to explore the beauty of God's Word that you might be freed to become the beautiful creation God calls you to be. Supported by our prayer and encouraged by our fellowship, go seek together the meaning of God's saving Word. May it sustain you until the day when you can feast with us at the table of his Body and his Blood. Go in peace.**

All process to where the dismissal session will take place. The catechist holds the Lectionary in a reverent manner. The assembly may sing an acclamation to accompany the procession.

Centering

Upon reaching the place where the dismissal occurs, place the Lectionary on the ambo, lectern, or other dignified place (or hold the book reverently). Light the candle that is in the place of gathering and reread Mark 6:1–6 in order to refocus the group's attention. Consider singing the Responsorial Psalm or have a recording of it available to use as part of the centering, either before or after the reading.

Reflection and Discussion

The following "script" may be used or adapted to help facilitate discussion on today's readings. Begin the discussion by asking the catechumens if any words or phrases from today's readings spoke to them.

Jesus taught in the synagogue and many were amazed at his teaching. We participate in the Liturgy of the Word each Sunday. We hear the same teaching his followers heard centuries ago.

◈ What astonishes you about Jesus' teaching? Jesus' wisdom?

◈ What amazes you about the wondrous deeds he performs?

The hometown folks are amazed at Jesus' teaching. The next step would be for them to affirm or deny their faith in him.

◈ Are their hearts softened enough by his teaching to accept him?

The hometown folks' hearts are not softened. They could not grasp the fact that the Messiah seems to be an ordinary person, a carpenter in their neighborhood. Further, they know his relatives well and, presumably, these people were not remarkable in their eyes. Ironically, the people who think they know him fail to recognize him.

◈ Why might people not accept Jesus' teaching?

◕ Why might they not accept him?

◕ Have there been times when you have not accepted Jesus and his Word?

Jesus was in the synagogue of his hometown when he experienced rejection. Rejection often hits close to home. Seemingly not upset by this, Jesus simply moved on to the next town, resigned to the fact that he only was able to cure a few sick people, yet amazed at the absence of faith among the people of his hometown.

◕ Would Jesus be amazed at the lack of faith today? Why? In what situation(s)?

In the First Reading, God sent Ezekiel to instruct people he knew would not listen to God's Word. They were stubborn, obstinate, and recalcitrant. These adjectives all describe the Israelites who had rebelled against God and had chosen to worship other gods. Ezekiel undertook his prophetic calling only to face rejection. The Lord's words at the conclusion of the First Reading remind us, though, that all was not lost for Ezekiel, nor is all lost for us when we speak God's Word to people who are not ready to hear it. The Israelites indeed knew that in Ezekiel a prophet was among them.

◕ When have you spoken or witnessed someone speak God's Word to a stubborn-hearted people?

Serving as a prophet and spreading God's Word is sometimes not an easy calling. It is a vocation to which those who choose to be baptized are called. In Baptism, each son and daughter of God is anointed to live out his or her priestly, prophetic, and kingly mission. St. Paul describes the hardship and persecution he faced as he proclaimed the Gospel. Facing this suffering, Paul approached the Lord asking it to go away. The Lord's response was straightforward: "My grace is sufficient for you" (2 Corinthians 12:9).

◕ What challenges have you faced on your journey toward initiation?

◕ How has the Lord's grace allowed you to move forward?

One thing that Paul's words are not saying to us is that as Christians we are to go out and seek suffering and persecution. In the Gospel, Jesus did not seek out rejection. In other words, we are not "better" Christians because we endure suffering. What Paul's words and example do teach us is that we can rely on God's grace when difficult times come our way or when other people choose to deride us for our faith or simply do not understand us. God's power is wholly active in our weakness. God makes his mercy completely available to us—even when our own hearts are stubborn and unchangeable.

◕ When have you needed to ask for God's mercy because you found your own heart closed to his grace?

◕ What about God's grace leaves you amazed each time you experience it?

Wrapping It Up   *Consider these points to conclude the dismissal. Integrate the thoughts and ideas that surfaced during the discussion.*

- God works in amazing and mysterious ways in each of our lives. Jesus instructs us with his wisdom and works mighty deeds that impact us in amazing ways. Ours is the choice to respond in either negative or positive amazement. Will our faith grow? Or will our faith response be found lacking?

- Ezekiel was no doubt amazed and perhaps even in shock when God called him to be a prophet to a people with hardened hearts. God calls us to be prophets in our families, in our places of work, in our neighborhoods, and in our world. We will experience rebellious people, yet Ezekiel's example shows us that in time everyone will know God has been among his people through us.
- In our weakness is our strength. God's grace will never be found lacking. We might not immediately sense its presence when we face hardships, but Christ's power always dwells with us. How remarkable, astonishing, wonderful, and yes, amazing is this!

Closing Prayer

Conclude with prayer. If time permits, sing the psalm refrain a few times before or after the following prayer.

God of Wisdom,
you called Ezekiel as your prophet to a rebellious people
and instilled in him the confidence to proclaim your merciful Word.
You invite us to announce your amazing Word in the world today.
Though we might experience rejection in own house
and among our own friends and families,
we know that you remain with us.
When we become disheartened by others' response to us,
reassure us with your grace so that our faith might flourish
and others might see in us your love present in Jesus Christ our Lord.
Who lives and reigns with you for ever and ever.
Amen.

Readings for the Next Dismissal

Provide catechumens with a list of the readings for the next dismissal session. Consult the liturgical calendar on page xvi to find out what day will be observed next week. Give catechumens the questions below to guide their reflection through the week.

- What connections are you seeing in the readings of this liturgical season? As you pray with the readings, around what themes do your thoughts seem to be coming together?
- Where do the readings intersect with your journey of faith? What questions do they raise for you?

Extended Catechesis

Based on today's readings and liturgical observance, the following topics may be covered for extended catechesis:

- Grace
- Wisdom
- Prophet
- Anointed for priestly, prophetic, and kingly mission in Baptism
- God's call to proclaim his prophetic Word *today*
- Suffering in faith
- Power of Christ
- God's mercy

FIFTEENTH SUNDAY IN ORDINARY TIME

Focus: To preach regardless of the reception.

Lectionary #104B

Catechist's Preparation

Overview of the Sunday

By his example, Jesus has shown us how to preach prophetic words and offer life to others through healing. We have seen how amazement filled the people who heard him teach and witnessed his healing miracles. By faith, some accepted him. Lacking faith, others—even those in his hometown—rejected him. We hear on this Sunday how leaders bullied the prophet Amos for the words of justice he spoke. God had called Amos from his ordinary life as a shepherd to speak prophetic words. In the Gospel reading, Jesus gives his authority to preach repentance, exorcise demons, and heal the sick to the Twelve. They, too, will experience both acceptance and rejection. In Christ Jesus, they will have everything they need for their mission. Redemption and salvation in Christ is all we need, too, for we belong to God.

Scripture Background

Amos 7:12–15 Around the year 750 BC, Amos, a herdsman from Judah (the Southern Kingdom) who also tended sycamore trees, hears God calling him to prophesy to the Northern Kingdom (Israel) at the royal sanctuary in Bethel. Amos travels to Bethel to proclaim God's judgment on the prosperous north for its failure to act with justice toward the poor. Amaziah, priest of Bethel, banishes him because he has dared to call into question the fidelity of the king and his people to God's covenant in their dealings with the poor and needy. In an attempt to undermine his words of judgment, Amos is accused of profiting from his prophetic vocation. Amos responds by letting Amaziah know that this prophetic task was not his choice but God's. He is not a prophet that can be bought by priests or kings to make religiously or politically convenient pronouncements. Rather, Amos' only loyalty is to God who called him and to the words that God commissioned him to speak to an unjust and oppressive people.

Psalm 85:9–10, 11–12, 13–14 (8) Psalm 85 expresses the longing of a suffering and deprived community for restoration, justice, and peace. Such longing is linked to God's covenant love and fidelity, which the community recalls and seeks to respond to. God is the only one who can help them, and they turn to his promises for assurance and fulfillment. God's covenant qualities—loving-kindness, truth, justice, and peace—are personified to act on behalf of the people and the land, restoring both economic prosperity and communal well-being. Renewed attentiveness to covenant promises focuses the community's hope and anticipates restoration. God will animate those qualities and send them forth to restore the people.

Ephesians 1:3–14 or 1:3–10 This powerful message to the Ephesians is an extended act of praise to God, stressing the Trinitarian nature of God and extolling him for the great love by which we were chosen in Christ "before the foundation of the world" (1:4). In Christ, we were chosen for adoption, for filial relationship with God, "to be holy and without blemish before him" (1:4). God's endless choice and love were manifested through Christ, in whose Blood we are redeemed. That filial relationship, made possible through Christ, makes us privy to God's eternal plan of salvation for all humanity. The promised Holy Spirit, given to all at Baptism, is the "first installment of our inheritance" (4:14) as children of God. All this calls forth from us is blessings and praise of God to be shared with all creation. In Baptism, God gifts us with the Spirit, choosing us to be children and heirs, and empowers us to be living witnesses of Christ. All are chosen by God for love and intimacy. Knowing this, we are called to share that knowledge with others so that all may become aware of God's deep mysterious love and enter deeply into it.

Mark 6:7–13 Mark's account of Jesus sending forth the Twelve two by two emphasizes Jesus' desire to send out his followers to continue his mission. Mark's Jesus has come to announce and bring into being God's reign by confronting the powers of evil in whatever way they manifest themselves. Sickness, death, and possession by demons were all manifestations of the power of evil at work. In sending out his followers, Jesus gives them "authority over unclean spirits" (Mark 6:7), the same mission that he has initiated by his presence among them. In sending them off, Jesus instructs them to let go of things that could prevent them from being effective ministers. To travel light, to trust and depend on others, and to be content with what others offer are all necessary components of mission. Jesus further warns them that rejection will be a component of their ministry experience. When rejection occurs, they are to "shake the dust off [their] feet" (6:11) and move on.

The Twelve go forth, successful in preaching repentance, healing, anointing, and driving out demons. Like them, we are commissioned to reconcile, heal, and drive out evil. When we are faithful to Jesus' guidance and instruction, we become instruments through which God's care and love are actualized in the world. By carrying on the work of proclaiming and activating God's reign, we become living witnesses to Jesus.

Reflection Questions for the Catechist

- What was it like when God called you forth from your everyday life to serve as a dismissal catechist?
- When have you not been welcomed and your words not listened to? When have you been welcomed and your words listened to? Where was God present in those experiences?
- Who accompanies you as you participate in the catechumenate ministry?

Catechist's Guide

Objectives

- ▷ To discern how Jesus sends you out in mission as a catechumen.
- ▷ To recognize the many different ways God calls us to preach a prophetic word to the world.
- ▷ To appreciate the fact that God sends us out in mission not alone, but with one another as his sons and daughters.

Dismissal and Procession

Following the homily, the priest celebrant picks up the Lectionary and invites the catechumens to come forward with the catechist(s) who will lead today's dismissal session. Holding the Lectionary so that all can see, the priest celebrant sends the catechumens and catechist(s) forward using RCIA, 67, his own words, or the following:

PRIEST: **My dear friends, you have shared with us at the table of God's Word. Supported by our prayer and encouraged by our fellowship, go seek together the meaning of God's saving Word. May it sustain you until the day when you can feast with us at the table of his Body and his Blood. Go in peace.**

All process to where the dismissal session will take place. The catechist holds the Lectionary in a reverent manner. The assembly may sing an acclamation to accompany the procession.

Centering

Upon reaching the place where the dismissal occurs, place the Lectionary on the ambo, lectern, or other dignified place (or hold the book reverently). Light the candle that is in the place of gathering and reread Amos 7:12–15 in order to refocus the group's attention. Consider singing the Responsorial Psalm or have a recording of it available to use as part of the centering, either before or after the reading.

Reflection and Discussion

The following "script" may be used or adapted to help facilitate discussion on today's readings. Begin the discussion by asking the catechumens if any words or phrases from today's readings spoke to them.

The prophet Amos' message challenged the status quo. The Word of the Lord he spoke put unjust kings and rulers on edge. In the First Reading, we hear Amaziah, priest of Bethel, send Amos off from Bethel to Judah because the Lord's vision of justice was incompatible with Amaziah's hold on the people.

- How do the Lord's words of justice and kindness test the status quo of leaders in today's world?
- Have you or someone you know been asked to move on and spread the Lord's Word to someone else?

The prophet Amos did not belong to the ruling class. In response to Amaziah, Amos even tries to disavow his identity as a prophet because he never belonged to the prophetic class. No one from among the prophets made Amos undertake his mission. Rather, God calls Amos from his life as a shepherd to serve as a prophet. Out of this ordinary, day-to-day life God chose Amos to preach his Word. Amos probably thought he was not qualified to be a prophet, yet he accepted God's call. He probably knew the Word he preached would not receive a positive reception from the ruling class.

⑨ From where does God call you to go and preach his prophetic Word?

⑨ How does God's prophetic call make you feel: afraid, concerned, under-qualified, worried about how others will respond to you?

In the Gospel reading, Jesus sends the Twelve out on mission to preach, heal, and exorcise. His directions are practical. They do not need to pack anything, for each of them will only need a walking stick, a pair of sandals, and the tunic on his back. Jesus' Word and authority are sufficient for the journey.

⑨ What have you taken with you on your faith journey as you learn about and reflect on Jesus' Word?

⑨ Have you brought too much? Too little? How have you come to know that Jesus' Word and authority are sufficient?

Jesus offers more practical advice to the Twelve about what to do when people neither welcome nor listen to them. Neither should they ruminate about why they were rejected, nor should they spend more time in that place. The urgency in their mission remains, so they must move on. The message of repentance and the need for healing the sick and exorcising demons was so pressing they must preach the Good News to people in another locale.

⑨ What enables you to press forward after you have experienced rejection?

⑨ Where do you see the urgent need for proclaiming Jesus' message?

Jesus sent the Twelve forth together to companion each other on their mission. God's call to us to preach the Good News is a personal call. We choose individually whether or not to follow Jesus. When we do choose to follow and live out the Good News, we always do so within the context of the Church. Others companion us in faith. Your sponsors companion you in this catechumenate journey. Catechists accompany you. We are not disciples on our own, but together we serve as a community of disciples. We are God's beloved, adopted sons and daughters through Jesus Christ as St. Paul reminds us in the Second Reading.

⑨ Who are some of the people who companion you on your faith journey?

⑨ How are you already companioning others?

⑨ How do you encourage others and receive encouragement to move on when you/ they share the Word but others neither welcome you/them nor listen to you/them?

In Christ and with Christ's Word, we have all we need to lead holy lives. Our destiny is salvation and redemption.

Wrapping It Up

Consider these points to conclude the dismissal. Integrate the thoughts and ideas that surfaced during the discussion.

- It does not matter where we are in our faith journey. Neither does our state in life nor our chosen life's profession matter. Jesus sends us forth in mission from this unique point in time and our unique place in the world to preach repentance and bring life to others.

- The word of salvation in Jesus Christ and redemption through him is the Word we preach. We preach repentance, life, and love. The ways we do this are many and unique to our situation in life. Ours is the responsibility, through prayer and participation in the life of the Church, to discern how God calls us to bring his prophetic word to those we meet.

- We accompany each other as we preach. We buoy each other up in faith when we experience rejection. We share in one another's joys when we see God's prophetic word accepted and acted upon. We celebrate our call to mission in the Church and await the day when we will be strengthened in mission through the sacraments.

Closing Prayer

Conclude with prayer. If time permits, sing the psalm refrain a few times before or after the following prayer.

> Loving God,
> you destined us to be your sons and daughters through Jesus Christ.
> Through the example of your prophet Amos,
> we have come to know the courage it takes to speak
> your prophetic word of justice, humility, and tenderness.
> In Jesus, we have seen the Good News of forgiveness and life
> preached everyone regardless of their response.
> Make us strong through the redemption of your Son
> to proclaim and live the Good News.
> Hold out to us the grace we need to accompany each other
> as you send us forth in mission.
> Through Christ our Lord.
> Amen.

Readings for the Next Dismissal

Provide catechumens with a list of the readings for the next dismissal session. Consult the liturgical calendar on page xvi to find out what day will be observed next week. Give catechumens the questions below to guide their reflection through the week.

🌀 What connections are you seeing in the readings of this liturgical season? As you pray with the readings, around what themes do your thoughts seem to be coming together?

🌀 Where do the readings intersect with your journey of faith? What questions do they raise for you?

Extended Catechesis

Based on today's readings and liturgical observance, the following topics may be covered for extended catechesis:

✷ The mission of a prophet

✷ God's sons and daughters chosen in Christ

✷ Redemption and salvation

✷ The Twelve and their authority

✷ Accepting our mission

✷ Threefold commission received in Baptism: priestly, prophetic, and kingly

SIXTEENTH SUNDAY IN ORDINARY TIME

Focus: To follow the True Shepherd.

Lectionary #107B

Catechist's Preparation

Overview of the Sunday

Jesus shepherds us. He is the righteous shoot of Davidic lineage whom God raised up. His care, compassion, and justice show us how to live. His peace is the message of peace he commissions us to preach. Our mission, like that of the prophet Jeremiah, and the Apostles, is not easy. Jesus never said it would be. Many will come desiring to know what this peace is about and why we find fulfillment in Jesus. Why does this shepherd leave us wanting for nothing? When we follow the True Shepherd, even though he invites us to rest from the demands of our mission with him, he continues to minister to us, teaching us his ways of justice, love, and peace.

Scripture Background

Jeremiah 23:1–6 The Hebrew word for *shepherd* shares a root with the verb "to rule." Kings were called shepherds because their primary responsibility was to manifest care for all and to rule with justice. Jeremiah rants against kings for their failure to care for God's people, resulting in the Exile, which scattered God's people from their land. Jeremiah warns the kings that God will deal with them in the same fashion they dealt with the people. God will then take over the king's responsibilities, restoring the people to the land and ruling them with justice and peace.

Jeremiah then articulates poetically the hope that one day God would "raise up a righteous shoot to David" (23:5). Such a king would rule wisely and justly, and do "right in the land" (23:5). Peace, security, and right relationship would be so evident under this "righteous shoot" (23:5) that they would name him "the LORD, our justice" (23:6). Christians believe that this "righteous shoot" is Jesus (23:5), who perfectly epitomizes God's justice and compassion toward all. Jesus, the Good Shepherd, knows us and cares for us. Should we not listen deeply to his voice?

Psalm 23:1–3, 3–4, 5, 6 (1) Psalm 23 presents the Lord as a shepherd who cares for the sheep. The shepherd leads the sheep to food and water, protects the sheep from enemies, and guides them. The psalmist experiences that same care and concern from God, with a secure space and table in the very sight of his enemies. All this is possible because God's covenant love, God's goodness and loving kindness, follow us at all times. We are thus assured of an everlasting relationship with God.

Nothing could be more secure than to be with the shepherd. In return, we must trust in God. Listening to and being guided by the Lord will always lead to security, harmony, and right relationship with all. For Christians, Jesus is that Good Shepherd who models care and concern for all, and calls us to the same mission.

Ephesians 2:13–18 The author of Ephesians tackles the division that divided the early followers of Christ between Jews and Gentiles who accepted Christ as their Lord and Messiah. Because of their different traditions, teachings, and rituals, Christian Jews lived differently from Christian Gentiles. This division led some Christian Jews to advocate that the only correct way to follow Christ was through the Jewish Torah and rituals. The letter to the Ephesians addresses and corrects this mistaken notion.

The blood of Christ has saved all humanity, restoring unity between God and humanity, as well as between all people. Christ is "our peace," who in his body "broke down the dividing wall of enmity" (2:14). Those who were near, the Jews, and those who were far, the Gentile Ephesians, are united as one in the sacrifice of Christ, who destroyed death and all that divided humanity. Because of Christ, all now have access to God through the power of the Spirit.

Mark 6:30–34 After the Apostles' successful mission to preach and heal, Jesus instructs them to rest away from the ever-present crowd. They set out in a boat to find such a place, but the crowds notice where they are heading. When Jesus and the Apostles arrive, the crowd is there already. Even Jesus and the Apostles they are frustrated in their attempt to find rest, Jesus is moved with pity for crowd and begins "to teach them many things" (6:34). Mark provides this setting to articulate some strongly held beliefs of his community. Jesus is the true shepherd who is not only attuned to the people's needs, but also is willing to sacrifice his own needs for theirs. Unlike the leadership of his day, Jesus leads by instructing the community in the ways of the Lord, as well as providing for their physical needs. This deserted place is Mark's setting for the feeding of the five thousand, another clear manifestation of the shepherd's care for the people. The hope of Jeremiah for a true shepherd is fulfilled for Christians in the person of Christ.

Reflection Questions for the Catechist

- When have you experienced being misled by a "shepherd" you trusted?
- How do you extend Christ's peace to others?
- Where does Jesus lead you to come away with him and rest? How do you rest when you need to in your catechumenate ministry?

Catechist's Guide

Objectives

- ▷ To accept Jesus' invitation to follow him to a place of rest.
- ▷ To discover how the Lord shepherds you in your daily life.
- ▷ To sense the peace of Christ at work in you and in the community of faith in which you participate.

Dismissal and Procession

Following the homily, the priest celebrant picks up the Lectionary and invites the catechumens to come forward with the catechist(s) who will lead today's dismissal session. Holding the Lectionary so that all can see, the priest celebrant sends the catechumens and catechist(s) forward using RCIA, 67, his own words, or the following:

PRIEST: **My dear friends, you have shared with us at the table of God's Word. Supported by our prayer and encouraged by our fellowship, go seek together the meaning of God's saving Word. May it sustain you until the day when you can feast with us at the table of his Body and his Blood. Go in peace.**

All process to where the dismissal session will take place. The catechist holds the Lectionary in a reverent manner. The assembly may sing an acclamation to accompany the procession.

Centering

Upon reaching the place where the dismissal occurs, place the Lectionary on the ambo, lectern, or other dignified place (or hold the book reverently). Light the candle that is in the place of gathering and reread Mark 6:30–34 in order to refocus the group's attention. Consider singing the Responsorial Psalm or have a recording of it available to use as part of the centering, either before or after the reading.

Reflection and Discussion

The following "script" may be used or adapted to help facilitate discussion on today's readings. Begin the discussion by asking the catechumens if any words or phrases from today's readings spoke to them.

We find a twofold message in Jeremiah's prophetic words in the First Reading. He gives a stern warning to those who mislead and do not care for God's people. God will punish those who inflict harm upon his people.

- When have you experienced being misled or not cared for by someone in control?

God's flock (his people) has been scattered to various lands. God promises to gather the flock back together and that their numbers will increase and multiply. From among them, God will raise up shepherds who will truly guide them. And, from among them God will raise "a righteous shoot" (Jeremiah 23:5b) a true shepherd, from David's lineage, to be king. He will be Lord, and he will lead with justice.

- How have you experienced or seen the Lord shepherd with justice?
- How did the Lord shepherd you in your experience of being misled or not cared for? Did you know that the Lord was shepherding you at the time, or are you now able to look back and see how the Lord guided you?

Jesus shepherded the Twelve and then sent them off in mission. In last Sunday's Gospel we heard how Jesus commissioned the Twelve to preach repentance, heal the sick, and exorcise demons. This Sunday, the Twelve return from their adventures and report their experiences to Jesus. Evidently they must have worked hard because Jesus invites them to come away to a deserted place.

🌀 What is the deserted place where you find respite?

People are so hungry for the Good News and to know healing through Jesus that they approach Jesus and the Twelve in huge numbers. The Apostles and Jesus cannot even get a bite to eat, so they try to move on to their deserted place by boat.

🌀 When do you experience desperately wanting and needing rest, but people still surround you?

🌀 What do you do to find your deserted place with the Lord?

The crowds find Jesus on the other shore. Out of compassion, Jesus responds to their needs. He sees how much they desire a true shepherd, so he teaches them his ways of mercy, healing, love, and justice—all that he had previously taught in the synagogues and towns. The text of the Gospel reading does not tell us that the Twelve responded to the crowd at the water's edge. It's as if Jesus was still shepherding them as well, teaching them the importance of balancing rest and extending compassion.

🌀 How does Jesus continue you to teach you when you are drained and exhausted and needing rest?

🌀 What helps you to consciously realize that Jesus is at work in your daily life, shepherding you at work, at home, and at play?

St. Paul's words in the Second Reading convey the truth that Christ is our peace. He preached peace to all people. He destroyed the wall of hate between peoples and the wall of sin between peoples and God, once and for all. In Christ, all is reconciled to God. His peace reaches people far and near.

🌀 What is the peace that Jesus Christ the True Shepherd brings to you? To the Church? To the world?

🌀 How will you bring the peace of Christ to people both far and near to you this week?

🌀 What walls do we build that prevent Christ's peace from spreading throughout the world?

The words of the well-known refrain from Psalm 23 sung as today's Responsorial Psalm communicate to us that the Lord is *your* Shepherd. There is no one the Lord does not shepherd. *You* will want for nothing in the Lord.

🌀 How does your prayer life and the prayer of the Church enable you to recognize the Lord is your Shepherd? To experience the gift of his peace? To fortify you so you can extend this peace to others?

Wrapping It Up   *Consider these points to conclude the dismissal. Integrate the thoughts and ideas that surfaced during the discussion.*

- Our mission never completely stops. Yet there are times when Jesus invites us to rest in him. For some, those times might be daily occurrences, and for others, they might be after a lengthy time of service or a challenging period in life.

- The Lord is our true Shepherd not just on Sundays, and not just when we are consciously at prayer or discussing the Scripture readings, but in every moment of our lives—when we are at work and at play, when we are having a family discussion or trying to discern a new direction for our lives, when we attempt to enact justice in the world. The Lord indeed shepherds us.

- Christ is our peace. He preached peace in his earthly life. It was central to his mission. Now peace is our mission.

Closing Prayer   *Conclude with prayer. If time permits, sing the psalm refrain a few times before or after the following prayer.*

God our Shepherd,
through the prophet Jeremiah's words,
corrupt rulers came to know your justice as the sign of a true shepherd.
You raised up Jesus to shepherd us all in the ways of justice, love, and peace.
Embolden us to continue his mission to the people
throughout the neighborhoods, cities, and countryside of our world
in need of his healing justice and peace.
Through Christ our Lord, the True Shepherd.
Amen.

Readings for the Next Dismissal   *Provide catechumens with a list of the readings for the next dismissal session. Consult the liturgical calendar on page xvi to find out what day will be observed next week. Give catechumens the questions below to guide their reflection through the week.*

- What connections are you seeing in the readings of this liturgical season? As you pray with the readings, around what themes do your thoughts seem to be coming together?

- Where do the readings intersect with your journey of faith? What questions do they raise for you?

Extended Catechesis   *Based on today's readings and liturgical observance, the following topics may be covered for extended catechesis:*

※ The Lord, our Shepherd   ※ Peace of Christ

※ Following the True Shepherd   ※ Resting in the Lord

※ Divine justice   ※ Our mission of justice and peace

SEVENTEENTH SUNDAY IN ORDINARY TIME

Focus: The Lord feeds us.

Lectionary #110B

Catechist's Preparation

Overview of the Sunday

Jesus sends us forth on a mission to preach, heal, and drive out demons. What a difficult and challenging mission this is! We never know whether our mission will be accepted or rejected by others. Whichever response we will encounter, we do know we will need nourishment to continue the journey. God will provide food for us. Elisha's prophetic words in the First Reading attest to the abundance of food that the Lord will give us. The multiplication of loaves and fish in the Gospel reading serves to reaffirm the plenty that is ours in Jesus. Nourished on the food the Son of Man provides, we live by the virtues of the Lord's call Paul enumerates in the Second Reading.

Scripture Background

2 Kings 4:42–44 Elisha, the disciple of Elijah, is a prophet attending to the people and the Lord at the place of worship, the tent made during the Exodus. An offering of twenty barley loaves from the harvest's first fruits, the best of the crop, is offered to the Lord. The bread is to be placed before the Lord and later consumed by those who served at the Lord's tent. Instead of offering it to the Lord, Elisha commands that it be given to the people to eat, most likely because there is famine in the land, and these hundred people need food.

The servant alerts Elisha that the loaves will not be enough for so many people. Elisha insists that the loaves be shared, and that God would make certain that there would be more than enough. Elisha's words become reality when bread is left over after all have been satisfied. This event becomes the prototype for the Gospel feeding stories. Our God knows our needs and works with what is available to provide abundantly for all our needs.

Psalm 145:10–11, 15–16, 17–18 (see 16) The refrain from Psalm 145 highlights the fact that "the hand of the Lord feeds us; he answers all our needs." This praise psalm is replete with reasons for calling upon all people to praise God. Foremost among those reasons is that God is always faithful and can be relied upon whenever anyone calls. All who trust in the Lord never go away empty or unsatisfied, for the Lord feeds us and "answers all our needs" (refrain). God is always openhanded in response to our needs.

The last stanza emphasizes two qualities of God that need remembering and deserve praise. The Lord is just in all things, seeking right relationship with all of creation and providing all that is needed for life. The holiness of the Lord suffuses all of creation and everything that God does. This covenant love is what enables us to trust and call upon God in our need, and what enables God to draw near to all who call. Praise of God is therefore fitting, just, and proper.

Ephesians 4:1–6 Many New Testament letters contain ethical exhortations, practical suggestions for living that flow from the author's theological and doctrinal presentation. Chapters 4 through 6 of Ephesians provide such an ethical exhortation. Given the divisions between Jews and Gentiles that plagued Jesus' early followers, the letter to the Ephesians emphasizes unity and oneness. Through his life and death, Jesus broke down the barriers that divide us, calling all to be one through the power of his Spirit.

To do this well, Ephesians exhorts us to live "with all humility and gentleness, . . . bearing with one another through love" (4:2). Unity is based on the "one body and one Spirit" (4:4) that bonds Jesus' followers. Sharing "one hope, . . . one Lord, one faith, one baptism, one God and Father of all" (4:4-6) should unite us. Our Trinitarian God is one, totally powerful and fully present in us and in all of creation. In imitation of and obedience to God, we strive toward unity and oneness.

John 6:1–15 The Gospel passages for this Sunday and the next four Sundays focus on chapter 6 of John's account of the Gospel, known as the Bread of Life discourse. The miracle of feeding the multitudes is the only one that appears in all four accounts of the Gospel. The accounts are suffused with language that directly relates to the Eucharistic action of Jesus' followers.

John's version is replete with Eucharistic themes that connect back to Moses, Passover, manna, Elisha, and barley loaves. The emphasis throughout is on God's constant desire to provide for all living things. With a large crowd following him, Jesus articulates his desire to feed them, thus offering another sign that communicates his identity and mission.

"Five barley loaves and two fish" (6:5) become signs of God's transforming power among us. Jesus takes charge by directing that people recline as he takes, gives thanks, and personally distributes the bread and the fish till all "had their fill" (6:12). Twelve baskets are left over.

The sign clearly underscores Jesus' identity as the divine one, ever generous, openhanded, and always ready to nourish us. To follow Jesus is to perceive his identity and to understand his mission. In John's account of the Gospel, signs are done so that all may see and believe. In seeing and believing, we become living witnesses to God's transforming power in our lives. We make Jesus' mission our own by loving others as he loved us and by being willing to give of ourselves so that others may be fed.

Reflection Questions for the Catechist

- How does the Lord feed you when you experience hunger as you live out the mission of a disciple?
- How does the Lord invite you to feed others with the abundant food he offers?
- Where do you see members of your faith community offering nourishment to the catechumens in their midst?

Catechist's Guide

Objectives

- ▷ To acknowledge the times when the Lord feeds us.
- ▷ To consider how our hands can feed those in need with the abundant food the Lord provides us.
- ▷ To reflect on how the way Jesus nourishes leads us to understand more deeply who he is.

Dismissal and Procession

Following the homily, the priest celebrant picks up the Lectionary and invites the catechumens to come forward with the catechist(s) who will lead today's dismissal session. Holding the Lectionary so that all can see, the priest celebrant sends the catechumens and catechist(s) forward using RCIA, 67, his own words, or the following:

PRIEST: **My dear friends, you have shared with us at the table of God's Word. Now, you go forth to explore the beauty of God's Word that you might be freed to become the beautiful creation God calls you to be. Supported by our prayer and encouraged by our fellowship, go seek together the meaning of God's saving Word. May it sustain you until the day when you can feast with us at the table of his Body and his Blood. Go in peace.**

All process to where the dismissal session will take place. The catechist holds the Lectionary in a reverent manner. The assembly may sing an acclamation to accompany the procession.

Centering

Upon reaching the place where the dismissal occurs, place the Lectionary on the ambo, lectern, or other dignified place (or hold the book reverently). Light the candle that is in the place of gathering and reread John 6:1–15 in order to refocus the group's attention. Consider singing the Responsorial Psalm or have a recording of it available to use as part of the centering, either before or after the reading.

Reflection and Discussion

The following "script" may be used or adapted to help facilitate discussion on today's readings. Begin the discussion by asking the catechumens if any words or phrases from today's readings spoke to them.

Philip was the pragmatist. He responded to Jesus' question about where they could buy enough food to feed everyone in the large crowd simply stating the fact that it would take two-hundred-days' wages to have enough even to provide a small amount of food to each person. Andrew, on the other hand, also interested in facts, stated that there was a boy who had five loaves of bread and two fish. But, he too, wondered what good those few provisions could do. Andrew, though, must have seen something of a possibility in the boy's food.

🌀 Which disciple do you think you are more like?

Seeing what is possible in a situation that seems impossible is part of what it means to have faith in Jesus, who feeds us. With God, everything is possible. In Jesus, we have food for our faith journey.

🌀 How does Jesus feed you on your faith journey when you are hungry?

Jesus was a conservationist, too. He wanted nothing to go to waste, so he had his disciples collect the leftovers. What abundance Jesus had produced out of the five loaves and two fish! Even his disciples thought something good surely could not come out of the small amount of food they had at the start!

🌀 When have you been amazed at the abundance of food Jesus provides? When have you had more than enough to eat?

The people in the crowd came to know who Jesus was through the multiplication of the loaves and fish. They identified him as "the Prophet, the one who is to come into the world" (John 6:14).

🌀 How does being fed by Jesus help you to understand and testify to who he is?

The story of Elisha and the man from Baal-shalishah with twenty barley loaves is also a story of the abundance with which God feed us. The question of Elisha's servant parallels that of the disciples in the Gospel reading. The servant asks how twenty loaves can feed a hundred people. On Elisha's order, the servant feeds the people, and the Lord proclaims the abundance of leftovers there will be to feed even more people.

🌀 How will you feed others with the abundance you have received from the Lord?

We are fed through God's Word in the Scriptures that we hear proclaimed at each liturgy. You look forward to the day when the Eucharist will nourish you. We all feast now on the abundance of God's grace in Jesus Christ. We are learning to know and follow the Way of the Cross as Jesus' disciples. This is the call we have received. In the passage from Paul's letter to the Ephesians, we hear today God's call in involves living out the virtues of humility, gentleness, patience, and love. When we live these virtues, we nourish other people in faith.

🌀 Which of the virtues is relatively easy for you to live out? Which poses the most difficulty?

🌀 What role does the one body of faith, the community of the Church, play in encouraging you to live these virtues?

As there is one body of Jesus Christ, one Spirit, and one God, there is the one hope of our call to live as disciples. By our words and actions we seek to uphold the unity of the one God and one faith.

🌀 How do your words and actions feed others and witness to the unity of the Body and the Spirit?

Wrapping It Up

Consider these points to conclude the dismissal. Integrate the thoughts and ideas that surfaced during the discussion.

- The Lord will feed us even when we think there is a lack of food. God will provide, and provide abundantly.

- Out of the abundance with which the Lord feeds us, we must decide how we will share the "leftovers." This, too, is part of our mission. As you hunger for the Eucharist, know also that ours is the mission to bring the Eucharist to bear on our life in the world. Receiving Christ's Body and Blood nourishes us to continue our journey of faith.

- Each time Christ feeds us, we come to know who he is at a deeper level. In gratitude and prayer, contemplate how you understand Jesus each time he nourishes you. He truly is the One God promised to send into the world for its salvation.

Closing Prayer

Conclude with prayer. If time permits, sing the psalm refrain a few times before or after the following prayer.

God of abundant food,

you provide for us so that we will never be weary from hunger.

May your food strengthen us to live with humility, gentleness, patience, and love.

May your food sustain as we work to preserve the unity of our faith

and offer the abundance of your grace to those who hunger in the world,

for you are one God and Father of us all in Jesus Christ the Lord,

whose one Spirit abounds throughout all of creation,

and who lives and reigns with you for ever and ever.

Amen.

Readings for the Next Dismissal

Provide catechumens with a list of the readings for the next dismissal session. Consult the liturgical calendar on page xvi to find out what day will be observed next week. Give catechumens the questions below to guide their reflection through the week.

- What connections are you seeing in the readings of this liturgical season? As you pray with the readings, around what themes do your thoughts seem to be coming together?

- Where do the readings intersect with your journey of faith? What questions do they raise for you?

Extended Catechesis

Based on today's readings and liturgical observance, the following topics may be covered for extended catechesis:

- ❋ God's providence
- ❋ Abundance
- ❋ Providing and nourishing others
- ❋ One faith, one Baptism, one God

- ❋ One Spirit
- ❋ One Body in Christ
- ❋ Virtues we espouse when living God's call
- ❋ Jesus, the One God sent into the world

EIGHTEENTH SUNDAY IN ORDINARY TIME

Focus: Jesus is the Bread from heaven, the Bread of Life.

Lectionary #113B

Catechist's Preparation

Overview of the Sunday

Jesus multiplied the loaves and fish and fed thousands. The abundance was so great that there were leftovers a plenty. This Sunday the Scriptures reveal to us that the One who fed others is the Bread of Life, the true bread from heaven that the Lord promised Moses and the Israelites would rain down from above. We will never hunger or thirst if we come to Jesus, the Bread of Life. He is our food now and eternally. In him, Paul reminds us, we are a new creation. Our new righteous and holy selves will live forever in Jesus.

Scripture Background

Exodus 16:2–4, 12–15 God delivers the Hebrew people from slavery in Egypt through their leader, Moses. Despite this, the people complain to Moses and God at every difficulty they encounter in the desert. Each time God responds with a gift. When they complain they have neither bread nor meat, quails cover the ground in the evening, and manna covers the ground like dew in the early morning. "What is it?" (16:15; in Hebrew, *man hu* or "manna"), the people ask, and Moses answers, "It is the bread that the Lord has given you to eat" (16:15). There may be a natural explanation for how the Israelites are fed in the wilderness, but nothing seems to fit the exact description of whatever fell on the ground like "fine flaky substance, as fine as frost" (16:14). When the people gather the "bread from heaven" (16:4), they have as much as they need. Whatever the means God used, the miracles suggest that God provides for the people at every stage on their journey. The answer to "What is it?" is "God's providence." Even so, the people continue to ask, "Is the Lord among us or not?" (17:7). Each time God answers, "I am."

Psalm 78:3–4, 23–24, 25, 54 (24b) This psalm was written after the fall of the Northern Kingdom of Israel, but before the fall of Judah, the Southern Kingdom. It is a didactic psalm, drawing new meaning from the past. Each stanza recalls an incident in which God acted on behalf of the people and their ungrateful response of sin and rebellion. Despite God's gracious care of his people in the desert, they spoke against him, saying, "Can God spread a table in the wilderness?" (78:19). The lessons learned in the past must be taught by the older generation so "the next generation might know them" (78:6). If Judah makes the same mistakes that Israel made, they will not avoid their fate.

Ephesians 4:17, 20–24 Ephesus was a seaport with a way of life and values that were far from those who followed Christ. This letter insists "that is not the way you learned Christ!" (4:20). Christians "must no longer live as the Gentiles live" (4:17). Enlightened by Baptism, they must put away their former corrupt lives and clothe themselves in "righteousness and holiness" (4:24). By the renewal of their minds, they will acquire a fresh, spiritual way of thinking. When Christians join together as one with Christ as the head, the whole Church grows by "building itself up in love" (4:16).

John 6:24–35 After the multiplication of loaves in the wilderness, the crowds respond to the sign by saying, "This is indeed the prophet who is to come into the world" (6:14). When they try to carry Jesus off and make him king, he flees to the mountain while his disciples cross the lake in a boat. The crowds realize Jesus and his disciples have left, and they go around the lake to meet them when the boat arrives on the opposite shore. Jesus knows they are not looking for him but for the bread he gave them to eat. He tells them, "Do not work for the food that perishes, but for the food that endures for eternal life" (6:27). The people demand another sign (John's word for Jesus' miraculous acts) such as Moses gave the people in the wilderness. Although they saw the sign, they miss the reality to which it points, God's providential presence in Jesus. By seeking signs, they are missing the true nourishment that God wants to give them. Jesus uses the divine name given to Moses, YHWH, when he says, "I am the bread of life" (6:35). The discourse that follows is a combination of several Old Testament quotations from Exodus and Psalms. In the same way that the Scriptures offered their teaching and nourished all who accepted it, Jesus offers the bread of understanding to all who put their faith in him.

Reflection Questions for the Catechist	⑤ When have you grumbled to the Lord because you were unhappy with your situation in life? At that time, how did you hear the Lord's promise that the Lord would rain down bread from heaven to nourish you?
	⑤ How do you experience Christ as the Bread of Life?
	⑤ What will you do as you lead the catechumens in their reflection on this Sunday's Word to help them discern their own hunger and thirst for the Eucharist?

Catechist's Guide

Objectives	▷ To recognize that God does not abandon us when we grumble or complain but responds by renewing and feeding us with new life.
	▷ To consider how Christ offers us food that is imperishable and eternal.
	▷ To come to Christ as the Bread of Life and believe in him as the bread come down from heaven sent from the Father.

Dismissal and Procession

Following the homily, the priest celebrant picks up the Lectionary and invites the catechumens to come forward with the catechist(s) who will lead today's dismissal session. Holding the Lectionary so that all can see, the priest celebrant sends the catechumens and catechist(s) forward using RCIA, 67, his own words, or the following:

PRIEST: **My dear friends, you have shared with us at the table of God's Word. Now, you go forth to explore the beauty of God's Word that you might be freed to become the beautiful creation God calls you to be. Supported by our prayer and encouraged by our fellowship, go seek together the meaning of God's saving Word. May it sustain you until the day when you can feast with us at the table of his Body and his Blood. Go in peace.**

All process to where the dismissal session will take place. The catechist holds the Lectionary in a reverent manner. The assembly may sing an acclamation to accompany the procession.

Centering

Upon reaching the place where the dismissal occurs, place the Lectionary on the ambo, lectern, or other dignified place (or hold the book reverently). Light the candle that is in the place of gathering and reread Exodus 16:2–4, 12–15 in order to refocus the group's attention. Consider singing the Responsorial Psalm or have a recording of it available to use as part of the centering, either before or after the reading.

Reflection and Discussion

The following "script" may be used or adapted to help facilitate discussion on today's readings. Begin the discussion by asking the catechumens if any words or phrases from today's readings spoke to them.

The Israelites, fearing they would die from hunger in the desert, grumble against Moses and Aaron. Thankless, although the Lord had rescued them from slavery, they express their preference that they would have just died in Egypt, for at least there they had food.

⑤ When have you grumbled to another person of faith or to the Lord himself?

The Lord, of course, heard the grumbling of the Israelites and in response, assured Moses that bread would rain down from heaven to satisfy the people.

⑤ How did the Lord respond to your grumbling?

⑤ What food has the Lord provided you?

In the Gospel reading, again from John, the crowd sets out to find Jesus and the disciples. They locate them in Capernaum. Upon encountering Jesus, they question him, wanting to know when it was he arrived. Jesus' response begins his solemn teaching contained in what we title the Bread of Life discourse. Jesus accurately reflects that the crowd sought him out because they ate the loaves for which he had given thanks and distributed to them. Jesus had fed them, and they returned desiring more.

⑨ When have you returned to Jesus and sought him out, wanting more of the bread he offers?

Jesus instructs the crowds to not work for perishable food but for food that brings eternal life. The people respond with another question about what they can do to achieve God's works. All that is necessary, Jesus responds, is to believe in him whom God sent. Believe in Jesus.

⑨ What does it mean to you to believe in Christ as the One whom the Father sent?

⑨ What connections do you see between the bread from heaven God provided the Israelites in the desert after they complained and Christ teaching to the crowds that the Father gives them the true bread from heaven?

Life comes from Christ, the Bread of God come down from heaven. He is the Bread of Life. Come to Christ and believe. You will never hunger and never thirst.

⑨ How does Jesus satisfy your hunger and quench your thirst?

⑨ What life does Jesus bring to you? To the Church? To the world?

Catholics believe that when we receive the Body and Blood of Christ in the Eucharist, we receive the Bread and Wine of Life. In the Eucharist, we participate in the life that Christ gives us. We are fed and nourished for our faith journey and to go out into the world proclaim the Bread of Life to others who hunger and thirst for food, for justice, for love, and for faith. Christ is the One the Father sent from heaven to offer life to the world—not just in the future but here and now. The gift of eternal life begins today, when we come to Christ and believe.

⑨ How would you describe your hunger for participating in the Eucharist and receiving the Bread of Life in this sacrament at this point in your faith journey?

⑨ What do you see as the responsibility of those who receive the Eucharist to live as the Body of Christ in the world today? To help others know Christ as the Bread of Life?

When we believe in Christ, we put away our old self, our former way of life, and put on a new self. Our new self believes in Christ, the Bread of Life the Father sent from heaven. In Baptism, we become a new creation. With God's grace, we actualize this new self. We will still grumble at times because we are human. Empowered by God, we will not resign ourselves to futility when we face situations that cause us to hunger and thirst. Our faith leads us to Christ, the Bread of Life.

⑨ Who or what will guide you back to Christ, the Bread of Life, the Bread of Heaven, when you hunger or thirst?

Wrapping It Up

Consider these points to conclude the dismissal. Integrate the thoughts and ideas that surfaced during the discussion.

- God responds to our grumblings and cries for help. God does not abandon us but accompanies us to the point of sending God's Son into the world to be the bread from heaven, the Bread of Life for us. We must only approach him in faith and believe in him. He will satisfy our spiritual hunger and quench our holy thirst.
- In Christ is the gift of eternal life. The food he gives us is food for the entire world. He never ceases to feed us. Day after day, Christ offers us himself as Life for us now, in the future, and forever.
- Christ invites us to approach him believing that he is the Bread of Life and that in him we will never grow hungry. Some days we might find it difficult to approach him. Other days we might experience Christ as very near to us. No matter the day, our faith gives us the confidence to trust that we can come to Christ as the righteous and holy persons we are and he will feed us with his life and grace.

Closing Prayer

Conclude with prayer. If time permits, sing the psalm refrain a few times before or after the following prayer.

Father of Life,
you rained down manna from heaven to feed the Israelites
who grumbled about perishing from famine in the desert
after you freed them from slavery's bonds.
You sent Jesus Christ, your Son and the Son of Man,
as the true bread from heaven, the Bread of Life.
Bless us with your grace so we might come to him and believe
that he will satisfy our many hungers and thirsts.
Open our hearts in holiness so that we might invite others
to come to him and feast on the food of eternal life.
Through Christ our Lord, our Bread of Life.
Amen.

Readings for the Next Dismissal

Provide catechumens with a list of the readings for the next dismissal session. Consult the liturgical calendar on page xvi to find out what day will be observed next week. Give catechumens the questions below to guide their reflection through the week.

- What connections are you seeing in the readings of this liturgical season? As you pray with the readings, around what themes do your thoughts seem to be coming together?
- Where do the readings intersect with your journey of faith? What questions do they raise for you?

Extended Catechesis

Based on today's readings and liturgical observance, the following topics may be covered for extended catechesis:

- Bread from Heaven, Bread of Life
- Son of Man sent from the Father
- Eternal Life
- Spiritual hunger and thirst
- Receiving the Bread of Life in the Eucharist
- Living the Eucharist in the World
- Belief
- Christ, Bread of Life for the World
- New creation and putting on new self in Baptism

Nineteenth Sunday in Ordinary Time

Focus: Christ is our source of nourishment.

Lectionary #116B

Catechist's Preparation

Overview of the Sunday

We must eat and drink on the journey, for it is long and tiresome. The angel of the Lord reminds Elijah of this in the First Reading. We need strength. We need nourishment to carry out the mission on which God sends us. Without nourishment, we find it difficult to live virtuous lives. Malice and bitterness take over. Being imitators of God becomes impossible. But when we realize our nourishment comes from Christ, the One whom the Father sent, we shall live. Life forever is ours. Life for the world is Christ's gift.

Scripture Background

1 Kings 19:4–8 This event in the Elijah narratives takes place soon after Elijah has overcome the prophets of Baal on Mount Carmel. Furious at Elijah, King Ahab and his wife Jezebel are determined to kill him. Fleeing to the desert, Elijah becomes despondent and dejected, asking God for death. The prophetic vocation is fraught with opposition, rejection, and persecution, and Elijah has had enough for one lifetime. But God has other plans. Resting under a broom tree, Elijah twice experiences an angel waking him and ordering him to eat. Elijah eats and drinks from the hearth cake and water miraculously provided. Nourished and refreshed, Elijah is again energized, walking forty days and nights to encounter the Lord at Horeb, or Mount Sinai.

Like Moses, Elijah journeys through the desert to encounter the Lord and to be reenergized for service to God and others. Like Moses and the people in their desert journey, God does not give up on Elijah, but nourishes and sustains him. Christians affirm that God nourishes us on our life's journey through Christ, the living bread that came down from heaven.

Psalm 34:2–3, 4–5, 6–7, 8–9 (9a) Psalm 34 is a psalm of praise to God who has rescued the psalmist from danger, fear, and affliction. The psalmist invites all to trust and have confidence in God, who hears our pleas and responds to our calls for help. The "angel of the LORD" (34:8), a euphemism for God, actually "encamps" (34:8) around those who call upon the Lord and "delivers" them (34:8). The psalmist again invites all to put trust in God by playing on the image of food. Taste and you will see, or experience, the goodness of the Lord.

Ephesians 4:30—5:2 Using baptismal imagery, this passage from Ephesians exhorts the community to live in imitation of God, as exemplified in Christ. Anything that disrupts the love, unity, and harmony of the community grieves the Spirit of God (see 4:30). Rather, all bitterness, rivalry, and anger must be replaced by kindness, compassion, and forgiveness. In imitation of God who has forgiven us in Christ, we are called to forgive one another.

Christ was willing to sacrifice himself completely for our sake. Through our Baptism, we are called to give of ourselves for others. In so doing, we become living witnesses to Jesus, through the power of the Spirit. Like Jesus, we too become "a fragrant aroma" (5:2) to God and to all we encounter. In the Spirit, we become more like Jesus, the source of all our growth, nourishment, and right living.

John 6:41–51 The Gospel continues Jesus' argument with an unbelieving crowd after his declaration in being the bread that came down from heaven. The crowd, in murmuring reminiscent of the Exodus desert experience, responds that they know Jesus' parentage, so how can he claim heavenly origins. Jesus responds that to know him demands that they be open to being drawn to him by the Father, who is the true teacher in all matters of faith. If they were open to the Father's actions in their lives, they would come to know and accept Jesus, the "bread of life" (6:48).

Jesus continues to instruct them by affirming that to know him is to know the Father. Since he is the bread of life, whoever believes in him will have eternal life. The desert manna that came down from heaven did not provide eternal life. Rather, Jesus, the "living bread that came down from heaven," (6:51) is true bread that provides eternal life to all who believe and partake, "whoever eats this bread will live forever" (6:51).

Jesus, our true source of nourishment, specifies that the bread he will give is his "flesh for the life of the world" (6:51). Partaking of Jesus, the "bread of life" (6:48), calls the partakers to give of themselves for the life of the world. We are nourished by Jesus so that we can nourish others both physically and spiritually. Jesus came to model how we are to be nourishment for one another: by partaking of the rich nourishment that the Father has given us in Christ.

Reflection Questions for the Catechist

- When have you rested like Elijah and awoke finding the nourishment you needed to move on right in front of you?
- How does Christ the Living Bread from heaven nourish you in your daily life?
- In what areas of your life and ministry do you love as Christ has loved you? In what areas do you find it difficult to do so, where you need to draw closer to Christ the Living Bread for nourishment?

Catechist's Guide

Objectives

▷ To recognize that Christ is the source of our nourishment every step of the way in our faith journey.

▷ To discern how Christ the Living Bread brings life to us and to the world here and now.

▷ To explore how we can companion others by loving as Christ loves us and bring them to know Christ as the source of their nourishment.

Dismissal and Procession

Following the homily, the priest celebrant picks up the Lectionary and invites the catechumens to come forward with the catechist(s) who will lead today's dismissal session. Holding the Lectionary so that all can see, the priest celebrant sends the catechumens and catechist(s) forward using RCIA, 67, his own words, or the following:

PRIEST: **My dear friends, you have shared with us at the table of God's Word. Now, you go forth to explore the beauty of God's Word that you might be freed to become the beautiful creation God calls you to be. Supported by our prayer and encouraged by our fellowship, go seek together the meaning of God's saving Word. May it sustain you until the day when you can feast with us at the table of his Body and his Blood. Go in peace.**

All process to where the dismissal session will take place. The catechist holds the Lectionary in a reverent manner. The assembly may sing an acclamation to accompany the procession.

Centering

Upon reaching the place where the dismissal occurs, place the Lectionary on the ambo, lectern, or other dignified place (or hold the book reverently). Light the candle that is in the place of gathering and reread 1 Kings 19:4–8 in order to refocus the group's attention. Consider singing the Responsorial Psalm or have a recording of it available to use as part of the centering, either before or after the reading.

Reflection and Discussion

The following "script" may be used or adapted to help facilitate discussion on today's readings. Begin the discussion by asking the catechumens if any words or phrases from today's readings spoke to them.

- When have you cried to the Lord in prayer that you have had enough of the journey?

Elijah expressed his frustration and exhaustion with his prophetic journey when he cried out to the Lord in desperation and then fell asleep beneath the broom tree. All seemed lost. But was it? God visited Elijah through an angel's touch. The angel not only encouraged Elijah, but also ordered him to eat and drink.

- How did God respond to your prayer? Who encouraged you to take nourishment?

Elijah rested after eating and drinking the first time only to experience the Lord's angel visiting him again and commanding him a second time to eat and drink more, fostering in him the strength and courage to continue on the arduous, lengthy journey of forty days and nights. God never leaves those on the journey. The choice is ours to continue.

◕ How have you known God's presence throughout your faith journey? What were the points where you needed to decide again to eat and drink so you could continue on?

In the Gospel reading, Christ affirms for us once again that he is the Bread of Life, the Bread who is come down from heaven. He is our source of nourishment—eternal nourishment. His promise to us is that if we eat the bread he gives, we will live forever.

◕ What draws you or makes you curious about this eternal bread that Christ offers?

Some among the people whispered about Christ's identity. They thought they knew Christ—and they did. They knew his earthly mother and father, Mary and Joseph, but they were not quite grasping how Christ could have come down from heaven. Jesus responds to them by teaching about his unique relationship with the Father. The Father draws believers to Christ, the Bread of Life.

◕ How do you find God the Father drawing and leading you to his Son?

◕ What place does the Father have in your life of prayer?

When we listen and learn from God, we will be led closer to our source of nourishment, Christ the Bread of Life. We will come to know how Christ came down from heaven, loved us, and gave himself as an offering for us so that we might receive the gift of life and love that comes through him.

As we continue to hear from St. Paul's letter to the Ephesians, the passage today expresses the depth of Christ's love for us. St. Paul instructs us to follow Christ's example and to live in love. We are God's beloved children. We are to imitate God. The Christian tradition speaks of *imitatio Christi*, living in imitation of Christ. As Christ is the source of our nourishment, we are to nourish and sustain others.

◕ Where is God calling you to live in imitation of Christ by nourishing others? By inviting them to find the source of their nourishment in the Bread of Life?

◕ How do you live in love as Christ loved you, forgiving as God forgives you in Christ?

The words of the psalm writer in today's Responsorial Psalm refrain invite us to taste and see the Lord's goodness. May we be mindful of all the goodness that is around us—in nature, in our friends and families and neighbors, in the Church—in all communities of faith in which we honor all that is good and true and beautiful.

◕ What will help you to be consciously aware of the Lord's goodness around you this week? Of the countless ways the Lord makes his nourishment available to you? Of Christ, who is the source of our nourishment?

Wrapping It Up

Consider these points to conclude the dismissal. Integrate the thoughts and ideas that surfaced during the discussion.

- Whether we go a day's journey in the desert like Elijah or whether we murmur about who Christ is, like some of the people in the Gospel reading, Christ is always our source of nourishment. Ours is the responsibility to believe, to listen to the Father and learn what God teaches.

- We do not have to wait on Christ's gift of life. He is the Bread of Life at work in our lives and in the world here and now. He is the source of nourishment for those who participate in the communion of the Church, especially in the sacrament of the Eucharist, to which our journey might lead. He gave his life for the sake of the world, and for the world he continues to be the source of nourishment.

- In our hunger for the Bread of Life, we companion others on their journey. When we love as Christ taught us, others see his life in us. As we imitate God by living in love, we too bring others to faith in Christ. When we feed God's hungry people with food, not just with love and kindness, we show them the way to Christ, the Bread of Life.

Closing Prayer

Conclude with prayer. If time permits, sing the psalm refrain a few times before or after the following prayer.

God of the hungry,
your angel directed the weary Elijah to feast on the food and drink within his reach
so he would be strengthened to walk forty days and nights.
Over and over again, you teach us that Christ is the source of our nourishment,
and that we need not look far for him,
for his life and love are available to us in a multitude of places.
As we have come to know Christ as the Bread of Life within this faith community,
nourish us with his love so that we might accompany others on the road of faith
and to recognize the gift of eternal life he offers,
where he lives and reigns for ever and ever.
Amen.

Readings for the Next Dismissal

Provide catechumens with a list of the readings for the next dismissal session. Consult the liturgical calendar on page xvi to find out what day will be observed next week. Give catechumens the questions below to guide their reflection through the week.

- What connections are you seeing in the readings of this liturgical season? As you pray with the readings, around what themes do your thoughts seem to be coming together?
- Where do the readings intersect with your journey of faith? What questions do they raise for you?

Extended Catechesis

Based on today's readings and liturgical observance, the following topics may be covered for extended catechesis:

- Believing in Jesus
- Jesus' sacrifice for the life of the world
- Eucharist as the source of nourishment for the journey
- Imitating God by living in love
- Imitation of Christ
- The relationship between the Father and Jesus (the Son)
- Eternal life
- Mass and mission

TWENTIETH SUNDAY IN ORDINARY TIME

Focus: Come, eat and drink of the Lord.

Lectionary #119B

Catechist's Preparation

Overview of the Sunday

On this Sunday, Wisdom offers us another invitation to feast on her food and drink. She invites us to leave foolishness behind and share in her Wisdom. Paul's summons to us is the same: live as wise, not foolish persons, feasting on the Spirit and praising the Lord, who the Gospel reading once again reminds us is the Living Bread from heaven. Christ, too, offers us an invitation. He desires that we share in his life by feeding on him. How much life-giving food is available to us when accept the invitation to come, eat and drink of the Lord.

Scripture Background

Proverbs 9:1–6 Wisdom, personified as a woman, is pictured making preparations for a rich feast of meat and wine. Her home set upon seven columns indicates both lavishness and the universal appeal of her dwelling, seven being a perfect or universal number. She sends out her maidens to invite the "simple" (6:4) and those who lack understanding to come and feast in her house. Those who accept her invitation will learn wisdom and live enriched lives that "forsake foolishness" (9:6).

The invitation to the "simple" (6:4) indicates the necessity for a childlike innocence and openness to seeing, learning, and believing. The arrogant and those who think they know all find the invitation useless. The appeal is universal, addressed to all who are open to learning. The rewards are life guided by Wisdom, something that endures no matter what life brings.

Food and drink that nourishes for a lifetime is what Wisdom offers. This passage provides a backdrop to the Bread of Life discourse in chapter 6 of John's account of the Gospel, which we continue to proclaim on this Sunday. Christians believe Jesus is the wisdom of God who invites us to partake of his flesh and blood, food that nourishes for eternal life.

Psalm 34:2–3, 4–5, 6–7 (9a) Praising and thanking God for help in time of need summarizes these verses, most of which we also sang last Sunday, from Psalm 34, a thanksgiving psalm with strong wisdom motifs. Within the context of a liturgical setting, the psalmist invites the community to "glorify the LORD" (34:3) for delivering the psalmist from "all my fears" (34:5). The psalmist continues with a call to look to the Lord at all times, for the Lord hears and answers the call of the poor and lowly.

Ephesians 5:15–20 This moral exhortation, or *parenesis*, addressed to the Ephesians is full of wisdom language and instruction. The community is admonished to live wisely, for wisdom is constantly challenged by the evil and disruption around them. Living wisely demands an attunement to the "will of the Lord" (5:17), leading to understanding and God-centered living, in contrast to ignorance infected by the powers of evil. Drunkenness and debauchery are signs of a life lived in foolishness and ignorance.

One who lives life in wisdom is "filled with the Spirit" (5:18), giving thanks to God in the name of Jesus for all of life. *Eucharistia*, the Greek word for thanksgiving, is to be expressed both communally and holistically "in psalms and hymns and spiritual songs, singing and playing to the Lord in your hearts" (5:19). The heart of any Christian wisdom community is the offering of thanksgiving to our Trinitarian God, in all places and at all times.

John 6:51–58 Today's reading the Bread of Life discourse from chapter 6 of John's account of the Gospel, focuses the various strands of the discourse on the meaning and significance of the Christian community's Eucharistic gathering. Picking up from last Sunday's reading, we hear Jesus assert once again that he is the living bread from heaven. Those who partake of this bread, Jesus' flesh given for the life of the world, will live forever. The crowd, thinking literally, cannot comprehend Jesus' words. Jesus begins to elaborate rather clearly and repeatedly his intended meaning.

Four times, in clear and direct speech, Jesus affirms that "my flesh is true food, and my blood is true drink" (6:55). If we desire to have eternal life and be one with Christ, as he is one with the Father, then we are to eat his flesh and drink his blood, that same incarnate flesh and blood that was given "for the life of the world" (6:51). We do not become one with Christ through our minds or hearts. We become one with him by feeding on his body and blood, thus allowing him to remain with us and allowing us to be one with him. This sacramental indwelling unites all those who partake, forming one body and one mind. To be Christian is to be deeply one with God by partaking of Jesus, our true food and true drink.

Reflection Questions for the Catechist

⑨ How does Wisdom speak her invitation to you to come eat and drink of the food and wine she has to offer?

⑨ What is the foolishness you need to leave behind?

⑨ How does eating and drinking of the Lord lead you to draw closer to him? To have life because of him? To be filled with the Spirit?

Catechist's Guide

Objectives

▷ To reflect on what it means to eat and drink of the Lord.

▷ To ponder the foolishness in our lives we need to leave behind to participate more fully in Wisdom's feast.

▷ To appreciate how the Spirit leads us to celebrate the life we have when we feast on the Lord, whose flesh is true food and blood is true drink.

Dismissal and Procession

Following the homily, the priest celebrant picks up the Lectionary and invites the catechumens to come forward with the catechist(s) who will lead today's dismissal session. Holding the Lectionary so that all can see, the priest celebrant sends the catechumens and catechist(s) forward using RCIA, 67, his own words, or the following:

PRIEST: **My dear friends, you have shared with us at the table of God's Word. Now, you go forth to explore the beauty of God's Word that you might be freed to become the beautiful creation God calls you to be. Supported by our prayer and encouraged by our fellowship, go seek together the meaning of God's saving Word. May it sustain you until the day when you can feast with us at the table of his Body and his Blood. Go in peace.**

All process to where the dismissal session will take place. The catechist holds the Lectionary in a reverent manner. The assembly may sing an acclamation to accompany the procession.

Centering

Upon reaching the place where the dismissal occurs, place the Lectionary on the ambo, lectern, or other dignified place (or hold the book reverently). Light the candle that is in the place of gathering and reread Proverbs 9:1–6 in order to refocus the group's attention. Consider singing the Responsorial Psalm or have a recording of it available to use as part of the centering, either before or after the reading.

Reflection and Discussion

The following "script" may be used or adapted to help facilitate discussion on today's readings. Begin the discussion by asking the catechumens if any words or phrases from today's readings spoke to them.

Imagine you receive an invitation to participate in a luscious feast of food and drink. Consider what food would be on the table, what drink available to quench thirsts. Think about who would be invited and why they would be asked to "come." Now ponder Wisdom's feast described in the First Reading.

⑨ What connections do you see between the feast you visualize and the description of Wisdom's feast?

⑨ What do you need to leave behind in order to be fully present at the feast?

Wisdom's food and drink are practical knowledge and insights and understanding into how to live God's ways in the midst of our own foolishness and the world's foolishness.

⑨ How ready are you to receive Wisdom's gift of knowledge? To feast at her table?

🌀 Where do you need to replace foolishness in your life with Wisdom?

Wisdom's bounty presents itself to everyone. When we feast at Wisdom's table, we will live. God's life will be our life. We will become wise in the Lord's ways. We will taste and see the Lord's goodness, as the refrain from Psalm 34 again tells us.

🌀 When have you experienced life in God more deeply because you have chosen to live by Wisdom?

The Second Reading, from Ephesians, describes the opportunity we have to live as wise persons and what it entails. The Spirit fills us and makes us wise. We gather together to sing the Lord's praise and to give thanks for the Lord for everything that is his and all he has done in Jesus Christ.

🌀 How do you sense the Spirit filling you and empowering you to live a wisdom-filled life?

🌀 Where and when do you gather in the company of others seeking Wisdom to praise and thank the Lord?

The feast to which Wisdom invites us in the First Reading fully realizes itself in the Gospel, where we find Jesus teaching the crowds that his flesh is "true food" and his blood "true drink" (John 6:55). Jesus invites us to eat and drink his body and blood so that we might have eternal life. He is the Wisdom of God made flesh. When we accept his invitation to feast on his life, his life will reside in us.

🌀 When do you eat and drink of Christ's wisdom?

🌀 What is it like to experience his life within you?

The goodness of God's Wisdom present in Christ, the Living Bread, amazes us so much that we want to express our thanks to God and summon others to the feast.

🌀 Who will you invite to Wisdom's feast? To feast on Christ's wisdom?

🌀 How have others noticed Wisdom present in you since you have been involved on the catechumenate journey?

Christ promises that those who eat and drink will be raised up by him on the last day. What a feast this shall be when all who have died in Christ will be raised up together.

🌀 What is the hope of Christ's promise of sharing in his Resurrection mean to you? To those you know?

🌀 How do you envision the celebration that will occur on the last day?

🌀 What impact does Christ's promise have on you as you live your life now?

May our response to Wisdom's invitation to "Come, eat and drink of the Lord" be a joyful yes. May our yes express our thanks for the abundance of the Lord's goodness we taste and see all around us.

Wrapping It Up
Consider these points to conclude the dismissal. Integrate the thoughts and ideas that surfaced during the discussion.

- The Lord invites us to receive the nourishment he offers in his Word and in our life together as a communion of persons journeying together in faith. He extends his gift of life to us in many ways as we grow in our relationship with him and prepare to participate in the Eucharist. For the many ways the Lord is present, we give thanks.

- God invites us to grow in Wisdom and knowledge of his Son, Jesus Christ, and to leave behind those foolish habits that can be called sin and the foolishness that would separate us from believing in Christ as the Bread of Life. Let us let God fill us with the Spirit to encourage us to live as wise persons.

- Liturgy and worship unite us in praise of the Lord for the life he offers us through his own Body and Blood. Filled with the Spirit, we come together as a community of faith to give thanks for everything we have in Jesus Christ.

Closing Prayer

Conclude with prayer. If time permits, sing the psalm refrain a few times before or after the following prayer.

God of all creation,

you are the Author of Wisdom,

who invites us to eat of her food and drink of her wine.

Grant us insight so that we might accept the invitation to Wisdom's feast

and renounce the foolishness that entices us.

Encourage us to bring Wisdom's invitation

to your people in neighborhoods, cities, and villages everywhere.

Fill us with the Spirit, and lead us to give thanks to you

for everything that is ours in the name of Jesus Christ,

the living and true bread from heaven,

where you live and reign for ever and ever.

Amen.

Readings for the Next Dismissal

Provide catechumens with a list of the readings for the next dismissal session. Consult the liturgical calendar on page xvi to find out what day will be observed next week. Give catechumens the questions below to guide their reflection through the week.

⑥ What connections are you seeing in the readings of this liturgical season? As you pray with the readings, around what themes do your thoughts seem to be coming together?

⑥ Where do the readings intersect with your journey of faith? What questions do they raise for you?

Extended Catechesis

Based on today's readings and liturgical observance, the following topics may be covered for extended catechesis:

※ Wisdom

※ Our share in divine Wisdom

※ Living as a wise person in faith

※ Discerning the Lord's will

※ Being filled with the Holy Spirit

※ Liturgy and worship

※ Eucharist as giving praise and thanks, meal, and sacrifice

※ Holy Communion is the Body and Blood of Christ

TWENTY-FIRST SUNDAY IN ORDINARY TIME

Focus: We shall serve the Lord.

Lectionary #122B

Catechist's Preparation

Overview of the Sunday

Eating is not a selfish act. It is an act that provides nourishment to serve the Lord and others. In the First Reading, Joshua lays out the choice that he and his household have made. They will serve the Lord. Will we? When we choose to serve the Lord, we choose to live to extend the same liberating love God extended to the Israelites and now to us. This is the main point in the Second Reading, from Ephesians. The Gospel reading, again from John, makes our choice clear: either we choose to remain with Jesus or we choose to desert him and abandon the journey we began. In Jesus, we have ample nourishment for the journey of love.

Scripture Background

Joshua 24:1–2, 15–17, 18b Some biblical archaeologists suspect that Israel had help conquering Canaan. What had been thought of as an invasion may have been more of a revolution from within. The oppressed rural Canaanites saw the radical religion and politics of their new neighbors who had escaped Egypt and immediately identified with them. Together they overthrew the ruling urban Canaanite city states. Our reading is a record of the covenant made between those loosely federated tribes from Egypt and the native tribes of Canaan. This covenant formed what we know today as the people of Israel.

Joshua puts this covenant in terms of a choice. For the tribes who had come from bondage in Egypt, it was a chance to renew the covenant they had made at Sinai. Joshua was smart to do this. Most of the first generation had passed away and the current generation needed to decide for themselves. Will they serve the gods of their new land, the gods of the Canaanite rulers, or the God who had rescued their parents from Egypt? For the Canaanite revolutionaries, this was a chance to show their new allegiance to the liberating God of the Exodus. It cemented relations between the tribes and made a peaceful settlement of the land possible.

That same choice is still before us. Will we serve the gods of the powerful (possessions, status, money, security) or will we serve the liberating God we know in Christ? Joshua says that making the choice is a challenge. Living it is even more so.

Psalm 34:2–3, 16–17, 18–19, 20–21 (9a) On this third and final time we sing from Psalm 34 on a Sunday this year, we reach the final strophe in the psalmist's song. In it, the psalmist offers us a choice like the one Joshua offered. Are we among the righteous (willing to stand up for our faith even in the face of opposition) or are we among the evildoers (living as if there is no God)? Again, the choice is ours, but the psalmist wants us to understand the consequences. The righteous, he says, have a special relationship to God.

That doesn't necessarily mean life will be less of a challenge for them. Like everyone else, the righteous suffer affliction. But, the psalmist explains, when the righteous cry for help, God hears them. God is near to them and will redeem their lives. Evildoers, however, are cut off. God does not even remember them. In the end, they stand condemned, slain by their own evil.

Ephesians 5:21–32 or 5:2a, 25–32 The household code in Ephesians offers us a perfect example of second-century Christianity's struggle to retain the radical teaching and practice of Jesus while also gaining acceptance in wider society. Such household codes were a common Hellenistic Greek literary form, but the author of Ephesians has added some surprisingly radical elements.

As expected, he begins by assigning people into a hierarchy. "Wives," he says, "be subject to your husbands" (5:22). This is the part he borrowed. But note what else the author says. "Be subject to one another out of reverence for Christ" (5:21). This introduces a new element of equality unheard of in traditional society. "Husbands, love your wives as Christ loved the Church and gave himself up for her" (5:25). This, too, is new. It gives husbands an example of servanthood which undermines any ideas they may have had about being traditional heads of household.

The author's words reflect an old hierarchy, but his examples reflect a radical reinterpretation of human relations. For those in authority, the lordship of Christ means giving up power over people. For those on the lower rungs of society, the lordship of Christ means giving up victimization. It means respecting each other, caring for each other, cherishing each other just as Christ cherishes us. The challenge before us is to live this new way in the midst of a culture that constantly pulls us into old patterns of injustice.

John 6:60-69 Once Jesus claims that he is the "living bread that came down from heaven," John says, the crowds who followed him dwindle. When Jesus begins to talk about ascending to heaven, even his disciples leave. Eventually, only the Twelve are left. "Do you also wish to go away?" Jesus asks (6:67). Speaking for the rest, Peter replies, "To whom shall we go? You have the words of eternal life" (6:68). It was a confession of faith much like the one at Caesarea Philippi, which Matthew and Mark record. In typical Johannine fashion, Peter confesses, "We have believed, and have come to know that you are the Holy One of God."

Once again, faith presents us with a choice. In John's language, do we believe Jesus is the Holy One of God or not? That is John's challenge. Many in his day did not accept it, but his Church did (which is probably why they remembered this story). Many in our day will not accept it either. The question is What do we say?

Reflection Questions for the Catechist

⑨ How have you and your household chosen to serve the Lord?

⑨ When life in Jesus begins to get difficult, what enables you to continue to follow him?

⑨ Where do you see God offering liberating love in your life? In the lives of the catechumens?

⑨ Where is God calling you to extend his liberating love to others in the Church? In your neighborhoods? In the world?

Catechist's Guide

Objectives

▷ To consider the enormity of the choice we have to serve the Lord or not.

▷ To ponder the commitment God invites us to make to continue to walk with Jesus to Jerusalem.

▷ To recognize that serving the Lord requires us to serve others in love as the Lord loves us.

Dismissal and Procession

Following the homily, the priest celebrant picks up the Lectionary and invites the catechumens to come forward with the catechist(s) who will lead today's dismissal session. Holding the Lectionary so that all can see, the priest celebrant sends the catechumens and catechist(s) forward using RCIA, 67, his own words, or the following:

PRIEST: My dear friends, Jesus calls us to follow him, to take times of silence, and to live lives worthy of the Gospel. As you reflect upon his Word, may you be strengthened in your attempts to bear fruit and grow stronger in your faith. May you never be discouraged, and may you find the strength to turn to God in your need. Take heart, knowing that God can do great things when we cannot. Find your hope in him now. Go in peace.

All process to where the dismissal session will take place. The catechist holds the Lectionary in a reverent manner. The assembly may sing an acclamation to accompany the procession.

Centering

Upon reaching the place where the dismissal occurs, place the Lectionary on the ambo, lectern, or other dignified place (or hold the book reverently). Light the candle that is in the place of gathering and reread John 6:60–69 in order to refocus the group's attention. Consider singing the Responsorial Psalm or have a recording of it available to use as part of the centering, either before or after the reading.

Reflection and Discussion

The following "script" may be used or adapted to help facilitate discussion on today's readings. Begin the discussion by asking the catechumens if any words or phrases from today's readings spoke to them.

As if we did not already realize it, this Sunday's Gospel reading makes obvious how difficult the life of a disciple is. Many, not just some, among Christ's disciples left him to return to their prior life. They were unable to accept Christ's teaching that he was the Living Bread come down from heaven and those who believe in will have eternal life. They just could not grasp the magnitude of the gift Christ invited them to accept.

- ⑨ At what point are you at in terms of accepting Christ's teaching that he is the Bread of Life, the Bread come down from heaven?

- ⑨ What about the Christian faith is the most challenging for you to accept or believe in?

Many of the disciples returned to their former way of life. Christ did not stop them. After they left, Christ asked the Twelve who were left in his inner circle if they also wanted to leave. He was giving them an out. The decision lay with each of them individually. Simon Peter, knowing there was no one else to whom they could go, responded with a rhetorical question and then an affirmation that Christ's words were indeed the words of eternal life. Speaking for the group, Simon Peter acknowledged that they had all come to believe. They knew Christ to be the one sent from God, the "Holy One of God" (John 6:69).

- ⑨ How would you articulate your response to Christ's question, "Do you also want to leave" (John 6:67)?

- ⑨ What keeps you from leaving and returning to your life before you began your catechumenate journey?

Believing in Christ also includes following him. It consists of embracing his way of life—the way of preaching repentance and the Good News of the Kingdom of God, the way of healing, the way of overcoming evil, the way of choosing wisdom over foolishness, and the way of living out justice in the world. In the First Reading, we hear Joshua's address to God's people. In candid terms, Joshua challenges the people to see that they have a choice: they can serve the Lord or not. Joshua's household chooses to serve the Lord. The people respond that they, too, will serve the Lord, for all that the Lord has done for them is clear. The Lord saved them from slavery and watched over them in their journey. They acclaim the Lord as God.

- ⑨ What is your choice?

- ⑨ On what basis do you make that choice?

- ⑨ How would you put into a few sentences how God has been at work in your life?

Serving the Lord entails serving others, and for us as Christians, serving as Christ did. It entails loving as Christ loves us and as Christ loves the Church. It involves a mutual love for one another that respects everyone as a son or daughter of God, as a person created in the image and likeness of God.

- ⑨ How do you serve the Lord?

- ⑨ How does your love for others reflect Christ's love?

Our service to the Lord and others reflects God's goodness. Through our love, we reflect the goodness of the Lord. We lead others to taste the Lord's goodness. We know the road of serving the Lord as disciples brings us to the Cross, and that not every day will be easy. Christ never promises this. Surely, if his sayings were hard to accept, his actions were too.

- ⑨ What keeps you intent on remaining with Christ when you have a difficult experience or a tough day?

- What role does the faith community play in helping you keep your commitment to live as a disciple?
- How do prayer and the Church's liturgy assist you in serving the Lord?

Wrapping It Up

Consider these points to conclude the dismissal. Integrate the thoughts and ideas that surfaced during the discussion.

- Whether or not we choose to serve the Lord is the major decision on which this Sunday's readings have asked us to reflect. It is a decision that will change our lives. It is a decision we might make one day and then struggle with at other times, as the disciples in today's Gospel reading did. We in the community of faith are here to support one another each time the immensity of the choice to follow Christ appears central in our lives.
- Will we follow Christ all the way to the Cross? Or, will we be among the disciples who want to leave and return to our former way of life? These questions will arise at some point in our faith journey. Praying with them is the work of the heart. It is the work of love, not judgment, of ourselves and others who embrace the life of faith.
- When we decide to serve the Lord, we also decide to serve others as the Lord served us. As Christ freed, fed, and healed, so we too must free, feed, and heal. As Christ loved, so must we love.

Closing Prayer

Conclude with prayer. If time permits, sing the psalm refrain a few times before or after the following prayer.

God of freedom,
you liberated your people in the exodus
and called them to serve you as Lord.
Give us the courage to believe in Jesus Christ
and the boldness to continue to live as his disciples.
Grace us with the audacity to love ourselves and others and you.
Through Christ our Lord.
Amen.

Readings for the Next Dismissal

Provide catechumens with a list of the readings for the next dismissal session. Consult the liturgical calendar on page xvi to find out what day will be observed next week. Give catechumens the questions below to guide their reflection through the week.

- What connections are you seeing in the readings of this liturgical season? As you pray with the readings, around what themes do your thoughts seem to be coming together?
- Where do the readings intersect with your journey of faith? What questions do they raise for you?

Extended Catechesis

Based on today's readings and liturgical observance, the following topics may be covered for extended catechesis:

- Serving the Lord
- Loving as Christ loves the Church
- The relationships between Christ and the Church
- The challenges of discipleship

TWENTY-SECOND SUNDAY IN ORDINARY TIME

Focus: "Be doers of the Word" (James 1:22).

Lectionary #125B

Catechist's Preparation

Overview of the Sunday

The Lord's commandments belong not to us, but to the Lord. They are ours neither to write nor to edit. On this Twenty-Second Sunday in Ordinary Time, we hear Moses instruct the people to observe the commandments and James instruct Christians to be "doers of the Word" (James 1:22). Hearing the Word and the Lord's commandments is not the end of the story. Putting them into action, or in other words, living the Word, is. In response to the Pharisees who question Jesus about his disciples not observing ritual purity laws, Jesus articulates the importance of God's commandments over human tradition. What is in a disciple's heart is what matters most. Enacting justice—caring for orphans and widows—is the work of the heart, the work of God's commandments.

Scripture Background

Deuteronomy 4:1–2, 6–8 Before entering the Promised Land, Moses admonishes the Israelites to hear the Lord's statutes and decrees. Only active attentiveness to God's Word will lead to fullness of life and possession of the land God promised. Not adding to or subtracting from God's commands, a common stipulation in the laws of the ancient world, insured fidelity to what had been communicated.

Two reasons are given for attentiveness and fidelity to God's commands. Observance of God's law insures God's blessings on the land and the people. Secondly, the wisdom and intelligence of God's laws will be evident to all nations through the Israelites' manner of living. Their closeness to God and the wisdom of God's commands manifested when they live lives of justice will be admired and envied by all nations.

Psalm 15:2–3, 3–4, 4–5 (1a) Psalm 15 has temple and ritual worship as its backdrop. Some have called it an entrance liturgy for pilgrims or anyone desiring to know the requirements for temple worship. The response given by the temple priests is both an instruction in living and an examination of the life path one has chosen to walk. Living in the presence of the Lord demands a life lived justly, exercising right relationship with all in thought, word, and deed.

Specific examples of right relationship are offered to the worshipper who desires temple entrance. These include doing justice, speaking truth and not slander, causing harm to no one, fearing the Lord, not charging interest on money lent (usury), and not accepting bribes. Living thusly will bring about communal harmony and peace, along with personal well-being and integrity. Choosing this path insures God's blessings, for it integrates God's commands with everyday living and enables authentic communal worship.

James 1:17–18, 21b–22, 27 For the next five Sundays, the Second Reading will proclaim selections from the Letter of James. The letter is better characterized as a moral exhortation to the baptized, those given "birth by the word of truth" who are the "firstfruits" (1:18) of God's creative activity. James begins by highlighting his image of God. God, the source of all goodness, showers us with abundant blessings. Since God is changeless, God can be relied upon eternally. God desires to recreate the world, with those baptized into Christ being the "firstfruits" (1:18) of God's creative love.

James exhorts God's "firstfruits" (1:18) to welcome God's Word with humility and to become "doers of the word and not hearers only." Warning that we can easily delude ourselves, James specifies what is required to stand before God "pure and undefiled" (1:27). Care and concern for all powerless and defenseless people, "orphans and widows" (1:27), is foremost. "Doers of the word" (1:22) are ever diligent about removing all that would prevent them from serving God and others. James exhorts all to be and do justice.

Mark 7:1–8, 14–15, 21–23 This Sunday's return to Mark's account of the Gospel has Jesus being confronted by some religious authorities who question his disciples' fidelity to religious laws, especially ritual purity. Since Mark writes primarily for a non-Jewish audience, he spells out some of the pharisaic regulations concerning ritual purity. Jesus responds to their questions by quoting from Isaiah, who criticized the people of his day for external show in worship without internal conviction, and for elevating human precepts to the level of doctrine.

Jesus challenges the Pharisees and scribes by asserting that defilement has its source not in external actions but in interior disposition. One cannot judge merely on the basis of external actions. Rather, one has to search the heart and one's interior disposition to adequately and justly judge external actions. The list of vices, a common catalogue in moral exhortations, is used as examples of actions that manifest an interior disposition averse to God and neighbor. True defilement begins in the heart.

Jesus is not saying that laws and regulations have no value. Rather, Jesus is emphasizing the necessity of establishing laws and traditions that enhance, not minimize or distort, a person's relationship to God and others. They should help all be effective "doers of the word and not hearers only" (James 1:22).

Reflection Questions for the Catechist

- When do you find it most challenging to be both hearer and doer of the Word?
- In what ways do you cling to human tradition and disregard God's commandments?
- How does your heart reflect the heart of Jesus?

Catechist's Guide

Objectives

- ▷ To affirm our responsibility to enact God's Word of justice and care for those who suffer in the world.
- ▷ To recognize whether the orientation of our heart is to evil and malice or to God's commandment of love.
- ▷ To discern what causes us to let human traditions become more important than God's commandments.

Dismissal and Procession

Following the homily, the priest celebrant picks up the Lectionary and invites the catechumens to come forward with the catechist(s) who will lead today's dismissal session. Holding the Lectionary so that all can see, the priest celebrant sends the catechumens and catechist(s) forward using RCIA, 67, his own words, or the following:

PRIEST: **My dear friends, Jesus calls us to follow him, to take times of silence, and to live lives worthy of the Gospel. As you reflect upon his Word, may you be strengthened in your attempts to bear fruit and grow stronger in your faith. May you never be discouraged, and may you find the strength to turn to God in your need. Take heart, knowing that God can do great things when we cannot. Find your hope in him now. Go in peace.**

All process to where the dismissal session will take place. The catechist holds the Lectionary in a reverent manner. The assembly may sing an acclamation to accompany the procession.

Centering

Upon reaching the place where the dismissal occurs, place the Lectionary on the ambo, lectern, or other dignified place (or hold the book reverently). Light the candle that is in the place of gathering and reread James 1:17–18, 21b–22, 27 in order to refocus the group's attention. Consider singing the Responsorial Psalm or have a recording of it available to use as part of the centering, either before or after the reading.

Reflection and Discussion

The following "script" may be used or adapted to help facilitate discussion on today's readings. Begin the discussion by asking the catechumens if any words or phrases from today's readings spoke to them.

Enacting God's Word is all about life—giving and receiving life. James instructs his brothers and sisters *both* to hear God's Word *and* to be doers of God's Word. Often when we hear the Word, especially on Sundays, we do not know how to act on it during the week, or we forget the Word, or we simply choose not to live God's Word on a particular day or week. James invites us to humbly welcome the Word God has placed in us.

- How can we humbly welcome the Word and invite it to grow in us?

⑨ Where have you seen someone enact the Word of God in his or her life that had a profound impact on you?

James specifically references our duty to care for orphans and widows and to keep ourselves unstained by the world as we embody the Word. People considered orphans and widows to be among the least in society at the time James wrote.

⑨ Who are the least among us now that God's Word calls us to care for?

⑨ What does it imply for us to remain unstained or untarnished by the world today?

In the First Reading, Moses instructs the Israelites that following the commandments of the Lord is all about life. Moses reduces it to a simple equation: observing the commandments as God gives them equals life and entering the Promised Land. The Israelites should neither add nor subtract from the side of the equation that contains the Lord's commandments.

⑨ How has being a "doer of the Word" (James 1:22) and following the Lord's commandments been a source of life for you?

⑨ Where are you tempted to add or subtract, or edit, God's commandments to suit your needs or to make them easier to follow?

God's Word is Wisdom. As Moses tells the Israelites, when they live God's Word, others will know their wisdom and intelligence. Theirs is a practical wisdom—wisdom for daily life that allows them to know the joy of life in the Lord. Theirs is the wisdom of justice that leads them to live in the Lord's presence. It is not with human wisdom, but divine wisdom that God fills them. Recall from the First Reading two Sundays ago that it is knowledge and understanding that we feast on when we participate in Wisdom's banquet.

⑨ In what ways have other Christians (members of your faith community, friends, family, others) affected you? Changed you?

Understanding the meaning of God's commandments in the twenty-first century is not always easy. It's about listening to the Spirit, to the guidance of the Church, and faithfully discerning how to enact the Word today within the communion of believers. In the Gospel reading, the Pharisees try to manipulate Jesus into admitting that his disciples were doing wrong by not following the tradition of the elders and observing ritual purity before they ate. Jesus, the embodiment of Wisdom, does not fall for their trap. Rather, he quotes from Isaiah and speaks about the hypocrites who only follow human tradition, but not God's law.

⑨ When have you seen human tradition take precedence over God's law in your life? In the lives of others? In the life of the faith community?

⑨ What happens when human tradition is more important the God's commandment?

Wisdom comes from the heart. When God's wisdom meets our hearts, love, justice, and mercy reign. We are able to hear and live God's Word of love. Evil thoughts do not defile us as they did the Pharisees.

⑨ What is the evil in your heart that you need God's mercy to forgive?

⑨ What is the Word of God that you need to enter your heart today?

Wrapping It Up   *Consider these points to conclude the dismissal. Integrate the thoughts and ideas that surfaced during the discussion.*

- God's Word is clear: those of us who love the Lord will live the Lord's Word. Our actions matter. We have the obligation to make our actions reflect the love for the most vulnerable that we hear in God's Word.

- Living God's commandments involves being in right relationship with God, others, Creation, and ourselves. This is the work of the heart. This is the work of asking God to forgive our sinful ways and to help orient our hearts to love.

- James instructs us to "humbly welcome the word" (James 1:21) that God has placed in us for our salvation. In all humility, we let our prayer be to let God's Word reign over any human traditions that we want to hang onto so tightly that they interfere with us bringing God's Word to bear on our world today.

Closing Prayer   *Conclude with prayer. If time permits, sing the psalm refrain a few times before or after the following prayer.*

> Just and merciful God,
> you give us the commandments of your Living Word
> to bring us wisdom, not foolishness,
> to bring us life, not death.
> Open our hearts to the change we need to make in order
> to live as doers of your Word,
> to let go of our human habits and traditions
> that interfere with the justice your Word beckons us to extend
> to those who suffer injustice and oppression.
> May we know the gift life and salvation that comes as we live the Word.
> Through Christ our Lord.
> Amen.

Readings for the Next Dismissal   *Provide catechumens with a list of the readings for the next dismissal session. Consult the liturgical calendar on page xvi to find out what day will be observed next week. Give catechumens the questions below to guide their reflection through the week.*

- What connections are you seeing in the readings of this liturgical season? As you pray with the readings, around what themes do your thoughts seem to be coming together?

- Where do the readings intersect with your journey of faith? What questions do they raise for you?

Extended Catechesis   *Based on today's readings and liturgical observance, the following topics may be covered for extended catechesis:*

❋ God's commandments	❋ Tradition of the Church
❋ Hearing and living the Word	❋ Sense of the faithful
❋ Humility	❋ Aligning our heart and will with God's will
❋ The relationship between Church law and the Word	❋ Jesus as the Word/Wisdom of God (second person of the Trinity)

Twenty-Third Sunday in Ordinary Time

Focus: Be open to the Lord.

Lectionary #128B

Catechist's Preparation

Overview of the Sunday

Serving the Lord, listening to the Word, and being a doer of the Lord's commandments requires openness to the Lord. The Lord will direct our actions, but we must let the Lord into our hearts. Today's readings show us that the Lord comes in a myriad of different ways. Many will surprise us! The Lord will come in a poor person no less than in a rich person. The Lord will come to open eyes to the joy salvation brings and empower the lame to dance in happiness for this gift. The Lord will overcome fear with strength. In Jesus, the blind and deaf will see and hear! The gift of new life in Jesus is ours, too. Are we open to the Lord? Are we open to hear and proclaim his saving Word and deeds?

Scripture Background

Isaiah 35:4–7a Isaiah's salvation proclamation begins with a call to "be strong, fear not" (Isaiah 35:4). No matter what struggles surround or overwhelm us with fear, trust that God comes to save. God's salvation is for all, most especially for those suffering any physical infirmity that would prevent them from full participation in religious, cultural, and communal involvement. The blind, the deaf, the lame, and the mute will experience God's saving power, enabling them to become full and active members of the community. Creation will also be renewed with new life and fertility as deserts teem with life from streams and rivers that overflow in abundance. Both human beings and nature will experience the life-giving power of God that restores and renews. Isaiah firmly asserts that God does not and will not give up on us no matter how bad things may appear. All are called to be open to the saving power of God, a power that is attuned to the weak and the powerless, the frightened and those bereft of life. Christians believe that in the person of Jesus, God's salvation has come, healing, renewing, and restoring all to newness of life.

Psalm 146:7, 8–9, 9–10 (1b) This psalm calls the entire community to praise the Lord with all their being (soul). Such total praise is due because God "keeps faith forever" (146:6), secures justice, feeds the hungry, and liberates the captives. The Lord heals and restores the blind and those bowed down. The stranger, the fatherless, and the widow—all those socially and economically powerless and marginalized—are cared for by God's empowering love. Our faithful God is attuned to all who are in need of healing, care, protection, and fullness of life. We are called to be people who imitate God in our dealings with all, most especially those in need. A life of justice challenges us to work toward establishing right relationship with all. To be open to God operating in our lives demands that we be open to all who are in need of God's healing touch and renewing love.

James 2:1–5 James counsels all followers of Christ to live lives that manifest love for all, most especially the poor and those that society easily marginalizes because of their looks, appearance, or social status. The assembly of believers is not to operate according to the standards of those who discriminate based on wealth or possessions. James refers to these people as "judges with evil designs" (2:4). We have been called by God to be brothers and sisters in the Lord. In Christian communities, all are treated equally, with preferential option given to the poor. The poor are especially close to the Lord because they are more attuned to depending on God and trusting God above all else. The rich tend to put their trust in other objects besides God. Ultimately, James states that God chose the poor to be "rich in faith and heirs of the kingdom" (2:5). We are to imitate God in love of the poor, caring for them as they challenge us by their deep trust and love of God.

Mark 7:31–37 This healing of the deaf and mute man is unique to Mark and is unique in the manner in which Jesus performs the miracle. Jesus' way of touching this man (inserting fingers in his ears and placing saliva on his tongue) is not his usual manner of healing. Mark communicates lessons through this narrative that are instructive for discipleship. The locale places Jesus in Gentile territory. For Mark, Jesus' mission is not exclusively for Jews, but for all people. Jesus breaks boundaries so that all might experience God's saving power. Gentiles are open to approaching Jesus, a Jew, to request healing. Jesus does not shrink from touching, going out of his way to use fingers, saliva, groaning, and a word of command—*Ephphatha*, "be opened"—to heal and restore the person to wholeness.

Made whole by becoming able to speak and hear, the healed man becomes a sign of God's reign and saving power, realized and activated through Jesus. Isaiah's salvation oracle in the First Reading is being fulfilled in the person of Jesus. The forces of evil are being defeated through Jesus' life-giving touch. Both Jew and Gentile, along with disciples then and now, are made aware that Jesus opens ears and mouths, enabling all to hear God's words and to speak God's praises. We, too, are made whole, in order to reach out to others and make them whole with God's help. Like the crowd, we, too, are "exceedingly astonished" (7:37), for Jesus "has done all things well" (7:37).

Reflection Questions for the Catechist

- What helps you open yourself to the Lord?
- When have you experienced the Lord helping you to hear and see more clearly?
- How has openness to the Lord empowered you to recognize God's presence in those who are poor?

Catechist's Guide

Objectives

- ▷ To ponder what helps us open ourselves to the Lord and what prevents us from assuming the posture of openness to the divine.
- ▷ To name and celebrate the times the Lord has opened us to his saving grace.
- ▷ To open ourselves to accept God's invitation to show no partiality as we live our faith.

Dismissal and Procession

Following the homily, the priest celebrant picks up the Lectionary and invites the catechumens to come forward with the catechist(s) who will lead today's dismissal session. Holding the Lectionary so that all can see, the priest celebrant sends the catechumens and catechist(s) forward using RCIA, 67, his own words, or the following:

PRIEST: **My dear friends, Jesus calls us to follow him, to take times of silence, and to live lives worthy of the Gospel. As you reflect upon his Word, may you be strengthened in your attempts to bear fruit and grow stronger in your faith. May you never be discouraged, and may you find the strength to turn to God in your need. Take heart, knowing that God can do great things when we cannot. Find your hope in him now. Go in peace.**

All process to where the dismissal session will take place. The catechist holds the Lectionary in a reverent manner. The assembly may sing an acclamation to accompany the procession.

Centering

Upon reaching the place where the dismissal occurs, place the Lectionary on the ambo, lectern, or other dignified place (or hold the book reverently). Light the candle that is in the place of gathering and reread Mark 7:31–37 in order to refocus the group's attention. Consider singing the Responsorial Psalm or have a recording of it available to use as part of the centering, either before or after the reading.

Reflection and Discussion

The following "script" may be used or adapted to help facilitate discussion on today's readings. Begin the discussion by asking the catechumens if any words or phrases from today's readings spoke to them.

We are a society of doers. Last Sunday, we focused on St. James' instruction to us to not only hear God's Word, but to "be doers of the Word" (James 1:22). Jesus exemplifies to us in today's Gospel how to live the Word. He enacts the Word in a personal encounter with the deaf man with a speech impediment whom others had brought to him. Jesus heals the man.

- How are we open to the very Word made flesh in Jesus?

The Gospel reading does not tell us whether the people who brought the deaf man to Jesus were the man's friends, bystanders, or complete strangers. Sometimes we need others to show us the way to Jesus, to accompany us to him for healing.

- Has there been a time in your life when someone helped you to see your need for healing?

- What is your story of approaching Jesus so that he could open you to new life in him?

The deaf and mute man needed to do nothing to receive healing from Jesus. Sometimes doing nothing is the hardest thing for those of us who have to do so much all day at work and at home. Just receiving life and goodness can be a challenge.

- What is it like for you to know you do not need to do anything to be made whole in Jesus? To experience new life in him?

The people who witnessed Jesus open the deaf man's ears and restore his speech could not help themselves. Despite Jesus' order, they had to proclaim the Good News of what they saw happen.

- When Jesus opens your ears to hear his Word and gives you the ability to plainly speak his Word, how do you respond? Do you tell others about what happened and about who Jesus is?

The poetry that are the Lord's words in the First Reading from the prophet Isaiah, paints a beautiful picture of what will happen when the Lord comes to save us. The Lord will open eyes and ears. Those unable to walk will dance. Those unable to speak will sing. Even the desert will bloom. Sands will turn to water. Jesus is the fulfillment of this amazing prophecy! The refrain for the Responsorial Psalm provides the short and simple response to this abundant goodness: "Praise the Lord, my soul!"

- Where has Jesus come into your life? Where do you see his presence in the Church? In the world?

- What is the song of praise in your heart and on your lips in response to Jesus' presence?

The Second Reading from St. James, directly instructs us to "show no partiality" (James 2:1) as we follow our faith in Jesus Christ. In the way we live, people should see no partiality, no distinction between rich and poor. Human distinctions hold no merit in God. Neither should they hold sway for a person of faith. God's salvation in Jesus Christ is available to all. God's love knows no borders. Healing and wholeness, new life and boundless love are God's gifts to everyone.

- Where do you struggle to show no partiality?

- Where do you see partiality based on human distinctions in the world that needs to be replaced with God's mercy and love?

- What is one action you can take this week to be open to the Lord and his presence everywhere and in all people?

Wrapping It Up *Consider these points to conclude the dismissal. Integrate the thoughts and ideas that surfaced during the discussion.*

- Jesus healed the deaf man in a personal encounter. The man did not have to do anything to receive wholeness. There is nothing we can do to earn the gift of wholeness and salvation in Jesus Christ. All we need do is receive the love of Christ in pure openness to his grace.

- The people responded to Jesus' healing of the deaf man with astonishment. They proclaimed to others the goodness he did. May the psalmist's song of praise on this Sunday be ours as well. From the depths of our soul, may we sing "Praise the Lord!" (refrain, Psalm 146) and may our lives reflect the joy of our new life in Christ.

- When we practice our faith in Jesus Christ, we do so by following his example to the best of our ability. As God shows no partiality in offering the grace of his Kingdom to rich and poor alike, so we are to do. In all our personal encounters this week, may our kindness and generosity mirror God's, for richness comes through faith, not money.

Closing Prayer

Conclude with prayer. If time permits, sing the psalm refrain a few times before or after the following prayer.

> God of healing,
> you promised your people that you would come
> to open the eyes of the blind
> and the ears of the deaf,
> and that those physically challenged would be able to leap and dance.
> Your Son indeed came and brought wholeness to the deaf man
> who had difficulty speaking.
> The gift of wholeness he received is the gift of salvation
> your Son makes available to all people.
> Help us set aside any fears we have as we seek
> to open ourselves to your healing grace.
> Lead us to praise you with songs of "Alleluia"
> for the wonders performed by Christ the Lord.
> Who lives and reigns for ever.
> Amen.

Readings for the Next Dismissal

Provide catechumens with a list of the readings for the next dismissal session. Consult the liturgical calendar on page xvi to find out what day will be observed next week. Give catechumens the questions below to guide their reflection through the week.

- What connections are you seeing in the readings of this liturgical season? As you pray with the readings, around what themes do your thoughts seem to be coming together?

- Where do the readings intersect with your journey of faith? What questions do they raise for you?

Extended Catechesis

Based on today's readings and liturgical observance, the following topics may be covered for extended catechesis:

- Prayer and discernment
- God's saves us and makes us whole
- Proclaiming Jesus' as the Messiah
- God chooses all and shows no partiality
- God comes to us through all people and through all of creation
- Signs of God's coming in the world

Twenty-Fourth Sunday in Ordinary Time

Focus: God comes to the aid of the faithful.

Lectionary #131B

Catechist's Preparation

Overview of the Sunday

On the Twenty-Third Sunday in Ordinary Time, we rejoiced with the deaf man when Jesus opened his ears to hear. This Sunday, the First Reading begins with the prophet's words proclaiming how God opene his ears. What Good News this is for us who serve the Lord and face difficulties, suffering, and persecution. The message is clear and consistent: God cares for his people! God in Jesus Christ is our help. God gives life to us! But, Jesus brings two questions to us in the Gospel reading: "Who do we say that Jesus is?" and, "Are we willing to follow him and take up his Cross?" When we follow Jesus, we will know life. When we take up the Cross, we will know our salvation. We do not earn salvation by the works we do to follow Jesus, James tells us in the Second Reading. But the good works we do are our response to the gift of faith and grace and life we have in God through Jesus Christ. And what a gift that is we can present to others by the good we do!

Scripture Background

Isaiah 50:5–9a Popular preaching often makes an association between sin and suffering, or between holiness and good fortune. Those links cannot be legitimated by using the Old Testament, much less the New Testament. Throughout scriptural history, the prophets suffer for remaining faithful to their vocation, and the psalms often depict the innocent as undergoing unjust punishments. In today's reading, from the third of four sections of Isaiah known as Servant Songs, Isaiah describes the servant of God as one who is willing to undergo torment.

As we ponder this reading, there is no indication of who is inflicting the suffering. The central characters are the testifying servant and God. Unlike the complaints we hear from prophets in some prophetic books (Jeremiah 20), the servant of Isaiah 50 expresses nothing but gratitude. He recognizes God as the one who opens his ears, who keeps him from disgrace and from being proven wrong. This is the song of a disciple who values a faithful relationship with God above all else.

Psalm 116:1–2, 3–4, 5–6, 8–9 (9) This psalm of thanksgiving follows the First Reading from one of the Servant Song in beautiful harmony. Whereas the servant proclaimed that his ear was opened by God, we are invited to join the psalmist in singing the praise of the

God who gives ear to our cries. There is no doubt that the psalmist knew mortal danger as well as near despair. But, the plea "Lord, save my life" (116:4), shows that even in the midst of a living nightmare, one can both have and express faith.

The third strophe of our psalm speaks in a particular way to the theme proclaimed by the servant. As it expresses God's special concern for the little ones and those brought low, it emphasizes the fact that, although we frequently forget it, before God we are all little and lowly. The gratitude this psalm expresses reminds us that only when we recognize our own frailty can we become aware of the immense privilege of walking in the sight of God in the land of the living.

James 2:14–18 Our selection from James fits well with today's other readings. It responds to the question of what it means to have faith. James insists that genuine faith in Christ is more than intellectual. Real faith is demonstrated through Christ-like actions, such as caring for the needy. The teaching in this reading from James leads us into our Gospel reading, where Peter is told that authentic faith in Jesus as Messiah implies a readiness to accept and share his Cross.

Mark 8:27–35 This incident takes place during Jesus' final journey with the disciples (Mark 8:27—10:45). They are entering into a long period in which Jesus tries to teach them who he is and what it means to be his follower. Today's Gospel provides a summary statement of each of those points.

Jesus asks, "Who do you say that I am?" (8:27). This question touches the central theme of Mark's account of the Gospel. While Peter's response, "You are the Christ" (8:29), sounded very good, his understanding of what that implied had little in common with Jesus' own understanding of himself and his mission. That is why Jesus ordered the disciples not to tell anyone about him: they didn't know what they were talking about!

Faced with their lack of understanding, Jesus had to shatter their expectations. Mark tells us that "he began" (8:31) to teach them. That "beginning" would last through the rest of the Gospel. It was beyond their imagination that a Messiah would be rejected and killed. The job of a warrior Messiah was to route Israel's enemies, not suffer at their hands. The job of a priestly Messiah was to rebuild or renew the Temple, not be rejected by all the religious leaders.

Jesus' retort to Peter's rebuke underlined the problem they had to deal with. Peter had pulled Jesus aside to plead against the fate he predicted. When Jesus called Peter "Satan" (8:33), the effect was not to say he was a devil, but rather a tempter. The phrase "get behind me" (8:33), pointed out that Jesus, not Peter, was the teacher.

The place for a disciple was following the master's lead, not vice versa.

Jesus had discerned God's plan. He knew that his confrontation with evil would lead evil to lash out at him. Peter's perspective focused on safety and triumph. Jesus knew that his prophetic ministry would bring him suffering, but he also trusted that God would see him through. That was and still is a hard message to communicate.

Reflection Questions for the Catechist

⑨ WWhen have you faced suffering yet not turned your back on the Lord when there were others who wanted to tear you down?

⑨ How would you describe the relationship between faith and works in your own life?

⑨ Who do you say Jesus is? How has the way you identify him changed over the course of your life's journey of faith?

Catechist's Guide

Objectives

▷ To reflect on how we take up the Cross of Jesus in our lives and the ways God comes to our aid when the Cross seems too much to carry.

▷ To consider who we say Jesus is and to consider how the way we understand who he is has changed or deepened throughout our life.

▷ To think about how we live out the relationship between faith and works in our lives.

Dismissal and Procession

Following the homily, the priest celebrant picks up the Lectionary and invites the catechumens to come forward with the catechist(s) who will lead today's dismissal session. Holding the Lectionary so that all can see, the priest celebrant sends the catechumens and catechist(s) forward using RCIA, 67, his own words, or the following:

PRIEST: **My dear friends, who seek to know the Lord more fully, and who strive to develop this relationship in the Church, be active builders of the Kingdom in all that you do. We pray that you continue your journey of faith with a lively concern for your neighbor and for creation and that you have a willing desire to follow God's will. May the Word, which you share this day, grow within you. We look forward to the day when you will participate fully with us at the Lord's table. Go in peace.**

All process to where the dismissal session will take place. The catechist holds the Lectionary in a reverent manner. The assembly may sing an acclamation to accompany the procession.

Centering

Upon reaching the place where the dismissal occurs, place the Lectionary on the ambo, lectern, or other dignified place (or hold the book reverently). Light the candle that is in the place of gathering and reread Isaiah 50:5–9a in order to refocus the group's attention. Consider singing the Responsorial Psalm or have a recording of it available to use as part of the centering, either before or after the reading.

Reflection and Discussion

The following "script" may be used or adapted to help facilitate discussion on today's readings. Begin the discussion by asking the catechumens if any words or phrases from today's readings spoke to them.

Despite torment and suffering, and notwithstanding opposition and even confrontation, Isaiah remained faithful. God opened his ears to receive and embrace his prophetic call. God gave him the courage to preach the divine Word and to act righteously.

- What struggles have you faced in life? Have there been times when you have encountered resistance to your faith?

The beautiful words of Isaiah's poetry attest to the constancy of God's help. They express the faithful prophet's confidence that God is always by his side ready to come to his aid. Isaiah's words exemplify a person's ideal response of faith to challenges that arise. At times when we are in the midst of struggle and suffering, we might not respond confidently that God is with us, that God is indeed our help.

- With what level of confidence have you expressed your faith that God is your help when you have struggled through a difficult situation?

- What benefits your confidence level and trust in God's presence during challenging times?

Peter's confession of Jesus as the Christ in today's Gospel reading is a turning point in the Gospel according to Mark. As part of their conversation on the way to Caesarea Philippi, Jesus asked the disciples who they thought he was. Most related Jesus to one of the prophets or to John the Baptist, but Peter acknowledged him as the Messiah.

- Who is Jesus to you? Why have you chosen to follow him?

Mark has Jesus warn the disciples not to say anything about his identity going forward. This is because Mark wants Jesus' identity as the Christ centered on the Cross and Resurrection.

- What has taught you the most about Jesus' identity?

Jesus explains to his disciples the rejection, suffering, and death he must face at the hands of religious and political leaders, but that he will rise after three days. Perhaps Peter did not hear the last part about Jesus' Resurrection, because he was clearly upset with Jesus' words. Peter's thinking was limited by his human nature. He could not grasp how God would offer salvation, coming to the aid of his people, in an amazing and astonishing way!

- What place does Jesus' suffering, Death, and Resurrection have in your life of faith?

- How can it help you to know that during your own times of suffering God's profound offer of help is present for you in the suffering, Death, and Resurrection of Jesus, the Christ?

If we follow him, Jesus instructs us, we must take up the Cross. We must lose our life for his sake. When we take up our own cross in solidarity with Jesus, we choose to extend God's help to those in need. This is the work of faith. It is not work done as if it could earn our salvation. It is the work done out of gratitude for the help and life God gives us. It is our recognition that others deserve the same, and that through our actions we can help them hear and see God, to know that God is their help too.

- How do you take up the Cross as you follow Jesus?

- How is your life lost for Jesus and then saved?

- What do you see as your responsibility in demonstrating faith—the faith of the Cross—through works?

Wrapping It Up

Consider these points to conclude the dismissal. Integrate the thoughts and ideas that surfaced during the discussion.

- God is our help. This we know. Isaiah acclaimed this twice in the First Reading. Our life stories reflect the ways God comes to our aid when the Cross seems unbearable. We might not realize God's help at the time, but as we continue the journey, we often see and hear more clearly the times when God has helped us in the past.

- Peter identified Jesus as the Christ, the Messiah. This is a turning point in Mark's account of the Gospel. Suffering, rejection, and death would envelop Jesus' journey to the Cross. As people of faith, we know this is not the end of the story. God's help comes through the Cross. Each day, we must be willing to follow and take up Jesus' Cross. Each day we must respond to the question "Who do I say Jesus is?"

We accompany each other on the road of faith—in the faith that God our help is Jesus Christ who suffered, died, and rose for us. Yet faith is not merely a set of propositions. It is a life-giving gift. It is our responsibility to respond in kind to this gift. We do so by engaging in works of faith.

Closing Prayer

Conclude with prayer. If time permits, sing the psalm refrain a few times before or after the following prayer.

> God of grace and mercy,
> in times of desperation you helped your people of old.
> In your Son, Jesus, who shouldered the burden of the Cross,
> you relieve the suffering of people for all time.
> Open our ears to hear Peter's confession that Jesus is the Christ
> and our mouths to proclaim him as Messiah.
> Form us now and always into a people of the Cross.
> Let our works of kindness and justice reflect gratitude for the life you have given us.
> Through Christ our Lord.
> Amen.

Readings for the Next Dismissal

Provide catechumens with a list of the readings for the next dismissal session. Consult the liturgical calendar on page xvi to find out what day will be observed next week. Give catechumens the questions below to guide their reflection through the week.

- What connections are you seeing in the readings of this liturgical season? As you pray with the readings, around what themes do your thoughts seem to be coming together?

- Where do the readings intersect with your journey of faith? What questions do they raise for you?

Extended Catechesis

Based on today's readings and liturgical observance, the following topics may be covered for extended catechesis:

- ※ Suffering, persecution, and the Way of the Cross

- ※ Calling on the Lord in time of need

- ※ The relationship between faith and works

- ※ The gift of salvation

- ※ Jesus as the Christ, the Messiah

- ※ The relationship between the Cross and discipleship

- ※ Caring for people's material needs as a faith response

- ※ Stations of the Cross (devotion)

TWENTY-FIFTH SUNDAY IN ORDINARY TIME

Focus: To value humility.

Lectionary #134B

Catechist's Preparation

Overview of the Sunday

We always want to be first, to be on top of the heap, to be the greatest. Jesus turns this human wisdom upside down in today's Gospel as he tells the disciples that whoever wants to be first, that person shall serve others and put themselves last. To receive a child is to receive Jesus and the One who sent him. Humility is the core Christian value reflected not only in the Gospel reading, but also in the First Reading, from Wisdom. In it, we hear how the wicked strongly desire to put the just one to death. In all humility, Jesus will accept his death, but death will not have the last word. Rather, life will reign triumphant in his Resurrection! As we continue to proclaim from James, we hear the many fruits of wisdom, which we could summarize as living a life of compassion and humility, all the while cultivating peace. Doing so embodies the consistent message of Ordinary Time—that life and love triumph!

Scripture Background

Wisdom 2:12, 17–20 The words that we hear in today's First Reading are neither the words of God nor of anyone who speaks for God. They are the words of the wicked, as seen by the author of the Book of Wisdom. This author, often called "the Sage," wrote in Greek shortly before the birth of Jesus. His purpose was to justify the God of Israel in the eyes of sophisticated Jewish students who were often tempted to devalue their Jewish beliefs in favor of secular culture. Aware and appreciative of the positive insights of Hellenistic culture, the Sage is nevertheless firm in his conviction that the true meaning of life will only be realized through the revelation of Israel's God.

As the wicked speak in today's reading, they reveal the ignorance that leads them astray. They attack the "just one" (2:12) because he does not agree with their philosophy. They seek to revile and torture him in order to test whether he possesses the particular virtues they promote. "Gentleness" and "patience" (2:19) were virtues celebrated by Greek ethical teachers such as Epictetus. These Hellenistic virtues are contrasted to the beliefs of the just one who trusts that "God will take care of him" (2:20). Even though the just one's belief in God is ridiculed by the wicked, the reader knows that such a belief is true. The Sage uses the disdain of the wicked to make his point: one can study the philosophy of this world, but true wisdom is found by trusting in the power of God.

Psalm 54:3–4, 5, 6–8 (6b) Psalm 54 clearly echoes the belief of the Sage: the truth of human existence can only be found in relationship with the true God. This brief psalm is an individual prayer for help. The reason for confidence is grounded in God's faithfulness to the one who prays.

James 3:16—4:3 This reading presents a catalogue of virtues and vices. Purity, peace, gentleness, compliancy, and mercy all flow from true wisdom. Coveting, envy, fighting, and killing all result from the war that rages within our passions. James may have drawn the virtues offered here from the list composed by the Sage who authored today's First Reading (see Wisdom 7:21–28).

The virtues are not only important in themselves. Although the list of virtues and vices describes what we should and should not do, James wants us to understand why we should do one and avoid the other. In the verses before the Lectionary selection (see James 3:13–15) James criticizes his readers because they are unwise and immature. Their stance toward the poor demonstrates that they have not yet replaced the worldly evaluation of power and importance with God's perspective. Following virtues and avoiding vices must flow from adopting that perspective. This requires humility (see James 3:13). The Sage of the Book of Wisdom would fully agree. So will Jesus in the Gospel.

Mark 9:30–37 Jesus teaches that we must redefine greatness. We are important not when we place ourselves first, but when we assume the last place. Greatness is not found in an exalted position but in service. Contrary to the assumptions of our society, humility is true power. Humility is not negating ourselves, but immersing ourselves in the truth that God has revealed. Jesus enacts a parable by embracing a child. In the ancient world, children were those without legal standing and societal influence. Jesus shows us that when we identify with those who are marginalized and vulnerable, we are glorified in God's sight. This is how we adopt the divine perspective that both the Sage of Wisdom and the author of James promote. When we humbly embrace the last place, we are standing in Christ's place.

Reflection Questions for the Catechist

- In what areas in your life do you find yourself seeking worldly power and prestige rather than humbly serving others?
- Which of the virtues in the Second Reading do you find most challenging?
- How does Jesus' teaching about humility apply to your life at this point?

Catechist's Guide

Objectives

▷ To know the humility required of a disciple who imitates Jesus' example of service to the least among us.

▷ To consider the profound impact of Jesus' reversal of worldly wisdom.

▷ To discern willingness to follow Jesus after his second prediction of his Passion, Death, and Resurrection.

Dismissal and Procession

Following the homily, the priest celebrant picks up the Lectionary and invites the catechumens to come forward with the catechist(s) who will lead today's dismissal session. Holding the Lectionary so that all can see, the priest celebrant sends the catechumens and catechist(s) forward using RCIA, 67, his own words, or the following:

PRIEST: **My dear friends, who seek to know the Lord more fully, and who strive to develop this relationship in the Church, be active builders of the Kingdom in all that you do. We pray that you continue your journey of faith with a lively concern for your neighbor and creation and have a willing desire to follow God's will. May the Word, which you share this day, grow within you. We look forward to the day when you will participate fully with us at the Lord's table. Go in peace.**

All process to where the dismissal session will take place. The catechist holds the Lectionary in a reverent manner. The assembly may sing an acclamation to accompany the procession.

Centering

Upon reaching the place where the dismissal occurs, place the Lectionary on the ambo, lectern, or other dignified place (or hold the book reverently). Light the candle that is in the place of gathering and reread Mark 9:30–37 in order to refocus the group's attention. Consider singing the Responsorial Psalm or have a recording of it available to use as part of the centering, either before or after the reading.

Reflection and Discussion

The following "script" may be used or adapted to help facilitate discussion on today's readings. Begin the discussion by asking the catechumens if any words or phrases from today's readings spoke to them.

The disciples chose not to question Jesus about his second prediction of the Son of Man's Passion, Death, and Resurrection. They were afraid, fearful of what it might mean for them.

- What was a time when you were afraid to ask someone—or even to ask Jesus—about what you heard?
- Why did fear paralyze you?

Rather than ask questions to clarify what Jesus meant, the disciples chose to argue about who among them was the greatest. And, oh, are they surprised when Jesus calls them together to reorient their thought processes. Jesus teaches that greatness for those who follow him does not lie in what the world understands as greatness. Power, prestige, climbing the corporate latter, when all done just to topple others and gain access to self-serving greatness, will not lead one to be first in the eyes of God. Serving others will, as will welcoming a child and others who the world considers among the least. This is the wisdom of Jesus.

- What connection do you see between Jesus' wisdom and what is happening in the world today?
- What personal call to discipleship do you hear for yourself in Jesus' words?

Much of the reason the religious and political authorities of Jesus' time plotted to put him death lies in his wisdom teaching. In it, Jesus reversed the status quo. In Jesus' call to servanthood there is an obvious turning upside down of human desire for self-aggrandizement.

- Where do you come face-to-face with the desire to be on top or even the desire to simply win an argument?

Jesus will lead his disciples all the way to the Cross, where he perfectly enacts his teaching on humility. He humbles himself even to the point of death. But for those of us who know the end of the story, we know and believe that his Death on the Cross did not have the final say. The final, once-and-for-all reversal of worldly wisdom came in his Resurrection. Death no longer has the final say. Death that comes from self-aggrandizement and not welcoming others will no longer triumph. Life that comes through Jesus will. Life lived in humility and in service to others is seen as a life of pure love.

- Where does God take care of you, as God took care of Jesus, when you face suffering and even death for your actions or beliefs?
- What does it require of you to live your life with humility and in service of others?

The virtues described in the Second Reading from James, help us to grasp in more detail the meaning of Jesus' wisdom. Purity, peace, gentleness, compliance, mercy, righteousness, sincerity—these constitute part of living out Jesus' wisdom and humility in our own lives.

- Which one of these virtues do you find the simplest to live out? Which one seems to pose the most challenges?
- Where are the conflicts that divide you from others? That divides us as a Christian community? That divides us in the world?

Jesus' second prediction of his Passion, Death, and Resurrection provides us an opportunity to step back and reflect on where we are at in our relationship with him. It gives us pause to consider the seriousness of our decision to follow him, a decision that we should not take lightly. Might it be that the disciples' fear—the fear that kept them from asking Jesus about the meaning of his talk about suffering and Death—had been based in their own fear about where the Cross would lead?

- How willing are you to carry the cross of suffering, death, and humility in today's world?
- How will you need God to take care of you as you follow his Son, Jesus?

Wrapping It Up

Consider these points to conclude the dismissal. Integrate the thoughts and ideas that surfaced during the discussion.

- Humility does not mean disregarding our own needs. If we are to serve the least among us in humility, we must take care of ourselves and allow others to accompany us on the journey to the Cross. Humility does mean not seeking power and prestige when our achievements will denigrate others and only serve to make us look good. Humility is welcoming the goodness in all people and seeing that together with Jesus we make the journey of faith as a community of disciples, equal in the wisdom of faith.

- When we believe in Jesus, we accept his wisdom as true, as non-negotiable. Receive and welcome all as children of God. Serve others rather than seeking worldly glory.

- Many of the religious authorities in Jesus' time despised him for the wisdom that he taught and lived. This led to his suffering and Death. Jesus had been clear all along that his disciples must express willingness to carry the Cross, too. The intensity heightened today as we heard the second prediction of Jesus' Passion and Death. Prayerful consideration of the extent to which we are willing to follow Jesus stands as an important task for us this week and in the weeks ahead.

Closing Prayer

Conclude with prayer. If time permits, sing the psalm refrain a few times before or after the following prayer.

God of Wisdom,
the wicked ones of old sought to do you harm,
yet into their midst you sent your Son, Jesus, whose humility to the point of Death enacted the ultimate reversal of earthly, human wisdom.
Create in our hearts a willingness not to join in condemning him to death
by seeking power and prestige, but to be the servant of all,
but by welcoming and receiving all people with gentleness, justice, and peace.
Through Christ our Lord.
Amen.

Readings for the Next Dismissal

Provide catechumens with a list of the readings for the next dismissal session. Consult the liturgical calendar on page xvi to find out what day will be observed next week. Give catechumens the questions below to guide their reflection through the week.

- What connections are you seeing in the readings of this liturgical season? As you pray with the readings, around what themes do your thoughts seem to be coming together?

- Where do the readings intersect with your journey of faith? What questions do they raise for you?

Extended Catechesis

Based on today's readings and liturgical observance, the following topics may be covered for extended catechesis:

- ❄ Christian humility and other Christian virtues

- ❄ Christian service

- ❄ Jesus' identity as the Son of Man

- ❄ Jesus' Passion, Death, and Resurrection—the Paschal Mystery

- ❄ Jesus' Wisdom as the reversal of earthly wisdom

- ❄ Welcoming all people is welcoming of God—Father, Son, and Holy Spirit

Twenty-Sixth Sunday in Ordinary Time

Focus: To live as faithful disciples.

Lectionary #137B

Catechist's Preparation

Overview of the Sunday

Faithful disciples are always hard at work teaching and living what they have learned from Jesus. Humility, as we saw last Sunday, is one of the greatest virtues for a disciple to practice. In our practice of humility, we express in the confidence of faith that God will uphold us. Today, we see how the Lord bestows the Spirit on the elders. The Spirit touched not only those in the gathering, but also Eldad and Medad, who had remained in camp. Joshua wanted to stop Eldad and Medad from proclaiming God's Word, but Moses taught that all are to be prophets. Jesus message in the Gospel reading is consistent: do not prevent people from driving out demons and bringing life. Should our words and actions prevent goodness, perhaps we should to look at ourselves and see where we need God's mercy to help us live as faithful disciples.

Scripture Background

Numbers 11:25-29 Moses seems to be overwhelmed by the responsibilities of leading the people and calls upon God for help. God takes some of the spirit that was on Moses and bestows it on seventy elders who will assist him. The ritual is to take place at the meeting tent outside the camp. Two of the seventy elders, Eldad and Medad, do not attend the ritual but remain in the camp. Yet, they too receive the spirit and prophesy. Joshua tells Moses to stop them since they were not at the tent ritual, thus are not officially appointed elders. Moses refuses, allowing God to dispense the spirit on whomever he desires.

Moses has learned that God knows better than we do who has the gifts to assist in building up the community. Like Joshua, some want God to act in an orderly matter, going through the right channels. But God's spirit moves where it wills. Our task is to attune ourselves to the presence of God's spirit wherever and whenever it is experienced.

Psalm 19:8, 10, 12-13, 14 (9a) Psalm 19 celebrates God by focusing on two images that guide us in living faithfully to him. The first seven verses are a hymn to the sun which, as an image of God, provides light, warmth, and life to all of creation. Creation responds by gloriously praising God for this wondrous gift. God contin-

ues to guide creation by revealing the divine name and by giving the Law or Torah to the people. Verses 8-12 sing the praises of God's Law. Like the sun, the Law gives light, teaching us how to live in fidelity to God. The Law is perfect and trustworthy, dispensing wisdom to all, even the simple. The Law is just and God's ordinances are true. The last few verses address the possibility that even though we strive to live faithfully according to the Law, we might not be aware of our own weaknesses.

James 5:1-6 James presents one of the strongest condemnations of the rich in the New Testament. Like other prophets before him, James accuses the rich of injustices against workers who have toiled but have not been justly compensated. He charges that the rich have become so by cheating and taking advantage of workers whose rights and dignity they consistently violate. Thus, the wealthy do not live faithfully according to God's wisdom. Rather, they live to please and satisfy only themselves. James warns the rich that God has heard the cry of the abused workers. Like other prophets, James guarantees God will right injustice, if not in this life, then definitely in the next.

Mark 9:38-43, 45, 47-48 Part of what prevents humans from living faithfully according to God's desires is our consistent temptation to want things our way, to control life. This temptation is the root of all sinfulness and leads to prejudice, blindness, lack of openness, insincerity, lack of compassion and understanding, injustice, and many other ills. Jesus addresses these issues in today's reading from the Gospel.

Jesus reprimands John for desiring to control who can or cannot act compassionately toward others. Because a particular person is not one of Jesus' followers, John wants him prevented from acting in Jesus' name. Like Moses in the First Reading, Jesus does not stop, but rather welcomes any and all who would live and act in accordance to God's wishes and designs. Such a manifestation of faithful living expressed in compassionate concern for the other should be welcomed and encouraged. Rather than controlling, we should be attentive to the surprising ways in which God directs others to act, even if different from our way of acting.

Reflection Questions for the Catechist

🌀 Where does the Spirit lead you to prophesy God's Word?

🌀 What is an occasion on which you attempted to prevent someone from prophesying or enacting goodness over evil?

🌀 How do you already see the catechumens to whom you minister as a dismissal catechist living as faithful disciples?

Catechist's Guide

Objectives

▷ To accept without jealousy that God's Spirit fills everyone.

▷ To recognize that all who work for what is good and life-giving in Jesus' name are not against us, but for us.

▷ To appreciate that sometimes, in order to grow in faithfulness, disciples need to examine their own hearts and consciences to see what causes them to sin.

Dismissal and Procession

Following the homily, the priest celebrant picks up the Lectionary and invites the catechumens to come forward with the catechist(s) who will lead today's dismissal session. Holding the Lectionary so that all can see, the priest celebrant sends the catechumens and catechist(s) forward using RCIA, 67, his own words, or the following:

PRIEST: My dear friends, who seek to know the Lord more fully, and who strive to develop this relationship in the Church, be active builders of the Kingdom in all that you do. We pray that you continue your journey of faith with a lively concern for your neighbor and creation and have a willing desire to follow God's will. May the Word, which you share this day, grow within you. We look forward to the day when you will participate fully with us at the Lord's table. Go in peace.

All process to where the dismissal session will take place. The catechist holds the Lectionary in a reverent manner. The assembly may sing an acclamation to accompany the procession.

Centering

Upon reaching the place where the dismissal occurs, place the Lectionary on the ambo, lectern, or other dignified place (or hold the book reverently). Light the candle that is in the place of gathering and reread Numbers 11:25–29 in order to refocus the group's attention. Consider singing the Responsorial Psalm or have a recording of it available to use as part of the centering, either before or after the reading.

Reflection and Discussion

The following "script" may be used or adapted to help facilitate discussion on today's readings. Begin the discussion by asking the catechumens if any words or phrases from today's readings spoke to them.

Living as a prophetic witness to the Lord's Word is a calling not reserved for a few, but is for all upon whom the Lord's spirit rests. The First Reading, from Numbers, makes this clear. While we humans might want to decide who is a legitimate prophet based on whether they are insiders or outsiders to a gathering, this is not how the Lord works. Jealousy, as was the case with Joshua, son of Nun, will get us nowhere. Moses desires that all of the Lord's people serve as prophets.

🌀 Who do you see as the Lord's prophets? Why do you consider them prophets?

🌀 What "qualifies" a person to be a prophet?

🌀 How is the Lord's Spirit already present in you, teaching you to live as prophet?

🌀 How would you define a faithful prophet?

This Sunday is the last time we will read from the letter of James in Ordinary Time. James saves for his final chapter his harshest words against the rich who have lived in wanton luxury at the expense of others. Their oppressive habits have led to their death. Eternal life surely will not be theirs. They have put the just one to death. They have truly not been faithful disciples.

🌀 What message do you take from James' stark criticism of the actions of the rich?

🌀 What prophetic words are disciples called to speak in light of the Second Reading?

🌀 How do James' words impact the way you live your life? What you do with your financial and material resources?

The Gospel reading also centers on faithful action. Faithful action and prophetic witness do not belong to just a few. In response to John's attempt to prevent someone from outside of the group of Jesus' disciples from exorcising demons in his name, Jesus speaks of an inclusive mission. Anyone performing a "mighty deed" (Mark 9:39) in his name proclaims his goodness. They are collaborating with Jesus and his disciples in their mission.

🌀 What makes a faithful disciple?

🌀 Who does God call us to work together with as faithful disciples of Jesus?

🌀 Sometimes we fall short of what it means to live as a faithful disciple. We do not always make choices that are consistent with being a follower of Jesus. We do not always see as God sees or hear as God hears. We need our eyes and ears opened by Jesus as he opened the eyes of ears of those who were blind and deaf. What is a time when you have fallen short of living as a faithful disciple?

Jesus' warning to John and the rest of the disciples is stern. It would be better to have physical challenges than to have a fully functioning body that leads us to sin and destines us for Gehenna rather than God's Kingdom. It would be better to remain faithful and, when sin leads us astray, to seek God's mercy. A perfect life of faithfulness is impossible alone, but it is possible through God's mercy. With God's grace, we can have a place at the banquet table in the Kingdom of God. Our prophetic witness includes even admitting in all humility when we have sinned and need God's forgiveness.

🌀 What do you take away from Jesus' stern warning to his disciples?

🌀 How can the recognition of our need for God's mercy be a prophetic witness to others? How does it help us to remain faithful disciples?

Wrapping It Up

Consider these points to conclude the dismissal. Integrate the thoughts and ideas that surfaced during the discussion.

- God's Spirit fills everyone, regardless of where they are in life, regardless of where they are from, and regardless of the place in which they prophesy. Speaking God's words of wisdom in the world is the responsibility of all who call themselves faithful disciples. The Spirit enables us to prophesy God's life-giving words.

- Many will do good works in Jesus' name. Many will help others to overcome poverty, to feed the hungry, and to live in humility and service to others. They are with us as we extend the Gospel of life. When we prevent people from doing good, we deny Christ acting in the world today.

- We have limitations. We sometimes make choices that are not life-giving for us or for others. Our hands, feet, and eyes cause us to sin. Yet God continues to call us to live as faithful disciples. We grow in our faithfulness when we reach out to God for forgiveness and mercy in the face of our sin.

Closing Prayer

Conclude with prayer. If time permits, sing the psalm refrain a few times before or after the following prayer.

God of mercy and love,
you sent your Spirit upon the people Moses led
to proclaim your Word of life and justice everywhere.
Fill us with the same Spirit to empower us to speak out against evil and injustice
and bring life in the name of your Son, Jesus Christ.
Guide our actions so that others may see how living in luxury
and pleasure for its own sake brings harm, not good.
Lead us back to a life of faithful discipleship when sin befalls us.
Through Christ our Lord.
Amen.

Readings for the Next Dismissal

Provide catechumens with a list of the readings for the next dismissal session. Consult the liturgical calendar on page xvi to find out what day will be observed next week. Give catechumens the questions below to guide their reflection through the week.

🌀 What connections are you seeing in the readings of this liturgical season? As you pray with the readings, around what themes do your thoughts seem to be coming together?

🌀 Where do the readings intersect with your journey of faith? What questions do they raise for you?

Extended Catechesis

Based on today's readings and liturgical observance, the following topics may be covered for extended catechesis:

❋ The gift of the Holy Spirit

❋ Called to prophesy / Called to be prophets

❋ Sin

❋ Preferential option for the poor

❋ Faithfulness and who is included in the community of faithful disciples

❋ Economic justice

❋ Ecumenical and interreligious dialogue/relationships

TWENTY-SEVENTH SUNDAY IN ORDINARY TIME

Focus: To love each other in community.

Lectionary #140B

Catechist's Preparation

Overview of the Sunday

Faithful disciples are prophetic disciples. This was the focus on the Twenty-Sixth Sunday in Ordinary Time. This Sunday the readings convey to us how disciples love one another and welcome each other as people called on the journey to God's Kingdom. We belong to a community of disciples who love as Jesus taught us to love. The First Reading describes the relationship of love between human beings, and between human beings and creation. For the Second Reading, we transition this Sunday to the letter to the Hebrews, in which we hear of Jesus' solidarity with our humanity. His love for us is so deep and profound, he entered completely into the experience of suffering and death. He is our brother, and we are united with him as brothers and sisters. God joins human beings together in love through Jesus Christ, whose love embraced all people.

Scripture Background

Genesis 2:18–24 There are two creation accounts in Genesis. This reading comes from the second or older creation account. Here a human being, the heart of creation, is created first, and then everything else is created for the good of the human. The passage begins with God expressing the insight that it is not good for the man to be alone. God goes about finding a suitable partner for him by creating animals. When none prove to be suitable partners, the first human being is put to sleep and God creates another human being from the rib of the first.

When the man sees the woman, two significant truths are expressed about the meaning of being human. First, the truth of difference, namely man is different from woman. Second, the truth of oneness, namely that each has a desire to be one with the other. This desire for unity amid differences is the heart of human community. God created us for community; we need one other. Marriage is the most explicit expression of this unity, "the two of them become one flesh" (2:24). But desire for unity with God and others is true for all humans, even when they do not marry.

Psalm 128:1–2, 3, 4–5, 6 (see 5) Wisdom literature affirms that fear of the Lord is the beginning of wisdom. This pilgrimage psalm begins with a blessing on all those who fear the Lord. Most likely, the blessing would have been given as pilgrims began their return home from pilgrimage. Fear is understood as awe and reverence of the gracious and mighty deeds the Lord has done. Those who reverence the Lord are blessed and favored by him. The best manifestation of God's blessing in this life is the harmony, peace, and fruitfulness of family life, where abundance of children is present.

From the family, blessings such as peace are extended to the tribe and to all of Israel. Community has its source in God and becomes the source of personal, familial, and national strength and blessing.

Hebrews 2:9–11 This Sunday begins a series of readings from the letter to the Hebrews. Today's selection focuses on the affirmation that God, in Jesus, became one of us. As a human being, Jesus entered into solidarity with all humanity in every way save sin. This was the only way to communicate how much God desired to be with us and to repair the ruptured relationship that had been caused by humans.

The rupture is ultimately repaired through the suffering, Death, and Resurrection of Jesus. Not only was Jesus willing to empty himself of divinity, but he was also willing to give all as a human being, even to empty himself by suffering and dying, so all could live once more in communion with God. This restoration to communion with God affirms once again God's intention for all humanity to be one with him through our life in community with others. Because all have God as their origin, Jesus, by becoming one of us, restores the familial relationship between us and God, not ashamed to identify with us as brothers and sisters.

Mark 10:2–16 or 10:2–12 Linked to the Genesis account of creation, this passage from Mark's account of the Gospel focuses on God's intentions for humanity. Marriage becomes the example par excellence of the community relationship God intended from the beginning. But what happens if there is a rupture in that communal relationship? This is the question that the Pharisees present to Jesus. God's Law is the context within which the question "Is it lawful . . . ?" is posed (10:2).

Moses may have allowed divorce for a husband, but it was not what God originally intended. Quoting Genesis, Jesus affirms marriage as God's intention from the very beginning. Once humans become one flesh, united so by God, there is to be no separation between them. Divorce and remarriage to another by either husband or wife is adultery and violates what God originally intended.

In teaching this, Jesus affirms two truths. One truth states both man and woman are equals in establishing community among themselves, and thus are to be treated as equals. The other truth states both are responsible for maintaining and preserving the union they have formed.

Jesus' ministry was a model of how human beings can begin to work out the differences in relationships. The self-emptying that Jesus modeled is a way to maintain unity. Willingness to trust, to be open, to depend on and include others, particularly children, also contributes greatly to maintaining community.

Reflection Questions for the Catechist

⑥ How does Jesus call you to love others in the community of faith?

⑥ What do you do to work out differences you experience in the community of faith?

⑥ How does Jesus' self-emptying love serve as an example for you in your relationships?

Catechist's Guide

Objectives

▷ To ponder how love is central to our relationships and our life together in the community of faith.

▷ To reflect on how we negotiate differences and points of conflict in our relationship at home, in our parish community, and in the world.

▷ To identify how Jesus' example of love serves as the basis for relationships among disciples.

Dismissal and Procession

Following the homily, the priest celebrant picks up the Lectionary and invites the catechumens to come forward with the catechist(s) who will lead today's dismissal session. Holding the Lectionary so that all can see, the priest celebrant sends the catechumens and catechist(s) forward using RCIA, 67, his own words, or the following:

PRIEST: My dear friends, who seek to know the Lord more fully, and who strive to develop this relationship in the Church, be active builders of the Kingdom in all that you do. We pray that you continue your journey of faith with a lively concern for your neighbor and creation and have a willing desire to follow God's will. May the Word, which you share this day, grow within you. We look forward to the day when you will participate fully with us at the Lord's table. Go in peace.

All process to where the dismissal session will take place. The catechist holds the Lectionary in a reverent manner. The assembly may sing an acclamation to accompany the procession.

Centering

Upon reaching the place where the dismissal occurs, place the Lectionary on the ambo, lectern, or other dignified place (or hold the book reverently). Light the candle that is in the place of gathering and reread Genesis 2:18–24 in order to refocus the group's attention. Consider singing the Responsorial Psalm or have a recording of it available to use as part of the centering, either before or after the reading.

Reflection and Discussion

The following "script" may be used or adapted to help facilitate discussion on today's readings. Begin the discussion by asking the catechumens if any words or phrases from today's readings spoke to them.

God knew that we could not survive alone. God created us to be in relationship with each other and with all of creation. Most of us have probably tried to go it alone at some point in life. Perhaps we experienced difficulties along the way. Perhaps we enjoyed our solo time on life's journey. In our friends and our spouses God is present partnering with us in all we do.

꧁ What was a time when you travelled life's journey alone? What was that time like?

꧁ Where was God for you during that time?

꧁ How is God present in your friendships and significant relationships?

God is the source and origin of our creation. We are God's holy children. In the Second Reading, from Hebrews, we learn that God is also the source and origin of Jesus Christ. In him, we are all brothers and sisters, part of God's family in the community of faith.

꧁ How do you experience your community of faith as a family of brothers and sisters in the Lord?

꧁ What impact does it have on you to realize your identity as Jesus' brother or sister?

Jesus tasted death for everyone—for each one of us gathered here today. The fullness of his humanity allowed him to know the depths of human suffering. Together with the fullness of his divinity, Jesus leads us to our salvation, our share in the Kingdom of God.

꧁ What effect does Jesus' humanity have on your relationship with him?

꧁ How does the fullness of Jesus' humanity help you to see his presence in yourself and others?

Relationships are never perfect. Community is never ideal. We struggle to come together in our differences. Sometimes our differences in background, in material wealth, in opinions, and in beliefs cause us to move apart from one another. We are human. In the Gospel reading, Jesus speaks to the ideal of a Marriage in which two people never part ways. We always hope that the unity among people in faith communities will never fracture. We hope the bonds of friendship will never dissolve. But they do. Even human community centered in the Lord faces the challenge of our humanity.

꧁ Where do you perceive the need to strengthen the bonds of love in your significant relationships? In your community of faith?

꧁ What differences do you consider to be potentially divisive?

꧁ Where is the Lord present helping to solidify relationships and offer compassion in light of broken bonds of friendship and love?

The Gospel reading concludes with Jesus rebuking the disciples for trying to prevent people from bringing children to him, to be part of his community circle. Jesus' communicates to them his desire that the Kingdom of God belongs to everyone who approaches him like a child. A child's humility stands as the basis for how we enter into relationships and community. A child comes simply as he or she is. When a child stands before us, Jesus sees him or her as a child of God. This is how we are to see each other in our relationships and in the communities to which we belong.

꧁ What does it take for you as an adult to approach your relationships, and your belonging to the community of faith, like a child?

꧁ How do you experience Jesus' embrace and blessing in your relationships and community of faith?

꧁ Who are you called to not prevent from approaching Jesus and experiencing welcome into God's Kingdom?

Wrapping It Up

Consider these points to conclude the dismissal. Integrate the thoughts and ideas that surfaced during the discussion.

- God created us for community. God desires that we embrace friendship and love with him and with one another. The path of discipleship is travelled in communion with other disciples, not alone.

- Ideally, separation would not happen in relationships. The reality is that it does. Spousal love falls short. Friends part ways. Members of the faith community see things differently and can struggle to come together. Unity among churches has fractured throughout history. Jesus' words continue to call us back together in love, to welcome each other, to humbly accept the unifying vision of God's Kingdom as he welcomes children.

- Jesus' love is a self-emptying love. He makes us holy and knows us as his brothers and sisters. He calls us to embody his self-giving love in our relationships. He is not asking us to lose ourselves and forget that we have needs, but rather to give of our best selves.

Closing Prayer

Conclude with prayer. If time permits, sing the psalm refrain a few times before or after the following prayer.

God of love,
you yourself are a community of persons—Father, Son, and Holy Spirit.
You created us to live in partnership with each other and with all of creation.
Through the example of your Son's self-giving love,
direct us to love as he did.
Help us to love through our differences and conflicts,
trusting that you made us to live in unity
and when the Lord's day comes all will be forever one in the Kingdom,
where you live and reign for ever and ever.
Amen.

Readings for the Next Dismissal

Provide catechumens with a list of the readings for the next dismissal session. Consult the liturgical calendar on page xvi to find out what day will be observed next week. Give catechumens the questions below to guide their reflection through the week.

⑥ What connections are you seeing in the readings of this liturgical season? As you pray with the readings, around what themes do your thoughts seem to be coming together?

⑥ Where do the readings intersect with your journey of faith? What questions do they raise for you?

Extended Catechesis

Based on today's readings and liturgical observance, the following topics may be covered for extended catechesis:

※ God as the source of all creation

※ God makes us holy

※ Christian community

※ Jesus' self-emptying love

※ The Sacrament of Matrimony

※ The Church's teaching on divorce and annulment

※ The fullness of Jesus' divinity and humanity

Twenty-Eighth Sunday in Ordinary Time

Focus: To know our salvation is possible for God.

Lectionary #143B

Catechist's Preparation

Overview of the Sunday

Prudence and wisdom come through prayer. Wisdom leads us to experience good things in community with her. One of the most profound teachings we learn from Wisdom is that salvation is impossible for us. We cannot merit salvation by anything we do. But as Jesus says to his disciples in the Gospel reading, our salvation is only impossible for us, but not for God. Yes, we must follow Jesus and even give up all we have to live as his disciples. Yet we do this not to earn new life in him, but simply to receive it and hold out its possibility to others we encounter along the journey. As disciples, we make God's Word known to those who are open to its wisdom—God's Word that is living and effective in Jesus Christ.

Scripture Background

Wisdom 7:7–11 We can see common themes from the wisdom tradition throughout this reading. Wisdom is equated with obedience to the law. It is linked to righteous conduct. Wisdom is pictured as a gift of God that we can seek. It is pictured as above price. It is assumed to bring blessings to those who seek it. It is also pictured as worth seeking for its own sake as well as for the good that it brings.

These verses do not have much struggle in them nor do they raise particularly hard questions. Apparently, the author has found the help he needs as he struggles with the questions of life. He has found wisdom. His experience, however, contrasts with that of the rich man in the Gospel, who chose to keep his many possessions and in the end "went away sorrowfully" (see 1:13).

Psalm 90:12–13, 14–15, 16–17 (14) Psalm 90 is a corporate lament seeking divine deliverance from national tragedy and travail. It begins with a hymn-like introduction comparing God's eternity with human mortality. It continues with a reflection on the sorrow inherent in the human condition. The psalmist prays that people might learn from this sorrow, and then concludes with a prayer for Israel's deliverance from trouble.

This psalm is the only one in the psalter to be attributed to Moses. Most scholars doubt that the historical Moses wrote these verses, but given his role as a mediator in the Exodus story, the attribution is appropriate. Not only did Moses speak on God's behalf, he was often called upon to speak on behalf of the people as well. In a way, Moses straddled the gulf between divine and human that is pictured here by the psalmist. More than once he managed to talk God out of "consuming" (see 90:7, 11) the people with divine anger.

The psalmist presents us with at least two hard questions. The first is his assumption that God is angry and full of wrath. Second is his assumption that calamity is often God's punishment for sin. For centuries, both of those assumptions, and the questions that accompany them, have troubled those who seek to live God's ways. The psalmist concludes that life is a struggle and God cares very much about the choices we make in dealing with it.

Hebrews 4:12–13 The reading is short and to the point. In it, the author begins to conclude this long series of exhortations by reflecting on the power of God's Word. This Word, which for the author encompasses all of God's intention and not just the written Word, is very decisive. It sees into the soul and cuts right through all human pretension. Such an idea was not new, even in the author's day. The sword as a symbol for the Word of God can also be found in Wisdom, Ephesians, and Revelation. The image of God as all-seeing and all-knowing is also common throughout the Scriptures.

In this reading, the author shows us that the struggle to seek God's ways is a serious one. Not only do we live that struggle guided by discerning the Word of God, we must attend to the struggle with the sharpness that God's word provides, pondering deeply the thoughts of our hearts for what is true and what is not.

Mark 10:17–30 or 10:17–27 The passage has three distinct sections. The first is the story of the rich man who comes to Jesus inquiring about eternal life. This story is also recorded by Matthew and Luke, but with some interesting changes. Only Luke, for instance, says the man was a ruler. Only Matthew says he was young. Mark remains deliberately ambiguous. For Mark, it was enough that the man was rich. All three record that the man clearly lived a life in obedience to the law. Yet something was still lacking. Jesus wasted no time getting to the point. It was the man's possessions which held him back from experiencing the eternal life he desired. Get rid of those, Jesus said, and he would have what he sought.

The second part of this passage begins as the rich man walks away sadly. The disciples, shocked that a man of his stature and means would be unable to obtain eternal life, question Jesus. Jesus answers their surprise with several sayings on wealth that Mark has collected for the occasion.

The third section is another collection of originally independent sayings on the rewards of discipleship, particularly for those disciples who, like the Twelve, have given up much to follow Jesus. They will receive back what they have relinquished, he assures them, and more besides.

This reading vividly illustrates the hard choices that confront those who are successes in this world when they try to live the way of God. The rich man knew enough to realize that his strict adherence to the law was not going to save him. At the same time, he was not ready to do what would save him. The disciples are obviously struggling in this passage, too. Unlike the rich man, they have chosen to live God's ways but the ways of the world apparently still tug at them. They look at the successful rich man and wonder: Did we make the right choice in giving up everything to follow Jesus? Jesus assures them that they did.

Not everyone needs to give up all they own; only those for whom their possessions are an impediment to eternal life. We are called to discern the impediments that we need to be rid of or find ways of making them part of the path to eternal life.

Reflection Questions for the Catechist

⑥ If you were to ask Jesus what you need to do to inherit eternal life, how would he respond to you at this point in your life?

⑥ When do you try to do too much and forget that God companions you and makes all things possible?

⑥ What is the wisdom you pray for as you lead the dismissal sessions?

Catechist's Guide

Objectives

▷ To identify the Wisdom present in the Word of God.

▷ To accept that we do not earn our salvation, but that God makes it possible.

▷ To discern what we must do to inherit eternal life.

Dismissal and Procession

Following the homily, the priest celebrant picks up the Lectionary and invites the catechumens to come forward with the catechist(s) who will lead today's dismissal session. Holding the Lectionary so that all can see, the priest celebrant sends the catechumens and catechist(s) forward using RCIA, 67, his own words, or the following:

PRIEST: My dear friends, we pray that you continue your journey of faith with a lively concern for your neighbor and creation and have a willing desire to follow God's will. May the Word, which you share this day, grow within you. Go in peace.

All process to where the dismissal session will take place. The catechist holds the Lectionary in a reverent manner. The assembly may sing an acclamation to accompany the procession.

Centering

Upon reaching the place where the dismissal occurs, place the Lectionary on the ambo, lectern, or other dignified place (or hold the book reverently). Light the candle that is in the place of gathering and reread Mark 10:17–27 or Mark 10:17–30 in order to refocus the group's attention. Consider singing the Responsorial Psalm or have a recording of it available to use as part of the centering, either before or after the reading.

Reflection and Discussion

The following "script" may be used or adapted to help facilitate discussion on today's readings. Begin the discussion by asking the catechumens if any words or phrases from today's readings spoke to them. The man's question to Jesus is perhaps our question. What must we do to inherit eternal life? Just when we think we are doing everything we have to do by following the commandments, we find out we lack one thing. Our material possessions, what we can consider our earthly treasure, will not lead us to heaven. Only knowing and living in a way that reflects the treasure we have in God and the gift that will be ours in the Kingdom will carry us through on the journey of discipleship.

- What is your response to Jesus saying to the man, "You are lacking in one thing" (Mark 10:21), and then hearing that the man must sell everything he has and give to the poor?

- What might Jesus' response be if you asked him the same question?

Notice that Jesus does not belittle the man for asking him and that Jesus knows how difficult it is to do what he will ask the man to do. The Gospel reading tells us that before Jesus instructs the man in the one thing he lacks, Jesus looks at him and loves him. Jesus will not leave him if he chooses to leave everything behind and follow him. Nor will Jesus ever abandon us.

- How have you experienced Jesus' love as you have made changes in your life to follow him?

- When have been the times when you have thought what Jesus is asking of you is just too difficult and you want to walk away sad like the rich man did in the Gospel reading?

Jesus teaches his disciples just how difficult it is to enter the Kingdom of God. A camel will find it easier to pass through the eye of a needle than we will to enter God's Kingdom. Surely, in light of this impossibility, we can wonder along with the disciples about who then can be saved. Then we hear Jesus make his point: "All things are possible for God" (Mark 10:27). Our salvation is in God's hands. Nothing we can or do will earn us this free gift of amazing and astonishing life!

- When have you thought everything was in your hands and forgotten that everything is possible in God?

- What is it like to let go of control of your own salvation and place it in God's hands?

- How do you view the relationship between your actions as a disciple and God's work of salvation?

Peter justifiably affirms to Jesus that the disciples have given up everything to follow him. Jesus responds with words of hope. Those who change their lives completely and who give up everything of earthly value will indeed know eternal life. All is not lost in following Jesus. Rather, we gain so much more than what we hand. Wisdom is priceless!

- What have you had to change and/or give up in your life to follow Jesus?

- What have you gained already since choosing to follow Jesus on the road to celebrating the sacraments of initiation?

Being a person of faith requires Wisdom. Being a disciple requires Wisdom. The First Reading begins with the author of Wisdom reflecting on how the result of his prayer and pleading was prudence and wisdom. Wisdom helps us discern how God's Word is "living and effective" (Hebrews 4:12) in our life and in the world around us. The Second Reading, from Hebrews, speaks about how the sharpness of the Lord's Word penetrates our soul and spirit and enters our bodies in between our joins and marrow. The Lord's Word knows and guides our heart.

🌀 Where do you pray for prudence and the spirit of wisdom?

🌀 How is the Word of God "living and effective" (Hebrews 4:12) in your body, soul, and spirit?

Wrapping It Up

Consider these points to conclude the dismissal. Integrate the thoughts and ideas that surfaced during the discussion.

- The Word of God offers us practical Wisdom for daily living. It enters into our mind, soul, and spirit and guides us to make decisions based on faith. It gives our heart a healthy beat so that we might live God's law in Word and deed.

- Wisdom leads us to live just and humble lives of love. It also deeply penetrates us so that we know there is nothing we do that will earn us salvation. Salvation is God's work in Jesus Christ.

- As Jesus' disciples, our responsibility lies not in earning salvation, but in responding to God's gift of life that is ours in Jesus. Our response must be total, complete, and unequivocal. Everything we have and all we are belongs to Jesus. Our life as a disciple is a life for Jesus and the Gospel. It is a life for others.

Closing Prayer

Conclude with prayer. If time permits, sing the psalm refrain a few times before or after the following prayer.

God of Life and Wisdom,
all good things come to those who seek you.
Your Word lives in us and in the world that surrounds us.
Companion us as we rid ourselves of everything we have to follow your Son.
You alone are the author of salvation.
May we reach out to others, especially the poor, as disciples of your Son.
Who lives and reigns for ever and ever.
Amen.

Readings for the Next Dismissal

Provide catechumens with a list of the readings for the next dismissal session. Consult the liturgical calendar on page xvi to find out what day will be observed next week. Give catechumens the questions below to guide their reflection through the week.

🌀 What connections are you seeing in the readings of this liturgical season? As you pray with the readings, around what themes do your thoughts seem to be coming together?

🌀 Where do the readings intersect with your journey of faith? What questions do they raise for you?

Extended Catechesis

Based on today's readings and liturgical observance, the following topics may be covered for extended catechesis:

❈ Wisdom comes through prayer   ❈ The commitment to follow Jesus

❈ Word of God as a Living Word   ❈ Giving up everything to be a disciple

❈ The commandments   ❈ Salvation comes from God as a free, unmerited gift

Twenty-Ninth Sunday in Ordinary Time

Focus: Grace comes to all who hope in God's kindness.

Lectionary #146B

Catechist's Preparation

Overview of the Sunday

Who would want to commit to following Jesus as a disciple? The readings over the course of the past Sundays have presented seemingly increasing demands of discipleship. Today's readings prove no exception. The two brief verses of the First Reading, from the fourth "Suffering Servant Song" in Isaiah, speak of how the servant gave his life as a sin offering and through his death justified many. The Second Reading, from Hebrews, presents Jesus as the high priest, who in his humanity was able to sympathize with our weaknesses. From these two readings, we see how, without a doubt, suffering has a place in a disciple's life. In the Gospel reading, Jesus could not be more candid about this truth. He invites his disciples to share in his baptism and drink the cup of his Blood he will pour out in his suffering and Death. Suffering is not the end for Jesus or his disciples, but hope in God's kindness and grace is.

Scripture Background

Isaiah 53:10–11 These short verses are found toward the end of the last of the four "Suffering Servant Songs" in Isaiah (see 52:13—53:12). Using both the voice of God and that of a narrator, the song presents two originally opposite appraisals of the servant and his suffering. In the beginning, the narrator describes an innocent victim whose affliction left him frighteningly marred and finally dead and buried among the wicked. Meanwhile, God's voice presents the victim as "my servant" (53:11) who will prosper and be exalted. In the beginning, the narrator assumed that the victim must be guilty of some sin fitting his punishment. Eventually it became clear that "it was our infirmities he bore, / our sufferings that he endured" (53:4). In this, the servant can be compared to Moses and the prophets who suffered at and for the sin of their people.

Although the opening line of today's selection sounds exceptionally harsh, the point is not that God is pleased with pain; rather, God is pleased with the faithfulness of the servant in spite of and through the course of his suffering. As the early Church struggled to interpret Jesus' Death and Resurrection, this servant song was particularly helpful. It seemed to be a perfect description of how Jesus suffered at the hands of sinful people and bore their guilt, and how God vindicated him and brought salvation through him.

Psalm 33:4–5, 18–19, 20, 22 (22) Psalm 33 is a thoroughgoing song of praise. It begins by praising God's Word and works—God's self-revelation to us. Then it recognizes that God's justice is expressed in kindness. The next verse reminds us that God's loving gaze is ever upon us, ready to deliver us from all evil. In the final strophe, it proclaims our faith that God is our only source of safety, the only one worth counting on. The refrain sums up and deepens our appreciation of the prayer as we beg for God's mercy and proclaim and promise our trust.

Hebrews 4:14–16 These few verses from the Letter to the Hebrews introduce themes that the author will develop significantly in later parts of the letter. One of the most important of these is the image of Christ as the merciful and final High Priest. The key function of the Jewish high priest was to approach the altar of God on the Day of Atonement. He would enter the Holy of Holies with sacrifices on behalf of the people. After the sacrifice he would return wearing a different robe, representing God who was purifying the people. The allusion here is that Jesus' exaltation was his passing into the presence of God with the result that belief in him would bring salvation from sin.

As the author speaks of Jesus as Son of God, the emphasis is on divine compassion. The Son of God, far from being aloof, sympathizes with each human creature and, as we proclaimed in the psalm, offers mercy and grace whenever we are in need.

Mark 10:35–45 or 10:42–45 Last week, we heard Jesus promise one hundredfold rewards, along with persecution, to his faithful followers. Now we hear two of the principal disciples make an appeal for even greater rewards and honors with no mention of the suffering. Jesus' reply, "You do not know what you are asking," could hardly have been more pointed. In the verses we skip between these two Sunday Gospel readings, Jesus predicted his Passion for a third time, again to the utter incomprehension of his chosen disciples. Now, in his reply to James and John, Jesus refers to his ultimate self-giving as a cup and a baptism, a strong reminder to the Christian community about the meaning of their sacraments. Jesus then critiqued their understanding of himself and his mission. Following his previous references to the Kingdom of God, Jesus now used the rulers of the world as a contrast to the divine. James and John had fallen into the trap of aspiring to be "great ones." What they missed was how their own Lord was leading them and giving them an example. As they were aspiring to the power of the world, Jesus tried to show them that real power, divine power, expresses itself in loving service, in giving oneself for others. Not unlike the rich man of last week's Gospel, the disciples had not yet understood that the only real security and power come from trust in God. Neither wealth nor power can prevent or survive death.

Reflection Questions for the Catechist

⑨ What role has suffering played in your faith life?

⑨ How does God lead you to hope in his kindness and trust in his grace in the midst of struggle?

⑨ How have you seen the catechumens' confidence to approach God for mercy and grace increase over the past months and weeks?

Catechist's Guide

Objectives

▷ To express hope in God's merciful kindness.

▷ To ponder the presence of God's grace in the midst of suffering.

▷ To consider how Jesus enables us to approach the "throne of grace" with confidence (Hebrews 4:16).

Dismissal and Procession

Following the homily, the priest celebrant picks up the Lectionary and invites the catechumens to come forward with the catechist(s) who will lead today's dismissal session. Holding the Lectionary so that all can see, the priest celebrant sends the catechumens and catechist(s) forward using RCIA, 67, his own words, or the following:

PRIEST: My dear friends, who seek to know the Lord more fully, and who strive to develop this relationship in the Church, be active builders of the Kingdom in all that you do. We pray that you continue your journey of faith with a lively concern for your neighbor and creation and have a willing desire to follow God's will. May the Word, which you share this day, grow within you. We look forward to the day when you will participate fully with us at the Lord's table. Go in peace.

All process to where the dismissal session will take place. The catechist holds the Lectionary in a reverent manner. The assembly may sing an acclamation to accompany the procession.

Centering

Upon reaching the place where the dismissal occurs, place the Lectionary on the ambo, lectern, or other dignified place (or hold the book reverently). Light the candle that is in the place of gathering and reread Hebrews 4:14–16 in order to refocus the group's attention. Consider singing the Responsorial Psalm or have a recording of it available to use as part of the centering, either before or after the reading.

Reflection and Discussion

The following "script" may be used or adapted to help facilitate discussion on today's readings. Begin the discussion by asking the catechumens if any words or phrases from today's readings spoke to them.

⑨ As you heard the passage from Hebrews read again, what stood out for you in the description of Jesus?

⑨ How might it impact your prayer life to know Jesus sympathizes with our weaknesses and suffering?

The author of Hebrews speaks of Jesus in this passage as a "great high priest" (Hebrews 4:14). The high priesthood of Jesus is one of the primary themes of this letter. Jesus is the "great high priest" because his offering of himself on the Cross for us is a once and for all sin offering that no priest will ever have to repeat. We remember Jesus' sacrificial offering in the sacrifice of the Mass.

- How does Jesus offer you the confidence to approach God and receive grace and mercy in times of suffering and struggle?

Christians see in Jesus the Suffering Servant in Isaiah's servant songs, the one proclaimed in the First Reading today and in the other three suffering servant songs found in this prophetic book. Sometimes we tend to distort our faith when we see in Jesus' suffering a glorification of suffering for its own sake. God does not will us to suffer. Neither does God want us to seek out suffering. Enough of life's challenges will come our way simply as we live day-to-day. What the short passages from Isaiah and Hebrews do is direct us to the truth that God's grace is present in suffering. We can have confidence and hope in the midst of life's challenges because Jesus has justified us, or, in other words, aligned our relationship with God aright.

- How do you experience God present with you in suffering?
- When you find your confidence waning in the face of life's challenges and struggles, who or what helps reorient you to find strength in God? Who and what helps you to experience God's loving kindness and mercy?

In the Gospel reading, the disciples ask Jesus to sit by his side and share in his glory. Jesus responds by asking them if they are willing to drink the cup that he will drink and be baptized in his baptism. We know that he is asking the disciples whether or not they are able to share in his suffering and death on the way to receiving eternal life. Mark does not let us know whether the disciples understand Jesus to mean this or not. But what we do know is that the disciples respond, apparently without hesitation, that they can do what Jesus asks of them.

- How willing are you to drink of the cup from which Jesus' drinks? To share in his baptism?
- Does our willingness depend on the day or the week or on what is happening in your life?

Most of us will not be asked to give our life for others as Jesus did. Yet Jesus asks all of us to live a life of service. The Gospel reading continues with Jesus teaching what it takes to be truly great. Do not lord power or authority over others, he says. But instead, serve others. Live as a servant. Imitate Jesus' own life of service with your own life of service. Perhaps we could think of a life of service as a way of expressing our hope and confidence in God's own kindness. Through our kindness we can reflect God's love and lead others to God in Jesus Christ.

- How do you already live a life of service?
- When has someone else's life of service reflected God's kindness to you?
- How might our life of service lead others to have confidence and hope in God's kindness?

Wrapping It Up

Consider these points to conclude the dismissal. Integrate the thoughts and ideas that surfaced during the discussion.

- God's mercy and kindness are available to all who seek him. In struggle and suffering we can still place our trust in the Lord and call upon him to let his grace and mercy be upon us.

- God's grace is always present in the midst of struggle and suffering. Sometimes we find it difficult to identify exactly where God's grace is. Often it is easier to see the presence of divine grace only when we look back on life's tough times. But in the moment, simply living in the hope of faith is enough.

- Jesus sympathizes with our struggles. He knows the pain of human suffering, although he is without sin, since he has experienced the highs and lows of human life. This in itself helps us to approach God to receive grace and mercy.

Closing Prayer

Conclude with prayer. If time permits, sing the psalm refrain a few times before or after the following prayer.

God of grace,
you sent your Son, one like us in all things but sin,
to show us the way to you.
In suffering and death, he is our high priest,
who leads us to your mercy.
Grace us with the gift of hope.
Empower us with the courage to serve as he served others
and the strength to participate in his baptism
so that we might also share one day in his glory,
where he lives and reigns for ever and ever.
Amen.

Readings for the Next Dismissal

Provide catechumens with a list of the readings for the next dismissal session. Consult the liturgical calendar on page xvi to find out what day will be observed next week. Give catechumens the questions below to guide their reflection through the week.

- What connections are you seeing in the readings of this liturgical season? As you pray with the readings, around what themes do your thoughts seem to be coming together?

- Where do the readings intersect with your journey of faith? What questions do they raise for you?

Extended Catechesis

Based on today's readings and liturgical observance, the following topics may be covered for extended catechesis:

- Grace

- Hope

- Jesus as the suffering servant

- Jesus' high priesthood

- Humanity and divinity of Jesus

- Participation in Jesus' Death and Resurrection in Baptism

- Jesus' example of service and the disciple's responsibility to serve

- Jesus gave his life as a "ransom for many" (Mark 10:45)

THIRTIETH SUNDAY IN ORDINARY TIME

Focus: Take courage, Jesus is calling.

Lectionary #149B

Catechist's Preparation

Overview of the Sunday

God restores the people. This is the joyful and beautiful hope described in the First Reading, from the prophet Jeremiah. God consoles the people when they face hardship and gives them drink when they thirst. The most vulnerable God notices with particular care. As we continue to hear from the letter to the Hebrews in the Second Reading, the author once more asserts Jesus' everlasting high priesthood. In the Gospel reading, we see again how Jesus fulfills the hope of Jeremiah's prophetic words. As Jesus instructs the disciples to invite Bartimaeus to "take courage" (Mark 10:49) and come to him for healing and salvation, so they invitation to hear Jesus' calling presents itself to us.

Scripture Background

Jeremiah 31:7–9 The selection we read today is part of the rebuilding of the people, also called the "Book of Comfort" (see Jeremiah 30:1—33:26), which promised a return from exile. What we hear today from the Book of Comfort is an exuberant cry of gratitude for God's restoration of the people. Addressed to a people in exile, refugees scattered "to the ends of the world" (31:8), it underlines the great contrast between the weakness of the people and God's strength and faithfulness. Their restoration has nothing to do with their merit and everything to do with God's great love. Jeremiah offers us an image of God as a consoler, a shepherd who leads the people to refreshing streams, a road-building father who is careful to see that no one stumbles along the way.

Psalm 126:1–2, 2–3, 4–5, 6 (3) This psalm reflects both remembrance of God's saving actions and hope that the same will happen in the future. In recalling the return of the exiles from Babylon, it emphasizes the way God creates something new and wonderful out of disastrous circumstances. Although God's punishment may have been harsh, the people also know the appropriateness of joyous laughter in God's presence. Because their dreams were once fulfilled, they have confidence that God will again restore their fortunes and fill them with joy.

Hebrews 5:1–6 After God instructed Moses to appoint Aaron and his sons as priests, the priesthood became a hereditary office (Exodus 28:1–5, 29:29). Thus, because Jesus was not of the priestly class, the author of the Letter to the Hebrews insists that his priesthood, like Aaron's, was specifically appointed by God. While we can see some similarity between Aaron and Jesus, there is even greater contrast between them. Repeating a citation from Hebrews 1:1–13, which extols Christ's all-surpassing greatness, the author uses a phrase from Psalm 2:7, "You are my son: / this day I have begotten you," insisting that Christ is far more than Aaron: truly God's begotten Son. Finally, we have a citation from Psalm 110:4, "You are a priest forever / according to the order of Melchizedek." That same phrase will be cited in Hebrews 6:20, 7:17, and 21. Although there was no "order" of priests in the line of Melchizedek, Hebrews will indicate that Melchizedek ranked over even Abraham, and because no one knew his ancestry, his priesthood was forever (7:3). The point the author makes over and again is that Christ's priesthood is superior to any other; it is eternal and it is God the Father who has given him his glory.

Mark 10:46–52 Bartimaeus hears that Jesus is nearby and begins to call to him for help. By using the title "Son of David," he acknowledges Jesus as a successor to Israel's most important king, the first to whom the words "you are my son: / this day I have begotten you" (Psalm 2:7) were addressed. Although the crowds attempted to silence him, Bartimaeus' hope in Jesus proved more powerful than their objections. The very people who tried to suppress his shouts were sent to tell him to take courage because Jesus was calling him. In his encounter with Jesus, Bartimaeus modeled the faith that the disciples had been failing to attain. Asking for healing rather than money, he responded to Jesus with the insight and courage to become disciple and join him on the fateful road to Jerusalem.

Reflection Questions for the Catechist

- Where do you find your courage to respond to Jesus' call?
- How have you come to know wholeness through your faith?
- How has God restored you? Where do you see God at work restoring your faith community? The world around you?

Catechist's Guide

Objectives

- ▷ To recognize the ways Jesus is calling us to have courage and approach him.
- ▷ To how Jesus makes us whole through faith.
- ▷ To discern how we will respond to our faith saving us.

Dismissal and Procession

Following the homily, the priest celebrant picks up the Lectionary and invites the catechumens to come forward with the catechist(s) who will lead today's dismissal session. Holding the Lectionary so that all can see, the priest celebrant sends the catechumens and catechist(s) forward using RCIA, 67, his own words, or the following:

PRIEST: **My dear friends, who seek to know the Lord more fully, and who strive to develop this relationship in the Church, be active builders of the Kingdom in all that you do. We pray that you continue your journey of faith with a lively concern for your neighbor and creation and have a willing desire to follow God's will. May the Word, which you share this day, grow within you. We look forward to the day when you will participate fully with us at the Lord's table. Go in peace.**

All process to where the dismissal session will take place. The catechist holds the Lectionary in a reverent manner. The assembly may sing an acclamation to accompany the procession.

Centering

Upon reaching the place where the dismissal occurs, place the Lectionary on the ambo, lectern, or other dignified place (or hold the book reverently). Light the candle that is in the place of gathering and reread Mark 10:46–52 in order to refocus the group's attention. Consider singing the Responsorial Psalm or have a recording of it available to use as part of the centering, either before or after the reading.

Reflection and Discussion

The following "script" may be used or adapted to help facilitate discussion on today's readings. Begin the discussion by asking the catechumens if any words or phrases from today's readings spoke to them.

The blind man and beggar, Bartimaeus, cried out for healing to Jesus not once, but twice. People rebuked Bartimaeus after they heard him call to Jesus for pity the first time, but this did not stop Bartimaeus. Jesus heard him call and asked people to encourage Bartimaeus to have courage and approach him.

- When have you cried out to Jesus for mercy? Have others tried to stop you?
- How did you find the courage to respond to Jesus' invitation to come to him? What role did others play in bolstering your courage to approach Jesus?

Jesus does not immediately offer healing to Bartimaeus. He begins his encounter with the blind man by asking him a personal question about what it is that Bartimaeus wants him to do. Bartimaeus knows exactly what he wants and needs: to see! Jesus answers his request by instructing him to go forth because his faith saved him. Jesus restored his sight.

- What do you want Jesus to do for you?
- In what ways does Jesus respond to you so you know your faith makes you whole?

Bartimaeus, with newly restored sight, follows Jesus not alone, but as part of the disciples and the large crowd who are already with Jesus. This is his response to the gift of salvation. Surely, Bartimaeus was filled with the joy the writer of Psalm 126 experienced as he recounted the great things the Lord has done for the people.

- What is your response to Jesus' gift of salvation?
- How do you follow Jesus together with others who are also on the journey of faith to deepen their relationship with him?
- What role does community play in nurturing your relationship with Jesus?

How God restores the people in the First Reading, from Jeremiah, holds out to us the possibility that we can show others the way to healing in Jesus. God's care for the most vulnerable among the people, including the blind, the lame, the mothers, the pregnant women, those who mourn, and those who thirst, provides an example of how we are to help others know God's healing in Jesus. It shows us how we are to be present in our relationships with those we know and with those strangers who need care. For our song of joy—sung because we have known healing and salvation—compels us to extend God's love to others that they might truly know that God has destroyed death in his Son.

- In what ways, small or large, can you bring God's healing and restoration to those in need?
- Where are you in need of courage to reach out to those you ordinarily would not?

God is always calling us to come to him through his Son, Jesus. Chances are there will be times in our lives when we will, for whatever reason, decide not to immediately spring to our feet to approach Jesus as Bartimaeus did. And when we do approach Jesus, we might even struggle to articulate what we want him to do. We are often like the disciples in the Gospel according to Mark who misunderstood what Jesus was saying more often than not. Or, in the least, they did not want to hear and accept the demands of discipleship. Yet some of the disciples still followed Jesus rather than return to their former life. However limited, they had the courage of faith, a faith that saves.

- What keeps you on the journey of faith with Jesus even when your courage needs to be reinforced?
- What is the song you sing when you are filled with joy and gratitude for all the Lord has done for you on the journey?

Wrapping It Up

Consider these points to conclude the dismissal. Integrate the thoughts and ideas that surfaced during the discussion.

- Jesus continuously invites us to approach him. Others invite us to respond to Jesus' call. Sometimes we invite others to see how Jesus is calling them. We need each other to draw on their courage to approach Jesus for mercy and wholeness. This is the work of Christian disciples who support one another in faith and life. We all know what it is like to need God's mercy.
- Faith in Jesus saves us. Jesus' words to Bartimaeus make this clear. Bartimaeus had the courage to approach Jesus and ask for what he needed. As we go forth today, may we have the courage to ask Jesus for the sight we need.

- Jesus instructed Bartimaeus to go on his way. Once he received his sight, he chose to follow Jesus. When Jesus heals us, will we chose to follow him? Following Jesus ever more closely is a response of gratitude for all the great things he has done for us.

Closing Prayer

Conclude with prayer. If time permits, sing the psalm refrain a few times before or after the following prayer.

God of healing and wholeness,
you restored the people to you and consoled them when they were in tears.
You sent your Son as high priest to bring salvation to us
through the sacrifice of his own life.
When we cry out to you for mercy,
send others to bolster our courage to approach Jesus.
Saved by our faith in your Son,
may we go forth to follow him
and gift others with the courage of faith that others have shared with us.
Through Christ our Lord.
Amen.

Readings for the Next Dismissal

Provide catechumens with a list of the readings for the next dismissal session. Consult the liturgical calendar on page xvi to find out what day will be observed next week. Give catechumens the questions below to guide their reflection through the week.

- What connections are you seeing in the readings of this liturgical season? As you pray with the readings, around what themes do your thoughts seem to be coming together?
- Where do the readings intersect with your journey of faith? What questions do they raise for you?

Extended Catechesis

Based on today's readings and liturgical observance, the following topics may be covered for extended catechesis:

- Faith and salvation
- Jesus' high priesthood
- The relationship between the Father and the Son
- The courage and faith to approach Jesus for healing
- Living as a community of disciples who encourage one another
- Jesus as the fulfillment of Old Testament prophecies
- Anointed for priestly, prophetic, and kingly mission in Baptism
- Sacrament of Holy Orders

THIRTY-FIRST SUNDAY IN ORDINARY TIME

Focus: To love God and to love your neighbor as yourself.

Lectionary #152B

Catechist's Preparation

Overview of the Sunday

As we arrive at the final weeks of the liturgical year, the readings this Sunday give us a summary-like statement of what living as a disciple entails. Moses extols the people to keep God's commandments, to know the Lord alone is God, and to love the Lord with their whole heart, soul, and strength. In the Gospel reading, Jesus repeats this part of the Shema' in response to a scribe who asks which commandment is the first of all the commandments, as any faithful follower of Jewish law would do. Jesus adds a second commandment: to "love your neighbor as yourself" (Mark 12:31). This three-fold love is the centerpiece of discipleship. Embracing this law of love places us not far from the Kingdom of God.

Scripture Background

Deuteronomy 6:2–6 Deuteronomy, the title of which is translated as "second law-giving," reads as if it were three long homilies in which Moses interpreted the law. It is presented as his final message. The centerpiece of today's reading begins with "Hear, O Israel! The Lord is our God . . ." (6:4). This is the beginning of the Shema, the prayer spoken by devout Jews every evening and morning, in times of danger, and when they are on their deathbed (see Deuteronomy 6:4–9).

As the core of the Law, the Shema reminds the people that the God who has entered their history is the only God. To love that loving God with their heart means to love God with their intellect, remembering God's great deeds. To love God with the soul means to love him with their affect. To love God with all one's strength means not only with physical strength, but with all they possess as well. Loving God in this way, they will be faithful in every dimension of their personal life. That is the injunction they are to take to heart.

Psalm 18:2–3, 3–4, 47, 51 (2) As the psalm praises God's Law, it reminds us that rather than being legalistic, the Law is a source of wisdom, of joy, of enlightenment; it puts us on the route to justice. As we remember all of that, we joyfully exclaim with the refrain, "I love you, Lord, my strength!"

Hebrews 7:23–28 Today's passage from Hebrews continues the theme of the absolute superiority of Jesus' priesthood. The author cites three reasons for that: Jesus' singular priesthood is eternal, his self-sacrifice was once-for-all, and he was appointed by God's own oath (see 7:20–21). As a result of that, Jesus is "always able to save" (7:25) and forever "makes intercession" (7:25) for those who approach God through him. In that continual priestly role, Christ is not only the high priest representing his own before God, but also the representative of God whose concern for humanity never ceases.

Mark 12:28b–34 The scribe who asks Jesus about the first or greatest of the commandments seems to be motivated more sympathetically than most. What we witness here appears to be a conversation about faith between two men who loved their tradition. Replying to the scribe's question, Jesus recited the Shema, something he had presumably done twice a day since he had first learned to pray. Much like a creed, the Shema reminded the people of their special relationship to the one true God. That, of course, helped them maintain their unique identity in times of occupation by foreigners, exile, or other threats to their life as a people of faith. As usually happened, Jesus deepened the scribe's original question. Not stopping with the issue of the first commandment, he immediately added the injunction of Leviticus 19:18b: "You shall love your neighbor as yourself: I am the Lord." Recognizing that reference, Jesus' audience would have immediately understood Jesus' teaching: love of God necessarily expresses itself in love of neighbor.

Upon hearing Jesus' reply, the scribe did something quite unusual in the Gospel: he agreed and added to Jesus' own explanation by repeating the prophetic teaching that care for others is more important than any amount of sacrifice. As the scene closes, Jesus tells the man he is not far from the kingdom of God. Given what has gone before this, especially the Gospel passages we have heard in the past few weeks, that statement seems to have put the scribe ahead of the pain-avoiding, infighting disciples as well as those who clung to their wealth. This is one of the very few moments in which we see Jesus speaking heart to heart with someone who shares and accepts his teaching.

Reflection Questions for the Catechist

- How do you love the Lord your God with all your heart, soul, and strength?
- How do you love yourself? Your neighbor?
- Which of the three components of the law of love do you find most challenging to live out as a disciple?

Catechist's Guide

Objectives

- ▷ To acknowledge how you love God with you whole heart, soul, and strength.
- ▷ To see how you love your neighbor as yourself.
- ▷ To understand how Jesus' sacrifice of love reflects his eternal priesthood and the gift of salvation available to all people.

Dismissal and Procession

Following the homily, the priest celebrant picks up the Lectionary and invites the catechumens to come forward with the catechist(s) who will lead today's dismissal session. Holding the Lectionary so that all can see, the priest celebrant sends the catechumens and catechist(s) forward using RCIA, 67, his own words, or the following:

PRIEST: **My dear friends, who seek to know the Lord more fully, and who strive to develop this relationship in the Church, be active builders of the Kingdom in all that you do. We pray that you continue your journey of faith with a lively concern for your neighbor and creation and have a willing desire to follow God's will. May the Word, which you share this day, grow within you. We look forward to the day when you will participate fully with us at the Lord's table. Go in peace.**

All process to where the dismissal session will take place. The catechist holds the Lectionary in a reverent manner. The assembly may sing an acclamation to accompany the procession.

Centering

Upon reaching the place where the dismissal occurs, place the Lectionary on the ambo, lectern, or other dignified place (or hold the book reverently). Light the candle that is in the place of gathering and reread Mark 12:28b–34 in order to refocus the group's attention. Consider singing the Responsorial Psalm or have a recording of it available to use as part of the centering, either before or after the reading.

Reflection and Discussion

The following "script" may be used or adapted to help facilitate discussion on today's readings. Begin the discussion by asking the catechumens if any words or phrases from today's readings spoke to them.

In the Gospel according to Mark, Jesus is the Master, the great teacher. At the beginning of today's passage, a scribe looks to Jesus for direction. This scribe, in contrast to others in Mark's account, merely desires Jesus' wisdom. He seeks understanding and is not out to entrap Jesus with his question about the first of all the commandments.

- What do you see as the relationship between these two commandments of love and the other commandments from the Old Testament?
- What do you see as the relationship between loving God and loving others as you love yourself?

The scribe affirms Jesus' answer regarding the foremost of the commandments. Jesus, then, acknowledges the scribe's understanding of the importance of the commandments of love and tells him he is not far from the Kingdom of God. Neither the scribe, nor anyone else present, asks Jesus a follow-up question. However, if the scribe was not far from the Kingdom, but not quite there yet, one wonders if Jesus was saying to him that knowledge of the greatest of the commandments is not enough. Living the commandments through a life of love helps to bring one to the precipice of the Kingdom and opens one to the gift of salvation from the One who is true Love—Jesus Christ.

- How do you close the gap between understanding the commandments of love and enacting them in your life?

- What do you understand as the relationship between loving God with your heart, soul, and strength and loving your neighbor as yourself?

Jesus' whole life proves that one cannot follow him and love God without at the same time loving one's neighbor. Moreover, loving one's neighbor, for Jesus, includes loving the poor, the sick, those possessed by demons, indeed loving all those whom the powerful would leave by the roadside. To love one another, Jesus teaches, means to be a humble servant. It means to welcome the children and let them come to him. It means proclaiming the Good News of life in him to all people. It means feeding the hungry, even when the available food seems to be inadequate for the masses. It means taking up the Cross and encouraging others to follow Jesus to Jerusalem and beyond.

- How have you grown in your love of God, others, and self over the course of the past liturgical year?

- Where do you still need to work on living the commandments of love?

- Where do you find Jesus' example of love embodied in the Christian community?

- How do you already contribute to the love present in your faith community?

One of the ways we express our love for God and acclaim God as the one Lord is through prayer—both in the Church's liturgy and in personal prayer. When we pray, no matter where we are or what we are doing, we always pray in communion with the Church. Many of the poems found in the Book of Psalms communicate the psalm writer's love for God. Psalm 18, today's psalm is an excellent example of this. The refrain, taken from verse 2 of the psalm, simply states the psalm writer's love for God and attests to how God is his strength.

- How do you express your love for God?

- Do you have a short saying or mantra that you use to center yourself in God's love and acknowledge your love for God? What could be some examples of a short mantra?

Wrapping It Up

Consider these points to conclude the dismissal. Integrate the thoughts and ideas that surfaced during the discussion.

- We are called to love God with our whole being. With everything we have and all of who God created us to be, our life returns in love to God what God has graciously given us.

- Love of neighbor and love of self go hand in hand. When we love our neighbors, they are often able to reflect love back to us and help us love ourselves. When we love ourselves and acknowledge the goodness within us, we are able to love our neighbor without reservation. We are able to see the image of God in them.

- In Jesus' life, suffering, and Death on the Cross is the example par excellence of love. In him, we see how to love God, love neighbor, love self, and love the created world. This is why there is no need for any other priests of the old law to offer sacrifices day after day for the people's sins. Once and for all, his sacrifice of love freed us from the death sin brings. In Jesus, is life forever. In Jesus is our way to the Kingdom of God.

Closing Prayer

Conclude with prayer. If time permits, sing the psalm refrain a few times before or after the following prayer.

> God of love,
> you alone are Lord.
> Through your Son's sacrificial love in his life and on the Cross,
> you showed us how to love.
> Strengthen us with the deepest resolve to love you
> and to love our neighbors as we love ourselves.
> Reveal to us the path of that leads to your Kingdom
> when sin causes us to choose hate over love.
> Through Christ our Lord.
> Amen.

Readings for the Next Dismissal

Provide catechumens with a list of the readings for the next dismissal session. Consult the liturgical calendar on page xvi to find out what day will be observed next week. Give catechumens the questions below to guide their reflection through the week.

⑨ What connections are you seeing in the readings of this liturgical season? As you pray with the readings, around what themes do your thoughts seem to be coming together?

⑨ Where do the readings intersect with your journey of faith? What questions do they raise for you?

Extended Catechesis

Based on today's readings and liturgical observance, the following topics may be covered for extended catechesis:

❊ The commandment to love God, neighbor, self, and the created world

❊ Entering the Kingdom of God

❊ The relationship between Jesus' high priesthood and Roman Catholic priesthood

❊ Jesus' example of love

❊ Love within the divine communion of persons: Father, Son, and Holy Spirit

❊ Discipleship and love

❊ Various liturgies of the Church

THIRTY-SECOND SUNDAY IN ORDINARY TIME

Focus: To act out of love as Christ did.

Lectionary #155B

Catechist's Preparation

Overview of the Sunday

The two great commandments of love were the focus of the readings for the Thirty-First Sunday in Ordinary Time. As we draw ever closer to the Solemnity of Our Lord Jesus Christ, King of the Universe, our readings show us what it truly means to act out of love. God offered his Son once and for all to take away sin. His sacrifice is a true act of love. In the interim before Christ's Second Coming, ours is the call to love like the poor widow in today's Gospel reading who gives from her poverty, not from her surplus as the rich people do. Our love is not self-serving like that of most of the scribes who seek places of honor. Our love reflects God's love for the widow who trusted in Elijah's prophetic words and thus feasted from a flour jar and oil jug that never went empty.

Scripture Background

1 Kings 17:10–16   Both Elijah and Elisha are called "man of God." As prophets, they were the mouthpiece of God, revealing messages of divine import and significance. Here, God speaks through the prophet and brings his words to fulfillment, bestowing blessing. We must not take for granted the fact that God is acting here; the prophet is the spokesman, but it is God who acts. Another piece of information brings a touch of color to this passage: the widow's coming from Zarephath suggests that she is a Gentile. Already in these historical books we see the dawning of a universalism in which God extends a hand of compassion and mercy to draw in all people, demonstrating the love of the one who is Creator of all.

Psalm 146:7, 8–9, 9–10 (1b)   Psalm 146 acknowledges and repeats the teaching of the preceding passage: our Creator and God cares for all, the work of divine hands. This psalm expresses so well God's care for the oppressed, the hungry, prisoners, the blind, the stranger, and the widow and orphan (a connection with the First Reading). This stance is understood as divine justice, affirming the right relationship that underlies authentic righteous behavior. When the thwarted plans of the wicked are described at the end of the psalm, it subtly cries out for us to act justly, as God does.

Hebrews 9:24–28   The significance of this passage cannot be understood without a consideration of Leviticus 16, which describes Yom Kippur (the Day of Atonement).

Yom Kippur was and still is considered the holiest day of the year for Jews. On this day, the high priest would enter the Holy of Holies with the blood of goats and bulls, and sprinkle it upon the mercy seat. From that mercy seat, God's forgiveness would go out to the four corners of the earth and bring forgiveness and reconciliation with God. This passage in Hebrews tells us that Jesus, our perfect and blameless High Priest, has now taken his own blood and entered the heavenly sanctuary to bring about our forgiveness and reconciliation. He has become the mercy seat of the new law, from which has come our eternal redemption. Another important allusion to the Old Testament is found in the final verse of this passage where it reads, "offered once to take away the sins of many" (9:28). In the fourth song of the servant in Second Isaiah (read on Good Friday), we find reference to the redemptive death of the servant, which brings about the forgiveness of sins (see Isaiah 53:11–12). The author of Hebrews saw Jesus as the fulfillment of both these Old Testament images (the High Priest and the Servant). The author of Hebrews makes the point that this one perfect sacrifice of Jesus need never be repeated, for it has surpassed and completed what the Old Law never envisioned could be accomplished. When Christ appears again, this time it will be to bestow salvation at the end of time.

Mark 12:38–44 or 12:41–44   Throughout the Scriptures, the biblical authors portray God as caring for the poor. The widow, the orphan, the foreigner, and all who are in need are the concern of God and his people. In the psalms, the king, who is expected to be God's representative on earth, bears the responsibility of caring for those in need (see Psalm 72:1–2, 4, 12–14). The Gospel shows Jesus in this same light, having a heart open to the needs of the poor, bringing them healing of body and consolation of spirit. The religious leaders fail to show or appreciate the kind of compassion expected of God's ambassadors to the poor. Rather, their religious practice is for show and self-aggrandizement. They understand neither their calling nor their deepest responsibility. Earlier in this chapter of Mark's account of the Gospel (see 12:28–34), Jesus teaches about the great commandment: love of God and neighbor. Does not the widow exemplify this teaching for all to see?

Reflection Questions for the Catechist

- What enables you to act out of love even when you have little to give?
- When has God provided for you out of love when you thought you would not have enough?
- How is Jesus' act of love on the Cross central to your faith?

Catechist's Guide

Objectives

▷ To acknowledge that Christian love requires action, not just words.

▷ To discover how acting out of love requires us to give even when we might be uncomfortable doing so.

▷ To praise God for God's abundant act of love in Jesus.

Dismissal and Procession

Following the homily, the priest celebrant picks up the Lectionary and invites the catechumens to come forward with the catechist(s) who will lead today's dismissal session. Holding the Lectionary so that all can see, the priest celebrant sends the catechumens and catechist(s) forward using RCIA, 67, his own words, or the following:

PRIEST: **My dear friends, who seek to know the Lord more fully, and who strive to develop this relationship in the Church, be active builders of the Kingdom in all that you do. We pray that you continue your journey of faith with a lively concern for your neighbor and creation and have a willing desire to follow God's will. May the Word, which you share this day, grow within you. We look forward to the day when you will participate fully with us at the Lord's table. Go in peace.**

All process to where the dismissal session will take place. The catechist holds the Lectionary in a reverent manner. The assembly may sing an acclamation to accompany the procession.

Centering

Upon reaching the place where the dismissal occurs, place the Lectionary on the ambo, lectern, or other dignified place (or hold the book reverently). Light the candle that is in the place of gathering and reread 1 Kings 17:10–16 in order to refocus the group's attention. Consider singing the Responsorial Psalm or have a recording of it available to use as part of the centering, either before or after the reading.

Reflection and Discussion

The following "script" may be used or adapted to help facilitate discussion on today's readings. Begin the discussion by asking the catechumens if any words or phrases from today's readings spoke to them.

What love God has for his people—for us! In the First Reading, from 1 Kings, Elijah asks a widow for a small cup of water to drink and a piece of bread to eat. The widow truthfully responds to his requests by telling him she has little, only a handful of flour and a smidgeon of oil. Yet Elijah replies that neither will the flour run out nor the oil dry up until the Lord sends rain upon the earth. The widow trusts in the Lord's words the prophet spoke.

- When have you trusted in the Lord to provide for you in your need?
- How have you provided for others because of what the Lord gave you?
- How do you experience the Lord's love in your life?

The Gospel reading begins with another stern warning from Jesus. In this warning, he speaks out against the hypocrisy of the scribes. The hypocritical scribes believe and teach the great commandment to love God with one's whole heart, soul, and strength. Yet they go around seeking power and prestige at the expense of others, including those most vulnerable in society, the widows.

⑥ Where do you struggle with inconsistency between what you believe about the commandments of love and your actions?

The Lord's love is not ours to keep for ourselves. It is, rather, ours to give to others. When we do so, we contribute to the building up of the common good. We enact our faith. We embody Christ's love for us. Certainly, the widow in the Gospel reading is an example of how to live the commandments of love we heard last Sunday. She loves God and others by contributing her whole livelihood. She gives of herself. This is true self-giving love. The widow's love contrasts mightily with the insincere love of the rich people who gave only from their surplus.

⑥ How and when do you give from your whole livelihood in love?

⑥ When might it be easier to merely give as the rich people gave?

The examples of the two widows in today's readings direct us to God's act of love in Jesus on the Cross. His whole life of selfless service, preaching and embodying the Kingdom of God, is consistent with his sacrifice on the Cross and his Resurrection.

⑥ How will you live in love this day as you await Christ's Second Coming?

⑥ How will your love reflect Christ's love in his Death and Resurrection?

In today's psalm, we praise the Lord for the justice he brings to the oppressed, the food he gives to the hungry, the freedom he grants to captives, the sight he gives to the blind, and the protection he gives to strangers. For the sustenance the Lord provides the fatherless and the widows, for the love he extends to the just, we praise the Lord. For upending the evil ways of the wicked, we praise the Lord. It seems like the list of reasons to praise the Lord continues on and on! In the last verse we declare the Lord's everlasting reign through all generations. Would that our acts of love mirror in some small way these acts of God's love.

⑥ If you were to choose one of the acts of God's love noted in Psalm 146 to mirror, which one would it be?

The call of the Christian disciple is to let his or her life be a reflection of God's love in Christ Jesus. In other words, our life of love as a disciple is to be one beautiful song of praise to God in return for the love that is ours in Jesus.

Wrapping It Up
Consider these points to conclude the dismissal. Integrate the thoughts and ideas that surfaced during the discussion.

- A disciple's words of love to God and others are significant. Yet a true disciple also puts these words into action. The example of the poor widow who gave all she had contrasts starkly with that of the rich people who gave large sums of money out of their surplus. Her love genuinely reflected how she followed the commandments of love. The actions of the rich people bordered on hypocrisy. How will your actions of love this week be consistent with your understanding of the commandments of love?

- Perhaps the widow was uncomfortable giving all that she had. Surely it was a stretch for her to do so. The love a disciple is called to give is never easy. This love requires emptying ourselves for the good of others as a reflection of God's love for us and our love for God. When Christ comes again, how we love God and others in word and deed will affect the final judgment.

- The fitting response to God's love for us in Jesus is praise. God's love for the widow who trusted Elijah's prophetic word was evident in the lasting abundance God provided her. In Jesus' act of love on the Cross, we see a boundless offering love for eternity.

Closing Prayer

Conclude with prayer. If time permits, sing the psalm refrain a few times before or after the following prayer.

Life-giving God,

you provided for the widow as Elijah foretold.

In the act of unselfish love of your Son on the Cross,

you gave life to the world.

Gift us with the compassion to give from ourselves—

to contribute from our whole livelihood as the poor widow did.

Make us steadfast in our love of you and of others

as we eagerly await the Second Coming of Christ our Lord,

who lives and reigns in the heavenly Kingdom for ever and ever.

Amen.

Readings for the Next Dismissal

Provide catechumens with a list of the readings for the next dismissal session. Consult the liturgical calendar on page xvi to find out what day will be observed next week. Give catechumens the questions below to guide their reflection through the week.

⑨ What connections are you seeing in the readings of this liturgical season? As you pray with the readings, around what themes do your thoughts seem to be coming together?

⑨ Where do the readings intersect with your journey of faith? What questions do they raise for you?

Extended Catechesis

Based on today's readings and liturgical observance, the following topics may be covered for extended catechesis:

※ God's providential care for us

※ Selfless giving

※ Second Coming of Christ

※ Contributing to the common good

※ Heaven

※ Sincerity in faith/consistency between our beliefs and our actions

※ Final judgment

THIRTY-THIRD SUNDAY IN ORDINARY TIME

Focus: To recognize the goodness of creation.

Lectionary #158B

Catechist's Preparation

Overview of the Sunday

On this final Sunday before the Solemnity of Our Lord Jesus Christ, King of the Universe, the Lectionary directly speaks of the end times, when those who have died will be raised. The First Reading, from Daniel, brings to mind the passages about divine Wisdom we heard proclaimed earlier in Ordinary Time. The splendor of the wise and those who have pursued justice will shine brightly with the goodness of all creation. In the Gospel reading, Jesus instructs his disciples about the time of tribulation by describing what they will see in nature. The Son of Man will come in the clouds to gather the faithful ones from the four winds. The fig tree will grow leaves. All will pass away except the Lord's Word.

Scripture Background

Daniel 12:1–3 Today's First Reading expresses the Jewish belief in the resurrection of the dead: "Many of those who sleep in the dust of the earth shall awake" (12:2). This belief developed late in Jewish history, largely as a result of the terrible persecution of Antiochus IV in 168 BC. Even when so many of Israel's best and most faithful believers were wantonly slaughtered in that horrible persecution, Jews refused to conclude that God was unfaithful. Since those who were martyred could not experience victory in this life, the belief arose that God would give them new life on the last day.

It is crucial to appreciate how such life was envisioned. The Jewish tradition did not settle for a spiritual afterlife. It asserted that God would raise the just up to a new bodily existence. God's gift would not be heaven but resurrection. Bodily resurrection flowed from the Jewish view of creation. Hellenistic culture devalued material realities in favor of the spiritual. The Jewish tradition was different. It saw all of creation as God's gift. It was confident that God would stand by the gift that was given. Therefore, material creation would certainly be a part of whatever future life God would offer. God had made the human body, and so God would raise up the just in a bodily manner. Jewish faith gave birth to bodily resurrection because it believed in a God who would never give up on creation. The good material world would always be a part of God's plan.

Psalm 16:5, 8, 9–10, 11 (1) Psalm 16 is a prayer of unshakable confidence in the Lord. That confidence is grounded early in the psalm in the relationship between the psalmist and God: "you are my Lord, / you are my only good" (16:2). Because of this relationship, the psalmist's whole being—heart, soul, and body—is secure.

This trust remains firm even in the face of death. Commentators debate whether the psalmist's statement, "you will not abandon my soul to the netherworld" (16:10), is expressing a belief in an afterlife. It is possible that the psalmist is praying that God will forestall death until the end of a long earthly life. What is not debatable, however, is the source of the psalmist's hope: his closeness to the Lord. So intimate is the psalmist's connection to God, that he cannot imagine a future without God's presence. It is such intimate faith that in time leads to the belief in the Resurrection.

Hebrews 10:11–14, 18 The author of Hebrews continues to draw out the superiority of Jesus' sacrifice. Yet although Jesus' one sacrifice is perfect, it is not complete. Jesus must return to bring history to fulfillment. Although the author continues to present the work of Christ in Hellenistic categories, his belief in the end time indicates that he does not reject Jewish apocalyptic thought.

As Jesus sits at the right hand of God, "he waits until his enemies are made his footstool" (10:13). His enemies are all the evils of the world: injustice, hatred, poverty, and disease. On the last day, Jesus will come again. On that day, all these evils will be made subject to his authority. At the Second Coming, the perfect sacrifice will attain the perfect ending.

Mark 13:24–32 Chapter 13 of Mark's account of the Gospel is often called "The Little Apocalypse." It is a discourse by Jesus about the end of time, displaying many of the characteristics of apocalyptic literature. It is important, therefore, to read this kind of writing correctly. The upheaval in the sun, moon, and stars is not simply meant to indicate destruction. It is a way to illustrate the transformation of the present world into God's Kingdom. The text is not about demolition, but recreation.

Christian faith sees the resurrection of the dead as part of God's re-creation of the world. This belief is an inheritance from Judaism. When God remakes all that is good according to God's good design, we too will be raised up bodily in God's presence. Because we believe that this is our future, it should increase our appreciation for the material world. Because we will be resurrected from the dead, we should never ignore or abuse our bodies. Because our world will be transformed, we should commit ourselves to be good stewards of God's creation. The material world was good when God made it, and it will retain that goodness in God's Kingdom. God will never abandon or discard the world around us. Neither should we. All that we see and touch is the handiwork of God. We must treasure it. It is the material of the new creation.

Reflection Questions for the Catechist	
	⑨ Where does the Lord come in your life?
	⑨ How does creation reflect the presence of God to you?
	⑨ What wisdom have you yet to learn as this liturgical year comes to a close?

Catechist's Guide

Objectives

▷ To cherish the beauty and goodness of creation around us.

▷ To seek wisdom and justice so as to shine with the stars.

▷ To ponder the coming of the Son of Man at the end of time.

Dismissal and Procession

Following the homily, the priest celebrant picks up the Lectionary and invites the catechumens to come forward with the catechist(s) who will lead today's dismissal session. Holding the Lectionary so that all can see, the priest celebrant sends the catechumens and catechist(s) forward using RCIA, 67, his own words, or the following:

PRIEST: My dear friends, who seek to know the Lord more fully, and who strive to develop this relationship in the Church, be active builders of the Kingdom in all that you do. We pray that you continue your journey of faith with a lively concern for your neighbor and creation and have a willing desire to follow God's will. May the Word, which you share this day, grow within you. We look forward to the day when you will participate fully with us at the Lord's table. Go in peace.

All process to where the dismissal session will take place. The catechist holds the Lectionary in a reverent manner. The assembly may sing an acclamation to accompany the procession.

Centering

Upon reaching the place where the dismissal occurs, place the Lectionary on the ambo, lectern, or other dignified place (or hold the book reverently). Light the candle that is in the place of gathering and reread Daniel 12:1–3 in order to refocus the group's attention. Consider singing the Responsorial Psalm or have a recording of it available to use as part of the centering, either before or after the reading.

Reflection and Discussion

The following "script" may be used or adapted to help facilitate discussion on today's readings. Begin the discussion by asking the catechumens if any words or phrases from today's readings spoke to them.

We often hear gloom and doom stories about the signs of the end times. The First Reading, from Daniel, begins by noting the distress of peoples and nations. But the second half of the reading paints a hopeful picture for those who have lived faithfully. Many will share in the resurrection of the dead. The wise and the just will shine brightly with the stars.

⑨ What are your images of the end time?

⑨ What concerns you about the end time?

⑨ What makes you hopeful about the end time?

The Gospel reading begins similarly to the First Reading. Jesus tells his disciples that trials and tribulations will occur. He will give us ominous warning signs in the skies. But then the Son of Man will come. His power and glory will be self-evident. Angels will come. He will gather together the elect, the chosen faithful ones. We will see new life in nature.

🌀 What signs of death and life are occurring in nature already?

🌀 Where is the power and glory of the Son of Man present around us now?

Both heaven and earth will pass away, Jesus says in his solemn teaching, but his words will remain.

🌀 What words of Jesus do you recall from the past liturgical year?

Since we do not know the day or hour when Christ will come again, we continue to live as his disciples each day. Each day we awake, we have the opportunity to choose the path of discipleship. We seek to be among the wise and the just who will shine like the stars forever.

🌀 How will you choose to live in the time before Christ comes again?

🌀 What wisdom do you still need to learn as this liturgical year comes to a close?

This is also the final Sunday we hear from the letter to the Hebrews. Once again, the author repeats his teaching about the uniqueness of Jesus' priesthood. Jesus sacrificed for our sins and now sits forever at God's right hand.

🌀 Where do you experience Jesus' forgiveness in your life?

🌀 How do you offer Jesus' forgiveness to others?

God's goodness is all around us. In the beginning God created everything good. God created us in his image and likeness. What God created good will be good at the end time. God's promises of restoration and deliverance and salvation will be fulfilled when the Son of Man comes. As people of faith, we look forward to that day not in fear, but in hope. Ours is the hope that we will share in Christ's Resurrection and live forever with him in God's Kingdom surrounded by the glorious beauty and bounty of all creation.

🌀 If you were to draw or paint your image of sharing in the Resurrection of the dead in God's Kingdom and being surround by the goodness of all creation, what would it look like?

🌀 Where is God in your image?

Wrapping It Up

Consider these points to conclude the dismissal. Integrate the thoughts and ideas that surfaced during the discussion.

- Take walks outside this week at different times of the day. Notice the beauty and goodness of creation around you. Observe what is dying in creation and where there are signs of life. God's presence is all around us in creation. God is Lord over all.

- Wisdom and justice are two cornerstones of a faithful life—a life lived in love for creation and for all people.

- Trials and tribulations will face the world's peoples, and creation will show signs of struggle. But when the Son of Man comes, he will bring new life to all. His word of healing, hope, and life will remain where evil will pass away. Everything God created good will still be beautiful in God's eyes when the hour of the Son of Man's coming arrives.

Closing Prayer

Conclude with prayer. If time permits, sing the psalm refrain a few times before or after the following prayer.

> God of all creation,
> your beauty surrounds us.
> Strengthen us to look forward in hope to the hour
> when the Son of Man will come again.
> Calm our fears when signs of the end time appear.
> Grace us with hope that we will share in the Resurrection of the dead on the last day.
> Make us into people of wisdom and justice who care for all of creation.
> Through Christ our Lord.
> Amen.

Readings for the Next Dismissal

Provide catechumens with a list of the readings for the next dismissal session. Consult the liturgical calendar on page xvi to find out what day will be observed next week. Give catechumens the questions below to guide their reflection through the week.

⑨ What connections are you seeing in the readings of this liturgical season? As you pray with the readings, around what themes do your thoughts seem to be coming together?

⑨ Where do the readings intersect with your journey of faith? What questions do they raise for you?

Extended Catechesis

Based on today's readings and liturgical observance, the following topics may be covered for extended catechesis:

❊ Goodness of creation

❊ Resurrection of the Dead

❊ Second Coming of Christ

❊ Forgiveness of sin

❊ End Times

❊ Apocalyptic literature in the Bible

SOLEMNITY OF OUR LORD JESUS CHRIST, KING OF THE UNIVERSE

Last or Thirty-Fourth Sunday in Ordinary Time

Focus: To transform the world into God's Kingdom.

Lectionary #161B

Catechist's Preparation

Overview of the Sunday

We have arrived at the end of the liturgical year. On this day, we celebrate the universal kingship of Jesus Christ. He is the fulfillment of the vision of the Son of Man coming in the First Reading from Daniel. Dominion and glory are his as he reigns over all peoples and nations. He is the beginning and the end, as we hear in the Second Reading, from Revelation. His Kingdom does not belong to this world, he tells Pilate in the Gospel reading from John. Pilate names him a king, though Jesus did not identify himself as such. Truth is the basis of Jesus' Kingdom—a far different basis than that of earthly kings and rulers. As his followers, we belong to the truth. The truth of Jesus is the basis on which we can work to transform the world so it more closely mirrors God's Kingdom of love and justice here and now.

Scripture Background

Daniel 7:13–14 Chapter 7 of the Book of Daniel presents the great dream vision of the prophet. It is the most important chapter of the book, both by its position and content. The vision deals with power. It seeks to establish who will rule the earth. Four terrible beasts representing the kingdoms of the Babylonians, Medes, Persians, and Greeks are all destroyed. This leads to the Lectionary passage in which the Ancient One (God) grants true and ultimate power to "one like a Son of man" (7:13).

The Son of Man has been understood as a heavenly figure similar to the archangel Michael, a human ruler on whom God bestows divine authority, or a collective person representing faithful Israel. All of these interpretations agree, however, that it is through the Son of Man that God will conform the world to the divine will. Justice will be established and evil will be destroyed. Daniel's vision was written for faithful Jews experiencing dreadful persecution under the Syrian king, Antiochus IV (168–164 BC). By giving ultimate power to the Son of Man, Daniel is assuring his readers that the evil political rulers under whom they suffer will ultimately be defeated by God's power.

Psalm 93:1, 1–2, 5 (1a) Psalm 93 is also about power—the power of God. Aware that God cannot be visualized, the psalmist robes the Almighty not with physical garments but with splendor. Strength is to God what rich vestments are to earthly kings. God's rule is connected to the act of creation. It was God who drove back the waters of chaos and established the inhabitable world. The act of creation established God as the King of creation, and God's continuing kingship is the guarantee that the world will endure. This is what the psalm means when it says God's "throne stands firm" (93:2).

Yet God's authority is not limited to the material stuff of creation. It extends to the human heart. This is why the psalm ends praising God's decrees that guide the ordering of human society. Both the material world of earth, sea, and sky and the human world of justice, goodness, and peace flow from God's strength and glory.

Revelation 1:5–8 Having considered the Son of Man and the Lord as King, we reflect on the role of Jesus Christ. This passage from the beginning of the Book of Revelation makes two astounding claims: Jesus is the firstborn of the dead and the ruler of the kings of the earth. The two claims are connected. It was through the victory of his Resurrection that God has bestowed ultimate authority upon him.

The profession that Jesus "is coming amid the clouds" (1:7) is a reference to the Son of Man vision of Daniel 7. The author of Revelation sees Jesus as the Son of Man. As the Son of Man, Jesus is to destroy every force that is opposed to God's will. Through his Resurrection, God's authority is now exercised over all things. God's claim to be "the Alpha and the Omega" expresses the scope of the power. Alpha is the first letter of the Greek alphabet and Omega is the last. Therefore, God's power, now active in Jesus, extends from the beginning to the end of all things.

John 18:33b–37 On this Solemnity of Christ the King, the Gospel has obviously been chosen because it gives to Jesus the title, "King." As Jesus describes his kingdom to Pilate, though, it might appear that Jesus' reign differs from the earlier readings of this Sunday. Daniel, Psalm 93, and Revelation all refer to a kingship that destroys the evil of the world. But Jesus tells Pilate that his kingdom does not belong to this world.

This incongruity disappears, however, when we examine Jesus' words more closely. When Jesus says his kingdom does not belong to this world, we should not suppose that Jesus intends to establish his kingdom in some heavenly realm. Jesus is not talking about location. He is talking about power. He does not intend to abandon this world but to transform it. His mission is to change the world by destroying every evil that is contrary to God's purpose. "[T]his world" will become something new—the Kingdom of God (see 18:36–37).

We who follow Christ the King are called to share in his mission. We are not to turn our backs to the world around us and yearn for a heavenly escape. We hasten God's Kingdom by our commitment to justice and peace. In this way, we will demonstrate our allegiance to Christ and help to extend his rule to every person and place.

Reflection Questions for the Catechist

⑥ Where do you see signs of God's Kingdom in your life and in the world around you?

⑥ How do you herald God's Kingdom?

⑥ How would you recap your faith journey of this past year? What do you look forward to in Advent?

Catechist's Guide

Objectives

▷ To recognize our responsibility to transform the world into God's Kingdom.

▷ To affirm Jesus as King over our hearts and King of the Universe.

▷ To celebrate the Lord's glory present all around us.

Dismissal and Procession

Following the homily, the priest celebrant picks up the Lectionary and invites the catechumens to come forward with the catechist(s) who will lead today's dismissal session. Holding the Lectionary so that all can see, the priest celebrant sends the catechumens and catechist(s) forward using RCIA, 67, his own words, or the following:

PRIEST: My dear friends, who seek to know the Lord more fully, and who strive to develop this relationship in the Church, be active builders of the Kingdom in all that you do. We pray that you continue your journey of faith with a lively concern for your neighbor and creation and have a willing desire to follow God's will. May the Word, which you share this day, grow within you. We look forward to the day when you will participate fully with us at the Lord's table. Go in peace.

All process to where the dismissal session will take place. The catechist holds the Lectionary in a reverent manner. The assembly may sing an acclamation to accompany the procession.

Centering

Upon reaching the place where the dismissal occurs, place the Lectionary on the ambo, lectern, or other dignified place (or hold the book reverently). Light the candle that is in the place of gathering and reread John 18:33b–37 in order to refocus the group's attention. Consider singing the Responsorial Psalm or have a recording of it available to use as part of the centering, either before or after the reading.

Reflection and Discussion

The following "script" may be used or adapted to help facilitate discussion on today's readings. Begin the discussion by asking the catechumens if any words or phrases from today's readings spoke to them.

In the Gospel reading, from John, Pilate interrogates Jesus about his kingship. It is obvious from the back and forth between Pilate and Jesus that Pilate just does not understand what Jesus is saying. Pilate's conceptions of a king and kingdom are *of* this world. They are focused on earthly power that oppresses people and nations and exists for its own sake. Pilate's model of kingship is a self-serving one. This is far from the truth about who Jesus is as King and his Kingdom, and is why Jesus says that his "kingdom does not belong to this world" (John 18:36).

🌀 What are differences between Pilate's conception of an earthly kingdom and the Kingdom of God?

🌀 From the Scriptures we have heard proclaimed over the course of the past year, what would you say characterizes Jesus' Kingdom? The people who would belong to Jesus' Kingdom?

Pilate identifies Jesus as a king according to Pilate's interpretation of what a king is. Jesus never acknowledges himself as a king. Instead, he speaks about the truth which he came to speak and he talks about those who belong to the truth and those who listen to his voice. Belonging to the truth is about drawing close to Jesus. It is about believing in him, following him, and choosing to live as his disciple.

🌀 How does a disciple belong to the truth?

🌀 How does a disciple listen to Jesus' voice?

Belonging to the truth, belonging to Jesus, is about nurturing a relationship with him. It is about growing in understanding about who he is and how we are to live as disciples. It is about belonging to a community of faith, a community of disciples who commit themselves to the Truth and to living lives of justice, compassion, and love. It is about transforming those areas of the world in need of change so they better reflect the values of God's Kingdom.

🌀 What are the areas in your own life in need of transformation so you might better reflect the Kingdom of God?

🌀 What areas in your family, your faith community, and in the world need to change to mirror the truth of God's Kingdom?

The Lord is the beginning and the end. In Christ, God's reign lasts forever. The truth about the work of transforming this world into God's Kingdom is that we do not do this work alone. This is God's work, but we are coworkers with God bringing about the reality of God's Kingdom now. As we do this, we recognize that's God's Kingdom will never be fully realized on earth by anything that we do. God's Kingdom of truth is already here, but it is yet to fully come. We look forward in joyful hope to this day when the Kingdom fully comes. As we companion each other on the work of the journey of faith to the Kingdom, we place Jesus Christ in our hearts. He is the Truth who guides us forward. He is Priest, Prophet, and King. We are his disciples.

🌀 What will be your prayer this week as you prepare yourself to enter another year of discipleship with Christ the King?

Wrapping It Up

Consider these points to conclude the dismissal. Integrate the thoughts and ideas that surfaced during the discussion.

- We are accountable to God for how we live our lives as disciples of his Son. Jesus' Kingdom might not belong to the world as the world understands earthly kingdoms, but it is in the world. As his disciples, our task is to live out all the wisdom he has taught us throughout this past year. He sends us forth in mission to preach, to heal, to do away with evil, to live justly, and to love—love God and love neighbor as we love ourselves. This is what his Kingdom is about. This is the Kingdom we herald and help create here on earth. Our lives can and do reflect the glory of Christ the King.

- Jesus' glory reigns in our hearts. He directs us, guides us, and helps us to discern our vocation as his disciples. We can come away with him to rest when we need to rejuvenate ourselves for our mission or when we need to understand more clearly how it is he is calling us to reflect his glory. Our relationship with him is one where heart speaks to heart. This strengthens us as we enter another year in our faith journey.

- The Lord's glory is in us and all around us. We celebrate this truth today! As we go through the day and week, notice the many ways the Lord is present around you. Take time to breathe in the glory that surrounds you. Praise God for the glory and splendor of Jesus Christ, King of the Universe!

Closing Prayer

Conclude with prayer. If time permits, sing the psalm refrain a few times before or after the following prayer.

Lord of all,
on this Solemnity of Our Lord Jesus Christ, King of the Universe,
we express our gratitude for your glory and dominion present in your Son.
Lead us ever closer to the truth of his Kingdom.
Empower us to uphold this truth and live as heralds of the Kingdom here on earth
so that all peoples and nations might know your ways of justice, peace, and love.
Enable us to serve as good stewards of the stunning glory of your creation.
Grace us with hope that one day we will share forever in Christ's glory
in the Kingdom of truth,
where you live and reign for ever and ever.
Amen.

Readings for the Next Dismissal

⑥ What connections are you seeing in the readings of this liturgical season? As you pray with the readings, around what themes do your thoughts seem to be coming together?

⑥ Where do the readings intersect with your journey of faith? What questions do they raise for you?

Extended Catechesis

Based on today's readings and liturgical observance, the following topics may be covered for extended catechesis:

- ❄ Kingdom of God
- ❄ Transforming and building up the Kingdom of God on earth
- ❄ Jesus' truth
- ❄ Jesus Christ, King of the Universe

- ❄ Divine glory
- ❄ Coming of the Son of Man
- ❄ End of the liturgical year
- ❄ Advent

INTRODUCTION TO THE SOLEMNITIES AND FEASTS OF THE LORD AND SOLEMNITIES OF THE SAINTS

Overview of the Solemnities and Feasts of the Lord and Solemnities of the Saints

Throughout the liturgical year, the Church celebrates the mysteries, events in the life of Our Lord and his Blessed Mother, events in the life of the Church, saints, angels, and all the faithful departed with solemnities, feasts, commemorations, and memorials—optional or not. A few of these days are kept as Holydays of Obligation, to be celebrated by all in the territories where they have been so designated. Most of these days are celebrated on their appointed dates unless they fall on a Sunday or within the Sacred Triduum or the Octave of Easter. The Solemnities of the Most Holy Trinity and the Most Holy Body and Blood of Christ are permanently affixed to the first two Sundays of Ordinary Time after Pentecost. And a few others are deemed of such importance to the life and memory of the Church that when they fall on Sundays of Ordinary Time they supersede the Sunday. Only those days which have the potential to supersede Sunday are included in this resource.

Preparing a Seasonal Environment

When preparing the environment for the solemnities and feasts of the Lord and the saints, you will want to keep the seasonal environment apparent in the space you use for dismissal catechesis. You may add the color of the day, often white for a solemnity or feast, to the environment. If the solemnity celebrates a particular saint, consider including an icon or statue of the saint as part of the environment. Take some time during the session to discuss the environment and how it reflects the liturgical celebration of the day. You might ask the catechumens: How does the environment help to form our spirituality and life of faith on this day?

In everything you do to create the environment for a solemnity or feast in the dismissal space, take your lead from the environment in the sanctuary of the main assembly. Consistency between what the catechumens see in the environment in that space and in the environment in the dismissal space is important. You do not want to create divergent messages about the day and season and thus generate unnecessary questions or confusion within the group. Keep the environment simple but not simplistic, understated but not minimized. Colors, light, and images or icons, should all assist the catechumens in their reflection on the significance of the day and the Word of God.

As with the environment for the liturgical seasons, have a prominent space for the Lectionary (or the Bible) such as a lectern or table. Place a candle near the Lectionary (or Bible) to highlight and honor the Word of God. Have the Lectionary (or Bible) open to the passage you have chosen to read during the dismissal session.

Overview of the Readings

The readings for solemnities and feasts are proper to the day. To say a set of Lectionary readings is "proper" to a particular solemnity or feast means that the readings have been specifically selected to correspond to the dogmatic teaching or event in Christ's life, which we celebrate. For example, the readings selected for the Feast of the Exaltation of the Holy Cross remind us of how our salvation comes through Jesus' Death on the Cross. In Jesus, the Cross is no longer a symbol of death, but of victory and of eternal life. On the Solemnity of All Saints, the First Reading gives us an opportunity to reflect on the ones whose robes have been made white from the Lamb's blood. We are reminded of our Baptism and our call to live a holy life. The Gospel reading, which is always Matthew's version of the Beatitudes, describes the blessedness to which God calls us. This is the blessedness of a disciple's life that leads us to the Kingdom of Heaven.

"Proper" readings for a solemnity of a saint reflect particular charisms of that saint and guide us to see why a particular saint is important in the life of the Church. On the Solemnity of Sts. Peter and Paul, the Gospel reading from Matthew highlights Simon Peter's response to Jesus' question "But who do you say that I am?" Peter's confession of Jesus as the Christ, the Son of the living God, helps us acknowledge that it is Peter's faith that shows us the way as we grow in our own faith. Peter's faith is why the Church acknowledges him as the first shepherd, the first leader of the faithful. On this solemnity, the Second Reading, from 2 Timothy, attests to the strength the Lord gave Paul as he faced suffering and persecution. After his conversion, Paul's hope was only in the Lord as he proclaimed the Gospel of Christ. He knew a new "crown of righteousness" awaited him in heaven.

Some solemnities such as the Most Holy Trinity and Most Holy Body and Blood of Christ have proper readings for each liturgical year, whether Year A, Year B, or Year C. For other solemnities such as All Saints, Assumption, and the Immaculate Conception, we proclaim the same set of Lectionary readings each time we celebrate the solemnity. For the Commemoration of All the Faithful Departed, while the Lectionary provides many options from which to choose, the editors and authors of this resource have provided recommendations for the readings you should select. However, you will want to check with the director of liturgy or pastor to see which readings will be proclaimed in your parish's liturgy on this day. You can adapt the dismissal session accordingly, as many of the themes for All Souls' are consistent among the reading options.

The Lectionary readings for the solemnities and feasts are singularly important. Treat these days as you would treat each Sunday. They are formative for the faith of catechumens and formative for your own faith as a dismissal catechist, parish leader, or participant on the initiation team. Let the readings speak deeply and widely into your hearts and the hearts of your catechumens. As always, keep a reflective tone for your dismissal sessions on these days so that the Word penetrates everyone and will remain with them the entire week.

SOLEMNITY OF THE MOST HOLY TRINITY

Sunday after Pentecost
Focus: To live the apostolic witness.
Lectionary #165B

Catechist's Preparation

Overview of the Solemnity

The essential component of being in relationship with our Trinitarian God is to allow that relationship to impact all that we say and do. We are to preach at all times both in our words and actions. Today's Gospel has Jesus send us on a mission to all nations, witnessing to the many wonders that God has done on our behalf. To be disciples of the Lord is to live according to Jesus' values and lifestyle and to model for others what relationship with God entails. Our mission is to do for others what Jesus had done for us, both in his words and deeds, but most especially in his loving outreach to all. Blessed are we for having been chosen to be apostolic witnesses to all.

Scripture Background

Deuteronomy 4:32–34, 39–40 This reading ostensibly comes from a sermon of Moses and can be considered a summary of the whole book of Deuteronomy. Moses is presented as a preacher who wants to both instruct and persuade his people. His homily begins with the invitation to look at everything that has happened since the creation. He asks his people what has ever happened that could possibly compare with what their God has done for them.

Moses reminds them that God has spoken directly to them. Beyond that, they have been formed as a nation that belongs to God and God alone. God has rescued them from their enemies, proving to them that this God who enters their history is the one true God in heaven and on earth. The only fitting response to this is to keep the commandments and to enjoy the benefits of belonging to such a God.

Psalm 33:4–5, 6, 9, 18–19, 20, 22 (12b) In response to Moses' teaching, we cry out, "Blessed the people the Lord has chosen to be his own" (refrain). As we pray the psalm, we begin with praise of God's dependability, fairness, and kindness. We then marvel at the power of God's Word and works: the visible extensions of God's very being. Finally, recalling what it means to be God's own People, we sing in joy for the God who takes note of our hope and preserves our life. We promise to wait for the Lord and discern the everyday signs of God's kindness.

Romans 8:14–17 Paul adds to what Moses proclaimed to the Israelites in the desert. Moses recalled God's historical activity; Paul reminds his listeners of God's activity within them. All that the people can do in response is allow themselves to be led by that Spirit who makes them heirs, not of a land or a tradition, but of God, the Father of Jesus. Unlike Moses who promised the security of a "long life on the land," Paul reminds his fellow believers that if they are led by the Spirit of God, they will share in Jesus' fate.

Matthew 28:16–20 These last four verses of Matthew's account of the Gospel are filled with symbolic meaning. They summarize the entire Gospel in the moment when Jesus definitively hands over his mission to the disciples. The fact that Jesus meets the disciples on a mountain recalls other mountain events, including Jesus' third temptation, the Sermon on the Mount, the Transfiguration, and Jesus' arrest. As it was in the Old Testament, the mountain was an important meeting spot between God and humanity.

Matthew's description of Baptism in the name of the Father, Son, and Spirit is unique in the New Testament. Doing something "in the name of" implies solidarity, or identity with the one named. In calling for a Trinitarian Baptism as the expression of discipleship, Matthew summarizes his teaching about Jesus as the Son of the Father and the one through whom God's Spirit was at work. Finally, that Baptism is a sign of commitment to "do everything I have commanded you" (28:20), implying that belief is not an intellectual assertion, but an entire way of life. Taken together, these readings remind us of God's ongoing presence to us and our responsibility to proclaim the Gospel by the way we allow the Spirit to lead us in action.

Reflection Questions for the Catechist	⑥ How do you witness to the Lord by your life, words, and actions?
	⑥ How are you challenged in your call to be an apostolic witness to others?
	⑥ What obstacles have you encountered in your mission to be an apostolic witness?
	⑥ What advice would you give to others as they embark on a life of apostolic witness to all?

Catechist's Guide

Objectives	▷ To realize what being disciples of the Lord entails.
	▷ To acknowledge both the challenges and the rewards of apostolic witnessing.
	▷ To recall daily that no matter the challenge, God has promised to journey with us till the end of time.

Dismissal and Procession

Following the homily, the priest celebrant picks up the Lectionary and invites the catechumens to come forward with the catechist(s) who will lead today's dismissal session. Holding the Lectionary so that all can see, the priest celebrant sends the catechumens and catechist(s) forward using RCIA, 67, his own words, or the following:

> PRIEST: My dear friends, in his Word, the Lord reveals to us a God of perfect relationship that has no end. As we send you forth to reflect more deeply on this mystery, may your developing relationship with God—Father, Son, and Holy Spirit—begin to bear witness to his presence and dominion in the world. Go in peace.

All process to where the dismissal session will take place. The catechist holds the Lectionary in a reverent manner. The assembly may sing an acclamation to accompany the procession.

Centering

Upon reaching the place where the dismissal occurs, place the Lectionary on the ambo, lectern, or other dignified place (or hold the book reverently). Light the candle that is in the place of gathering and reread Matthew 28:16–20 in order to refocus the group's attention. Consider singing the Responsorial Psalm or have a recording of it available to use as part of the centering, either before or after the reading.

Reflection and Discussion

The following "script" may be used or adapted to help facilitate discussion on today's readings. Begin the discussion by asking the catechumens if any words or phrases from today's readings spoke to them.

With Moses, we marvel at how God has chosen to be with us from the first moment of creation, accompanying us along the way and always acting on our behalf. The only fitting response to such love and care is to love in return by aligning ourselves with all that God desires of us. By so doing, we manifest that we value our relationship with God, that we want it to continue forever, and that we are willing to witness to that love relationship with all we encounter.

⑥ How do you witness to the love relationship that you have with the Lord?

⑥ How has that love relationship led you to the faith journey that you are undertaking as a catechumen?

Before departing from his disciples, Jesus commissions them to go out into the world and make the love relationship that he formed with them real and active in the world. They are to live, act, speak, and witness to all that they have seen and experienced while with Jesus.

In so doing, they will make Jesus known and they will be the living witnesses to his continued presence among us, in and through the Spirit of God with which they and we have been gifted.

- ⑨ How do you cultivate your love relationship with the Lord so that you can become a most effective witness to others?

- ⑨ Name things that you do daily or on a fairly regular basis to deepen your relationship with and understanding of what the Lord requires.

Paul affirms that if we are led by the Spirit of God then we are children of God, for in Christ, God has adopted us as both children and heirs. Such an intimate relationship does not remove the suffering and trials that are part of being fully human. Jesus encountered those in his life and so will we. Fidelity to God in the midst of suffering is what led to Jesus' glorification. Paul assures us that through our faith and fidelity in Christ we too will experience glorification with him.

- ⑨ In cultivating your familial relationship with the Lord, how do you deal with the trials and suffering that are an inevitable part of our lives?

- ⑨ How can suffering, when aligned with Christ, become an opportunity not only for deeper faith and trust in the Lord, but also to witness to others about how to deal with daily trials and suffering in a loving faith context?

God chooses to be in relationship with all people, not just a few. Such inclusivity is essential for any disciple. We are called to be apostolic witness to all the nations, inviting them believe in the Lord and cultivate that love relationship in every aspect of their lives.

- ⑨ How do you insure that your apostolic witness is not exclusive but always as inclusive as God's is?

- ⑨ How do you cultivate that inclusivity on your faith journey to Baptism?

Wrapping It Up   *Consider these points as you conclude the session. Integrate the thoughts and ideas that surfaced in your discussion with the catechumens as you conclude your time together.*

- Our baptismal commitment calls us to live as apostolic witnesses to all that we have come to know about God in and through the Word, actions, and life of Christ. In living out our baptismal call, it is essential that we cultivate our relationship to God in Christ so that we can be living, effective witnesses.

- Challenges, trials, and suffering will always be an integral part of life. Yet God journeys with us, ensuring us that they will not overwhelm us if we maintain our trust and confidence in the Lord. In our witnessing, Jesus' gift of the Spirit guides and strengthens us. We are assured that the Spirit of the Lord is always present and active in our lives and world.

- Our intimacy with the Lord is one of familial and never-ending love. Such realization moves us to respond in love by continually aligning ourselves with God's wishes and desires. In so doing we witness to that love in our lives and invite others to share in the richness that we have found therein.

Closing Prayer

Conclude with prayer. If time permits, sing the psalm refrain a few times before or after the following prayer.

O Creator God of fidelity and love,
we praise and exalt you.
You have chosen us to be yours from the beginning of time.
You have called us into relationships
and have done such marvels on our behalf.
Be with us as we respond to your love call.
Empower us to cultivate that relationship always
so we can become your living witnesses in the world
and to all we encounter.
Through Christ our Lord.
Amen.

Readings for the Next Dismissal

Provide catechumens with a list of the readings for the next dismissal session. Consult the liturgical calendar on page xvi to find out what day will be observed next week. Give catechumens the questions below to guide their reflection through the week.

- As you pray with the readings, around what themes do your thoughts seem to be coming together?

- Where do the readings intersect with your journey of faith? What questions do they raise for you?

Extended Catechesis

Based on today's readings and liturgical observance, the following topics may be covered for extended catechesis:

- ✳ God always acts on our behalf
- ✳ Our baptismal call
- ✳ God, our Abba, Father

- ✳ Handling suffering
- ✳ The demands of apostolic witnessing
- ✳ Jesus as God with Us

Solemnity of the Most Holy Body and Blood of Christ (Corpus Christi)

Sunday after the Solemnity of the Most Holy Trinity (Second Sunday after Pentecost)

Focus: To share in Christ's life and sacrifice.

Lectionary #168B

Catechist's Preparation

Overview of the Solemnity

As Christians we are called to share in Christ's life and sacrifice. On this Solemnity of the Most Holy Body and Blood of Christ, traditionally known as Corpus Christi, we delve into Christ's willingness to sacrifice himself for others. God becoming human in Christ was the beginning of a life devoted to others. In celebrating this solemnity, we focus on blood, the ultimate symbol of life that Christ was willing to shed for us. Beginning with our Baptism and every time we celebrate Eucharist, we commit ourselves to sharing in Christ's life and sacrifice. We feed on Christ who gives of himself for us so that we might be ready to give of ourselves for others.

Scripture Background

Exodus 24:3–8 In this scene in the Sinai desert the people already have a significant history with God. They knew their God as the one who had heard their cries (see Exodus 3:7), who led them out of Egypt, and who gave them bread and water in the desert. They understood themselves as a people special to the Lord. As this scene begins, they had already promised obedience to God's Word (see 19:8). They had seen the effects of God's presence (see 20:18) and had received the law. Now as they repeat their acceptance of God's Law, Moses formalizes the covenant with a sacrifice.

Scholars say that the Hebrew verb for *covenant* means "to bond" or "to eat bread with." In this case, Moses symbolizes that bonding by sprinkling blood, first on the altar of the Divine Presence, and then, after reading the law, on the people. Because blood was a symbol of life, the sprinkling expressed a profound sharing of life between God and the people. This was a precursor of temple sacrifices, especially the ritual for the annual Day of Atonement.

Psalm 116:12–13, 15–16, 17–18 (13) This hymn of thanksgiving is sung by someone who God rescued from the danger of death. When the psalmist calls the death of God's faithful ones "precious," the phrase intends to explain that the death of the faithful costs a great deal to the God of life. The "cup of salvation," which may have

originally been part of a sacrifice (see Exodus 29:40), leads us to meditate on our communion with the Blood of Christ. Praying this psalm helps us share in the experience of Israel in the desert, giving thanks for deliverance, and promising to be faithful and to give witness.

Hebrews 9:11–15 The epistle to the Hebrews is not so much a letter as it is a homily about the significance of Christ. Reflecting on Israel's sacrificial liturgies, the author presents Jesus as the definitive high priest whose sacrifice accomplishes deliverance from transgressions. In the liturgy for the Day of Atonement, the high priest passed into the Holy of Holies with the blood of a goat. He would sprinkle that blood on the mercy seat, which represented the divine presence. When he came back out, he came as a representative of God to sprinkle the people and bring atonement or the righting of all that had gone wrong in creation. According to the author of Hebrews, Jesus accomplished the final sacrifice by offering himself through the Spirit to God. He is the priest who established the New Covenant (see Jeremiah 31:31–34) that will never end.

Sequence This Sunday, the Church sings one of four sequences—ancient, poetic songs that precede the singing of the Gospel Acclamation. The sequence for the Most Holy Body and Blood of Christ, Lauda Sion, is ascribed to St. Thomas Aquinas. The sixth stanza of the sequence reminds us of the history of the Eucharistic feast.

Mark 14:12–16, 22–26 The details of Mark's account of the Last Supper communicate some surprising things. First of all, the disciples asked Jesus where they should prepare the Passover "for you" rather than "for us" (14:20). He sent them off to ask their mysterious host where to find the room where Jesus would eat with his disciples. Because this meal is going to summarize the life of Jesus and the meaning of discipleship, Mark makes it a point to show that the disciples who have resisted understanding Jesus' impending suffering (see Mark 8:31, 9:32, 10:32) still resist the idea of participating in his Passover.

Mark explains that Jesus took the bread and blessed it and broke it. The blessing Jesus pronounced would have included prayers thanking God for key events in the course of salvation history. Jesus' identification of his body with the bread made a tremendous and potentially shocking theological statement; he was inserting his life into the traditional history of salvific events.

Finally, he gave them the cup and interpreted it as the sacrifice of his own blood in a New Covenant. But as Mark tells it, Jesus invited them to take the cup, they all drank, and only then did he explain what it meant. Just as he had asked them earlier if they could drink his cup (see 10:38), now he shared it with them both as gift and call to communion with his self-giving. All that he had done with them led to what this moment symbolized: as ignorant as they were willing, they were being ushered into the New Covenant.

Reflection Questions for the Catechist

⑥ How is Christ's life of sacrifice on behalf of others, the model for your life?

⑥ How does sharing in Christ's life help you deal with life's difficulties and challenges?

⑥ What lessons do you draw from the way Christ faced suffering and death?

⑥ How is our willingness to share in Christ's sacrifice redemptive for ourselves, for others, and for all of creation?

Catechist's Guide

Objectives

▷ To acknowledge the lengths that Christ was willing to go to for our sakes.

▷ To realize the demands of sharing in Christ's life and sacrifice.

▷ To ponder the lengths that we are willing to go to for the sake of others and all creation.

Dismissal and Procession

Following the homily, the priest celebrant picks up the Lectionary and invites the catechumens to come forward with the catechist(s) who will lead today's dismissal session. Holding the Lectionary so that all can see, the priest celebrant sends the catechumens and catechist(s) forward using RCIA, 67, his own words, or the following:

PRIEST: **My dear friends, you have shared with us at the table of God's Word. As you go to reflect more deeply on this Word, this community sends you forth with prayers and encouragement. We look forward to the day when you remain with us to share at the table of the Eucharist. Go in peace.**

All process to where the dismissal session will take place. The catechist holds the Lectionary in a reverent manner. The assembly may sing an acclamation to accompany the procession.

Centering

Upon reaching the place where the dismissal occurs, place the Lectionary on the ambo, lectern, or other dignified place (or hold the book reverently). Light the candle that is in the place of gathering and reread Mark 14:12–16, 22–26 in order to refocus the group's attention. Consider singing the Responsorial Psalm or have a recording of it available to use as part of the centering, either before or after the reading.

Reflection and

The following "script" may be used or adapted to help facilitate discussion on today's readings. Begin the discussion by asking the catechumens if any words or phrases from today's readings spoke to them.

Moses seals the covenant relationship of the people with God by sprinkling the blood of sacrificed animals on the people. By means of blood, the symbol of life, the people commit themselves to God and one another. Bonded to God, they are now connected and responsible to God and to each other.

⑥ How does your willingness to commit yourself to God connect with your relationship to others and to all of creation?

🌀 What does such a commitment entail?

🌀 How far are you willing to go in living out the responsibilities of being in relationship with God?

Psalm 116 offers thanksgiving to God for having been rescued from death. God is attuned to those in need and responds, no matter the cost. God is our nearest kin, willing to pay the cost to release the faithful one from bondage. We are precious in God's eyes. Being related to God calls us to act in the same manner.

🌀 Do you consider yourself precious in God's eyes? Why?

🌀 When has God responded to your cry for help?

🌀 How do you expect God to act when you call out for help?

🌀 How do you act when others cry out to you for help?

The letter to the Hebrews speaks of Christ's obtaining our redemption not through animal sacrifice but through the shedding of his own blood. His sacrifice on our behalf reconciles us to God and establishes a new, eternal covenant. By sharing in his life and sacrifice, we become eternally bonded to God in Christ.

🌀 As a disciple of Christ, how ready are you to give of yourself in service of others?

🌀 In imitation of Christ, how willing are you to be a source of reconciliation and healing for others, especially those you might not like?

The disciples in Mark's account of the Gospel find it difficult to accept the reality that sharing in Christ's life will demand a share in his sacrifice as well. They often misunderstand, reject, or run away from what is required of discipleship. Yet Christ remains constant in being willing to give of himself so that other may live. The Last Supper is the clearest lesson that Jesus offers to his disciples. If we are to be united to him, we must be willing not only to live as he did but to sacrifice of ourselves as he did.

🌀 How do you struggle with the demands of discipleship?

🌀 What gives you strength and courage in the midst of the struggle?

🌀 How does Christ nourish you in your struggles?

🌀 How willing and ready will you be to drink of the cup that Christ was willing to shed on your behalf?

🌀 As you share in Christ's life, how willing are you to share in Christ's sacrifice? What will it demand of you?

Wrapping It Up

Consider these points as you conclude the session. Integrate the thoughts and ideas that surfaced in your discussion with the catechumens as you conclude your time together.

- Discipleship calls for sharing not only in Christ's life but also a willingness to share in Christ's sacrifice. In order to do this well, we must cultivate intimacy with God in Christ through prayer and action. The more we model ourselves on Christ, the more we become intimate with God and others.

- Sharing in Christ's life and sacrifice is not easy. It demands an attitude toward others that does not come naturally to us. As Christ struggled in carrying out his relationship to God and others, we too struggle in being faithful to God's way of thinking and acting. Yet Christ, fully human like us, walked that journey and brought about new life and meaning for all. As disciples of Christ, we share in that mission and strive to be Christ to all.

- Christ was willing to shed his Blood so that we could be reconciled to God and all creation. As disciples we are asked to give of ourselves, even to the shedding of our blood if necessary, so that others may live and come to know God's loving presence within them.

Closing Prayer

Conclude with prayer. If time permits, sing the psalm refrain a few times before or after the following prayer.

> O God of intimacy and life,
> we thank you always for initiating
> an enduring covenant relationship with us.
> Christ's willingness to shed his Blood for us
> has reconciled us to you and to one another.
> As we strive to be faithful disciples of Christ,
> give us the strength and courage to share
> not only in his life but his sacrifice as well.
> Who lives and reigns for ever.
> Amen.

Readings for the Next Dismissal

Provide catechumens with a list of the readings for the next dismissal session. Consult the liturgical calendar on page xvi to find out what day will be observed next week. Give catechumens the questions below to guide their reflection through the week.

⑨ As you pray with the readings, around what themes do your thoughts seem to be coming together?

⑨ Where do the readings intersect with your journey of faith? What questions do they raise for you?

Extended Catechesis

Based on today's readings and liturgical observance, the following topics may be covered for extended catechesis:

※ Covenant relationship with God

※ The demands of discipleship

※ Christ as the cup of salvation

※ Baptism as sharing in Christ's life

※ Eucharist as sharing in Christ's sacrifice

※ Disciples as reconcilers

FEAST OF THE PRESENTATION OF THE LORD

February 2

Focus: To proclaim Christ as light to the nations.

Lectionary #524

Catechist's Preparation

Overview of the Feast

Forty days after Christmas (the Solemnity of the Nativity of the Lord), we celebrate Christ as light to the nations as evident in Simeon's prayer in today's Gospel text. Recognizing Christ as our light developed over the centuries into the ritual practice of blessing candles and processing with them during today's liturgy, also known as Candlemas.

The Feast of the Presentation of the Lord is rooted in everyday life. In faithful observance of the law of Moses, Mary and Joseph present Jesus in the Temple to consecrate him to the Lord. There they met the righteous Simeon and the prophet Anna, for whom Temple worship was part of everyday life. According to Luke's account of the Gospel, Simeon recognized Jesus as the Messiah in the Temple and declared him "a light for revelation to the Gentiles, and glory for your people Israel" (Luke 2:32). God rewarded their fidelity by allowing them to see the one who was Savior and to hold him in their arms. When the ceremony of presentation was completed, Mary and Joseph and Jesus returned to their hometown. There, they created a home and a family life. There, Jesus grew up, becoming strong and wise, and the grace of God was upon him.

Scripture Background

Malachi 3:1–4 An anonymous prophet wrote the Book of Malachi (Hebrew for "my messenger"), the last book in the Old Testament. After the Babylonian Exile and the rebuilding of the Temple (515 BC), the practices of the priest and the community did not live up to the standards of the covenant. The prophet denounces the priests, who failed to instruct the people. He reproaches the people for offering polluted food and blemished animals, which the priests accepted for sacrifice (see Malachi 1:7–8). God's response to this unfaithfulness is the "Day of the Lord." Unlike a day of victory and rejoicing, it will be a time of judgment. God will purify the people just as a refiner purifies gold with fire. God will enter the Temple, but the people may be unable to endure this encounter. A faithful community will then offer a "pure offering" as they did in earlier days, "from the rising of the sun to its setting" (3:11; a phrase that appears in Eucharistic Prayer III). If the people do not heed the message of the prophet, God will send another messenger. Christians see this hope fulfilled in Christ whose messenger was Elijah (see 4:5, Mark 1:4).

Psalm 24:7, 8, 9, 10 (10b) This psalm was sung during a procession, perhaps when the ark of the covenant was carried through the city into the Temple. As the people welcomed rulers into the city gates, God is greeted as the "King of glory" (24:8). The gates are too low; they must raise them so God can enter. Unlike the mood of Malachi, here the presence of God brings rejoicing.

Hebrews 2:14–18 The author of Hebrews writes for Jewish Christians. Hebrews is the only book in the Bible in which Christ is portrayed as the great high priest. Israel considered the daily and yearly sacrifices in the Temple as the only way to ensure permanent reconciliation with God. Unlike other high priests, Jesus had no need to offer sacrifices day after day. In Christ's sacrificial Death on the Cross, he did this "once for all" (7:27), reconciling all of humanity to God. Christ's Death is not the death of some spiritual being, but the "flesh and blood" (7:14) death of a human being. Through his humanity, Christ's obedience to God defeats death and restores creation to its original intent. Christ understands the human struggle to remain faithful (see 2:18). As "descendants of Abraham" (2:16) through faith, all people are helped by Christ in their trials and difficulties.

Luke 2:22–40 or 2:22–32 In Christ's Presentation, God enters the Temple in Jerusalem. As in Malachi, God's coming is a day of joy and of judgment (see Malachi 3:1–2). As Jews faithful to the Law of Moses, Mary and Joseph bring the infant Jesus to the Temple for the rite of purification (see Leviticus 12:2–8). Like Samuel, his parents dedicate Jesus to the service of God (see 1 Samuel 1:24–28). In the Temple are two of God's faithful servants, Simeon and Anna, who await the deliverance of Israel through the coming Messiah. Simeon praises God for allowing him to see the one who brings salvation, the one who will be the revealing "light to the nations" (2:32). In this child, God's Word is fulfilled. Jesus will be a sign of contradiction. Some will accept his message, and others will reject him. The words of Simeon to Mary pierce her to the heart. Already, at the beginning of Luke's account of the Gospel, the Cross is revealed.

Reflection Questions for the Catechist

- In what ways is Christ the light of your life?
- How do you proclaim Christ as light to the nations?
- How is Christ a "sign of contradiction" for the world?
- What light does Christ shed on your life journey when darkness overtakes you and the path is difficult to discern?

Catechist's Guide

Objectives

- ▷ To identify Christ as the ultimate source of light to all nations.
- ▷ To cultivate Christ as the light that directs our life's journey.
- ▷ To become disciples through whom Christ's light always shines.

Dismissal and Procession

Following the homily, the priest celebrant picks up the Lectionary and invites the catechumens to come forward with the catechist(s) who will lead today's dismissal session. Holding the Lectionary so that all can see, the priest celebrant sends the catechumens and catechist(s) forward using RCIA, 67, his own words, or the following:

PRIEST: **My dear friends, in today's readings, the Lord Jesus is revealed as the long-awaited hope of Israel. As you go forth to reflect more deeply upon this mystery, may you recognize his glory shining in your hearths and in the hearts of those who seem least important among us. May his Word enlighten your way to the day when you will share with us the sacrament of his Body and Blood. Go in peace.**

All process to where the dismissal session will take place. The catechist holds the Lectionary in a reverent manner. The assembly may sing an acclamation to accompany the procession.

Centering

Upon reaching the place where the dismissal occurs, place the Lectionary on the ambo, lectern, or other dignified place (or hold the book reverently). Light the candle that is in the place of gathering and reread Luke 2:22–40 in order to refocus the group's attention. Consider singing the Responsorial Psalm or have a recording of it available to use as part of the centering, either before or after the reading.

Reflection and Discussion

The following "script" may be used or adapted to help facilitate discussion on today's readings. Begin the discussion by asking the catechumens if any words or phrases from today's readings spoke to them.

The prophet Malachi sees the Lord's coming as one of purification and refining fire. Once refined and purified of all that separates them from God, they will please the Lord with their lives and sacrifices. This call to conversion at the Lord's coming is crucial yet always challenging.

- What areas of your life would you like the Lord to help you refine and purify?
- How are you pleasing to the Lord?
- How would you react if you knew the Lord was coming today? What would you say or do?

Psalm 24 asks us to recognize and acknowledge the King of Glory, the one who rules and guides our life. Having acknowledged the Lord as our King of Glory, we are now tasked with the privilege of lifting up both lintels and portals so as to prepare a fitting entrance for the King into the temple of our lives.

🌀 How is the Lord the King of Glory of your life?

🌀 How do you lift the lintels and portals of your life so as to prepare a more fitting entrance for the Lord?

🌀 How would others know that the Lord is the King of Glory of your life? What could you point to and why?

The letter to the Hebrews proclaims that God became fully human in Christ so that we might be reconciled through Christ's pure sacrifice. Christ was tested in every way through his suffering, yet remained faithful and merciful. Because of this, he is able to be our help and support whenever we are tested, and thus light our way whenever darkness envelops us.

🌀 How has the Lord walked with you whenever you were tested by life?

🌀 How do you react when you hear that Christ was tested by life and suffering the same way that you are?

🌀 How is Christ the font of mercy and fidelity in your life? How does this help you to be merciful and understanding towards others, especially those you don't like?

Luke tells us that forty days after his birth, Jesus was consecrated to God in the Temple and was recognized as the long awaited Messiah by both Simeon and Anna. Simeon proclaims the child as the light of the nations and Anna praises God for the redemption that will be wrought through the child. Jesus returns home, grows in wisdom, and the favor of the Lord was upon him. At your Baptism, you will be given a candle symbolizing that the light of Christ should always guide our life, helping us grow in wisdom and knowledge of the Lord.

🌀 How have you come to recognize Christ as the light of your world?

🌀 Name several aspects of Christ's light that affects you personally. How do those aspects affect the way you relate to others and the world?

🌀 After you are baptized, how will you care for the light of Christ so that it helps you grow in wisdom and intimacy with the Lord?

Wrapping It Up *Consider these points as you conclude the session. Integrate the thoughts and ideas that surfaced in your discussion with the catechumens as you conclude your time together.*

- God, becoming fully human in Christ, has entered the temple of our lives and world and transformed them. Christ brought much needed light into the world, enabling all nations to know God's desires. Tested like us in every way, most especially through suffering, Christ remained faithful and merciful. He is the light that the world still sorely needs.

- By acknowledging Christ as the light to the nations, we strive to live in that light faithfully and full of mercy. The baptismal candle that the catechumens will receive at their Baptism becomes a living reminder of Christ, the light that should guide our life. As disciple we are called to keep that light brightly lit for ourselves and to share it with others.

- Joy and constant lifting of the lintels and portals of our life and world should be the overwhelming response to Christ, the light who brightens our world and offers us hope. Whenever we acknowledge Christ as our light, we bring more light into our lives and our world.

Closing Prayer

Conclude with prayer. If time permits, sing the psalm refrain a few times before or after the following prayer.

> O most gentle and loving God,
> you have blessed us with such rich gifts.
> The gift of your Son, Christ Jesus, one like us in all things,
> has entered the temple of our lives and world,
> and we are forever transformed.
> As light to the nations, Christ guides us and all creation
> on our journey to you.
> Help us to live always in that light,
> with fidelity and mercy towards all.
> Through Christ our Lord and light.
> Amen.

Readings for the Next Dismissal

Provide catechumens with a list of the readings for the next dismissal session. Consult the liturgical calendar on page xvi to find out what day will be observed next week. Give catechumens the questions below to guide their reflection through the week.

⑨ As you pray with the readings, around what themes do your thoughts seem to be coming together?

⑨ Where do the readings intersect with your journey of faith? What questions do they raise for you?

Extended Catechesis

Based on today's readings and liturgical observance, the following topics may be covered for extended catechesis:

❋ Christ, the light to the nations

❋ Rites of Baptism and Confirmation

❋ Baptismal candle

❋ Paschal candle

❋ Mercy as essential to discipleship

❋ The day of the Lord

❋ Christ as one like us in all things

Solemnity of the Nativity of St. John the Baptist

June 24

Focus: To respond to God's call from our mother's womb.

Lectionary #587 (Mass during the Day)

Catechist's Preparation

Overview of the Solemnity

Throughout the liturgical year, the Church celebrates the birthdays of only three people: Jesus on December 25, Mary on September 8, and John the Baptist on June 24. All other observances typically celebrate the death of the saint, the person's *dies natalis*, their "birthday into heaven." Today's solemnity highlights God's intimate connection with us from the moment of our conception. Our God knows us and calls us forth from our mother's womb. As disciples we are called forth to know the Lord, grow in intimacy with the Lord, and to manifest the Lord to the world. John the Baptist models what discipleship is all about. We are to serve the Lord by preparing the way so that others come to see and know the Lord for themselves. The joy in this calling far outweighs the challenges, which are often many, as they were for John.

Scripture Background

Isaiah 49:1–6 The First Reading is the second "servant song" from Second Isaiah. Some scripture scholars suggest the image refers to Israel and how she is called to act in response to her covenant. Others suggest that they refer to an individual, such as an ideal king who is anointed by God and acts as God would to the poor and lowly. Prophets, too, were alluded to as servants of God. The images are also referenced as a prediction of the Messiah who would be the true one to witness in God's name. In any case, the reading suggests that the servant is called by name even before birth to act in God's name. This servant will trust in God completely, despite difficulty or even death, for "my reward is with the Lord, / my recompense is with my God" (49:4). In placing this reading on the feast of John the Baptist, the Church recognizes both John's legacy of calling people to return to God and also his willingness to point toward the coming Messiah who would fulfill all the hope of Israel for a king who would act with righteousness and justice. Both Elizabeth and Zechariah announce John's name in the Gospel, the name given to him by God before his birth.

Psalm 139:1b–3, 13–14ab, 14c–15 (14) The psalm used for today's celebration of the birth of John the Baptist speaks of God's intimate knowledge of us from the time we were made in our mother's womb. The psalmist says that God so lovingly and tenderly probes, knows, and understands us that it is as if our very being was formed by God, knit together and wonderfully made. The final verses of the psalm, which we do not hear on this solemnity, speak of how fiercely we must be willing to do what God requires. "Do I not hate, Lord, those who hate you? / Those who rise against you, do I not loathe? / With fierce hatred I hate them, / enemies I count as my own" (139:21–22). Our response to being so lovingly made is to defend our God with all the power we have within us. John the Baptist did just that with his preaching, witness, and eventual death at the hands of the enemies of God's Word and God's Son.

Acts of the Apostles 13:22–26 John is mentioned in the reading from Acts of the Apostles as the prophet who heralded the coming Messiah and who in humility declared his own unworthiness to fasten the sandals of Jesus. John had been called by name from birth by God, and he was aware of his identity as a servant of the Lord, but not as the Messiah. He knew that the one coming after him was the true Messiah who would be the salvation of the world. John is the precursor, the preparer, the herald, the servant of the Lord. He points the way. We, too, are called by name to do the same by living lives of witness and proclamation to the coming reign of God. We are called to serve God as faithfully as John did.

Luke 1:57–66, 80 Though this Gospel story from Luke is all about the wonders and miracles at the birth and naming of John the Baptist, it leads directly to the action of God. "All who heard these things took them to heart, saying, 'What, then, will this child be?' For surely the hand of the Lord was with him" (1:66). John the Baptist was certainly of God. The readings on this solemnity emphasize how a servant of God is formed in the womb and called by God. Despite hardship or suffering, a servant is confident in God's presence and clear about his mission. John was clear. He was to call attention to the one who was to come after him. In the First Reading, the passage from Isaiah says this about the suffering servant:

"I will make you a light to the nations, / that my salvation may reach to the ends of the earth" (Isaiah 49:6). John knows this truth, and his proclamation about the coming Messiah is a message to the entire world that the light that has come is the Christ. John's eventual martyrdom happens because he chose to continue in his role, announcing the coming of Christ and to point to the Lord as the salvation of the world. God called John before he was born and sent him on a mission to proclaim the coming of the Lord. John is a faithful witness to present-day disciples who are also called to testify to the light of the world now. John's testimony was strong and clear, as ours must be as well.

Reflection Questions for the Catechist

⑨ When and how did you first hear the Lord call your name?

⑨ What would you include in a job description for one called to be a servant of the Lord?

⑨ How does John the Baptist help you in clarifying what your role as a catechist is all about?

Catechist's Guide

Objectives

▷ To realize that the Lord knows us and calls us by name from our mother's womb.

▷ To discern how to best respond to the Lord's call and invitation to intimacy and service.

▷ To learn from John the Baptist how to live out God's call, no matter the challenges.

Dismissal and Procession

Following the homily, the priest celebrant picks up the Lectionary and invites the catechumens to come forward with the catechist(s) who will lead today's dismissal session. Holding the Lectionary so that all can see, the priest celebrant sends the catechumens and catechist(s) forward using RCIA, 67, his own words, or the following:

PRIEST: **Nothing stirs the Church like the victory song of the Lamb, slain but now risen in glory. Yet your desire to bond yourself to Christ and to join the ranks of his saints fills heaven with splendid joy and swells the sound of the angelic chorus. Let God's Word be your nourishment and our fellowship be your bond that a special place has been prepared for you in the Kingdom in which we all hope to rejoice with the One who conquered death and called us to himself. Go in peace.**

All process to where the dismissal session will take place. The catechist holds the Lectionary in a reverent manner. The assembly may sing an acclamation to accompany the procession.

Centering

Upon reaching the place where the dismissal occurs, place the Lectionary on the ambo, lectern, or other dignified place (or hold the book reverently). Light the candle that is in the place of gathering and reread Isaiah 49:1–6 in order to refocus the group's attention. Consider singing the Responsorial Psalm or have a recording of it available to use as part of the centering, either before or after the reading.

Reflection and Discussion

The following "script" may be used or adapted to help facilitate discussion on today's readings. Begin the discussion by asking the catechumens if any words or phrases from today's readings spoke to them.

God creates out of love. All of creation is loved into existence by God. God knows us and invites us into relationship with him and into service from the time we were fashioned into being in our mother's womb. We are to discern ways of coming to know and respond to God's call. We are created with gifts and talents. How will we use them in service of the Lord? John the Baptist models for us the vocation that is incumbent on all who claim to be disciples.

⑨ How and when did you hear God calling you to intimacy and discipleship?

⑨ What are some of the specifics that you feel God is asking of you in your life?

⑨ How are you doing in your attempt to respond to what you feel God is asking of you?

Psalm 139 pictures God as one familiar "with all my ways" (139:3b), knowing everything about me. At the same time, the psalmist thanks God for being "fearfully, wonderfully made" for "wonderful are all your works" (139:14). Who we are is a result of God's love, and everything that God creates is good.

⑨ How do you react to the realization that God knows everything about you, both the good and the not so good?

⑨ What feelings and thoughts surface within you?

⑨ Does such awareness draw you closer to God or make you hesitant?

⑨ What conversations would you have with God in light of this awareness?

In Acts of the Apostles, Paul calls John the Savior's herald, preparing the way for Christ by calling people to repentance. Even more importantly, John consistently pointed to the Lord and not to himself. The nature of discipleship demands that we first prepare ourselves to be true servants by taking on the mind and heart of Christ. Once so clothed, we too, like John, are to consistently point others to the Lord and not to ourselves.

⑨ As a disciple, how has taking on the mind and heart of Christ transformed your life? What would you point to as clear indicators of this transformation?

⑨ How do you point others to Christ? What obstacles need to be worked on so that others see you pointing to Christ and not to yourself?

The conception and birth of John the Baptist are seen as God's gifts of mercy and love toward his parents. More importantly, John is known by God from his mother's womb, symbolic of the name given and of his servant role as the Lord's herald. All acknowledge that the hand of the Lord is with John, though they do not yet know who or what he will become.

⑨ How do you see your life as a gift flowing from God's mercy and love?

⑨ Do you believe that God knew you and called you from your mother's womb?

⑨ Name some feeling that flow from this belief. How has the hand of the Lord been with you both in the past and today? What is God calling you to?

Wrapping It Up   *Consider these points as you conclude the session. Integrate the thoughts and ideas that surfaced in your discussion with the catechumens as you conclude your time together.*

- God's love brings us into existence and keeps us in existence. From the beginning God is with us, knows us, and calls us to service on behalf of others. As disciples we attune ourselves to God's love and call. Cultivating that love in our lives enables us to respond to God's call and carry it out as best we can.

- The core of God's call is to make known God's ways to all. Christ lived among us and modeled what God desires. As Christ's disciples, our call and ministry is to point others to Christ by living like him so that others may clearly see him in us. Like John, we prepare the way for Christ by the way we live so that we may be authentic witnesses to Christ, the Savior.

- Being wonderfully made by God, our only adequate response is praise and thanksgiving. God knows us intimately and loves us always, no matter what we do or say. Such intimate love is overwhelming to comprehend, yet such is our God. We are called to respond in love and to model that love to all.

Closing Prayer

Conclude with prayer. If time permits, sing the psalm refrain a few times before or after the following prayer.

O Gracious God of intimacy and love,
you know us and call us forth from our mother's womb.
We praise and thank you for being wonderfully made.
You sent your Son, Christ Jesus, to be the full expression of your love
and to teach us how to live and love as you do.
Strengthen us in our desire to be like Christ,
that we might become his heralds,
and, like John the Baptist, point him out to others.
Through Christ our Lord and Savior.
Amen.

Readings for the Next Dismissal

Provide catechumens with a list of the readings for the next dismissal session. Consult the liturgical calendar on page xvi to find out what day will be observed next week. Give catechumens the questions below to guide their reflection through the week.

⑥ As you pray with the readings, around what themes do your thoughts seem to be coming together?

⑥ Where do the readings intersect with your journey of faith? What questions do they raise for you?

Extended Catechesis

Based on today's readings and liturgical observance, the following topics may be covered for extended catechesis:

※ God creates out of love

※ God's call and our response

※ The essence of ministry

※ The beauty of God's creation and the environment

※ The hand of God with us

※ Heralds of God

SOLEMNITY OF STS. PETER AND PAUL, APOSTLES

June 29

Focus: To proclaim the Good News, no matter the cost.

Lectionary #591 (Mass during the Day)

Catechist's Preparation

Overview of the Solemnity

Today's solemnity celebrates two pillars of the Church, Peter and Paul, who play key roles in the New Testament as proclaimers of the Good News of Jesus Christ. They remain faithful to their discipleship and ministry despite the suffering they endured. We celebrate their lives as living models of discipleship's demands and joys. Each was willing to give of themselves fully for the sake of the Gospel, imitating the Lord even to the point of death. Tradition holds that they both died in Rome under Emperor Nero around AD 65. A famous icon has them meeting and embracing as each is being led to their respective deaths. Such is the model they offer us today.

Scripture Background

Acts of the Apostles 12:1–11 The story of Peter's release from prison reads like a supernatural play. The "background music" introduced by the author (see 12:5) is the community's prayer on Peter's behalf. The whole escape has an unreal, dreamlike quality: shining light, oblivious guards, dropping chains, and opening gates. The threat that the Jesus movement represented is underscored by the size of the contingent assigned to guard Peter -four squads of four guards each.

The one who stands to benefit from Peter's death is King Herod Agrippa I, the grandson of Herod the Great. Educated in Rome, Herod Agrippa grew up with the children of the emperor and in childhood became good friends with the future emperor Caligula. His contacts enabled him to succeed his father and rule a large territory that included Judea. He maintained his power there by supporting Pharisaic Judaism. No doubt his persecution of followers of Jesus endeared him to the Pharisees who feared the "heretical sect" that followed Jesus.

The solemn celebration of Passover precludes Herod from immediately presenting Peter to the people for trial and certain death. Like Jesus, Peter faced death at Passover, the feast that commemorates liberation from Pharaoh. Like Jesus, Peter is saved by God. Peter's rescue parallels both Christ's Resurrection and the Exodus. To the early Christians, who thought the return of Christ was at hand, this Passover rescue of Peter is a significant and hopeful sign.

Psalm 34:2–3, 4–5, 6–7, 8–9 (5) This psalm addresses the just and encourages them to join the psalmist in praising the God who rescues them. The initial verses exhort the hearer to glorify the Lord (see 34:1–4). Then the psalmist expresses gratitude to the Lord for being rescued from danger. The psalmist has called out and the Lord has heard. Echoing the reading from Acts of the Apostles, the psalmist acknowledges the "angel of the Lord [who] encamps around those who fear him, and delivers them" (34:7). The psalmist calls upon the hearer to "taste and see" (34:9)—that is, experience—the goodness of the Lord. Those who "fear the Lord" will want for nothing (34:10).

2 Timothy 4:6–8, 17–18 The excerpt from 2 Timothy speaks of Paul's imminent death. The metaphor of libation refers to the Hellenistic ritual by which meals were concluded with the sacrifice of a cup of wine poured out in respect to the gods. Clearly, Paul sees his death as a sacrifice, a fitting end to a life of service to God.

Matthew 16:13–19 This reading focuses directly on the essence of Jesus' identity and the Church. Jesus asks his followers who people say he is (see 16:13). It is a question Matthew's Church must answer as well. The responses Jesus receives all reflect the respect the people have for Jesus. Some think he is John the Baptist, a prophet or the resurrected Elijah or the suffering Jeremiah (only Matthew mentions Jeremiah, perhaps a hint of Christ's Passion).

The answers also reveal that the people have not recognized Jesus as their Messiah. Matthew differs from Mark in using "Son of Man" rather than "I" in Jesus' question (see 16:13). The emphasis is on the human Jesus. With Peter's inspired proclamation, Matthew refers to the "Son of the living God" (16:16), a title which shifts the image of the Messiah from a nationalistic and military one to a familial relationship—a new idea to the expectant Jews.

Many scholars believe that Peter's revelation is actually post-Resurrection in context. This passage serves as a foundation story for the post-Easter Church and the line of authority. Just as Peter named Jesus, Jesus named Peter. Jesus assumes what hitherto had been God's role—changing someone's name, Abram to Abraham, and Sarai to Sarah, for example. Simon becomes *Kepha* (Aramaic) or *Petros* (Greek). Abram was the foundation of the people of Israel and the rock from whom the people were carved (see Isaiah 51:1–2). Peter the rock is the foundation stone of the Church, the new people of God. (The reference to the Church as *ekklesia* is one of only two in the four Gospel accounts and refers to the assembly of the people.)

The ritual handing on of the keys of the kingdom clearly designates the Church as the mediator between earth and heaven. Peter is given authority to determine what is permissible as a follower of Jesus and who is part of the community. "Binding and loosing" is a Semitic expression for rendering a decision that either imposes or releases an obligation (see 16:19). The Church is the ultimate witness to God's vision revealed through Jesus, the "Son of the living God" (16:16).

Reflection Questions for the Catechist

- How are Peter and Paul living models for your ministry of proclaiming the Word?
- What are some of the joys that you experience in your ministry?
- What are some of the challenges and difficulties you face in being faithful to your ministry?
- How does your intimate relationship to the Lord help you in carrying out your ministry?

Catechist's Guide

Objectives

- ▷ To realize that discipleship and ministry entails both great joys and many challenges.
- ▷ To know that the Lord journeys with us through our joys and challenges.
- ▷ To nourish our intimate relationship with the Lord, who calls us to discipleship and ministry.

Dismissal and Procession

Following the homily, the priest celebrant picks up the Lectionary and invites the catechumens to come forward with the catechist(s) who will lead today's dismissal session. Holding the Lectionary so that all can see, the priest celebrant sends the catechumens and catechist(s) forward using RCIA, 67, his own words, or the following:

PRIEST: **My dear catechumens, let God's Word be your nourishment and our fellowship be your bond that a special place has been prepared for you in the Kingdom in which we all hope to rejoice with the One who conquered death and called us to himself. Go in peace.**

All process to where the dismissal session will take place. The catechist holds the Lectionary in a reverent manner. The assembly may sing an acclamation to accompany the procession.

Centering

Upon reaching the place where the dismissal occurs, place the Lectionary on the ambo, lectern, or other dignified place (or hold the book reverently). Light the candle that is in the place of gathering and reread Acts 12:1–11 in order to refocus the group's attention. Consider singing the Responsorial Psalm or have a recording of it available to use as part of the centering, either before or after the reading.

Reflection and Discussion

The following "script" may be used or adapted to help facilitate discussion on today's readings. Begin the discussion by asking the catechumens if any words or phrases from today's readings spoke to them.

Peter, in proclaiming the Lord openly, faces many challenges—even imprisonment. Yet Peter does not waver in his call, for he knows that the Lord is with him. Peter's faith helps him face the difficulties of ministry, and the Lord responds by aiding Peter and all disciples to be faithful. Angels, representing God's special care and love, always act on our behalf, aiding us in our call to serve.

- How has your life changed as a result of your desire to respond to God's call?

- What are the joys and challenges that you face in your call to be a disciple?

- How have families and friends reacted to your desire to respond to God's call?

- Where do you find support and encouragement to be faithful to God's call?

Psalm 34 is the grateful praise of one who cried out to the Lord and was heard. God's love, care, and concern, represented by angels, are always there whenever one trusts in and cries out to the Lord. Drawing near to God and continually trusting in the Lord makes discipleship fruitful and rewarding, no matter the difficulties.

- How often do you praise and thank the Lord for all the care and blessings showered upon you?

- Name times when you called out to the Lord in your need and were heard. How did it make you feel? How did you respond to the Lord? How did it deepen your relationship to the Lord?

Paul often speaks of the challenges of being called to be a disciple to the Gentiles. Yet despite all the difficulties, Paul remained faithful to his ministry, always knowing and trusting in the Lord, who called him and never abandoned him. No matter how difficult the race, Paul asserts that "I have competed well; I have finished the race; I have kept the faith" (2 Timothy 4:7). How? For Paul, the answer always is: "The Lord stood by me and gave me strength" (2 Timothy 4:17).

- How does the Lord stand by you and give you strength as you strive to respond to God's call?

- How are you, like Paul, competing against those things that might distract you from being faithful to God's call?

- How do you, like Paul, keep the faith, no matter the cost?

- How do you cultivate intimacy and trust in God's loving care when things do not go well?

Peter's profession of Jesus as "the Christ, the Son of the living God" (Matthew 16:16), is the essential affirmation of discipleship. Like Peter, we make this profession with the help of God. It becomes the basis for gathering as a community to celebrate and live out our call and discipleship. In so doing, we align ourselves with God's ways and thoughts.

- Recall when you, like Peter, professed Jesus as "the Christ, the Son of the living God." What did you hear Jesus saying to you?

- How did your profession of faith in Jesus impact your life and relationships? How does that profession of faith continue to impact you today?

Wrapping It Up

Consider these points as you conclude the session. Integrate the thoughts and ideas that surfaced in your discussion with the catechumens as you conclude your time together.

- God continually calls us to discipleship and ministry modeled on Jesus, the Christ. God is always there, standing by us, strengthening and supporting us in our proclamation of the Good News. Our intimacy with and trust in God empower us to run the race and keep the faith, no matter the cost.

- The challenges of discipleship and ministry are real. They can distract or sidetrack us on our journey of faith. But God's love, care, and concern, symbolically represented by angels, are always there to help us in our need. We are assured of being heard whenever we trust in and call upon the Lord.

- Our profession of faith in Jesus as the Christ, the Son of the living God, demands that we come to know the Lord more intimately and model ourselves on him. This attracts others to come together as a community, to celebrate and live out that profession in mutual love, support, and care for one another and for all of God's creation. This is Church.

Closing Prayer

Conclude with prayer. If time permits, sing the psalm refrain a few times before or after the following prayer.

O Attentive and Caring God,
we praise and thank you for standing by us,
for listening and responding to us whenever we call upon you,
most especially in our times of need.
We ask that you continue to be with us
as we strive to be faithful disciples.
Like Sts. Peter and Paul, help us in proclaiming your Good News to all,
not counting the cost, nor overwhelmed by the challenges.
Through Christ our Lord.
Amen.

Readings for the Next Dismissal

Provide catechumens with a list of the readings for the next dismissal session. Consult the liturgical calendar on page xvi to find out what day will be observed next week. Give catechumens the questions below to guide their reflection through the week.

⑥ As you pray with the readings, around what themes do your thoughts seem to be coming together?

⑥ Where do the readings intersect with your journey of faith? What questions do they raise for you?

Extended Catechesis

Based on today's readings and liturgical observance, the following topics may be covered for extended catechesis:

❋ God's call and our response

❋ Meaning of Church

❋ Angels as signs of God's love

❋ Joys and challenges of ministry

❋ Profession of faith

❋ Keeping the faith

FEAST OF THE TRANSFIGURATION OF THE LORD

August 6

Focus: The power of God is made known.

Lectionary #614

Catechist's Preparation

Overview of the Feast

The Transfiguration of the Lord refers to a mysterious event during which Jesus is changed or transfigured in the presence of three of his disciples, Peter, James, and John. Moses and Elijah, two Old Testament figures representing the Law and the Prophets, appear and converse with Jesus. The event highlights Jesus' divinity and glory that was hidden from the world but now revealed to his closest disciples. Jesus is the fulfillment and completion of the Old Testament promises. This brief glimpse into Jesus' hidden power, divinity, and glory would be fully revealed in the Resurrection once the journey of suffering and Death had been accomplished.

Scripture Background

Daniel 7:9–10, 13–14 At about the time that Daniel was written, the Jewish people lived under the rule of Antiochus Epiphanes. Antiochus wanted to impose Greek culture and religion on his Jewish subjects. The dreams and visions described in chapters seven through twelve are addressed to persecuted people, particularly those persecuted by Antiochus. In the verses that precede the reading, four mythical beasts emerge from an abyss. These beasts can be identified as empires that ruled over the people of Israel: Assyria, Babylon, Persia, and Greece. These beasts terrorize and destroy people (see 7:5). Amid this destruction comes "an Ancient One" (7:9), taking his throne of fiery flames. God appears and judges the beasts, in particular a beast's horn that represented Antiochus.

The horn is destroyed (see 7:11), and on the horizon a new vision arises. A being in human form appears before the Ancient One and receives authority over the world for eternity (see 7:13–14). For the people undergoing persecution, this vision promises that God, not human rulers, reigns over the world and throughout history.

The Book of Daniel promises that faith will triumph: the good and righteous will be saved and the wicked destroyed. Later Christians interpreted the one given authority to be Jesus Christ, whose power comes from God and whose rule is eternal.

Psalm 97:1–2, 5–6, 9 (1a, 9a) Psalm 97 celebrates the reign of God over Israel. The people experience God as a mysterious force, like "clouds and thick darkness" (97:2). God's reign is founded on justice (see 97:2), and God's power is overwhelming. The highest points on earth dissolve in the presence of the mighty one (see 97:5). The psalm proclaims that no god is eater than the God of Israel (see 97:9).

2 Peter 1:16–19 The early Christians, who once believed that Christ would return soon, became confused as the years progressed. Some people began to teach that belief in Christ's return was one of several "cleverly devised myths" (1:16). The Second Letter of Peter addresses these false teachers.

The passage defends belief in Christ's return with an appeal to the Apostles' experience of the Transfiguration. According to the author, the experience of Jesus' transformation and the words spoken from heaven revealed him to be the one from God. The Transfiguration is like a window offering a view into the reality to come. Present time is compared to darkness, but Christ's reappearance will mark the dawn of a new day. Until then, believers must stand firm in their faith founded on the Apostles' witness.

Mark 9:2–10 The Transfiguration is a mysterious event that revealed Jesus' divine nature and the glory that would be his after the Resurrection and Ascension into heaven. Peter, James, and John, the same disciples who will accompany Jesus to the garden at Gethsemane, are led to a mountain to see Jesus transform into a being of light. Two great leaders, Elijah and Moses, also appear. Moses and Elijah both experienced the glory of the Lord on a high mountain: Moses received the Law (see Exodus 19–34) and Elijah heard the voice of God (see 1 Kings 19:8–14). They may represent the Law and the words of the prophets that Jesus has fulfilled.

In all three Gospel accounts, the Transfiguration immediately follows Jesus telling his followers that discipleship involves denying oneself and taking up the cross (see Mark 8:34–38). The Gospel accounts teach that if the disciples persevere through suffering and trial, they will also share a glorious encounter with God.

Reflection Questions for the Catechist

- How do you understand the meaning and significance of Jesus' Transfiguration?
- When have you experienced the power of God working in your life?
- How are God's power and glory an overwhelming reality in your life?
- How do you make known to others the power of God that is operative in your faith and ministry?

Catechist's Guide

Objectives

- ▷ To recognize that God's power and glory have been revealed to us in Jesus.
- ▷ To acknowledge Jesus as the full revelation among us of God's power and glory.
- ▷ To make known God's power and glory to others by our faithful living as disciples of Jesus.

Dismissal and Procession

Following the homily, the priest celebrant picks up the Lectionary and invites the catechumens to come forward with the catechist(s) who will lead today's dismissal session. Holding the Lectionary so that all can see, the priest celebrant sends the catechumens and catechist(s) forward using RCIA, 67, his own words, or the following:

PRIEST: **My dear friends, on the holy mountain the Lord was transfigured in glory, and his radiance continues to shine brightly in our world. As you go forth to reflect more deeply on this mystery, may you too be transfigured and your relationship with God and the Church be strengthened as you continue your journey to the Eucharistic banquet. Go in peace.**

All process to where the dismissal session will take place. The catechist holds the Lectionary in a reverent manner. The assembly may sing an acclamation to accompany the procession.

Centering

Upon reaching the place where the dismissal occurs, place the Lectionary on the ambo, lectern, or other dignified place (or hold the book reverently). Light the candle that is in the place of gathering and reread Mark 9:2–10 in order to refocus the group's attention. Consider singing the Responsorial Psalm or have a recording of it available to use as part of the centering, either before or after the reading.

Reflection and Discussion

The following "script" may be used or adapted to help facilitate discussion on today's readings. Begin the discussion by asking the catechumens if any words or phrases from today's readings spoke to them.

In the midst of life's difficulties, we are asked to trust in the power of God present and working in and through our human condition. God is attuned to our needs and acts on our behalf, even when we can't see it or understand why things happen. God does respond. We are asked to trust that God's ways will ultimately win out. Name times when your faith in God was tested by life's circumstances.

- How is Jesus a model of trust and confidence in God when life overwhelms?
- What helps you to trust in God when events in life disappoint?

Psalm 97 proclaims that "The Lord is king, the most high over all the earth" (refrain). Such acclaim comes from trust and faith in God who acts with justice. All creation acknowledges that God's power and glory is manifested through justice bringing about right relationship with God, ourselves, others, and all creation. God's power and glory is fully revealed in Jesus' life of justice and right relationship with all.

- ⑨ How do you show by your words and actions that the Lord is the king of your life?

- ⑨ How is justice, the virtue of working towards right relationship with all, a key component of your life as a disciple?

- ⑨ Name times when you were treated with justice. How did it make you feel?

Some find it difficult to acknowledge God's existence. Others acknowledge God's existence but have difficulty placing faith and trust in God. We cannot prove God's existence or our faith. We choose to believe. For Christians, we choose to believe that Jesus is the living manifestation of God's power, glory, and presence among us. We choose to live like Jesus because we believe that God intends us to live in harmonious relationship with all creation. By modeling Jesus, we make God present with the hope that others might choose to believe and allow God, the king of justice, to rule their lives.

- ⑨ How do you respond when people challenge your belief in God?

- ⑨ What reasons do you give for why you believe?

- ⑨ How is your life a source of light to others who might be living in dark places?

Jesus' divinity and power are fully revealed only in the Resurrection. The Transfiguration is a glimpse into his identity offering his followers hope, trust, and confidence. Such trust will be challenged by Jesus' Passion and Death, the only path to Resurrection. Will they continue to trust and believe when it really counts? This is the dilemma of all disciples.

- ⑨ How does Jesus help you walk through the various sufferings of your life?

- ⑨ How does Jesus make known God's power and glory in your life?

- ⑨ What glimpse of God's power and glory do you receive from being intimately connected to Jesus?

Wrapping It Up   *Consider these points as you conclude the session. Integrate the thoughts and ideas that surfaced in your discussion with the catechumens as you conclude your time together.*

- God's power and glory are revealed to us in Jesus. Like his disciples, we are given glimpses of that power and glory as we journey in this life. Such glimpses help us to maintain trust and hope in our Loving God, giving us strength to endure when life's difficulties challenge us.

- The Lord is king over all creation. As king over our lives, God calls us to practice justice, modeling ourselves on Jesus, who promoted right relationship with all. As Jesus' disciples, we are called to make known to others God's power and glory visibly manifested by our words and actions.

- God's power and glory manifested in our lives is only a small portion of what awaits us when we are finally united with our loving God. Jesus ultimate power and glory were manifested when he fully embraced our human condition and walked our journey. Jesus models for us what faith entails, both its challenges and its life-giving power.

Closing Prayer

Conclude with prayer. If time permits, sing the psalm refrain a few times before or after the following prayer.

> O Loving God of Power and Might,
> we praise and bless you, as our King and Lord.
> Justice and right relationship with all creation
> are the hallmarks of your power and glory.
> You sent your Son, Christ Jesus, to manifest your power and glory
> by practicing justice toward all.
> Modeling ourselves on your Son, we ask for the grace to live justly,
> so that your power and glory may be made known to all.
> Through Christ our Lord.
> Amen.

Readings for the Next Dismissal

Provide catechumens with a list of the readings for the next dismissal session. Consult the liturgical calendar on page xvi to find out what day will be observed next week. Give catechumens the questions below to guide their reflection through the week.

🌀 As you pray with the readings, around what themes do your thoughts seem to be coming together?

🌀 Where do the readings intersect with your journey of faith? What questions do they raise for you?

Extended Catechesis

Based on today's readings and liturgical observance, the following topics may be covered for extended catechesis:

❊ Justice as right relationship

❊ Justice as God's power and might

❊ Jesus, God's justice

❊ Faith amid life's challenges

❊ Why do you choose to believe?

❊ Perseverance in faith

SOLEMNITY OF THE ASSUMPTION OF THE BLESSED VIRGIN MARY

August 15

Focus: Mary rejoices in the Lord.

Lectionary #622 (Mass during the Day)

Catechist's Preparation

Overview of the Solemnity

Because Mary attuned herself to God's Word and will in her life, she actively cooperated with God in gifting the world with Jesus, God-with-us. Mary greatly rejoiced in her humble role as the Mother of God. Her role as *Theotokos*, the "God-bearer" or "Mother of God," enabled Jesus to carry out his mission of intimately connecting all humanity with God. For her courageous discipleship, God blessed Mary during her difficult life and at her death, God assumed her bodily into heaven, where she now enjoys full union with her Lord. Mary, as one of us, points to what awaits the Church and all disciples who wait in hope for full union with God. While not in Scripture, Mary's bodily Assumption into heaven is an ancient Church belief. The solemnity not only celebrates Mary's Assumption, but as the primary symbol of the Church, Mary's Assumption points to the fullness of salvation that will be given to the entire Church with the Lord's Second Coming.

Scripture Background

Revelation 11:19a; 12:1–6a, 10ab John sees a vision of the Temple opened and of the Ark of the Covenant fully displayed. The ark of the covenant was in the Holy of Holies, which the high priest could enter only on the Day of Atonement. The ark was a reminder of God's faithfulness to the covenant with Israel, whatever terror yet to come. John sees another vision, with details drawn from many sources. The Babylonians frequently depicted their goddesses as crowned with the twelve signs of the zodiac. The woman's twelve-star crown also represents the twelve tribes of Israel of the Old Covenant and the Twelve Apostles of the New Covenant. She is the mother of the Church and the mother of the Messiah. She is in labor about to bear a child who is destined to "rule all the nations with a rod of iron" (12:5, see Psalm 2:9, a messianic psalm). When the child is born, he is rescued from the attack of the dragon, an ancient image for Satan, by being taken up to the throne of God in heaven, a reference to Christ's Ascension. The woman, too, escapes the attack of the dragon by being taken into the desert (a biblical place of refuge, see Jesus' instruc-

tions to his disciples, Mark 13:14). The reference to "one thousand two hundred sixty days" (Revelation 12:6b) is roughly the length of persecution of Israel by Antiochus Epiphanes IV (also "forty-two months," three and one-half years, see Revelation 11:2). A voice from heaven proclaims Christ's victory over Satan: "Now have come the salvation and the power and the kingdom of our God and the authority of his Messiah" (11:10a).

Psalm 45:10, 11, 12, 16 (10bc) Psalm 45 was originally written to celebrate the marriage of the king of Israel. The king's pursuit "for the cause of truth and to defend the right" (45:4) is recalled and celebrated. Later traditions have seen another level of meaning in the psalm. Jews understand it as the relationship between the royal Messiah and his people Israel. Christians see it as celebrating the union of Christ and the Church (often portrayed as a marriage, see Ephesians 5:21–23). The psalmist delights in the wedding procession as "they are led in with glad and joyous acclaim; they enter the palace of the king" (Psalm 45:15).

1 Corinthians 15:20–27 The Feast of the Passover had more than one meaning. It commemorated the deliverance of Israel from Egypt, but it also was a harvest festival. The law required that the firstfruits of the harvest be brought to the priest as an offering to the Lord (see Leviticus 23:10–11). For Paul, the firstfruits were a sign of the Resurrection of Jesus and a sign of the resurrection of all believers. At Christ's final coming, he will return to the Father like a conqueror returning home. Christ will hand "over the kingdom to God," and put "all his enemies under his feet" (1 Corinthians 15:24, 25; it was the custom of a king to place his foot on the back of his vanquished enemy, see Psalm 110: 1). Death will be the last enemy to defeat. Then there will be nothing outside God's redeeming power and love.

Luke 1:39–56 As a sign to Mary that she would be the mother of the Messiah, the angel Gabriel tells her that her kinswoman Elizabeth conceived a son in her old age. Mary is the obedient servant of the Lord who travels four days to the hill country of Judah to assist her cousin. On hearing Mary's greeting, Elizabeth's unborn child leaps for joy in her womb, recalling David's dance before the Lord when the Ark of the Covenant was brought to Jerusalem (see 2 Samuel 6:9,14). Elizabeth expresses her unworthiness of being visited by Mary, the Ark bearing the New Covenant, her divine son Jesus. Elizabeth rejoices in Mary's privileged role. Mary is "blessed . . . among women" (Luke 1:42) for believing that God's promises to her would be fulfilled. In an exultant hymn of praise, Mary rejoices in God's saving promises, (see the canticle of Hannah, 1 Samuel 2:1–10). God casts down the powerful and raises up the poor. Mary recognizes her own lowliness before her mighty God. She is God's humble handmaid, "servant Israel" (Luke 1:54), obedient to the Lord's command. All Christians hope to be "lifted up" (1:52) by God one day to join Mary and her son in heaven.

Reflection Questions for the Catechist

⑨ How do you articulate your belief concerning Mary's bodily Assumption into heaven?

⑨ How is Mary's active cooperation with God in her life a model for you as a disciple of Jesus?

⑨ How do you attune yourself to God's Word and allow it to take flesh in your life the way Mary did?

⑨ How does Mary challenge you in the way you respond to the Lord in your life?

Catechist's Guide

Objectives

▷ To imitate Mary in attuning ourselves to God's Word and actions in our life as disciples.

▷ To rejoice in the Lord always as Mary does, no matter the challenge or life's complications.

▷ To acknowledge God's graciousness toward all creation in gifting us with Jesus, God-with-us.

Dismissal and Procession

Following the homily, the priest celebrant picks up the Lectionary and invites the catechumens to come forward with the catechist(s) who will lead today's dismissal session. Holding the Lectionary so that all can see, the priest celebrant sends the catechumens and catechist(s) forward using RCIA, 67, his own words, or the following:

PRIEST: **My dear friends, the Blessed Virgin Mary was raised body and soul into heaven and saved by the corruption wrought by sin. As you go forth to reflect more deeply upon this mystery, may you chase after our Mother by living a life of holiness and glorifying God's name in all that you say and do. Go in peace.**

All process to where the dismissal session will take place. The catechist holds the Lectionary in a reverent manner. The assembly may sing an acclamation to accompany the procession.

Centering

Upon reaching the place where the dismissal occurs, place the Lectionary on the ambo, lectern, or other dignified place (or hold the book reverently). Light the candle that is in the place of gathering and reread Luke 1:39–56 in order to refocus the group's attention. Consider singing the Responsorial Psalm or have a recording of it available to use as part of the centering, either before or after the reading.

Reflection and Discussion

The following "script" may be used or adapted to help facilitate discussion on today's readings. Begin the discussion by asking the catechumens if any words or phrases from today's readings spoke to them.

Mary, as God bearer, cooperated with God in bringing up the child Jesus, teaching him God's ways and ultimately letting him go to complete the mission to which he was called. Mary rejoiced in her role, despite the difficulties. For this, God prepared a special place for Mary so that she could abide fully with her Lord and God.

🌀 What meaning and significance does the solemnity of Mary's Assumption into heaven have for you in your faith life?

🌀 What does this solemnity say about us who, like Mary, strive to attune ourselves to God's ways?

Psalm 45, a royal wedding song, speaks of the intimacy between two people who love each other and desire to be always in each other's presence. Each is so attuned to the other that nothing else matters. Mary cultivated a similar relationship with God and in this she becomes a model of what discipleship entails.

🌀 How is Mary a model of discipleship for you as you commit yourself to God?

🌀 How do you, like Mary, continuously cultivate greater and deeper intimacy with God?

🌀 How do you, like Mary, strive to cooperate with God to bring Jesus to birth in your life?

God choosing to become human in Jesus elevated and dignified all of creation. Like Mary, we take great joy in God's graciousness and love. Fidelity to the Father's ways led Jesus to be crucified. The Father raised Jesus up, assuring that all faithful disciples of Jesus will also be raised with him. The specialness that God granted Mary, a faithful disciple of Jesus, is the same as that which is granted to all disciples.

🌀 How does Mary's specialness in God's eyes help you to rejoice in your own specialness to God?

🌀 How does Jesus' life, Death, and Resurrection enable you, like Mary, to be connected with God for all time?

🌀 Do you believe that God has prepared a special place for you, as he did for Mary?

In her Magnificat, Mary rejoices in her Lord for allowing her to cooperate in bringing about Jesus' birth and mission. In so doing, Mary knows that the world's ways will be upended and that a new way of thinking and acting will prevail. Concern for the poor, the oppressed, and the powerless is the image of God that Mary elevates and praises, as she commits herself to teach her son those very values.

🌀 How do you cooperate with God to advocate and promote concern for the poor, the outcast, and the stranger?

🌀 How does Mary's Magnificat clue you into what Jesus' mission and ministry are all about?

🌀 How do you continue to carry on Jesus' mission and ministry through your life as a disciple?

Wrapping It Up

Consider these points as you conclude the session. Integrate the thoughts and ideas that surfaced in your discussion with the catechumens as you conclude your time together.

- Mary heard God's Word, reflected on it, and allowed it to literally take flesh in her. Because of her willing cooperation, intimacy with God through Jesus is now a reality for all creation. Mary was the first to benefit from the intimacy by being bodily assumed into heaven. In Jesus, we are all called to the same intimacy, as we await the day when we will be united with God for all time.

- Like Mary, we are called to listen to God's Word and flesh it out in the daily events of our lives. Like Mary, we strive to cultivate a deep intimacy with God. Jesus is the path to God, and Mary the disciple shows us how to walk that path.

- Mary fully rejoices in her Lord, who is faithful and keeps Old Testament promises. God is the mighty one who is always attuned to the needs of the poor, the oppressed, the outcast, and the stranger. The world's values are realigned to manifest God's ways. Like Mary, we disciples are called to rejoice in the Lord, who does wondrous things for us.

Closing Prayer

Conclude with prayer. If time permits, sing the psalm refrain a few times before or after the following prayer. Consider also praying the Magnificat.

> O Gracious and Loving God,
> we rejoice in your loving plan
> to gift us with your Son, in and through
> the active and willing cooperation of Mary.
> We pray that as you blessed her
> with complete intimacy with you through her Assumption,
> we too, as Jesus' disciples,
> may come to the same intimacy with you for all eternity.
> Through Christ our Lord.
> Amen.

Readings for the Next Dismissal

Provide catechumens with a list of the readings for the next dismissal session. Consult the liturgical calendar on page xvi to find out what day will be observed next week. Give catechumens the questions below to guide their reflection through the week.

- As you pray with the readings, around what themes do your thoughts seem to be coming together?

- Where do the readings intersect with your journey of faith? What questions do they raise for you?

Extended Catechesis

Based on today's readings and liturgical observance, the following topics may be covered for extended catechesis:

- ❄ God's creation as holy
- ❄ Mary as the first disciple
- ❄ Mary as one of us
- ❄ Mary, truly our sister
- ❄ Mary as Theotokos
- ❄ Theological implications of the Magnificat

FEAST OF THE EXALTATION OF THE HOLY CROSS

September 14

Focus: To be free of fear.

Lectionary #638

Catechist's Preparation

Overview of the Feast

The Feast of the Exaltation (or Triumph) of the Cross is an ancient feast dating to AD 335, when tradition attributes Helena, the mother the Roman emperor Constantine, with the finding of Christ's Cross. John's account of the Gospel promotes the Cross not as Jesus' degradation but as the ultimate symbol of love. Jesus' sacrificial love for the world turned the Cross into a symbol of triumph over fear, sin, and ultimately death itself. John's account of the Gospel connects Jesus being lifted up on the Cross to his Resurrection. Jesus' willingness to give of his life for others out of love exalts the Cross as the key symbol of what discipleship entails and the only true path to exaltation and Resurrection.

Scripture Background

Numbers 21:4–9 According to Scripture, the people of Israel spent most of their sojourn in the desert complaining. This passage contains one of the last such complaints recorded by the author of Numbers. This time, however, their complaint is not only against Moses, it is also against God. "Why have you brought us out of Egypt to die in the wilderness?" they cry (21:5). "There is no food and no water" (21:5). Incensed, God again plans to punish the murmuring people by sending poisonous snakes to bite them. As usual, Moses intervenes, God relents, and the people are saved, this time by looking at a statue of a bronze serpent.

The imagery in these verses is particularly rich. Among Israel's neighbors, the serpent was an object of worship. Indeed, in Canaan snakes were often connected to the healing arts. In Israel, the serpent as symbol evoked mixed messages. On the one hand, the serpent reminded them of the plagues of Egypt, which had contributed to their liberation from slavery. On the other hand, serpents were religiously suspicious, for they reminded the people of rival religions, particularly those of Canaan.

Christian tradition has added another layer of meaning to the images of this passage by associating it with the Cross of Jesus. In each case, God has taken what is usually harmful (poisonous snakes and methods of execution) and used them as means of healing.

Psalm 78:1bc–2, 34–35, 36–37, 38 (see 7b) This historical psalm comes out of the wisdom tradition. Probably composed for use in festivals, Psalm 78 recounts the sacred history of God's care for the people. The psalmist focuses primarily on Israel's disobedience and ingratitude in the face of God's continual loving kindness, most likely in an effort to warn the psalmist's generation against similar behavior. In a way, the psalmist here is remembering the "good old days," ending his narrative at the time of David, even though the psalm itself was probably written down during the period of the exile. The message is clear, "Do not forget God's loving-kindness" (78:7). We can hear a similar message: "Do not forget the Cross. It is our sign of God's loving-kindness."

Philippians 2:6–11 Philippians was written around the middle of the first century AD by Paul to a Church he had founded in Macedonia. The letter is amazingly upbeat considering that Paul was in prison at the time of its writing. Paul had several purposes in writing this letter. He wanted to thank the Philippians for their concern and for the gifts they sent him. He wanted to warn them about unscrupulous preachers who might lead them away from the Gospel Paul had preached to them. And he wanted to encourage the Philippians to be "of the same mind" in Christ (2:2).

It is this last concern that we see in this passage. In it, Paul exhorts the Philippians to live together in unity by practicing Christ's example of being obedient to God even to death, particularly death on a cross. Although it may not sound like it in English, the words Paul used are from an ancient hymn. (The Philippians would have easily recognized this hymn even though Paul changed it a bit to make it more Christian.) Like the reading from Numbers, this reading gives us a somewhat rare interpretation of the cross. It speaks of the cross not in terms of atonement, but in terms of Jesus' willingness to obey God perfectly. On the Cross, Paul says, Jesus gave up every claim to the authority and power which by rights were his from the beginning of creation. He did exactly what God wanted him to do, and as a result, God exalted him and gave him "the name which is above every name" (2:9).

John 3:13–17 Like the reading from Philippians, this reading represents a large shift in literary and theological context. While Mark is the earliest of the canonical Gospel accounts, John is the latest, written probably around the year 90. Mark portrays Jesus as the suffering Son of God, but John pictures Jesus as the mysterious and divine Son of Man. And while Mark saw the Cross as the decisive battle between evil and good, John saw the Cross as the exaltation of the Son of Man.

This reading highlights that exaltation. In the first part of the reading, John describes the work of Christ on the Cross in terms of descending and ascending. While at first this may seem strange, it resembles imagery Paul used in his letter to the Philippians, but with a distinctly Johannine twist. Like Paul, John pictures Jesus' sojourn on earth as a deliberate giving up of power, in this case by descending to earth. John then turns to the crucifixion itself, when Jesus ascends and is lifted up, much like the serpent in the reading from Numbers. On the Cross, John says, Jesus is like that bronze serpent. Just meditating on him is enough to bring repentance, healing, and most importantly, eternal life. In the second part of the reading, John describes the benefits believers derive from the Cross. Those who believe, he says, will "not perish but have eternal life" (3:16).

Reflection Questions for the Catechist	⑥ How do you articulate the meaning and significance of the Cross in your life?
	⑥ How does the Cross help you clarify what discipleship entails?
	⑥ How does Jesus' death on the Cross free you for fear, violence and ultimately death?
	⑥ How does love of others help you in taking up the various crosses that you face in your life?

Catechist's Guide

Objectives

▷ To perceive the Cross as a symbol of victory and power and not one of defeat and failure.

▷ To hold up the Cross as the ultimate expression of God's total self-giving love for all humanity.

▷ To value the Cross as the key symbol of what following Jesus entails and demands.

Dismissal and Procession

Following the homily, the priest celebrant picks up the Lectionary and invites the catechumens to come forward with the catechist(s) who will lead today's dismissal session. Holding the Lectionary so that all can see, the priest celebrant sends the catechumens and catechist(s) forward using RCIA, 67, his own words, or the following:

PRIEST: My dear friends, you have shared with us at the table of God's Word. As you go forth to reflect more deeply on this Word, this community sends you forth with prayers and encouragement. May you see the Cross as a sign of the Church's only hope, trusting that the power of death has been destroyed forever. We look forward to the day when you remain with us to share at the table of the Eucharist. Go in peace.

All process to where the dismissal session will take place. The catechist holds the Lectionary in a reverent manner. The assembly may sing an acclamation to accompany the procession.

Centering

Upon reaching the place where the dismissal occurs, place the Lectionary on the ambo, lectern, or other dignified place (or hold the book reverently). Light the candle that is in the place of gathering and reread Philippians 2:6–11 in order to refocus the group's attention. Consider singing the Responsorial Psalm or have a recording of it available to use as part of the centering, either before or after the reading.

Reflection and Discussion

The following "script" may be used or adapted to help facilitate discussion on today's readings. Begin the discussion by asking the catechumens if any words or phrases from today's readings spoke to them.

In their desert sojourn, the Jewish people complained to God and Moses about their wretched existence. They did not seem grateful at all for their freedom from slavery and death. Even though God punished them, their pleas for forgiveness reach the ears of God, who relents and offers healing.

- How often do you complain to God about the negative aspects of life without being grateful for all the positive things in life?

- How has God been a source of healing and strength for you when you asked for forgiveness and healing?

- How have you been a source of healing and strength for others when they reached out to you for forgiveness and healing?

The refrain to Psalm 78 pleads with us not to forget "the works of the Lord." Human beings tend to take God's gracious works for granted, being neither grateful nor attentive to God's love. Yet God is always there, waiting for us to return, to be mindful and to be grateful. It is up to us to respond to God's love and to remember all that God has and does for us. Name some of "the works of the Lord" operative in your life.

- How are you attentive to "the works of the Lord"? What helps you to be attentive and grateful to God?

Paul's well-known Philippian hymn asks us to take on the mind and heart of Christ, who did not cling to his divinity, nor hesitated to humble himself for our sake, even to the point of dying on the Cross. As a result, God greatly exalted him. Thus, Jesus becomes our Savior and the model for how we are challenged to live as disciples.

- How do you strive to take on the mind and heart of Christ in all your interactions with others?

- How hard is it for you to think of others and not only yourself whenever you make any decisions in life?

- How is Jesus the Lord of your life? How far are you willing to sacrifice for the sake of others, even those you do not like?

Like us, Nicodemus struggles to understand what it takes to live the way God intends. Jesus affirms that God's ways are caught up in love of the world, even when the world fails to love in return. Belief in Jesus leads to eternal life by way of the Cross, the way of self-giving love for the sake of others. God does not condemn us but loves us and desires that we love one another in the same fashion and to the same depth that we have been loved.

- How is Jesus the model for the way you love and interact with others?

- How willing are you to pay the price for loving the way Jesus loved us?

- How does your judgment of others often block your willingness to love them as Jesus does?

- How can you counteract this human tendency?

Wrapping It Up

Consider these points as you conclude the session. Integrate the thoughts and ideas that surfaced in your discussion with the catechumens as you conclude your time together.

- God is love, and the ultimate expression of that love was to become fully human. Jesus' life incarnated God's love for all humanity, not judging or condemning but always acting in total self-giving love. Even Death on the Cross did not lead Jesus to retract his love stance but remained faithful to it. For this reason, God raised him up and made him the Savior and model for all humanity.
- Even though he did not come to die on the Cross, Jesus accepted such a cruel death in order to show the power of love and to model for us how to be free from fear, violence, and even death. Christians have venerated and exalted the Cross as the ultimate symbol of love, freedom, and life.
- As Jesus' disciples, our baptismal call is to take on the mind and heart of Christ. We model ourselves on the total self-giving love of Christ, loving ourselves and others the way God loves us. We willingly love all so that others may live and experience the love with which we are loved.

Closing Prayer

Conclude with prayer. If time permits, sing the psalm refrain a few times before or after the following prayer.

O Gracious God of Love and Source of all Life,
we offer thanks and praise to you for the gift of your Son.
He willingly lived and died so that we might live
no longer in fear of suffering and death.
Death on the Cross was his path
to resurrected glory and new life.
Help us to model ourselves on his self-giving love,
so that we might love and give of ourselves to others
as he has given of himself totally for us.
Who lives and reigns for ever.
Amen.

Readings for the Next Dismissal

Provide catechumens with a list of the readings for the next dismissal session. Consult the liturgical calendar on page xvi to find out what day will be observed next week. Give catechumens the questions below to guide their reflection through the week.

- As you pray with the readings, around what themes do your thoughts seem to be coming together?
- Where do the readings intersect with your journey of faith? What questions do they raise for you?

Extended Catechesis

Based on today's readings and liturgical observance, the following topics may be covered for extended catechesis:

- The demands of love
- Virtue of humility
- Costly freedom
- Sin as refusal to love
- Rite of Acceptance and the Cross (see also page 313)
- True path to power and glory

Solemnity of All Saints

Focus: To be like him, for we shall see him as he is.

Lectionary #667

Catechist's Preparation

Overview of the Solemnity

Today's Solemnity of All Saints celebrates those who have committed themselves to Christ and striven to be like him. It includes all who are living and all "who have gone before us with the sign of faith" (Eucharistic Prayer I). In a more restrictive sense, it refers to those whom the Church names as saints and all those unnamed who are with the Lord. Paul's letters typically use the word "saints" to address those who commit themselves to follow Christ Jesus. We publically commit ourselves to Christ at our Baptism and join a community that strives to follow Christ in all things. Therefore, today, as we celebrate all those who are with God already, our hope is that we too, by being faithful to our baptismal call, may one day join them in complete union with God.

Scripture Background

Revelation 7:2–4, 9–14 Apocalyptic books such as Revelation use symbols, numbers, and colors to convey their message. The difficulty of establishing the significance of such literary characteristics, however, opens these texts to a wide range of misunderstandings. The number 144,000, which is mentioned in today's reading, aptly illustrates this danger. The number is used to characterize those who have been washed in the blood of the Lamb and therefore stand in God's favor. But what is the number telling us? Some interpreters read the number quantitatively, concluding that there will only be 144,000 people found to stand in God's grace. This interpretation results in a narrow and pessimistic view of salvation. It is better to read the number qualitatively. It is the perfect square of twelve, multiplied by one thousand (12 × 12 × 1,000). Twelve clearly refers to the twelve tribes of God's Chosen People. The enlarged number speaks the perfection of the new people that God is forming. Rather than limiting salvation, 144,000 tells us of the excellence of those who belong to God—perfection to the thousandth level.

What will God do for this new people? God will protect them. They will be marked with a seal on their foreheads. The image is drawn from Ezekiel 9:1–7, where an angel marks the forehead of those who honor God's Law in order to protect them from destruction. God's People will not be forgotten. The mark on their foreheads will always remind them of God's commitment to save them from harm.

Psalm 24:1bc–2, 3–4ab, 5–6 (see 6) The immense scope of the 144,000 is confirmed by Psalm 24. God is addressed as the Creator to whom all that is belongs. The psalmist does not see God as an aloof "first mover," but as an active possessor of "the earth and its fullness; / the world and those who dwell in it" (24:1). In the midst of creation, there is a community that knows God and seeks to serve God. These people pray this psalm. They sing God's praises and ascend to worship the Creator. They are God's people, set apart by their faith, "seek[ing] the face of the God of Jacob" (24:6).

1 John 3:1–3 The First Letter of John deepens the relationship between God and the people God has chosen. It reveals a personal connection between God and us. We are not only those who God saves. We are also God's children. God not only protects us, but also loves us.

Moreover, our present status is only a beginning. We are promised a future in which "we shall be like him, for we shall see him as he is" (1 John 3:2). Protected as God's children, we are on the way to something better. The contours of that greater gift are expressed in today's Gospel.

Matthew 5:1–12a Jesus' Beatitudes single out various groups of people and assert that they are "blessed." The Greek word for "blessed" could just as easily be translated as "happy" or "fortunate." But why would the poor, hungry, mourning, or meek be fortunate? Jesus is certainly not teaching that poverty, hunger, grief, or lowliness are good things in which we should rejoice.

He is rather saying that all of those who are now experiencing these burdens are destined for a better future. The tense of the verbs is crucial to the Beatitudes. Those who are grieving or hungry now, will be comforted and satisfied then. The blessed future will be realized in the kingdom of God. The Beatitudes, therefore, assert that God is establishing a kingdom in which every evil will be destroyed. Those who are a part of God's people—however burdened they might be—are blessed, because God's Kingdom will be theirs. In that Kingdom, every evil will be replaced with good.

The connection of this passage to today's solemnity is founded on one word. The last Beatitude changes the "blessed are they" to "blessed are you." The "you" is plural. Jesus is telling us that we are blessed as the community of his followers. We are blessed because God will protect us, because we are God's children, and because we have been promised the kingdom. But, the Solemnity of All Saints allows us to add another reason. We are blessed because we are a Church, because we have one another. Even though it is God who establishes the Kingdom, we work with each other to hasten its coming. We support each other in our burdens and work to lighten them. We are blessed because God has given us to one another. We do not need to face the challenges of life alone.

Reflection Questions for the Catechist

- What is your definition of *saint* and how restrictive or inclusive is it?

- Do you see yourself as a saint? If yes, why? If no, why not?

- How are the saints named by the Church models for your life of discipleship?

- How do you imagine and picture eternal life with God? How does that make you feel?

Catechist's Guide

Objectives

▷ To acknowledge all disciples of Christ Jesus as saints, both living and dead.

▷ To realize that intimacy and eternal life with God begins here on earth.

▷ To know that our intimacy and relationship with God begun at our Baptism will endure beyond death and forever.

Dismissal and Procession

Following the homily, the priest celebrant picks up the Lectionary and invites the catechumens to come forward with the catechist(s) who will lead today's dismissal session. Holding the Lectionary so that all can see, the priest celebrant sends the catechumens and catechist(s) forward using RCIA, 67, his own words, or the following:

PRIEST: **Nothing stirs the Church like the victory song of the Lamb, slain but now risen in glory. Yet your desire to bond yourself to Christ and to join the ranks of his saints fills heaven with splendid joy and swells the sound of the angelic chorus. Let God's Word be your nourishment and our fellowship be your bond that a special place has been prepared for you in the kingdom in which we all hope to rejoice with the One who conquered death and called us to himself. Go in peace.**

All process to where the dismissal session will take place. The catechist holds the Lectionary in a reverent manner. The assembly may sing an acclamation to accompany the procession.

Centering

Upon reaching the place where the dismissal occurs, place the Lectionary on the ambo, lectern, or other dignified place (or hold the book reverently). Light the candle that is in the place of gathering and reread Matthew 5:1–12a in order to refocus the group's attention. Consider singing the Responsorial Psalm or have a recording of it available to use as part of the centering, either before or after the reading.

Reflection and Discussion

The following "script" may be used or adapted to help facilitate discussion on today's readings. Begin the discussion by asking the catechumens if any words or phrases from today's readings spoke to them.

The scene from Revelation pictures saints as those marked with the seal of the living God. They consist of a great multitude "from every nation, race, people, and tongue" (Revelation 7:9). Included are all those who suffered martyrdom. Baptism marks us with the seal of the living God as we join the company of all those saints who have gone before us.

- What difference does, or will, being marked with the seal of the living God make in your life?

- How inclusive are you regarding all those whom God welcomes into eternal life?

- Who else would you like to see God welcome into eternal life with you?

Psalm 24 speaks of people's longing to see God's face. Love always longs for the beloved and will not rest till satisfied. Ultimate union consists of clearing the obstacles that divert or distract our longing. Sinless hands, clean hearts, and right desires all help us in achieving that for which we long, assured that our beloved is always there supporting and guiding us.

- How do you work at removing obstacles in your life that might divert or distract you from being like Christ Jesus?

- How does prayer help you to develop greater intimacy with Christ so that the road to God becomes less cluttered?

- What advice would you give to others who long for greater intimacy with Christ?

We are children of a loving God here and now. God has called us into existence and continues to love us in existence. We are created in the image of God, and our hope is to be with him for all time. What that will look like, we do not know. But when the time arrives we will see the Lord fully and dwell in that intimacy and warmth forever.

- How do you reflect the image of God in your interactions with others?

- What does it mean to you to be called a child of God? How does that reality impact the way you live and act?

- When you meet God, how do you envision that encounter? Name your hopes, thoughts, and feelings.

The Beatitudes envision interactions and attitudes from God's perspective and not ours. The value system they promote is the stuff of saints, of people striving to be more Christ-like. They challenge the status quo and offer an alternate worldview that guides us in our relationship with God and others. Name the virtues and values that the Beatitudes espouse and how they guide you on your journey to God.

- How do the Beatitudes help you become more like Christ?

- How do the Beatitudes challenge you?

- Which in particular presents the greatest challenge to you and why?

Wrapping It Up

Consider these points as you conclude the session. Integrate the thoughts and ideas that surfaced in your discussion with the catechumens as you conclude your time together.

- God creates us out of love to be in intimate relationship, inviting us to respond in love. As children of God we are called to cultivate that intimacy always by becoming more like Jesus, God-with-us. Saints are those who continually strive to take on more fully the mind and heart of Christ. As saints of God, our hope is to be other Christs both in this world and always.

- Those who strive to be like Christ offer light to a world that often walks in darkness. The Beatitudes are our lampposts lighting the way on our journey to God. They provide guidance and assurance of becoming more Christlike in our attitudes and behavior. Saints are made out of such substance.

- We know that if we conform ourselves to Christ in this life, we will be fully united with him in the next. Our constant hope is to enjoy eternal life with God in the company of all the saints who have gone before us marked with the seal of the living God. What that will look like, we do not yet know. But when we are with God we will know fully and revel in that intimacy for all eternity.

Closing Prayer

Conclude with prayer. If time permits, sing the psalm refrain a few times before or after the following prayer.

O Creator God, our Father and source of life,
you created us out of love and called us your children.
Your love for us is unbounding.
We long always to return that love
by becoming more like Jesus, your Son.
Grant us, we pray, the privilege
not only to be intimate with you in this life,
but to share that intimacy for all eternity
with you and all the saints who have gone before us.
Through Christ our Lord.
Amen.

Readings for the Next Dismissal

Provide catechumens with a list of the readings for the next dismissal session. Consult the liturgical calendar on page xvi to find out what day will be observed next week. Give catechumens the questions below to guide their reflection through the week.

⑨ As you pray with the readings, around what themes do your thoughts seem to be coming together?

⑨ Where do the readings intersect with your journey of faith? What questions do they raise for you?

Based on today's readings and liturgical observance, the following topics may be covered for extended catechesis:

- ※ Marked with the seal of the living God
- ※ A saint's job description
- ※ Beatitudes related to happiness
- ※ Eternal life with God
- ※ Communion of Saints
- ※ Becoming Christ-like
- ※ To know God as we are known
- ※ Christian character
- ※ Christian discipleship

COMMEMORATION OF ALL THE FAITHFUL DEPARTED (ALL SOULS' DAY)

November 2

Focus: The Lord, is our light and our salvation.

Lectionary #668

❦ Please note that there are many options for readings in the Lectionary for All Souls' Day. The following dismissal session is based on readings suggested by the editorial team at Liturgy Training Publications. Consult your parish staff to see which readings will be used at Mass.

Catechist's Preparation

Overview of the Commemoration

Today we remember and pray for all those who have died. We do not know for certain what happens after death, but we live in hope of eternal union with our loving God initiates a love relationship with us at our birth and continually invites us to respond. How we respond to God in our lifetime will determine if our life beyond death will be in union with God or separate from God. Thus, we believe that our love relationship with God endures for all eternity, with God always ready to welcome and embrace us. We also believe that death does not separate the living from those who have died. Just as we ask each other for prayers during our lifetime, we continue that practice even beyond death. So today we pray for each other.

Scripture Background

Isaish 25:6–9 This Sunday's reading from Isaiah comes from the Apocalypse of Isaiah found in chapters 24–27. Believing that God's action in human history would someday eliminate the suffering and death that began in the Genesis story, the prophet proclaimed the future time when God's people would die no more. God's people needed to practice patience and trust in God's action. Isaiah's images give a hope-filled sense of this future certainty: the Lord will provide, the veil of death will be destroyed, tears will be wiped away, and reproach will be removed. God will save, and all God's people will rejoice. Today is the day when we remind ourselves of the mercy of God upon all who have died, and this message from Isaiah is fitting. Those who have died will rise in new life. God's mercy endures forever. Death has no power. Along with Isaiah's listeners, we proclaim: "Let us rejoice and be glad that he has saved us!" (25:9).

Psalm 27:1, 4, 7, 8B, 9A, 13–14 The possible readings for the celebration of All Souls' Day are also those that may be used for Masses for the Dead, including Psalm 27. This psalm offers hope even at the most desper-ate of times. All that we need is God. With God as an anchor, whom should we fear? In the psalm, the singer takes an active role: I seek, I gaze at God, I contemplate, I wait with courage, I believe, I ask. I do all these things because God is my light and my salvation. Recognizing the power of this light over darkness, destruction, ter-ror, sin, and even death, the believer trusts that God's presence is enough. As we look through the eyes of the New Testament and the stories of Jesus in the Gospel, we know that God dwelt among us. It gives special power to our desire to seek God's face and find an eternal dwelling place with God.

2 Corinthians 5:1, 6–10 Paul's image to the Corinthians of "our earthly dwelling, a tent" (2 Corinthians 5:1) is a reference to our earthly body, which Paul understood to be temporary until we dwelt with God in heaven. Paul gives believers a reason to wait for the Lord to come: God will replace our earthly body and give us a new body. Earth is a temporary place for all, and death comes to everyone, even to God's own beloved Son. Jesus' own passage through death to new life gives all humans the authentic path to come to dwell in God's house, the way to follow for eternal life. Trust in God as Jesus did, and do the Father's bidding. If we live this way of faith and discipleship then we will be ready, Paul says, to go home to God.

Luke 7:11–17 Today's reading from the Gospel accord-ing to Luke consoles us as we remember those who have gone before us. They shall be told to arise and will be given new life. Those who mourn will be comforted, and God will be praised and glorified. In Luke's story, Jesus is moved with pity, or compassion, for a widow whose only son died. In his culture the loss of a husband and son, who would have provided for her, meant that her pro-tection was gone. Jesus knew that this could mean that she might be homeless with no one to care for her. He demonstrates his belief that God's presence eliminates all fear and mourning in his invitation to the young man to arise. This is how it will be in God's reign: death has no power and there will be no more distress or pain. Everything that Jesus did continually pointed to the day when God's reign would cover the whole earth. The crowd not only recognizes Jesus as a prophet, but also sees that this miracle expresses the intimate presence of God among them. God does indeed visit his people.

Reflection Questions for the Catechist

- Why do you pray for those who have died?
- How do you respond to those who claim that prayers for the dead are useless?
- How do you envision your encounter with God upon your death?
- How does the manner in which Jesus faced death help you in dealing with death in general?

Catechist's Guide

Objectives

- ▷ To realize that death is not the end of life but the beginning of a deeper life with God.
- ▷ To trust in God as ever life-giving and never death-dealing.
- ▷ To learn how to face death with the same trust in God that Jesus did.

Dismissal and Procession

Following the homily, the priest celebrant picks up the Lectionary and invites the catechumens to come forward with the catechist(s) who will lead today's dismissal session. Holding the Lectionary so that all can see, the priest celebrant sends the catechumens and catechist(s) forward using RCIA, 67, his own words, or the following:

PRIEST: **My dear friends, you have shared with us at the table of God's Word. As you go forth to reflect more deeply on this word, this community sends you forth with prayers and encouragement. We look forward to the day when you remain with us to share at the table of the Eucharist. Go in peace.**

All process to where the dismissal session will take place. The catechist holds the Lectionary in a reverent manner. The assembly may sing an acclamation to accompany the procession.

Centering

Upon reaching the place where the dismissal occurs, place the Lectionary on the ambo, lectern, or other dignified place (or hold the book reverently). Light the candle that is in the place of gathering and reread Luke 7:1–17 in order to refocus the group's attention. Consider singing the Responsorial Psalm or have a recording of it available to use as part of the centering, either before or after the reading.

Reflection and Discussion

The following "script" may be used or adapted to help facilitate discussion on today's readings. Begin the discussion by asking the catechumens if any words or phrases from today's readings spoke to them.

Isaiah pictures God as loving and merciful, the one who will wipe away all that limits us and separates us from each other and from him. God is our Savior, the one in whom we can trust and who will never let us down. Suffering, the unknown, and even death will be wiped away. We rejoice in the Lord, who creates us out of love and continues to shower that love upon us for all eternity.

- How does your image of God compare with the one that Isaiah presents?
- Is your image of God as loving and merciful as that of Isaiah, even with regards to death?
- What is your vision of what God intended in creating us? What are we created for?

Psalm 27 affirms that with God as our light and salvation, there is nothing to fear. As we seek and cultivate a deeper relationship with the Lord, our desire is to be with the Lord always. We learn to trust the Lord, calling upon the Lord in our need, knowing that the Lord hears us and responds. Our God abides in the land of the living, and we trust that this is where we will see the Lord.

🌀 How do you experience the Lord as your light and salvation?

🌀 How do you seek and cultivate a deeper relationship with the Lord?

🌀 How deep is your trust that you will see the Lord in the land of the living?

St. Paul states that "we walk by faith, not by sight" (2 Corinthians 5:7). Despite not knowing what will happen to us in death, we trust and have faith in the Lord that a dwelling has been prepared for us. In our bodies, we are still limited in the way we can experience and relate to the Lord. We desire to know the Lord more fully, and our desires will not be frustrated.

🌀 How do you understand Paul's claim that we walk by faith and not by sight?

🌀 How do you envision your dwelling place with God? What kind of dwelling do you think the Lord has prepared for you?

Jesus pictured the Father as always loving and merciful, a giver of life. In his encounters, Jesus encouraged others to come to the Lord, who is ever ready to sustain us in life. Jesus' raising up the widow of Nain's son is understood by others as God visiting the people. Thus, God is understood as one who desires life and never death. Jesus believed that, acted on it, and ultimate placed his Death in God's hands as well.

🌀 How do you relate to God when life presents its many challenges, disappointments, and sufferings?

🌀 How does Jesus help you deal with life's death-dealing experiences?

🌀 How does Jesus' image of God and ultimate trust in God help you on your faith journey to God?

🌀 How does it help you to deal with and ultimately face death?

Wrapping It Up   *Consider these points as you conclude the session. Integrate the thoughts and ideas that surfaced in your discussion with the catechumens as you conclude your time together.*

- God created us out of love, sustains that love throughout our lives, and deepens that love even more in our final union through death. Death is not the end of life but the beginning of a deeper and transformed life with God. The Church has traditionally celebrated the day of our earthly death as the *dies natalis,* the day of our birth into full and eternal life with God.

- As we remember those who have died, we pray for them as they continue to pray for us. God binds us all together into a faith community and death does not separate us from one another. As we cared for and prayed for one another in this life, we continue to do so even in death.

- God is always the God of life and not of death. In Jesus, death has been defeated and we are freed from the sting of death. By modeling ourselves on Jesus and his complete faith, trust and confidence in God, we too can face death with serenity and a sense of peace.

Closing Prayer

Conclude with prayer. If time permits, sing the psalm refrain a few times before or after the following prayer.

> O Loving God of Life and All the Living,
> we praise you for giving us life.
> We know that death is not the end of life
> but the beginning of a deeper transformed life with you.
> Give us the grace and strength to face
> the many death experiences of life
> with the same sense of faith, trust, and confidence
> that your Son, Christ Jesus, modeled for us.
> Who lives and reigns for ever.
> Amen.

Readings for the Next Dismissal

Provide catechumens with a list of the readings for the next dismissal session. Consult the liturgical calendar on page xvi to find out what day will be observed next week. Give catechumens the questions below to guide their reflection through the week.

- As you pray with the readings, around what themes do your thoughts seem to be coming together?

- Where do the readings intersect with your journey of faith? What questions do they raise for you?

Extended Catechesis

Based on today's readings and liturgical observance, the following topics may be covered for extended catechesis:

- The theological concept of *dies natalis*
- Praying for the dead
- Love as eternal
- Care of the dead
- Funeral rites
- Baptism and death
- God as life-giving, never death-dealing
- Corporal and Spiritual Works of Mercy

FEAST OF THE DEDICATION OF THE LATERAN BASILICA

November 9

Focus: We are living temples of God's Spirit.

Lectionary #671

Catechist's Preparation

Overview of the Feast

Today's feast celebrates the Mother Church of all churches in the city of Rome and the world. St. John Lateran is the cathedral church of the bishop of Rome, the pope, given to him by the Roman Emperor Constantine in AD 324. Its yearly celebration is focused not so much on the building but on the people who gather therein. What we celebrate today is the definition of Church retrieved by the Second Vatican Council, that of the Church as the pilgrim people of God (see *Lumen gentium*, chapter 7). We are the Church, the living temples of God's Spirit, called to make Christ's presence real in our lives and be living signs of that presence in the world. God's healing spirit flows through us to the world.

Scripture Background

Ezekiel 47:1-2, 8-9, 12 This last part of the book of Ezekiel was written as Israel languished in exile. Ezekiel had seen the exile coming. He had seen the glory of God take leave of even the Temple itself. As the prophet sits among his fellow exiles, a new vision emerges. This time he sees the Temple's eventual restoration. Is is a new and improved model, far surpassing the old Temple of the exiles' now fading memories.

The most significant improvement is the addition of a sacred river. The sacred river was a popular religious symbol among the Canaanites and other Mesopotamian people, but it was not unknown in Israel. Joel (3:18) and Zechariah (14:8) mention it. For Ezekiel, however, this river is particularly special. Not only does it originate from the very throne of God, this river's living waters also bring life to everything they touch: trees, crops, even the salt water of the Dead Sea.

Ezekiel's sacred river gives our theme a slightly different twist than we might have expected. Rather than concentrating on the Temple itself, it focuses instead on the life-giving water flowing out of the Temple and into the world. This, too, is a perfect image for the Christian life. Not only are we living Temples of God's Spirit, we are also meant to be like that sacred river, which flows from the heart of God and heals all it touches.

Psalm 46:2-3, 5-6, 8-9 (5) This psalm, which might have been written after one of David's many victories, encourages us to trust that God is with us in the worst of times. It is the first of the Zion Temple hymns, praising God for his presence to his people (see Psalms 48, 76, 84, 87, 122). Though Jerusalem itself is not situated on a river, the psalmist uses the expression "a river whose streams" as a symbol of the divine presence as in today's First Reading (see also Isaiah 33:21; Ezekiel 47:1-12; Joel 4:18; Zechariah 14:8; Revelation 22:12). Because God is present, dwelling in Jerusalem, the city will be at peace, war will cease, and weapons will be destroyed. In its place, the stream of life-giving water will cause the city to rejoice. We today who are the temple of the living God can also rejoice because God is present with and in us.

1 Corinthians 3:9c-11, 16-17 Paul again responds to reports of divisions and factions developing in the Corinthian Church. He reminds the Corinthians that the personality (or even the charisma) of their various leaders is not the point. What is important is the Gospel of Jesus Christ. If that foundation is solid, he says, it will not matter who builds; the building will be still be sound. Then, to drive home his point, Paul suddenly shifts the metaphor. "You are God's temple," he says. Today, we are so used to hearing that "you" in the singular, that we often miss Paul's real intent. He is not talking about "you" the individual believer being God's temple (although that is certainly the case). He is talking about "you" the Church. It is the Church, believers together, that is the temple he has in mind. It is in the body of Christ collectively that the Spirit dwells, which is why the kind of party spirit exhibited by the Corinthians is so destructive. It harms the very place where the Spirit of God has chosen to live.

John 2:13-22 Thousands of pilgrims are gathered for the Passover festival amid the din of street vendors and money changers (who exchanged Roman money with its blasphemous picture of Caesar for money acceptable within the Temple precincts). It is a thrilling sight and the long-awaited fulfillment of every pilgrim's dream.

Into this bustling scene strides Jesus. According to John, it is early in Jesus' ministry and already battle lines with the religious establishment are being drawn. Taking a whip and quoting the prophet Zechariah, Jesus "poured out the coins of the money changers and overturned their tables." When the authorities challenge his right to behave in such a way, Jesus shocks them all by claiming, "Destroy this Temple, and in three days I will build it up." It is no wonder they're shocked. Even the renovations to the Temple begun by King Herod several decades before were not yet complete!

John, of course, has a lot more in mind than construction projects and overturned tables. Most important for our purposes today, John is establishing Jesus' authority over the Temple. In light of our theme, this has at least two implications. First, it reminds us that, as living temples of God's Spirit, we are also under the authority of Jesus. Second, like the Temple in our passage, we, too, are meant for prayer, not commerce (in spite of what the ads on TV might tell us to the contrary).

Reflection Questions for the Catechist

⑨ What are the implications of naming the Church "the pilgrim people of God"?

⑨ What role and function does your diocesan cathedral church play in gathering the people of God to celebrate their identity and mission?

⑨ How are you a full, conscious, and active participant in building up the Church, the people of God?

⑨ How does your catechetical ministry contribute to making Christ present in the world?

Catechist's Guide

Objectives

▷ To celebrate our identity and mission as Church, the pilgrim people of God.

▷ To become full, conscious, and active participants in building up the Church of God.

▷ To realize fully the implications of our vocation as living temples of the Lord's healing presence in the world.

Dismissal and Procession

Following the homily, the priest celebrant picks up the Lectionary and invites the catechumens to come forward with the catechist(s) who will lead today's dismissal session. Holding the Lectionary so that all can see, the priest celebrant sends the catechumens and catechist(s) forward using RCIA, 67, his own words, or the following:

PRIEST: **My dear friends, the Church is the living stones out of which is built a Temple to give praise and glory to God's holy name. As you go forth to reflect upon the Word of God may you continue to realize the gifts that flow from his abundant love. Go in peace.**

All process to where the dismissal session will take place. The catechist holds the Lectionary in a reverent manner. The assembly may sing an acclamation to accompany the procession.

Centering

Upon reaching the place where the dismissal occurs, place the Lectionary on the ambo, lectern, or other dignified place (or hold the book reverently). Light the candle that is in the place of gathering and reread 1 Corinthians 3:9c–11, 16–17 in order to refocus the group's attention. Consider singing the Responsorial Psalm or have a recording of it available to use as part of the centering, either before or after the reading.

Reflection and Discussion

The following "script" may be used or adapted to help facilitate discussion on today's readings. Begin the discussion by asking the catechumens if any words or phrases from today's readings spoke to them.

Ezekiel pictures a rebuilt Temple from which water flows, healing all with which it comes into contact, making all things living, providing food and medicine. Such rich symbolism focuses not so much on the building as on what comes out of the building—namely, the people who gather there full of God's Spirit, reaching out to others as sources of nourishment and healing.

- As a living Temple, how are you a source of nourishment and healing for others?
- How are others a source of nourishment and healing in your life?
- How does gathering and celebrating with other community members reinforce your identity and mission as Church?

Psalm 46 speaks of God's dwelling among the people as a source of refuge and strength who can be relied upon when all else fails. God's holy dwelling is with the people, both in supportive presence and in might acts done on the people's behalf. We are called to acknowledge and celebrate God's dwelling in our midst.

- How do you make room for God in the living Temple that is your life?
- How is your relationship to God a source of refuge and strength?
- How is God a true and living presence in your life?
- How does God's present and active dwelling within you challenge you as a disciple?

Paul states boldly that we are God's building. If so, then our sure foundation has to be Christ. In building the living Temple of our lives, we must insure that Christ is the one and only blueprint that we use in constructing our lives. As living Temples, God's Spirit dwells within us, and we are made holy.

- How are you going about constructing the living building of your life that is God's dwelling?
- How do you insure that Christ is the only true foundation of your life?
- How do you react to Paul's assertion that as God's living Temple, you are holy?
- What thoughts and feelings surface for you?

In cleansing the Temple, Jesus knew that at times, holy places and things can be misused for our own purposes. In so doing, they cease being sources of nourishment and healing for others. As St. Paul states, Jesus is the true foundation to God's building. In constructing our dwelling place for God, our eyes should always be on Jesus, the source of God's nourishing and healing presence among us.

- How does zeal in constructing your life as God's dwelling place consume you?
- How is Jesus the true model of constructing the living temple of your life?
- How do you remove all that might distract you from focusing on Christ?
- How is Christ the source of God's nourishing and healing presence in your life?

Wrapping It Up

Consider these points as you conclude the session. Integrate the thoughts and ideas that surfaced in your discussion with the catechumens as you conclude your time together.

- St. Paul asserts that we are God's living Temples, wherein God desires to dwell among us. As such we are the holy people of God, called to be sources of nourishment and healing for the world. Whenever we gather as the people of God, we celebrate our identity as the Church, the pilgrim people of God, and our mission as sources of God's nourishment and healing for the world.

- Both Ezekiel and Psalm 24 speak of living streams that flow from God's Temple, bringing life and healing to all they touch. We are those streams flowing from our lives as God's living Temples. Our challenge is to become full, conscious, and active participants in making God's nourishing and healing presence real and active in our lives and in the world.
- In being God's living Temples, our building has to be sound and firm. Building on Christ and establishing him as our firm foundation is essential. We must actively cultivate a strong relationship to Christ, modeling ourselves on him and being willing to do for others what he has done and continues to do for us.

Closing Prayer

Conclude with prayer. If time permits, sing the psalm refrain a few times before or after the following prayer.

O nourishing and healing God,
source of our life and true fountain of our love.
We are indeed blessed to have you dwell among us and within us.
You have chosen us as your living Temples
from which you make nourishing and healing waters flow into the world.
Help us to build our living Temples on Christ,
the full manifestation of your presence among us,
and the only true and solid foundation of our lives.
Through Christ our Lord.
Amen.

Readings for the Next Dismissal

Provide catechumens with a list of the readings for the next dismissal session. Consult the liturgical calendar on page xvi to find out what day will be observed next week. Give catechumens the questions below to guide their reflection through the week.

- As you pray with the readings, around what themes do your thoughts seem to be coming together?
- Where do the readings intersect with your journey of faith? What questions do they raise for you?

Extended Catechesis

Based on today's readings and liturgical observance, the following topics may be covered for extended catechesis:

- Our lives as streams of living water
- Called to be holy
- Church as the pilgrim people of God
- Call to full, conscious, and active participation
- Church as sign and sacrament of Christ
- Role and function of the diocesan cathedral

SOLEMNITY OF THE IMMACULATE CONCEPTION OF THE BLESSED VIRGIN MARY

December 8

Focus: To cooperate with God as Mary did.

Lectionary #689

Catechist's Preparation

Overview of the Solemnity

Today's solemnity celebrates our belief that Mary was free from Original Sin from the moment of her conception. This solemnity is often confused with the virginal birth of Jesus, since the Gospel speaks of the angel's Annunciation to Mary that she is to have a child while still remaining a virgin. While not in Scripture, belief in Mary's Immaculate Conception goes back to the early Church and in 1854 was declared an infallible doctrine of the Church by Pope Pius IX. The doctrine affirms that Mary was full of God's grace from the moment of her conception. Because of this, Mary freely and willingly cooperated actively with God's plan to become fully human. Mary had free will to choose otherwise, but she chose to cooperate with God's plans and desires. In this manner, Mary becomes a model of discipleship.

Scripture Background

Genesis 3:9–15, 20 An old Christmas carol proclaimed, "Nova! Nova! Ave fit ex Eva." The Latin word *nova* morphed into the French *noël*. It means "good news," but it has come to mean Christmas itself. The rest of that carol's title is a play on words in Latin: Ave comes from Eva. In Latin, the name of the first woman in the Book of Genesis, Eve, is *Eva*. When you twist those letters backward, you get in Latin the word that the angel Gabriel used to greet the symbolic first woman of Luke's account of the Gospel: *Ave*, or "Hail, full of grace." Today's readings have in mind this contrast between Eve and Mary. Unfair as it is to pin the blame for all sin upon Eve, the point is that Mary became an instrument in God's plan of salvation. Eve foreshadows Mary, who became the mother of the Living One. Where our first parents said no, Mary said yes.

Psalm 98:1, 2–3, 3–4 (1a) The psalmist praises God for possessing and exercising power. God's power is matched by his kindness and faithfulness. The psalmist personally and Israel collectively have benefited from God's might. Not everyone likes to sing new songs. Most people like the old ones. But sometimes something so wonderful happens that it requires new notes and a new voice. The old songs do not always fit new circumstances. We have to change our tune.

In the Immaculate Conception, God has worked something tremendously powerful and totally new: creating a human being conceived without sin. God had the power to do this, and God exercised this power not just on Mary's behalf, but for the sake of us all. Only a new song can hope to tell the wondrous deeds of God.

Ephesians 1:3–6, 11–12 God chose Abraham, his wife, and their descendants to be a special people for a historic covenant. So, God has chosen the followers of Jesus Christ to be a special people for an eternal covenant. This mystery of God's choice is the subject of an early Christian hymn preserved in the Letter to the Ephesians. We may not feel worthy of this relationship with God, and we are not. However, God makes us worthy. God chose us to be holy and without blemish.

The first covenant was made to an extended family. But in Christ, God has willed to extend the boundaries of this family through a spiritual adoption. This reading especially fits the celebration of the Immaculate Conception because of our belief that God chose Mary for a special ministry in the history of salvation. God preserved her from sin, making her holy and without blemish for all time. Still, all of us have been chosen "in accord with the purpose of the One who accomplishes all things according to the intention of his will" (1:5). We do not perform the same role that Mary did, but we each play a part in the great drama of God's good plan for the salvation of the world.

Luke 1:26–38 God's miraculous powers are evident in the announcement Gabriel makes to Mary. She who is full of grace will become the mother of God's Son, and her elderly kinswoman has also conceived. Miracle upon miracle appears.

Today's solemnity concerns the earliest miracle of the series: the immaculate conception of Mary. From the moment her parents conceived her, Mary was preserved from all sin. We believe this in part because of the way Gabriel greets her: "full of grace" (1:28). Gabriel announces that Mary, though a virgin, will become a

307

mother. We commonly call this second miracle of the series the virgin birth of Christ. The words Immaculate Conception refer to Mary, not to Jesus. The miracle of Jesus' virginal conception was preceded by the miracle of Mary's Immaculate Conception.

As if that were not enough, Gabriel announces yet another miracle. Elizabeth, Mary's relative, a woman advanced in years, has also conceived a son. One reason for this miracle was to reassure Mary that "nothing will be impossible for God" (1:38). Mary first found the angel's announcement preposterous. How can a virgin conceive? But she had to rethink the news in the light of another miracle. How can an elderly woman conceive? Nothing is impossible for God.

This solemnity celebrates the triumph of God's power. It consoles us in our weakness and sin, in our misfortune and misjudgment. God is more powerful than we are, and God has proven it throughout the course of time, miracle upon miracle.

Reflection Questions for the Catechist

⟳ How do you explain the Immaculate Conception to those not familiar with the doctrine?

⟳ What impact does belief in the Immaculate Conception have on your faith life?

⟳ How is Mary's willing and active cooperation with God a model for your life of discipleship?

⟳ How have you been called to cooperate with God in bringing Jesus to birth in our world?

Catechist's Guide

Objectives

▷ To differentiate between the Mary's Immaculate Conception and the virginal birth of Jesus.

▷ To recognize Mary as fully one of us, who cultivated and cooperated with God's grace and presence in her life.

▷ To recall that as disciples, we too, like Mary, are invited daily to cooperate with God in bringing Jesus to birth in our lives and world.

Dismissal and Procession

Following the homily, the priest celebrant picks up the Lectionary and invites the catechumens to come forward with the catechist(s) who will lead today's dismissal session. Holding the Lectionary so that all can see, the priest celebrant sends the catechumens and catechist(s) forward using RCIA, 67, his own words, or the following:

PRIEST: **My dear friends, in the fullness of time, the Son of God was born of a woman, and so entered our world as a gesture of unconditional love. As you go forth to reflect more deeply on the Word, may you imitate more fully the humble obedience of Mary and bring glory to the Lord's name. Go in peace.**

All process to where the dismissal session will take place. The catechist holds the Lectionary in a reverent manner. The assembly may sing an acclamation to accompany the procession.

Centering

Upon reaching the place where the dismissal occurs, place the Lectionary on the ambo, lectern, or other dignified place (or hold the book reverently). Light the candle that is in the place of gathering and reread Luke 1:26–38 in order to refocus the group's attention. Consider singing the Responsorial Psalm or have a recording of it available to use as part of the centering, either before or after the reading.

Reflection and Discussion

The following "script" may be used or adapted to help facilitate discussion on today's readings. Begin the discussion by asking the catechumens if any words or phrases from today's readings spoke to them.

God created us to be in harmonious relationship with God, one another, and all creation. We chose otherwise desiring to have things our way. The reading from Genesis points out the result of our refusal to cooperate, namely "enmity" (Genesis 3:15) and lack of harmonious relationship with God, one another and all creation.

🌀 Why do you think God created?

🌀 How do you deal with the tension between desiring to cooperate with God and desiring to do your own thing apart from God?

🌀 How can Mary be a model for you in your desire to cooperate with God?

Psalm 98 calls us to sing a new song to the Lord because of the wondrous deeds that God has done on our behalf. This solemnity celebrates God's greatest deed in choosing to become human through the willing cooperation of Mary. Mary, one of us, shows us that active cooperation with God's ways is possible. Mary sings God justice and faithfulness in her Magnificat (see Luke 1:46–55). Like her, we are called to sing a new song to the Lord.

🌀 Why are we being encouraged by the psalmist to sing a new song?

🌀 When have you found yourself joyful in song because of what God has done for you?

🌀 How do you see God's justice and faithfulness operative in your life and world?

Ephesians proclaims that, like Mary, we too have been chosen by God "to be holy and without blemish" (Ephesians 5:27). Through Christ, we are adopted children of God, called to cooperate with God's ways and continually praise God by our lives. Mary cooperated with God in birthing Christ so that God's ultimate desire of intimate relationship with us and all creation might be accomplished through him.

🌀 How do you feel about being chosen by God "to be holy and without blemish" (Ephesians 5:27)?

🌀 What excites you about this? What challenges you? What gives you hope?

🌀 How can Mary's way of responding to God be a guide for our response to God?

While today's Gospel announces the conception of Jesus (Annunciation), the solemnity itself celebrates our belief that Mary was free from Original Sin from the moment of her conception. This solemnity is often confused with the virginal birth of Jesus, since the Gospel speaks of the angel's Annunciation to Mary that she is to have a child while still remaining a virgin. While not in Scripture, belief in Mary's Immaculate Conception goes back to the early Church and in 1854 was declared an infallible doctrine of the Church by Pope Pius IX. The doctrine affirms that Mary was full of God's grace from the moment of her conception. Because of this, Mary freely and willingly cooperated actively with God's plan to become fully human. Mary had free will to choose otherwise, but she chose to cooperate with God's plans and desires. In this manner, Mary becomes a model of discipleship.

In today's Gospel, Mary's response to God's invitation is a manifestation of the way Mary cultivated God's grace and presence with her from her conception. Through Christ, we too are blessed with God's grace and presence at our Baptism. Like Mary, we too are to cultivate God's grace and presence in order to cooperate always with God's invitation.

🌀 How do you cultivate God's grace and presence in your life?

- How can Mary be a model for you? Is our baptismal call to holiness the motivating factor in your life of discipleship? If yes, how does it affect the way you think and act? If not, why not?
- How can reflection on this solemnity help you focus more on how to respond to God's presence in your life?

Wrapping It Up

Consider these points as you conclude the session. Integrate the thoughts and ideas that surfaced in your discussion with the catechumens as you conclude your time together.

- Mary's Immaculate Conception asserts that God's grace and presence was with Mary from her conception. In Baptism, God's grace and presence are with us also through Christ. Like Mary, God calls us to cooperate with God's desire to bring Jesus to birth in our lives and in our world. Our baptismal call is our lifetime adventure of bringing Christ to birth. God creates us out of love and asks us to respond in love.
- Mary heard God's Word, willingly cooperated with it, reflected on it, and allowed it to take flesh in her life. As one of us, Mary models for us the essence of discipleship. We too are called to hear God's Word, willingly cooperate with it, reflect on it, and ultimately allow it to take flesh in our lives and world.

Closing Prayer

Conclude with prayer. If time permits, sing the psalm refrain a few times before or after the following prayer.

O God of Kindness and Faithfulness,
we thank you for creating us out of love
and inviting us to share in your divine life.
You gifted Mary with your grace and presence,
which she cultivated and nourished,
allowing her to cooperate willingly and actively
in your desire to become fully one with us in Christ.
Like Mary, help us to nourish and cultivate your presence within us
so that we too may cooperate in giving birth to Christ in our lives.
Who lives and reigns forever and ever.
Amen.

Readings for the Next Dismissal

Provide catechumens with a list of the readings for the next dismissal session. Consult the liturgical calendar on page xvi to find out what day will be observed next week. Give catechumens the questions below to guide their reflection through the week.

- As you pray with the readings, around what themes do your thoughts seem to be coming together?
- Where do the readings intersect with your journey of faith? What questions do they raise for you?

Extended Catechesis

Based on today's readings and liturgical observance, the following topics may be covered for extended catechesis:

- Proper understanding of Original Sin
- Our baptismal call to holiness
- Theological shift in our understanding of God's grace
- Mary as symbol of the Church
- Mary as one of us
- Vatican II teaching on Mary in *Lumen gentium*, chapter 8

Appendix:
The Rite of Christian Initiation
of Adults

Overview of the Appendix

Throughout the initiation process, catechumens and the elect participate in public rituals that mark the various stages in their journey toward the Easter sacraments (see RCIA, 75.3). It is important that catechists provide catechumens and the elect with an opportunity to reflect upon their experience of these rites. A dismissal guide has been prepared for the following rituals:

Rite of Acceptance into the Order of Catechumens The initiation process formally begins with the celebration of the Rite of Acceptance into the Order of Catechumens, but the Period of Evangelization and Precatechumenate that precedes it is crucial. During this time, which may begin long before an individual approaches the Christian community, God touches the heart and draws the person to seek to know him through Jesus Christ. During the Rite of Acceptance into the Order of Catechumens, inquirers declare to the Christian community their intention to become members of the Church, and the Church accepts them as such. This ritual changes the status of the person undergoing it from an outsider to an insider, from a guest to a member of the household, from an inquirer to a catechumen.

Rite of Sending Catechumens for Election This optional rite is particular to the Church in the United States. It takes place at the end of the Period of the Catechumenate and is used as a means for the local parish community to take a particular part in the process of the catechumens being elected for full initiation at the next Easter Vigil. The Catholic bishops of the United States approved this rite since the majority of the parish community will not go to the cathedral for the Rite of Election. For this reason, the Rite of Sending for Election closely resembles the Rite of Election itself, and it gives "the local community the opportunity to express its approval for the catechumens and to send them forth to the celebration of election assured of the parish's care and support" (RCIA, 107). It normally takes place on the First Sunday of Lent.

Rite of Election or Enrollment of Names The third period of formation, which usually coincides with Lent, is called Purification and Enlightenment. During this time the prayers of the Church purify the elect from whatever is keeping them from following Christ, and enlighten and strengthen all the good that is drawing them forward toward the waters of Baptism. The journey begins with the Rite of Election or Enrollment of Names. At this time the Church declares that those who have begun their formation are to be numbered among the "elect"—that is, among the new "chosen people" of God. The Rite of Election usually takes place on the First Sunday of Lent.

First, Second, and Third Scrutiny The three Scrutinies take place on the Third, Fourth, and Fifth Sundays of Lent. The Scrutinies are rites of self-searching and repentance. They have, above all, a spiritual purpose: "to uncover, then heal all that is weak, defective, or sinful in the hearts of the elect; to bring out, then strengthen, all that is upright, strong, and good. For the Scrutinies are celebrated in order to deliver the elect from the power of sin and Satan, to protect them against temptation, and to give them strength in Christ" (RCIA, 141). These are rites of purification in which the Church asks for strength for the elect as they enter into the final preparation for Baptism, Confirmation, and Eucharist. They help the elect achieve the "intimate knowledge of Christ and his Church" (RCIA, 142) needed for the sacraments of initiation and help the elect progress in genuine self-knowledge through serious examination of their lives and true repentance. Through this progressive self-examination and deepening self-knowledge, the elect gradually learn about the mystery of sin and increase their desire to be delivered from it.

Preparing the Environment

When discussing and reflecting upon the various rites, continue to use the environment for the season in which an individual rite takes place. For example, the Rite of Acceptance may take place at any time during the year. If it takes place during Ordinary Time, you will want the dismissal environment to incorporate aspects of that season. Refer to the seasonal overviews in this book for seasonal environment ideas.

In everything you do to create the environment for the dismissal space, take your lead from the environment in the sanctuary of the main assembly. Consistency between what the catechumens see in the environment in that space and in the environment in the dismissal space is important. You do not want to create divergent messages about the day and season and thus generate unnecessary questions or confusion within the group. Keep the environment simple, but not simplistic, understated, but not minimized. Colors, light, images, and other added elements should all assist the catechumens in their reflection on the significance of the day, the Word of God, and the initiation rituals that are celebrated.

RITE OF ACCEPTANCE INTO THE ORDER OF CATECHUMENS

May occur on most Sundays of the year.

Focus: God has called, and you have answered.

RCIA, #41-74

Catechist's Preparation

Overview of the Rite

This session on the Rite of Acceptance should be used on the Sunday(s) it occurs. The intention is for catechists to add this topic to the Sunday dismissal Scripture discussion.

The Rite of Acceptance into the Order of Catechumens is the first public rite of the catechumenal process. This rite is the moment when those who have been inquiring about the faith and how it is lived out publicly declare their intention to prepare to become disciples of Christ and members of his Church. In return, the community of believers accepts the inquirers as catechumens and commits to helping them follow Christ and learn to live as Christians. It usually takes place at the beginning of Sunday Mass. This is fitting because it is literally an Introductory Rite. Those inquirers seeking to become catechumens gather at the door of the church, or even outside the church. Ideally, the assembly (or at least some members) goes outside the worship space to greet them. This symbolizes that the Church is sent into the world to call all people to Christ. It is also a sign of the joy the Church experiences in receiving those who come seeking him.

When the celebrant greets the inquirers and their sponsors, he expresses this joy on behalf of the community. He then asks the inquirers their name and what they ask of the Church.

The giving of the name serves two purposes: it introduces the assembly to those who will be catechumens, and it indicates that God calls us and knows us by name. Our faith is shared and lived out in community, but each person professes their faith individually and walks their journey with God.

The asking of what they want of the Church indicates that they are seeking what the Church can give: Baptism, faith, and eternal life. It ritually ascertains that they are coming with the proper intent. Of course, this would have been discussed during the Period of the Precatechumenate.

The celebrant then asks if the inquirers are ready to listen to the Gospel and learn to pattern their lives on it. After a positive response, the sponsors and all assembled are asked if they are prepared to help them find and follow Christ.

Those seeking to become catechumens are then signed with the Cross, indicating that they have been claimed by Christ. The signing may be done on the forehead alone, but the option to sign them on several parts of the body (ears, eyes, lips, heart, shoulders, hands, and feet) indicates more fully that Christ claims every aspect of their lives. The prayer concluding the signing is the first time that they are referred to as catechumens.

The catechumens are then invited to listen to the Word of God. Following the homily, intercessions for the catechumens are prayed. Then they are dismissed in a kindly manner (unless this cannot be done for some serious reason). They then process out of the church to the place where the dismissal session will take place.

The new catechumens may be presented with a cross or a Bible or both during this rite; these presentations are optional. Some parishes ritually present the Lectionary or *Book of the Gospels* to the catechumens after the homily; some also include the book in the procession as the catechumens are dismissed.

🌀 What does it mean to you that you bear the Sign of the Cross on your body?

🌀 How does listening to the Word of God proclaimed deepen your relationship with Christ?

🌀 How has the community of faith helped you to understand what it means to be a disciple of Christ?

Catechist's Guide

Objectives

▷ To reflect on the meaning of the Gospel and the Cross.

▷ To appreciate what it means to be claimed by Christ.

▷ To understand more deeply the meaning of the Rite of Acceptance and to look forward to the Period of the Catechumenate.

Dismissal, Procession, and Centering

The dismissal, procession, and centering happens as usual. Consider rereading one of the prayers from the rite, such as (RCIA, 57A):

> Lord,
> we have signed these catechumens
> with the sign of Christ's cross.
> Protect them by its power
> so that, faithful to the grace which has begun in them;
> they may keep your commandments
> and come to the glory of rebirth in baptism.
> Through Christ our Lord.
> Amen.

Reflection and Discussion

The following suggestions may be used and adapted to help facilitate discussion on the Rite of Acceptance. It may be added to your discussion on today's readings.

Allow the new catechumens to talk about their experience of the rite they just celebrated. Have them stay with descriptions of their own experience and listen to the experiences of the others. Encourage them with such questions as:

🌀 What did you experience in the ritual we just celebrated? Does any particular moment stand out in your mind? Did any word or phrase speak to you in a particular way?

🌀 What did you feel at any part of it? How did you feel before the rite? During? Now?

Focus the discussion more on specific areas. For example, if the liturgy began outside the church, ask what it felt like to gather there rather than inside.

🌀 What did it feel like when the priest and ministers approached? (*Or if they gathered in the back of the church, what did it feel like when the assembly turned to face them?*)

Have them share and discuss the answers they gave to the questions that were asked during the rite ("What do you ask of the Church? What does that offer you?" and "How did you decide on that answer as you prepared for this rite beforehand"?)

Two important aspects of the Christian life are at the heart of the Rite of Acceptance. The first is the centrality of the Gospel as the way of faith, the way to come to know and love Christ. The catechist might refer to the language in RCIA, 52C, which offers three examples of how to ask those seeking to follow Christ if they are ready to accept the Gospel. Be ready to repeat the words that the priest celebrant used to elicit their response, such as:

> This is eternal life: to know the one true God and Jesus Christ, whom he has sent. Christ has been raised from the dead and appointed by God as the Lord of life and ruler of all things, seen and unseen.

> If, then, you wish to become his disciples and members of his Church, you must be guided to the fullness of the truth that he has revealed to us. You must learn to make the mind of Christ Jesus your own. You must strive to pattern your life on the teachings of the Gospel and so to love the Lord your God and your neighbor. For this was Christ's command and he was its perfect example.

> Is each of you ready to accept these teachings of the Gospel (RCIA, 52C)?

Discuss what these words (or whichever the priest celebrant used) might mean as a guide for the time that they are catechumens. Point out that to follow the Gospel is not just to know the teachings, but to pattern our lives on them, with Jesus as the perfect example of love.

The second important aspect follows on this example of love: the Cross. Ask the catechumens about the experience of having received the Sign of the Cross on their foreheads (and the rest of their body, if this was done). Listen to what they say. Talk about the meaning of Christ's Cross, his death and Resurrection. Explain this as the deepest sign of his love for us, his willingness to die so that sin's grasp on humanity could be broken. Be sure that they understand it as a sign of his absolute faithfulness to God, in the face of the forces of sin and death, and that the Cross is always viewed through the lens of the Resurrection. Jesus' life, suffering, Death, and Resurrection are understood as one great truth, the Paschal Mystery. As followers of Christ they are called to love to the point of suffering and perhaps even to Death, but the great promise of Resurrection is also theirs. By being signed with the Cross, the catechumens are claimed by Christ as his own, as being embraced by this mystery. If the signing was done on their whole body, it may be good to note that this is a sign that everything they are and do has been claimed by Christ.

By becoming part of the Church, they become part of the Body of Christ active and visible in his Church. Faith in Christ is an individual faith, but it is lived and learned in the community of other believers. Through this community, they will hear the Word of God proclaimed and preached, see what faith looks like when it is lived out, receive support and sustenance through prayer and fellowship, and learn to witness to the Gospel in word and deed. As a catechumen, they are members of the household; through Baptism, they will become brothers and sisters with all those whom God has claimed as his children through Christ.

Wrapping It Up/Closing Prayer

Consider these points to conclude your discussion. Integrate the thoughts and ideas that surfaced in your discussion. Close with the prayer from the appropriate Sunday dismissal guide.

- The Rite of Acceptance sums up the journey of the elect toward faith in Christ so far. By making this step, they commit themselves to learning to follow Christ through his Word.

- The rituals of the Church carry deep meaning. They are not empty actions, but acts of God carried out through the Church, the Body of Christ.

- The Paschal Mystery is at the heart of the Church, which expresses it in every act, every teaching, and every ritual action, especially the sacraments.

Rite of Sending of the Catechumens for Election

Usally occurs on the First Sunday of Lent.

Focus: This community recommends you.

RCIA, #106–117

Catechist's Preparation

Overview of the Rite

This session on the Rite of Sending should be used on the Sunday it occurs. The intention is for catechists to add this topic to the Sunday dismissal Scripture discussion. Refer to the Sunday dismissal guide for additional Scripture backgrounds.

The Rite of Sending of the Catechumens for Election sums up the Period of the Catechumenate for those who hope to be elected, or chosen, to celebrate the sacraments of initiation at the next Easter Vigil. This is an optional rite, preparatory to the Rite of Election, which is celebrated on or near the First Sunday of Lent and is normally presided over by the bishop (see page 319 for this rite).

Representatives of the parishes, such as the catechists and pastors, usually accompany the catechumens and their godparents to the Rite of Election and affirm their testimony that the catechumens are ready for initiation. The Rite of Sending offers the entire parish the opportunity to attest to their readiness so that when the godparents and others speak on their behalf, they speak in the name of the community that has accompanied them.

Before the Rite of Election and before the Rite of Sending, the catechists, pastors, sponsors, and others discern whether the catechumens are indeed ready. This is a discernment of readiness for the sacraments, not just for the Rite of Election. The Rite of Sending brings this discernment to the parish community for ratification.

The priest, speaking in the name of the community, asks these questions of the godparents (see RCIA, 112):

- "Have these catechumens taken their formation in the Gospel and in the Catholic way of life seriously?"

- "Have they given evidence of their conversion by the example of their lives?"

- "Do you judge them to be ready to be presented to the bishop for the rite of election?"

He may also ask the assembly for a sign of their approval. Once the affirmations are given, the priest informs the catechumens that "this community gladly recommends you to the bishop, who, in the name of Christ, will call you to the Easter sacraments" (RCIA, 112).

This is the essential difference between the Rite of Sending and the Rite of Election. In the Rite of Sending, the priest receives the recommendation of the community and affirms that it will be conveyed to the bishop. At the Rite of Election, the community's representatives speak to the bishop (or other presider), who, having listened to them, declares that "the Church in the name of Christ accepts their judgment and calls you to the Easter sacraments" (RCIA, 132). The whole process together is a discernment of whether the catechumens have been called by Christ for initiation into his Church at this time. It is a marvelous sign that Christ speaks to and through his Church.

The signing of the Book of the Elect may take place at this time if the signing does not take place during the Rite of Election itself. By inscribing their names, the elect (or soon-to-be elect) state finally their desire to be baptized and acknowledge their election, their having been chosen by God. As at the Rite of Acceptance, the individual's name is important. Even though the proclamation of election is made to the group, each individual name is written in the book. On the day of their initiation, they will be baptized and confirmed individually, addressed by name as they receive the sacraments.

Those baptized candidates who may be preparing for reception into the full communion of the Catholic Church are technically not supposed to sign the Book of the Elect (although different dioceses have different practices). The fact that they are already baptized indicates that they were elected long ago. It may help to encourage them and all members of the parish community to reflect on their election by Christ.

Reflection Questions for the Catechist

🌀 How do you perceive that you were chosen by Christ to be part of his Church, even if it happened before you can remember?

🌀 If you were baptized as a child, do you remember making a conscious decision later that you wanted to be part of the Church?

🌀 How has choosing to respond to Christ's election of you made a difference in your life?

Catechist's Guide

Objectives

▷ To help the catechumens recognize the role that the parish community has had in their journey.

▷ To help them see the changes in themselves and their growth in the Christian life during the Period of the Catechumenate.

▷ To affirm the catechumens in their readiness for election for the sacraments of initiation.

Dismissal, Procession, and Centering

The dismissal, procession, and centering happens as usual. Consider rereading one of the prayers from the rite, such as (RCIA, 115):

Father of love and power,
it is your will to establish everything in Christ
and to draw us into his all-embracing love.
Guide these catechumens in the days and weeks ahead:
strengthen them in their vocation,
build them into the kingdom of your Son,
and seal them with the Spirit of your promise.
Through Christ our Lord.
Amen.

Reflection and Discussion

The following suggestions may be used and adapted to help facilitate discussion on the Rite of Sending. It may be added to your discussion on today's readings.

Allow the catechumens to talk about their experience of the rite that they just celebrated. Have them stay with descriptions of their own experience and listen to the experiences of the others. Encourage them with such questions as:

🌀 What did you experience in the ritual we just celebrated? Does any particular moment stand out in your mind? Did any word or phrase speak to you in a particular way?

🌀 What did you feel at any part of it? How did you feel before the rite? During? Now?

Point out to them that they, for the most part, didn't have a whole lot to do in this rite. They were there to hear what the community has to say about them. In a way, this rite recapitulates their experience of the catechumenate as they lived it out in this community. It might be good to have them reflect on that period in light of this rite. Ask them to recall the first time they were publically part of a liturgy, at the Rite of Acceptance.

🌀 What was it like to enter into a church full of people that you didn't know? (*For most of them it was probably a bit uncomfortable.*)

🌀 What was it was like this time, after so many months or longer of sitting among this community for the Liturgy of the Word, being prayed over and dismissed, to process in (if they did) and sit among the assembly?

🌀 Are there stories of how you got to know some of the people who were there? Are there people you still don't know personally but recognize and feel supported by?

🌀 Do you feel at home among the assembly now? Why?

Recall the questions that their godparents were asked about the catechumens (see RCIA, 112; see also the introductory comments on page 316). If the godparents or other members of the assembly were given an opportunity to respond in their own words, ask the catechumens to react to what they said and to affirm and accept it. Ask them to answer the questions about themselves and about each other. Ask them to reflect on how they took the preparation to heart, how they felt a deepening sense of faith, a deeper understanding of God's love, a deeper relationship with Jesus Christ.

🌀 Have you seen changes in yourself, or have others told you that they see changes in you? Do you feel ready to be presented to the bishop at the Rite of Election—not perfect, but ready—to make the next step on this journey?

The catechist and others in the session should be ready to affirm them and offer examples of their progress. If the signing of the Book of the Elect took place at this rite, ask them to describe the moment that they signed.

🌀 Did the signing help make the moment more concrete?

Mention that the names of those who had been elected for years in the past are in the book, and that future elect will also sign that book. Point out to the catechumens that other catechumens from many parishes throughout the diocese will be participating with them in the Rite of Election. Catechumens will be gathering at cathedrals around the world on this same day for this same purpose. Encourage them to listen to the names and parishes, and perhaps notice the different languages and cultures, of the catechumens who will be elected and soon initiated, as they will be. Reflect with them how they are becoming members of the universal—Catholic—Church, to be one with people of every race and language, and every time in history, in Jesus Christ.

Describe the role of the bishop in this rite. He asks the members of the Church for their testimony and, having listened, declares the catechumens to be elect. He is the visible sign that all the parishes of the diocese are one. He and all the other bishops around the world, united to the pope, the Bishop of Rome, is the visible sign that the whole Church is one in Jesus Christ.

Wrapping It Up/Closing Prayer

Consider these points to conclude your discussion. Integrate the thoughts and ideas that surfaced in your discussion. Close with the prayer from the appropriate Sunday dismissal guide.

- The catechumens have been called by Christ for membership in his Church and they have responded.

- The community that has been there throughout their time of preparation shares the joy of this day and will continue to welcome them.

- The catechumens' journey of faith will continue in the context of the universal Church.

RITE OF ELECTION OR ENROLLMENT OF NAMES

Ususally occurs on the First Sunday of Lent.

Focus: You are chosen in the Lord.

RCIA, #118–137

Catechist's Preparation

Overview of the Rite

This session on the Rite of Election should be used on the Sunday it occurs. The intention is for catechists to add this topic to the Sunday dismissal Scripture discussion. Refer to that Sunday dismissal guide for additional Scripture backgrounds.

The Rite of Election or Enrollment of Names is the second step, or major transition, between periods of the catechumenal process. It closes the Period of the Catechumenate, during which the catechumens have been catechized, immersed in the Christian community's way of life, formed by the Church's prayer life, and engaged in the apostolic work of the Church through the witness of their lives (see RCIA, 75). The Rite of Election is the setting in which the diocesan bishop (or another celebrant designated by him) receives the testimony of the godparents and other members of the community that the work of the Period of the Catechumenate has taken root in the catechumens and that they are sufficiently prepared to be chosen for the sacraments of initiation at the coming Easter. The testimony of the godparents and others is based on the discernment of their catechists, pastors, sponsors, godparents, and others that they have "undergone a conversion in mind and in action and . . . have developed a sufficient acquaintance with Christian teaching as well as a spirit of faith and charity" (RCIA, 120). This discernment is the final discernment before initiation; readiness for election is readiness for the sacraments.

The term *election* in this context means God's choosing; the Church discerns God's choice by observing the changes that have taken place in the catechumen's life. The bishop asks the godparents (RCIA, 131B):

- "Have they faithfully listened to God's word proclaimed by the Church?"
- "Have they responded to that word and begun to walk in God's presence?"
- "Have they shared the company of their Christian brothers and sisters and joined with them in prayer?"

And then the bishop addresses the rest of the assembly:

- "Are you ready to support the testimony expressed about these catechumens and include them in your prayer and affection as we move toward Easter?"

The bishop, after hearing the outcome of this discernment, declares in the name of Christ's Church that these catechumens are now elect. After having done so, the bishop invites the newly elect to inscribe their names as a sign of their desire for the sacraments; this is the *enrollment*. It may have already taken place in the parish prior to the Rite of Election (see page 316), but it is acknowledged and received at the Rite of Election.

The Rite of Election, like all the Church's liturgies, is a celebration of the whole Church, but it is a particularly powerful sign of that reality. It usually takes place at the cathedral and is presided over by the diocesan bishop. The rite gathers clergy, catechists, and other members of the faithful, as well as the catechumens, from throughout the diocese. In many dioceses this means that Catholics of many cultures, races, and languages are united as the Body of Christ present in one local Church. In addition, dioceses around the world are celebrating this same rite on the same day, offering a sign of the meaning of Catholic: universal.

The Rite of Election normally takes place at the beginning of Lent, the time of preparation for the annual celebration of the Paschal Mystery at the Triduum, the three days commemorating the suffering, Death, and Resurrection of the Lord Jesus Christ. Lent is also the usual time for the final preparation for the reception of the sacraments of initiation, by which the elect are immersed in the Paschal Mystery of Jesus Christ. Having been declared "elect," those to be initiated at the Easter Vigil, the high point of the Sacred Paschal Triduum and the whole liturgical year, enter into spiritual preparation for the event, the Period of Purification and Enlightenment.

Reflection Questions for the Catechist

- What changes have you seen in the catechumens during the Period of the Catechumenate?
- What has God's choosing you for the sacraments of initiation and membership in Christ's Church meant in your own life?
- How do you understand your membership in the Universal Church?

Catechist's Guide

Objectives

- ▷ To help the elect understand what their election for the Easter sacraments means.
- ▷ To help the elect have a greater understanding of the Church into which they are being initiated.
- ▷ To help the elect acknowledge the growth and conversion they have undergone and increase their desire to prepare for and celebrate the sacraments of initiation.

Dismissal, Procession, and Centering

The dismissal, procession, and centering happens as usual. Consider rereading one of the prayers from the rite, such as (RCIA, 135B):

Father of love and power,
it is your will to establish everything in Christ
and to draw us into his all-embracing love.
Guide the elect of your Church:
strengthen them in their vocation,
build them into the Kingdom of your Son,
and seal them with the Spirit of your promise.
Through Christ our Lord.
Amen.

Reflection and Discussion

The following suggestions may be used and adapted to help facilitate discussion on the Rite of Election. It may be added to your discussion on today's readings.

Have the elect recall the Rite of Sending (if it was celebrated). Ask them:

- What was the trip to the cathedral like? Who did you travel with? How did you feel? What did you talk about? What did you experience as you entered the cathedral? Who else was there? What was the feeling in the church: excitement, nervousness, joy?
- Had you been to the cathedral before? What did you notice about the building?

The purpose of this discussion is to note that the cathedral belongs to everyone in the diocese; it is the mother Church of the diocese and therefore part of their heritage as members of the Church and of the diocese. Point out the bishop's chair *(cathedra)* and any other significant images or symbols in the building. Then ask about the rite:

- What did you hear from the Scripture proclamation and the homily that spoke to you on this occasion? Were you challenged, comforted, or surprised?
- How did it feel when your names were called as you were presented to the bishop?
- Did you notice anything about the others who were there to be elected, such as ages, other cultures, other languages? What did this say to you about our diocese and about the whole Church?

The purpose of this discussion is to help the elect realize more deeply the nature of the Catholic Church. As important as the parish community is, we are part of a universal Church. We have one set of teachings, we operate in communion with all the other parishes in our diocese and all the other bishops and dioceses of the country and around the world. After all those to be elected were presented, the bishop asked for testimony from their godparents (RCIA, 131B):

- ⑨ "Have they faithfully listened to God's word proclaimed by the Church?"

- ⑨ "Have they responded to that word and begun to walk in God's presence?"

- ⑨ "Have they shared the company of their Christian brothers and sisters and joined with them in prayer?"

Then ask the elect:

- ⑨ How did it feel to have your godparents affirm that you have done these things?

Have the elect reflect on each of these questions, discussing what they have heard in listening to the Word of God, how they have responded to it, and how they have begun to walk in God's presence. Ask them about their relations with other Christians, both in the parish and outside.

- ⑨ Has this experience led you to talk more freely about your faith? Has it changed the way you think about issues of everyday life, both personal and public?

- ⑨ How have you grown in participating in prayer with others?

The purpose of this discussion is to help them appreciate their growth through the catechumenate and embrace what the Church has declared: that they are ready. They may still have particular questions about some Church teachings and customs, but assure them that they will have the rest of their lives to deepen their understanding of these things. (Of course, if there are any burning questions, they can always ask a catechist.)

Ask them what they feel they need to prepare themselves for the sacraments. Explain to them that Lent exists primarily to prepare them for the sacraments and to prepare the whole community to celebrate with them and renew their own commitments. This time is called the Period of Purification and Enlightenment because during this time they, along with the rest of the Church, will focus on understanding sin and grace more deeply. For them, this will include the preparation and celebration of the scrutinies and the presentations of the Lord's Prayer and the Creed. The whole Church also prepares thorough the disciplines of prayer, fasting, and almsgiving. Be sure to make them aware of the Lenten prayers and other parish events. They may want to participate as a group as they are able.

Wrapping It Up/Closing Prayer

Consider these points to conclude your discussion. Integrate the thoughts and ideas that surfaced in your discussion. Close with the prayer from the appropriate Sunday dismissal guide.

- The Catholic Church is a world-wide communion of people who believe in Jesus Christ and act in his name. Their parish and diocese are part of that communion.

- The sacraments of initiation will make them fully part of that communion.

- The elect are ready for Baptism, Confirmation, and Eucharist, and the next few weeks will help them prepare spiritually for the reception of those sacraments.

THE FIRST SCRUTINY

Third Sunday of Lent

Focus: To thirst for living water.

RCIA, #141–146, 150–156

Catechist's Preparation

Overview of the Rite

The Scrutinies are the major feature of the Period of Purification and Enlightenment. They are primarily spiritual preparation for the celebration of the sacraments of initiation. They prepare the elect to respond to the renunciation of sin that precedes the Profession of Faith in the celebration of Baptism (see The Roman Missal Easter Vigil, 55):

- "Do you renounce Satan?"
- "And all his works?"
- "And all his empty show?"

They are "meant to uncover, then heal all that is weak, defective, or sinful in the hearts of the elect; to bring out, then strengthen all that is upright, strong, and good" (RCIA, 141). They deepen the awareness of the reality of "the mystery of sin, from which the whole world and every person longs to be delivered" (RCIA, 143) and increase their reliance on the forgiveness and mercy of God. During the Period of Precatechumenate, those who are making final preparation for the Easter sacraments certainly encountered the Church's teachings, the scriptural references, and their own experiences regarding sin and forgiveness. These rites prepare them to speak aloud the defining choice of Baptism: to refuse the power of sin and to accept the power of God to direct their lives. There are three Scrutinies because the depth of the reality of sin is great and renouncing it completely is not done easily.

The members of the assembly are also catechized by these scrutinies. Although they are baptized, they must still resist the lure of evil. These rites help them shake off any blindness toward sin or compliance with it that may have crept into their lives. Participating in these rites may serve as an invitation and impetus for the baptized to celebrate the Sacrament of Penance.

The three Scrutinies are rooted in the Liturgy of the Word using the readings of the Third, Fourth, and Fifth Sundays of Lent of Year A, no matter which year of the liturgical cycle is currently being celebrated. The Gospel readings of these Sundays are all from the Gospel according to John; they have been used as preparation for Baptism for centuries.

For the First Scrutiny, the Gospel, John 4:5–42, recounts the story of Jesus' meeting with a Samaritan woman at Jacob's well; it is proclaimed in tandem with Exodus 17:3–7, in which Moses strikes a rock to provide water to the Israelites, offering the images of dryness and water with which to ponder sin and grace. The homily should reflect these readings, explain the meaning of the scrutiny, and echo the imagery of the readings.

Following the homily, the elect are called forward for a period of silent prayer followed by intercessory prayer focusing on the elect's deliverance from the power of sin through acceptance of Christ. These intercessions might well be composed by those who have helped prepare the elect for the scrutiny by reflecting together on the nature of sin as thirst and dryness and their hope in Christ, who brings life-giving water.

After the intercessions, a solemn, two-part prayer of exorcism, which includes a laying-on of hands in silence, is prayed. Two options for this prayer are given in the RCIA, both of which reference the desire of the Samaritan woman and Jesus as the font of living water. An appropriate psalm or hymn may be sung, after which the elect are dismissed from the assembly as usual.

Refer to page 55 for more background on the Year A readings for the Third Sunday of Lent.

Reflection Questions for the Catechist

- How have you experienced the living water of Christ in times of sin or dryness?
- Have you ever experienced the presence of Christ in an unexpected place or circumstance?
- How have you helped people come to know that Jesus is the savior of the world?

Catechist's Guide

Objectives

- ▷ To reflect on the reality of sin and grace through the images of thirst and water.
- ▷ To unfold the meaning of the Scrutiny.
- ▷ To connect the approaching Baptism of the elect with salvation history.

Dismissal, Procession, and Centering

The dismissal, procession, and centering happens as usual. Consider rereading one of the prayers from the rite, such as (RCIA, 154A):

God of power,
you sent your Son to be our Savior.
Grant that these catechumens,
who, like the woman of Samaria, thirst for living water,
may turn to the Lord as they hear his word
and acknowledge the sins and weaknesses that weigh them down.
Protect them from vain reliance on self
and defend them from the power of Satan.
Free them from the spirit of deceit,
so that, admitting the wrong they have done,
they may attain purity of heart
and advance on the way to salvation.
Through Christ our Lord.
Amen.

Reflection and Discussion

The following suggestions may be used and adapted to help facilitate discussion on the First Scrutiny. It may be added to your discussion on today's readings.

The Scrutiny can be a powerful, even emotional experience, for the elect. Allow them time to describe their experience of the various moments of the rite: coming forward with their godparents or sponsors, standing or kneeling in silent prayer, the intercessory prayers, the prayer of exorcism, the laying on of hands. You might ask these questions:

- What did you hear, feel, experience? What emotions were raised? Did any words or phrases touch you?

Recount the story of the Samaritan woman. Note all the details: She's a Samaritan, considered a heretic by the Jewish people, a woman, an adulterer. Clearly Jesus already knows this about her; it does not stop him from inviting her to know the true God and worship him. Indeed, he says, "the Father seeks such people to worship him" (John 4:23). Some Scripture scholars say the "five husbands" (John 4:18) refers to the five foreign gods that the Samaritans came to know about and worship when they were conquered by other nations.

The woman knows that she desires something more than her current way of life is offering her. When Jesus tells her that he can give water that will be "a spring of life welling up to eternal life" (John 4:14), she asks to be given it. Jesus then asks about her husband. This issue seems to be what is preventing her from receiving what she asks for. Once she acknowledges the truth of her situation, she is able to speak on a deeper level about what she desires to know, and to hear what Jesus wants her to know.

Point out that in the Gospel reading, Jesus speaks to the woman first. In the Exodus reading, God promises to stand with Moses as he strikes the rock to show them that God cares for them. Before we turn to God, God is there waiting, inviting, ready to receive us. The antiphon for the Responsorial Psalm instructs, "If today you hear his voice, harden not your hearts." Ask the elect:

- What keeps you from turning to the God who is waiting to receive us?

- Why do we harden our hearts?

- What concerns, problems, habits, distractions, addictions get in the way of knowing what God wants of us and doing it?

- How does it feel when we put our lives into proper order, with knowing and worshiping the one true God at the center and everything else ordered around it?

- How does a proper relationship with God order our other relationships?

At the Easter Vigil, when the elect are baptized, they will be asked to renounce Satan and all his works and all his empty show. Ask if today's Scripture, liturgy, and discussion have given them any insight into what that means.

- Where in your lives have you experienced the empty promises that sin seems to offer?

- Where in our world today do you see the empty show of false gods, false ideas, and sinful attraction?

Ask the elect to recall how the woman acts after hearing the Good News that Jesus is the long-awaited Messiah. (*Catechists should note that if the shorter version of the Gospel was proclaimed at Mass, it would be good to read at least the missing part, if not the whole.*) Notice that she puts down her water jar and proclaims to the whole town that she has seen the Christ, and that he has seen and known her.

- How does it feel to be known and forgiven by God?

Point out that because of her conversion, others listened to Jesus and came to believe. Note that just as they may know people who were changed by coming to faith, their journey to Christ and the Church will likely influence others to seek him or draw more closely to him.

The elect should prepare for next week's Scrutiny. They will hear the Gospel proclamation of the healing of the man born blind. Preparation for the Second Scrutiny will focus on images of light and darkness, blindness and sight.

Wrapping It Up/Closing Prayer

Consider these points to conclude your discussion. Integrate the thoughts and ideas that surfaced in your discussion. Close with the prayer from the appropriate Sunday dismissal guide.

- The celebration of the Scrutinies prepares us to renounce Satan at Baptism by focusing on where sin is present in our lives.

- Sin keeps us from what we truly desire, from living as God wants us to live.

- God is always ready to forgive and embrace those who turn from sin.

THE SECOND SCRUTINY

Fourth Sunday of Lent

Focus: To see through the light of Christ.

RCIA, #141–146, 164–170

Catechist's Preparation

Overview of the Rite

The Scrutinies are the major feature of the Period of Purification and Enlightenment. They are primarily spiritual preparation for the celebration of the Sacraments of Initiation. They prepare the elect to respond to the renunciation of sin that precedes the Profession of Faith in the celebration of Baptism (see *The Roman Missal*, Easter Vigil, 55):

- "Do you renounce Satan?"
- "And all his works?"
- "And all his empty show?"

They are "meant to uncover, then heal all that is weak, defective, or sinful in the hearts of the elect; to bring out, then strengthen all that is upright, strong, and good" (RCIA, 141). They deepen the awareness of the reality of "the mystery of sin, from which the whole world and every person longs to be delivered" (RCIA, 143) and increase their reliance on the forgiveness and mercy of God. During the Period of Precatechumenate, those who are making final preparation for the Easter sacraments certainly encountered the Church's teachings, the scriptural references, and their own experiences regarding sin and forgiveness. These rites prepare them to speak aloud the defining choice of Baptism: to refuse the power of sin and to accept the power of God to direct their lives. There are three Scrutinies because the depth of the reality of sin is great and renouncing it completely is not done easily.

The members of the assembly are also catechized by these scrutinies. Although they are baptized, they must still resist the lure of evil. These rites help them shake off any blindness toward sin or compliance with it that may have crept into their lives. Participating in these rites may serve as an invitation and impetus for the baptized to celebrate the Sacrament of Penance.

The three Scrutinies are rooted in the Liturgy of the Word using the readings of the Third, Fourth, and Fifth Sundays of Lent of Year A, no matter which year of the liturgical cycle is currently being celebrated. The Gospel readings of these Sundays are all from the Gospel according to John; they have been used as preparation for Baptism for centuries.

For the Second Scrutiny, the Gospel, John 9:1–41, which recounts the story of Jesus' healing of a blind man and its repercussions, is proclaimed. The First Reading is 1 Samuel 16:1b, 6–7, 10–13a, in which the Prophet Samuel chooses the shepherd David as king after the prophet is reminded, "Not as man sees does God see, because man sees the appearance but the LORD looks into the heart" (1 Samuel 16:7). Together these readings point to images of blindness (refusal to see) and sight that help us ponder sin and grace. The Second Reading, Ephesians 5:8–14, reinforces those images with its admonition to "live as children of light." The homily should reflect these readings, explain the meaning of the scrutiny, and echo the imagery of the readings.

Following the homily, the elect are called forward for a period of silent prayer followed by intercessory prayer focusing on the elects' deliverance from the power of sin through acceptance of Christ. These intercessions might well be composed by those who have helped prepare the elect for the scrutiny by reflecting together on the nature of sin—as darkness and refusal to see—and on their hope in Christ, who brings life-giving light and true sight.

After the intercessions, a solemn, two-part prayer of exorcism, which includes a laying on of hands in silence, is prayed. Two options for this prayer are given in the RCIA, both of which reference our desire for truth and sight and for Jesus as the source of light. An appropriate psalm or hymn may be sung, after which the elect are dismissed from the assembly, as usual.

Refer to page 63 for more background on the Year A readings for the Fourth Sunday of Lent.

⑨ What or who in our society do we choose not to see?

⑨ What helps us see and understand more deeply who Jesus is?

⑨ What does our profession of faith cost us?

Catechist's Guide

Objectives

▷ To reflect on the reality of sin and grace through the images of darkness and light.

▷ To unfold the meaning of the Scrutiny.

▷ To connect the approaching Easter Vigil and Baptism of the elect with the image of the Light of Christ, which we are to bring to the world.

Dismissal, Procession, and Centering

The dismissal, procession, and centering happens as usual. Consider rereading one of the prayers from the rite, such as (RCIA, 168B):

Lord Jesus,
at your own baptism
the heavens were opened
and you received the Holy Spirit
to empower you to proclaim the Good News to the poor
and restore sight to the blind.
Pour out the same Holy Spirit on these elect,
who long for your sacraments.
Guide them along the path of right faith,
safe from error, doubt, and unbelief,
so that with eyes unsealed
they may come to see you face to face.
Who live and reign for ever and ever.
Amen.

Reflection and Discussion

The following suggestions may be used and adapted to help facilitate discussion on the First Scrutiny. It may be added to your discussion on today's readings.

The Scrutiny can be a powerful, even emotional experience, for the elect. Allow them time to describe their experience of the various moments of the rite: coming forward with their godparents or sponsors, standing or kneeling in silent prayer, the intercessory prayers, the prayer of exorcism, the laying on of hands. You might ask these questions:

⑨ What did you hear, feel, experience?

⑨ What emotions were raised?

⑨ Did any words or phrases touch you?

⑨ Was this experience different from the first Scrutiny? If so, how?

Recount the story of the healing of the blind man. Note all the details: Jesus is very clear that there is no sin involved in the man's blindness. This is important in this discussion—physical blindness is not equated with sin. Jesus is clear, particularly at the end of the Gospel reading that the sin is *choosing* not to see. A second detail is that Jesus acts to heal the man without being asked. He does it because "we have to do the works of the one who sent me while it is day" (John 9:4). The healing is a work done to show forth God's glory and to teach the disciples that they must do God's work while they can. Notice, too, that Jesus brings about the healing through the use of natural materials, mud, and water. While he certainly could have healed the man by a simple word or touch, he chose to use earthly signs, as we do in the sacraments. God is able to work and be glorified through creation.

While Jesus, the light of the world, heals the man, the forces of darkness begin to cast doubt on the healing, threatening the man and his family, denying what was obvious, and finally throwing the man out when he insisted several times that Jesus healed him and was certainly from God, even a prophet. If the religious leaders had acknowledged that the healing had actually occurred and that Jesus had indeed been sent by God, they would then have been obliged to listen to him and follow his teachings. Their position as people of authority and, therefore, of power would be threatened, so they deny what their own eyes have seen. For this, Jesus judges them as sinful, choosing darkness and denial over the light of faith.

In this Gospel, the sin exists not in the blind man but in the community around him: in the leaders who have something to lose, and in the parents and others who are afraid of the leaders and are intimidated into denial or silence

It is easy for us to choose not to see something we don't want to see. We don't want to get involved, or it's none of our business, or we're frightened for our own safety or that of our family. We may feel it's none of our business if we know a child who may be being bullied, a coworker who is behaving unethically, or a person who is being abused by a spouse. We may choose not to acknowledge that illegal activities seem to be taking place in our neighborhood, or that a family may need some help.

- ⑨ When have you chosen not to see something, or not to acknowledge what you've seen? Why?

- ⑨ When have you seen something you knew was wrong and acted on it? What was the result?

- ⑨ Have you ever been in need and felt invisible, as if no one could see you? Or have you been in need and been seen and helped? Or have you ever tried to be of help or to get help for someone in need, only to be ridiculed or ignored?

As people of faith we are called to be light for the world, to be the presence of Christ on earth, to overcome the darkness of sin, the "night . . . when no one can work" (John 9:4). Notice that as the blind man comes to grips with his new-found sight, he becomes more and more certain of what he had experienced and who Jesus was. The increasing opposition to his witness did not dissuade him, but actually strengthened his faith. The first steps into living our faith as a public witness may be difficult, but like the blind man, we must trust that what Jesus tells us will bring us light and hope. We, in turn, bring that light and hope to others, to help them see and act and grow confident.

In the Easter Vigil, the image of Christ the Light will be prominent. It is in his light that you will see clearly, to renounce evil and embrace Christ in the Sacraments of Baptism, Confirmation, and Eucharist, when you will become children of light.

Wrapping It Up/Closing Prayer

Consider these points to conclude your discussion. Integrate the thoughts and ideas that surfaced in your discussion. Close with the prayer from the appropriate Sunday dismissal guide.

- The celebration of the Scrutinies prepares us to see the light of Christ that we might renounce sin follow Christ.

- Sin keeps us from seeing and acknowledging the truth, and from acting as Christ in the world.

- God is always ready to forgive and embrace those who turn from sin.

THE THIRD SCRUTINY

Fifth Sunday of Lent

Focus: Jesus is the Resurrection and the Life.

RCIA, #141–146, 171–177

Catechist's Preparation

Overview of the Rite

The Scrutinies are the major feature of the Period of Purification and Enlightenment. They are primarily spiritual preparation for the celebration of the Sacraments of Initiation. They prepare the elect to respond to the renunciation of sin that precedes the Profession of Faith in the celebration of Baptism (see *The Roman Missal*, Easter Vigil, 55):

- "Do you renounce Satan?"

- "And all his works?"

- "And all his empty show?"

They are "meant to uncover, then heal all that is weak, defective, or sinful in the hearts of the elect; to bring out, then strengthen all that is upright, strong, and good" (RCIA, 141). They deepen the awareness of the reality of "the mystery of sin, from which the whole world and every person longs to be delivered" (RCIA, 143) and increase their reliance on the forgiveness and mercy of God. During the Period of Precatechumenate, those who are making final preparation for the Easter sacraments certainly encountered the Church's teachings, the scriptural references, and their own experiences regarding sin and forgiveness. These rites prepare them to speak aloud the defining choice of Baptism: to refuse the power of sin and to accept the power of God to direct their lives. There are three Scrutinies because the depth of the reality of sin is great and renouncing it completely is not done easily.

The members of the assembly are also catechized by these scrutinies. Although they are baptized, they must still resist the lure of evil. These rites help them shake off any blindness toward sin or compliance with it that may have crept into their lives. Participating in these rites may serve as an invitation and impetus for the baptized to celebrate the Sacrament of Penance.

The three Scrutinies are rooted in the Liturgy of the Word using the readings of the Third, Fourth, and Fifth Sundays of Lent of Year A, no matter which year of the liturgical cycle is currently being celebrated. The Gospel readings of these Sundays are all from the Gospel according to John; they have been used as preparation for Baptism for centuries.

For the Third Scrutiny, the Gospel, John 11:1–45, which recounts the story of Jesus raising his friend Lazarus from death, is proclaimed. The First Reading is Ezekiel 37:12–14, in which the prophet Ezekiel speaks of God's promise to a dispirited, exiled people that they shall rise from their graves and live in the land God gave them. Together these readings point to images of death and life with which to ponder sin and grace. The Second Reading, Romans 8:8–11, reinforces those images with its promise that "the one who raised Christ from the dead will give life to your mortal bodies also, through his Spirit dwelling in you" (Romans 8:11). The homily should reflect these readings, explain the meaning of the scrutiny, and echo the imagery of the readings.

Following the homily, the elect are called forward for a period of silent prayer followed by intercessory prayer focusing on the elect's deliverance from the power of sin through acceptance of Christ. These intercessions might well be composed by those who have helped prepare the elect for the scrutiny by reflecting together on the nature of sin as the bringer of death and on their hope in Christ, who brings life eternal.

After the intercessions, a solemn, two-part prayer of exorcism, which includes a laying on of hands in silence, is prayed. Two options for this prayer are given in the RCIA, both of which reference our desire for freedom from sin and death and Jesus as the source of life. An appropriate psalm or hymn may be sung, after which the elect are dismissed from the assembly as usual.

Refer to page 71 for more background on the Year A readings for the Fifth Sunday of Lent.

Reflection Questions for the Catechist

🌀 Where have you seen the power of sin bring death and the power of Christ bring life?

🌀 Another wording of one of the renunciations before Baptism asks, "Do you renounce the lure of evil, so that sin may have no mastery over you?" What do you understand by the lure of evil?

🌀 How can we bring life to a situation, a nation, a world that seems to be headed for death?

Catechist's Guide

Objectives

▷ To reflect on the reality of sin and grace through the images of death and life.

▷ To prepare the elect to renounce Satan and all his works, including the works of bringing death and destruction.

▷ To prepare the elect to profess faith in Jesus Christ, who was raised from the dead and is seated at the right hand of the Father.

Dismissal, Procession, and Centering

The dismissal, procession, and centering happens as usual. Consider rereading one of the prayers from the rite, such as (RCIA, 175B, second option):

> Lord Jesus Christ,
> you commanded Lazarus to step forth alive from his tomb
> and by your own resurrection freed all people from death.
> We pray for these your servants,
> who eagerly approach the waters of new birth
> and hunger for the banquet of life.
> Do not let the power of death hold them back,
> for, by their faith,
> they will share in the triumph of your resurrection.
> Who live and reign for ever and ever.
> Amen.

Reflection and Discussion

The following suggestions may be used and adapted to help facilitate discussion on the First Scrutiny. It may be added to your discussion on today's readings.

The Scrutiny can be a powerful, even emotional experience, for the elect. Allow them time to describe their experience of the various moments of the rite: coming forward with their godparents or sponsors, standing or kneeling in silent prayer, the intercessory prayers, the prayer of exorcism, the laying on of hands. You might ask these questions:

🌀 What did you hear, feel, experience?

🌀 What emotions were raised?

🌀 Did any words or phrases touch you?

🌀 Was this experience different from the first Scrutiny? If so, how?

Recount the story of the raising of Lazarus. Jesus delays responding to Mary and Martha's message that Lazarus is sick, seemingly knowing that he would die. Jesus himself faces death simply by going back to Judea, where attempts on his life had already been made. Jesus is deliberately, publicly choosing to face death in "the light of this world" (John 11:9), so that he may reveal who he is, to the glory of God.

Note that Thomas bravely encourages his fellow disciples to accompany Jesus "to die with him" (John 11:16). This is the same man who gets the unfortunate title "Doubting Thomas" from his refusal to believe that Jesus has been raised until he sees for himself; this Gospel story will be proclaimed the Second Sunday of Easter. In this reading, Thomas seems to have internalized Jesus' stance that death is not to be given the power to prevent us from doing what God asks of us.

The purpose of the celebration of the Scrutinies is to help the elect deepen their understanding of sin and their faith in the power of Christ over sin. Review with the elect the view of sin derived from the first two scrutinies, which looked at sin as dryness and Christ as living water, sin as refusal to see and Christ as light.

In this scrutiny we look at death and Christ, the Resurrection and the Life. In today's Gospel, the sin is not in the fact that Lazarus died, or in the fact that his grieving sisters were unhappy with the Lord for not preventing it from happening. We look at sin itself as the cause of death, harkening back to the Genesis story of Adam and Eve's disobedience in eating of the one tree forbidden to them, even though they had been warned that they would die if they did. Jesus grieves with Mary and the other mourners, and he finds himself deeply moved ("he became perturbed" [John 11:33], which indicates a great depth of emotion), which leads him to restore Lazarus to life. He does this very publicly, addressing his Father so that all who witness this event will understand that God sent him.

This raising of Lazarus is not the same as the Resurrection of Christ. Lazarus is restored to his human life; he will undergo death at a later time. But Jesus has given a sign of his power over life and death, which is the power of God. In his Resurrection he completely shatters the power of death over all people. Because of his absolute obedience to God, death, the fruit of human disobedience, is replaced with the promise of eternal life.

⑨ How has your faith in the Resurrection of Christ and the hope of eternal life changed how you view death?

Today's Gospel reading ends, "Now many of the Jews who had come to Mary and seen what he had done began to believe in him" (John 11:45). But the story continues, "But some of them went to the Pharisees and told them what Jesus had done" (John 11:46). The result is that the religious leaders convened and decided that Jesus had to die so that the people would not believe in him and bring down the wrath of the Romans on the nation.

In Baptism, the elect will die with Christ and be united with his Resurrection.

⑨ What does it mean for you to know that in Baptism, you will die with Christ and be united with his Resurrection?

⑨ What powers still seek to bring death into the world? (*Possible answers: drugs, war, urban violence, physical and mental abuse, lack of respect and hospitality to immigrants, racism, bigotry, misogyny, etc.*)

⑨ What difference does the power of Christ make?

⑨ What can Christians, who have died with Christ in Baptism, bring to these situations?

Wrapping It Up/Closing Prayer

Consider these points to conclude your discussion. Integrate the thoughts and ideas that surfaced in your discussion. Close with the prayer from the appropriate Sunday dismissal guide.

- The celebration of the Scrutinies prepares us to see the light of Christ that we might renounce sin follow Christ.

- Sin keeps us from seeing and acknowledging the truth and from acting as Christ in the world.

- Through Jesus' Death and Resurrection, the power of death has been broken and we may die to sin and be reborn to eternal life.